Gastrointestinal

Diseases and Disorders

SOURCEBOOK

Third Edition

Health Reference Series

Third Edition

Gastrointestinal
Diseases and Disorders
SOURCEBOOK

*Basic Consumer Health Information about the Upper and
Lower Gastrointestinal (GI) Tract, Including the Esophagus,
Stomach, Intestines, Rectum, Liver, and Pancreas, with Facts
about Gastroesophageal Reflux Disease, Gastritis, Appendicitis,
Ulcers, Celiac Disease, Diverticulitis, Irritable Bowel Syndrome,
Hemorrhoids, Gallstones, and Other Diseases and Disorders
Related to the Digestive Process*

*Along with Information about Cancers of the Gastrointestinal
Tract, Food Intolerances, and Commonly used Diagnostic and
Surgical Procedures, Statistics, a Glossary, and Resources
for Additional Help and Information*

OMNIGRAPHICS

155 W. Congress, Suite 200 Detroit, MI 48226

Bibliographic Note

Because this page cannot legibly accommodate all the copyright notices, the Bibliographic Note portion of the Preface constitutes an extension of the copyright notice.

* * *

Omnigraphics, Inc.

Editorial Services provided by Omnigraphics, Inc.,
a division of Relevant Information, Inc.

Keith Jones, *Managing Editor*

* * *

Copyright © 2016 Relevant Information, Inc.

ISBN 978-0-7808-1457-8
E-ISBN 978-0-7808-1458-5

Library of Congress Cataloging-in-Publication Data

Names: Omnigraphics, Inc.

Title: Gastrointestinal diseases and disorders sourcebook : basic consumer health information about the upper and lower gastrointestinal (GI) tract, including the esophagus, stomach, intestines, rectum, liver, and pancreas, with facts about gastroesophageal reflux disease, gastritis, hernias, ulcers, celiac disease, diverticulitis, irritable bowel syndrome, hemorrhoids, gastrointestinal cancers, and other diseases and disorders related to the digestive process; along with information about commonly used diagnostic and surgical procedures, statistics, reports on current research initiatives and clinical trials, a glossary, and resources for additional help and information.

Description: Third edition. | Detroit, MI : Omnigraphics, Inc., [2016] | Series: Health reference series | Includes bibliographical references and index.

Identifiers: LCCN 2015044229 (print) | LCCN 2015044765 (ebook) | ISBN 9780780814578 (hardcover : alk. paper) | ISBN 9780780814585 (ebook)

Subjects: LCSH: Gastrointestinal system--Diseases--Popular works.

Classification: LCC RC806 .G37 2016 (print) | LCC RC806 (ebook) | DDC 616.3/3--dc23

LC record available at http://lccn.loc.gov/2015044229

Table of Contents

Part III: Disorders of the Upper Gastrointestinal Tract

Part IV: Disorders of the Lower Gastrointestinal Tract

Part V: Disorders of the Digestive System's Solid Organs: The Liver and Pancreas

Part VI: Cancers of the Gastrointestinal Tract

Part VII: Food Intolerances and Infectious Disorders of the Gastrointestinal Tract

Part VIII: Additional Help and Information

Preface

About This Book

The gastrointestinal tract includes the stomach, intestines, and other organs related to digestion—the process by which food and drink are changed into molecules of nutrients that can be carried to the body's cells. Disorders that interfere with this process affect an estimated 60 to 70 million Americans and account for more than 48.3 million doctor visits every year. According to the National Institute of Diabetes and Digestive and Kidney Diseases (NIDDK), researchers have only recently begun to understand many gastrointestinal diseases and disorders. As a result, the process of helping people set aside common misconceptions about the causes of symptoms and turn to scientifically-based treatments instead of folkloric remedies is progressing only gradually.

Gastrointestinal Diseases and Disorders Sourcebook, Third Edition, provides readers with updated health information about the causes, symptoms, diagnosis, and treatment of diseases and disorders affecting the esophagus, stomach, intestines, appendix, gall bladder, liver, and pancreas. It also describes how the gastrointestinal tract can be affected by food intolerances, infectious diseases, and various cancers. The structure and function of the digestive system, common diagnostic methods, medical treatments, surgical procedures, and current research initiatives are described. The book concludes with a glossary of related terms and directory of resources for further help and information.

How to Use This Book

This book is divided into parts and chapters. Parts focus on broad areas of interest. Chapters are devoted to single topics within a part.

Part I: Introduction to the Digestive System begins with a look at the anatomy and physiology of the digestive system. It describes commonly experienced symptoms and discusses how the gastrointestinal tract can be impacted by tobacco use.

Part II: Diagnostic and Surgical Procedures Used for Gastrointestinal Disorders provides a detailed look at endoscopic procedures and other types of tests used to diagnose gastrointestinal disorders. It also discusses common gastrointestinal surgical procedures.

Part III: Disorders of the Upper Gastrointestinal Tract looks at disorders of the esophagus and the stomach. It describes the risk factors, symptoms, and treatment options for a variety of disorders of the upper gastrointestinal tract including dyspepsia, gastroesophageal reflux disease, swallowing disorders, and gastroparesis.

Part IV: Disorders of the Lower Gastrointestinal Tract describes the risk factors, symptoms, and treatment options for disorders affecting the large and small intestines, appendix, gall bladder, anus, and rectum. Disorders including IBS, Crohn's disease, appendicitis, gallstones, and hemorrhoids are discussed.

Part V: Disorders of the Digestive System's Solid Organs: The Liver and the Pancreas offers current information about the risk factors, symptoms, and treatment options for pancreatitis, hepatitis, cirrhosis of the liver, and other liver disorders.

Part VI: Cancers of the Gastrointestinal Tract provides a detailed look at the different cancers that affect the gastrointestinal tract. Each chapter reports on risk factors, symptoms, diagnostic methods, staging information, treatment options, and clinical trials.

Part VII: Food Intolerances and Infectious Disorders of the Gastrointestinal Tract discusses lactose intolerance, food-and water-borne diseases, celiac disease, rotavirus, and diseases transmitted by viral, bacterial, or parasitic contamination of food or drinking water.

Part VIII: Additional Help and Information provides a glossary of gastrointestinal terms and a directory of organizations that can provide further information.

Bibliographic Note

This volume contains documents and excerpts from publications issued by the following U.S. government agencies: Centers for Disease Control and Prevention (CDC); Genetic and Rare Diseases Information Center (GARD); Genetics Home Reference (GHR); National Cancer Institute (NCI); National Heart, Lung, and Blood Institute (NHLBI); National Institute of Allergy and Infectious Diseases (NIAID); National Institute of Child Health and Human Development (NICHD); National Institute of Diabetes and Digestive and Kidney Diseases (NIDDK); Office on Women's Health (OWH); U.S. Food and Drug Administration (FDA); and U.S. Department of Veterans Affairs (VA).

It may also contain original material produced by Omnigraphics, Inc. and reviewed by medical consultants.

About the Health Reference Series

The *Health Reference Series* is designed to provide basic medical information for patients, families, caregivers, and the general public. Each volume takes a particular topic and provides comprehensive coverage. This is especially important for people who may be dealing with a newly diagnosed disease or a chronic disorder in themselves or in a family member. People looking for preventive guidance, information about disease warning signs, medical statistics, and risk factors for health problems will also find answers to their questions in the *Health Reference Series*. The *Series*, however, is not intended to serve as a tool for diagnosing illness, in prescribing treatments, or as a substitute for the physician/patient relationship. All people concerned about medical symptoms or the possibility of disease are encouraged to seek professional care from an appropriate health care provider.

A Note about Spelling and Style

Health Reference Series editors use *Stedman's Medical Dictionary* as an authority for questions related to the spelling of medical terms and the *Chicago Manual of Style* for questions related to grammatical structures, punctuation, and other editorial concerns. Consistent adherence is not always possible, however, because the individual volumes within the *Series* include many documents from a wide variety of different producers, and the editor's primary goal is to present material from each source as accurately as is possible. This sometimes means that information in different chapters or sections may follow other guidelines and alternate spelling authorities.

Medical Review

Omnigraphics contracts with a team of qualified, senior medical professionals who serve as medical consultants for the *Health Reference Series*. As necessary, medical consultants review reprinted and originally written material for currency and accuracy. Citations including the phrase,

"Reviewed (month, year)" indicate material reviewed by this team. Medical consultation services are provided to the *Health Reference Series* editors by:

Dr. Vijayalakshmi, MBBS, DGO, MD
Dr. Senthil Selvan, MBBS, DCH, MD

Our Advisory Board

We would like to thank the following board members for providing initial guidance to the development of this series:

- Dr. Lynda Baker, Associate Professor of Library and Information Science, Wayne State University, Detroit, MI

- Nancy Bulgarelli, William Beaumont Hospital Library, Royal Oak, MI

- Karen Imarisio, Bloomfield Township Public Library, Bloomfield Township, MI

- Karen Morgan, Mardigian Library, University of Michigan-Dearborn, Dearborn, MI

- Rosemary Orlando, St. Clair Shores Public Library, St. Clair Shores, MI

Health Reference Series *Update Policy*

The inaugural book in the *Health Reference Series* was the first edition of *Cancer Sourcebook* published in 1989. Since then, the *Series* has been enthusiastically received by librarians and in the medical community. In order to maintain the standard of providing high-quality health information for the layperson the editorial staff at Omnigraphics felt it was necessary to implement a policy of updating volumes when warranted.

Medical researchers have been making tremendous strides, and it is the purpose of the *Health Reference Series* to stay current with the most recent advances. Each decision to update a volume is made on an individual basis. Some of the considerations include how much new information is available and the feedback we receive from people who use the books. If there is a topic you would like to see added to the update list, or an area of medical concern you feel has not been adequately addressed, please write to:

Managing Editor
Health Reference Series
Omnigraphics, Inc.
155 W. Congress, Suite 200
Detroit, MI 48226

Part One

Introduction to the Digestive System

Chapter 1

Your Digestive System and How It Works

What is the digestive system?

The digestive system is made up of the gastrointestinal (GI) tract—also called the digestive tract—and the liver, pancreas, and gallbladder. The GI tract is a series of hollow organs joined in a long, twisting tube from the mouth to the anus. The hollow organs that make up the GI tract are the mouth, esophagus, stomach, small intestine, large intestine—which includes the rectum—and anus. Food enters the mouth and passes to the anus through the hollow organs of the GI tract. The liver, pancreas, and gallbladder are the solid organs of the digestive system. The digestive system helps the body digest food.

Bacteria in the GI tract, also called gut flora or microbiome, help with digestion. Parts of the nervous and circulatory systems also play roles in the digestive process. Together, a combination of nerves, hormones, bacteria, blood, and the organs of the digestive system completes the complex task of digesting the foods and liquids a person consumes each day.

Text in this chapter is excerpted from "Your Digestive System and How It Works," National Institute of Diabetes and Digestive and Kidney Diseases (NIDDK), September 2013.

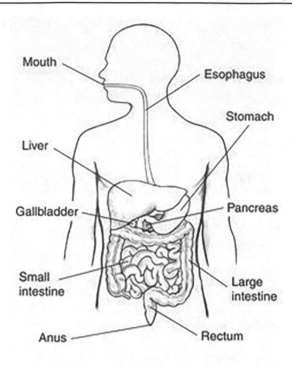

Figure 1.1. *The digestive system*

Why is digestion important?

Digestion is important for breaking down food into nutrients, which the body uses for energy, growth, and cell repair. Food and drink must be changed into smaller molecules of nutrients before the blood absorbs them and carries them to cells throughout the body. The body breaks down nutrients from food and drink into carbohydrates, protein, fats, and vitamins.

Carbohydrates. Carbohydrates are the sugars, starches, and fiber found in many foods. Carbohydrates are called simple or complex, depending on their chemical structure. Simple carbohydrates include sugars found naturally in foods such as fruits, vegetables, milk, and milk products, as well as sugars added during food processing. Complex carbohydrates are starches and fiber found in whole-grain breads and cereals, starchy vegetables, and legumes. The *Dietary Guidelines for Americans* recommends that 45 to 65 percent of total daily calories come from carbohydrates.

Protein. Foods such as meat, eggs, and beans consist of large molecules of protein that the body digests into smaller molecules called amino acids. The body absorbs amino acids through the small intestine into the blood, which then carries them throughout the body. The *Dietary Guidelines for Americans* recommends that 10 to 35 percent of total daily calories come from protein.

Fats. Fat molecules are a rich source of energy for the body and help the body absorb vitamins. Oils, such as corn, canola, olive, safflower, soybean, and sunflower, are examples of healthy fats. Butter, shortening, and snack foods are examples of less healthy fats. During digestion, the body breaks down fat molecules into fatty acids and glycerol. The *Dietary Guidelines for Americans* recommends that 20 to 35 percent of total daily calories come from fat.

Vitamins. Scientists classify vitamins by the fluid in which they dissolve. Water-soluble vitamins include all the B vitamins and vitamin C. Fat-soluble vitamins include vitamins A, D, E, and K. Each vitamin has a different role in the body's growth and health. The body stores fat-soluble vitamins in the liver and fatty tissues, whereas the body does not easily store water-soluble vitamins and flushes out the extra in the urine.

Table 1.1. The Digestive Process

Organ	Movement	Digestive Juices Used	Food Particles Broken Down
Mouth	Chewing	Saliva	Starches
Esophagus	Swallowing	None	None
Stomach	Upper muscle in stomach relaxes to let food enter and lower muscle mixes food with digestive juice	Stomach acid	Protein
Small intestine	Peristalsis	Small intestine digestive juice	Starches, protein, and carbohydrates
Pancreas	None	Pancreatic juice	Starches, fats, and protein
Liver	None	Bile acids	Fats

How does digestion work?

Digestion works by moving food through the GI tract. Digestion begins in the mouth with chewing and ends in the small intestine. As food passes through the GI tract, it mixes with digestive juices, causing large molecules of food to break down into smaller molecules. The body then absorbs these smaller molecules through the walls of the small intestine into the bloodstream, which delivers them to the rest of the body. Waste products of digestion pass through the large intestine and out of the body as a solid matter called stool.

Table 1.1 shows the parts of the digestive process performed by each digestive organ, including movement of food, type of digestive juice used, and food particles broken down by that organ.

How does food move through the GI tract?

The large, hollow organs of the GI tract contain a layer of muscle that enables their walls to move. The movement of organ walls—called peristalsis—propels food and liquid through the GI tract and mixes the contents within each organ. Peristalsis looks like an ocean wave traveling through the muscle as it contracts and relaxes.

Esophagus. When a person swallows, food pushes into the esophagus, the muscular tube that carries food and liquids from the mouth to the stomach. Once swallowing begins, it becomes involuntary and proceeds under the control of the esophagus and brain. The lower esophageal sphincter, a ringlike muscle at the junction of the esophagus and stomach, controls the passage of food and liquid between the esophagus and stomach. As food approaches the closed sphincter, the muscle relaxes and lets food pass through to the stomach.

Stomach. The stomach stores swallowed food and liquid, mixes the food and liquid with digestive juice it produces, and slowly empties its contents, called chyme, into the small intestine. The muscle of the upper part of the stomach relaxes to accept large volumes of swallowed material from the esophagus. The muscle of the lower part of the stomach mixes the food and liquid with digestive juice.

Small intestine. The muscles of the small intestine mix food with digestive juices from the pancreas, liver, and intestine and push the mixture forward to help with further digestion. The walls of the small

6

intestine absorb the digested nutrients into the bloodstream. The blood delivers the nutrients to the rest of the body.

Large intestine. The waste products of the digestive process include undigested parts of food and older cells from the GI tract lining. Muscles push these waste products into the large intestine. The large intestine absorbs water and any remaining nutrients and changes the waste from liquid into stool. The rectum stores stool until it pushes stool out of the body during a bowel movement.

How do digestive juices in each organ of the GI tract break down food?

Digestive juices contain enzymes—substances that speed up chemical reactions in the body—that break food down into different nutrients.

Salivary glands. Saliva produced by the salivary glands moistens food so it moves more easily through the esophagus into the stomach. Saliva also contains an enzyme that begins to break down the starches from food.

Glands in the stomach lining. The glands in the stomach lining produce stomach acid and an enzyme that digests protein.

Pancreas. The pancreas produces a juice containing several enzymes that break down carbohydrates, fats, and proteins in food. The pancreas delivers digestive juice to the small intestine through small tubes called ducts.

Liver. The liver produces a digestive juice called bile. The gallbladder stores bile between meals. When a person eats, the gallbladder squeezes bile through the bile ducts, which connect the gallbladder and liver to the small intestine. The bile mixes with the fat in food. The bile acids dissolve fat into the watery contents of the intestine, much like how detergents dissolve grease from a frying pan, so the intestinal and pancreatic enzymes can digest the fat molecules.

Small intestine. Digestive juice produced by the small intestine combines with pancreatic juice and bile to complete digestion. The body completes the breakdown of proteins, and the final breakdown of starches produces glucose molecules that absorb into the blood. Bacteria in the small intestine produce some of the enzymes needed to digest carbohydrates.

What happens to the digested food molecules?

The small intestine absorbs most digested food molecules, as well as water and minerals, and passes them on to other parts of the body for storage or further chemical change. Specialized cells help absorbed materials cross the intestinal lining into the bloodstream. The bloodstream carries simple sugars, amino acids, glycerol, and some vitamins and salts to the liver. The lymphatic system, a network of vessels that carry white blood cells and a fluid called lymph throughout the body, absorbs fatty acids and vitamins.

How is the digestive process controlled?

Hormone and nerve regulators control the digestive process.

Hormone Regulators

The cells in the lining of the stomach and small intestine produce and release hormones that control the functions of the digestive system. These hormones stimulate production of digestive juices and regulate appetite.

Nerve Regulators

Two types of nerves help control the action of the digestive system: extrinsic and intrinsic nerves.

Extrinsic, or outside, nerves connect the digestive organs to the brain and spinal cord. These nerves release chemicals that cause the muscle layer of the GI tract to either contract or relax, depending on whether food needs digesting. The intrinsic, or inside, nerves within the GI tract are triggered when food stretches the walls of the hollow organs. The nerves release many different substances that speed up or delay the movement of food and the production of digestive juices.

Chapter 2

Common Gastrointestinal Symptoms

Chapter Contents

Section 2.1

Bleeding in the Digestive Tract

Text in this section is excerpted from "Bleeding in the Digestive
Tract," National Institute of Diabetes and Digestive and Kidney
Diseases (NIDDK), July 2014.

What is bleeding in the digestive tract?

Bleeding in the digestive tract is any type of bleeding that starts
in the digestive tract. Bleeding in the digestive tract is a symptom of
a disease rather than a disease itself. Health care providers describe
two types of bleeding:

- acute bleeding—sudden and sometimes severe bleeding

- chronic bleeding—slight bleeding that lasts for a long time or
  may come and go

What is the digestive tract?

The digestive tract, also called the gastrointestinal (GI) tract,
is a series of hollow organs joined in a long, twisting tube from
the mouth to the anus. Food enters the mouth and passes to the
anus through the hollow organs of the GI tract. The upper GI tract
includes the mouth, esophagus, stomach, and duodenum. The duodenum is the first part of the small intestine. The lower GI tract
consists of the large intestine—which includes the colon and rectum—and anus.

The digestive tract, also called the GI tract, is a series of hollow
organs joined in a long, twisting tube from the mouth to the anus.

What causes bleeding in the digestive tract?

A variety of conditions can cause bleeding in the digestive tract.
Locating the source of bleeding is an important step to help the health
care provider find the cause of the bleeding. Different conditions can
cause bleeding in the upper or lower GI tract.

Causes of bleeding in the upper GI tract may include,

- peptic ulcers
- esophageal varices
- a Mallory-Weiss tear
- gastritis
- esophagitis

Causes of bleeding in the lower GI tract may include,

- hemorrhoids or fissures
- diverticular disease
- colitis
- angiodysplasia
- colon polyps

Causes of bleeding in both the lower and upper GI tract may include,

- benign tumors and cancer

What are the signs and symptoms of bleeding in the digestive tract?

The signs and symptoms of bleeding in the digestive tract depend on the location and severity of bleeding.

Signs and symptoms of bleeding in the upper or lower GI tract may include,

- acute bleeding, which may include abdominal cramps
- black or tarry stool
- bright red blood in vomit
- dark or bright red blood mixed with stool
- dizziness or faintness
- fatigue, or feeling tired
- paleness
- shortness of breath
- vomit that looks like coffee grounds
- weakness

A person with acute bleeding may go into shock, which is an emergency condition. A person in shock may have additional signs and symptoms that may include,

- a rapid pulse

- a drop in blood pressure

- little or no urine output

- unconsciousness

When a person has any signs or symptoms of shock, 911 should be called immediately.

Chronic bleeding. A person with chronic bleeding may develop anemia, a condition in which red blood cells are fewer than normal, which prevents the body's cells from getting enough oxygen. Symptoms of anemia may include fatigue and shortness of breath, which can develop over time.

Some people may have occult bleeding. Occult bleeding may be a sign of inflammation or a disease such as colorectal cancer. A simple lab test can detect occult blood in the stool.

How is the cause of bleeding in the digestive tract diagnosed?

To diagnose bleeding in the digestive tract, the health care provider will first determine the site of the bleeding based upon the following:

- medical and family history

- physical exam

- lab tests

- nasogastric lavage

- upper GI endoscopy, enteroscopy, and capsule endoscopy

- colonoscopy and flexible sigmoidoscopy

- imaging tests

- other tests

Medical and Family History

Taking a medical and family history is one of the first things a health care provider may do to help determine the cause of digestive tract bleeding. Patients should report all medications they are taking to their health care provider.

Physical Exam

A physical exam may help diagnose the cause of bleeding in the digestive tract. During a physical exam, a health care provider usually

- examines a patient's body
- uses a stethoscope to listen to sounds in the abdomen
- taps on specific areas of the patient's body

Lab Tests

The health care provider may use the following lab tests to help determine the cause of digestive tract bleeding:

- **Stool test.** A stool test is the analysis of a sample of stool. The health care provider will give the patient a container for catching and storing the stool. The patient will return the sample to the health care provider or a commercial facility that will send the sample to a lab for analysis. Stool tests can show occult bleeding.

- **Blood test.** A blood test involves drawing blood at a health care provider's office or a commercial facility and sending the sample to a lab for analysis. The blood test can help determine the extent of the bleeding and whether the patient has anemia.

Nasogastric Lavage

During this procedure, a health care provider uses a nasogastric tube to remove the stomach contents. The health care provider will spray a numbing medication on the back of the patient's throat before the procedure. The health care provider inserts a nasogastric tube through the nose or mouth, down the esophagus, and into the stomach. The procedure helps determine the cause of upper GI tract bleeding. A health care provider performs a nasogastric lavage in an outpatient center or a hospital.

Upper Gastrointestinal Endoscopy, Enteroscopy, and Capsule Endoscopy

- **Upper GI endoscopy.** This procedure involves using an endo-scope—a small, flexible tube with a light—to see the upper GI

13

tract. A gastroenterologist—a doctor who specializes in digestive diseases—performs the test at a hospital or an outpatient center. The gastroenterologist carefully feeds the endoscope down the esophagus and into the stomach and duodenum. A small camera mounted on the endoscope transmits a video image to a monitor, allowing close examination of the intestinal lining. A health care provider may give a patient a liquid anesthetic to gargle or may spray anesthetic on the back of the patient's throat. A health care provider will place an intravenous (IV) needle in a vein in the arm to administer a sedative or general anesthesia.

During the procedure, a gastroenterologist may obtain a biopsy to help diagnose the bleeding. A biopsy is a procedure in which a tiny piece of the GI tract lining is removed for examination with a microscope. The endoscopy may show the source of bleeding, such as an ulcer or esophageal varices. When the health care provider cannot see the source of the bleeding during the endoscopy, the patient has obscure bleeding. The gastroenterologist may repeat the endoscopy or use other procedures to find the cause of obscure bleeding.

- **Enteroscopy.** This procedure examines the small intestine with a special, longer endoscope. A gastroenterologist usually performs the test at an outpatient center or a hospital. The gastroenterologist carefully feeds the endoscope down the esophagus, into the stomach and duodenum, and then into the small intestine. Types of enteroscopy procedures may include

  - push enteroscopy, which uses a long endoscope to examine the upper portion of the small intestine

  - single- or double-balloon enteroscopy, which use balloons to help move the endoscope through the entire small intestine

  - spiral enteroscopy, which uses a tube attached to an enteroscope that is rotated and acts as a cork screw to move the instrument into the small intestine

- **Capsule endoscopy.** Although this procedure can examine the entire digestive tract, it is used mostly to examine the small intestine. The patient swallows a capsule containing a tiny camera. As the capsule passes through the GI tract, the camera will transmit and record images to a small receiver device worn by the patient. When the recording is done, the images stored in the receiver are downloaded to a video monitor and reviewed by a gastroenterologist.

Colonoscopy and Flexible Sigmoidoscopy

- **Colonoscopy.** Colonoscopy is a procedure that uses a long, flexible, narrow tube with a light and tiny camera on one end, called a colonoscope, to look inside the rectum and entire colon. Colonoscopy can show irritated and swollen tissue, ulcers, and polyps. A gastroenterologist performs this procedure at a hospital or an outpatient center. In most cases, light anesthesia and pain medication help patients relax for the test. Health care providers will monitor patients' vital signs and try to make patients as comfortable as possible.

A health care provider places an IV needle in a vein in the arm to give the patient a sedative or anesthesia. For the test, the patient will lie on a table while the gastroenterologist inserts a colonoscope into the anus and slowly guides it through the rectum and into the colon. The scope inflates the large intestine with air to give the gastroenterologist a better view. The camera sends a video image of the intestinal lining to a video monitor, allowing the gastroenterologist to carefully examine the intestinal tissues. The gastroenterologist may move the patient several times and adjust the scope for better viewing. Once the scope has reached the opening to the small intestine, the gastroenterologist slowly withdraws it and examines the lining of the large intestine again. The gastroenterologist can see and treat any bleeding in the lower GI tract during a colonoscopy.

- **Flexible sigmoidoscopy.** Flexible sigmoidoscopy is a test that uses a flexible, narrow tube with a light and tiny camera on one end, called a sigmoidoscope, to look inside the rectum and the lower, or sigmoid, colon. A gastroenterologist performs a flexible sigmoidoscopy at a health care provider's office, a hospital, or an outpatient center. The patient usually does not need anesthesia. For the test, the patient will lie on a table while the gastroenterologist inserts a sigmoidoscope into the anus and slowly guides it through the rectum and into the sigmoid colon. The scope inflates the large intestine with air to give the gastroenterologist a better view. The camera sends video images of the intestinal lining to a video monitor, allowing the gastroenterologist to carefully examine the tissues lining the sigmoid colon and rectum. The gastroenterologist can see and treat any bleeding in the sigmoid colon and rectum during a flexible sigmoidoscopy.

Imaging Tests

To help find the cause of digestive tract bleeding, a health care provider may order one or more of the following imaging tests. An X-ray technician performs these tests in an outpatient center or a hospital, and a radiologist—a doctor who specializes in medical imaging—interprets the images. Patients do not need anesthesia.

- **Abdominal computerized tomography (CT) scan.** An abdominal CT scan uses a combination of X-rays and computer technology to create images. For a CT scan, a health care provider may give the patient a solution to drink and an injection of a special dye, called contrast medium. CT scans require the patient to lie on a table that slides into a tunnel-shaped device where the technician takes X-rays. Abdominal CT scans can help find the cause of digestive tract bleeding.

- **Lower GI series.** A lower GI series is an X-ray exam that a health care provider uses to look at the large intestine. The health care provider may provide written bowel prep instructions to follow at home before the test. The health care provider may ask the patient to follow a clear liquid diet for 1 to 3 days before the procedure. A patient may need to use a laxative or an enema before the test. A laxative is medication that loosens stool and increases bowel movements. An enema involves flushing water or laxative into the rectum using a special squirt bottle.

For the test, the patient will lie on a table while the radiologist inserts a flexible tube into the patient's anus. The X-ray technician will fill the large intestine with barium, a chalky liquid, making the signs of underlying problems show up more clearly on X-rays. The test can show problems with the large intestine that are causing the bleeding.

Barium liquid in the GI tract causes white or light-colored stools for several days or longer. Enemas and repeated bowel movements may cause anal soreness. A health care provider will provide specific instructions about eating and drinking after the test.

- **Upper GI series.** This test is an X-ray exam that provides a look at the shape of the upper GI tract to help determine the cause of digestive tract bleeding. A patient should not eat or drink before the procedure, as directed by the health care provider. Patients should ask their health care provider about how to prepare for an upper GI series.

During the procedure, the patient will stand or sit in front of an X-ray machine and drink barium. Barium coats the esophagus, stomach, and small intestine so the radiologist and a gastroenterologist can see the organs' shapes more clearly on X-rays. A patient may experience bloating and nausea for a short time after the test. For several days afterward, barium liquid in the GI tract causes white or light-colored stools. A health care provider will give the patient specific instructions about eating and drinking after the test.

Other Tests

A health care provider also may order one or more of the following tests to determine the cause of digestive tract bleeding:

- **Angiogram.** An angiogram is a special kind of X-ray in which an interventional radiologist—a specially trained radiologist— threads a thin, flexible tube called a catheter through the large arteries, often from the groin, to the artery of interest. The radiologist injects contrast medium through the catheter so the artery and site of bleeding show up more clearly on the X-ray. During the procedure, the interventional radiologist can inject medications or other materials to stop some types of bleeding. The interventional radiologist performs the procedure and interprets the images in a hospital or an outpatient center. A patient does not need anesthesia, though a light sedative may help reduce a patient's anxiety during the procedure. This test can help diagnose the cause of digestive tract bleeding.

- **Exploratory procedures.** When a patient has acute bleeding that cannot be controlled and none of the other tests helps the health care provider diagnose the source of the bleeding, a surgeon may perform one of two operations called an exploratory laparotomy or laparoscopy.

- During a laparotomy, a surgeon will make a cut, or incision, in the abdomen and explore the abdomen to find the cause of the bleeding. During the operation, the surgeon can treat the problems that cause the bleeding. The patient receives general anesthesia.

- During a laparoscopy, a surgeon makes several small incisions in the abdomen and inserts special tools and a camera to try to locate and treat the source of the bleeding. The patient will receive general anesthesia.

- **Radionuclides scan.** A radionuclides scan can help find the cause of digestive tract bleeding. A specially trained technician performs this scan in an outpatient center or a hospital. The technician takes a sample of the patient's blood, mixes it with radioactive material and injects it back into the patient's body to highlight the area in the body that is bleeding. The dose of radioactive chemicals is small, so the chance of causing damage to cells is low. A special camera takes pictures that highlight the radioactive material. The patient does not need anesthesia.

How is bleeding in the digestive tract treated?

Treatment depends on the cause or location of the bleeding. During a laparotomy, a colonoscopy, or an endoscopy, a gastroenterologist can stop the bleeding by inserting tools through the endoscope or colonoscope to

- inject medications into the bleeding site

- treat the bleeding site and surrounding tissue with a heat probe, an electric current, or a laser

- close affected blood vessels with a band or clip

An interventional radiologist can use an angiogram to inject medications or other materials into blood vessels to stop some types of bleeding. When infections or ulcers cause the bleeding, health care providers prescribe medications to treat the problem. When a person has severe acute bleeding or bleeding that does not stop, a surgeon may need to perform a laparoscopy or laparotomy to stop the bleeding.

How can bleeding in the digestive tract be prevented?

Health care providers can prevent bleeding in the digestive tract by treating the conditions that cause the bleeding. People can prevent some of the causes of digestive tract bleeding by

- limiting the amount of Nonsteroidal anti-inflammatory drugs (NSAIDs) they take or by talking with a health care provider about other medication options

- following a health care provider's recommendations for treatment of GER

Eating, Diet, and Nutrition

People can prevent digestive tract bleeding by avoiding foods and triggers, such as alcoholic drinks and smoking, that can increase stomach acids and lead to ulcers. People who have a history of diverticular disease, anal fissures, and hemorrhoids should follow the diet their health care provider recommends to help prevent repeat bleeding.

Section 2.2

Gas in the Digestive Tract

Text in this section is excerpted from "Gas in the Digestive Tract," National Institute of Diabetes and Digestive and Kidney Diseases (NIDDK), November 2012.

What is gas?

Gas is air in the digestive tract—the large, muscular tube that extends from the mouth to the anus, where the movement of muscles, along with the release of hormones and enzymes, allows for the digestion of food. Gas leaves the body when people burp through the mouth or pass gas through the anus.

Gas is primarily composed of carbon dioxide, oxygen, nitrogen, hydrogen, and sometimes methane. Flatus, gas passed through the anus, may also contain small amounts of gasses that contain sulfur. Flatus that contains more sulfur gasses has more odor.

Everyone has gas. However, many people think they burp or pass gas too often and that they have too much gas. Having too much gas is rare.

What causes gas?

Gas in the digestive tract is usually caused by swallowing air and by the breakdown of certain foods in the large intestine by bacteria.

Everyone swallows a small amount of air when eating and drinking. The amount of air swallowed increases when people

- eat or drink too fast
- smoke

- chew gum

- suck on hard candy

- drink carbonated or "fizzy" drinks

- wear loose-fitting dentures

Burping allows some gas to leave the stomach. The remaining gas moves into the small intestine, where it is partially absorbed. A small amount travels into the large intestine for release through the anus.

The stomach and small intestine do not fully digest some carbohydrates—sugars, starches, and fiber found in many foods. This undigested food passes through the small intestine to the large intestine. Once there, undigested carbohydrates are broken down by bacteria in the large intestine, which release hydrogen and carbon dioxide in the process. Other types of bacteria in the large intestine take in hydrogen gas and create methane gas or hydrogen sulfide, the most common sulfur gas in flatus.

Studies have detected methane in the breath of 30 to 62 percent of healthy adults. A larger percentage of adults may produce methane in the intestines, but the levels may be too low to be detected. Research suggests that people with conditions that cause constipation are more likely to produce detectable amounts of methane. More research is needed to find out the reasons for differences in methane production and to explore the relationship between methane and other health problems.

Some of the gas produced in the intestines is absorbed by the bloodstream and carried to the lungs, where it is released in the breath.

Normally, few bacteria live in the small intestine. Small intestinal bacterial overgrowth is an increase in the number of bacteria or a change in the type of bacteria in the small intestine. These bacteria can produce excess gas and may also cause diarrhea and weight loss. Small intestinal bacterial overgrowth is usually related to diseases or disorders that damage the digestive system or affect how it works, such as Crohn's disease—an inflammatory bowel disease that causes inflammation, or swelling, and irritation of any part of the gastrointestinal (GI) tract—or diabetes.

Which foods cause gas?

Most foods that contain carbohydrates can cause gas. In contrast, fats and proteins cause little gas. Foods that produce gas in one person may not cause gas in someone else, depending on how well individuals digest carbohydrates and the type of bacteria present in the intestines.

Some foods that may cause gas include,

- beans
- vegetables such as broccoli, cauliflower, cabbage, brussels sprouts, onions, mushrooms, artichokes, and asparagus
- fruits such as pears, apples, and peaches
- whole grains such as whole wheat and bran
- sodas; fruit drinks, especially apple juice and pear juice; and other drinks that contain high-fructose corn syrup, a sweetener made from corn
- milk and milk products such as cheese, ice cream, and yogurt
- packaged foods—such as bread, cereal, and salad dressing—that contain small amounts of lactose, a sugar found in milk and foods made with milk
- sugar-free candies and gums that contain sugar alcohols such as sorbitol, mannitol, and xylitol

What are the symptoms of gas?

The most common symptoms of gas are burping, passing gas, bloating, and abdominal pain or discomfort. However, not everyone experiences these symptoms.

Burping. Burping, or belching, once in a while, especially during and after meals, is normal. However, people who burp frequently may be swallowing too much air and releasing it before the air enters the stomach.

Some people who burp frequently may have an upper GI disorder, such as gastroesophageal reflux disease—a chronic condition in which stomach contents flow back up into the esophagus. People may believe that swallowing air and releasing it will relieve the discomfort, and they may intentionally or unintentionally develop a habit of burping to relieve discomfort.

Passing gas. Passing gas around 13 to 21 times a day is normal. Flatulence is excessive gas in the stomach or intestine that can cause bloating and flatus. Flatulence may be the result of problems digesting certain carbohydrates.

Bloating. Bloating is a feeling of fullness and swelling in the abdomen, the area between the chest and hips. Problems digesting carbohydrates may cause increased gas and bloating. However, bloating is not always caused by too much gas. Bloating may result from diseases that affect how gas moves through the intestines, such as rapid gastric emptying, or from diseases that cause intestinal obstruction, such as colon cancer. People who have had many operations, internal hernias, or bands of internal scar tissue called adhesions may experience bloating.

Disorders such as irritable bowel syndrome (IBS) can affect how gas moves through the intestines or increase pain sensitivity in the intestines. IBS is a functional GI disorder, meaning that the symptoms are caused by changes in how the digestive tract works. The most common symptoms of IBS are abdominal pain or discomfort, often reported as cramping, along with diarrhea, constipation, or both. IBS may give a sensation of bloating because of increased sensitivity to normal amounts of gas.

Eating a lot of fatty food can delay stomach emptying and cause bloating and discomfort, but not necessarily too much gas.

Abdominal pain and discomfort. People may feel abdominal pain or discomfort when gas does not move through the intestines normally. People with IBS may be more sensitive to gas and feel pain when gas is present in the intestines.

How is the cause of gas found?

People can try to find the cause of gas on their own by keeping a diary of what they eat and drink and how often they burp, pass gas, or have other symptoms. A diary may help identify specific foods that cause gas.

A health care provider should be consulted if,

- symptoms of gas are bothersome

- symptoms change suddenly

- new symptoms occur, especially in people older than age 40

- gas is accompanied by other symptoms, such as constipation, diarrhea, or weight loss

The health care provider will ask about dietary habits and symptoms and may ask a person to keep a food diary. Careful review of diet and the amount of burping or gas passed may help relate specific foods to symptoms and determine the severity of the problem. Recording gas symptoms can help determine whether the problem is too much gas in the intestines or increased sensitivity to normal amounts of gas.

If milk or milk products are causing gas, the health care provider may perform blood or breath tests to check for lactose intolerance, the inability or insufficient ability to digest lactose. Lactose intolerance is caused by a deficiency of the enzyme lactase, which is needed to digest lactose. The health care provider may suggest avoiding milk products for a short time to see if symptoms improve.

The health care provider may perform a physical exam and order other types of diagnostic tests, depending on a person's symptoms. These tests can rule out serious health problems that may cause gas or symptoms similar to those of gas.

How is gas treated?

Gas can be treated by reducing swallowed air, making dietary changes, or taking over-the-counter or prescription medications. People who think they have too much gas can try to treat gas on their own before seeing a health care provider. Health care providers can provide advice about reducing gas and prescribe medications that may help.

Reducing swallowed air. Swallowing less air may help reduce gas, especially for people who burp frequently. A health care provider may suggest eating more slowly, avoiding gum and hard candies, or checking with a dentist to make sure dentures fit correctly.

Making dietary changes. People may be able to reduce gas by eating less of the foods that cause gas. However, many healthy foods may cause gas, such as fruits and vegetables, whole grains, and milk products. The amount of gas caused by certain foods varies from person to person. Effective dietary changes depend on learning through trial and error which foods cause a person to have gas and how much of the offending foods one can handle.

While fat does not cause gas, limiting high-fat foods can help reduce bloating and discomfort. Less fat in the diet helps the stomach empty faster, allowing gases to move more quickly into the small intestine.

Taking over-the-counter medications. Some over-the-counter medications can help reduce gas or the symptoms associated with gas:

- Alpha-galactosidase (Beano), an over-the-counter digestive aid, contains the sugar-digesting enzyme that the body lacks to digest the sugar in beans and many vegetables. The enzyme comes in liquid and tablet form. Five drops are added per serving or one tablet is swallowed just before eating to break down the gas-producing sugars. Beano has no effect on gas caused by lactose or fiber.

- Simethicone (Gas-X, Mylanta Gas) can relieve bloating and abdominal pain or discomfort caused by gas.

- Lactase tablets or drops can help people with lactose intolerance digest milk and milk products to reduce gas. Lactase tablets are taken just before eating foods that contain lactose; lactase drops can be added to liquid milk products. Lactose-free and lactose-reduced milk and milk products are available at most grocery stores.

Taking prescription medications. Health care providers may prescribe medications to help reduce symptoms, especially for people with small intestinal bacterial overgrowth or IBS.

Eating, Diet, and Nutrition

People's eating habits and diet affect the amount of gas they have. For example, eating and drinking too fast may increase the amount of air swallowed, and foods that contain carbohydrates may cause some people to have more gas.

Tracking eating habits and symptoms can help identify the foods that cause more gas. Avoiding or eating less of these foods may help reduce gas symptoms.

Section 2.3

Abdominal Pain

Commonly known as stomach pain, tummy ache, belly ache, or cramps, abdominal pain refers to a minor or major ache or discomfort in the stomach area (from below the chest to the pelvic area). It is quite common, and most adults have experienced abdominal pain at some point in their lives. However, abdominal pain is also among the most misdiagnosed conditions in emergency rooms. Stomach discomfort encompasses a wide variety of symptoms that can indicate more than one condition and thus can be misleading. For instance, a severe pain or feeling of bloating in the belly may have a cause that is relatively harmless, such as indigestion or menstrual cramping. On the other hand, a minor ache may disguise a serious condition, such as appendicitis. Therefore, it is important to distinguish between the different kinds of abdominal pain and seek medical care when required.

Types of Abdominal Pain

There are several different types of abdominal pain, each of which may indicate a different set of possible medical conditions.

- Sharp, local pain

  This type of pain is probably the most serious and may require immediate medical attention. It occurs as an intense ache in a particular part of the stomach and may result from inflammation or trauma to an internal organ. Among the common conditions that cause sharp, localized pain are appendicitis, pancreatitis, diverticulitis, hernia, and colon cancer.

- Dull ache

  This type of pain is common and usually felt over a large part of the belly. The likely causes include indigestion, gas, or a stomach virus.

- Cramping

  This type of pain is usually a result of gas in the intestinal tract and is not generally worrisome unless it persists for a few days or is accompanied by diarrhea, vomiting, or fever. In this case, it may be food poisoning or gastroenteritis—intestinal inflammation caused by a virus, bacterium, or parasite.

- Pain that comes and goes

  This kind of pain mostly occurs in the upper abdomen. It is usually intense and may start and stop suddenly. Possible causes include kidney stones or gallstones, which require immediate medical attention.

Causes of Abdominal Pain

A host of conditions can result in abdominal pain. Many of the possible causes are simple problems like overeating, constipation, gas, or nerves, and the symptoms may disappear by themselves over a short period of time. Sometimes, however, abdominal pain may signal a critical condition that warrants urgent medical attention. Some of the more serious causes of abdominal pain may include food allergies, appendicitis, pancreatitis, diverticulitis, irritable bowel syndrome, kidney stones, gallstones, ulcers, colon cancer, or pregnancy-related complications. Abdominal pain occasionally may be related to problems outside the abdomen. Stomach aches can be a symptom of heart attack, pneumonia, or problems in the pelvis or groin.

It can be difficult to determine whether abdominal pain is symptomatic of a more serious medical condition. A person who experiences any of the following conditions should contact their medical practitioner:

- Your belly feels rigid and is overly sensitive to touch. You also have a fever and are vomiting blood, passing dark, tarry stools, or have bloody diarrhea. These symptoms could be a sign of appendicitis, diverticulitis, or bowel obstruction.

- You have sudden, intense pain in the back that slowly descends to the groin. It could be a sign of a kidney- or bladder-related complication.

- You are pregnant and have abdominal pain along with bleeding or vaginal discharge. You may be having a miscarriage or a tubal pregnancy.

- You have pain in the lower right abdomen and are passing stools tinged with blood or mucus. It may be due to inflammation of the colon or large intestine.

- Your pain starts in the upper abdomen and moves around to the back, or the pain is more pronounced after a fatty meal. These symptoms may indicate gallstones.

- You have mild pain in the lower abdomen and discomfort or a burning sensation while urinating. These could be signs of a urinary tract infection called cystitis.

- You are a woman and have a constant, dull ache in the lower abdomen along with vaginal discharge. These symptoms may indicate Pelvic Inflammatory Disease, an infection surrounding the ovaries, uterus, and fallopian tubes.

- You have diarrhea along with fever, nausea, or vomiting that lasts more than two days. It may be a case of gastroenteritis. Although most people recover without treatment, prolonged gastroenteritis can lead to dehydration, especially in children.

Diagnosis of Abdominal Pain

To diagnose a patient suffering from abdominal pain, a medical practitioner will take a medical history, perform a physical examination, and conduct investigative tests based on presenting symptoms in order to determine the underlying cause.

When taking the patient's history, the physician will inquire about the nature of the pain (sharp or dull, localized or general), its location, timing (before or after a meal, or related to a particular activity), and duration, past occurrences and symptoms, and factors that aggravate or alleviate the pain. It is important that patients provide accurate information in their case histories.

During the physical examination, the physician will feel the patient's abdomen for signs of tenderness or rigidity. The pelvis and rectum may also be examined for blood or other abnormalities. Next, the physician may order diagnostic tests to pinpoint or rule out certain conditions. Some of the tests that may be conducted include ultrasound, X-ray, CT scan, endoscopy, colonoscopy, blood tests, urine or stool examination, electrocardiogram, or barium enema.

Special Cases of Abdominal Pain

The diagnosis and treatment of abdominal pain may vary depending on the patient's age, gender, and underlying health conditions. Some circumstances that can affect the causes and symptoms of abdominal pain include:

- During pregnancy

  Most pregnant women feel some kind of abdominal pain as a consequence of the physiological and hormonal changes that occur during pregnancy. Although it is usually mild and harmless, severe or prolonged pain—or pain accompanied by bleeding—could be an indication of a life-threatening complication such as preeclampsia, miscarriage, or ectopic pregnancy. Immediate medical attention is required in such cases.

- In infants

  Abdominal pain with gas may be a result of colic. Other signs of colic include fussiness, inconsolable crying, and pulling the legs up to the abdomen. Though distressful, colic is a relatively harmless condition that goes away as the child gets older. It is important to consult a pediatrician, however, to rule out any other causes of abdominal pain.

- In children

  Stomach aches are quite common among young children and are usually a result of minor ailments like constipation, gas, or stomach flu. In these cases, the symptoms generally go away on their own within a few days. However, if the pain worsens with time, or if the child also has fever and nausea, it could be a sign of something more serious that warrants medical attention.

- In teenage girls

  Sharp pain or dull aches in the lower abdomen or lower back may be related to menstrual cramps.

- In cancer patients

  People undergoing chemotherapy for cancer treatment may often feel cramping or dull aches in the abdomen because chemotherapy affects the working of the intestines. It can either slow down or speed up the passage of stool through the bowel, thereby causing constipation or diarrhea and resulting in cramping. Chemotherapy also affects digestion and can cause gas. Some cancer medications can also cause ulcers or other abdominal complications. Cancer patients should seek medical attention if the pain is severe and prolonged, and accompanied by other symptoms like fever, vomiting, or sudden swelling of the abdomen.

- Peritonitis

  Peritonitis is a serious condition involving inflammation or infection of the tissue lining the inner wall of the abdominal cavity. It can be caused by the perforation or rupture of an abdominal organ or the leakage of bodily fluids like blood, urine, or gastric juices into the peritoneal cavity. Left untreated, peritonitis can cause potentially fatal damage to the liver, kidneys, and other organs. Symptoms of peritonitis include constant, severe abdominal pain that is aggravated by a slight touch or impact.

Prevention and Treatment

To prevent indigestion and abdominal pain, it is important to drink plenty of water and limit the consumption of carbonated beverages. Since dietary fiber aids in digestion and helps prevent constipation, a diet rich in whole grains, fruits, and vegetables can also help people avoid stomach aches. Other tips include eating small meals at regular intervals rather than overeating at a single meal, and limiting the intake of fatty, greasy, and high-sodium foods.

There are a variety of home remedies and over-the-counter medications available to provide relief from abdominal pain caused by indigestion or constipation. Additional treatments include lying down and taking deep breaths, placing a heating pad or hot water bottle on the belly, and eating mild foods like bananas, rice, applesauce, and toast. It is important to avoid taking aspirin or other anti-inflammatory drugs, unless prescribed by a doctor, as they may irritate the stomach and worsen symptoms.

References

1. American Academy of Family Physicians. "Abdominal Pain, Short-term." FamilyDoctor.org, 1996.

2. U.S. National Library of Medicine. "Abdominal Pain." MedlinePlus, 2014.

Section 2.4

Diarrhea

Text in this section is excerpted from "What I Need to Know about Diarrhea," National Institute of Diabetes and Digestive and Kidney Diseases (NIDDK), November 25, 2013.

What is diarrhea?

Diarrhea is frequent, loose, and watery bowel movements. Bowel movements, also called stools, are body wastes passed through the rectum and anus. Stools contain what is left after your digestive system absorbs nutrients and fluids from what you eat and drink. If your body does not absorb the fluids, or if your digestive system produces extra fluids, stools will be loose and watery. Loose stools contain more water, salts, and minerals and weigh more than solid stools.

Diarrhea that lasts a short time is called acute diarrhea. Acute diarrhea is a common problem and usually lasts only 1 or 2 days, but it may last longer. Diarrhea that lasts for at least 4 weeks is called chronic diarrhea. Chronic diarrhea symptoms may be continual or they may come and go.

What causes diarrhea?

Causes of diarrhea include

- bacteria from contaminated food or water

- viruses that cause illnesses such as the flu

- parasites, which are tiny organisms found in contaminated food or water

- medicines such as antibiotics

- problems digesting certain foods

- diseases that affect the stomach, small intestine, or colon, such as Crohn's disease

- problems with how the colon functions, caused by disorders such as irritable bowel syndrome

Sometimes no cause can be found. As long as diarrhea goes away within 1 to 2 days, finding the cause is not usually necessary.

What other symptoms might I have with diarrhea?

In addition to passing frequent, loose stools, other possible symptoms include

- cramps or pain in the abdomen—the area between the chest and hips
- an urgent need to use the bathroom
- loss of bowel control

You may feel sick to your stomach or become dehydrated. If a virus or bacteria is the cause of your diarrhea, you may have fever and chills and bloody stools.

Dehydration

Being dehydrated means your body does not have enough fluid to work properly. Every time you have a bowel movement, you lose fluids. Diarrhea causes you to lose even more fluids. You also lose salts and minerals such as sodium, chloride, and potassium. These salts and minerals affect the amount of water that stays in your body.

Dehydration can be serious, especially for children, older adults, and people with weakened immune systems.

Signs of dehydration in adults are

- being thirsty
- urinating less often than usual
- having dark-colored urine
- having dry skin
- feeling tired
- feeling dizzy or fainting

Signs of dehydration in babies and young children are

- having a dry mouth and tongue
- crying without tears

- having no wet diapers for 3 hours or more
- having sunken eyes, cheeks, or soft spot in the skull
- having a high fever
- being more cranky or drowsy than usual

Also, when people are dehydrated, their skin does not flatten back to normal right away after being gently pinched and released.

When should adults with diarrhea see a health care provider?

You should see a health care provider if you have any of the following symptoms:

- signs of dehydration
- diarrhea for more than 2 days
- severe pain in your abdomen or rectum
- a fever of 102 degrees or higher
- stools containing blood or pus
- stools that are black and tarry

Diarrhea often goes away by itself, but it may be a sign of a more serious problem.

When should children with diarrhea see a health care provider?

Take your child to a health care provider right away if your child has any of the following symptoms:

- signs of dehydration
- diarrhea for more than 24 hours
- a fever of 102 degrees or higher
- stools containing blood or pus
- stools that are black and tarry

Children with diarrhea become dehydrated much more easily than adults. Getting treatment quickly is most important if your baby is 6 months old or younger.

How is the cause of diarrhea diagnosed?

To find the cause of diarrhea, the health care provider may

- perform a physical exam
- ask about any medicines you are taking
- test your stool or blood to look for bacteria, parasites, or other signs of disease or infection
- ask you to stop eating certain foods to see whether your diarrhea goes away

If you have chronic diarrhea, your health care provider may perform other tests to look for signs of disease.

How is diarrhea treated?

Diarrhea is treated by replacing lost fluids, salts, and minerals to prevent dehydration.

Taking medicine to stop diarrhea can be helpful in some cases. Medicines you can buy over the counter without a prescription include loperamide (Imodium) and bismuth subsalicylate (Pepto-Bismol, Kaopectate). Stop taking these medicines if symptoms get worse or if the diarrhea lasts more than 2 days. If you have bloody diarrhea, you should not use over-the-counter diarrhea medicines. These medicines may make diarrhea last longer. The health care provider will usually prescribe antibiotics instead.

Over-the-counter medicines for diarrhea may be dangerous for babies and children. Talk with the health care provider before giving your child these medicines.

Eating, Diet, and Nutrition

To prevent dehydration when you have diarrhea, it is important to drink plenty of water, but you also need to drink fluids that contain sodium, chloride, and potassium.

- Adults should drink water, fruit juices, sports drinks, sodas without caffeine, and salty broths.
- Children should drink oral rehydration solutions—special drinks that contain salts and minerals to prevent dehydration. These drinks include Pedialyte, Naturalyte, Infalyte, and CeraLyte. These drinks are sold in most grocery stores and drugstores.

If you have diarrhea, eat soft, bland foods such as

- bananas
- plain rice
- boiled potatoes
- toast
- crackers
- cooked carrots
- baked chicken without the skin or fat

Once the diarrhea stops, you can go back to eating your regular foods.

If a certain food is the cause of diarrhea, try to avoid it.

While you wait for the diarrhea to end, avoid foods that can make it worse:

- drinks with caffeine, such as coffee and cola
- high-fat or greasy foods, such as fried foods
- foods with a lot of fiber, such as citrus fruits
- sweet foods, such as cakes and cookies

During or after an episode of diarrhea, some people have trouble digesting lactose, the sugar in milk and milk products. However, you may be able to digest yogurt. Eating yogurt with active, live bacterial cultures may even help you feel better faster.

When babies have diarrhea, continue breastfeeding or formula feeding as usual.

After you have had diarrhea caused by a virus, problems digesting lactose may last up to 4 to 6 weeks. You may have diarrhea for a short time after you eat or drink milk or milk products.

Can diarrhea be prevented?

Two types of diarrhea can be prevented—rotavirus diarrhea and traveler's diarrhea.

Rotavirus Diarrhea

Two vaccines, RotaTeq and Rotarix, protect against rotavirus—a common virus that causes diarrhea in babies and children. RotaTeq is given to babies in three doses at 2, 4, and 6 months of age. Rotarix is given in two doses. The first dose is given when the baby is 6 weeks old, and the second is given at least 4 weeks later but before the baby is 24 weeks old. To learn more about rotavirus vaccines, talk with your child's health care provider.

RotaTeq and Rotarix only prevent diarrhea caused by rotavirus. Children who have been vaccinated may still get diarrhea from another cause.

Traveler's Diarrhea

People may develop traveler's diarrhea while visiting developing areas of the world such as Latin America, Africa, and southern Asia. Traveler's diarrhea is caused by eating food or drinking water that contains harmful bacteria, viruses, or parasites.

You can prevent traveler's diarrhea by being careful:

- Do not drink tap water, use tap water to brush your teeth, or use ice cubes made from tap water.

- Do not eat or drink unpasteurized milk or milk products.

- Do not eat raw fruits and vegetables unless they can be peeled and you peel them yourself.

- Do not eat raw or rare meat and fish.

- Do not eat meat or shellfish that is not hot when served to you.

- Do not eat food sold by street vendors.

You can drink bottled water, carbonated soft drinks, and hot drinks such as coffee and tea.

Before traveling outside the United States, talk with your health care provider. Your health care provider may suggest taking medicine with you. In some cases, taking antibiotics before traveling can help prevent traveler's diarrhea. And early treatment with antibiotics can shorten an episode of traveler's diarrhea.

Section 2.5

Constipation

Text in this section is excerpted from "Constipation," National
Institute of Diabetes and Digestive and Kidney Diseases (NIDDK),
November 13, 2014.

Definition and Facts for Constipation

What is Constipation?

Constipation is a condition in which you typically have:

- fewer than three bowel movements a week

- bowel movements with stools that are hard, dry, and small,
  making them painful or difficult to pass

Some people think they are constipated if they don't have a bowel
movement every day. However, people can have different bowel movement patterns. Some people may have three bowel movements a day.
Other people may only have three bowel movements a week.

Constipation most often lasts for only a short time and is not dangerous. You can take steps to prevent or relieve constipation.

How common is constipation?

Constipation is one of the most common gastrointestinal (GI) problems, affecting about 42 million people in the United States.

Who is more likely to become constipated?

Constipation is common among all ages and populations in the
United States, yet certain people are more likely to become constipated, including

- women, especially during pregnancy or after giving birth

- older adults

- non-Caucasians

- people with lower incomes
- people who just had surgery
- people taking medicines to treat depression or to relieve pain from things such as a broken bone, a pulled tooth, or back pain

What are the complications of constipation?

Chronic, or long-lasting, constipation can lead to health problems such as hemorrhoids, anal fissures, rectal prolapse, or fecal impaction.

Hemorrhoids

Hemorrhoids are swollen and inflamed veins around your anus or in your lower rectum. You can develop hemorrhoids if you strain to have a bowel movement. If you have hemorrhoids, you may have bleeding in your rectum. You have bleeding in the rectum when you see bright red blood in your stool, on toilet paper, or in the toilet after a bowel movement.

Anal fissures

Anal fissures are small tears in your anus that may cause itching, pain, or bleeding.

Rectal prolapse

Rectal prolapse happens when your rectum slips so that it sticks out of your anus. Rectal prolapse can happen if you strain during bowel movements, among other reasons. Rectal prolapse may cause mucus to leak from your anus. Rectal prolapse is most common in older adults with a history of constipation, and is also more common in women than men, especially postmenopausal women.

Fecal impaction

Fecal impaction happens when hard stool packs your intestine and rectum so tightly that the normal pushing action of your colon is not enough to push the stool out. Fecal impaction occurs most often in children and older adults.

Symptoms and Causes of Constipation

What are the symptoms of constipation?

The most common symptoms of constipation are

- fewer-than-normal bowel movements
- stool that is difficult or painful to pass
- pain or bloating in your abdomen

What causes constipation?

Constipation can happen for many reasons, and constipation may have more than one cause at a time. Among the most common causes of constipation are

- slow movement of stool through the colon

- delayed emptying of the colon from pelvic disorders, especially in women

- a form of irritable bowel syndrome (IBS) that has symptoms of both IBS and constipation, also called IBS with constipation, or IBS-C.

Constipation may become worse because of the following factors:

Diets low in fiber

Fiber helps stool stay soft. Drink liquids to help fiber keep stool soft. Older adults commonly have constipation because of limited dietary fiber, lack of physical activity, and medications.

Lack of physical activity

If you don't exercise or move around regularly you may get constipated. For example, people may be less active because they

- have other health problems

- sit all day and don't exercise regularly

- have to stay in bed most of the time because of an illness or accident

Medicines

Some medicines that doctors prescribe to treat other health problems can cause constipation. Medicines that can cause constipation include

- antacids—used to neutralize stomach acid—that contain aluminum and calcium

- anticholinergics—used to treat muscle spasms in the intestines

- anticonvulsants—used to decrease abnormal electrical activity in the brain to prevent seizures

- antispasmodics—used to reduce muscle spasms in the intestines

- calcium channel blockers—used to treat high blood pressure and heart disease

- diuretics—used to help the kidneys remove fluid from the blood
- iron supplements—used to build up higher iron levels in the blood
- medicines used to treat Parkinson's disease
- narcotics—used to treat severe pain
- some medicines used to treat depression

Life changes or daily routine changes

Constipation can happen when your life or daily routine changes. For example, your bowel movements can change

- when you travel
- if you become pregnant
- as you get older

Ignoring the urge to have a bowel movement

If you ignore the urge to have a bowel movement, over time, you may stop feeling the need to have one. You may delay having a bowel movement because you do not want to use toilets outside of your home, do not have access to a toilet, or may feel you are too busy. This habit can lead to constipation.

Certain health problems

Some health problems can make stool move more slowly through your colon, rectum, or anus, causing constipation. These health problems include

- disorders that affect your brain and spine, such as Parkinson's disease
- spinal cord or brain injuries
- diabetes
- hypothyroidism

Gastrointestinal (GI) tract problems

Problems in your GI tract that compress or narrow your colon and rectum can cause constipation. These problems include

- tumors
- inflammation, or swelling, such as diverticulitis or inflammatory bowel disease

Functional GI disorders

Functional GI disorders happen when your GI tract behaves in an abnormal way, yet without evidence of damage due to a disease. For example, IBS is a common functional GI disorder, and many people with IBS can have IBS with constipation.

Treatment for Constipation

How do doctors treat constipation?

Treatment for constipation depends on

- what's causing your constipation
- how bad your constipation is
- how long you've been constipated

Treatment for constipation may include the following:

Changes in eating, diet, and nutrition

Changes in your eating, diet, and nutrition can treat constipation. These changes include

- drinking liquids throughout the day. A health care professional can recommend how much and what kind of liquids you should drink.
- eating more fruits and vegetables.
- eating more fiber.

Exercise and lifestyle changes

Exercising every day may help prevent and relieve constipation.

You can also try to have a bowel movement at the same time each day. Picking a specific time of day may help you have a bowel movement regularly. For example, some people find that trying to have a bowel movement 15 to 45 minutes after breakfast helps them have a bowel movement. Eating helps your colon move stool. Make sure you give yourself enough time to have a bowel movement. You should also use the bathroom as soon as you feel the urge to have a bowel movement.

Over-the-counter medicines

Your doctor may suggest using a laxative for a short time if you're doing all the right things and are still constipated. Your doctor will tell you what type of laxative is best for you. Over-the-counter laxatives come in many forms, including liquid, tablet, capsule, powder, and granules.

If you're taking an over-the-counter or prescription medicine or supplement that can cause constipation, your doctor may suggest you stop taking it or switch to a different one.

Bulk-forming agents. Bulk-forming agents absorb fluid in your intestines, making your stool bulkier. Bulkier stool helps trigger the bowel to contract and push stool out. Be sure to take bulk-forming agents with water or they can cause an obstruction or a blockage in your bowel. They can also cause bloating and pain in your abdomen. Brand names include

- Citrucel
- FiberCon
- Konsyl
- Metamucil
- Serutan

Osmotic agents. Osmotic agents help stool retain fluid. Stools with more fluid increase your number of bowel movements and soften stool. Older adults and people with heart or kidney failure should be careful when taking osmotic agents. They can cause dehydration or a mineral imbalance. Brand names include

- Cephulac
- Fleet Phospho-Soda
- Milk of Magnesia
- Miralax
- Sorbitol

Stool softeners. Stool softeners help mix fluid into stools to soften them. Doctors recommend stool softeners for people who should avoid straining while having a bowel movement. Doctors often recommend stool softeners after surgery or for women after childbirth. Brand names include

- Colace
- Docusate
- Surfak

Lubricants. Lubricants work by coating the surface of stool, which helps the stool hold in fluid and pass more easily. Lubricants are simple, inexpensive laxatives. Doctors may recommend lubricants for people with anorectal blockage. Brand names include

- Fleet
- Zymenol

If these laxatives don't work for you, your doctor may recommend other types of laxatives, including

Stimulants. Stimulant laxatives cause the intestines to contract, which moves stool. You should only use stimulants if your constipation is severe or other treatments have not worked. Brand names include

- Correctol
- Dulcolax
- Purge
- Senokot

People should not use stimulant laxatives containing phenolphthalein. Phenolphthalein may increase your chances of cancer. Most laxatives sold in the United States do not contain phenolphthalein. Make sure to check the ingredients on the medicine's package or bottle.

If you've been taking laxatives for a long time and can't have a bowel movement without taking a laxative, talk with your doctor about how you can slowly stop using them. If you stop taking laxatives, over time, your colon should start moving stool normally.

Prescription medicines

If over-the-counter medicines do not relieve your symptoms, your doctor may prescribe one of the following medicines:

Chloride channel activator. If you have irritable bowel syndrome (IBS) with long-lasting or idiopathic—meaning the cause is not known—constipation, your doctor may prescribe lubiprostone (Amitiza). Lubiprostone is a chloride channel activator available with a prescription. Research has shown lubiprostone to be safe when used for 6 to 12 months. This type of medicine increases fluid in your GI tract, which helps to

- reduce pain or discomfort in your abdomen

- make your stool softer

- reduce your need to strain when having a bowel movement

- increase how often you have bowel movements

Guanylate cyclase-C agonist. If you have IBS with long-lasting or idiopathic constipation, your doctor may prescribe linaclotide (Linzess) to help make your bowel movements regular. Linaclotide is a guanylate cyclase-C agonist that eases pain in your abdomen and speeds up how often you have bowel movements.

Biofeedback

If you have problems with the muscles that control bowel movements, your doctor may recommend biofeedback to retrain your muscles. Biofeedback uses special sensors to measure bodily functions. A video monitor shows the measurements as line graphs, and sounds from the equipment tell you when you're using the correct muscles. By watching the monitor and listening to the sounds, you learn how to change the muscle function. Practicing at home can improve muscle function. You may have to practice for 3 months before you get all the benefit from the training.

Surgery

You may need surgery to treat an anorectal blockage caused by rectal prolapse if other treatments don't work. You may need surgery to remove your colon if your colon muscles don't work correctly. Your doctor can tell you about the benefits and risks of surgery.

How do doctors treat complications of constipation?

Doctors can treat or tell you how to treat complications of constipation. Hemorrhoids, anal fissures, rectal prolapse, and fecal impaction all have different treatments.

Hemorrhoids

You can treat hemorrhoids at home by

- making dietary changes to prevent constipation
- taking warm tub baths
- applying over-the-counter hemorrhoid cream to the area or using suppositories—a medicine you insert into your rectum—before bedtime

Talk with your doctor about hemorrhoids that do not respond to at-home treatments.?

Anal fissures

You can treat anal fissures at home by

- making changes in your diet to prevent constipation
- applying over-the-counter hemorrhoid cream to numb the area or relax your muscles

43

- using stool softeners

- taking warm tub baths

Your doctor may recommend surgery to treat anal fissures that don't heal with at-home treatments.

Rectal prolapse

Your doctor may be able to treat your rectal prolapse in his or her office by manually pushing the rectum back through your anus. If you have a severe or chronic—long-lasting—rectal prolapse, you may need surgery. The surgery will strengthen and tighten your anal sphincter muscle and repair the prolapsed lining. You can help prevent rectal prolapse caused by constipation by not straining during a bowel movement.

Fecal impaction

You can soften a fecal impaction with mineral oil that you take by mouth or through an enema. After softening the impaction, a health care professional may break up and remove part of the hardened stool by inserting one or two gloved, lubricated fingers into your anus.

Section 2.6

Fecal Incontinence

Text in this section is excerpted from "Fecal Incontinence," National Institute of Diabetes and Digestive and Kidney Diseases (NIDDK), November 27, 2013

What is fecal incontinence?

Fecal incontinence, also called a bowel control problem, is the accidental passing of solid or liquid stool or mucus from the rectum. Fecal incontinence includes the inability to hold a bowel movement until reaching a toilet as well as passing stool into one's underwear without being aware of it happening. Stool, also called feces, is solid waste that is passed as a bowel movement and includes undigested food, bacteria, mucus, and dead cells. Mucus is a clear liquid that coats and protects tissues in the digestive system.

Fecal incontinence can be upsetting and embarrassing. Many people with fecal incontinence feel ashamed and try to hide the problem. However, people with fecal incontinence should not be afraid or embarrassed to talk with their health care provider. Fecal incontinence is often caused by a medical problem and treatment is available.

Who gets fecal incontinence?

Nearly 18 million U.S. adults—about one in 12—have fecal incontinence. People of any age can have a bowel control problem, though fecal incontinence is more common in older adults. Fecal incontinence is slightly more common among women. Having any of the following can increase the risk:

- diarrhea, which is passing loose, watery stools three or more times a day

- urgency, or the sensation of having very little time to get to the toilet for a bowel movement

- a disease or injury that damages the nervous system

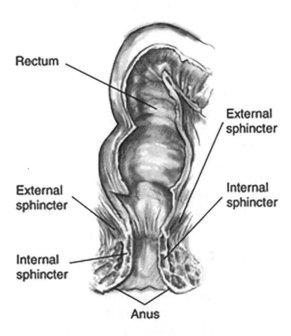

Figure 2.1. *The external and internal anal sphincter muscles*

- poor overall health from multiple chronic, or long lasting, illnesses

- a difficult childbirth with injuries to the pelvic floor—the muscles, ligaments, and tissues that support the uterus, vagina, bladder, and rectum

What causes fecal incontinence?

Fecal incontinence has many causes, including

- diarrhea

- constipation

- muscle damage or weakness

- nerve damage

- loss of stretch in the rectum

- childbirth by vaginal delivery

- hemorrhoids and rectal prolapse

- rectocele

- inactivity

Diarrhea

Diarrhea can cause fecal incontinence. Loose stools fill the rectum quickly and are more difficult to hold than solid stools. Diarrhea increases the chance of not reaching a bathroom in time.

Constipation

Constipation can lead to large, hard stools that stretch the rectum and cause the internal sphincter muscles to relax by reflex. Watery stool builds up behind the hard stool and may leak out around the hard stool, leading to fecal incontinence.

Muscle Damage or Weakness

Injury to one or both of the sphincter muscles can cause fecal incontinence. If these muscles, called the external and internal anal sphincter muscles, are damaged or weakened, they may not be strong enough to keep the anus closed and prevent stool from leaking.

Nerve Damage

The anal sphincter muscles won't open and close properly if the nerves that control them are damaged. Likewise, if the nerves that sense stool in the rectum are damaged, a person may not feel the urge to go to the bathroom. Both types of nerve damage can lead to fecal incontinence.

Loss of Stretch in the Rectum

Normally, the rectum stretches to hold stool until a person has a bowel movement. Rectal surgery, radiation treatment, and inflammatory bowel diseases—chronic disorders that cause irritation and sores on the lining of the digestive system—can cause the rectal walls to become stiff. The rectum then can't stretch as much to hold stool, increasing the risk of fecal incontinence.

Childbirth by Vaginal Delivery

Childbirth sometimes causes injuries to muscles and nerves in the pelvic floor. The risk is greater if forceps are used to help deliver the baby or if an episiotomy—a cut in the vaginal area to prevent the baby's head from tearing the vagina during birth—is performed. Fecal incontinence related to childbirth can appear soon after delivery or many years later.

Hemorrhoids and Rectal Prolapse

External hemorrhoids, which develop under the skin around the anus, can prevent the anal sphincter muscles from closing completely. Rectal prolapse, a condition that causes the rectum to drop down through the anus, can also prevent the anal sphincter muscles from closing well enough to prevent leakage. Small amounts of mucus or liquid stool can then leak through the anus.

Rectocele

Rectocele is a condition that causes the rectum to protrude through the vagina. Rectocele can happen when the thin layer of muscles separating the rectum from the vagina becomes weak. For women with rectocele, straining to have a bowel movement may be less effective because rectocele reduces the amount of downward force through the anus. The result may be retention of stool in the rectum. More research is needed to be sure rectocele increases the risk of fecal incontinence.

Inactivity

People who are inactive, especially those who spend many hours a day sitting or lying down, have an increased risk of retaining a large amount of stool in the rectum. Liquid stool can then leak around the more solid stool. Frail, older adults are most likely to develop constipation-related fecal incontinence for this reason.

How is fecal incontinence diagnosed?

Health care providers diagnose fecal incontinence based on a person's medical history, physical exam, and medical test results. In addition to a general medical history, the health care provider may ask the following questions:

- When did fecal incontinence start?

- How often does fecal incontinence occur?

- How much stool leaks? Does the stool just streak the underwear? Does just a little bit of solid or liquid stool leak out or does complete loss of bowel control occur?

- Does fecal incontinence involve a strong urge to have a bowel movement or does it happen without warning?

- For people with hemorrhoids, do hemorrhoids bulge through the anus? Do the hemorrhoids pull back in by themselves, or do they have to be pushed in with a finger?

- How does fecal incontinence affect daily life?

- Is fecal incontinence worse after eating? Do certain foods seem to make fecal incontinence worse?

- Can passing gas be controlled?

People may want to keep a stool diary for several weeks before their appointment so they can answer these questions. A stool diary is a chart for recording daily bowel movement details.

The person may be referred to a doctor who specializes in problems of the digestive system, such as a gastroenterologist, proctologist, or colorectal surgeon, or a doctor who specializes in problems of the urinary and reproductive systems, such as a urologist or urogynecologist. The specialist will perform a physical exam and may suggest one or more of the following tests:

- anal manometry

- anal ultrasound

- magnetic resonance imaging (MRI)

- defecography

- flexible sigmoidoscopy or colonoscopy

- anal electromyography (EMG)

Keeping a Food Diary

A food diary can help identify foods that cause diarrhea and increase the risk of fecal incontinence. A food diary should list foods eaten, portion size, and when fecal incontinence occurs. After a few days, the diary may show a link between certain foods and fecal incontinence. Eating less of foods linked to fecal incontinence may improve symptoms. A food diary can also be helpful to a health care provider treating a person with fecal incontinence.

Common foods and drinks linked to fecal incontinence include

- dairy products such as milk, cheese, and ice cream

- drinks and foods containing caffeine

- cured or smoked meat such as sausage, ham, and turkey

- spicy foods

- alcoholic beverages

- fruits such as apples, peaches, and pears

- fatty and greasy foods

- sweeteners in diet drinks and sugarless gum and candy, including sorbitol, xylitol, mannitol, and fructose

How is fecal incontinence treated?

Treatment for fecal incontinence may include one or more of the following:

- eating, diet, and nutrition

- medications

- bowel training

- pelvic floor exercises and biofeedback
- surgery
- electrical stimulation

Eating, Diet, and Nutrition

Dietary changes that may improve fecal incontinence include

Eating the right amount of fiber. Fiber can help with diarrhea and constipation. Fiber is found in fruits, vegetables, whole grains, and beans. Fiber supplements sold in a pharmacy or in a health food store are another common source of fiber to treat fecal incontinence. The Academy of Nutrition and Dietetics recommends consuming 20 to 35 grams of fiber a day for adults and "age plus five" grams for children.

Table 2.1. Examples of Foods That Have Fiber

Beans, cereals, and breads	Fiber
½ cup of beans (navy, pinto, kidney, etc.), cooked	6.2–9.6 grams
½ cup of shredded wheat, ready-to-eat cereal	2.7–3.8 grams
? cup of 100% bran, ready-to-eat cereal	9.1 grams
1 small oat bran muffin	3.0 grams
1 whole-wheat English muffin	4.4 grams
Fruits	
1 small apple, with skin	3.6 grams
1 medium pear, with skin	5.5 grams
½ cup of raspberries	4.0 grams
½ cup of stewed prunes	3.8 grams
Vegetables	
½ cup of winter squash, cooked	2.9 grams
1 medium sweet potato, baked in skin	3.8 grams
½ cup of green peas, cooked	3.5–4.4 grams
1 small potato, baked, with skin	3.0 grams
½ cup of mixed vegetables, cooked	4.0 grams
½ cup of broccoli, cooked	2.6–2.8 grams
½ cup of greens (spinach, collards, turnip greens), cooked	2.5–3.5 grams

A 7-year-old child, for example, should get "7 plus five," or 12, grams of fiber a day. American adults consume only 15 grams a day on average.2 Fiber should be added to the diet slowly to avoid bloating.

- **Getting plenty to drink**. Drinking eight 8-ounce glasses of liquid a day may help prevent constipation. Water is a good choice. Drinks with caffeine, alcohol, milk, or carbonation should be avoided if they trigger diarrhea.

Medications

If diarrhea is causing fecal incontinence, medication may help. Health care providers sometimes recommend using bulk laxatives, such as Citrucel and Metamucil, to develop more solid stools that are easier to control. Antidiarrheal medications such as loperamide or diphenoxylate may be recommended to slow down the bowels and help control the problem.

Bowel Training

Developing a regular bowel movement pattern can improve fecal incontinence, especially fecal incontinence due to constipation. Bowel training involves trying to have bowel movements at specific times of the day, such as after every meal. Over time, the body becomes used to a regular bowel movement pattern, thus reducing constipation and related fecal incontinence. Persistence is key to successful bowel training. Achieving a regular bowel control pattern can take weeks to months.

Pelvic Floor Exercises and Biofeedback

Exercises that strengthen the pelvic floor muscles may improve bowel control. Pelvic floor exercises involve squeezing and relaxing pelvic floor muscles 50 to 100 times a day. A health care provider can help with proper technique. Biofeedback therapy may also help a person perform the exercises properly. This therapy also improves a person's awareness of sensations in the rectum, teaching how to coordinate squeezing of the external sphincter muscle with the sensation of rectal filling. Biofeedback training uses special sensors to measure bodily functions. Sensors include pressure or EMG sensors in the anus, pressure sensors in the rectum, and a balloon in the rectum to produce graded sensations of rectal fullness. The measurements are displayed on a video screen as sounds or line graphs. The health care provider uses the information to help the person modify or change abnormal function. The person practices the exercises at home. Success with pelvic floor exercises depends on the cause of fecal incontinence, its severity, and the person's motivation and ability to follow the health care provider's recommendations.

Surgery

Surgery may be an option for fecal incontinence that fails to improve with other treatments or for fecal incontinence caused by pelvic floor or anal sphincter muscle injuries.

- **Sphincteroplasty,** the most common fecal incontinence surgery, reconnects the separated ends of a sphincter muscle torn by childbirth or another injury. Sphincteroplasty is performed at a hospital by a colorectal, gynecological, or general surgeon.

- **Artificial anal sphincter** involves placing an inflatable cuff around the anus and implanting a small pump beneath the skin that the person activates to inflate or deflate the cuff. This surgery is much less common and is performed at a hospital by a specially trained colorectal surgeon.

- **Nonabsorbable bulking agents** can be injected into the wall of the anus to bulk up the tissue around the anus. The bulkier tissues make the opening of the anus narrower so the sphincters are able to close better. The procedure is performed in a health care provider's office; anesthesia is not needed. The person can return to normal physical activities 1 week after the procedure.

- **Bowel diversion** is an operation that reroutes the normal movement of stool out of the body when part of the bowel is removed. The operation diverts the lower part of the small intestine or colon to an opening in the wall of the abdomen—the area between the chest and hips. An external pouch is attached to the opening to collect stool. The procedure is performed by a surgeon in a hospital and anesthesia is used.

Electrical Stimulation

Electrical stimulation, also called sacral nerve stimulation or neuromodulation, involves placing electrodes in the sacral nerves to the anus and rectum and continuously stimulating the nerves with electrical pulses. The sacral nerves connect to the part of the spine in the hip area. A battery-operated stimulator is placed beneath the skin.

Based on the person's response, the health care provider can adjust the amount of stimulation so it works best for that person. The person can turn the stimulator on or off at any time. The procedure is performed in an outpatient center using local anesthesia.

What are some practical tips for coping with fecal incontinence?

Fecal incontinence can cause embarrassment, fear, and loneliness. Taking steps to cope is important. The following tips can help:

- carrying a bag with cleanup supplies and a change of clothes when leaving the house.
- finding public restrooms before one is needed.
- using the toilet before leaving home.
- wearing disposable underwear or absorbent pads inserted in the underwear.
- using fecal deodorants—pills that reduce the smell of stool and gas. Although fecal deodorants are available over the counter, a health care provider can help people find them.

Eating tends to trigger contractions of the large intestine that push stool toward the rectum and also cause the rectum to contract for 30 to 60 minutes. Both these events increase the likelihood that a person will pass gas and have a bowel movement soon after eating. This activity may increase if the person is anxious. People with fecal incontinence may want to avoid eating in restaurants or at social gatherings, or they may want to take antidiarrheal medications before eating in these situations.

What if a child has fecal incontinence?

A child with fecal incontinence who is toilet trained should see a health care provider, who can determine the cause and recommend treatment. Fecal incontinence can occur in children because of a birth defect or disease, but in most cases it occurs because of constipation.

Children often develop constipation as a result of stool withholding. They may withhold stool because they are stressed about toilet training, embarrassed to use a public bathroom, do not want to interrupt playtime, or are fearful of having a painful or unpleasant bowel movement.

As in adults, constipation in children can cause large, hard stools that get stuck in the rectum. Watery stool builds up behind the hard stool and may unexpectedly leak out, soiling a child's underwear. Parents often mistake this soiling as a sign of diarrhea.

Anal Discomfort

The skin around the anus is delicate and sensitive. Constipation and diarrhea or contact between skin and stool can cause pain or itching. The following steps can help relieve anal discomfort:

- **Washing the anal area after a bowel movement.** Washing with water, but not soap, can help prevent discomfort. Soap can dry out the skin, making discomfort worse. Ideally, the anal area should be washed in the shower with lukewarm water or in a sitz bath—a special plastic tub that allows a person to sit in a few inches of warm water. No-rinse skin cleansers, such as Cavilon, are a good alternative. Wiping with toilet paper further irritates the skin and should be avoided. Premoistened, alcohol-free towelettes are a better choice.

- **Keeping the anal area dry.** The anal area should be allowed to air dry after washing. If time doesn't permit air drying, the anal area can be gently patted dry with a lint-free cloth.

- **Creating a moisture barrier.** A moisture barrier cream that contains ingredients such as dimethicone—a type of silicone—can help form a barrier between skin and stool. The anal area should be cleaned before applying barrier cream. However, people should talk with their health care provider before using anal creams and ointments because some can irritate the anus.

- **Using nonmedicated powders.** Nonmedicated talcum powder or cornstarch can also relieve anal discomfort. As with moisture barrier creams, the anal area should be clean and dry before use.

- **Using wicking pads or disposable underwear.** Pads and disposable underwear with a wicking layer can pull moisture away from the skin.

- **Wearing breathable clothes and underwear.** Clothes and underwear should allow air to flow and keep skin dry. Tight clothes or plastic or rubber underwear that blocks air can worsen skin problems.
- **Changing soiled underwear as soon as possible.**

Chapter 3

Cyclic Vomiting Syndrome

What is cyclic vomiting syndrome?

Cyclic vomiting syndrome, sometimes referred to as CVS, is an increasingly recognized disorder with sudden, repeated attacks—also called episodes—of severe nausea, vomiting, and physical exhaustion that occur with no apparent cause. The episodes can last from a few hours to several days. Episodes can be so severe that a person has to stay in bed for days, unable to go to school or work. A person may need treatment at an emergency room or a hospital during episodes. After an episode, a person usually experiences symptom-free periods lasting a few weeks to several months. To people who have the disorder, as well as their family members and friends, cyclic vomiting syndrome can be disruptive and frightening.

The disorder can affect a person for months, years, or decades. Each episode of cyclic vomiting syndrome is usually similar to previous ones, meaning that episodes tend to start at the same time of day, last the same length of time, and occur with the same symptoms and level of intensity.

What causes cyclic vomiting syndrome?

The cause of cyclic vomiting syndrome is unknown. However, some experts believe that some possible problems with bodily functions may contribute to the cause, such as the following:

Text in this chapter is excerpted from "Cyclic Vomiting Syndrome," National Institute of Diabetes and Digestive and Kidney Diseases (NIDDK), February 2014.

- gastrointestinal motility—the way food moves through the digestive system

- central nervous system function—includes the brain, spinal cord, and nerves that control bodily responses

- autonomic nervous system function—nerves that control internal organs such as the heart

- hormone imbalances—hormones are a chemical produced in one part of the body and released into the blood to trigger or regulate particular bodily functions

- in children, an abnormal inherited gene may also contribute to the condition

Specific conditions or events may trigger an episode of cyclic vomiting:

- emotional stress, anxiety, or panic attacks—for example, in children, common trig7gers of anticipatory anxiety are school exams or events, birthday parties, holidays, family conflicts, or travel

- infections, such as a sinus infection, a respiratory infection, or the flu

- eating certain foods, such as chocolate or cheese, or additives such as caffeine, nitrites—commonly found in cured meats such as hot dogs—and monosodium glutamate, also called MSG

- hot weather

- menstrual periods

- motion sickness

- overeating, fasting, or eating right before bedtime

- physical exhaustion or too much exercise

How common is cyclic vomiting syndrome?

Cyclic vomiting syndrome is more common in children than adults, although reports of the syndrome in adults have increased in recent years. Usually, children are about 5 years old when diagnosed with cyclic vomiting syndrome, which occurs in every three out of 100,000 children.

Who is more likely to develop cyclic vomiting syndrome?

Children who suffer from migraines—severe, throbbing headaches with nausea, vomiting, and sensitivity to light and sound—are more likely to develop cyclic vomiting syndrome. Up to 80 percent of children and 25 percent of adults who develop cyclic vomiting syndrome also get migraine headaches. People with a family history of migraines may be more likely to develop the syndrome.

People with a history of chronic marijuana use may also be more likely to develop cyclic vomiting syndrome.

What are the symptoms of cyclic vomiting syndrome?

The main symptoms of cyclic vomiting syndrome are severe nausea and sudden vomiting lasting hours to days. A person may also experience one or more of the following symptoms:

- retching, or making an attempt to vomit
- heaving or gagging
- lack of appetite
- abdominal pain
- diarrhea
- fever
- dizziness
- headache
- sensitivity to light

Intensity of symptoms will vary as a person cycles through four distinct phases of an episode:

- **Prodrome phase.** During the prodrome phase, the person feels that an episode of nausea and vomiting is about to start. Often marked by intense sweating and nausea—with or without abdominal pain—this phase can last from a few minutes to several hours. The person may appear unusually pale.

- **Vomiting phase.** This phase consists of intense nausea, vomiting, and retching. Periods of vomiting and retching can last 20 to 30 minutes at a time. The person may be subdued and responsive, immobile and unresponsive, or writhing and moaning with intense abdominal pain. An episode can last from hours to days.

- **Recovery phase.** This phase begins when the vomiting and retching stop and the nausea subsides. Improvement of symptoms during the recovery phase can vary. Healthy color, appetite, and energy return gradually or right away.

- **Well phase.** This phase occurs between episodes when no symptoms are present.

What are the complications of cyclic vomiting syndrome?

The severe vomiting and retching that define cyclic vomiting syndrome increase the chance of developing several complications, including dehydration, esophagitis, a Mallory-Weiss tear, and tooth decay.

- Dehydration may occur when a person does not replace fluids that were lost because of vomiting and diarrhea. When dehydrated, the body lacks enough fluid and electrolytes—minerals in salts, including sodium, potassium, and chloride—to function properly. Severe dehydration may require intravenous (IV) fluids and hospitalization.

- Esophagitis—inflammation or irritation of the esophagus—can result from the stomach acid that exits through the esophagus during vomiting.

- A Mallory-Weiss tear—a tear in the lower end of the esophagus—is caused by severe vomiting. A person with bloody vomit and stool should see a health care provider right away.

- Tooth decay or corroding tooth enamel is damage caused by stomach acid.

How is cyclic vomiting syndrome diagnosed?

A specific test to diagnose cyclic vomiting syndrome does not exist; instead, a health care provider will rule out other conditions and diagnose the syndrome based upon

- a medical and family history

- a physical exam

- a pattern or cycle of symptoms

- blood tests

- urine tests

- imaging tests

- upper GI endoscopy

- a gastric emptying test

Often, it is suspected that one of the following is causing their symptoms:

- gastroparesis—a disorder that slows or stops the movement of food from the stomach to the small intestine

- gastroenteritis—inflammation of the lining of the stomach, small intestine, and large intestine

A diagnosis of cyclic vomiting syndrome may be difficult to make until the person sees a health care provider. A health care provider will suspect cyclic vomiting syndrome if the person suffers from repeat episodes of vomiting.

Medical and Family History

Taking a medical and family history is one of the first things a health care provider may do to help diagnose cyclic vomiting syndrome. He or she will ask the patient to provide a medical and family history.

Physical Exam

A physical exam may help diagnose other conditions besides cyclic vomiting syndrome. During a physical exam, a health care provider usually

- examines a patient's body

- taps on specific areas of the patient's body

Pattern or Cycle of Symptoms in Children

A health care provider will often suspect cyclic vomiting syndrome in a child when the child

- has at least five separate episodes, or at least three separate episodes over 6 months

- has episodes of intense nausea and vomiting lasting 1 hour to 10 days and occurring at least 1 week apart

- has episodes that are similar to previous ones—they tend to start at the same time of day, last the same length of time, and occur with the same symptoms and level of intensity

- vomits during episodes at least four times per hour for at least 1 hour

- vomits and it is not attributed to another disorder

- has absence of nausea and vomiting between episodes

Pattern or Cycle of Symptoms in Adults

A health care provider will often suspect cyclic vomiting syndrome in adults when the following is present for at least 3 months and the symptoms started more than 6 months ago:

- Each episode of cyclic vomiting syndrome is usually similar to previous ones, meaning that episodes tend to start at the same time of day and last the same length of time—less than 1 week.

- Three or more separate episodes in the past year.

- Absence of nausea or vomiting between episodes.

Blood Tests

A nurse or technician will draw blood samples at a health care provider's office or a commercial facility and send the samples to a lab for analysis. The blood test can tell the health care provider if the patient has any signs of dehydration or other problems.

Urine Tests

Urinalysis involves testing a urine sample. The patient collects a urine sample in a special container in a health care provider's office or a commercial facility. A health care provider tests the sample in the same location or sends the sample to a lab for analysis. A urinalysis can rule out kidney problems or an infection.

Imaging Tests

The health care provider decides which test to order based on the symptoms, medical history, and physical exam.

Upper GI series. A health care provider may order an upper GI series to look at the upper GI tract. A radiologist—a doctor who specializes in medical imaging—performs this test at a hospital or an outpatient center. This test does not require anesthesia. During the procedure, the patient will stand or sit in front of an X-ray machine and drink barium, a chalky liquid. Infants lie on a table and a health care provider gives them barium through a tiny tube placed in the nose that runs into the stomach. Barium coats the GI tract, making signs of obstruction or other problems that can cause vomiting show up more clearly on X-rays. A patient may experience bloating and nausea for a short time after the test. The upper GI series can show other problems that may be causing symptoms, such as an ulcer or obstruction.

Abdominal ultrasound. A health care provider may order an ultrasound to look at the organs in the abdomen. A technician uses a device, called a transducer, that bounces safe, painless sound waves off organs to create an image of their structure.

Upper Gastrointestinal Endoscopy

This procedure involves using an endoscope—a small, flexible tube with a light—to see the upper GI tract. A gastroenterologist—a doctor who specializes in digestive diseases—performs the test at a hospital or an outpatient center. A health care provider may give a patient a liquid anesthetic to gargle or may spray anesthetic on the back of the patient's throat. A nurse or technician will place an IV needle in a vein in the arm to administer sedation or anesthesia.

Gastric Emptying Test

Also called gastric emptying scintigraphy, this test involves eating a bland meal—such as eggs or an egg substitute—that contains a small amount of radioactive material. A specially trained technician performs the test in a radiology center or hospital, and a radiologist interprets the results; the patient does not need anesthesia.

How is cyclic vomiting syndrome treated?

A health care provider may refer patients to a gastroenterologist for treatment.

People with cyclic vomiting syndrome should get plenty of rest and take medications to prevent a vomiting episode, stop an episode in progress, speed up recovery, or relieve associated symptoms.

The health care team tailors treatment to the symptoms experienced during each of the four cyclic vomiting syndrome phases:

- **Prodrome phase treatment.** The goal during the prodrome phase is to stop an episode before it progresses. Taking medication early in the phase can help stop an episode from moving to the vomiting phase or becoming severe; however, people do not always realize an episode is coming. For example, a person may wake up in the morning and begin vomiting. A health care provider may recommend the following medications for both children and adults:

- ondansetron (Zofran) or lorazepam (Ativan) for nausea

- ibuprofen for abdominal pain

- ranitidine (Zantac), lansoprazole (Prevacid), or omeprazole (Prilosec, Zegerid) to control stomach acid production

- sumatriptan (Imitrex)—prescribed as a nasal spray, an injection, or a pill that dissolves under the tongue—for migraines

- **Vomiting phase treatment.** Once vomiting begins, people should call or see a health care provider as soon as possible. Treatment usually requires the person to stay in bed and sleep in a dark, quiet room. A health care provider may recommend the following for both children and adults:

  - medication for pain, nausea, and reducing stomach acid and anxiety

  - anti-migraine medications such as sumatriptan to stop symptoms of a migraine or possibly stop an episode in progress

  - hospitalization for severe nausea and vomiting

  - IV fluids and medications to prevent dehydration and treat symptoms

  - IV nutrition if an episode continues for several days

- **Recovery phase treatment.** During the recovery phase, drinking and eating will replace lost electrolytes. A person may need IV fluids for a period of time. Some people find their appetite returns to normal right away, while others start by drinking clear liquids and then moving slowly to other liquids and solid food. A health care provider may prescribe medications during the recovery phase and well phase to prevent future episodes.

- **Well phase treatment.** During the well phase, a health care provider may use medications to treat people whose episodes are frequent and long lasting in an effort to prevent or ease future episodes. A person may need to take a medication daily for 1 to

2 months before evaluating whether it helps prevent episodes. A health care provider may prescribe the following medications for both children and adults during the well phase to prevent cyclic vomiting syndrome episodes, lessen their severity, and reduce their frequency:

- amitriptyline (Elavil)

- propranolol (Inderal)

- cyproheptadine (Periactin)

How can a person prevent cyclic vomiting syndrome?

A person should stay away from known triggers, especially during the well phase, as well as

- get adequate sleep to prevent exhaustion

- treat sinus problems or allergies

- scck help on reducing stress and anxiety

- avoid foods that trigger episodes or foods with additives

Eating, Diet, and Nutrition

During the prodrome and vomiting phases of cyclic vomiting syndrome, a person will generally take in little or no nutrition by mouth. During the recovery phase, the person may be quite hungry as soon as the vomiting stops. As eating resumes, a person or his or her family should watch for the return of nausea. In some cases, a person can start with clear liquids and proceed slowly to a regular diet.

During the well phase, a balanced diet and regular meals are important. People should avoid any trigger foods and foods with additives. Eating small, carbohydrate-containing snacks between meals, before exercise, and at bedtime may help prevent future attacks. A health care provider will assist with planning a return to a regular diet.

Chapter 4

Smoking and Your Digestive System

Smoking and the Digestive System

Smoking affects the entire body, increasing the risk of many life-threatening diseases—including lung cancer, emphysema, and heart disease. Smoking also contributes to many cancers and diseases of the digestive system. Estimates show that about one-fifth of all adults smoke, and each year at least 443,000 Americans die from diseases caused by cigarette smoking.

Does smoking increase the risk of cancers of the digestive system?

Smoking has been found to increase the risk of cancers of the

- mouth
- esophagus
- stomach
- pancreas

Text in this chapter is excerpted from "Smoking and the Digestive System," National Institute of Diabetes and Digestive and Kidney Diseases (NIDDK), March 2013.

Research suggests that smoking may also increase the risk of cancers of the

- liver
- colon
- rectum

What are the other harmful effects of smoking on the digestive system?

Smoking contributes to many common disorders of the digestive system, such as heartburn and gastroesophageal reflux disease (GERD), peptic ulcers, and some liver diseases. Smoking increases the risk of Crohn's disease, colon polyps, and pancreatitis, and it may increase the risk of gallstones.

How does smoking affect heartburn and GERD?

Smoking increases the risk of heartburn and GERD. Heartburn is a painful, burning feeling in the chest caused by reflux, or stomach contents flowing back into the esophagus—the organ that connects the mouth to the stomach. Smoking weakens the lower esophageal sphincter, the muscle between the esophagus and stomach that keeps stomach contents from flowing back into the esophagus. The stomach is naturally protected from the acids it makes to help break down food. However, the esophagus is not protected from the acids. When the lower esophageal sphincter weakens, stomach contents may reflux into the esophagus, causing heartburn and possibly damaging the lining of the esophagus.

GERD is persistent reflux that occurs more than twice a week. Chronic, or long lasting, GERD can lead to serious health problems such as bleeding ulcers in the esophagus, narrowing of the esophagus that causes food to get stuck, and changes in esophageal cells that can lead to cancer.

How does smoking affect peptic ulcers?

Smoking increases the risk of peptic ulcers. Peptic ulcers are sores on the inside lining of the stomach or duodenum, the first part of the small intestine. The two most common causes of peptic ulcers are infection with a bacterium called *Helicobacter pylori (H. pylori)* and long-term use of nonsteroidal anti-inflammatory drugs such as aspirin and ibuprofen.

Researchers are studying how smoking contributes to peptic ulcers. Studies suggest that smoking increases the risk of *H. pylori* infection, slows the healing of peptic ulcers, and increases the likelihood that peptic ulcers will recur. The stomach and duodenum contain acids, enzymes, and other substances that help digest food. However, these substances may also harm the lining of these organs. Smoking has not been shown to increase acid production. However, smoking does increase the production of other substances that may harm the lining, such as pepsin, an enzyme made in the stomach that breaks down proteins. Smoking also decreases factors that protect or heal the lining, including

- blood flow to the lining

- secretion of mucus, a clear liquid that protects the lining from acid

- production of sodium bicarbonate—a saltlike substance that neutralizes acid—by the pancreas

The increase in substances that may harm the lining and decrease in factors that protect or heal the lining may lead to peptic ulcers.

How does smoking affect liver disease?

Smoking may worsen some liver diseases, including

- primary biliary cirrhosis, a chronic liver disease that slowly destroys the bile ducts in the liver

- nonalcoholic fatty liver disease (NAFLD), a condition in which fat builds up in the liver

Researchers are still studying how smoking affects primary biliary cirrhosis, NAFLD, and other liver diseases.

Liver diseases may progress to cirrhosis, a condition in which the liver slowly deteriorates and malfunctions due to chronic injury. Scar tissue then replaces healthy liver tissue, partially blocking the flow of blood through the liver and impairing liver functions.

The liver is the largest organ in the digestive system. The liver carries out many functions, such as making important blood proteins and bile, changing food into energy, and filtering alcohol and poisons from the blood. Research has shown that smoking harms the liver's ability to process medications, alcohol, and other toxins and remove them from the body. In some cases, smoking may affect the dose of medication needed to treat an illness.

How does smoking affect Crohn's disease?

Current and former smokers have a higher risk of developing Crohn's disease than people who have never smoked.

Crohn's disease is an inflammatory bowel disease that causes irritation in the GI tract. The disease, which typically causes pain and diarrhea, most often affects the lower part of the small intestine; however, it can occur anywhere in the GI tract. The severity of symptoms varies from person to person, and the symptoms come and go. Crohn's disease may lead to complications such as blockages of the intestine and ulcers that tunnel through the affected area into surrounding tissues. Medications may control symptoms. However, many people with Crohn's disease require surgery to remove the affected portion of the intestine.

Among people with Crohn's disease, people who smoke are more likely to

- have more severe symptoms, more frequent symptoms, and more complications

- need more medications to control their symptoms

- require surgery

- have symptoms recur after surgery

The effects of smoking are more pronounced in women with Crohn's disease than in men with the disease.

Researchers are studying why smoking increases the risk of Crohn's disease and makes the disease worse. Some researchers believe smoking might lower the intestines' defenses, decrease blood flow to the intestines, or cause immune system changes that result in inflammation. In people who inherit genes that make them susceptible to developing Crohn's disease, smoking may affect how some of these genes work.

How does smoking affect colon polyps?

People who smoke are more likely to develop colon polyps. Colon polyps are growths on the inside surface of the colon or rectum. Some polyps are benign, or noncancerous, while some are cancerous or may become cancerous.

Among people who develop colon polyps, those who smoke have polyps that are larger, more numerous, and more likely to recur.

How does smoking affect pancreatitis?

Smoking increases the risk of developing pancreatitis. Pancreatitis is inflammation of the pancreas, which is located behind the stomach and close to the duodenum. The pancreas secretes digestive enzymes that usually do not become active until they reach the small intestine. When the pancreas is inflamed, the digestive enzymes attack the tissues of the pancreas.

How does smoking affect gallstones?

Some studies have shown that smoking may increase the risk of developing gallstones. However, research results are not consistent and more study is needed.

Gallstones are small, hard particles that develop in the gallbladder, the organ that stores bile made by the liver. Gallstones can move into the ducts that carry digestive enzymes from the gallbladder, liver, and pancreas to the duodenum, causing inflammation, infection, and abdominal pain.

Can the damage to the digestive system from smoking be reversed?

Quitting smoking can reverse some of the effects of smoking on the digestive system. For example, the balance between factors that harm and protect the stomach and duodenum lining returns to normal within a few hours of a person quitting smoking. The effects of smoking on how the liver handles medications also disappear when a person stops smoking. However, people who stop smoking continue to have a higher risk of some digestive diseases, such as colon polyps and pancreatitis, than people who have never smoked.

Quitting smoking can improve the symptoms of some digestive diseases or keep them from getting worse. For example, people with Crohn's disease who quit smoking have less severe symptoms than smokers with the disease.

Eating, Diet, and Nutrition

Eating, diet, and nutrition can play a role in causing, preventing, and treating some of the diseases and disorders of the digestive system that are affected by smoking, including heartburn and GERD, liver diseases, Crohn's disease, colon polyps, pancreatitis, and gallstones.

Part Two

Diagnostic and Surgical Procedures Used for Gastrointestinal Disorders

Chapter 5

Endoscopic Procedures and Related Concerns

Chapter Contents

Section 5.1

Colonoscopy

Text in this section is excerpted from "Colonoscopy," National
Institute of Diabetes and Digestive and Kidney Diseases (NIDDK),
November 13, 2014.

What is Colonoscopy?

Colonoscopy is a procedure in which a trained specialist uses a long,
flexible, narrow tube with a light and tiny camera on one end, called
a colonoscope or scope, to look inside your rectum and colon. Colonoscopy can show irritated and swollen tissue, ulcers, polyps, and cancer.

How is virtual colonoscopy different from colonoscopy?

Virtual colonoscopy and colonoscopy are different in several ways.
Virtual colonoscopy is an X-ray test, takes less time, and doesn't
require a doctor to insert a colonoscope into the entire length of your
colon. However, virtual colonoscopy may not be as effective as colonoscopy at detecting certain polyps. Also, doctors cannot treat problems
during virtual colonoscopy, while they can treat some problems during
colonoscopy. Your health insurance coverage for virtual colonoscopy
and colonoscopy may also be different.

Why do doctors use colonoscopy?

A colonoscopy can help a doctor find the cause of unexplained symptoms, such as

- changes in your bowel activity
- pain in your abdomen
- bleeding from your anus
- unexplained weight loss

Doctors also use colonoscopy as a screening tool for colon polyps and
cancer. Screening is testing for diseases when you have no symptoms.

Screening may find diseases at an early stage, when a doctor has a better chance of curing the disease.

Screening for Colon and Rectal Cancer

Your doctor will recommend screening for colon and rectal cancer at age 50 if you don't have health problems or other factors that make you more likely to develop colon cancer.

Risk factors for colorectal cancer include

- someone in your family has had polyps or cancer of the colon or rectum

- a personal history of inflammatory bowel disease, such as ulcerative colitis and Crohn's disease

- other factors, such as if you weigh too much or smoke cigarettes

If you are at higher risk for colorectal cancer, your doctor may recommend screening at a younger age, and you may need to be tested more often.

If you are older than 75, talk with your doctor about whether you should be screened.

Government health insurance plans, such as Medicare, and private health insurance plans sometimes change whether and how often they pay for cancer screening tests. Check with your insurance plan to find out how often your insurance will cover a screening colonoscopy.

How do I prepare for a colonoscopy?

To prepare for a colonoscopy, you will need to talk with your doctor, arrange for a ride home, clean out your bowel, and change your diet.

Talk with your doctor

You should talk with your doctor about any medical conditions you have and all prescribed and over-the-counter medicines, vitamins, and supplements you take, including:

- aspirin or medicines that contain aspirin

- nonsteroidal anti-inflammatory drugs such as ibuprofen or naproxen

- arthritis medicines
- blood thinners
- diabetes medicines
- vitamins that contain iron or iron supplements

Arrange for a ride home

For safety reasons, you can't drive for 24 hours after the procedure, as the sedatives or anesthesia used during the procedure needs time to wear off. You will need to make plans for getting a ride home after the procedure.

Clean out your bowel and change your diet

A health care professional will give you written bowel prep instructions to follow at home before the procedure. A health care professional orders a bowel prep so that little to no stool is present in your intestine. A complete bowel prep lets you pass stool that is clear. Stool inside your colon can prevent your doctor from clearly seeing the lining of your intestine.

You may need to follow a clear liquid diet for 1 to 3 days before the procedure and avoid drinks that contain red or purple dye. The instructions will provide specific direction about when to start and stop the clear liquid diet. In most cases, you may drink or eat the following:

- fat-free bouillon or broth
- strained fruit juice, such as apple or white grape—doctors recommend avoiding orange juice
- water
- plain coffee or tea, without cream or milk
- sports drinks in flavors such as lemon, lime, or orange
- gelatin in flavors such as lemon, lime, or orange

Your doctor will tell you before the procedure when you should have nothing by mouth.

A health care professional will ask you to follow the directions for a bowel prep before the procedure. The bowel prep will cause diarrhea, so you should stay close to a bathroom.

Different bowel preps may contain different combinations of laxatives, pills that you swallow or powders that you dissolve in water and other clear liquids, and enemas. Some people will need to drink a large amount, often a gallon, of liquid laxative over a scheduled amount of time—most often the night before the procedure. You may find this part of the bowel prep difficult; however, completing the prep is very important. Your doctor will not be able to see your colon clearly if the prep is incomplete.

Call a health care professional if you have side effects that prevent you from finishing the prep.

How do doctors perform a colonoscopy?

A trained specialist performs a colonoscopy in a hospital or an outpatient center.

A health care professional will place an intravenous (IV) needle in a vein in your arm to give you sedatives, anesthesia, or pain medicine so you can relax during the procedure. The health care staff will monitor your vital signs and keep you as comfortable as possible.

For the procedure, you'll be asked to lie on a table while the doctor inserts a colonoscope into your anus and slowly guides it through your rectum and into your colon. The scope pumps air into your large intestine to give the doctor a better view. The camera sends a video image of the intestinal lining to a monitor, allowing the doctor to examine your intestinal tissues. The doctor may move you several times on the table to adjust the scope for better viewing. Once the scope has reached the opening to your small intestine, the doctor slowly withdraws it and examines the lining of your large intestine again.

During the procedure, the doctor may remove polyps and send them to a lab for testing. Colon polyps are common in adults and are harmless in most cases. However, most colon cancer begins as a polyp, so removing polyps early is an effective way to prevent cancer.

The doctor may also perform a biopsy. You won't feel the biopsy.

Colonoscopy typically takes 30 to 60 minutes.

What should I expect after a colonoscopy?

After a colonoscopy, you can expect the following:

- You'll stay at the hospital or outpatient center for 1 to 2 hours after the procedure.

- You may have abdominal cramping or bloating during the first hour after the procedure.

- The sedatives or anesthesia takes time to wear off completely.

- You should expect a full recovery by the next day, and you should be able to go back to your normal diet.

- After the procedure, you—or a friend or family member—will receive instructions on how to care for yourself after the procedure. You should follow all instructions.

- A friend or family member will need to drive you home after the procedure.

If the doctor removed polyps or performed a biopsy, you may have light bleeding from your anus. This bleeding is normal. Some results from a colonoscopy are available right after the procedure. After the sedatives or anesthesia has worn off, the doctor will share results with you or, if you choose, with your friend or family member. A pathologist will examine the biopsy tissue. Biopsy results take a few days or longer to come back.

What are the risks of colonoscopy?

The risks of colonoscopy include

- bleeding

- perforation of the colon

- abnormal reaction to the sedative, including respiratory or cardiac problems

- abdominal pain

- death, although this risk is rare

Bleeding and perforation are the most common complications from colonoscopy. Most cases of bleeding occur in patients who have polyps removed. The doctor can treat bleeding that occurs during the colonoscopy right away. However, you may have delayed bleeding up to 2 weeks after the procedure. The doctor diagnoses and treats delayed bleeding with a repeat colonoscopy. The doctor may need to treat perforation with surgery.

A study of screening colonoscopies found roughly two serious complications for every 1,000 procedures.

Seek Care Right Away

If you have any of the following symptoms after a colonoscopy, seek medical care right away:

- severe abdominal pain
- fever
- continued bloody bowel movements or continued bleeding from the anus
- dizziness
- weakness

Section 5.2

Virtual Colonoscopy

Text in this section is excerpted from "Virtual Colonoscopy," National Institute of Diabetes and Digestive and Kidney Diseases (NIDDK), September 2013.

What is virtual colonoscopy?

Virtual colonoscopy, also called computerized tomography (CT) colonography, is a procedure that uses a combination of X-rays and computer technology to create images of the rectum and entire colon. Virtual colonoscopy can show irritated and swollen tissue, ulcers, and polyps—extra pieces of tissue that grow on the lining of the intestine.

This procedure is different from colonoscopy, which uses a long, flexible, narrow tube with a light and tiny camera on one end, called a colonoscope or scope, to look inside the rectum and entire colon.

Why is a virtual colonoscopy performed?

A virtual colonoscopy is performed to help diagnose

- changes in bowel habits
- abdominal pain
- bleeding from the anus
- weight loss

A gastroenterologist—a doctor who specializes in digestive diseases—may also order a virtual colonoscopy as a screening test for colon cancer. Screening is testing for diseases when people have no symptoms. Screening may find a disease at an early stage, when a gastroenterologist has a better chance of curing the disease. However, while some gastroenterologists use a virtual colonoscopy to screen for colon cancer, not enough evidence exists to fully assess its effectiveness as a screening tool. Instead, the U.S. Preventive Services Task Force recommends fecal occult blood testing, sigmoidoscopy, or colonoscopy for colon cancer screening.

The American College of Gastroenterology recommends screening for colon cancer

- at age 50 for people who are not at increased risk of the disease

- at age 45 for African Americans because they have an increased risk of developing the disease

A gastroenterologist may recommend earlier screening for people with a family history of colon cancer, a personal history of inflammatory bowel disease—a long-lasting disorder that causes irritation and sores in the GI tract—or other risk factors for colon cancer.

Medicare and private insurance companies sometimes change whether and how often they pay for cancer screening tests. People should check with their insurance company to find out how often they can get a screening virtual colonoscopy that their insurance will cover.

How does a person prepare for a virtual colonoscopy?

Preparation for a virtual colonoscopy includes the following steps:

- **Talk with a gastroenterologist.** When people schedule a virtual colonoscopy, they should talk with their gastroenterologist about medical conditions they have and all prescribed and over-the-counter medications, vitamins, and supplements they take, including

  - aspirin or medications that contain aspirin

  - nonsteroidal anti-inflammatory drugs such as ibuprofen or naproxen

  - arthritis medications

  - blood thinners

- diabetes medications

- vitamins that contain iron or iron supplements

- **Cleanse the bowel.** The gastroenterologist will give written bowel prep instructions to follow at home. A gastroenterologist orders a bowel prep so that little to no stool is present inside the person's intestine. A complete bowel prep lets the person pass stool that is clear. Stool inside the colon can prevent the CT scanner from taking clear images of the intestinal lining. Instructions may include following a clear liquid diet for 1 to 3 days before the procedure and avoiding drinks that contain red or purple dye. The instructions will provide specific direction about when to start and stop the clear liquid diet. People may drink or eat the following:

  - fat-free bouillon or broth

  - strained fruit juice, such as apple or white grape—orange juice is not recommended

  - water

  - plain coffee or tea, without cream or milk

  - sports drinks in flavors such as lemon, lime, or orange

  - gelatin in flavors such as lemon, lime, or orange

- The person needs to take laxatives and enemas the night before a virtual colonoscopy. A laxative is medication that loosens stool and increases bowel movements. An enema involves flushing water or laxative into the rectum using a special wash bottle. Laxatives and enemas can cause diarrhea, so the person should stay close to a bathroom during the bowel prep.

- Laxatives are usually swallowed in pill form or as a powder dissolved in water. Some people will need to drink a large amount, usually a gallon, of liquid laxative at scheduled times. People may find this part of the bowel prep difficult; however, it is very important to complete the prep. The images will not be clear if the prep is incomplete.

- People should call the gastroenterologist if they are having side effects that are preventing them from finishing the prep.

- **Drink contrast medium.** The night before the procedure, the person will drink a liquid that contains a special dye, called contrast medium. Contrast medium is visible on X-rays and can help distinguish between stool and polyps.

How is a virtual colonoscopy performed?

A radiologist—a doctor who specializes in medical imaging—performs a virtual colonoscopy at an outpatient center or a hospital. A person does not need anesthesia.

For the test, the person will lie on a table while the radiologist inserts a thin tube through the anus and into the rectum. The tube inflates the large intestine with air for a better view. The table slides into a tunnel-shaped device where the radiologist takes the X-ray images. The radiologist may ask the person to hold his or her breath several times during the test to steady the images. The radiologist will ask the person to turn over on the side or stomach so the radiologist can take different images of the large intestine. The procedure lasts about 10 to 15 minutes.

What can a person expect after a virtual colonoscopy?

After a virtual colonoscopy, a person can expect

- cramping or bloating during the first hour after the test
- to resume regular activities immediately after the test
- to return to a normal diet

After the test, a radiologist interprets the images, evaluates the results to find any abnormalities, and sends a report to the gastroenterologist. If the radiologist finds abnormalities, a gastroenterologist may perform a colonoscopy the same day or at a later time.

Seek Help for Emergency Symptoms

People who have any of the following symptoms after a virtual colonoscopy should seek immediate medical attention:

- severe abdominal pain
- fever
- bloody bowel movements or bleeding from the anus
- dizziness
- weakness

What are the risks of virtual colonoscopy?

The risks of virtual colonoscopy include

* exposure to radiation

* perforation—a hole or tear in the lining of the colon

Radiation exposure can cause cancer. However, though the level of radiation exposure that leads to cancer is unknown, the risk from these types of tests is thought to be small. Inflating the colon with air has a small risk of perforating the intestinal lining. Perforation may need to be treated with surgery.

Virtual colonoscopy shows the entire abdomen—the area between the chest and the hips—and can show abnormalities outside of the GI tract. These findings may lead to additional testing, cost, and anxiety.

Work with a Gastroenterologist to Determine the Best Screening Method

Virtual colonoscopy has several advantages and disadvantages when compared with a colonoscopy. The advantages of virtual colonoscopy include the following:

* Virtual colonoscopy does not require the insertion of a colonoscope into the entire length of the colon.
* People do not need anesthesia. People can return to their normal activities or go home after the procedure without the help of another person.
* Virtual colonoscopy takes less time than colonoscopy.
* The radiologist can use a virtual colonoscopy to view the inside of a colon that is narrowed because of inflammation or the presence of a polyp.

The disadvantages of virtual colonoscopy include the following:

* People require bowel prep and the insertion of a tube into the rectum.
* The radiologist cannot remove tissue samples or polyps or stop bleeding if a perforation occurs.
* If a virtual colonoscopy shows a polyp or cancer, a colonoscopy may be needed to confirm or treat the abnormality;

---

with a colonoscopy, treatment can occur at the same time as diagnosis.

- Virtual colonoscopy may not be as effective as colonoscopy at detecting certain polyps.

- Virtual colonoscopy may interfere with personal medical devices. People should tell the gastroenterologist about any implanted medical devices.

- Medicare and private insurance companies sometimes change whether and how often they pay for cancer screening tests. People should check with their insurance company to find out how often they can get a screening virtual colonoscopy that their insurance will cover.

- Virtual colonoscopy is a newer technology and not all medical facilities make this procedure available.

- Gastroenterologists do not recommend techniques that use X-ray radiation for pregnant women because the radiation may harm the fetus.

Section 5.3

Upper GI Endoscopy

Text in this section is excerpted from "Upper GI Endoscopy,"
National Institute of Diabetes and Digestive and Kidney Diseases
(NIDDK), November 13, 2014.

What is upper gastrointestinal (GI) endoscopy?

Upper GI endoscopy is a procedure in which a doctor uses an endoscope—a long, flexible tube with a camera—to see the lining of your upper GI tract. A gastroenterologist, surgeon, or other trained health care provider performs the procedure, most often while you receive light sedation. Your doctor may also call the procedure an EGD or esophagogastroduodenoscopy.

Why do doctors use upper GI endoscopy?

Upper GI endoscopy can help find the cause of unexplained symptoms, such as

- persistent heartburn
- bleeding
- nausea and vomiting

- pain
- problems swallowing
- unexplained weight loss

Upper GI endoscopy can also find the cause of abnormal lab tests, such as

- anemia
- nutritional deficiencies

Upper GI endoscopy can identify many different diseases

- anemia
- gastroesophageal reflux disease
- ulcers
- cancer
- inflammation, or swelling
- precancerous abnormalities
- celiac disease
- During upper GI endoscopy, a doctor obtains biopsies by passing an instrument through the endoscope to obtain a small piece of tissue. Biopsies are needed to diagnose conditions such as
- cancer
- celiac disease
- gastritis

Doctors also use upper GI endoscopy to

- treat conditions such as bleeding ulcers
- dilate strictures with a small balloon passed through the endoscope
- remove objects, including food, that may be stuck in the upper GI tract

How do I prepare for an upper GI endoscopy?

Talk with your doctor

You should talk with your doctor about medical conditions you have and all prescribed and over-the-counter medicines, vitamins, and supplements you take, including

- aspirin or medicines that contain aspirin

- arthritis medicines

- nonsteroidal anti-inflammatory drugs such as ibuprofen and naproxen

- blood thinners

- blood pressure medicines

- diabetes medicines

Arrange for a ride home

For safety reasons, you can't drive for 24 hours after the procedure, as the sedatives used during the procedure need time to wear off. You will need to make plans for getting a ride home after the procedure

Do not eat or drink before the procedure

The doctor needs to examine the lining of your upper GI tract during the procedure. If food or drink is in your upper GI tract when you have the procedure, the doctor will not be able to see this lining clearly. To make sure your upper GI tract is clear, the doctor will most often advise you not to eat, drink, smoke, or chew gum during the 8 hours before the procedure.

How do doctors perform an upper GI endoscopy?

A doctor performs an upper GI endoscopy in a hospital or an out-patient center. An intravenous (IV) needle will be placed in your arm to provide a sedative. Sedatives help you stay relaxed and comfortable during the procedure. In some cases, the procedure can be performed without sedation. You will be given a liquid anesthetic to gargle or spray anesthetic on the back of your throat. The anesthetic numbs your throat and calms the gag reflex. The health care staff will monitor your vital signs and keep you as comfortable as possible.

You'll be asked to lie on your side on an exam table. The doctor will carefully feed the endoscope down your esophagus and into your stomach and duodenum. A small camera mounted on the endoscope will send a video image to a monitor, allowing close examination of the lining of your upper GI tract. The endoscope pumps air into your stomach and duodenum, making them easier to see.

During the upper GI endoscopy, the doctor may

- perform a biopsy of tissue in your upper GI tract. You won't feel the biopsy.

- stop any bleeding.

- perform other specialized procedures, such as dilating strictures.

The procedure most often takes between 15 and 30 minutes. The endoscope does not interfere with your breathing, and many people fall asleep during the procedure.

What should I expect from an upper GI endoscopy?

After an upper GI endoscopy, you can expect the following:

- to stay at the hospital or outpatient center for 1 to 2 hours after the procedure so the sedative can wear off

- bloating or nausea for a short time after the procedure

- a sore throat for 1 to 2 days to go back to your normal diet once your swallowing has returned to normal

- to rest at home for the remainder of the day

Following the procedure, you—or a friend or family member who is with you if you're still groggy—will receive instructions on how to care for yourself following the procedure. You should follow all instructions.

Some results from an upper GI endoscopy are available right away after the procedure. After the sedative has worn off, the doctor will share these results with you or, if you choose, with your friend or family member. A pathologist will examine the biopsy tissue to help confirm a diagnosis. Biopsy results take a few days or longer to come back.

What are the risks of an upper GI endoscopy?

The risks of an upper GI endoscopy include

- bleeding from the site where the doctor took the biopsy or removed a polyp

- perforation in the lining of your upper GI tract
- an abnormal reaction to the sedative, including respiratory or cardiac problems

Bleeding and perforation are more common in endoscopies used for treatment rather than testing. Bleeding caused by the procedure often stops without treatment. Research has shown that serious complications occur in one out of every 1,000 upper GI endoscopies. A doctor may need to perform surgery to treat some complications. A doctor can treat an abnormal reaction to a sedative with medicines or IV fluids during or after the procedure.

Seek Care Right Away

If you have any of the following symptoms after an upper GI endoscopy, seek medical care right away:

- chest pain
- problems breathing
- problems swallowing or throat pain that gets worse
- vomiting—particularly if your vomit is bloody or looks like coffee grounds
- pain in your abdomen that gets worse
- bloody or black, tar-colored stool
- fever

Section 5.4

Flexible Sigmoidoscopy

Text in this section is excerpted from "Flexible Sigmoidoscopy," National Institute of Diabetes and Digestive and Kidney Diseases (NIDDK), April 2014.

What is flexible sigmoidoscopy?

Flexible sigmoidoscopy is a test that uses a flexible, narrow tube with a light and tiny camera on one end, called a sigmoidoscope or scope, to look inside the rectum and the lower, or sigmoid, colon. Flexible sigmoidoscopy can show irritated or swollen tissue, ulcers, and polyps—extra pieces of tissue that grow on the inner lining of the intestine. A health care provider performs the procedure during an office visit or at a hospital or an outpatient center.

Get Screened for Colon Cancer

The American College of Gastroenterology recommends screening for colon cancer

- at age 50 for people who are not more likely to develop the disease
- at age 45 for African Americans because they are more likely to develop the disease

A health care provider may recommend earlier screening if a person has a family history of colon cancer, a personal history of inflammatory bowel disease—long-lasting disorders that cause irritation and sores in the GI tract—or other risk factors for colon cancer.

Colonoscopy is the preferred screening method for colon cancer because it shows the entire colon. However, preparing for and performing a flexible sigmoidoscopy usually requires less time.

Medicare and private insurance companies sometimes change whether and how often they pay for cancer screening tests. People should check with their insurance company to find out how often their coverage will allow a screening flexible sigmoidoscopy.

Why is a flexible sigmoidoscopy performed?

A health care provider performs a flexible sigmoidoscopy to help diagnose

- changes in bowel habits
- abdominal pain
- bleeding from the anus
- weight loss

A health care provider may also perform a flexible sigmoidoscopy as a screening test for colon cancer. Screening is testing for a disease when a person has no symptoms. Screening may find diseases at an early stage, when there may be a better chance of curing the disease.

How does a person prepare for a flexible sigmoidoscopy?

A person prepares for a flexible sigmoidoscopy by

- **talking with a health care provider.** A person should talk with his or her health care provider about medical conditions he or she has and all prescribed and over-the-counter medications, vitamins, and supplements he or she takes, including
  - arthritis medications
  - aspirin or medications that contain aspirin
  - blood thinners
  - diabetes medications
  - nonsteroidal anti-inflammatory drugs such as ibuprofen or naproxen
  - vitamins that contain iron or iron supplements
- **cleansing the bowel.** The health care provider will give written bowel prep instructions to follow at home. A health care

provider orders a bowel prep so that little to no stool is present inside the person's intestine. A complete bowel prep lets the person pass stool that is clear. Stool inside the colon can prevent the health care provider from clearly seeing the lining of the intestine. Instructions may include following a clear liquid diet for 1 to 3 days before the procedure and avoiding drinks that contain red or purple dye. The instructions will provide specific direction about when to start and stop the clear liquid diet. During this diet, people may drink or eat the following:

- fat-free bouillon or broth
- gelatin in flavors such as lemon, lime, or orange
- plain coffee or tea, without cream or milk
- sports drinks in flavors such as lemon, lime, or orange
- strained fruit juice, such as apple or white grape—orange juice is not recommended
- water

- The person needs to take laxatives and enemas the night before and several hours before a flexible sigmoidoscopy. A laxative is medication that loosens stool and increases bowel movements. An enema involves flushing water or laxative into the rectum using a special wash bottle. Laxatives and enemas can cause diarrhea, so the person should stay close to a bathroom during the bowel prep.

Laxatives are usually swallowed in pill form or as a powder dissolved in water. Some people will need to drink a large amount, usually a gallon, of liquid laxative over the course of the bowel prep at scheduled times. People may find this part of the prep difficult; however, it is important to complete the prep. The health care provider will not be able to see the sigmoid colon clearly if the prep is incomplete.

People should call the health care provider if they are having side effects that make them feel they can't finish the prep.

How is a flexible sigmoidoscopy performed?

A health care provider performs a flexible sigmoidoscopy during an office visit or at a hospital or an outpatient center. A person usually does not need anesthesia, and the procedure takes about 20 minutes.

For the test, the person will lie on a table while the health care provider inserts a sigmoidoscope into the anus and slowly guides it through the rectum and into the sigmoid colon. The scope inflates the large intestine with air to give the health care provider a better view. The camera sends a video image of the intestinal lining to a computer screen, allowing the health care provider to examine the tissues lining the sigmoid colon and rectum. The health care provider may ask the person to move several times so he or she can adjust the scope for better viewing. Once the scope has reached the transverse colon, the health care provider withdraws it slowly while examining the lining of the colon again.

For the test, the person will lie on a table while the health care provider inserts a sigmoidoscope into the anus and slowly guides it through the rectum and into the sigmoid colon.

The health care provider can remove polyps during flexible sigmoidoscopy and send them to a lab for testing. Polyps are common in adults and are usually harmless. However, most colon cancer begins as a polyp, so removing polyps early is an effective way to prevent cancer.

The health care provider may also perform a biopsy, a procedure that involves taking a small piece of intestinal lining for examination with a microscope. The person will not feel the biopsy. A pathologist—a doctor who specializes in diagnosing diseases—will examine the tissue.

The health care provider may pass tiny tools through the scope to remove polyps and take a sample for biopsy. If bleeding occurs, the health care provider can usually stop it with an electrical probe or special medications passed through the scope. If the health care provider finds polyps or other abnormal tissues, he or she may suggest examining the rest of the colon with a colonoscopy.

What can a person expect after a flexible sigmoidoscopy?

After a flexible sigmoidoscopy, a person can expect

- abdominal cramps or bloating during the first hour after the test.

- to resume regular activities immediately after the test.

- to return to a normal diet.

- a member of the health care team to review the discharge instructions with the person and provide a written copy. The person should follow all instructions given.

Some results from a flexible sigmoidoscopy are available immediately after the procedure, and the health care provider will share results with the person. Biopsy results take a few days to come back.

What are the risks of flexible sigmoidoscopy?

The risks of flexible sigmoidoscopy include

- bleeding.
- perforation—a hole or tear in the lining of the colon.
- severe abdominal pain.
- diverticulitis—a condition that occurs when small pouches in the colon, called diverticula, become irritated, swollen, and infected.
- cardiovascular events, such as a heart attack, low blood pressure, or the heart skipping beats or beating too fast or too slow.
- death, although this risk is rare.

Bleeding and perforation are the most common complications from flexible sigmoidoscopy. Most cases of bleeding occur in people who have polyps removed. The health care provider can treat bleeding that occurs during the flexible sigmoidoscopy right away. However, a person may have delayed bleeding up to 2 weeks after the test. The health care provider diagnoses delayed bleeding with a colonoscopy or repeat flexible sigmoidoscopy and treats it with an electrical probe or special medication. A person may need surgery to treat perforation.

Seek Immediate Care

People who have any of the following symptoms after a flexible sigmoidoscopy should seek immediate care:

- severe abdominal pain
- fever
- continued bloody bowel movements or continued bleeding from the anus
- dizziness
- weakness

- Flexible sigmoidoscopy is a test that uses a flexible, narrow tube with a light and tiny camera on one end, called a sigmoidoscope or scope, to look inside the rectum and the lower, or sigmoid, colon.

- Flexible sigmoidoscopy can show irritated or swollen tissue, ulcers, and polyps—extra pieces of tissue that grow on the inner lining of the intestine.

- A health care provider performs a flexible sigmoidoscopy to help diagnose

  - changes in bowel habits

  - abdominal pain

  - bleeding from the anus

  - weight loss

- The health care provider will give written bowel prep instructions to follow at home. A health care provider orders a bowel prep so that little to no stool is present inside the person's intestine.

- People should call the health care provider if they are having side effects that make them feel they can't finish the prep.

- A health care provider performs a flexible sigmoidoscopy during an office visit or at a hospital or an outpatient center. A person usually does not need anesthesia, and the procedure takes about 20 minutes.

- After a flexible sigmoidoscopy, a person can expect

  - abdominal cramps or bloating during the first hour after the test.

  - to resume regular activities immediately after the test.

  - to return to a normal diet.

  - a member of the health care team to review the discharge instructions with the person and provide a written copy. The person should follow all instructions given.

- People who have any of the following symptoms after a flexible sigmoidoscopy should seek immediate care:

  - severe abdominal pain

  - fever

  - continued bloody bowel movements or continued bleeding from the anus

  - dizziness

  - weakness

Section 5.5

Endoscopic Retrograde Cholangiopancreatography (ERCP)

Text in this section is excerpted from "ERCP (Endoscopic Retrograde Cholangiopancreatography)," National Institute of Diabetes and Digestive and Kidney Diseases (NIDDK), June 2012. Reviewed December 2015.

What is ERCP?

Endoscopic retrograde cholangiopancreatography is a procedure that combines upper gastrointestinal (GI) endoscopy and X-rays to treat problems of the bile and pancreatic ducts. ERCP is also used to diagnose problems, but the availability of non-invasive tests such as magnetic resonance cholangiography has allowed ERCP to be used primarily for cases in which it is expected that treatment will be delivered during the procedure.

What is upper gastrointestinal (GI) endoscopy?

Upper GI endoscopy is a procedure that uses a lighted, flexible endoscope to see and perform procedures inside the upper GI tract. The upper GI tract includes the esophagus, stomach, and duodenum—the first part of the small intestine.

What are the bile and pancreatic ducts?

Ducts are tubelike structures in the body that carry fluids. The bile ducts carry bile, a liquid the liver makes to help break down food. A group of small bile ducts—called the biliary tree—in the liver empties bile into the larger common bile duct. Between meals, the common bile duct closes and bile collects in the gallbladder—a pear-shaped sac next to the liver.

The pancreatic ducts carry pancreatic juice, a liquid the pancreas makes to help break down food. A group of small pancreatic ducts in the pancreas empties into the main pancreatic duct.

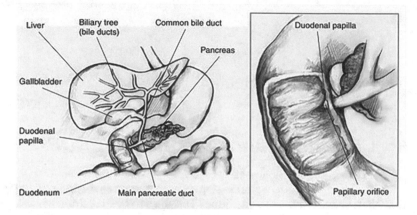

Figure 5.1. *Bile and pancreatic ducts*

The common bile duct and the main pancreatic duct join before emptying their contents into the duodenum through the papillary orifice at the end of the duodenal papilla—a small, nipplelike structure that extends into the duodenum.

When is ERCP used?

ERCP is used when it is suspected a person's bile or pancreatic ducts may be narrowed or blocked due to

- tumors

- gallstones that form in the gallbladder and become stuck in the ducts

- inflammation due to trauma or illness, such as pancreatitis— inflammation of the pancreas

- infection

- valves in the ducts, called sphincters, that won't open properly

- scarring of the ducts, called sclerosis

- pseudocysts—accumulations of fluid and tissue debris

How does a person prepare for ERCP?

The health care provider usually provides written instructions about how to prepare for ERCP.

The upper GI tract must be empty. Generally, no eating or drinking is allowed 8 hours before ERCP. Smoking and chewing gum are also prohibited during this time.

Patients should tell their health care provider about all health conditions they have, especially heart and lung problems, diabetes, and allergies. Patients should also tell their health care provider about all medications they take. Patients may be asked to temporarily stop taking medications that affect blood clotting or interact with sedatives, which are usually given during ERCP to help patients relax and stay comfortable.

Medications and vitamins that may be restricted before and after ERCP include

- nonsteroidal anti-inflammatory drugs, such as aspirin, ibuprofen (Advil), and naproxen (Aleve)

- blood thinners

- high blood pressure medication

- diabetes medications

- antidepressants

- dietary supplements

Driving is not permitted for 12 to 24 hours after ERCP to allow the sedatives time to completely wear off. Before the appointment, patients should make plans for a ride home.

How is ERCP performed?

ERCP is conducted at a hospital or outpatient center by a doctor and assistants who have specialized training in this procedure. Patients receive a local anesthetic that is gargled or sprayed on the back of the throat. The anesthetic numbs the throat and calms the gag reflex.

An intravenous needle is inserted into a vein in the arm if sedatives will be given. Doctors and other medical staff monitor vital signs while patients are sedated.

During ERCP, patients lie on their back or side on an X-ray table. The doctor inserts an endoscope down the esophagus, through the stomach, and into the duodenum. Video is transmitted from a small camera attached to the endoscope to a computer screen within the doctor's view. Air is pumped through the endoscope to inflate the stomach and duodenum, making them easier for the doctor to examine.

When the doctor locates the duodenal papilla, a blunt tube called a catheter is slid through the endoscope and guided through the papillary opening. Once the catheter is inside the papilla, the doctor injects a dye into the ducts. The dye, also called contrast medium, allows the ducts to be seen on X-rays. X-rays are then taken to see the ducts and to look for narrowed areas or blockages.

Procedures to treat narrowed areas or blockages can be performed during ERCP. To see the ducts during treatment procedures, the doctor uses X-rays video, also called fluoroscopy. Special tools guided through the endoscope and into the ducts allow the doctor to open blocked ducts, break up or remove gallstones, remove tumors in the ducts, or insert stents. Stents are plastic or expandable metal tubes that are left in narrowed ducts to restore the flow of bile or pancreatic juice. A kind of biopsy called brush cytology allows the doctor to remove cells from inside the ducts using a brush that fits through the endoscope. The collected cells are later examined with a microscope for signs of infection or cancer.

Occasionally, ERCP is done after gallbladder surgery, if a surgical bile leak is suspected, to find and stop the leak with a temporary stent.

What does recovery from ERCP involve?

After ERCP, patients are moved to a recovery room where they wait for about an hour for the sedatives to wear off. Patients may not remember conversations with health care staff, as the sedatives reduce memory of events during and after the procedure. During this time, patients may feel bloated or nauseous. Patients may also have a sore throat, which can last a day or two.

Patients can go home after the sedatives wear off. Patients will likely feel tired and should plan to rest for the remainder of the day.

Some ERCP results are available immediately after the procedure. Biopsy results are usually ready in a few days.

Eating, Diet, and Nutrition

Unless otherwise directed, patients may immediately resume their normal diet and medications after having an ERCP. The health care provider can answer any specific questions about eating, diet, and nutrition.Some ERCP results are available immediately after the procedure. Biopsy results are usually ready in a few days.

What are the risks associated with ERCP?

Significant risks associated with ERCP include

- infection
- pancreatitis
- allergic reaction to sedatives
- excessive bleeding, called hemorrhage
- puncture of the GI tract or ducts
- tissue damage from radiation exposure
- death, in rare circumstances

When ERCP is performed by an experienced doctor, complications occur in about 6 to 10 percent of patients and these often require hospitalization. Patients who experience any of the following symptoms after ERCP should contact their health care provider immediately:

- swallowing difficulties
- throat, chest, or abdominal pain that worsens
- vomiting
- bloody or dark stool
- fever

Chapter 6

Upper and Lower GI Series

Chapter Contents

103

Section 6.1

Upper GI and Small Bowel Series (Barium Swallow)

Text in this section is excerpted from "Upper GI Series," National Institute of Diabetes and Digestive and Kidney Diseases (NIDDK), April 2014.

What is an upper gastrointestinal (GI) series?

An upper GI series, also called a barium swallow, uses X-rays and fluoroscopy to help diagnose problems of the upper GI tract. An X-ray is a picture created by using radiation and recorded on film or on a computer. Fluoroscopy is a form of X-rays that makes it possible to see the internal organs and their motion on a video monitor. To make the upper GI tract more visible on X-ray, a health care provider will fill the person's upper GI tract with a chalky liquid called barium. The two types of upper GI series are

- a standard barium upper GI series, which uses only barium during the test

- a double-contrast upper GI series, which uses a combination of air and barium to create a more detailed view of the stomach lining

What is the upper gastrointestinal tract?

The upper GI tract is the first part of the GI tract, which includes a series of hollow organs joined in a long, twisting tube from the mouth to the anus—a 1-inch-long opening through which stool leaves the body. The upper GI tract includes the mouth, esophagus, stomach, duodenum, and small intestine. The duodenum is the first part of the small intestine.

The esophagus carries food and liquids from the mouth to the stomach. The muscular layers of the esophagus are normally pinched together at both the upper and lower ends by muscles called sphincters. When a person swallows, the sphincters relax to let food or drink pass from the mouth into the stomach. The muscles then close rapidly to prevent the food or drink from leaking out of the stomach back into the esophagus. This process is automatic and people are usually not aware of it, though people sometimes feel food in their esophagus when they swallow something too large, try to eat too quickly, or drink very hot or cold liquids.

The stomach slowly pumps the food and liquids into the small intestine, which absorbs needed nutrients. The body digests food using the movement of the muscles in the GI tract, along with the release of hormones and enzymes.

Why is an upper gastrointestinal series performed?

An upper GI series can help diagnose the cause of

- abdominal pain
- nausea and vomiting
- problems swallowing
- unexplained weight loss

An upper GI series can also show

- abnormal growths.
- esophageal varices—abnormal, enlarged veins in the lower part of the esophagus.
- gastroesophageal reflux, which occurs when stomach contents flow back up into the esophagus.
- a hiatal hernia, or when the upper part of the stomach slips through the diaphragm and moves up into the chest. The diaphragm is the muscle wall that separates the stomach from the chest.
- inflammation, or swelling, of the GI tract.
- scars or strictures—abnormal narrowing of openings in the body.
- ulcers—sores on the stomach or intestinal lining.

How does a person prepare for an upper gastrointestinal series?

A person prepares for an upper GI series by:

- talking with a health care provider
- clearing the upper GI tract

Talking with a health care provider. A person should talk with his or her health care provider about:

- medical conditions he or she has

- all prescribed and over-the-counter medications, vitamins, and supplements he or she takes

Women should let their health care provider know if they may be pregnant to avoid potential risks to the developing baby. The health care provider will take special precautions to minimize the exposure to radiation, or he or she may suggest a different procedure.

Clearing the upper GI tract. This procedure uses X-ray images to examine the upper GI tract during the procedure. The X-ray can't show the lining of the organs clearly if food or drink is inside the upper GI tract. To ensure the upper GI tract is clear, health care providers usually advise people not to eat, drink, smoke, or chew gum during the 8 hours before the procedure.

How is an upper gastrointestinal series performed?

An X-ray technician and a radiologist—a doctor who specializes in medical imaging—perform an upper GI series at a hospital or an outpatient center. A person does not need anesthesia. The procedure usually takes about 2 hours to complete. However, if the barium moves slowly through the small intestine, the test may take up to 5 hours to complete.

For the test,

- the person stands or sits in front of an X-ray machine and drinks barium, which coats the lining of the upper GI tract

- the person lies on the X-ray table and the radiologist watches the barium move through the GI tract on the X-rays and fluoroscopy

- the technician may press on the abdomen—the area between the chest and hips—or ask the person to change positions to fully coat the upper GI tract with the barium

If a person has a double-contrast study, he or she will swallow gas-forming crystals, which activate when they mix with the barium. The gas expands the barium-coated stomach, filling it with air and exposing finer details of the upper GI tract lining. The technician will take additional X-rays.

What can a person expect after an upper gastrointestinal series?

After an upper GI series, a person can expect the following:

- bloating or nausea for a short time after the procedure
- to resume most normal activities after leaving the hospital or outpatient center
- barium in the GI tract that causes stools to be white or light colored for several days after the procedure

A person should carefully read and follow the discharge instructions, which will explain how to flush the remaining barium from the GI tract. The radiologist will interpret the images and send a report of the findings to the person's health care provider.

Seek Immediate Care

People who have any of the following symptoms after an upper GI series should seek immediate medical attention:

- failure to have a bowel movement within 2 days of the procedure
- fever
- inability to pass gas
- severe abdominal pain
- severe constipation

What are the risks of an upper gastrointestinal series?

The risks of an upper GI series include:

- constipation from the barium—the most common complication of an upper GI series.
- an allergic reaction to the barium or flavoring in the barium.
- bowel obstruction—partial or complete blockage of the small or large intestine. Although rare, bowel obstruction can be a life-threatening condition that requires emergency medical treatment.

Radiation exposure can cause cancer, although the level of radiation exposure that leads to cancer is unknown. Health care providers estimate the risk of cancer from this type of test to be small.

Section 6.2

Lower GI Series (Barium Enema)

Text in this section is excerpted from "Lower GI Series," National Institute of Diabetes and Digestive and Kidney Diseases (NIDDK), April 2014.

What is a lower gastrointestinal (GI) series?

A lower GI series, also called a barium enema, is an X-ray exam used to help diagnose problems of the large intestine. An X-ray is a picture created by using radiation and recorded on film or on a computer. To make the large intestine more visible on X-ray, a health care provider will fill the person's intestine with a chalky liquid called barium. The two types of lower GI series are

- a single-contrast lower GI series, which uses only barium during the test

- a double-contrast or air-contrast lower GI series, which uses a combination of barium and air to create a more detailed view of the large intestine

The health care provider and radiologist—a doctor who specializes in medical imaging—will work together to determine which exam to perform.

What is the large intestine?

The large intestine is part of the GI tract, a series of hollow organs joined in a long, twisting tube from the mouth to the anus—a 1-inch-long opening through which stool leaves the body. The body digests food using the movement of muscles in the GI tract, along with the release of hormones and enzymes. Organs that make up the GI tract are the mouth, esophagus, stomach, small intestine, large intestine—which includes the appendix, cecum, colon, and rectum—and anus. The intestines are sometimes called the bowel. The last part of the GI tract—called the lower GI tract—consists of the large intestine and anus.

The large intestine is about 5 feet long in adults and absorbs water and any remaining nutrients from partially digested food passed from the small intestine. The large intestine then changes waste from liquid to a solid matter called stool. Stool passes from the colon to the rectum. The rectum is 6 to 8 inches long in adults and is located between the last part of the colon—called the sigmoid colon—and the anus. The rectum stores stool prior to a bowel movement. During a bowel movement, stool moves from the rectum to the anus.

Why is a lower gastrointestinal series performed?

A lower GI series can help diagnose the cause of

- abdominal pain
- bleeding from the anus
- changes in bowel habits
- chronic diarrhea
- unexplained weight loss

A lower GI series can also show

- cancerous growths.
- diverticula—small pouches in the colon.
- a fistula—an abnormal passage, or tunnel, between two organs, called an internal fistula, or between an organ and the outside of the body, called an external fistula. Fistulas occur most often in the areas around the rectum and anus.
- inflammation, or swelling, of the intestinal lining.
- polyps—extra pieces of tissue that grow on the lining of the intestine.
- ulcers—sores on the intestinal lining.

How does a person prepare for a lower gastrointestinal series?

A person prepares for a lower GI series by

- talking with a health care provider
- cleansing the bowel

Talking with a health care provider. People should talk with their health care provider

- about medical conditions they have

- about all prescribed and over-thecounter medications, vitamins, and supplements they take

- if they've had a colonoscopy with a biopsy or polyp removal in the last 4 weeks

Women should let their health care provider know if they may be pregnant to avoid potential risks to the developing baby. The health care provider will take special precautions to minimize exposure to radiation, or he or she may suggest a different procedure.

Cleansing the bowel. The health care provider will give written bowel prep instructions to follow at home. The health care provider orders a bowel prep so that little to no stool is present inside the person's intestine. A complete bowel prep lets the person pass stool that is clear. Stool inside the colon can prevent the X-ray from making a clear image of the intestine. Instructions may include following a clear liquid diet for 1 to 3 days before the procedure and avoiding drinks that contain red or purple dye. The instructions will provide specific direction about when to start and stop the clear liquid diet. During this diet, people may drink or eat the following:

- fat-free bouillon or broth

- gelatin in flavors such as lemon, lime, or orange

- plain coffee or tea, without cream or milk

- sports drinks in flavors such as lemon, lime, or orange

- strained fruit juice, such as apple or white grape—orange juice is not recommended

- water

The person needs to take laxatives and enemas the night before a lower GI series. A laxative is medication that loosens stool and increases bowel movements. An enema involves flushing water or laxative into the rectum using a special wash bottle. Laxatives and enemas can cause diarrhea, so the person should stay close to a bathroom during the bowel prep.

A person may take laxatives swallowed as a pill or as a powder dissolved in water. Some people will need to drink a large amount, usually a gallon, of liquid laxative over the course of the bowel prep at scheduled times. People may find this step difficult; however, it is very important to complete the prep. The images will not be clear if the prep is incomplete.

People should call their health care provider if they are having side effects that make them feel they can't finish the prep.

How is a lower gastrointestinal series performed?

An X-ray technician and a radiologist perform a lower GI series at a hospital or an outpatient center. A person does not need anesthesia. The procedure usually takes 30 to 60 minutes.

For the test,

- the person lies on a table while the radiologist inserts a flexible tube into the person's anus and fills the large intestine with barium

- the radiologist prevents leaking of barium from the anus by inflating a balloon on the end of the tube

- the technician may ask the person to change position several times to evenly coat the large intestine with the barium

- if the health care provider has ordered a double-contrast lower GI series, the radiologist will inject air through the tube to inflate the intestine

During the test, the person may have some discomfort and feel the urge to have a bowel movement.

The person will need to hold still in various positions while the radiologist and technician take X-ray images and possibly X-ray video, called fluoroscopy. The radiologist and technician will view the large intestine from different angles.

When the imaging is complete, the radiologist or technician will deflate the balloon on the tube, and most of the barium will drain through the tube. The person will expel the remaining barium into a bedpan or nearby toilet. A nurse or technician may give the person an enema to further flush out the barium.

What can a person expect after a lower gastrointestinal series?

After a lower GI series, a person can expect the following:

- abdominal cramps and bloating that may occur for a short time after the procedure

- to resume most normal activities after leaving the hospital or outpatient center

- barium in the large intestine that causes stools to be white or light colored for several days after the procedure

A person should carefully read and follow the discharge instructions, which will explain how to flush the remaining barium from the intestine. The radiologist will interpret the images and send a report of the findings to the person's health care provider.

Seek Immediate Care

People who have any of the following symptoms after a lower GI series should seek immediate medical attention:

- severe abdominal pain
- bloody bowel movements or bleeding from the anus
- inability to pass gas
- fever
- severe constipation

What are the risks of a lower gastrointestinal series?

The risks of a lower GI series include:

- constipation from the barium enema—the most common complication of a lower GI series.

- an allergic reaction to the barium.

- bowel obstruction—partial or complete blockage of the small or large intestine. Although rare, bowel obstruction can be a life-threatening condition that requires emergency medical treatment.

- leakage of barium into the abdomen—the area between the chest and the hips—through an undetected tear or hole in the lining of the large intestine. This complication is rare; however, it usually requires emergency surgery to repair.

Radiation exposure can cause cancer, although the level of radiation exposure that leads to cancer is unknown. Health care providers estimate the risk of cancer from this type of test to be small.

Chapter 7

Diagnostic Liver Tests

Chapter Contents

Section 7.1

Understanding Liver Tests

Text in this section is excerpted from "Understanding Lab Tests:
Entire Lesson," U.S. Department of Veterans Affairs (VA), October
16, 2015.

Tests of the liver

If you have hepatitis C, most likely, your doctor will check blood
tests of your liver. There's a handful of liver tests and it is helpful to
know what each of them means.

- Liver panel
- Liver enzymes
- Liver function tests (LFT)
- ALT
- AST
- Bilirubin

- Albumin
- Prothrombin time
- Alkaline phosphatase
- INR
- Platelets
- Total protein

Liver panel

A "liver panel" usually refers to several lab tests performed
as a group. Depending on the physician or the laboratory, a liver
panel usually includes tests for AST, ALT, bilirubin, and alkaline
phosphatase.

Liver enzymes

Usually, the term "liver enzymes" refers to the AST and the ALT.

Liver function tests (LFTs)

The phrase "liver function tests" or "LFTs" is commonly used by
patients and physicians. Many patients and physicians use the term

to describe the AST and ALT. However, this is not correct—the AST and ALT do not measure the function of the liver.

The true function of the liver is actually best measured by the PT, INR and albumin. Therefore, if you are getting a PT, INR or albumin, these tests can determine how the liver is "functioning."

ALT (SGPT)

ALT, or alanine aminotransferase, is 1 of the 2 "liver enzymes." It is sometimes known as serum glutamic-pyruvic transaminase, or SGPT. It is a protein made only by liver cells. When liver cells are damaged, ALT leaks out into the bloodstream and the level of ALT in the blood is higher than normal.

Explanation of test results:

A high ALT level often means there is some liver damage, but it may not be related to hepatitis C. It is important to realize the ALT level goes up and down in most patients with hepatitis C. The ALT level does not tell you exactly how much liver damage there is, and small changes should be expected. Changes in the ALT level do not mean the liver is doing any better or any worse. The ALT level does not tell you how much scarring (fibrosis) is in the liver and it does not predict how much liver damage will develop.

Other things to know:

- Many patients with hepatitis C will have a normal ALT level.

- Patients can have very severe liver disease and cirrhosis and still have a normal ALT level.

- When a patient takes treatment for hepatitis C, it is helpful to see if the ALT level goes down.

AST (SGOT)

AST, or aspartate aminotransferase, is 1 of the 2 "liver enzymes." It is also known as serum glutamic-oxaloacetic transaminase, or SGOT. AST is a protein made by liver cells. When liver cells are damaged, AST leaks out into the bloodstream and the level of AST in the blood becomes higher than normal. AST is different from ALT because AST is found in parts of the body other than the liver—including the heart, kidneys, muscles, and brain. When cells in any of those parts of the body are damaged, AST can be elevated.

Explanation of test results:

A high AST level often means there is some liver damage, but it is not necessarily caused by hepatitis C. A high AST with a normal ALT may mean that the AST is coming from a different part of the body. It is important to realize that the AST level in most patients with hepatitis C goes up and down. The exact AST level does not tell you how much liver damage there is, or whether the liver is getting better or worse, and small changes should be expected. However, for patients receiving treatment for hepatitis C, it is helpful to see if the AST level goes down.

Other things to know:

• The AST level is not as helpful as the ALT level for checking the liver.

• Many patients with hepatitis C will have a normal AST level.

• Patients can have very severe liver disease or cirrhosis and still have a normal AST level.

Bilirubin

Bilirubin is a yellowish substance that is created by the breakdown (destruction) of hemoglobin, a major component of red blood cells.

Explanation of test results:

As red blood cells age, they are broken down naturally in the body. Bilirubin is released from the destroyed red blood cells and passed on to the liver. The liver excretes the bilirubin in fluid called bile. If the liver is not functioning correctly, the bilirubin will not be properly excreted. Therefore, if the bilirubin level is higher than normal, it may mean that the liver is not functioning correctly.

Other things to know:

• Levels of bilirubin in the blood go up and down in patients with hepatitis C.

• When bilirubin levels remain high for prolonged periods, it usually means there is severe liver disease and possibly cirrhosis.

- High levels of bilirubin can cause jaundice (yellowing of the skin and eyes, darker urine, and lighter-colored bowel movements).

- Elevated bilirubin levels can be caused by reasons other than liver disease.

- Total bilirubin is made up of 2 components: direct bilirubin and indirect bilirubin.

- Direct bilirubin + indirect bilirubin = total bilirubin.

Albumin

Albumin is a protein made by the liver. Albumin prevents fluid from leaking out of blood vessels into tissues.

Explanation of test results:

A low albumin level in patients with hepatitis C can be a sign of cirrhosis (advanced liver disease). Albumin levels can go up and down slightly. Very low albumin levels can cause symptoms of edema, or fluid accumulation, in the abdomen (called ascites) or in the leg.

Other things to know:

- A low albumin level can also come from kidney disease or malnutrition or acute illness.

- A low albumin level causing fluid overload is often treated with diuretic medications, or "water pills."

Prothrombin time

Prothrombin is a protein made by the liver. Prothrombin helps blood to make normal clots. The "prothrombin time" (PT) is one way of measuring how long it takes blood to form a clot, and it is measured in seconds (such as 13.2 seconds). A normal PT indicates that a normal amount of blood-clotting protein is available.

Explanation of test results:

When the PT is high, it takes longer for the blood to clot (17 seconds, for example). This usually happens because the liver is not making the right amount of blood clotting proteins, so the clotting process takes longer. A high PT usually means that there is serious liver damage or cirrhosis.

Other things to know:

- Some patients take a drug called Coumadin (warfarin), which elevates the PT for the purpose of "thinning" the blood. This is not related to having liver disease because it is the Coumadin causing the PT to be high.

- The test called INR measures the same factors as PT and is used instead of PT by many doctors.

Alkaline phosphatase

Alkaline phosphatase (often shortened to alk phos) is an enzyme made in liver cells and bile ducts. The alk phos level is a common test that is usually included when liver tests are performed as a group.

Explanation of test results:

A high alk phos level does not reflect liver damage or inflammation. A high alk phos level occurs when there is a blockage of flow in the biliary tract or a buildup of pressure in the liver—often caused by a gallstone or scarring in the bile ducts.

Other things to know:

- Many patients with hepatitis C have normal alk phos levels.

- Hepatitis C treatment usually does not affect alk phos levels.

- Alk phos is produced in other organs besides the liver—it is also found in the bones and the kidneys.

- If your alk phos level is high, your doctor will probably order additional tests to determine why.

INR (international normalized ratio)

International normalized ratio (INR) is blood-clotting test. It is a test used to measure how quickly your blood forms a clot, compared with normal clotting time.

Explanation of test results:

A normal INR is 1.0. Each increase of 0.1 means the blood is slightly thinner (it takes longer to clot). INR is related to the prothrombin time (PT). If there is serious liver disease and cirrhosis, the liver may not produce the normal amount of proteins and then the blood is not able to clot normally. When your doctor is evaluating the function of your liver, a high INR usually means that the liver is not working as well as it could because it is not making the blood clot normally.

Other things to know:

- Some patients take a drug called Coumadin (warfarin), which elevates the INR, for the purpose of "thinning" the blood.

- The INR is another way of measuring the blood-clotting time and it is easier to determine than the PT.

Platelets

Platelets are cells that help the blood to form clots. The platelet number or "platelet count" in the blood is measured as part of the complete blood count (CBC).

Explanation of test results:

Platelet counts in a patient who has cirrhosis are often low. But low platelet counts can also come from other causes, including certain medications. Interferon treatment can reduce platelet counts. When the platelet count is extremely reduced, this condition is known as "thrombocytopenia." If a platelet count is too low, the patient cannot make normal clots and may bruise more easily.

Other things to know:

- If the platelet count drops too low (below 50,000, for example) when a patient is receiving interferon, doctors may recommend that the interferon dosage be reduced.

Total protein

Total protein level is a measure of a number of different proteins in the blood. Total protein can be divided into the albumin and globulin fractions.

Explanation of test results:

Low levels of total protein in the blood can occur because of impaired function of the liver.

Section 7.2

Liver Biopsy

Text in this section is excerpted from "Liver Biopsy," National
Institute of Diabetes and Digestive and Kidney Diseases (NIDDK),
April 2014.

What is a liver biopsy?

A liver biopsy is a procedure that involves taking a small piece of
liver tissue for examination with a microscope for signs of damage or
disease. The three types of liver biopsy are the following:

- Percutaneous biopsy—the most common type of liver biopsy—
  involves inserting a hollow needle through the abdomen into the
  liver. The abdomen is the area between the chest and hips.

- Transvenous biopsy involves making a small incision in the neck
  and inserting a needle through a hollow tube called a sheath
  through the jugular vein to the liver.

- Laparoscopic biopsy involves inserting a laparoscope, a thin tube
  with a tiny video camera attached, through a small incision to
  look inside the body to view the surface of organs. The health
  care provider will insert a needle through a plastic, tubelike
  instrument called a cannula to remove the liver tissue sample.

What is the liver and what does it do?

The liver is the body's largest internal organ. The liver is called the
body's metabolic factory because of the important role it plays in metabolism—the way cells change food into energy after food is digested and
absorbed into the blood. The liver has many functions, including

- taking up, storing, and processing nutrients from food—including fat, sugar, and protein—and delivering them to the rest of
  the body when needed

- making new proteins, such as clotting factors and immune
  factors

- producing bile, which helps the body absorb fats, cholesterol, and fat-soluble vitamins

- removing waste products the kidneys cannot remove, such as fats, cholesterol, toxins, and medications

A healthy liver is necessary for survival. The liver can regenerate most of its own cells when they become damaged.

Why is a liver biopsy performed?

A health care provider will perform a liver biopsy to

- diagnose liver diseases that cannot be diagnosed with blood or imaging tests

- estimate the degree of liver damage, a process called staging

- help determine the best treatment for liver damage or disease

How does a person prepare for a liver biopsy?

A person prepares for a liver biopsy by

- talking with a health care provider

- having blood tests

- arranging for a ride home

- fasting before the procedure

Talking with a health care provider. People should talk with their health care provider about medical conditions they have and all prescribed and over-the-counter medications, vitamins, and supplements they take, including

- antibiotics

- antidepressants

- aspirin

- asthma medications

- blood pressure medications

- blood thinners

- diabetes medications

- dietary supplements

- nonsteroidal anti-inflammatory drugs such as ibuprofen and naproxen

The health care provider may tell the person to stop taking medications temporarily that affect blood clotting or interact with anesthesia, which people sometimes receive during a liver biopsy.

Having blood tests. A person will have a test to show how well his or her blood clots. A person will have a test to show how well his or her blood clots. A technician or nurse draws a blood sample during an office visit or at a commercial facility and sends the sample to a lab for analysis. People with severe liver disease often have blood-clotting problems that can increase their chance of bleeding after the biopsy. A health care provider may give the person a medication called clotting factor concentrates just before a liver biopsy to reduce the chance of bleeding.

Arranging for a ride home after the procedure. For safety reasons, most people cannot drive home after the procedure. A health care provider will ask a person to make advance arrangements for getting home after the procedure.

Fasting before the procedure. A health care provider will ask a person not to eat or drink for 8 hours before the procedure if the provider anticipates using anesthesia or sedation.

How is a liver biopsy performed?

A health care provider performs the liver biopsy at a hospital or an outpatient center and determines which type of biopsy is best for the person.

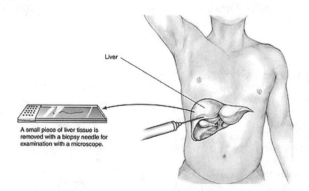

Figure 7.1. *Percutaneous liver biopsy is the most common type of liver biopsy.*

Percutaneous Liver Biopsy

A person lies face up on a table and rests the right hand above the head. A health care provider gives the person a local anesthetic on the area where he or she will insert the biopsy needle. If needed, the health care provider will give the person sedatives and pain medication.

The health care provider either taps on the abdomen to locate the liver or uses one of the following imaging techniques:

- **Ultrasound.** Ultrasound uses a device, called a transducer, that bounces safe, painless sound waves off organs to create an image of their structure.

- **Computerized tomography (CT) scan.** A CT scan uses a combination of X-rays and computer technology to create images. For a CT scan, a technician may give the person a solution to drink and an injection of a special dye, called contrast medium. CT scans require the person to lie on a table that slides into a tunnel-shaped device where the technician takes the X-rays.

Research has shown fewer complications after biopsy when health care providers use ultrasound to locate the liver compared with tapping on the abdomen. Health care providers may select ultrasound over a CT scan because it is quicker and less expensive, and can show the biopsy needle in real time.

The health care provider will

- make a small incision in the right side of the person's abdomen, either toward the bottom of or just below the rib cage

- insert the biopsy needle

- ask the person to exhale and hold his or her breath while the health care provider inserts the needle and quickly removes a sample of liver tissue

- insert and remove the needle several times if multiple samples are needed

- place a bandage over the incision

After the biopsy, the person must lie on his or her right side for up to 2 hours to reduce the chance of bleeding. Medical staff monitor the person for signs of bleeding for 2 to 4 more hours.

Transvenous Liver Biopsy

When a person's blood clots slowly or the person has ascites—a buildup of fluid in the abdomen—the health care provider may perform a transvenous liver biopsy.

For this procedure, the person lies face up on an X-ray table, and a health care provider applies local anesthetic to one side of the neck. The health care provider will give sedatives and pain medication if the person needs them.

The health care provider will

- make a small incision in the neck.

- insert a sheath into the jugular vein and thread the sheath down the jugular vein, along the side of the heart, and into one of the veins in the liver.

- inject contrast medium into the sheath and take an X-ray. The contrast medium makes the blood vessels and the location of the sheath clearly visible on the X-ray images.

- thread a biopsy needle through the sheath and into the liver and quickly remove a liver tissue sample.

- insert and remove the biopsy needle several times if multiple samples are needed.

- carefully withdraw the sheath and close the incision with a bandage.

Medical staff monitor the person for 4 to 6 hours afterwards for signs of bleeding.

Laparoscopic Liver Biopsy

Health care providers use this type of biopsy to obtain a tissue sample from a specific area or from multiple areas of the liver, or when the risk of spreading cancer or infection exists. A health care provider may take a liver tissue sample during laparoscopic surgery performed for other reasons, including liver surgery.

The person lies on his or her back on an operating table. A nurse or technician will insert an intravenous (IV) needle into the person's arm to give anesthesia.

The health care provider will

- make a small incision in the abdomen, just below the rib cage

- insert a cannula into the incision and fill the abdomen with gas to provide space to work inside the abdominal cavity and to see the liver

- insert a biopsy needle through the cannula and into the liver and quickly remove a liver tissue sample

- insert and remove the biopsy needle several times if multiple samples are needed

- remove the cannula and close the incisions with dissolvable stitches

The health care provider can easily spot any bleeding from the procedure with the camera on the laparoscope and treat it using an electric probe. The person stays at the hospital or an outpatient center for a few hours while the anesthesia wears off.

What can a person expect after a liver biopsy?

After a liver biopsy, a person can expect

- full recovery in 1 to 2 days.

- to avoid intense activity, exercise, or heavy lifting for up to 1 week.

- soreness around the biopsy or incision site for about a week. Acetaminophen (Tylenol) or other pain medications that do not interfere with blood clotting may help. People should check with their health care provider before taking any pain medications.

- a member of the health care team to review the discharge instructions with the person—or with an accompanying friend or family member if the person is still groggy—and provide a written copy. The person should follow all instructions given.

Seek Immediate Care

People who have any of the following symptoms after a liver biopsy should seek immediate medical attention:

- chest pain
- difficulty breathing

> - increasing abdominal pain
> - dizziness
> - bleeding from the incision or biopsy site
> - abdominal swelling or bloating
> - fever
> - swelling or redness at the incision or biopsy site
> - nausea or vomiting

Liver biopsy results take a few days to come back. The liver sample goes to a pathology lab where a technician stains the tissue. Staining highlights important details within the liver tissue and helps identify any signs of liver disease. The pathologist—a doctor who specializes in diagnosing diseases—looks at the tissue with a microscope and sends a report to the person's health care provider.

What are the risks of liver biopsy?

The risks of a liver biopsy include

- pain and bruising at the biopsy or incision site—the most common complication after a liver biopsy. Most people experience mild pain that does not require medication; however, some people need medications to relieve the pain.

- prolonged bleeding from the biopsy or incision site or internal bleeding. A person may require hospitalization, transfusions, and sometimes surgery or another procedure to stop the bleeding.

- infection of the biopsy site or incision site that may cause sepsis. Sepsis is an illness in which the body has a severe response to bacteria or a virus.

- pneumothorax, also called collapsed lung, which occurs when air or gas builds up in the pleural space. The pleural space is thin layers of tissue that wrap around the outside of the lungs and line the inside of the chest cavity. Pneumothorax may happen when the biopsy needle punctures the pleural space.

- hemothorax, or the buildup of blood in the pleural space.

- puncture of other organs.

Chapter 8

Other Diagnostic Tests of the Gastrointestinal Tract

Chapter Contents

Section 8.1

Celiac Disease Tests

Text in this section is excerpted from "Celiac Disease," National
Institute of Diabetes and Digestive and Kidney Diseases (NIDDK),
September 2014.

How is celiac disease diagnosed?

A health care provider diagnoses celiac disease with

- a medical and family history

- a physical exam

- blood tests

- an intestinal biopsy

- a skin biopsy

Medical and Family History

Taking a medical and family history may help a health care provider diagnose celiac disease. He or she will ask the patient or caregiver to provide a medical and family history, specifically if anyone in the patient's family has a history of celiac disease.

Physical Exam

A physical exam may help diagnose celiac disease. During a physical exam, a health care provider usually

- examines the patient's body for malnutrition or a rash

- uses a stethoscope to listen to sounds within the abdomen

- taps on the patient's abdomen checking for bloating and pain

Blood Tests

A blood test involves drawing blood at a health care provider's office or a commercial facility and sending the sample to a lab for analysis.

A blood test can show the presence of antibodies that are common in celiac disease.

If blood test results are negative and a health care provider still suspects celiac disease, he or she may order additional blood tests, which can affect test results.

Before the blood tests, patients should continue to eat a diet that includes foods with gluten, such as breads and pastas. If a patient stops eating foods with gluten before being tested, the results may be negative for celiac disease even if the disease is present.

Intestinal Biopsy

If blood tests suggest that a patient has celiac disease, a health care provider will perform a biopsy of the patient's small intestine to confirm the diagnosis. A biopsy is a procedure that involves taking a piece of tissue for examination with a microscope. A health care provider performs the biopsy in an outpatient center or a hospital. He or she will give the patient light sedation and a local anesthetic. Some patients may receive general anesthesia.

During the biopsy, a health care provider removes tiny pieces of tissue from the patient's small intestine using an endoscope—a small, flexible camera with a light. The health care provider carefully feeds the endoscope down the patient's esophagus and into the stomach and small intestine. A small camera mounted on the endoscope transmits a video image to a monitor, allowing close examination of the intestinal lining. The health care provider then takes the samples using tiny tools that he or she passes through the endoscope. A pathologist—a doctor who specializes in examining tissues to diagnose diseases—examines the tissue in a lab. The test can show damage to the villi in the small intestine.

Skin Biopsy

When a health care provider suspects that a patient has dermatitis herpetiformis, he or she will perform a skin biopsy. A skin biopsy is a procedure that involves removing tiny pieces of skin tissue for examination with a microscope. A health care provider performs the biopsy in an outpatient center or a hospital. The patient receives a local anesthetic; however, in some cases, the patient will require general anesthesia.

A pathologist examines the skin tissue in a lab and checks the tissue for antibodies that are common in celiac disease. If the skin tissue tests positive for the antibodies, a health care provider will perform blood tests to confirm celiac disease. If the skin biopsy and blood tests both suggest celiac disease, the patient may not need an intestinal biopsy for diagnosis.

Section 8.2

Esophageal Manometry and Esophageal Monitoring

Text in this section is excerpted from "Diagnosis of (GER) and (GERD)," National Institute of Diabetes and Digestive and Kidney Diseases (NIDDK), November 13, 2014.

Esophageal pH and impedance monitoring

The most accurate procedure to detect acid reflux is esophageal pH and impedance monitoring. Esophageal pH and impedance monitoring measures the amount of acid in your esophagus while you do normal things, such as eating and sleeping.

A gastroenterologist performs this procedure at a hospital or an outpatient center as a part of an upper GI endoscopy. Most often, you can stay awake during the procedure.

A gastroenterologist will pass a thin tube through your nose or mouth into your stomach. The gastroenterologist will then pull the tube back into your esophagus and tape it to your cheek. The end of the tube in your esophagus measures when and how much acid comes up your esophagus. The other end of the tube attaches to a monitor outside your body that records the measurements.

You will wear a monitor for the next 24 hours. You will return to the hospital or outpatient center to have the tube removed.

This procedure is most useful to your doctor if you keep a diary of when, what, and how much food you eat and your GERD symptoms are after you eat. The gastroenterologist can see how your symptoms, certain foods, and certain times of day relate to one another. The procedure can also help show whether acid reflux triggers any respiratory symptoms.

Bravo wireless esophageal pH monitoring

Bravo wireless esophageal pH monitoring also measures and records the pH in your esophagus to determine if you have GERD. A doctor temporarily attaches a small capsule to the wall of your esophagus during an upper endoscopy. The capsule measures pH levels in the esophagus and transmits information to a receiver. The receiver is about the size of a pager, which you wear on your belt or waistband.

You will follow your usual daily routine during monitoring, which usually lasts 48 hours. The receiver has several buttons on it that you will press to record symptoms of GERD such as heartburn. The nurse will tell you what symptoms to record. You will be asked to maintain a diary to record certain events such as when you start and stop eating and drinking, when you lie down, and when you get back up.

To prepare for the test talk to your doctor about medicines you are taking. He or she will tell you whether you can eat or drink before the procedure. After about seven to ten days the capsule will fall off the esophageal lining and pass through your digestive tract.

Esophageal manometry

Esophageal manometry measures muscle contractions in your esophagus. A gastroenterologist may order this procedure if you're thinking about anti-reflux surgery.

The gastroenterologist can perform this procedure during an office visit. A health care professional will spray a liquid anesthetic on the back of your throat or ask you to gargle a liquid anesthetic.

The gastroenterologist passes a soft, thin tube through your nose and into your stomach. You swallow as the gastroenterologist pulls the tube slowly back into your esophagus. A computer measures and records the pressure of muscle contractions in different parts of your esophagus.

The procedure can show if your symptoms are due to a weak sphincter muscle. A doctor can also use the procedure to diagnose other esophagus problems that might have symptoms similar to heartburn. A health care professional will give you instructions about eating, drinking, and taking your medicines after the procedure.

Section 8.3

Fecal Occult Blood Tests

Text in this chapter is excerpted from "Fecal Occult Blood," U.S. Food
and Drug Administration (FDA), June 5, 2014.

What does this test do?

This is a home-use test kit to measure the presence of hidden
(occult) blood in your stool (feces).

What is fecal occult blood?

Fecal occult blood is blood in your feces that you cannot see in your
stool or on your toilet paper after you use the toilet.

What type of test is this?

This is a qualitative test—you find out whether or not you have
occult blood in your feces, not how much is present.

Why should you do this test?

You should do this test, because blood in your feces may be an early
sign of a digestive condition, for example abnormal growths (polyps)
or cancer in your colon.

How often should you test for fecal occult blood?

The American Cancer Society recommends that you test for fecal
occult blood every year after you turn 50. Some doctors suggest that
you start testing at age 40, if your family is thought to be at increased
risk. Follow your doctor's recommendations about how often you test
for fecal occult blood.

How accurate is this test?

This test is about as accurate as the test your doctor uses, but you
must follow the directions carefully. For accurate results, you must
prepare properly for the test and get a good stool sample.

Does a positive test mean you have hidden blood in your stool?

A positive result means that the test has detected blood. This does not mean you have tested positive for cancer or any other illness. False positive results may be caused by diet or medications. Further testing and examinations should be performed by the physician to determine the exact cause and source of the occult blood in the stool.

If the test results are negative, can you be sure that you do not have a bowel condition?

No. You could still have bowel condition that you should know about. You should use this test again in a year.

How do you do this test?

There are several different methods for detecting hidden blood in the stool.

In one method, you collect stool samples and smear them onto paper cards in a holder. You then either send these cards to a laboratory for testing or test them at home. If you test them at home, you add a special solution from your test kit to the paper cards to see if they change color. If the paper cards change color, it means there was blood in the stool.

In another method, you put special paper in the toilet after a bowel movement. If the special paper changes color, it indicates there was blood in the toilet.

You will need to test your feces from three separate bowel movements. These bowel movements should be three in a row, closely spaced in time to minimize the time you need to be on the special diet. This is necessary because if you have polyps, they may not bleed all the time. You improve your chances of catching any bleeding if you sample three different bowel movements.

- Unless you use the method where you put a test solution into the toilet, it is best to catch your feces before it enters the toilet. You can do this by holding a piece of toilet paper in your hand. After you catch it, cut it apart in two places with the little wooden stick you get in the kit. Take a little bit of the feces from each place where you cut it apart and put these bits on one place in the cardboard in the kit. You use the second and third spots on the cardboard for other bowel movements.

What interferes with this test?

To get good results with this test, you have to follow the instructions. You may find it difficult because you need to things you do not ordinarily do.

Because the test is for blood, any source of blood will give a positive test. Blood from another source, like bleeding hemorrhoids or your menstrual period will interfere with the test, so you won't be able to tell what made the test positive.

Pay attention to your diet before the test:

- Eat a high fiber diet, such as one that has cereals and breads with bran.

- Cook your fruits and vegetables well.

- Don't eat raw turnips, radishes, broccoli, or horseradish. These foods can make it look like you have hidden blood when you don't.

- Don't eat red meat. (You may eat poultry or fish). Red meat in your diet can make it look like you have hidden blood when you don't.

Avoid the following drugs for the 7 days before the test—they can make it look like you have hidden blood when you don't:

- Aspirin

- Anti-inflammatory drugs, such as Motrin,

Don't take Vitamin C supplements for the 7 days before the test. Then can prevent the test from detecting your hidden blood.

Chapter 9

Gastrointestinal Surgical Procedures

Chapter Contents

Section 9.1

Gastric Banding (Gastric Bypass Surgery)

Text in this section is excerpted from "Gastric Banding," U.S. Food
and Drug Administration (FDA), July 28, 2015.

Gastric Banding (Gastric Bypass Surgery)

Gastric banding is a weight loss option for people who have not been
successful using non-surgical weight loss methods, such as supervised
diet, exercise or behavior modification.

Gastric banding is a surgical procedure to reduce the size of the
stomach for weight loss. In this procedure, a silicone band is placed
around the upper portion of the stomach to create a small pouch.
Afterwards, the stomach is smaller, so people feel full more quickly,
eat less and in many cases lose weight.

A gastric band is intended to be a long-term implant. Most people
lose weight with the gastric band, but a gastric band is not a permanent device. Many people require another operation to reposition,
replace or remove the gastric band due to complications or because
they have not lost weight.

Gastric banding requires a lifelong commitment to eating less and
following a doctor's recommendations. People who are not able to do
this may not be able to achieve or maintain weight loss, and may
experience severe complications.

Currently, there are two FDA approved gastric banding devices
on the market designed to treat obesity: Lap-Band Gastric Banding
System and Realize Gastric Band.

Patient Eligibility

Gastric banding devices are approved for patients with the following
characteristics:

- 18 years and older AND
- BMI of 40 or higher OR

- BMI between 30 and 40 with one or more obesity-related medical conditions, such as high blood pressure, heart disease, diabetes or sleep apnea

The FDA has not approved any gastric band for use in patients under 18 because the agency has not reviewed the safety and effectiveness of gastric bands in patients of this age.

People with certain stomach or intestinal disorders, those who take aspirin frequently, or those who regularly use alcohol and certain drugs should not have gastric banding.

Surgical Procedure

Before Surgery

If you are considering whether to have gastric banding surgery, the FDA recommends that you do the following:

- discuss your medical conditions and any medications you are currently taking with your surgeon.

- read the device patient labeling, which provides information about the risks and benefits. If your surgeon does not provide you with a copy of the patient labeling, ask for it.

- ask your surgeon any questions that you may have before you agree to the procedure.

During Surgery

Gastric banding is usually performed using laparoscopic surgery. The surgery is performed while the patient is asleep (general anesthesia). The surgeon makes one to five small cuts (incisions) in the abdomen. A small camera and surgical instruments are placed through the cuts into the abdominal cavity.

During the surgery, the surgeon places an adjustable silicone band around the upper part of the stomach to create a small pouch. The band is connected with tubing to a port near the skin. Once the device is in place, the camera and surgical instruments are removed and the cuts are closed with stitches.

The surgery usually takes about an hour to complete. Patients are usually sent home the same day as the procedure and are able to return to their normal activities, including returning to work, a few days later.

After Surgery

Following surgery, the doctor can adjust the band, without the need for additional surgery, by adding or removing fluid through the implanted port. These adjustments tighten or loosen the band, allowing less or more or food to fit in the stomach.

Risks of Gastric Banding

It is important that you know and understand the risks of gastric banding before deciding to have the procedure. Advertisements for a device or procedure may not include all of the risks, so it is important for you to read the patient labeling and talk to your doctor.

Any surgery involves risks, including death. There are risks from the surgical procedure and the medications or anesthesia used during surgery. Risks from surgery are greater when a patient is obese or has other serious health conditions.

In addition to the risks of surgery, you could experience any of the following complications after gastric banding surgery:

- nausea

- vomiting or spitting-up food you just ate

- difficulty swallowing

- gastroesophageal reflux disease (GERD)

- indigestion or upset stomach

- abdominal pain

- leaking of the gastric band

- stretching of the new stomach pouch, so it no longer restricts the amount of food you can eat

- moving of the gastric band from its original position, requiring another surgery to reposition it

- erosion of the band through the stomach wall, and into the stomach, requiring additional surgery

- stretching of the esophagus.

If you experience any of these complications, you should talk to your doctor right away. Some complications may lead to more operations or removal of the device.

Benefits of Gastric Banding

Gastric banding has demonstrated benefits for people who have not been successful using non-surgical weight loss methods. This surgical procedure may help patients lose weight and maintain the weight loss, and it may help improve their health.

Some patients who have received gastric banding have reported the following benefits:

- Weight-loss

- Decreased waist and hip circumference

- Improvements in obesity-related conditions, like diabetes, hypertension, and sleep apnea

- Improvements in general health

- Improvements in quality of life

Another benefit of gastric banding is that it can be performed in a minimally invasive manner using laparoscopic surgery. Compared to other surgeries used to treat obesity, laparoscopic gastric banding is less painful, uses smaller incisions, usually has a shorter surgery recovery time, and allows patients to go home from the hospital sooner after surgery.

Patients who are committed to making major, lifelong changes to their eating habits are likely to have better weight-loss outcomes with gastric banding than those who do not.

Lifestyle Changes after Gastric Banding Surgery

Gastric banding is not a "quick fix."

In order to be successful in losing weight with gastric banding, you must make major, long-term changes to your eating habits. The smaller pouch that is created at the top of your stomach will only be able to hold about a quarter cup of food at a time. If you eat too much, you may have complications such as nausea and vomiting.

For the first month or two after surgery you will be able to eat very little and will have to slowly add foods to your diet. Your surgeon and/or dietician will work with you to:

- make smart food choices

- teach you about changing how you chew and swallow your food

- advise you on what foods to avoid

- help you recognize when you are full

- increase your physical activity

In addition to making changes to your diet, you will need to make regular follow-up visits to your doctor to monitor your progress and make any adjustments to your band.

Section 9.2

Ostomy Surgery of the Bowel

Text in this chapter is excerpted from "Ostomy Surgery of the Bowel," National Institute of Diabetes and Digestive and Kidney Diseases (NIDDK), July 2014.

What is ostomy surgery of the bowel?

Ostomy surgery of the bowel, also known as bowel diversion, refers to surgical procedures that reroute the normal movement of intestinal contents out of the body when part of the bowel is diseased or removed. Creating an ostomy means bringing part of the intestine through the abdominal wall so that waste exits through the abdominal wall instead of passing through the anus.

Ostomy surgery of the bowel may be temporary or permanent, depending on the reason for the surgery. A surgeon specially trained in intestinal surgery performs the procedure in a hospital. During the surgery, the person receives general anesthesia.

Ostomy surgeries of the bowel include

- ileostomy

- colostomy

- ileoanal reservoir

- continent ileostomy

Why does a person need ostomy surgery of the bowel?

A person may need ostomy surgery of the bowel if he or she has

- cancer of the colon or rectum

- an injury to the small or large intestine

- inflammatory bowel disease—longlasting disorders, such as Crohn's disease and ulcerative colitis, that cause irritation or sores in the GI tract

- obstruction—a blockage in the bowel that prevents the flow of fluids or solids

- diverticulitis—a condition that occurs when small pouches in the colon called diverticula become inflamed, or irritated and swollen, and infected

What is a stoma?

During ostomy surgery of the bowel, a surgeon creates a stoma by bringing the end of the intestine through an opening in the abdomen and attaching it to the skin to create an opening outside the body. A stoma may be three-fourths of an inch to a little less than 2 inches wide. The stoma is usually located in the lower part of the abdomen, just below the beltline. However, sometimes the stoma is located in the upper abdomen. The surgeon and a wound, ostomy, and continence (WOC) nurse or an enterostomal therapist will work together to select the best location for the stoma. A removable external collection pouch, called an ostomy pouch or ostomy appliance, is attached to the stoma and worn outside the body to collect intestinal contents or stool. Intestinal contents or stool passes through the stoma instead of passing through the anus. The stoma has no muscle, so it cannot control the flow of stool, and the flow occurs whenever peristalsis occurs. Ileostomy and colostomy are the two main types of ostomy surgery of the bowel during which a surgeon creates a stoma.

What is an ileostomy?

An ileostomy is a stoma created from a part of the ileum. For this surgery, the surgeon brings the ileum through the abdominal wall to make a stoma. An ileostomy may be permanent or temporary. An ileostomy is permanent when the surgeon removes or bypasses the entire colon, rectum, and anus. A surgeon may perform a temporary ileostomy for a damaged or an inflamed colon or rectum that only needs time to rest or heal from injury or surgery. After the colon or rectum heals, the surgeon repairs the opening in the abdominal wall and reconnects the ileum so stool will pass into the colon normally. An ileostomy is the most common temporary bowel diversion. A surgeon performs an ileostomy most often to treat inflammatory bowel disease or rectal cancer.

What is a colostomy?

A colostomy is a stoma created from a part of the colon. For this surgery, the surgeon brings the colon through the abdominal wall and makes a stoma. A colostomy may be temporary or permanent. The colostomy is permanent when the surgeon removes or bypasses the lower end of the colon or rectum. A surgeon may perform a temporary colostomy for a damaged or an inflamed lower part of the colon or rectum that only needs time to rest or heal from injury or surgery. Once the colon or rectum heals, the surgeon repairs the opening in the abdominal wall and reconnects the colon so stool will pass normally. A surgeon performs a colostomy most often to treat rectal cancer, diverticulitis, or fecal incontinence—the accidental loss of stool.

What is an ileoanal reservoir?

An ileoanal reservoir is an internal pouch made from the ileum. This surgery is a common alternative to an ileostomy and does not have a permanent stoma. Also known as a J-pouch or pelvic pouch, the ileoanal reservoir connects to the anus after a surgeon removes the colon and rectum. Stool collects in the ileoanal reservoir and then exits the body through the anus during a bowel movement. An ileoanal

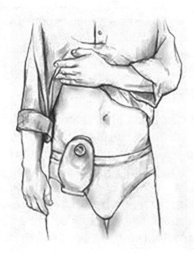

Figure 9.1. *An ostomy pouch*

142

reservoir is an option after removal of the entire large intestine when the anus remains intact and disease-free. The surgeon often makes a temporary ileostomy before or at the time of making an ileoanal reservoir. Once the ileoanal reservoir heals from surgery, the surgeon reconnects the ileum to the ileoanal pouch and closes the temporary ileostomy. A person does not need a permanent external ostomy pouch for an ileoanal reservoir.

A surgeon creates an ileoanal reservoir most often to treat ulcerative colitis or familial adenomatous polyposis. Familial adenomatous polyposis is an inherited disease characterized by the presence of 100 or more polyps in the colon. The polyps may lead to colorectal cancer if not treated. People with Crohn's disease usually are not candidates for this procedure.

What is a continent ileostomy?

A continent ileostomy is an internal pouch, sometimes called a Kock pouch, fashioned from the end of the ileum just before it exits the abdominal wall as an ileostomy. The surgeon makes a valve inside the pouch so that intestinal contents do not flow out. The person drains the pouch each day by inserting a thin, flexible tube, called a catheter, through the stoma. The person covers the stoma with a simple patch or dressing. A continent ileostomy is an option for people who are not

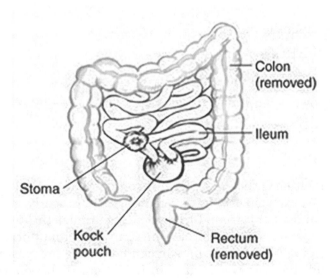

Figure 9.2. *Ileoanal reservoir and Continent ileostomy*

good candidates for an ileoanal reservoir because of damage to the rectum or anus and who do not want to wear an ostomy pouch.

Creating the Kock pouch is a delicate surgical procedure that requires a healthy bowel for proper healing. Therefore, a surgeon usually does not perform Kock pouch surgery during an acute attack of bowel disease. A continent ileostomy is now uncommon, and most hospitals do not have a specialist who knows how to perform this type of surgery. As with ileoanal reservoir surgery, the surgeon usually removes the colon and rectum to treat the original bowel disease, such as ulcerative colitis or familial adenomatous polyposis. People with Crohn's disease are not usually candidates for this procedure.

What are the complications of ostomy surgery of the bowel?

Complications of ostomy surgery of the bowel may include

- skin irritation
- stoma problems
- blockage
- diarrhea
- bleeding
- electrolyte imbalance
- infection
- irritation of the internal pouch, or pouchitis
- vitamin B12 deficiency
- phantom rectum
- short bowel syndrome
- rectal discharge

Skin Irritation

Skin irritation is the most common complication for people with an ostomy. If the external ostomy pouch does not fit properly, stool or stool contents can leak out around the stoma and under the pouch. When irritated, a person's skin will become itchy, red, and uncomfortable. When changing the pouch, a person can use an ostomy powder on the skin around the stoma to treat skin irritation. If the skin irritation does not improve, the person should talk with a WOC nurse or an enterostomal therapist—who are specially trained in ostomy care and rehabilitation—or another health care provider about the symptoms. Skin irritation may occur around the stoma for people who have an ileostomy or a colostomy. People who have ileoanal reservoir surgery may have skin irritation around the anus. Sometimes, using a barrier ointment to protect the skin around the anus can help treat and prevent irritation.

Stoma Problems

Stoma problems include the following:

- **Hernia.** A stoma hernia, seen as a bulge in the skin around the stoma, is a weakening of the abdominal wall around the stoma site. As with all hernias, a stoma hernia continues to increase in size and may eventually need surgical repair when it becomes too large. Rarely, the intestine gets trapped or kinked within the hernia and becomes blocked. A blocked intestine that loses its blood supply requires emergency surgery.

- **Prolapse.** A stoma prolapse occurs when the bowel pushes itself through the stoma. A person may be able to push the bowel back through the stoma and keep it in place with a stoma shield. If not, the stoma prolapse may require special care and a larger ostomy pouch. A stoma prolapse that becomes blocked or loses its blood supply requires surgical repair.

- **Narrowing of the stoma.** Narrowing of the stoma makes it difficult for stool to pass through the stoma. A narrowed stoma may need surgical repair.

Blockage

Occasionally, an ileostomy or a colostomy does not function for a short time. If the stoma has not passed intestinal content or stool for 4 to 6 hours and the person is experiencing cramping or nausea, the ileum or colon may be blocked. Blockage may occur when foods that are hard to digest get stuck in the ileum or colon.

Abdominal adhesions in the ileum or colon may cause blockage as well. Abdominal adhesions are bands of fibrous tissue that form between abdominal tissues and organs, causing them to kink or narrow. Most blockages get better without additional surgery by not eating food and drinking only clear liquids to rest the bowel for a short time.

Diarrhea

Diarrhea is loose, watery stools. A person has diarrhea if he or she passes loose stools three or more times a day. Diarrhea occurs when intestinal contents pass through the small intestine too quickly for fluid and mineral absorption. When fluids and minerals such as sodium and potassium are not absorbed, they leave the body. Diarrhea can lead to dehydration, malnutrition, and weight loss. Diarrhea is common, even normal, with an ileostomy or ileoanal reservoir. In most cases of diarrhea, the only treatment necessary is replacing lost fluids and electrolytes to prevent dehydration. Electrolytes are minerals in body fluids that are part of salts, including sodium, potassium, magnesium, and chloride. People should maintain good daily hydration by drinking plenty of water and liquids, such as fruit juices, sports drinks, caffeine-free soft drinks, and broths. In some cases of diarrhea, a health care provider may recommend changes in diet and may prescribe medications to treat diarrhea.

Bleeding

As with any major surgery, ostomy surgery may cause internal bleeding. If too much blood is lost, the person may require a blood transfusion. Bleeding may also occur through the stoma or through the anus after surgery.

Electrolyte Imbalance

The main function of the large intestine is to absorb water, nutrients, and electrolytes from partially digested food that enters from the ileum. When a surgeon removes the large intestine, absorption of electrolytes does not occur to the same extent, making electrolyte imbalance more likely. Diarrhea, excessive sweating, and vomiting can increase the chance of developing electrolyte imbalance. Symptoms of electrolyte imbalance may include

- fatigue, or feeling tired
- weakness
- nausea
- muscle problems such as spasms, weakness, uncontrolled twitching, and cramps
- dizziness and confusion

People with these symptoms require medical care and should contact a health care provider.

People who have had their large intestine removed should talk with a health care provider or dietitian about diets that help maintain electrolyte balance.

Infection

The GI tract is filled with bacteria that can leak out during ostomy surgery and infect areas inside the abdomen. Bacteria entering the body through the stoma or anus can also cause an infection. The person's skin around the stoma may also become infected with bacteria or skin fungus. Health care providers treat infections with antibiotics. Symptoms of infection may include

- fever
- back pain
- poor appetite
- nausea and vomiting

Irritation of the Internal Pouch, or Pouchitis

Pouchitis is an irritation or inflammation of the lining of an ileoanal reservoir or a continent ileostomy pouch. A health care provider treats pouchitis with antibiotics. For severe or chronic pouchitis, a health care provider may prescribe immunosuppressive medications, such as corticosteroids. Symptoms of pouchitis include

- frequent bowel movements with diarrhea
- an urgent need to have a bowel movement
- a feeling of pressure in the pouch
- abdominal pain
- cramping or bleeding
- dehydration
- low-grade fever
- a general unwell feeling

Vitamin B12 Deficiency

Ostomy surgery of the bowel may affect vitamin B12 absorption from food and result in a gradual drop in vitamin B12 levels in the body. Low levels of vitamin B12 can affect the body's ability to use nutrients and may cause anemia. Anemia is a condition in which red blood cells are fewer or smaller than normal, which prevents the body's cells from getting enough oxygen. Health care providers treat vitamin B12 deficiency with vitamin B12 supplements.

Phantom Rectum

Phantom rectum is the feeling of needing to have a bowel movement even though the rectum is not present. Phantom rectum is relatively common. Symptoms are usually mild and often go away without treatment. However, for some people, phantom rectum may occur for years after a surgeon removes the rectum. Some people with phantom rectum may feel pain. Health care providers treat rectal pain with medications such as pain relievers and sometimes antidepressants. To help control phantom rectum, a health care provider may recommend complementary therapies such as guided imagery and other relaxation techniques.

Short Bowel Syndrome

Short bowel syndrome is a group of problems related to inadequate absorption of nutrients after removal of part of the small intestine. People with short bowel syndrome cannot absorb enough water, vitamins, and other nutrients from food to sustain life. Diarrhea is the main symptom of short bowel syndrome. Other symptoms may include

- cramping
- bloating
- heartburn
- weakness and fatigue
- vomiting
- excessive gas
- foul-smelling stool

Short bowel syndrome is uncommon and can occur with Crohn's disease, trauma, or other conditions that lead to removal of a large amount of the small intestine.

A health care provider will recommend a treatment for short bowel syndrome based on a person's nutritional needs. Treatment may include nutritional support, medications, and surgery.

Rectal Discharge

People with an ileostomy or a colostomy whose lower colon, rectum, and anus are still present may experience a discharge of mucus from their rectum. Mucus is a clear fluid made by the GI tract that coats and protects the lining of the bowel. Mucus within the bypassed part of the colon may leak out of the rectum from time to time or gradually build up, forming a small, stoollike ball that passes out of the rectum. A person cannot control mucus production and rectal discharge. However, people who have rectal discharge can learn how to manage and cope with this problem.

Seek Immediate Care

People should seek immediate medical care if they have any of the following symptoms, as complications of ostomy surgery can become a medical emergency:

- continuous nausea and vomiting
- dramatic change in stoma size, shape, or color
- continuous bleeding at the junction between the stoma and the skin that does not stop by applying pressure
- obstruction, prolapse, or narrowing of the stoma
- a deep cut in the stoma
- no output of intestinal content or stool from the stoma for 4 to 6 hours, with cramping and nausea
- severe diarrhea with risk of dehydration
- excessive bleeding from the stoma opening

Living with an Ostomy

At first, living with an ostomy can be overwhelming and scary for some people. However, most people adjust and lead active and productive lives. A WOC nurse or an enterostomal therapist will provide education, support, and medical advice on topics that include the following:

- what to expect after ostomy surgery
- caring for an ostomy
- resuming normal activities after ostomy surgery

- maintaining personal relationships after ostomy surgery

- coping with practical, social, and emotional issues

What to Expect after Ostomy Surgery

Once the person is home from the hospital, the first week or two are considered an extension of the hospital stay. Most people will tire quite easily when they first come home. Getting enough rest is important. Gradually, stamina and strength will improve. Most people can return to work about 6 to 8 weeks after surgery. People may have certain GI issues—such as gas, diarrhea, and constipation—as the bowel heals, depending on the type of bowel diversion.

Ileostomy and colostomy. During the early weeks and months after surgery, people with an ileostomy or a colostomy may have excessive gas. This extra gas will decrease once the bowel has had time to heal and the person resumes a regular diet.

Ileoanal reservoir. People with an ileoanal reservoir initially have about six to 10 bowel movements a day. The newly formed ileoanal reservoir takes several months to stretch and adjust to its new function. After the adjustment period, bowel movements decrease to as few as four to six a day. People with an ileoanal reservoir may have mild fecal incontinence and may have to get up during periods of sleep to pass stool.

Continent ileostomy. Similar to people with an ileostomy or a colostomy, people with a continent ileostomy may have excessive gas during the early weeks and months after surgery.

Caring for an Ostomy

During the recovery in the hospital and at home, a person will learn to care for the ostomy. The type of care required depends on the type of ostomy surgery. A WOC nurse or an enterostomal therapist will teach a person about special care after ostomy surgery.

Ileostomy and colostomy. People with an ileostomy or a colostomy will to learn how to attach, drain, and change their ostomy pouch and care for the stoma and the surrounding skin. Ostomy pouches, or pouching systems, may be one piece or two pieces. They include a barrier, also called a wafer or flange, and a disposable plastic pouch. In a two-piece system, the pouch can be detached or replaced without removing the barrier. For both systems, the barrier attaches to the skin around the stoma and protects it from stool. The length of time the barrier stays sealed to the skin depends on many things, such as

- how well the barrier fits
- the condition of the skin around the stoma
- the person's level of physical activity
- the shape of the body around the stoma

Most people can leave the barrier on for 3 to 7 days. However, a person should change the barrier as soon as stool starts to go underneath it and onto the skin.

Most ostomy pouches empty through an opening in the bottom. Emptying the pouch several times a day reduces the chance of leakage and bulges underneath the person's clothing. A person should empty the pouch when it is about one-third full. He or she should rinse the pouch in a two-piece system before reattaching it to the skin barrier.

How often a person needs to change his or her pouching system depends on the type of system. Many pouching systems may be worn for 3 to 7 days. Some pouching systems are made to be changed every day. When changing a pouch system, the person should

- wipe away any mucus on the stoma
- clean the skin around the stoma with warm water and a washcloth
- rinse the skin thoroughly
- dry the skin completely

People may use mild soap to clean the skin. However, the soap should not have oils, perfumes, or deodorants, which may cause skin problems or keep the skin barrier from sticking. A WOC nurse or an enterostomal therapist can give advice if a person has problems attaching the skin barrier or keeping it attached.

When changing the pouching system, people should inspect the stoma and contact a health care provider about any dramatic changes in stoma size, shape, or color. People should look for blood and signs of skin irritation around the stoma. Sensitivities or allergies to ostomy products such as adhesives, skin barriers, pastes, tape, or pouch materials can cause skin irritation. People with pouching systems can test different products to see if their skin reacts to them. People should use only ostomy products recommended by their health care provider.

Ileoanal reservoir. People with an ileoanal reservoir will learn how to care for irritated skin around the anus resulting from frequent stools or fecal incontinence. A WOC nurse or an enterostomal therapist may recommend pelvic floor exercises to help strengthen the muscles around the anus.

Continent ileostomy. People with a continent ileostomy will learn how to insert a catheter through the stoma to drain the internal pouch. They can drain the pouch by standing in front of the toilet or by sitting on the toilet and then emptying the catheter. During the first few weeks after a continent ileostomy, the person needs to drain the internal pouch about every 2 hours. After a few weeks, the person is able to go 4 to 6 hours between pouch drainings. The person should wash his or her hands with soap and water after using a catheter. The person should clean the skin around the stoma with warm water and a washcloth and let the skin dry completely.

Resuming Normal Activities after Ostomy Surgery

After ostomy surgery, people should be able to resume their normal activities after healing completes and their strength returns. However, they may need to restrict activities, including driving and heavy lifting, during the first 2 to 3 weeks after surgery. Strenuous activities, such as heavy lifting, increase the chance of a stoma hernia. A person who has recovered from the ostomy surgery should be able to do most of the activities he or she enjoyed before the ostomy surgery, even swimming and other water sports. The only exceptions may be contact sports such as football or karate. People whose jobs include strenuous physical activities should talk with their health care provider and employer about making adjustments to job responsibilities.

People should avoid extreme physical exercise and sports activities for the first 3 months. Walking, biking, and swimming are fine and should be encouraged as long as they are not overly strenuous.

People with an ostomy should talk with their health care provider about when they can resume normal activities.

Maintaining Personal Relationships after Ostomy Surgery

People with an ostomy should be able to maintain personal relationships just as before their surgery. Some people may worry that friends and relatives will have negative reactions to their ostomy and stoma. Only a spouse, sexual partner, or primary caretaker needs to know the details of the ostomy surgery. People can choose how much they share with others about their health condition, including the ostomy.

People can still maintain a satisfying sexual relationship after ostomy surgery and may resume sexual activity as soon as the health care provider says it is safe to do so. People should talk with their health care provider about any concerns they have with maintaining sexual relations. For people with ostomies, the health care provider can also give information about ways to protect the stoma during sexual activity. People with ostomies may want to ask about specially designed apparel to enhance intimacy. Communicating with a sexual partner is essential. People should share their concerns and wishes and listen carefully to their partner's concerns.

Coping with Practical, Social, and Emotional Issues

Although ostomy surgery can bring great relief, many people have problems coping with the practical, social, and emotional issues related to having this type of surgery. Every person reacts differently. A person's emotions may change frequently during recovery. People with an ostomy adjust faster and experience fewer problems when they have help from their family members, partners, and health care providers. Community and online resources for support and education are available to help people with an ostomy cope with practical, social, and emotional issues. A WOC nurse and an enterostomal therapist can provide a list of resources and support groups.

Part Three

Disorders of the Upper Gastrointestinal Tract

Chapter 10

Dyspepsia

What is indigestion?

Indigestion, also known as dyspepsia, is a term used to describe one or more symptoms including a feeling of fullness during a meal, uncomfortable fullness after a meal, and burning or pain in the upper abdomen.

Indigestion is common in adults and can occur once in a while or as often as every day.

What causes indigestion?

Indigestion can be caused by a condition in the digestive tract such as gastroesophageal reflux disease (GERD), peptic ulcer disease, cancer, or abnormality of the pancreas or bile ducts. If the condition improves or resolves, the symptoms of indigestion usually improve.

Sometimes a person has indigestion for which a cause cannot be found. This type of indigestion, called functional dyspepsia, is thought to occur in the area where the stomach meets the small intestine. The indigestion may be related to abnormal motility—the squeezing or relaxing action—of the stomach muscle as it receives, digests, and moves food into the small intestine.

Text in this chapter is excerpted from "Indigestion," National Institute of Diabetes and Digestive and Kidney Diseases (NIDDK), October 30, 2013.

What are the symptoms of indigestion?

Most people with indigestion experience more than one of the following symptoms:

- **Fullness during a meal.** The person feels overly full soon after the meal starts and cannot finish the meal.

- **Bothersome fullness after a meal.** The person feels overly full after a meal—it may feel like the food is staying in the stomach too long.

- **Epigastric pain.** The epigastric area is between the lower end of the chest bone and the navel. The person may experience epigastric pain ranging from mild to severe.

- **Epigastric burning.** The person feels an unpleasant sensation of heat in the epigastric area.

Other, less frequent symptoms that may occur with indigestion are nausea and bloating—an unpleasant tightness in the stomach. Nausea and bloating could be due to causes other than indigestion.

Sometimes the term indigestion is used to describe the symptom of heartburn, but these are two different conditions. Heartburn is a painful, burning feeling in the chest that radiates toward the neck or back. Heartburn is caused by stomach acid rising into the esophagus and may be a symptom of GERD. A person can have symptoms of both indigestion and heartburn.

How is indigestion diagnosed?

To diagnose indigestion, the doctor asks about the person's current symptoms and medical history and performs a physical examination. The doctor may order X-rays of the stomach and small intestine.

The doctor may perform blood, breath, or stool tests if the type of bacteria that causes peptic ulcer disease is suspected as the cause of indigestion.

The doctor may perform an upper endoscopy. After giving a sedative to help the person become drowsy, the doctor passes an endoscope—a long, thin tube that has a light and small camera on the end—through the mouth and gently guides it down the esophagus into the stomach. The doctor can look at the esophagus and stomach with the endoscope to check for any abnormalities. The doctor may perform biopsies— removing small pieces of tissue for examination with a microscope—to look for possible damage from GERD or an infection.

Because indigestion can be a sign of a more serious condition, people should see a doctor right away if they experience

- frequent vomiting
- blood in vomit
- weight loss or loss of appetite
- black tarry stools
- difficult or painful swallowing
- abdominal pain in a nonepigastric area
- indigestion accompanied by shortness of breath, sweating, or pain that radiates to the jaw, neck, or arm
- symptoms that persist for more than 2 weeks

How is indigestion treated?

Some people may experience relief from symptoms of indigestion by

- eating several small, low-fat meals throughout the day at a slow pace
- refraining from smoking
- abstaining from consuming coffee, carbonated beverages, and alcohol
- stopping use of medications that may irritate the stomach lining—such as aspirin or anti-inflammatory drugs
- getting enough rest
- finding ways to decrease emotional and physical stress, such as relaxation therapy or yoga

The doctor may recommend over-the-counter antacids or medications that reduce acid production or help the stomach move food more quickly into the small intestine. Many of these medications can be purchased without a prescription. Nonprescription medications should only be used at the dose and for the length of time recommended on the label unless advised differently by a doctor. Informing the doctor when starting a new medication is important.

Antacids, such as Alka-Seltzer, Maalox, Mylanta, Rolaids, and Riopan, are usually the first drugs recommended to relieve symptoms of indigestion. Many brands on the market use different combinations of three basic salts—magnesium, calcium, and aluminum—with hydroxide or bicarbonate ions to neutralize the acid in the stomach. Antacids, however, can have side effects. Magnesium salt can lead to diarrhea, and aluminum salt may cause constipation. Aluminum and magnesium salts are often combined in a single product to balance these effects.

Calcium carbonate antacids, such as Tums, Titralac, and Alka-2, can also be a supplemental source of calcium, though they may cause constipation.

H2 receptor antagonists (H2RAs) include ranitidine (Zantac), cimetidine (Tagamet), famotidine (Pepcid), and nizatidine (Axid) and are available both by prescription and over-the-counter. H2RAs treat symptoms of indigestion by reducing stomach acid. They work longer than but not as quickly as antacids. Side effects of H2RAs may include headache, nausea, vomiting, constipation, diarrhea, and unusual bleeding or bruising.

Proton pump inhibitors (PPIs) include omeprazole (Prilosec, Zegerid), lansoprazole (Prevacid), pantoprazole (Protonix), rabeprazole (Aciphex), and esomeprazole (Nexium) and are available by prescription. Prilosec is also available in over-the-counter strength. PPIs, which are stronger than H2RAs, also treat indigestion symptoms by reducing stomach acid. PPIs are most effective in treating symptoms of indigestion in people who also have GERD. Side effects of PPIs may include back pain, aching, cough, headache, dizziness, abdominal pain, gas, nausea, vomiting, constipation, and diarrhea.

Prokinetics such as metoclopramide (Reglan) may be helpful for people who have a problem with the stomach emptying too slowly. Metoclopramide also improves muscle action in the digestive tract. Prokinetics have frequent side effects that limit their usefulness, including fatigue, sleepiness, depression, anxiety, and involuntary muscle spasms or movements.

If testing shows the type of bacteria that causes peptic ulcer disease, the doctor may prescribe antibiotics to treat the condition.

Chapter 11

Barrett's Esophagus

Definition and Facts

What is Barrett's Esophagus?

Barrett's esophagus is a condition in which tissue that is similar to the lining of your intestine replaces the tissue lining your esophagus. Doctors call this process intestinal metaplasia.

Are people with Barrett's esophagus more likely to develop cancer?

People with Barrett's esophagus are more likely to develop a rare type of cancer called esophageal adenocarcinoma.

The risk of esophageal adenocarcinoma in people with Barrett's esophagus is about 0.5 percent per year. Typically, before this cancer develops, precancerous cells appear in the Barrett's tissue. Doctors call this condition dysplasia and classify the dysplasia as low grade or high grade.

You may have Barrett's esophagus for many years before cancer develops.

Text in this chapter is excerpted from "Barrett's Esophagus," National Institute of Diabetes and Digestive and Kidney Diseases (NIDDK), November 13, 2014.

How common is Barrett's esophagus?

Experts aren't sure how common Barrett's esophagus is. Researchers estimate that it affects 1.6 to 6.8 percent of people.

Who is more likely to develop Barrett's esophagus?

Men develop Barrett's esophagus twice as often as women, and Caucasian men develop this condition more often than men of other races. The average age at diagnosis is 55. Barrett's esophagus is uncommon in children.

Symptoms and Causes

What are the symptoms of Barrett's esophagus?

While Barrett's esophagus itself doesn't cause symptoms, many people with Barrett's esophagus have

gastroesophageal reflux disease (GERD), which does cause symptoms.

What causes Barrett's esophagus?

Experts don't know the exact cause of Barrett's esophagus. However, some factors can increase or decrease your chance of developing Barrett's esophagus.

What factors increase a person's chances of developing Barrett's esophagus?

Having GERD increases your chances of developing Barrett's esophagus. GERD is a more serious, chronic form of gastroesophageal reflux, a condition in which stomach contents flow back up into your esophagus. Refluxed stomach acid that touches the lining of your esophagus can cause heartburn and damage the cells in your esophagus.

Between 5 and 10 percent of people with GERD develop Barrett's esophagus.

Obesity—specifically high levels of belly fat—and smoking also increase your chances of developing Barrett's esophagus. Some studies suggest that your genetics, or inherited genes, may play a role in whether or not you develop Barrett's esophagus.

What factors decrease a person's chances of developing Barrett's esophagus?

Having a *Helicobacter pylori (H. pylori)* infection may decrease your chances of developing Barrett's esophagus. Doctors are not sure how *H. pylori* protects against Barrett's esophagus. While the bacteria damage your stomach and the tissue in your duodenum, some researchers believe the bacteria make your stomach contents less damaging to your esophagus if you have GERD.

Researchers have found that other factors may decrease the chance of developing Barrett's esophagus, including

- frequent use of aspirin or other nonsteroidal anti-inflammatory drugs
- a diet high in fruits, vegetables, and certain vitamins

Diagnosis

How do doctors diagnose Barrett's esophagus?

Doctors diagnose Barrett's esophagus with an upper gastrointestinal (GI) endoscopy and a biopsy. Doctors may diagnose Barrett's esophagus while performing tests to find the cause of a patient's gastroesophageal reflux disease (GERD) symptoms.

Medical history

Your doctor will ask you to provide your medical history. Your doctor may recommend testing if you have multiple factors that increase your chances of developing Barrett's esophagus.

Upper GI endoscopy and biopsy

In an upper GI endoscopy, a gastroenterologist, surgeon, or other trained health care provider uses an endoscope to see inside your upper GI tract, most often while you receive light sedation. The doctor carefully feeds the endoscope down your esophagus and into your stomach and duodenum. The procedure may show changes in the lining of your esophagus.

The doctor performs a biopsy with the endoscope by taking a small piece of tissue from the lining of your esophagus. You won't feel the biopsy. A pathologist examines the tissue in a lab to determine whether Barrett's esophagus cells are present. A pathologist who has expertise in diagnosing Barrett's esophagus may need to confirm the results.

Barrett's esophagus can be difficult to diagnose because this condition does not affect all the tissue in your esophagus. The doctor takes biopsy samples from at least eight different areas of the lining of your esophagus.

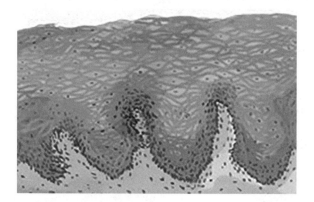

Figure 11.1. *Normal esophagus*

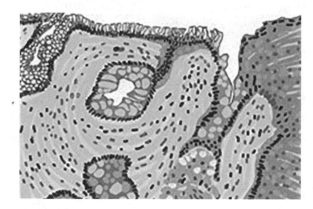

Figure 11.2. *Barrett's esophagus*

Treatment

How do doctors treat Barrett's esophagus?

Your doctor will talk about the best treatment options for you based on your overall health, whether you have dysplasia, and its severity.

Treatment options include medicines for GERD, endoscopic ablative therapies, endoscopic mucosal resection, and surgery.

Periodic surveillance endoscopy

Your doctor may use upper gastrointestinal endoscopy with a biopsy periodically to watch for signs of cancer development. Doctors call this approach surveillance.

Experts aren't sure how often doctors should perform surveillance endoscopies. Talk with your doctor about what level of surveillance is best for you. Your doctor may recommend endoscopies more frequently if you have high-grade dysplasia rather than low-grade or no dysplasia.

Medicines

If you have Barrett's esophagus and gastroesophageal reflux disease (GERD), your doctor will treat you with acid-suppressing medicines called proton pump inhibitors (PPIs). These medicines can prevent further damage to your esophagus and, in some cases, heal existing damage.

PPIs include

- omeprazole (Prilosec, Zegerid)
- lansoprazole (Prevacid)
- pantoprazole (Protonix)
- rabeprazole (AcipHex)
- esomeprazole (Nexium)
- dexlansoprazole (Dexilant)

All of these medicines are available by prescription. Omeprazole and lansoprazole are also available in over-the-counter strength.

Your doctor may consider anti-reflux surgery if you have GERD symptoms and don't respond to medicines. However, research has not shown that medicines or surgery for GERD and Barrett's esophagus lower your chances of developing dysplasia or esophageal adenocarcinoma.

Endoscopic ablative therapies

Endoscopic ablative therapies use different techniques to destroy the dysplasia in your esophagus. After the therapies, your body should begin making normal esophageal cells.

Radiologists perform these procedures at certain hospitals and outpatient centers. You will receive local anesthesia and a sedative. The most common procedures are the following:

- **Photodynamic therapy.** Photodynamic therapy uses a light-activated chemical called porfimer (Photofrin), an endoscope, and a laser to kill precancerous cells in your esophagus. A doctor injects porfimer into a vein in your arm, and you return 24 to 72 hours later to complete the procedure.

Complications of photodynamic therapy may include

- sensitivity of your skin and eyes to light for about 6 weeks after the procedure
- burns, swelling, pain, and scarring in nearby healthy tissue
- coughing, trouble swallowing, stomach pain, painful breathing, and shortness of breath.
- Radiofrequency ablation. Radiofrequency ablation uses radio waves to kill precancerous and cancerous cells in the Barrett's tissue. An electrode mounted on a balloon or an endoscope creates heat to destroy the Barrett's tissue and precancerous and cancerous cells.

Endoscopic mucosal resection

In endoscopic mucosal resection, your doctor lifts the Barrett's tissue, injects a solution underneath or applies suction to the tissue, and then cuts the tissue off. The doctor then removes the tissue with an endoscope. Gastroenterologists perform this procedure at certain hospitals and outpatient centers. You will receive local anesthesia to numb your throat and a sedative to help you relax and stay comfortable.

Before performing an endoscopic mucosal resection for cancer, your doctor will do an endoscopic ultrasound.

Complications can include bleeding or tearing of your esophagus. Doctors sometimes combine endoscopic mucosal resection with photodynamic therapy.

Surgery

Surgery called esophagectomy is an alternative to endoscopic therapies. Many doctors prefer endoscopic therapies because these procedures have fewer complications.

Esophagectomy is the surgical removal of the affected sections of your esophagus. After removing sections of your esophagus, a surgeon rebuilds your esophagus from part of your stomach or large intestine. The surgery is performed at a hospital. You'll receive general anesthesia, and you'll stay in the hospital for 7 to 14 days after the surgery to recover.

Surgery may not be an option if you have other medical problems. Your doctor may consider the less-invasive endoscopic treatments or continued frequent surveillance instead.

Eating, Diet, and Nutrition

How can your diet help prevent Barrett's esophagus?

Researchers have not found that diet and nutrition play an important role in causing or preventing Barrett's esophagus.

If you have gastroesophageal reflux (GER) or gastroesophageal reflux disease (GERD), you can prevent or relieve your symptoms by changing your diet. Dietary changes that can help reduce your symptoms include

- decreasing fatty foods

- eating small, frequent meals instead of three large meals

Avoid eating or drinking the following items that may make GER or GERD worse:

- chocolate

- coffee

- peppermint

- greasy or spicy foods

- tomatoes and tomato products

- alcoholic drinks

Chapter 12

Gastroesophageal Reflux Disease (GERD)

Chapter Contents

Section 12.1

Gastroesophageal Reflux (GER) and Gastroesophageal Reflux Disease (GERD) in Adults

Text in this section is excerpted from "Gastroesophageal Reflux (GER) and Gastroesophageal Reflux Disease (GERD) in Adults," National Institute of Diabetes and Digestive and Kidney Diseases (NIDDK), September 2013.

What is GER?

Gastroesophageal reflux (GER) occurs when stomach contents flow back up into the esophagus—the muscular tube that carries food and liquids from the mouth to the stomach.

GER is also called acid reflux or acid regurgitation because the stomach's digestive juices contain acid. Sometimes people with GER can taste food or acidic fluid in the back of the mouth. Refluxed stomach acid that touches the lining of the esophagus can cause heartburn. Also called acid indigestion, heartburn is an uncomfortable, burning feeling in the midchest, behind the breastbone, or in the upper part of the abdomen—the area between the chest and the hips.

Occasional GER is common. People may be able to control GER by

- avoiding foods and beverages that contribute to heartburn, such as chocolate, coffee, peppermint, greasy or spicy foods, tomato products, and alcoholic beverages

- avoiding overeating

- quitting smoking

- losing weight if they are overweight

- not eating 2 to 3 hours before sleep

- taking over-the-counter medications

What is GERD?

Gastroesophageal reflux disease (GERD) is a more serious, chronic—or long lasting—form of GER. GER that occurs more than twice a week for a few weeks could be GERD, which over time can lead to more serious health problems. People with suspected GERD should see a health care provider.

What causes GERD?

Gastroesophageal reflux disease results when the lower esophageal sphincter—the muscle that acts as a valve between the esophagus and stomach—becomes weak or relaxes when it should not, causing stomach contents to rise up into the esophagus.

Abnormalities in the body such as hiatal hernias may also cause GERD. Hiatal hernias occur when the upper part of the stomach moves up into the chest. The stomach can slip through an opening found in the diaphragm. The diaphragm is the muscle wall that separates the stomach from the chest. Hiatal hernias may cause GERD because of stomach acid flowing back up through the opening; however, most produce no symptoms.

Other factors that can contribute to GERD include

- obesity

- pregnancy

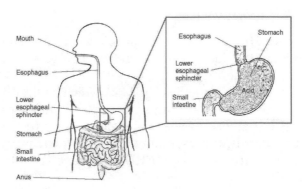

Figure 12.1. *GERD*

GERD results when the lower esophageal sphincter—the muscle that acts as a valve between the esophagus and stomach—becomes weak or relaxes when it should not, causing stomach contents to rise up into the esophagus.

- certain medications, such as asthma medications, calcium channel blockers, and many antihistamines, pain killers, sedatives, and antidepressants
- smoking, or inhaling secondhand smoke

People of all ages can develop GERD, some for unknown reasons.

What are the symptoms of GERD?

The main symptom of GERD is frequent heartburn, though some adults with GERD do not have heartburn. Other common GERD symptoms include

- a dry, chronic cough
- wheezing
- asthma and recurrent pneumonia
- nausea
- vomiting
- a sore throat, hoarseness, or laryngitis—swelling and irritation of the voice box
- difficulty swallowing or painful swallowing
- pain in the chest or the upper part of the abdomen
- dental erosion and bad breath

How is GERD diagnosed?

A health care provider may refer people with suspected GERD to a gastroenterologist—a doctor who specializes in digestive diseases—for diagnosis and treatment.

Lifestyle changes and medications are often the first lines of treatment for suspected GERD. If symptoms improve with these treatment methods, a GERD diagnosis often does not require testing. However, to confirm a diagnosis, a person may need testing if symptoms do not improve. People with possible GERD who have trouble swallowing also may require testing.

A completely accurate test for diagnosing GERD does not exist. However, several tests can help with diagnosis:

Upper GI series

While a gastroenterologist does not use an upper GI series to diagnose acid reflux or GERD, the test can provide a look at the shape of the upper GI tract. An X-ray technician performs this test at a hospital or an outpatient center, and a radiologist—a doctor who specializes in medical imaging—interprets the images. This test does not require anesthesia. People should check with their gastroenterologist about what to do to prepare for an upper GI series.

During the procedure, the person will stand or sit in front of an X-ray machine and drink barium, a chalky liquid. Barium coats the esophagus, stomach, and small intestine so the radiologist and gastroenterologist can see theses organs' shapes more clearly on X-rays. The barium shows problems related to GERD, such as hiatal hernias. While an upper GI series cannot detect mild irritation, the test can detect esophageal strictures— narrowing of the esophagus that can result from GERD—as well as ulcers, or sores.

A person may experience bloating and nausea for a short time after the test. For several days afterward, barium liquid in the GI tract causes white or light-colored stools. A health care provider will give the person specific instructions about eating and drinking after the test.

Upper endoscopy

A gastroenterologist may use an upper endoscopy, also known as an esophagogastroduodenoscopy, if a person continues to have GERD symptoms despite lifestyle changes and treatment with medications. An upper endoscopy is a common test used to evaluate the severity of GERD. This procedure involves using an endoscope—a small, flexible tube with a light—to see the upper GI tract.

A gastroenterologist performs this test at a hospital or an outpatient center. The person may receive a liquid anesthetic that is gargled or sprayed on the back of the throat.

If sedation is used, a health care provider will place an intravenous (IV) needle in the person's vein.

After the person receives sedation, the gastroenterologist carefully feeds an endoscope through the mouth and down the esophagus, then into the stomach and duodenum. A small camera mounted on the endoscope transmits a video image to a monitor, allowing close examination of the intestinal lining. The gastroenterologist uses the endoscope to take a biopsy, a procedure that involves taking a small piece of esophageal tissue. A pathologist —a doctor who specializes in diagnosing diseases—will examine the tissue with a microscope and determine the extent of inflammation.

A gastroenterologist diagnoses GERD when the test shows injury to the esophagus in a person who has had moderate to severe GERD symptoms.

Esophageal pH monitoring

The most accurate test to detect acid reflux, esophageal pH monitoring measures the amount of liquid or acid in the esophagus as the person goes about normal activities, including eating and sleeping. A gastroenterologist performs this test at a hospital or an outpatient center as a part of an upper endoscopy. The person can remain awake during the test. Sedation is not required for the test; however, it can be used if necessary.

A gastroenterologist will pass a thin tube, called a nasogastric probe, through the person's nose or mouth to the stomach. The gastroenterologist will then pull the tube back into the esophagus, where it will be taped to the person's cheek and remain in place for 24 hours. The end of the tube in the esophagus has a small probe to measure when and how much liquid or acid comes up into the esophagus. The other end of the tube, attached to a monitor outside the body, shows the measurements taken.

This test is most useful when combined with a carefully kept diary of when, what, and how much food the person eats and GERD symptoms that result. The gastroenterologist can see correlations between symptoms and certain foods or times of day. The procedure can also help show whether reflux triggers respiratory symptoms.

Esophageal manometry

Esophageal manometry measures muscle contractions in the esophagus. A gastroenterologist may order this test when considering a person for anti-reflux surgery. The gastroenterologist performs this test during an office visit. A person may receive anesthetic spray on the inside of the nostrils or back of the throat. The gastroenterologist passes a soft, thin tube through the person's nose into the stomach. The person swallows as the gastroenterologist pulls the tube slowly back into the esophagus. A computer measures and records the pressure of the muscle contractions in different parts of the esophagus. The test can show if symptoms are due to a weak sphincter muscle. A health care provider can also use the test to diagnose other disorders of the esophagus that might have similar symptoms as heartburn. Most people can resume regular activity, eating, and medications right after the test.

How is GERD treated?

Treatment for GERD may involve one or more of the following, depending on the severity of symptoms: lifestyle changes, medications, or surgery.

Lifestyle Changes

Some people can reduce GERD symptoms by

- losing weight, if needed
- wearing loose-fitting clothing around the stomach area, as tight clothing can constrict the area and increase reflux
- remaining upright for 3 hours after meals
- raising the head of the bed 6 to 8 inches by securing wood blocks under the bedposts—just using extra pillows will not help
- avoiding smoking and being around others who are smoking

Medications

People can purchase many GERD medications without a prescription; however, people with persistent symptoms should still see a health care provider.

- Antacids
- H2 blockers
- PPIs
- Prokinetics
- Antibiotics

Surgery

When a person cannot manage severe GERD symptoms through medication or lifestyle changes, a health care provider may recommend surgery. A health care provider may also recommend surgery for GERD that results from a physical abnormality or for GERD symptoms that lead to severe respiratory problems. Fundoplication is the standard surgical treatment for GERD and leads to long-term reflux control in most cases. A gastroenterologist or surgeon may also use endoscopic techniques to treat GERD. However, the success rates of endoscopic techniques are not completely known, as researchers have not tested them enough in clinical trials. People are more likely to develop complications from surgery than from medications. Anti-reflux surgery is most successful in people younger than 50.

Fundoplication is an operation to sew the top of the stomach around the esophagus to add pressure to the lower end of the esophagus and reduce reflux. A surgeon performs fundoplication using a laparoscope, a thin tube with a tiny video camera attached used to look inside the body. The surgeon performs the operation at a hospital or an outpatient center, and the person receives general anesthesia. People can leave the hospital or outpatient center in 1 to 3 days and return to their daily activities in 2 to 3 weeks.

Endoscopic techniques, such as endoscopic sewing and radiofrequency, help control GERD in a small number of people. Endoscopic sewing uses small stitches to tighten the sphincter muscle. adiofrequency creates heat lesions that help tighten the sphincter muscle. Surgery for both techniques requires an endoscope. A surgeon performs the operation at a hospital or an outpatient center, and the person receives anesthesia. Although the devices for these procedures are approved, results may not be as good as laparoscopic surgery, and these procedures are not commonly used.

What are the long-term complications of GERD?

Untreated GERD can sometimes cause serious complications over time, including

- esophagitis—irritation of the esophagus from refluxed stomach acid that damages the lining and causes bleeding or ulcers. Adults who have chronic esophagitis over many years are more likely to develop precancerous changes in the esophagus.
- strictures that lead to swallowing difficulties.
- respiratory problems, such as trouble breathing.
- Barrett's esophagus, a condition in which the tissue lining the esophagus is replaced by tissue similar to the lining of the intestine. A small number of people with Barrett's esophagus develop a rare yet often deadly type of cancer of the esophagus.

A health care provider should monitor a person with GERD to prevent or treat longterm complications.

Eating, Diet, and Nutrition

People with GERD can often reduce reflux by avoiding foods and drinks that worsen symptoms. Other dietary changes that can help reduce symptoms include decreasing fat intake and eating small, frequent meals instead of three large meals. People who are overweight can talk with a health care provider about dietary changes that can help them lose weight, which may decrease GERD symptoms.

Section 12.2

Gastroesophageal Reflux (GER) and Gastroesophageal Reflux Disease (GERD) in Children and Teens

Text in this section is excerpted from "Definition and Facts for GER and GERD in Children and Teens," National Institute of Diabetes and Digestive and Kidney Diseases (NIDDK), April 8, 2015.

Definition and Facts

How common is GER in children and teens?

Occasional GER is common in children and teens—ages 2 to 19— and doesn't always mean that they have gastroesophageal reflux disease (GERD).

What is the difference between GER and GERD?

GER that occurs more than twice a week for a few weeks could be GERD. GERD can lead to more serious health problems over time. If you think your child or teen has GERD, you should take him or her to see a doctor or a pediatrician.

How common is GERD in children and teens?

Up to 25 percent of children and teens have symptoms of GERD, although GERD is more common in adults.

What are the complications of GERD in children and teens?

Without treatment, GERD can sometimes cause serious complications over time, such as:

Esophagitis

Esophagitis may lead to ulcerations, a sore in the lining of the esophagus.

Esophageal Stricture

An esophageal stricture happens when a person's esophagus becomes too narrow. Esophageal strictures can lead to problems with swallowing.

Respiratory Problems

A child or teen with GERD might breathe stomach acid into his or her lungs. The stomach acid can then irritate his or her throat and lungs, causing respiratory problems or symptoms, such as

- asthma—a long-lasting lung disease that makes a child or teen extra sensitive to things that he or she is allergic to

- chest congestion, or extra fluid in the lungs

- a dry, long-lasting cough or a sore throat

- hoarseness—the partial loss of a child or teen's voice

- laryngitis—the swelling of a child or teen's voice box that can lead to a short-term loss of his or her voice

- pneumonia—an infection in one or both lungs—that keeps coming back

- wheezing—a high-pitched whistling sound that happens while breathing

A pediatrician should monitor children and teens with GERD to prevent or treat long-term problems.

Symptoms and Causes

What are the symptoms of GER and GERD in children and teens?

If a child or teen has gastroesophageal reflux (GER), he or she may taste food or stomach acid in the back of the mouth.

Symptoms of gastroesophageal reflux disease (GERD) in children and teens can vary depending on their age. The most common symptom of GERD in children 12 years and older is regular heartburn, a painful, burning feeling in the middle of the chest, behind the breastbone, and in the middle of the abdomen. In many cases, children with GERD who are younger than 12 don't have heartburn.

Other common GERD symptoms include

- bad breath
- nausea
- pain in the chest or the upper part of the abdomen
- problems swallowing or painful swallowing
- respiratory problems
- vomiting
- the wearing away of teeth

What causes GER and GERD in children and teens?

GER and GERD happen when a child or teen's lower esophageal sphincter becomes weak or relaxes when it shouldn't, causing stomach contents to rise up into the esophagus. The lower esophageal sphincter becomes weak or relaxes due to certain things, such as

- increased pressure on the abdomen from being overweight, obese, or pregnant
- certain medicines, including
  - those used to treat asthma—a long-lasting disease in the lungs that makes a child or teen extra sensitive to things that he or she is allergic to
  - antihistamines—medicines that treat allergy symptoms
  - painkillers
  - sedatives—medicines that help put someone to sleep
  - antidepressants—medicines that treat depression
- smoking,which is more likely with teens than younger children, or inhaling secondhand smoke

Other reasons a child or teen develops GERD include

- previous esophageal surgery
- having a severe developmental delay or neurological condition, such as cerebral palsy

When should I seek a doctor's help?

Call a doctor right away if your child or teen

- vomits large amounts
- has regular projectile, or forceful, vomiting
- vomits fluid that is
  - green or yellow
  - looks like coffee grounds
  - contains blood
- has problems breathing after vomiting
- has mouth of throat pain when he or she eats
- has problems swallowing or pain when swallowing
- refuses food repeatedly, causing weight loss or poor growth
- shows signs of dehydration, such as no tears when he or shes cries

Diagnosis

How do doctors diagnose GER in children and teens?

In most cases, a doctor diagnoses gastroesophageal reflux (GER) by reviewing a child or teen's symptoms and medical history. If symptoms of GER do not improve with lifestyle changes and anti-reflux medicines, he or she may need testing.

How do doctors diagnose GERD in children and teens?

If a child or teen's GER symptoms do not improve, if they come back frequently, or he or she has trouble swallowing, the doctor may recommend testing for gastroesophageal reflux disease (GERD).

The doctor may refer the child or teen to a pediatric gastroenterologist to diagnose and treat GERD.

What tests do doctors use to diagnose GERD?

Several tests can help a doctor diagnose GERD. A doctor may order more than one test to make a diagnosis.

Upper GI Series

An upper GI series looks at the shape of the child or teen's upper GI tract.

An X-ray technician performs this procedure at a hospital or an outpatient center. A radiologist reads and reports on the X-ray images. The child or teen doesn't need anesthesia.

During the procedure, the child or teen will drink liquid contrast (barium or gastrograffin) to coat the lining of the upper GI tract. The X-ray technician takes several X-rays as the contrast moves through the GI tract. The technician or radiologist will often change the position of the child or teen to get the best view of the GI tract. They may press on the child's abdomen during the X-ray procedure.

The upper GI series can't show mild irritation in the esophagus. It can find problems related to GERD, such as esophageal strictures, or problems with the anatomy that may cause symptoms of GERD.

Children or teens may have bloating and nausea for a short time after the procedure. For several days afterward, they may have white or light-colored stools from the barium. A health care professional will give you specific instructions about the child or teen's eating and drinking after the procedure.

Esophageal pH and impedance monitoring

The most accurate procedure to detect acid reflux is esophageal pH and impedance monitoring. Esophageal pH and impedance monitoring measures the amount of acid or liquid in a child or teen's esophagus while he or she does normal things, such as eating and sleeping.

A nurse or physician places a thin flexible tube through the child or teen's nose into the stomach. The tube is then pulled back into the esophagus and taped to the child or teen's cheek. The end of the tube in the esophagus measures when and how much acid comes up into the esophagus. The other end of the tube attaches to a monitor outside his or her body that records the measurements. The placement of the tube is sometimes done while a child is sedated after an upper endoscopy, but can be done while a child is fully awake.

The child or teen will wear a monitor for the next 24 hours. He or she will return to the hospital or outpatient center to have the tube removed. Children may need to stay in the hospital for the esophageal pH and impedancemonitoring.

This procedure is most useful to the doctor if you keep a diary of when, what, and how much food the child or teen eats and his or her GERD symptoms after eating. The gastroenterologist can see how the symptoms, certain foods, and certain times of day relate to one another.

The procedure can also help show whether acid reflux triggers any respiratory symptoms the child or teen might have.

Upper Gastro Intestinal (GI) endoscopy and biopsy

In an upper GI endoscopy, a gastroenterologist, surgeon, or other trained health care professional uses an endoscope to see inside a child or teen's upper GI tract. This procedure takes place at a hospital or an outpatient center.

An intravenous (IV) needle will be placed in the child or teen's arm to give him or her medicines that keep him or her relaxed and comfortable during the procedure. They may be given a liquid anesthetic to gargle or spray anesthetic on the back of his or her throat. The doctor carefully feeds the endoscope down the child or teen's esophagus then into the stomach and duodenum. A small camera mounted on the endoscope sends a video image to a monitor, allowing close examination of the lining of the upper GI tract. The endoscope pumps air into the child or teen's stomach and duodenum, making them easier to see.

The doctor may perform a biopsy with the endoscope by taking small pieces of tissue from the lining of the child or teen's esophagus, stomach, or duodenum. He or she won't feel the biopsy. A pathologist examines the tissue in a lab.

In most cases, the procedure only diagnoses GERD if the child or teen has moderate to severe symptoms.

Treatment

How do doctors treat GER and GERD in children and teens?

You can help control a child or teen's gastroesophageal reflux (GER) or gastroesophageal reflux disease (GERD) by having him or her

- not eat or drink items that may cause GER, such as greasy or spicy foods

- not overeat

- avoid smoking and secondhand smoke

- lose weight if he or she is overweight or obese

- avoid eating 2 to 3 hours before bedtime

- take over-the-counter medicines, such as Alka-Seltzer, Maalox, or Rolaids

How do doctors treat GERD in children and teens?

Depending on the severity of the child's symptoms, a doctor may recommend lifestyle changes, medicines, or surgery.

Lifestyle changes

Helping a child or teen make lifestyle changes can reduce his or her GERD symptoms. A child or teen should

- lose weight, if needed.
- eat smaller meals
- avoid high-fat foods
- wear loose-fitting clothing around the abdomen. Tight clothing can squeeze the stomach area and push the acid up into the esophagus.
- stay upright for 3 hours after meals and avoid reclining and slouching when sitting.
- sleep at a slight angle. Raise the head of the child or teen's bed 6 to 8 inches by safely putting blocks under the bedposts. Just using extra pillows will not help.
- If a teen smokes, help them quit smoking and avoid secondhand smoke.

Over-the-counter and prescription medicines

If a child or teen has symptoms that won't go away, you should take him or her to see a doctor. The doctor can prescribe medicine to relieve his or her symptoms. Some medicines are available over the counter.

All GERD medicines work in different ways. A child or teen may need a combination of GERD medicines to control symptoms.

- Antacids
- H2 blockers
- Proton pump inhibitors (PPIs)
- Prokinetics
- Antibiotics

Surgery

A pediatric gastroenterologist may recommend surgery if a child or teen's GERD symptoms don't improve with lifestyle changes or medicines. A child or teen is more likely to develop complications from surgery than from medicines.

Fundoplication is the most common surgery for GERD. In most cases, it leads to long-term reflux control.

A surgeon performs fundoplication using a laparoscope, a thin tube with a tiny video camera. During the operation, a surgeon sews the top of the stomach around the esophagus to add pressure to the lower end of the esophagus and reduce reflux.

The surgeon performs the operation at a hospital. The child or teen receives general anesthesia and can leave the hospital in 1 to 3 days. Most children and teens return to their usual daily activities in 2 to 3 weeks.

Endoscopic techniques, such as endoscopic sewing and radiofrequency, help control GERD in a small number of people. Endoscopic sewing uses small stitches to tighten the sphincter muscle. Radiofrequency creates heat lesions, or sores, that help tighten the sphincter muscle. A surgeon performs both operations using an endoscope at a hospital or an outpatient center, and the child or teen receives general anesthesia.

The results for endoscopic techniques may not be as good as those for fundoplication. Doctors don't use endoscopic techniques.

Eating, Diet, and Nutrition

How can diet help prevent or relieve GER or GERD in children and teens?

You can help a child or teen prevent or relieve their symptoms from gastroesophageal reflux (GER) or gastroesophageal reflux disease (GERD) by changing their diet. He or she may need to avoid certain foods and drinks that make his or her symptoms worse. Other dietary changes that can help reduce the child or teen's symptoms include

- decreasing fatty foods

- eating small, frequent meals instead of three large meals

What should a child or teen with GERD avoid eating or drinking?

He or she should avoid eating or drinking the following items that may make GER or GERD worse

- chocolate

- coffee

- peppermint

- greasy or spicy foods

- tomatoes and tomato products

What can a child or teen eat if they have GERD?

Eating healthy and balanced amounts of different types of foods is good for your child or teen's overall health. For more information about eating a balanced diet, visit Choose My Plate (www.choosemyplate.gov).

If your child or teen is overweight or obese, talk with a doctor or dietitian about dietary changes that can help with losing weight and decreasing the GERD symptoms.

Section 12.3

Gastroesophageal Reflux (GER) and Gastroesophageal Reflux Disease (GERD) in Infants

Text in this section is excerpted from "Gastroesophageal Reflux (GER) and Gastroesophageal Reflux Disease (GERD) in Infants," National Institute of Diabetes and Digestive and Kidney Diseases (NIDDK), April 8, 2015.

Definition and Facts

How common is GER in infants?

GER is common in infants. About half of all infants spit up, or regurgitate, many times a day in the first 3 months of their lives. In most cases, infants stop spitting up between the ages of 12 and 14 months.

What is the difference between GER and GERD?

Infants with symptoms that prevent them from feeding or those with GER that lasts more than 12 to 14 months may actually have GERD. If you think your infant has GERD, you should take him or her to see a doctor or a pediatrician.

How common is GERD in infants?

GERD is common in infants. Two-thirds of 4-month-olds have symptoms of GERD. By 1 year old, up to 10 percent of infants have symptoms of GERD.

Symptoms and Causes

What are the symptoms of GERD in infants?

The main symptom of gastroesophageal reflux disease (GERD) in infants is spitting up more than they normally do. Infants with GERD can also have some or all of the following recurring symptoms:

- arching of the back, often during or right after feeding
- colic—crying that lasts for more than 3 hours a day with no medical cause
- coughing
- gagging or trouble swallowing
- irritability, particularly after feeding
- pneumonia—an infection in one or both of the lungs
- poor feeding or refusal to feed
- poor growth and malnutrition
- poor weight gain
- trouble breathing
- vomiting
- weight loss
- wheezing—a high-pitched whistling sound that happens while breathing

What causes GER and GERD in infants?

Gastroesophageal reflux (GER) happens when an infant's lower esophageal sphincter is not fully developed, and the muscle lets the stomach contents back up the esophagus. Once the stomach contents move up into the esophagus, the infant will regurgitate, or spit up. Once an infant's sphincter muscle fully develops, he or she should no longer spit up.

GERD happens when an infant's lower esophageal sphincter muscle becomes weak or relaxes when it shouldn't. This weakness or relaxation lets the stomach contents come back up into the esophagus.

When should I seek a doctor's help?

Call a doctor right away if an infant

- vomits large amounts

- has regular projectile, or forceful, vomiting, particularly in infants younger than 2 months

- vomits fluid that is

    - green or yellow

    - looks like coffee grounds

    - contains blood

- has problems breathing after vomiting or spitting up

- often refuses feedings, causing weight loss or poor growth

- cries 3 or more hours a day and is more irritable than usual

- shows signs of dehydration, such as having dry diapers or extreme fussiness

Diagnosis

How do doctors diagnose GER in infants?

In most cases, a doctor diagnoses gastroesophageal reflux (GER) by reviewing an infant's symptoms and medical history. If symptoms of GER do not improve with feeding changes and anti-reflux medicines, he or she may need testing.

How do doctors diagnose GERD in infants?

The doctor may recommend testing for gastroesophageal reflux disease (GERD) if

- an infant's symptoms don't improve

- he or she is not gaining weight
- he or she is having lung problems

The doctor may refer the infant to a pediatric gastroenterologist to diagnose and treat GERD.

What tests do doctors use to diagnose GERD in infants?

Several tests can help a doctor diagnose GERD. A doctor may order more than one test to make a diagnosis.

Upper gastro intestinal (GI) endoscopy and biopsy

In an upper GI endoscopy, a gastroenterologist, surgeon, or other trained health care professional uses an endoscope to see inside an infant's upper GI tract. This procedure takes place at a hospital or an outpatient center. A health care professional will use an upper GI endoscopy especially if an infant has growth or breathing problems.

An intravenous (IV) needle is placed into one of the veins in the infant's arms, hands, or feet to give him or her medicines to keep him or her relaxed during the endoscopy procedure. The infant will receive extra oxygen throughout the procedure. The health care professional carefully feeds the endoscope down the infant's esophagus and into the stomach and duodenum. A small camera mounted on the endoscope sends a video image to a monitor, allowing close examination of the lining of the upper GI tract. The endoscope pumps air into the infant's GI tract, making them easier to see.

The doctor may perform a biopsy with the endoscope by taking a small piece of tissue from the lining of the infant's esophagus. He or she won't feel the biopsy. A pathologist examines the tissue in a lab.

In most cases, the procedure only diagnoses GERD if the infant has moderate to severe symptoms.

Upper GI series

An upper GI series looks at the shape of an infant's upper GI tract.

An X-ray technician performs this procedure at a hospital or an outpatient center. A radiologist reads and reports on the X-ray images. The infant doesn't need anesthesia.

During the procedure, a health care professional will give the infant liquid contrast (barium) in a bottle or mixed with food to coat the inner lining of the upper GI tract. The X-ray technician takes several X-rays as the contrast moves through the GI tract. The technician or radiologist will often change the position of the infant to get the best view of the GI tract. The barium shows up on the X-ray and can help find problems related to GERD.

For several days afterward, the infant may have white or light-colored stools from the barium. A health care professional will give you specific instructions about the infant's feeding and drinking after the procedure.

Esophageal pH and impedance monitoring

The most accurate procedure to detect acid reflux is esophageal pH and impedance monitoring. Esophageal pH and impedance monitoring measures the amount of acid or liquid in an infant's esophagus while he or she does normal things, such as eating and sleeping.

This procedure takes place at a hospital or outpatient center. A nurse or physician places a thin flexible tube through the infant's nose into the stomach. The tube is then pulled back into the esophagus and is secured in place with tape to the infant's cheek. The end of the tube in the esophagus measures when and how much acid or liquid comes into the esophagus from the stomach. The other end of the tube attaches to a monitor outside his or her body that records the measurements. The placement of the tube is sometimes done while a child is sedated after an upper endoscopy, but can be done while an infant is fully awake.

Most infants will stay overnight in the hospital for 24 hours after the tube is placed.

This procedure is most useful to the doctor if you keep a diary of when, what, and how much food the infant eats and his or her GERD symptoms after feeding. The gastroenterologist can see how the symptoms, certain foods, and certain times of day relate to one another. The procedure can also show whether or not reflux triggers any breathing problems.

Treatment

How do doctors treat GER in infants?

In most cases, gastroesophageal reflux (GER) in infants goes away before it becomes gastroesophageal reflux disease (GERD), so doctors don't treat GER in infants.

How do doctors treat GERD in infants?

Treatment for GERD depends on an infant's symptoms and age and may involve feeding changes, medicines, or surgery.

Feeding changes

A doctor may first recommend treating an infant's GERD by changing the way you feed him or her. The doctor may suggest that you

- add up to 1 tablespoon of rice cereal for every 2 ounces of formula in the infant's bottles. If the mixture is too thick, you can change the nipple size or cut a little "x" in the nipple to make the opening larger. Do not change formulas unless the doctor tells you to.

- add rice cereal to breast milk stored in a bottle for breastfed babies.

- burp infants after they have 1 to 2 ounces of formula, or burp breastfed infants after nursing from each breast.

- avoid overfeeding infants. Follow the amount of formula or breast milk recommended.

- hold infants upright for 30 minutes after feedings.

- try putting infants on a hydrolyzed protein formula for 2 to 4 weeks if the doctor thinks he or she may be sensitive to milk protein. The protein content of this type of formula is already broken down or "predigested."

Over-the-counter and prescription medicines

A doctor may recommend medicines that treat GERD by decreasing the amount of acid in the infant's stomach. The doctor will only prescribe a medicine if the infant still has regular GERD symptoms and if

- you have tried making feeding changes

- the infant has problems sleeping or feeding

- the infant does not grow properly

The doctor will often prescribe a medicine on a trial basis and will explain any possible complications. You shouldn't give an infant any medicines unless told to do so by a doctor.

H2 blockers. H2 blockers decrease acid production. They provide short-term or on-demand relief for infants with GERD symptoms. They can also help heal the esophagus.

A doctor may prescribe an H2 blocker, such as

- cimetidine (Tagamet HB)

- famotidine (Pepcid AC)

- nizatidine (Axid AR)

- ranitidine (Zantac 75)

Proton pump inhibitors (PPIs). PPIs lower the amount of acid the infant's stomach makes. PPIs are better at treating GERD symptoms than H2 blockers. They can heal the esophageal lining in infants. Doctors often prescribe PPIs for long-term GERD treatment.

An infant needs to be given these medicines on an empty stomach so that his or her stomach acid can make them work.

Several types of PPIs are available by a doctor's prescription, including

- esomeprazole (Nexium)

- lansoprazole (Prevacid)

- omeprazole (Prilosec, Zegerid)

- pantoprazole (Protonix)

- rabeprazole (AcipHex)

Surgery

A pediatric gastroenterologist will only use surgery to treat GERD in infants in severe cases. Infants must have severe breathing problems or a physical problem that causes GERD symptoms for surgery to be an option.

Eating, Diet, and Nutrition

How can diet prevent or relieve GER and GERD in infants?

An infant's doctor will first suggest feeding changes if the infant is not growing well or has malnutrition.

If feeding changes don't help an infant's GERD symptoms, the doctor may suggest a higher-calorie formula or tube feedings. For tube feedings, a doctor places a feeding tube through an infant's nose or mouth and into the stomach. An infant feeds from food, liquids, and medicines through the tube.

Chapter 13

Eosinophilic Gastrointestinal Disorders (EGIDs)

Eosinophilic gastrointestinal disorders (EGIDs) are a group of diseases in which eosinophils build up in the gastrointestinal tract. These disorders include

- Eosinophilic esophagitis (EoE), which involves the esophagus. This is the most common type of EGID.

- Eosinophilic gastritis, which involves the stomach

- Eosinophilic gastroenteritis, which affects both the stomach and small intestine

- Eosinophilic colitis, which affects the colon, or large intestine

In healthy people, small numbers of eosinophils may be found in all areas of the gastrointestinal tract except the esophagus. However, people with EGIDs have high eosinophil counts in the gastrointestinal tract.

The diagnosis of EGIDs, particularly EoE, is increasing in both adults and children. Health experts believe that this increase reflects changes in diagnostic practice as well as an actual increase in the

Text in this chapter is excerpted from "Eosinophilic Gastrointestinal Disorders," National Institute of Allergy and Infectious Diseases (NIAID), April 23, 2014.

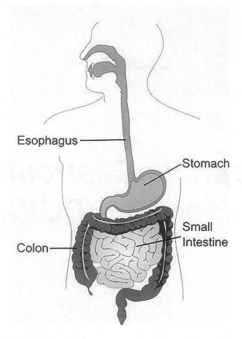

Figure 13.1. *Gastrointestinal tract organs of the digestive system that can be affected by eosinophilic gastrointestinal disorders.*

number of cases. According to the Registry for Eosinophilic Gastrointestinal, EoE may affect up to one in 1,000 people.

For most patients, EGIDs are life-long conditions. Early treatment and continued followup are important to decrease the long-term effects of these diseases.

Cause

Health experts are working to understand the factors that influence development of EGIDs. These disorders sometimes run in families, and scientists have identified several genetic variations associated with EoE.

Symptoms

Symptoms of EGIDs vary from person to person and depend on where in the gastrointestinal system eosinophils accumulate. Many signs of EGIDs closely resemble those of other gastrointestinal disorders, such as inflammatory bowel diseases.

Common EGID symptoms include

- Trouble swallowing
- A feeling that food is stuck in the throat or chest
- Chest or abdominal pain
- Heartburn or acid reflux that does not improve after taking appropriate medicine
- Nausea
- Vomiting
- Poor appetite
- Bloating

Diagnosis

Currently, the only clear-cut way for doctors to diagnose an EGID is by conducting an endoscopy with biopsy. In this procedure, a doctor uses an endoscope—a thin tube with a camera and light on the end—to look at the gastrointestinal tract and take small tissue samples called biopsies. A pathologist reviews the biopsies, looking for high levels of eosinophils and signs of tissue damage.

Treatment

Treatment with diet changes and/or medicines can alleviate EGID symptoms and prevent further damage to the gastrointestinal tract. Treatment options vary depending on the location of eosinophils and the severity of symptoms.

Diet changes

Many people with EoE respond well to diet changes, and dietary restrictions also may be helpful in treating those with other forms of EGID.

Sometimes, doctors will advise a "six food elimination diet," in which patients avoid all common allergenic foods, including milk, eggs, wheat, soy, peanuts and other nuts, and fish and shellfish.

Some people with EoE require a stricter diet called an elemental diet, which does not contain any whole or partial proteins for the immune system to recognize and respond to. People on an elemental diet consume prescription liquid formulas that contain amino acids (the building blocks of proteins), fats, sugars, vitamins, and minerals. Some people find it difficult to drink enough of the formula to maintain proper nutrition and may require tube feedings directly into the stomach.

Once EGID symptoms are under control, certain foods may be slowly added back into the diet under the guidance of a doctor and dietician.

Medicines

Because dietary management of EGIDs can be challenging, some patients choose medicines to treat their EGID. The Food and Drug Administration has not yet approved any medications for the treatment of EGIDs, but doctors may use certain drugs "off-label" to treat these disorders. Corticosteroids used to control asthma, such as fluticasone propionate or budesonide, may help suppress inflammation in people with EoE. While people with asthma typically take these medicines with an inhaler or nebulizer, those with EoE swallow the drugs so that the medicine comes in direct contact with the esophagus. Studies have shown that these drugs can resolve symptoms completely in some people with EoE, although symptoms return when medicine is stopped.

People with other types of EGIDs may take corticosteroids designed for delivery to specific parts of the gastrointestinal tract. In more severe cases, doctors may prescribe oral corticosteroids, such as prednisone, which deliver medicine to the whole body.

Chapter 14

Swallowing Disorders

Dysphagia

What is dysphagia?

People with dysphagia have difficulty swallowing and may even experience pain while swallowing (odynophagia). Some people may be completely unable to swallow or may have trouble safely swallowing liquids, foods, or saliva. When that happens, eating becomes a challenge. Often, dysphagia makes it difficult to take in enough calories and fluids to nourish the body and can lead to additional serious medical problems.

How do we swallow?

Swallowing is a complex process. Some 50 pairs of muscles and many nerves work to receive food into the mouth, prepare it, and move it from the mouth to the stomach. This happens in three stages. During the first stage, called the oral phase, the tongue collects the food or liquid, making it ready for swallowing. The tongue and jaw move solid food around in the mouth so it can be chewed. Chewing makes solid food the right size and texture to swallow by mixing the food with saliva. Saliva softens and moistens the food to make swallowing easier. Normally, the only solid we swallow without chewing is in the

---

Text in this chapter is excerpted from "Dysphagia," National Institute on Deafness and Other Communication Disorders (NIDCD), April 25, 2014.

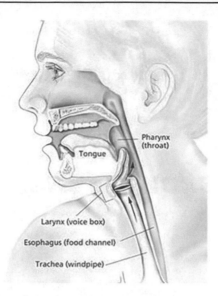

Figure 14.1. *Parts of the mouth and neck involved in swallowing*

form of a pill or caplet. Everything else that we swallow is in the form of a liquid, a puree, or a chewed solid.

The second stage begins when the tongue pushes the food or liquid to the back of the mouth. This triggers a swallowing response that passes the food through the pharynx, or throat (see figure 15.1). During this phase, called the pharyngeal phase, the larynx (voice box) closes tightly and breathing stops to prevent food or liquid from entering the airway and lungs.

The third stage begins when food or liquid enters the esophagus, the tube that carries food and liquid to the stomach. The passage through the esophagus, called the esophageal phase, usually occurs in about three seconds, depending on the texture or consistency of the food, but can take slightly longer in some cases, such as when swallowing a pill.

How does dysphagia occur?

Dysphagia occurs when there is a problem with the neural control or the structures involved in any part of the swallowing process. Weak tongue or cheek muscles may make it hard to move food around in the mouth for chewing. A stroke or other nervous system disorder may make it difficult to start the swallowing response, a stimulus that allows food and liquids to move safely through the throat. Another difficulty can occur when weak throat muscles, such as after cancer surgery, cannot move all of the food toward the stomach. Dysphagia may also result from disorders of the esophagus.

What are some problems caused by dysphagia?

Dysphagia can be serious. Someone who cannot swallow safely may not be able to eat enough of the right foods to stay healthy or maintain an ideal weight.

Food pieces that are too large for swallowing may enter the throat and block the passage of air. In addition, when foods or liquids enter the airway of someone who has dysphagia, coughing or throat clearing sometimes cannot remove it. Food or liquid that stays in the airway may enter the lungs and allow harmful bacteria to grow, resulting in a lung infection called aspiration pneumonia.

Swallowing disorders may also include the development of a pocket outside the esophagus caused by weakness in the esophageal wall. This abnormal pocket traps some food being swallowed. While lying down or sleeping, someone with this problem may draw undigested food into the throat. The esophagus may also be too narrow, causing food to stick. This food may prevent other food or even liquids from entering the stomach.

What causes dysphagia?

Dysphagia has many possible causes and happens most frequently in older adults. Any condition that weakens or damages the muscles and nerves used for swallowing may cause dysphagia. For example, people with diseases of the nervous system, such as cerebral palsy or Parkinson's disease, often have problems swallowing. Additionally, stroke or head injury may weaken or affect the coordination of the swallowing muscles or limit sensation in the mouth and throat.

People born with abnormalities of the swallowing mechanism may not be able to swallow normally. Infants who are born with an opening in the roof of the mouth (cleft palate) are unable to suck properly, which complicates nursing and drinking from a regular baby bottle.

In addition, cancer of the head, neck, or esophagus may cause swallowing problems. Sometimes the treatment for these types of cancers can cause dysphagia. Injuries of the head, neck, and chest may also create swallowing problems. An infection or irritation can cause narrowing of the esophagus. Finally, for people with dementia, memory loss and cognitive decline may make it difficult to chew and swallow.

How is dysphagia treated?

There are different treatments for various types of dysphagia. Medical doctors and speech-language pathologists who evaluate and treat swallowing disorders use a variety of tests that allow them to look at the stages of the swallowing process. One test, the Flexible Endoscopic Evaluation of Swallowing with Sensory Testing (FEESST), uses a lighted fiberoptic tube, or endoscope, to view the mouth and throat while examining how the swallowing mechanism responds to such stimuli as a puff of air, food, or liquids.

A videofluoroscopic swallow study (VFSS) is a test in which a clinician takes a videotaped X-ray of the entire swallowing process by having you consume several foods or liquids along with the mineral barium to improve visibility of the digestive tract. Such images help identify where in the swallowing process you are experiencing problems. Speech-language pathologists use this method to explore what changes can be made to offer a safe strategy when swallowing. The changes may be in food texture, size, head and neck posture, or behavioral maneuvers, such as "chin tuck," a strategy in which you tuck your chin so that food and other substances do not enter the trachea when swallowing. If you are unable to swallow safely despite rehabilitation strategies, then medical or surgical intervention may be necessary for the short-term as you recover. In progressive conditions such as amyotrophic lateral sclerosis (ALS, or Lou Gehrig's disease), a feeding tube in the stomach may be necessary for the long-term.

For some people, treatment may involve muscle exercises to strengthen weak facial muscles or to improve coordination. For others, treatment may involve learning to eat in a special way. For example, some people may have to eat with their head turned to one side or looking straight ahead. Preparing food in a certain way or avoiding certain foods may help in some situations. For instance, people who cannot swallow thin liquids may need to add special thickeners to their drinks. Other people may have to avoid hot or cold foods or drinks.

For some, however, consuming enough foods and liquids by mouth may no longer be possible. These individuals must use other methods to nourish their bodies. Usually this involves a feeding system, such as a feeding tube, that bypasses or supplements the part of the swallowing mechanism that is not working normally.

Chapter 15

Peptic Ulcers

Definition and Facts

What is a peptic ulcer?

A peptic ulcer is a sore on the lining of your stomach or duodenum. Rarely, a peptic ulcer may develop just above your stomach in your esophagus. Doctors call this type of peptic ulcer an esophageal ulcer.

Causes of peptic ulcers include

- long-term use of nonsteroidal anti-inflammatory drugs (NSAIDs), such as aspirin and ibuprofen

- an infection with the bacteria *Helicobacter pylori (H. pylori)*

- rare cancerous and noncancerous tumors in the stomach, duodenum, or pancreas—known as Zollinger-Ellison syndrome (ZES)

Who is more likely to develop peptic ulcers caused by NSAIDs?

People of any age who take NSAIDs every day or multiple times per week are more likely to develop a peptic ulcer than people who do not take them regularly. NSAIDs are a class of pain killers, such as aspirin and ibuprofen. Long-term use of NSAIDs can cause peptic ulcer disease.

Text in this chapter is excerpted from "Peptic Ulcer Disease," National Institute of Diabetes and Digestive and Kidney Diseases (NIDDK), November 13, 2014.

Your chance of having a peptic ulcer caused by NSAIDs, also called an NSAID-induced peptic ulcer, is increased if you

- are age 70 or older

- are female

- are taking more than two types of NSAIDs or have taken NSAIDs regularly for a long time

- have had a peptic ulcer before

- have two or more medical conditions or diseases

- are taking other medicines, such as corticosteroids and medicines to increase your bone mass

- drink alcohol or smoke

Who is more likely to develop peptic ulcers caused by H. pylori?

About 30 to 40 percent of people in the United States get an *H. pylori* infection. In most cases, the infection remains dormant, or quiet without signs or symptoms, for years. Most people get an *H. pylori* infection as a child.

Adults who have an *H. pylori* infection may get a peptic ulcer, also called an *H. pylori*-induced peptic ulcer. However, most people with an *H. pylori* infection never develop a peptic ulcer. Peptic ulcers caused by *H. pylori* are uncommon in children.

H. pylori are spiral-shaped bacteria that can damage the lining of your stomach and duodenum and cause peptic ulcer disease. Researchers are not certain how *H. pylori* spread. They think the bacteria may spread through

- unclean food

- unclean water

- unclean eating utensils

- contact with an infected person's saliva and other bodily fluids, including kissing

Researchers have found *H. pylori* in the saliva of some infected people, which means an *H. pylori* infection could spread through direct contact with saliva or other bodily fluids.

Who develops peptic ulcers caused by tumors?

People who have Zollinger-Ellison syndrome (ZES) develop peptic ulcers caused by tumors. Anyone can have ZES, yet it is rare and only occurs in about one in every 1 million people. However, ZES is more common among men 30 to 50 years old. A child who has a parent with multiple endocrine neoplasia type 1 is also more likely to have Zollinger-Ellison syndrome.

What other problems can a peptic ulcer cause?

A peptic ulcer can cause other problems, including

- bleeding from a broken blood vessel in your stomach or small intestine
- perforation of your stomach or small intestine
- a blockage that can stop food from moving from your stomach into your duodenum
- peritonitis

You may need surgery to treat these problems.

Symptoms and Causes

What are the symptoms of a peptic ulcer?

A dull or burning pain in your stomach is the most common symptom of a peptic ulcer. You may feel the pain anywhere between your belly button and breastbone. The pain most often

- happens when your stomach is empty—such as between meals or during the night
- stops briefly if you eat or if you take antacids
- lasts for minutes to hours
- comes and goes for several days, weeks, or months

Less common symptoms may include

- bloating
- burping
- feeling sick to your stomach

- poor appetite
- vomiting
- weight loss

Even if your symptoms are mild, you may have a peptic ulcer. You should see your doctor to talk about your symptoms. Without treatment, your peptic ulcer can get worse.

What causes a peptic ulcer?

Causes of peptic ulcers include

- long-term use of nonsteroidal anti-inflammatory drugs (NSAIDs), such as aspirin and ibuprofen
- an infection with the bacteria *Helicobacter pylori (H. pylori)*
- rare cancerous and noncancerous tumors in the stomach, duodenum, or pancreas—known as Zollinger-Ellison syndrome

Sometimes peptic ulcers are caused by both NSAIDs and *H. pylori*.

How do NSAIDs cause a peptic ulcer?

To understand how NSAIDs cause peptic ulcer disease, it is important to understand how NSAIDs work. Nonsteroidal anti-inflammatory drugs reduce pain, fever, and inflammation, or swelling.

Everyone has two enzymes that produce chemicals in your body's cells that promote pain, inflammation, and fever. NSAIDs work by blocking or reducing the amount of these enzymes that your body makes. However, one of the enzymes also produces another type of chemical that protects the stomach lining from stomach acid and helps control bleeding. When NSAIDs block or reduce the amount of this enzyme in your body, they also increase your chance of developing a peptic ulcer.

How do H. pylori cause a peptic ulcer and peptic ulcer disease?

H. pylori are spiral-shaped bacteria that can cause peptic ulcer disease by damaging the mucous coating that protects the lining of the stomach and duodenum. Once *H. pylori* have damaged the mucous coating, powerful stomach acid can get through to the sensitive lining. Together, the stomach acid and *H. pylori* irritate the lining of the stomach or duodenum and cause a peptic ulcer.

How do tumors from ZES cause peptic ulcers?

Zollinger-Ellison syndrome is a rare disorder that happens when one or more tumors form in your pancreas and duodenum. The tumors release large amounts of gastrin, a hormone that causes your stomach to produce large amounts of acid. The extra acid causes peptic ulcers to form in your duodenum and in the upper intestine.

When should you call or see a doctor?

You should call or see your doctor right away if you

- feel weak or faint
- have difficulty breathing
- have red blood in your vomit or vomit that looks like coffee grounds
- have red blood in your stool or black stools
- have sudden, sharp stomach pain that doesn't go away

These symptoms could be signs that a peptic ulcer has caused a more serious problem.

Diagnosis

How do doctors diagnose a peptic ulcer?

Your doctor will use information from your medical history, a physical exam, and tests to diagnose an ulcer and its cause. The presence of an ulcer can only be determined by looking directly at the stomach with endoscopy or an X-ray test.

Medical history

To help diagnose a peptic ulcer, your doctor will ask you questions about your medical history, your symptoms, and the medicines you take.

Be sure to mention medicines that you take without a prescription, especially nonsteroidal anti-inflammatory drugs (NSAIDs), such as

- aspirin (Bayer Aspirin)
- ibuprofen (Motri, Advil)
- naproxen (Aleve)

Physical Exam

A physical exam may help a doctor diagnose a peptic ulcer. During a physical exam, a doctor most often

- checks for bloating in your abdomen

- listens to sounds within your abdomen using a stethoscope

- taps on your abdomen checking for tenderness or pain

Lab tests

To see if you have a *Helicobacter pylori (H. pylori)* infection, your doctor will order these tests:

- Blood test

- Urea breath test

- Stool test

Upper gastrointestinal (GI) endoscopy and biopsy

In an upper GI endoscopy, a gastroenterologist, surgeon, or other trained health care professional uses an endoscope to see inside your upper GI tract. This procedure takes place at a hospital or an outpatient center.

An intravenous (IV) needle will be placed in your arm to provide a sedative. Sedatives help you stay relaxed and comfortable during the procedure. In some cases, the procedure can be performed without sedation. You will be given a liquid anesthetic to gargle or spray anesthetic on the back of your throat. The doctor will carefully feed the endoscope down your esophagus and into your stomach and duodenum. A small camera mounted on the endoscope sends a video image to a monitor, allowing close examination of the lining of your upper GI tract. The endoscope pumps air into your stomach and duodenum, making them easier to see.

The doctor may perform a biopsy with the endoscope by taking a small piece of tissue from the lining of your esophagus. You won't feel the biopsy. A pathologist examines the tissue in a lab.

Upper GI series

An upper GI series looks at the shape of your upper GI tract. An X-ray technician performs this test at a hospital or an outpatient center. A radiologist reads and reports on the X-ray images. You don't need anesthesia. A health care professional will tell you how to prepare for the procedure, including when to stop eating and drinking.

During the procedure, you'll stand or sit in front of an X-ray machine and drink barium, a chalky liquid. Barium coats your esophagus, stomach, and small intestine so your doctor can see the shapes of these organs more clearly on X-rays.

You may have bloating and nausea for a short time after the test. For several days afterward, you may have white or light-colored stools from the barium. A health care professional will give you instructions about eating and drinking after the test.

Computerized tomography (CT) scan

A CT scan uses a combination of X-rays and computer technology to create images. For a CT scan, a health care professional may give you a solution to drink and an injection of a special dye, which doctors call contrast medium. You'll lie on a table that slides into a tunnel-shaped device that takes the X-rays. An X-ray technician performs the procedure in an outpatient center or a hospital, and a radiologist interprets the images. You don't need anesthesia.

CT scans can help diagnose a peptic ulcer that has created a hole in the wall of your stomach or small intestine.

Treatment

How do doctors treat peptic ulcer disease?

There are several types of medicines used to treat a peptic ulcer. Your doctor will decide the best treatment based on the cause of your peptic ulcer.

How do doctors treat an NSAID-induced peptic ulcer?

If NSAIDs are causing your peptic ulcer and you don't have an *H. pylori* infection, your doctor may tell you to

- stop taking the NSAID
- reduce how much of the NSAID you take
- switch to another medicine that won't cause a peptic ulcer

Your doctor may also prescribe medicines to reduce stomach acid and coat and protect your peptic ulcer. Proton pump inhibitors (PPIs), histamine receptor blockers, and protectants can help relieve pain and help your ulcer heal.

PPIs

PPIs reduce stomach acid and protect the lining of your stomach and duodenum. While PPIs can't kill *H. pylori*, they do help fight the *H. pylori* infection.

PPIs include

- esomeprazole (Nexium)
- dexlansoprazole (Dexilant)
- lansoprazole (Prevacid)

- omeprazole (Prilosec, Zegerid)
- pantoprazole (Protonix)
- rabeprazole (AcipHex)

Histamine receptor blockers

Histamine receptor blockers work by blocking histamine, a chemical in your body that signals your stomach to produce acid. Histamine receptor blockers include

- cimetidine (Tagamet)
- famotidine (Pepcid)

- ranitidine (Zantac)
- nizatidine (Axid) Protectants

Protectants

Protectants coat ulcers and protect them against acid and enzymes so that healing can occur. Doctors only prescribe one protectant— sucralfate (Carafate) — for peptic ulcer disease.

Tell your doctor if the medicines make you feel sick or dizzy or cause diarrhea or headaches. Your doctor can change your medicines. If you smoke, quit. You also should avoid alcohol. Drinking alcohol and smoking slow the healing of a peptic ulcer and can make it worse.

What if I still need to take NSAIDs?

If you take NSAIDs for other conditions, such as arthritis, you should talk with your doctor about the benefits and risks of using NSAIDs. Your doctor can help you determine how to continue using an NSAID safely after your peptic ulcer symptoms go away. Your doctor may prescribe a medicine used to prevent NSAID-induced ulcers called Misoprosotol.

Tell your doctor about all the prescription and over-the-counter medicines you take. Your doctor can then decide if you may safely take NSAIDs or if you should switch to a different medicine. In either case, your doctor may prescribe a PPI or histamine receptor blocker to protect the lining of your stomach and duodenum.

If you need NSAIDs, you can reduce the chance of a peptic ulcer returning by

- taking the NSAID with a meal
- using the lowest effective dose possible
- quitting smoking
- avoiding alcohol

How do doctors treat an NSAID-induced peptic ulcer when you have an H. pylori infection?

If you have an *H. pylori* infection, a doctor will treat your NSAID-induced peptic ulcer with PPIs or histamine receptor blockers and other medicines, such as antibiotics, bismuth subsalicylates, or antacids.

PPIs reduce stomach acid and protect the lining of your stomach and duodenum. While PPIs can't kill *H. pylori*, they do help fight the *H. pylori* infection.

PPIs include

- esomeprazole (Nexium)
- dexlansoprazole (Dexilant)
- lansoprazole (Prevacid)
- omeprazole (Prilosec, Zegerid)
- pantoprazole (Protonix)
- rabeprazole (AcipHex)

Histamine receptor blockers

Histamine receptor blockers work by blocking histamine, a chemical in your body that signals your stomach to produce acid. Histamine receptor blockers include

- cimetidine (Tagamet)
- famotidine (Pepcid)
- ranitidine (Zantac)
- nizatidine (Axid)

Antibiotics

A doctor will prescribe antibiotics to kill *H. pylori*. How doctors prescribe antibiotics may differ throughout the world. Over time, some types of antibiotics can no longer destroy certain types of *H. pylori*.

Antibiotics can cure most peptic ulcers caused by *H. pylori* or *H. pylori*-induced peptic ulcers. However, getting rid of the bacteria can be difficult. Take all doses of your antibiotics exactly as your doctor prescribes, even if the pain from a peptic ulcer is gone.

Bismuth subsalicylates

Medicines containing bismuth subsalicylate, such as Pepto-Bismol, coat a peptic ulcer and protect it from stomach acid. Although bismuth subsalicylate can kill *H. pylori*, doctors sometimes prescribe it with antibiotics, not in place of antibiotics.

Antacids

An antacid may make the pain from a peptic ulcer go away temporarily, yet it will not kill *H. pylori*. If you receive treatment for an *H. pylori*-induced peptic ulcer, check with your doctor before taking antacids. Some of the antibiotics may not work as well if you take them with an antacid.

How do doctors treat an H.pylori-induced peptic ulcer?

Doctors may prescribe triple therapy, quadruple therapy, or sequential therapy to treat an *H. pylori*-induced peptic ulcer.

Triple therapy

For triple therapy, your doctor will prescribe that you take the following for 7 to 14 days:

- the antibiotic clarithromycin
- the antibiotic metronidazole or the antibiotic amoxicillin
- a PPI

Quadruple therapy

For quadruple therapy, your doctor will prescribe that you take the following for 14 days:

- a PPI
- bismuth subsalicylate
- the antibiotics tetracycline and metronidazole

Doctors prescribe quadruple therapy to treat patients who

- can't take amoxicillin because of an allergy to penicillin. Penicillin and amoxicillin are similar.

- have previously received a macrolide antibiotic, such as clarithromycin.

- are still infected with *H. pylori* after triple therapy treatment.

Doctors prescribe quadruple therapy after the first treatment has failed. In the second round of treatment, the doctor may prescribe different antibiotics than those that he or she prescribed the first time.

Sequential therapy

For sequential therapy, your doctor will prescribe that you take the following for 5 days:

- a PPI

- amoxicillin

Then the doctor will prescribe you the following for another 5 days:

- a PPI

- clarithromycin

- the antibiotic tinidazole

Triple therapy, quadruple therapy, and sequential therapy may cause nausea and other side effects, including

- an altered sense of taste

- darkened stools

- a darkened tongue

- diarrhea

- headaches

- temporary reddening of the skin when drinking alcohol

- vaginal yeast infections

Talk with your doctor about any side effects that bother you. He or she may prescribe you other medicines.

How do doctors treat peptic ulcers caused by ZES?

Doctors use medicines, surgery, and chemotherapy to treat Zollinger-Ellison syndrome.

What if a peptic ulcer doesn't heal?

Most often, medicines heal a peptic ulcer. If an *H. pylori* infection caused your peptic ulcer, you should finish all of your antibiotics and take any other medicines your doctor prescribes. The infection and peptic ulcer will heal only if you take all medicines as your doctor prescribes.

When you have finished your medicines, your doctor may do another breath or stool test in 4 weeks or more to be sure the *H. pylori* infection is gone. Sometimes, *H. pylori* bacteria are still present, even after you have taken all the medicines correctly. If the infection is still present, your peptic ulcer could return or, rarely, stomach cancer could develop. Your doctor will prescribe different antibiotics to get rid of the infection and cure your peptic ulcer.

Can a peptic ulcer come back?

Yes, a peptic ulcer can come back. If you smoke or take NSAIDs, peptic ulcers are more likely to come back. If you need to take an NSAID, your doctor may switch you to a different medicine or add medicines to help prevent a peptic ulcer. Peptic ulcer disease can return, even if you have been careful to reduce your risk.

How can I prevent a peptic ulcer?

To help prevent a peptic ulcer caused by NSAIDs, ask your doctor if you should

- stop using NSAIDs

- take NSAIDs with a meal if you still need NSAIDs

- take a lower dose of NSAIDs

- take medicines to protect your stomach and duodenum while taking NSAIDs

- switch to a medicine that won't cause ulcers

To help prevent a peptic ulcer caused by *H. pylori*, your doctor may recommend that you avoid drinking alcohol.

Eating, Diet, and Nutrition

How can your diet help prevent or relieve a peptic ulcer?

Researchers have not found that diet and nutrition play an important role in causing or preventing peptic ulcers. Before acid blocking drugs became available, milk was used to treat ulcers. However, milk is not an effective way to prevent or relieve a peptic ulcer.

Alcohol and smoking do contribute to ulcers and should be avoided.

Chapter 16

Gastroparesis

What is gastroparesis?

Gastroparesis, also called delayed gastric emptying, is a disorder that slows or stops the movement of food from the stomach to the small intestine. Normally, the muscles of the stomach, which are controlled by the vagus nerve, contract to break up food and move it through the gastrointestinal (GI) tract. The GI tract is a series of hollow organs joined in a long, twisting tube from the mouth to the anus. The movement of muscles in the GI tract, along with the release of hormones and enzymes, allows for the digestion of food. Gastroparesis can occur when the vagus nerve is damaged by illness or injury and the stomach muscles stop working normally. Food then moves slowly from the stomach to the small intestine or stops moving altogether.

What causes gastroparesis?

Most people diagnosed with gastroparesis have idiopathic gastroparesis, which means a health care provider cannot identify the cause, even with medical tests. Diabetes is the most common known cause of gastroparesis. People with diabetes have high levels of blood glucose, also called blood sugar. Over time, high blood glucose levels can damage the vagus nerve. Other identifiable causes of gastroparesis include

Text in this chapter is excerpted from "Gastroparesis," National Institute of Diabetes and Digestive and Kidney Diseases (NIDDK), June 2012.

intestinal surgery and nervous system diseases such as Parkinson's disease or multiple sclerosis. For reasons that are still unclear, gastroparesis is more commonly found in women than in men.

What are the symptoms of gastroparesis?

The most common symptoms of gastroparesis are nausea, a feeling of fullness after eating only a small amount of food, and vomiting undigested food—sometimes several hours after a meal. Other symptoms of gastroparesis include

- gastroesophageal reflux (GER), also called acid reflux or acid regurgitation—a condition in which stomach contents flow back up into the esophagus, the organ that connects the mouth to the stomach

- pain in the stomach area

- abdominal bloating

- lack of appetite

Symptoms may be aggravated by eating greasy or rich foods, large quantities of foods with fiber—such as raw fruits and vegetables—or drinking beverages high in fat or carbonation. Symptoms may be mild or severe, and they can occur frequently in some people and less often in others. The symptoms of gastroparesis may also vary in intensity over time in the same individual. Sometimes gastroparesis is difficult to diagnose because people experience a range of symptoms similar to those of other diseases.

How is gastroparesis diagnosed?

Gastroparesis is diagnosed through a physical exam, medical history, blood tests, tests to rule out blockage or structural problems in the GI tract, and gastric emptying tests. Tests may also identify a nutritional disorder or underlying disease. To rule out any blockage or other structural problems, the health care provider may perform one or more of the following tests:

- **Upper gastrointestinal (GI) endoscopy.** This procedure involves using an endoscope—a small, flexible tube with a light—to see the upper GI tract, which includes the esophagus, stomach, and duodenum—the first part of the small intestine. The test is performed at a hospital or outpatient center by a gastroenterologist—a doctor who specializes in digestive diseases. The endoscope is carefully fed down the esophagus and into the stomach and duodenum. A small camera mounted on the endoscope transmits a video image to a monitor, allowing close examination of the intestinal lining. A person may receive a liquid anesthetic that is gargled or sprayed on the back of the throat. An intravenous (IV) needle is placed in a vein in the arm if general anesthesia is given. The test may show blockage or large bezoars—solid collections of food, mucus, vegetable fiber, hair, or other material that cannot be digested in the stomach—that are sometimes softened, dissolved, or broken up during an upper GI endoscopy.

- **Upper GI series.** An upper GI series may be done to look at the small intestine. The test is performed at a hospital or outpatient center by an X-ray technician, and the images are interpreted by a radiologist—a doctor who specializes in medical imaging. Anesthesia is not needed. No eating or drinking is allowed for 8 hours before the procedure, if possible. If the person has diabetes, a health care provider may give different instructions about fasting before the test. During the procedure, the person will stand or sit in front of an X-ray machine and drink barium, a chalky liquid. Barium coats the small intestine, making signs of gastroparesis show up more clearly on X-rays. Gastroparesis is likely if the X-ray shows food in the stomach after fasting. A person may experience bloating and nausea for a short time after the test. For several days afterward, barium liquid in the GI tract causes stools to be white or light colored. A health care provider will give the person specific instructions about eating and drinking after the test.

- **Ultrasound.** Ultrasound uses a device, called a transducer, that bounces safe, painless sound waves off organs to create an image of their structure. The procedure is performed in a health care provider's office, outpatient center, or hospital by a specially trained technician, and the images are interpreted by a radiologist; anesthesia is not needed. The images can show whether gallbladder disease and pancreatitis could be the cause of a person's digestive symptoms, rather than gastroparesis.

- **Gastric emptying scintigraphy.** The test involves eating a bland meal—such as eggs or an egg substitute—that contains a small amount of radioactive material. The test is performed in a radiology center or hospital by a specially trained technician and interpreted by a radiologist; anesthesia is not needed. An external camera scans the abdomen to show where the radioactive material is located. The radiologist is then able to measure the rate of gastric emptying at 1, 2, 3, and 4 hours after the meal. If more than 10 percent of the meal is still in the stomach at 4 hours, the diagnosis of gastroparesis is confirmed.

- **SmartPill.** The SmartPill is a small electronic device in capsule form. The SmartPill test is available at specialized outpatient centers. The images are interpreted by a radiologist. The device is swallowed and moves through the entire digestive tract, sending information to a cell-phone-sized receiver worn around the person's waist or neck. The recorded information provides a detailed record of how quickly food travels through each part of the digestive tract.

- **Gastric emptying breath test.** With this test, the person eats a special test meal that includes a natural material with a special type of carbon in it. Then, breath samples are taken over a period of several hours to measure the amount of the material in the exhaled breath. The results allow the health care provider to calculate how fast the stomach is emptying.

How is gastroparesis treated?

Treatment of gastroparesis depends on the severity of the person's symptoms. In most cases, treatment does not cure gastroparesis, which is usually a chronic, or long-lasting, condition. Gastroparesis is also a relapsing condition—the symptoms can come and go for periods of time. Treatment helps people manage the condition so they can be as comfortable and active as possible.

Eating, Diet, And Nutrition

Changing eating habits can sometimes help control the severity of gastroparesis symptoms. A health care provider may suggest eating six small meals a day instead of three large ones. If less food enters the stomach each time a person eats, the stomach may not become overly full, allowing it to empty more easily. Chewing food well, drinking noncarbonated liquids with a meal, and walking or sitting for 2 hours after a meal—instead of lying down—may assist with gastric emptying.

A health care provider may also recommend avoiding high-fat and fibrous foods. Fat naturally slows digestion and some raw vegetables and fruits are more difficult to digest than other foods. Some foods, such as oranges and broccoli, contain fibrous parts that do not digest well. People with gastroparesis should minimize their intake of large portions of these foods because the undigested parts may remain in the stomach too long. Sometimes, the undigested parts form bezoars.

When a person has severe symptoms, a liquid or puréed diet may be prescribed. As liquids tend to empty more quickly from the stomach, some people may find a puréed diet helps improve symptoms. Puréed fresh or cooked fruits and vegetables can be incorporated into shakes and soups. A health care provider may recommend a dietitian to help a person plan meals that minimize symptoms and ensure all nutritional needs are met.

When the most extreme cases of gastroparesis lead to severe nausea, vomiting, and dehydration, urgent care may be required at a medical facility where IV fluids can be given.

Medications

Several prescription medications are available to treat gastroparesis. A combination of medications may be used to find the most effective treatment.

Metoclopramide (Reglan). This medication stimulates stomach muscle contractions to help with gastric emptying. Metoclopramide also helps reduce nausea and vomiting. The medication is taken 20 to 30 minutes before meals and at bedtime. Possible side effects of metoclopramide include fatigue, sleepiness, and depression. Currently, this is the only medication approved by the FDA for treatment of gastroparesis. However, the FDA has placed a black box warning on this medication because of rare reports of it causing an irreversible neurologic side effect called tardive dyskinesia—a disorder that affects movement.

Erythromycin. This antibiotic, prescribed at low doses, may improve gastric emptying. Like metaclopramide, erythromycin works by increasing the contractions that move food through the stomach. Possible side effects of erythromycin include nausea, vomiting, and abdominal cramps.

Other medications. Other medications may be used to treat symptoms and problems related to gastroparesis. For example, medications known as antiemetics are used to help control nausea and vomiting.

- Botulinum Toxin
- Gastric Electrical Stimulation
- Jejunostomy
- Parenteral Nutrition

How is gastroparesis treated if a person has diabetes?

An elevated blood glucose level directly interferes with normal stomach emptying, so good blood glucose control in people with diabetes is important. However, gastroparesis can make blood glucose control difficult. When food that has been delayed in the stomach finally enters the small intestine and is absorbed, blood glucose levels rise. Gastric emptying is unpredictable with gastroparesis, causing a person's blood glucose levels to be erratic and difficult to control.

The primary treatment goals for gastroparesis related to diabetes are to improve gastric emptying and regain control of blood glucose levels. In addition to the dietary changes and treatments already described, a health care provider will likely adjust the person's insulin regimen.

To better control blood glucose, people with diabetes and gastroparesis may need to

- take insulin more often or change the type of insulin they take
- take insulin after meals, instead of before
- check blood glucose levels frequently after eating and administer insulin when necessary

A health care provider will give specific instructions for taking insulin based on the individual's needs and the severity of gastroparesis.

In some cases, the dietitian may suggest eating several liquid or puréed meals a day until gastroparesis symptoms improve and blood glucose levels are more stable.

What Are the Problems of Gastroparesis?

The problems of gastroparesis can include

- severe dehydration due to persistent vomiting
- gastroesophageal reflux disease (GERD), which is GER that occurs more than twice a week for a few weeks; GERD can lead to esophagitis— irritation of the esophagus

- bezoars, which can cause nausea, vomiting, obstruction, or inter-fere with absorption of some medications in pill form
- difficulty managing blood glucose levels in people with diabetes
- malnutrition due to poor absorption of nutrients or a low calorie intake
- decreased quality of life, including work absences due to severe symptoms

Chapter 17

Other Diseases of the Upper Gastrointestinal Tract

Chapter Contents

Section 17.1

Gastritis

Text in this section is excerpted from "Gastritis," National
Institute of Diabetes and Digestive and Kidney
Diseases (NIDDK), September 2014.

What is gastritis?

Gastritis is a condition in which the stomachlining—known as the
mucosa—is inflamed, or swollen. The stomach lining contains glands
that produce stomach acid and an enzyme called pepsin. The stomach
acid breaks down food and pepsin digests protein. A thick layer of
mucus coats the stomach lining and helps prevent the acidic digestive
juice from dissolving the stomach tissue. When the stomach lining
is inflamed, it produces less acid and fewer enzymes. However, the
stomach lining also produces less mucus and other substances that
normally protect the stomach lining from acidic digestive juice.

Gastritis may be acute or chronic:

- Acute gastritis starts suddenly and lasts for a short time.

- Chronic gastritis is long lasting. If chronic gastritis is not
  treated, it may last for years or even a lifetime.

Gastritis can be erosive or nonerosive:

Erosive gastritis can cause the stomach lining to wear away, causing erosions—shallow breaks in the stomach lining—or ulcers—deep
sores in the stomach lining.

Nonerosive gastritis causes inflammation in the stomach lining;
however, erosions or ulcers do not accompany nonerosive gastritis.

A health care provider may refer a person with gastritis to a gastroenterologist—a doctor who specializes in digestive diseases.

What causes gastritis?

Common causes of gastritis include

- *Helicobacter pylori* (*H. pylori*) infection

- damage to the stomach lining, which leads to reactive gastritis

- an autoimmune response

What are the signs and symptoms of gastritis?

Some people who have gastritis have pain or discomfort in the upper part of the abdomen—the area between the chest and hips. However, many people with gastritis do not have any signs and symptoms. The relationship between gastritis and a person's symptoms is not clear. The term "gastritis" is sometimes mistakenly used to describe any symptoms of pain or discomfort in the upper abdomen.

When symptoms are present, they may include

- upper abdominal discomfort or pain

- nausea

- vomiting

Seek Help for Symptoms of Bleeding in the Stomach

Erosive gastritis may cause ulcers or erosions in the stomach lining that can bleed. Signs and symptoms of bleeding in the stomach include:

- shortness of breath
- dizziness or feeling faint
- red blood in vomit
- black, tarry stools
- red blood in the stool
- weakness
- paleness

A person with any signs or symptoms of bleeding in the stomach should call or see a health care provider right away.

What are the complications of chronic and acute gastritis?

The complications of chronic gastritis may include

- peptic ulcers. Peptic ulcers are sores involving the lining of the stomach or duodenum, the first part of the small intestine. NSAID use and H. pylori gastritis increase the chance of developing peptic ulcers.

- atrophic gastritis. Atrophic gastritis happens when chronic inflammation of the stomach lining causes the loss of the stomach lining and glands. Chronic gastritis can progress to atrophic gastritis.

- anemia. Erosive gastritis can cause chronic bleeding in the stomach, and the blood loss can lead to anemia. Anemia is a condition in which red blood cells are fewer or smaller than normal, which prevents the body's cells from getting enough oxygen. Red blood cells contain hemoglobin, an iron-rich protein that gives blood its red color and enables the red blood cells to transport oxygen from the lungs to the tissues of the body. Research suggests that H. pylori gastritis and autoimmune atrophic gastritis can interfere with the body's ability to absorb iron from food, which may also cause anemia.

- vitamin B12 deficiency and pernicious anemia. People with autoimmune atrophic gastritis do not produce enough intrinsic factor. Intrinsic factor is a protein made in the stomach and helps the intestines absorb vitamin B12. The body needs vitamin B12 to make red blood cells and nerve cells. Poor absorption of vitamin B12 may lead to a type of anemia called pernicious anemia.

- growths in the stomach lining. Chronic gastritis increases the chance of developing benign, or noncancerous, and malignant, or cancerous, growths in the stomach lining. Chronic H. pylori gastritis increases the chance of developing a type of cancer called gastric mucosa-associated lymphoid tissue (MALT) lymphoma.

In most cases, acute gastritis does not lead to complications. In rare cases, acute stress gastritis can cause severe bleeding that can be life threatening.

How is gastritis diagnosed?

A health care provider diagnoses gastritis based on the following:

- medical history

- physical exam

- upper GI endoscopy

- other tests, such as upper GI series, blood tests, stool test, and urea breath test

How is gastritis treated?

Health care providers treat gastritis with medications to

- reduce the amount of acid in the stomach
- treat the underlying cause

Reduce the Amount of Acid in the Stomach

The stomach lining of a person with gastritis may have less protection from acidic digestive juice. Reducing acid can promote healing of the stomach lining. Medications that reduce acid include

- antacids
- H2 blockers
- proton pump inhibitors (PPIs)

Treat the Underlying Cause

Depending on the cause of gastritis, a health care provider may recommend additional treatments.

- Treating *H. pylori* infection with antibiotics is important, even if a person does not have symptoms from the infection. Curing the infection often cures the gastritis and decreases the chance of developing complications, such as peptic ulcer disease, MALT lymphoma, and gastric cancer.
- Avoiding the cause of reactive gastritis can provide some people with a cure. For example, if prolonged NSAID use is the cause of the gastritis, a health care provider may advise the patient to stop taking the NSAIDs, reduce the dose, or change pain medications.
- Health care providers may prescribe medications to prevent or treat stress gastritis in a patient who is critically ill or injured. Medications to protect the stomach lining include sucralfate (Carafate), H2 blockers, and PPIs. Treating the underlying illness or injury most often cures stress gastritis.
- Health care providers may treat people with pernicious anemia due to autoimmune atrophic gastritis with vitamin B12 injections.

How can gastritis be prevented?

People may be able to reduce their chances of getting gastritis by preventing *H. pylori* infection. No one knows for sure how *H. pylori* infection spreads, so prevention is difficult. To help prevent infection, health care providers advise people to

- wash their hands with soap and water after using the bathroom and before eating

- eat food that has been washed well and cooked properly

- drink water from a clean, safe source

Eating, Diet, and Nutrition

Researchers have not found that eating, diet, and nutrition play a major role in causing or preventing gastritis.

Section 17.2

Ménétrier Disease

Text in this section is excerpted from "Ménétrier's Disease," National Institute of Diabetes and Digestive and Kidney Diseases (NIDDK), February 2014.

What is Ménétrier's disease?

Ménétrier's disease causes the ridges along the inside of the stomach wall—called rugae—to enlarge, forming giant folds in the stomach lining. The rugae enlarge because of an overgrowth of mucous cells in the stomach wall.

In a normal stomach, mucous cells in the rugae release protein-containing mucus. The mucous cells in enlarged rugae release too much mucus, causing proteins to leak from the blood into the stomach. This shortage of protein in the blood is known as hypoproteinemia. Ménétrier's disease also reduces the number of acid-producing cells in the stomach, which decreases stomach acid.

Ménétrier's disease is also called Ménétrier disease or hypoproteinemic hypertrophic gastropathy.

What causes Ménétrier's disease?

Scientists are unsure about what causes Ménétrier's disease; however, researchers think that most people acquire, rather than inherit, the disease. In extremely rare cases, siblings have developed Ménétrier's disease as children, suggesting a genetic link.

Studies suggest that people with Ménétrier's disease have stomachs that make abnormally high amounts of a protein called transforming growth factor-alpha (TGF-α).

TGF-α binds to and activates a receptor called epidermal growth factor receptor. Growth factors are proteins in the body that tell cells what to do, such as grow larger, change shape, or divide to make more cells. Researchers have not yet found a cause for the overproduction of TGF-α.

Some studies have found cases of people with Ménétrier's disease who also had *Helicobacter pylori (H. pylori)* infection. *H. pylori* is a bacterium that is a cause of peptic ulcers, or sores on the lining of the stomach or the duodenum, the first part of the small intestine. In these cases, treatment for *H. pylori* reversed and improved the symptoms of Ménétrier's disease.

Researchers have linked some cases of Ménétrier's disease in children to infection with cytomegalovirus (CMV). CMV is one of the herpes viruses. This group of viruses includes the herpes simplex viruses, which cause chickenpox, shingles, and infectious mononucleosis, also known as mono. Most healthy children and adults infected with CMV have no symptoms and may not even know they have an infection. However, in people with a weakened immune system, CMV can cause serious disease, such as retinitis, which can lead to blindness.

Researchers are not sure how *H. pylori* and CMV infections contribute to the development of Ménétrier's disease.

Who gets Ménétrier's disease?

Ménétrier's disease is rare. The disease is more common in men than in women. The average age at diagnosis is 55.

What are the signs and symptoms of Ménétrier's disease?

The most common symptom of Ménétrier's disease is pain in the upper middle part of the abdomen. The abdomen is the area between the chest and hips.

Other signs and symptoms of Ménétrier's disease may include

- nausea and frequent vomiting

- diarrhea

- loss of appetite

- extreme weight loss

- malnutrition

- low levels of protein in the blood

- swelling of the face, abdomen, limbs, and feet due to low levels of protein in the blood

- anemia—too few red blood cells in the body, which prevents the body from getting enough oxygen—due to bleeding in the stomach

People with Ménétrier's disease have a higher chance of developing stomach cancer, also called gastric cancer.

How is Ménétrier's disease diagnosed?

Health care providers base the diagnosis of Ménétrier's disease on a combination of symptoms, lab findings, findings on upper gastrointestinal (GI) endoscopy, and stomach biopsy results. A health care provider will begin the diagnosis of Ménétrier's disease by taking a patient's medical and family history and performing a physical exam. However, a health care provider will confirm the diagnosis of Ménétrier's disease through a computerized tomography (CT) scan, an upper GI endoscopy, and a biopsy of stomach tissue. A health care provider also may order blood tests to check for infection with *H. pylori* or CMV.

- Medical and family history
- Physical exam
- CT scan
- Upper GI endoscopy
- Biopsy
- Blood test

How is Ménétrier's disease treated?

Treatment may include medications, IV protein, blood transfusions, and surgery.

Medications

Health care providers may prescribe the anticancer medication cetuximab (Erbitux) to treat Ménétrier's disease. Studies have shown that cetuximab blocks the activity of epidermal growth factor receptor and can significantly improve a person's symptoms, as well as decrease the thickness of the stomach wall from the overgrowth of mucous cells. A person receives cetuximab by IV in a health care provider's office or an outpatient center. Studies to assess the effectiveness of cetuximab to treat Ménétrier's disease are ongoing. A health care provider also may prescribe medications to relieve nausea and abdominal pain.

In people with Ménétrier's disease who also have *H. pylori* or CMV infection, treatment of the infection may improve symptoms. Health care providers prescribe antibiotics to kill *H. pylori*. Antibiotic regimens may differ throughout the world because some strains of *H. pylori* have become resistant to certain antibiotics—meaning that an antibiotic that once destroyed the bacterium is no longer effective. Health care providers use antiviral medications to treat CMV infection in a person with a weakened immune system in order to prevent a serious disease from developing as a result of CMV. Antiviral medications cannot kill CMV; however, they can slow down the virus reproduction.

Intravenous Protein and Blood Transfusions

A health care provider may recommend an IV treatment of protein and a blood transfusion to a person who is malnourished or anemic because of Ménétrier's disease. In most cases of children with Ménétrier's disease who also have had CMV infection, treatment with protein and a blood transfusion led to a full recovery.

Surgery

If a person has severe Ménétrier's disease with significant protein loss, a surgeon may need to remove part or all of the stomach in a surgery called gastrectomy.

Surgeons perform gastrectomy in a hospital. The patient will require general anesthesia. Some surgeons perform a gastrectomy through laparoscopic surgery rather than through a wide incision in the abdomen. In laparoscopic surgery, the surgeon uses several smaller incisions and feeds special surgical tools through the incisions to remove the diseased part of the stomach. After gastrectomy, the surgeon may reconstruct the changed portions of the GI tract so that it may continue to function. Usually the surgeon attaches the small intestine to any remaining portion of the stomach or to the esophagus if he or she removed the entire stomach.

Eating, Diet, and Nutrition

Researchers have not found that eating, diet, and nutrition play a role in causing or preventing Ménétrier's disease. In some cases, a health care provider may prescribe a high-protein diet to offset the loss of protein due to Ménétrier's disease. Some people with severe malnutrition may require IV nutrition, which is called total parenteral nutrition (TPN). TPN is a method of providing an IV liquid food mixture through a special tube in the chest.

Section 17.3

Rapid Gastric Emptying (Dumping Syndrome)

Text in this section is excerpted from "Dumping Syndrome," National Institute of Diabetes and Digestive and Kidney Diseases (NIDDK), September 2013.

What is dumping syndrome?

Dumping syndrome occurs when food, especially sugar, moves too fast from the stomach to the duodenum—the first part of the small intestine—in the upper gastrointestinal (GI) tract. This condition is also called rapid gastric emptying. Dumping syndrome has two forms, based on when symptoms occur:

- early dumping syndrome—occurs 10 to 30 minutes after a meal

- late dumping syndrome—occurs 2 to 3 hours after a meal

What causes dumping syndrome?

Dumping syndrome is caused by problems with the storage of food particles in the stomach and emptying of particles into the duodenum. Early dumping syndrome results from rapid movement of fluid into the intestine following a sudden addition of a large amount of food from the stomach. Late dumping syndrome results from rapid movement of sugar into the intestine, which raises the body's blood glucose level and causes the pancreas to increase its release of the hormone insulin.

The increased release of insulin causes a rapid drop in blood glucose levels, a condition known as hypoglycemia, or low blood sugar.

Who is more likely to develop dumping syndrome?

People who have had surgery to remove or bypass a significant part of the stomach are more likely to develop dumping syndrome. Some types of gastric surgery, such as bariatric surgery, reduce the size of the stomach. As a result, dietary nutrients pass quickly into the small intestine. Other conditions that impair how the stomach stores and empties itself of food, such as nerve damage caused by esophageal surgery, can also cause dumping syndrome.

What are the symptoms of dumping syndrome?

The symptoms of early and late dumping syndrome are different and vary from person to person. Early dumping syndrome symptoms may include

- nausea
- vomiting
- abdominal pain and cramping
- diarrhea
- feeling uncomfortably full or bloated after a meal
- sweating
- weakness
- dizziness
- flushing, or blushing of the face or skin
- rapid or irregular heartbeat

The symptoms of late dumping syndrome may include
- hypoglycemia
- sweating
- weakness
- rapid or irregular heartbeat
- flushing
- dizziness

About 75 percent of people with dumping syndrome report symptoms of early dumping syndrome and about 25 percent report symptoms of late dumping syndrome. Some people have symptoms of both types of dumping syndrome.

How is dumping syndrome diagnosed?

A health care provider will diagnose dumping syndrome primarily on the basis of symptoms. A scoring system helps differentiate dumping syndrome from other GI problems. The scoring system assigns points to each symptom and the total points result in a score. A person with a score above 7 likely has dumping syndrome.

The following tests may confirm dumping syndrome and exclude other conditions with similar symptoms:

- A **modified oral glucose tolerance test** checks how well insulin works with tissues to absorb glucose. A health care provider performs the test during an office visit or in a commercial facility and sends the blood samples to a lab for analysis. The person should fast—eat or drink nothing except water—for at least 8 hours before the test. The health care provider will measure blood glucose concentration, hematocrit—the amount of red blood cells in the blood—pulse rate, and blood pressure before the test begins. After the initial measurements, the person drinks a glucose solution. The health care provider repeats the initial measurements immediately and at 30-minute intervals for up to 180 minutes. A health care provider often confirms dumping syndrome in people with

    - low blood sugar between 120 and 180 minutes after drinking the solution

    - an increase in hematocrit of more than 3 percent at 30 minutes

    - a rise in pulse rate of more than 10 beats per minute after 30 minutes

- A gastric emptying scintigraphy test involves eating a bland meal—such as eggs or an egg substitute—that contains a small amount of radioactive material. A specially trained technician performs this test in a radiology center or hospital, and a radiologist—a doctor who specializes in medical imaging—interprets the results. Anesthesia is not needed. An external camera scans the abdomen to locate the radioactive material. The radiologist measures the rate of gastric emptying at 1, 2, 3, and 4 hours after the meal. The test can help confirm a diagnosis of dumping syndrome.

How is dumping syndrome treated?

Treatment for dumping syndrome includes changes in eating, diet, and nutrition, medication; and, in some cases, surgery. Many people with dumping syndrome have mild symptoms that improve over time with simple dietary changes.

Eating, Diet, and Nutrition

The first step to minimizing symptoms of dumping syndrome involves changes in eating, diet, and nutrition, and may include

- eating five or six small meals a day instead of three larger meals

- delaying liquid intake until at least 30 minutes after a meal

- increasing intake of protein, fiber, and complex carbohydrates—found in starchy foods such as oatmeal and rice

- avoiding simple sugars such as table sugar, which can be found in candy, syrup, sodas, and juice beverages

- increasing the thickness of food by adding pectin or guar gum—plant extracts used as thickening agents

Some people find that lying down for 30 minutes after meals also helps reduce symptoms.

Medication

A health care provider may prescribe octreotide acetate (Sandostatin) to treat dumping syndrome symptoms. The medication works by slowing gastric emptying and inhibiting the release of insulin and other GI hormones. Octreotide comes in short- and long-acting formulas. The short-acting formula is injected subcutaneously—under the skin—or intravenously—into a vein—two to four times a day. A health care provider may perform the injections or may train the patient or patient's friend or relative to perform the injections. A health care provider injects the long-acting formula into the buttocks muscles once every 4 weeks. Complications of octreotide treatment include increased or decreased blood glucose levels, pain at the injection site, gallstones, and fatty, foul-smelling stools.

Surgery

A person may need surgery if dumping syndrome is caused by previous gastric surgery or if the condition is not responsive to other treatments. For most people, the type of surgery depends on the type of gastric surgery performed previously. However, surgery to correct dumping syndrome often has unsuccessful results.

Section 17.4

Zollinger-Ellison Syndrome

Text in this section is excerpted from "Zollinger-Ellison Syndrome,"
National Institute of Diabetes and Digestive and Kidney Diseases
(NIDDK), December 2013.

What is Zollinger-Ellison syndrome?

Zollinger-Ellison syndrome is a rare disorder that occurs when one or more tumors form in the pancreas and duodenum. The tumors, called gastrinomas, release large amounts of gastrin that cause the stomach to produce large amounts of acid. Normally, the body releases small amounts of gastrin after eating, which triggers the stomach to make gastric acid that helps break down food and liquid in the stomach. The extra acid causes peptic ulcers to form in the duodenum and elsewhere in the upper intestine.

The tumors seen with Zollinger-Ellison syndrome are sometimes cancerous and may spread to other areas of the body.

What are the stomach, duodenum, and pancreas?

The stomach, duodenum, and pancreas are digestive organs that break down food and liquid.

- The stomach stores swallowed food and liquid. The muscle action of the lower part of the stomach mixes the food and liquid with digestive juice. Partially digested food and liquid slowly move into the duodenum and are further broken down.

- The duodenum is the first part of the small intestine—the tube-shaped organ between the stomach and the large intestine—where digestion of the food and liquid continues.

- The pancreas is an organ that makes the hormone insulin and enzymes for digestion. A hormone is a natural chemical produced in one part of the body and released into the blood to trigger or regulate particular functions of the body. Insulin helps cells throughout the body remove glucose, also called sugar, from blood and use it for energy. The pancreas is located behind the stomach and close to the duodenum.

What causes Zollinger-Ellison syndrome?

Experts do not know the exact cause of Zollinger-Ellison syndrome. About 25 to 30 percent of gastrinomas are caused by an inherited genetic disorder called multiple endocrine neoplasia type 1 (MEN1). MEN1 causes hormone-releasing tumors in the endocrine glands and the duodenum. Symptoms of MEN1 include increased hormone levels in the blood, kidney stones, diabetes, muscle weakness, weakened bones, and fractures.

How common is Zollinger-Ellison syndrome?

Zollinger-Ellison syndrome is rare and only occurs in about one in every 1 million people. Although anyone can get Zollinger-Ellison syndrome, the disease is more common among men 30 to 50 years old. A child who has a parent with MEN1 is also at increased risk for Zollinger-Ellison syndrome.

What are the signs and symptoms of Zollinger-Ellison syndrome?

Zollinger-Ellison syndrome signs and symptoms are similar to those of peptic ulcers. A dull or burning pain felt anywhere between the navel and midchest is the most common symptom of a peptic ulcer. This discomfort usually

- occurs when the stomach is empty—between meals or during the night—and may be briefly relieved by eating food

- lasts for minutes to hours

- comes and goes for several days, weeks, or months

Other symptoms include

- diarrhea
- bloating
- burping
- nausea

- vomiting
- weight loss
- poor appetite

Some people with Zollinger-Ellison syndrome have only diarrhea, with no other symptoms. Others develop gastroesophageal reflux (GER), which occurs when stomach contents flow back up into the esophagus—a muscular tube that carries food and liquids to the stomach. In addition to nausea and vomiting, reflux symptoms include a painful, burning feeling in the midchest.

Seek Help for Emergency Symptoms

A person who has any of the following emergency symptoms should call or see a health care provider right away:

- chest pain
- sharp, sudden, persistent, and severe stomach pain
- red blood in stool or black stools
- red blood in vomit or vomit that looks like coffee grounds

These symptoms could be signs of a serious problem, such as

- internal bleeding—when gastric acid or a peptic ulcer breaks a blood vessel
- perforation—when a peptic ulcer forms a hole in the duodenal wall
- obstruction—when a peptic ulcer blocks the path of food trying to leave the stomach

How is Zollinger-Ellison syndrome diagnosed?

A health care provider diagnoses Zollinger-Ellison syndrome based on the following:

- medical history
- physical exam
- signs and symptoms

- blood tests
- upper gastrointestinal (GI) endoscopy
- imaging tests to look for gastrinomas
- measurement of stomach acid

Medical History

Taking a medical and family history is one of the first things a health care provider may do to help diagnose Zollinger-Ellison syndrome. The health care provider may ask about family cases of MEN1 in particular.

Physical Exam

A physical exam may help diagnose Zollinger-Ellison syndrome. During a physical exam, a health care provider usually

- examines a person's body
- uses a stethoscope to listen to bodily sounds
- taps on specific areas of the person's body

Signs and Symptoms

A health care provider may suspect Zollinger-Ellison syndrome if

- diarrhea accompanies peptic ulcer symptoms or if peptic ulcer treatment fails.
- a person has peptic ulcers without the use of nonsteroidal anti-inflammatory drugs (NSAIDs) such as aspirin and ibuprofen or a bacterial *Helicobacter pylori* (*H. pylori*) infection. NSAID use and H. pylori infection may cause peptic ulcers.
- a person has severe ulcers that bleed or cause holes in the duodenum or stomach.
- a health care provider diagnoses a person or the person's family member with MEN1 or a person has symptoms of MEN1.

Blood Tests

The health care provider may use blood tests to check for an elevated gastrin level. A technician or nurse draws a blood sample during an office visit or at a commercial facility and sends the sample to a lab for analysis. A health care provider will ask the person to fast for several hours prior to the test and may ask the person to stop acid-reducing medications for a period of time before the test. A gastrin level that is 10 times higher than normal suggests Zollinger-Ellison syndrome.

A health care provider may also check for an elevated gastrin level after an infusion of secretin. Secretin is a hormone that causes gastrinomas to release more gastrin. A technician or nurse places an intravenous (IV) needle in a vein in the arm to give an infusion of secretin. A health care provider may suspect Zollinger-Ellison syndrome if blood drawn after the infusion shows an elevated gastrin level.

Upper Gastrointestinal Endoscopy

The health care provider uses an upper GI endoscopy to check the esophagus, stomach, and duodenum for ulcers and esophagitis—a general term used to describe irritation and swelling of the esophagus. This procedure involves using an endoscope—a small, flexible tube with a light—to see the upper GI tract, which includes the esophagus, stomach, and duodenum. The gastroenterologist carefully feeds the endoscope down the esophagus and into the stomach and duodenum. A small camera mounted on the endoscope transmits a video image to a monitor, allowing close examination of the intestinal lining. A person may receive a liquid anesthetic that is gargled or sprayed on the back of the throat. A technician or nurse inserts an IV needle in a vein in the arm if anesthesia is given.

Imaging Tests

To help find gastrinomas, a health care provider may order one or more of the following imaging tests:

- **Computerized tomography (CT) scan.** A CT scan is an X-ray that produces pictures of the body. A CT scan may include the injection of a special dye, called contrast medium. CT scans use a combination of X-rays and computer technology to create images. CT scans require the person to lie on a table that slides into a tunnel-shaped device where an X-ray technician takes X-rays. A computer puts the different views together to create a model of the pancreas, stomach, and duodenum. The X-ray technician performs the procedure in an outpatient center or a hospital, and a radiologist—a doctor who specializes in medical imaging—interprets the images. The person does not need anesthesia. CT scans can show tumors and ulcers.

- **Magnetic resonance imaging (MRI).** MRI is a test that takes pictures of the body's internal organs and soft tissues without using X-rays. A specially trained technician performs the procedure in an outpatient center or a hospital, and a radiologist interprets the images. The person does not need anesthesia, though people with a fear of confined spaces may receive light sedation, taken by mouth. An MRI may include the injection of contrast medium. With most MRI machines, the person will lie on a table that slides into a tunnel-shaped device that may be open ended or closed at one end. Some machines allow the person to lie in a more open space. During an MRI, the person, although usually awake, remains perfectly still while the technician takes the images, which usually takes only a few minutes. The technician will take a sequence of images from different angles to create a detailed picture of the upper GI tract. During sequencing, the person will hear loud mechanical knocking and humming noises.

- **Endoscopic ultrasound.** This procedure involves using a special endoscope called an endoechoscope to perform ultrasound of the pancreas. The endoechoscope has a built-in miniature ultrasound probe that bounces safe, painless sound waves off organs to create an image of their structure. A gastroenterologist performs the procedure in an outpatient center or a hospital, and a radiologist interprets the images. The gastroenterologist carefully feeds the endoechoscope down the esophagus, through the stomach and duodenum, until it is near the pancreas. A person may receive a liquid anesthetic that is gargled or sprayed on the back of the throat. A sedative helps the person stay relaxed and comfortable. The images can show gastrinomas in the pancreas.

- **Angiogram.** An angiogram is a special kind of X-ray in which an interventional radiologist—a specially trained radiologist—threads a thin, flexible tube called a catheter through the large arteries, often from the groin, to the artery of interest. The radiologist injects contrast medium through the catheter so the images show up more clearly on the X-ray. The interventional radiologist performs the procedure and interprets the images in a hospital or an outpatient center. A person does not need anesthesia, though a light sedative may help reduce a person's anxiety during the procedure. This test can show gastrinomas in the pancreas.

- **Somatostatin receptor scintigraphy.** An X-ray technician performs this test, also called OctreoScan, at a hospital or an

241

outpatient center, and a radiologist interprets the images. A person does not need anesthesia. A radioactive compound called a radiotracer, when injected into the bloodstream, selectively labels tumor cells. The labeled cells light up when scanned with a device called a gamma camera. The test can show gastrinomas in the duodenum, pancreas, and other parts of the body.

Small gastrinomas may be hard to see; therefore, health care providers may order several types of imaging tests to find gastrinomas.

Stomach-Acid Measurement

Using a sample of stomach juices for analysis, a health care provider may measure the amount of stomach acid a person produces. During the exam, a health care provider puts in a nasogastric tube—a tiny tube inserted through the nose and throat that reaches into the stomach. A person may receive a liquid anesthetic that is gargled or sprayed on the back of the throat. Once the tube is placed, a health care provider takes samples of the stomach acid. High acid levels in the stomach indicate Zollinger-Ellison syndrome.

How is Zollinger-Ellison syndrome treated?

A health care provider treats Zollinger-Ellison syndrome with medications to reduce gastric acid secretion and with surgery to remove gastrinomas. A health care provider sometimes uses chemotherapy— medications to shrink tumors—when tumors are too widespread to remove with surgery.

Medications

A class of medications called proton pump inhibitors (PPIs) includes

- esomeprazole (Nexium)

- lansoprazole (Prevacid)

- pantoprazole (Protonix)

- omeprazole (Prilosec or Zegerid)

- dexlansoprazole (Dexilant)

PPIs stop the mechanism that pumps acid into the stomach, helping to relieve peptic ulcer pain and promote healing. A health care provider may prescribe people who have Zollinger-Ellison syndrome higher-than-normal doses of PPIs to control the acid production. Studies show that PPIs may increase the risk of hip, wrist, and spine fractures when a person takes them long term or in high doses, so it's important for people to discuss risks versus benefits with their health care provider.

Surgery

Surgical removal of gastrinomas is the only cure for Zollinger-Ellison syndrome. Some gastrinomas spread to other parts of the body, especially the liver and bones. Finding and removing all gastrinomas before they spread is often challenging because many of the tumors are small.

Chemotherapy

Health care providers sometimes use chemotherapy drugs to treat gastrinomas that cannot be surgically removed, including

- streptozotocin (Zanosar)
- 5-fluorouracil (Adrucil)
- doxorubicin (Doxil)

Eating, Diet, and Nutrition

Researchers have not found that eating, diet, and nutrition play a role in causing or preventing Zollinger-Ellison syndrome.

Chapter 18

Gastric Antral Vascular Ectasia (GAVE) – Watermelon Stomach

What is watermelon stomach?

Watermelon stomach is a condition in which the lining of the stomach bleeds, causing it to look like the characteristic stripes of a watermelon when viewed by endoscopy. Although it can develop in men and women of all ages, watermelon stomach is most commonly observed in older women (over age 70 years). Signs and symptoms of watermelon stomach include blood in stool, hematemesis (vomiting blood) and anemia. The exact cause of watermelon stomach is unknown; however, it is often diagnosed in people with other chronic (long-term) conditions such as cirrhosis (scarring of the liver and poor liver function), autoimmune disease, systemic sclerosis, and CREST syndrome. Treatment consists of surgery and/or medications to stop or control the bleeding.

What causes watermelon stomach?

The exact cause of watermelon stomach is unknown. However, it is often diagnosed in people with other chronic (long-term) conditions

---

Text in this chapter is excerpted from "Watermelon Stomach," Genetic and Rare Diseases Information Center (GARD), June 12, 2014.

such as cirrhosis (scarring of the liver and poor liver function), auto-immune disease, systemic sclerosis, and CREST syndrome.

What are the signs and symptoms of watermelon stomach?

Watermelon stomach is characterized primarily by gastrointestinal bleeding, which may result in the following signs and symptoms:

- anemia
- hematemesis (vomiting blood)
- blood in stool

How is watermelon stomach diagnosed?

A diagnosis of watermelon stomach is usually made when rows of flat, reddish stripes on the lining of the stomach (like the stripes of a watermelon) are seen on endoscopy. Other tests, such as a biopsy of the stomach lining, an endoscopic ultrasound (ultrasound probe on the tip of an endoscope), computed tomography (CT scan) and/or a tagged red blood cell scan, may be used to confirm the diagnosis.

How might watermelon stomach be treated?

Watermelon stomach is usually treated with endoscopic laser surgery or argon plasma coagulation. Both of these procedures are performed by endoscopy. Endoscopic laser surgery uses a laser light to treat bleeding blood vessels, while argon plasma coagulation uses argon gas and electrical current to seal irregular or bleeding tissue.

In some cases, people may be treated with certain medications that help stop or control the gastrointestinal bleeding. Corticosteriods, tranexamic acid, and hormone therapy (with estrogen and progesterone) have been used to treat watermelon stomach with some success.

Depending on the severity of the bleeding, blood transfusions may also be necessary at the time of diagnosis. Additional transfusions may be recommended if gastrointestinal bleeding can not be stopped or controlled.

Part Four

Disorders of the Lower Gastrointestinal Tract

Chapter 19

Irritable Bowel Syndrome (IBS)

Definition and Facts

What is irritable bowel syndrome (IBS)?

Irritable bowel syndrome (IBS) is a group of symptoms—including pain or discomfort in your abdomen and changes in your bowel movement patterns—that occur together. Doctors call IBS a functional gastrointestinal (GI) disorder. Functional GI disorders happen when your GI tract behaves in an abnormal way without evidence of damage due to a disease.

Does IBS have another name?

In the past, doctors called IBS colitis, mucous colitis, spastic colon, nervous colon, and spastic bowel. Experts changed the name to reflect the understanding that the disorder has both physical and mental causes and isn't a product of a person's imagination.

What are the four types of IBS?

Doctors often classify IBS into one of four types based on your usual stool consistency. These types are important because they

---

Text in this chapter is excerpted from "Irritable Bowel Syndrome," National Institute of Diabetes and Digestive and Kidney Diseases (NIDDK), February 23, 2015.

affect the types of treatment that are most likely to improve your symptoms.

The four types of IBS are

- IBS with constipation, or IBS-C
  - hard or lumpy stools at least 25 percent of the time
  - loose or watery stools less than 25 percent of the time
- IBS with diarrhea, or IBS-D
  - loose or watery stools at least 25 percent of the time
  - hard or lumpy stools less than 25 percent of the time
- Mixed IBS, or IBS-M
  - hard or lumpy stools at least 25 percent of the time
  - loose or watery stools at least 25 percent of the time
- Unsubtyped IBS, or IBS-U
  - hard or lumpy stools less than 25 percent of the time
  - loose or watery stools less than 25 percent of the time

How common is IBS?

Studies estimate that IBS affects 10 to 15 percent of U.S. adults. However, only 5 to 7 percent of U.S. adults have received a diagnosis of IBS.

Who is more likely to develop IBS?

IBS affects about twice as many women as men and most often occurs in people younger than age 45.

What other health problems do people with IBS have?

People with IBS often suffer from other GI and non-GI conditions. GI conditions such as gastroesophageal reflux disease and dyspepsia are more common in people with IBS than the general population.

Non-GI conditions that people with IBS often have include

- chronic fatigue syndrome
- chronic pelvic pain
- temporomandibular joint disorders

- depression
- anxiety
- somatoform disorders

Symptoms and Causes

What are the symptoms of IBS?

The most common symptoms of irritable bowel syndrome (IBS) include pain or discomfort in your abdomen and changes in how often you have bowel movements or how your stools look. The pain or discomfort of IBS may feel like cramping and have at least two of the following:

- Your pain or discomfort improves after a bowel movement.
- You notice a change in how often you have a bowel movement.
- You notice a change in the way your stools look.

IBS is a chronic disorder, meaning it lasts a long time, often years. However, the symptoms may come and go. You may have IBS if:

- You've had symptoms at least three times a month for the past 3 months.
- Your symptoms first started at least 6 months ago.

People with IBS may have diarrhea, constipation, or both. Some people with IBS have only diarrhea or only constipation. Some people have symptoms of both or have diarrhea sometimes and constipation other times. People often have symptoms soon after eating a meal.

Other symptoms of IBS are

- bloating
- the feeling that you haven't finished a bowel movement
- whitish mucus in your stool

Women with IBS often have more symptoms during their menstrual periods.

While IBS can be painful, IBS doesn't lead to other health problems or damage your gastrointestinal (GI) tract.

What causes IBS?

Doctors aren't sure what causes IBS. Experts think that a combination of problems can lead to IBS.

Physical Problems

Brain-Gut Signal Problems

Signals between your brain and the nerves of your gut, or small and large intestines, control how your gut works. Problems with brain-gut signals may cause IBS symptoms.

GI Motility Problems

If you have IBS, you may not have normal motility in your colon. Slow motility can lead to constipation and fast motility can lead to diarrhea. Spasms can cause abdominal pain. If you have IBS, you may also experience hyperreactivity—a dramatic increase in bowel contractions when you feel stress or after you eat.

Pain Sensitivity

If you have IBS, the nerves in your gut may be extra sensitive, causing you to feel more pain or discomfort than normal when gas or stool is in your gut. Your brain may process pain signals from your bowel differently if you have IBS.

Infections

A bacterial infection in the GI tract may cause some people to develop IBS. Researchers don't know why infections in the GI tract lead to IBS in some people and not others, although abnormalities of the GI tract lining and mental health problems may play a role.

Small Intestinal Bacterial Overgrowth

Normally, few bacteria live in your small intestine. Small intestinal bacterial overgrowth is an increase in the number or a change in the type of bacteria in your small intestine. These bacteria can produce extra gas and may also cause diarrhea and weight loss. Some experts think small intestinal bacterial overgrowth may lead to IBS. Research continues to explore a possible link between the two conditions.

Neurotransmitters (Body Chemicals)

People with IBS have altered levels of neurotransmitters—chemicals in the body that transmit nerve signals—and GI hormones. The role these chemicals play in IBS is unclear.

Younger women with IBS often have more symptoms during their menstrual periods. Post-menopausal women have fewer symptoms compared with women who are still menstruating. These findings suggest that reproductive hormones can worsen IBS problems.

Genetics

Whether IBS has a genetic cause, meaning it runs in families, is unclear. Studies have shown IBS is more common in people with family members who have a history of GI problems.

Food Sensitivity

Many people with IBS report that foods rich in carbohydrates, spicy or fatty foods, coffee, and alcohol trigger their symptoms. However, people with food sensitivity typically don't have signs of a food allergy. Researchers think that poor absorption of sugars or bile acids may cause symptoms.

Mental Health Problems

Psychological, or mental health, problems such as panic disorder, anxiety, depression, and post-traumatic stress disorder are common in people with IBS. The link between mental health and IBS is unclear. GI disorders, including IBS, are sometimes present in people who have reported past physical or sexual abuse. Experts think people who have been abused tend to express psychological stress through physical symptoms.

If you have IBS, your colon may respond too much to even slight conflict or stress. Stress makes your mind more aware of the sensations in your colon. IBS symptoms can also increase your stress level.

Diagnosis

How do doctors diagnose IBS?

Your doctor may be able to diagnose irritable bowel syndrome (IBS) based on a review of your medical history, symptoms, and physical exam. Your doctor may also order tests.

To diagnose IBS, your doctor will take a complete medical history and perform a physical exam.

Medical History

The medical history will include questions about

- your symptoms
- family history of gastrointestinal (GI) tract disorders
- recent infections

- medicines

- stressful events related to the start of your symptoms

Your doctor will look for a certain pattern in your symptoms. Your doctor may diagnose IBS if

- your symptoms started at least 6 months ago

- you've had pain or discomfort in your abdomen at least three times a month for the past 3 months

- your abdominal pain or discomfort has two or three of the following features:

  - Your pain or discomfort improves after a bowel movement.

  - You notice a change in how often you have a bowel movement.

  - You notice a change in the way your stools look.

Physical Exam

During a physical exam, your doctor usually

- checks for abdominal bloating

- listens to sounds within your abdomen using a stethoscope

- taps on your abdomen checking for tenderness or pain

What tests do doctors use to diagnose IBS?

In most cases, doctors don't need to perform tests to diagnose IBS. Your doctor may perform a blood test to check for other conditions or problems. Your doctor may perform more tests based on the results of the blood test and if you have

- a family history of celiac disease, colon cancer, or inflammatory bowel disease

- a fever

- anemia

- bleeding from your rectum

- weight loss

Blood Test

Doctors use blood tests to check for conditions or problems other than IBS. A health care professional sends your blood sample to a lab.

Stool Test

A stool test is the analysis of a sample of stool. Your doctor will give you a container for catching and holding a stool sample. You will receive instructions on where to send or take the kit for analysis, to check for blood or parasites. Your doctor may also check for blood in your stool by examining your rectum during your physical exam.

Flexible Sigmoidoscopy

Flexible sigmoidoscopy is a procedure that uses a flexible, narrow tube with a light and tiny camera (called a sigmoidoscope) on one end to look inside your rectum and lower colon.

This procedure can show signs of conditions or problems in the lower GI tract. During the procedure, the doctor can take a biopsy. You won't feel the biopsy.

Colonoscopy

Colonoscopy is a procedure that uses a long, flexible, narrow tube with a light and tiny camera (called a colonoscope) on one end to look inside your rectum and colon.

Colonoscopy can show irritated or swollen tissue, ulcers, polyps, and cancer. A trained specialist performs this procedure.

Lower GI Series

A lower GI series, also called a Barium Enema, uses X-rays to look at your large intestine.

During a lower GI series, you'll be asked to lie on a table while the doctor inserts a flexible tube into your anus. The doctor will fill your large intestine with barium. You may be asked to change positions several times during the test.

Treatment

How do doctors treat IBS?

Though irritable bowel syndrome (IBS) doesn't have a cure, your doctor can manage the symptoms with a combination of diet, medicines,

255

probiotics, and therapies for mental health problems. You may have to try a few treatments to see what works best for you. Your doctor can help you find the right treatment plan.

Changes in Eating, Diet, and Nutrition

Changes in eating, diet, and nutrition, such as following a FODMAP diet, can help treat your symptoms.

Medicines

Your doctor may recommend medicine to relieve your symptoms.

- Fiber supplements to relieve constipation when increasing fiber in your diet doesn't help.

- Laxatives to help with constipation. Laxatives work in different ways, and your doctor can recommend a laxative that's right for you.

- Loperamide to reduce diarrhea by slowing the movement of stool through your colon. Loperamide is an antidiarrheal that reduces diarrhea in people with IBS, though it doesn't reduce pain, bloating, or other symptoms.

- Antispasmodics, such as hyoscine, cimetropium, and pinaverium, help to control colon muscle spasms and reduce pain in your abdomen.

- Antidepressants, such as low doses of tricyclic antidepressants and selective serotonin reuptake inhibitors, to relieve IBS symptoms, including abdominal pain. In theory, because of their effect on colon transit, tricyclic antidepressants should be better for people with IBS with diarrhea, or IBS-D, and selective serotonin reuptake inhibitors should be better for people with IBS with constipation, or IBS-C, although studies haven't confirmed this theory. Tricyclic antidepressants work in people with IBS by reducing their sensitivity to pain in the gastrointestinal (GI) tract as well as normalizing their GI motility and secretion.

- Lubiprostone (Amitiza) for people who have IBS-C to improve abdominal pain or discomfort and constipation symptoms.

- Linaclotide (Linzess) for people who have IBS-C to relieve abdominal pain and increase how often you have bowel movements.

- The antibiotic rifaximin to reduce bloating by treating small intestinal bacterial overgrowth. However, experts are still debating and researching the use of antibiotics to treat IBS.

- Coated peppermint oil capsules to reduce IBS symptoms.

Follow your doctor's instructions when you use medicine to treat IBS. Talk with your doctor about possible side effects and what to do if you have them.

Some medicines can cause side effects. Ask your doctor and your pharmacist about side effects before taking any medicine.

Probiotics

Your doctor may also recommend probiotics. Probiotics are live microorganisms—tiny organisms that can be seen only with a microscope. These microorganisms, most often bacteria, are like the microorganisms that are normally present in your GI tract. Studies have found that taking large enough amounts of probiotics, specifically Bifidobacteria and certain probiotic combinations, can improve symptoms of IBS. However, researchers are still studying the use of probiotics to treat IBS.

You can find probiotics in dietary supplements, such as capsules, tablets, and powders, and in some foods, such as yogurt.

Discuss your use of complementary and alternative medical practices, including probiotics and dietary supplements, with your doctor.

Eating, Diet, and Nutrition

How can my diet treat the symptoms of IBS?

Eating smaller meals more often, or eating smaller portions, may help your irritable bowel syndrome (IBS) symptoms. Large meals can cause cramping and diarrhea if you have IBS.

Eating foods that are low in fat and high in carbohydrates, such as pasta, rice, whole-grain breads and cereals, fruits, and vegetables, may help.

Fiber may improve constipation symptoms caused by IBS because it makes stool soft and easier to pass. Fiber is a part of foods such as whole-grain breads and cereals, beans, fruits, and vegetables. The U.S. Department of Agriculture and U.S. Department of Health and Human Services state in its *Dietary Guidelines for Americans*, 2010 that adults should get 22 to 34 grams of fiber a day.

While fiber may help constipation, it may not reduce the abdominal discomfort or pain of IBS. In fact, some people with IBS may feel a bit more abdominal discomfort after adding more fiber to their diet. Add foods with fiber to your diet a little at a time to let your body get used to them. Too much fiber at once can cause gas, which can trigger symptoms in people with IBS. Adding fiber to your diet slowly, by 2 to 3 grams a day, may help prevent gas and bloating.

What should I avoid eating to ease IBS symptoms?

Certain foods or drinks may make symptoms worse, such as

- foods high in fat

- some milk products

- drinks with alcohol or caffeine

- drinks with large amounts of artificial sweeteners

- beans, cabbage, and other foods that may cause gas

To find out if certain foods trigger your symptoms, keep a diary and track

- what you eat during the day

- what symptoms you have

- when symptoms occur

Take your notes to your doctor and talk about which foods seem to make your symptoms worse. You may need to avoid these foods or eat less of them.

Your doctor may recommend that you try a special diet—called low FODMAP or FODMAP—to reduce or avoid certain foods containing carbohydrates that are hard to digest. Examples of high FODMAP foods and products you may reduce or avoid include

- fruits such as apples, apricots, blackberries, cherries, mango, nectarines, pears, plums, and watermelon, or juice containing any of these fruits

- canned fruit in natural fruit juice, or large quantities of fruit juice or dried fruit

- vegetables such as artichokes, asparagus, beans, cabbage, cauliflower, garlic and garlic salts, lentils, mushrooms, onions, and sugar snap or snow peas

- dairy products such as milk, milk products, soft cheeses, yogurt, custard, and ice cream
- wheat and rye products
- honey and foods with high-fructose corn syrup
- products, including candy and gum, with sweeteners ending in "–ol," such as
  - sorbitol
  - mannitol
  - xylitol
  - maltitol

Chapter 20

Inflammatory Bowel Diseases

Chapter Contents

Section 20.1

Understanding Inflammatory
Bowel Disease (IBD)

Text in this section is excerpted from "Inflammatory Bowel Disease
Fact Sheet," Office on Women's Health (OWH), July 16, 2012; and
text from "Inflammatory Bowel Disease (IBD)," Centers for Disease
Control and Prevention (CDC), May 5, 2014.

What is inflammatory bowel disease (IBD)?

Inflammatory bowel disease (IBD) is the name of a group of disorders in which the intestines (small and large intestines or bowels)
become inflamed (red and swollen). This inflammation causes symptoms such as:

- Severe or chronic (almost all of the time) pain in the abdomen
  (belly)

- Diarrhea—may be bloody

- Unexplained weight loss

- Loss of appetite

- Bleeding from the rectum

- Joint pain

- Skin problems

- Fever

Symptoms can range from mild to severe. Also, symptoms can come
and go, sometimes going away for months or even years at a time.
When people with IBD start to have symptoms again, they are said to
be having a relapse or flare-up. When they are not having symptoms,
the disease is said to have gone into remission.

The most common forms of IBD are ulcerative colitis and Crohn's disease. The diseases are very similar. In fact, doctors sometimes have a hard
time figuring out which type of IBD a person has. The main difference
between the two diseases is the parts of the digestive tract they affect.

Ulcerative colitis affects the top layer of the large intestine, next to where the stool is. The disease causes swelling and tiny open sores, or ulcers, to form on the surface of the lining. The ulcers can bleed and produce pus. In severe cases of ulcerative colitis, ulcers may weaken the intestinal wall so much that a hole develops. Then the contents of the large intestine, including bacteria, spill into the abdominal (belly) cavity or leak into the blood. This causes a serious infection and requires emergency surgery.

Crohn's disease can affect all layers of the intestinal wall. Areas of the intestines most often affected are the last part of the small intestine, called the ileum, and the first part of the large intestine. But Crohn's disease can affect any part of the digestive tract, from the mouth to the anus. Inflammation in Crohn's disease often occurs in patches, with normal areas on either side of a diseased area.

In Crohn's disease, swelling and scar tissue can thicken the intestinal wall. This narrows the passageway for food that is being digested. The area of the intestine that has narrowed is called a stricture. Also, deep ulcers may turn into tunnels, called fistulas, that connect different parts of the intestine. They may also connect to nearby organs, such as the bladder or vagina, or connect to the skin. And as with ulcerative colitis, ulcers may cause a hole to develop in the wall of the intestine.

IBD is not the same as irritable bowel syndrome (IBS), although the symptoms can be similar. Unlike inflammatory bowel disease, IBS does not cause inflammation or damage in the intestines.

In many people with IBD, medicines can control symptoms. But for people with severe IBD, surgery is sometimes needed. With treatment, most people with IBD lead full and active lives.

What causes inflammatory bowel disease?

No one knows for sure what causes inflammatory bowel disease (IBD). Experts think that abnormal action of a person's immune system may trigger IBD. The immune system is made up of various cells and proteins. Normally, the immune system protects the body from infections caused by viruses or bacteria. Once the infection has cleared up, the immune system "shuts off."

But in people with IBD, the immune system seems to overreact to normal bacteria in the digestive tract. And once it starts working, the immune system fails to "shut off." This causes the inflammation, which damages the digestive tract and causes symptoms.

IBD runs in families. This suggests that inherited factors called genes play a role in causing IBD. Experts think that certain genes may cause the immune system to overreact in IBD.

Stress and eating certain foods do not cause IBD. But both can make IBD symptoms worse.

How does IBD affect health?

In people with IBD the immune system mistakes food, bacteria, and other materials in the intestine for foreign substances and it attacks the cells of the intestines. In the process, the body sends white blood cells into the lining of the intestines where they produce chronic inflammation. IBD is a condition that gets worse over time and causes severe gastrointestinal symptoms that can affect quality of life.

Inflammatory bowel diseases such as ulcerative colitis and Crohn's disease should not be confused with irritable bowel syndrome (IBS), a disorder that affects the colon's muscle contractions. Intestinal inflammation is not a symptom of IBS which is a much less serious disease than ulcerative colitis or Crohn's disease.

Can inflammatory bowel disease cause health problems in parts of the body other than the digestive tract?

Yes. Inflammatory bowel disease (IBD) can cause a number of problems outside of the digestive tract.

One common problem that occurs because of loss of blood from the digestive tract is anemia. Anemia means that the amount of healthy red blood cells, which carry oxygen to organs, is below normal. This can make a person feel very tired.

Other health problems include:

- Arthritis and joint pain
- Weak bones and bone breaks
- Inflammation in the eye and other eye problems
- Liver inflammation
- Gallstones
- Red bumps or ulcers on the skin
- Kidney stones
- Delayed puberty and growth problems (in children and teens)
- In rare cases, lung problems

Some of these problems are caused by poor absorption of nutrients. Others are due to inflammation in parts of the body other than the digestive tract.

Some of these problems get better when the IBD is treated. Others must be treated separately.

How does inflammatory bowel disease interfere with digestion?

When the small intestine becomes inflamed, as in Crohn's disease, it is less able to absorb nutrients from food. These nutrients leave the body in the bowel movement. This is one reason why people with Crohn's disease don't get enough nutrients, along with not having much appetite. Also, the undigested food that goes into the large intestine makes water absorption harder. This causes a watery bowel movement, or diarrhea.

In ulcerative colitis, the small intestine absorbs nutrients as it should. But inflammation in the large intestine keeps it from absorbing water, causing diarrhea.

Who gets inflammatory bowel disease?

Although inflammatory bowel disease (IBD) can occur in any group of people, it is more common among:

- People who have a family member with IBD
- Jewish people of European descent
- White people
- People who live in cities
- People who live in developed countries

Smoking also seems to affect a person's risk of getting IBD. People who smoke are more likely to develop Crohn's disease but less likely to develop ulcerative colitis.

Experts think that as many as 1 million people in the United States have IBD. Most people with IBD begin to have symptoms between the ages of 15 and 30.

How is inflammatory bowel disease diagnosed?

If you think you have inflammatory bowel disease (IBD), talk to your doctor. She or he will use your health history, a physical exam, and different tests to ure out if you have IBD and, if so, which type.

Tests used to diagnose IBD include:

- Blood tests
- Stool sample
- Colonoscopy or sigmoidoscopy
- X-rays with barium
- Computerized axial tomography (CT or CAT scan)
- Capsule endoscopy

It often takes awhile for doctors to diagnose IBD. This is because IBD symptoms vary and are similar to those of many other problems.

Can I do anything to avoid getting inflammatory bowel disease?

Since doctors don't know what causes inflammatory bowel disease, there is no proven way to prevent it.

How is inflammatory bowel disease treated?

Treatments for inflammatory bowel disease (IBD) may include:

- Medicines
- Surgery
- Changes in the foods you eat — some people find following specific diets helps ease their symptoms.
- Nutritional supplements
- Reducing stress and getting enough rest

If you have IBD, your treatment will depend on:
Your symptoms and how severe they are

- Which part of your digestive tract is affected
- If you have health problems outside the digestive tract

Most people with IBD take medicine to control their symptoms. If medicines cannot control their disease, some people will need surgery.

What medicines are used to treat inflammatory bowel disease?

Medicines for treating inflammatory bowel disease (IBD) reduce the inflammation, relieve symptoms, and prevent flare-ups. Every patient is different. What may work for one person with IBD may not work for another. You may need to try several different medicines before you find one or more that work best for you. You should keep track of how well the drugs are working, any side effects, and report all details to your doctor. The following kinds of medicines are used to treat IBD:

- Aminosalicylates
- Corticosteroids
- Immunomodulators
- Biologic therapies
- Antibiotics
- Other treatments

What types of surgery are used to treat inflammatory bowel disease?

Sometimes severe inflammatory bowel disease (IBD) does not get better with medicine. In these cases, doctors may suggest surgery to fix or remove damaged parts of the intestine. There are different types of surgery used to treat IBD.

Surgery for ulcerative colitis

About 25 to 40 percent of people with ulcerative colitis need surgery at some point in their lives. Surgery that removes the entire large intestine can completely cure ulcerative colitis. After the large intestine is removed, surgeons perform one of two types of operations to allow the body to get rid of food waste:

- In one procedure, a small opening is made in the front of the abdominal wall. Then the end of the ileum is brought through the hole. This allows waste to drain out of the body. An external pouch is worn over the opening to collect the waste, and the patient empties the pouch several times a day.

- In another procedure, the surgeon attaches the ileum to the inside of the anus where the rectum was, creating an internal pouch. Waste is stored in the pouch and passes out of the anus in the usual manner.

Surgery for Crohn's disease

About 65 to 75 percent of people with Crohn's disease need surgery at some point in their lives. Surgery can relieve symptoms and correct problems like strictures, fistulae, or bleeding in the intestine. Surgery can help relieve Crohn's disease symptoms. But, since Crohn's disease occurs in patches, surgery cannot cure the disease. If a part of the small or large intestine is removed, the inflammation may then affect the part next to the section that was removed.

Types of surgery for Crohn's disease include:

Strictureplasty. In this surgery, the doctor widens the strictured, or narrowed, area without removing any part of the small intestine.

Bowel resection. In this surgery, the damaged part of the small or large intestine is removed and the two healthy ends are sewn back together.

Removal of the large intestine. This procedure is the same as that done for ulcerative colitis. But, people with Crohn's can't have an internal pouch for waste because it can become inflamed. Instead, surgeons use the external pouch procedure.

Inflammatory Bowel Disease – FAQs

I have inflammatory bowel disease and my doctor says that I should have surgery. Did I fail at managing my disease?

No. If medicines can no longer control your symptoms, you should consider surgery. Surgery can give lasting relief from symptoms and may reduce or even get rid of the need for medicine. Not every type of surgery is right for every person. People faced with the decision to have surgery should get as much information as they can from their doctors, nurses, and other patients.

Can changing the foods I eat help control inflammatory bowel disease?

No special eating plan has been proven effective for treating inflammatory bowel disease (IBD). But for some people, changing the foods they eat may help control the symptoms of IBD.

There are no blanket food rules. Changes that help one person with IBD may not relieve symptoms in another. Talk to your doctor and maybe a dietitian about which foods you should and should not be eating. Their suggestions will depend on the part of your intestine that is affected and which disease you have.

Your doctor may suggest some of the following changes:

- Taking specific nutritional supplements, including possibly vitamin and mineral supplements

- Avoiding greasy or fried foods
- Avoiding cream sauces and meat products
- Avoiding spicy foods
- Avoiding foods high in fiber, such as nuts and raw fruits and vegetables
- Eating smaller, more frequent meals

Even though you may have to limit certain foods, you should still aim to eat meals that give you all the nutrients you need.

Can stress make inflammatory bowel disease worse?

Although stress does not cause inflammatory bowel disease (IBD), some people find that stress can bring on a flare-up in their disease. If you think this is happening to you, try using relaxation techniques, such as slow breathing. Also, be sure to get enough sleep.

What new treatments for inflammatory bowel disease are being studied?

Researchers are studying many new treatments for inflammatory bowel disease (IBD). These include new medicines, such as new biologic therapies. Researchers are also studying whether fish or flaxseed oils can help fight the inflammation in IBD. Some evidence supports using probiotics to treat some types of diarrhea and a form of IBD called pouchitis. Probiotics are "good" bacteria that may improve the balance of bacteria in your digestive system. Some researchers are hoping to develop new therapies by studying probiotics.

With inflammatory bowel disease, do I have a higher chance of getting colon cancer?

Yes. Inflammatory bowel disease (IBD) can increase your chances of getting cancer of the colon, or large intestine. Even so, more than 90 percent of people with IBD do NOT get colon cancer.

What we know about colon cancer and inflammatory bowel disease (IBD) comes mostly from studying people with ulcerative colitis. Less is known about the link between Crohn's disease and cancer. But research suggests that Crohn's patients have an increased risk as well. For both diseases, the risk of colon cancer depends on:

- How long you have had IBD
- How much of your colon is affected by IBD

Also, people who have family members with colon cancer may have an even higher chance of getting the cancer.

For people with ulcerative colitis, the risk of colon cancer does not start to increase until they have had the disease for 8 to 10 years. People whose disease affects the entire colon have the highest risk of colon cancer. People whose disease affects only the rectum have the lowest risk.

People with inflammatory bowel disease (IBD) should talk to their doctors about when to begin checking for colon cancer, what tests to get, and how often to have them. Your doctor's suggestions will depend on how long you have had IBD and how severe it is.

In people who have had IBD for 8 to 10 years, most doctors recommend a colonoscopy with biopsies every 1 to 2 years. This test checks for early warning signs of cancer in the cells of the colon lining. When cancer is found early, it is easier to cure and treat.

Can my inflammatory bowel disease make it harder for me to get pregnant?

If you have ulcerative colitis, you can get pregnant as easily as other women. The same is true of Crohn's disease, if your disease is in remission. But if you are having a flare-up of Crohn's disease, you may have trouble getting pregnant.

I have inflammatory bowel disease. Is pregnancy safe for me?

You should talk with your doctor before getting pregnant. If you think you might be pregnant, call your doctor right away. Some of the medicines used to treat inflammatory bowel disease (IBD) can harm the growing fetus.

If possible, your disease should be in remission for 6 months before becoming pregnant. It is also best if you have not started a new treatment or are taking corticosteroids. If you are already pregnant, you should continue taking your medicines as your doctor has told you to take them. If you stop taking your medicines and your disease flares, it may be hard to get it back under control.

In some cases, IBD gets better during pregnancy. This is because of changes in the immune system and hormone levels that occur during pregnancy. Even so, you shouldn't get pregnant as a way of treating your IBD. That is better done with medicines and perhaps surgery.

Can my inflammatory bowel disease harm the fetus or affect delivery?

If you have ulcerative colitis, your chances of having a normal delivery and a healthy baby are the same as for women who do not have inflammatory bowel disease. If you have a flare-up of Crohn's disease during pregnancy, you have a slightly higher risk of miscarriage, protorm birth, and stillbirth

Can inflammatory bowel disease affect my monthly period?

Yes. Some women with inflammatory bowel disease (IBD) feel worse right before and during their menstrual periods than at other times. Diarrhea, abdominal pain, and other symptoms can be more severe during these times. Women with IBD and their doctors should keep track of these monthly changes in symptoms. This will prevent over-treating the disease.

If you have not been eating well and have lost a lot of weight, your menstrual cycles can become irregular or even stop entirely.

Can inflammatory bowel disease affect my sex life?

Yes, but there are steps you can take to have a healthy sex life.

Inflammatory bowel disease, as well as the surgery and medicines used to treat it, can all affect your sex life. Sometimes, you may just feel too tired to have sex. You may also have emotional issues related to the disease. For instance, you may not feel as confident about your body as you did before you got the disease. Even though it may be embarrassing, it is important to talk to your doctor if you are having sexual problems. She or he may have treatments that can help. For instance, if you are having pain during sex, your doctor may prescribe a hormonal cream or suppository for your vagina.

If you have an external pouch, here are some tips:

- Empty the pouch before sex.

- Use deodorizers — one in the pouch and perhaps a pill or liquid you take by mouth (ask you doctor about them).

- Make sure the pouch is secure.

- If the pouch is in the way or causes pain during sex, experiment with different positions.

- Cover up your pouch with a pouch cover or by wearing a short slip or nightie.

Talking with your partner about how having inflammatory bowel disease is affecting your sex life can help build intimacy and clear up misunderstandings. Talking with a counselor or therapist may also help you find ways to deal with your emotional issues.

Section 20.2

Crohn's Disease

Text in this section is excerpted from "Crohn's Disease," National Institute of Diabetes and Digestive and Kidney Diseases (NIDDK), September 2014.

What is Crohn's disease?

Crohn's disease is a chronic, or long lasting, disease that causes inflammation—irritation or swelling—in the gastrointestinal (GI) tract. Most commonly, Crohn's affects the small intestine and the beginning of the large intestine. However, the disease can affect any part of the GI tract, from the mouth to the anus.

Crohn's disease is a chronic inflammatory disease of the GI tract, called inflammatory bowel disease (IBD). Ulcerative colitis and microscopic colitis are the other common IBDs.

Crohn's disease most often begins gradually and can become worse over time. Most people have periods of remission—times when symptoms disappear—that can last for weeks or years.

Some people with Crohn's disease receive care from a gastroenterologist, a doctor who specializes in digestive diseases.

What causes Crohn's disease?

The exact cause of Crohn's disease is unknown. Researchers believe the following factors may play a role in causing Crohn's disease:

- autoimmune reaction
- genes
- environment

Autoimmune reaction. Scientists believe one cause of Crohn's disease may be an autoimmune reaction—when a person's immune system attacks healthy cells in the body by mistake. Normally, the immune system protects the body from infection by identifying and destroying bacteria, viruses, and other potentially harmful foreign substances. Researchers believe bacteria or viruses can mistakenly trigger the immune system to attack the inner lining of the intestines. This immune system response causes the inflammation, leading to symptoms.

Genes. Crohn's disease sometimes runs in families. Research has shown that people who have a parent or sibling with Crohn's disease may be more likely to develop the disease. Researchers continue to study the link between genes and Crohn's disease.

Environment. Some studies suggest that certain things in the environment may increase the chance of a person getting Crohn's disease, although the overall chance is low. Nonsteroidal anti-inflammatory drugs, antibiotics, and oral contraceptives may slightly increase the chance of developing Crohn's disease. A high-fat diet may also slightly increase the chance of getting Crohn's disease.

Some people incorrectly believe that eating certain foods, stress, or emotional distress can cause Crohn's disease. Emotional distress and eating certain foods do not cause Crohn's disease. Sometimes the stress of living with Crohn's disease can make symptoms worse. Also, some people may find that certain foods can trigger or worsen their symptoms.

Who is more likely to develop Crohn's disease?

Crohn's disease can occur in people of any age. However, it is more likely to develop in people

- between the ages of 20 and 29

- who have a family member, most often a sibling or parent, with IBD

- who smoke cigarettes

What are the signs and symptoms of Crohn's disease?

The most common signs and symptoms of Crohn's disease are

- diarrhea

- abdominal cramping and pain

- weight loss

Other general signs and symptoms include

- feeling tired

- nausea or loss of appetite

- fever

- anemia—a condition in which the body has fewer red blood cells than normal

Signs and symptoms of inflammation outside of the intestines include

- joint pain or soreness

- eye irritation

- skin changes that involve red, tender bumps under the skin

The symptoms a person experiences can vary depending on the severity of the inflammation and where it occurs.

How is Crohn's disease diagnosed?

A health care provider diagnoses Crohn's disease with the following:

- medical and family history

- physical exam

- lab tests

- computerized tomography (CT) scan

- intestinal endoscopy

The health care provider may perform a series of medical tests to rule out other bowel diseases, such as irritable bowel syndrome, ulcerative colitis, or celiac disease, that cause symptoms similar to those of Crohn's disease.

Medical and Family History

Taking a medical and family history can help a health care provider diagnose Crohn's disease and understand a patient's symptoms. He or she will ask the patient to describe his or her

- family history

- symptoms

- current and past medical conditions
- current medications

Physical Exam

A physical exam may help diagnose Crohn's disease. During a physical exam, the health care provider most often

- checks for abdominal distension, or swelling
- listens to sounds within the abdomen using a stethoscope
- taps on the abdomen to check for tenderness and pain and establish if the liver or spleen is abnormal or enlarged

Lab Tests

A health care provider may order lab tests, including blood and stool tests.

Blood tests. A blood test involves drawing blood at a health care provider's office or a lab. A lab technologist will analyze the blood sample. A health care provider may use blood tests to look for changes in

- red blood cells. When red blood cells are fewer or smaller than normal, a patient may have anemia.
- white blood cells. When the white blood cell count is higher than normal, a person may have inflammation or infection somewhere in his or her body.

Stool tests. A stool test is the analysis of a sample of stool. A health care provider will give the patient a container for catching and storing the stool at home. The patient returns the sample to the health care provider or to a lab. A lab technologist will analyze the stool sample. Health care providers commonly order stool tests to rule out other causes of GI diseases.

Computerized Tomography Scan

Computerized tomography scans use a combination of X-rays and computer technology to create images. For a CT scan, a health care provider may give the patient a solution to drink and an injection of a special dye, called contrast medium. CT scans require the patient to lie on a table that slides into a tunnel-shaped device where the X-rays are taken. An X-ray technician performs the procedure in an outpatient center or a hospital, and a radiologist interprets the images. The patient does not need anesthesia. CT scans can diagnose both Crohn's disease and the complications seen with the disease.

Intestinal Endoscopy

Intestinal endoscopies are the most accurate methods for diagnosing Crohn's disease and ruling out other possible conditions, such as ulcerative colitis, diverticular disease, or cancer. Intestinal endoscopies include

- upper GI endoscopy and enteroscopy

- capsule endoscopy

- colonoscopy

Upper GI endoscopy and enteroscopy. An upper GI endoscopy is a procedure that uses an endoscope—a small, flexible tube with a light—to directly visualize the lining of the upper GI tract. A health care provider performs the procedure at a hospital or an outpatient center. A nurse or technician may give the patient a liquid anesthetic to gargle or will spray the anesthetic on the back of a patient's throat. The anesthetic numbs the throat and calms the gag reflex. The nurse or technician will then place an intravenous (IV) needle in the person's arm or hand to provide a sedative. The health care provider carefully feeds the endoscope down the patient's esophagus and into the stomach. A small camera on the endoscope sends a video image to a monitor, allowing close examination of the GI tract.

During an enteroscopy, the health care provider examines the small intestine with a special, longer endoscope. The health care provider carefully feeds the endoscope into the small intestine using one of the following procedures:

- push enteroscopy, which uses a long endoscope to examine the upper portion of the small intestine

- single- or double-balloon enteroscopy, which use small balloons to help move the endoscope into the small intestine

- spiral enteroscopy, which uses a tube attached to an endocope that acts as a cork screw to move the instrument into the small intestine

The procedure most often takes between 15 and 60 minutes. The endoscope does not interfere with the patient's breathing, and many patients fall asleep during the procedure.

Capsule endoscopy. Although this procedure can examine the entire digestive tract, health care providers use it mostly to examine the small intestine. The patient swallows a capsule containing a tiny camera. As the capsule passes through the GI tract, the camera will record and transmit images to a small receiver device worn by the patient. When the recording is done, the health care provider downloads the images and reviews them on a video monitor. The camera capsule leaves the patient's body during a bowel movement and is safely flushed down the toilet.

Colonoscopy. Colonoscopy is a test that uses a long, flexible, narrow tube with a light and tiny camera on one end, called a colonoscope or scope, to look inside a patient's rectum and entire colon. In most cases, light anesthesia and pain medication help patients relax for the test. The medical staff will monitor a patient's vital signs and try to make him or her as comfortable as possible. A nurse or technician will place an IV needle in a vein in the patient's arm or hand to give anesthesia.

For the test, the patient will lie on a table or stretcher while the gastroenterologist inserts a colonoscope into the patient's anus and slowly guides it through the rectum and into the colon. The scope inflates the large intestine with air to give the gastroenterologist a better view. The camera sends a video image of the intestinal lining to a monitor, allowing the gastroenterologist to examine the tissues lining the colon and rectum. The gastroenterologist may move the patient several times and adjust the scope for better viewing. Once the scope has reached the opening to the small intestine, the gastroenterologist slowly withdraws it and examines the lining of the colon and rectum again.

A colonoscopy can show inflamed and swollen tissue, ulcers, and abnormal growths such as polyps—extra pieces of tissue that grow on the inner lining of the intestine. If the gastroenterologist suspects Crohn's disease, he or she will biopsy the patient's colon and rectum. A biopsy is a procedure that involves taking small pieces of tissue for examination with a microscope.

A health care provider will give patients written bowel prep instructions to follow at home before the test. The health care provider will also give patients information about how to care for themselves following the procedure.

How is Crohn's disease treated?

A health care provider treats Crohn's disease with

- medications
- bowel rest
- surgery

Which treatment a person needs depends on the severity of the disease and symptoms. Each person experiences Crohn's disease differently, so health care providers adjust treatments to improve the person's symptoms and induce, or bring about, remission.

Medications

While no medication cures Crohn's disease, many can reduce symptoms. The goals of medication therapy are

- inducing and maintaining remission
- improving the person's quality of life

Many people with Crohn's disease require medication therapy. Health care providers will prescribe medications depending on the person's symptoms:

- aminosalicylates
- corticosteroids
- immunomodulators
- biologic therapies
- other medications

Aminosalicylates are medications that contain 5-aminosalicyclic acid (5-ASA), which helps control inflammation. Health care providers use aminosalicylates to treat people newly diagnosed with Crohn's disease who have mild symptoms. Aminosalicylates include

- balsalazide
- mesalamine
- olsalazine
- sulfasalazine—a combination of sulfapyridine and 5-ASA

Some of the common side effects of aminosalicylates include

- abdominal pain
- diarrhea

- headaches
- heartburn
- nausea and vomiting

Corticosteroids, also known as steroids, help reduce the activity of the immune system and decrease inflammation. Health care providers prescribe corticosteroids for people with moderate to severe symptoms. Corticosteroids include

- budesonide
- hydrocortisone
- methylprednisone
- prednisone

Side effects of corticosteroids include

- acne
- a higher chance of developing infections
- bone mass loss
- high blood glucose
- high blood pressure
- mood swings
- weight gain

In most cases, health care providers do not prescribe corticosteroids for long-term use.

Immunomodulators reduce immune system activity, resulting in less inflammation in the GI tract. These medications can take several weeks to 3 months to start working. Immunomodulators include

- 6-mercaptopurine, or 6-MP
- azathioprine
- cyclosporine
- methotrexate

Health care providers prescribe these medications to help people with Crohn's disease go into remission or to help people who do not respond to other treatments. People taking these medications may have the following side effects:

- a low white blood cell count, which can lead to a higher chance of infection

- fatigue, or feeling tired

- nausea and vomiting

- pancreatitis

Health care providers most often prescribe cyclosporine only to people with severe Crohn's disease because of the medication's serious side effects. People should talk with their health care provider about the risks and benefits of cyclosporine.

Biologic therapies are medications that target a protein made by the immune system. Neutralizing this protein decreases inflammation in the intestine. Biologic therapies work quickly to bring on remission, especially in people who do not respond to other medications. Biologic therapies include

- adalimumab

- certolizumab

- infliximab

- natalizumab

- vedolizumab

Health care providers most often give patients infliximab every 6 to 8 weeks at a hospital or an outpatient center. Side effects may include a toxic reaction to the medication and a higher chance of developing infections, particularly tuberculosis.

Other medications to treat symptoms or complications may include

- acetaminophen for mild pain. People with Crohn's disease should avoid using ibuprofen, naproxen, and aspirin since these medications can make symptoms worse.

- antibiotics to prevent or treat infections and fistulas.

- loperamide to help slow or stop severe diarrhea. In most cases, people only take this medication for short periods of time since it can increase the chance of developing megacolon.

Bowel Rest

Sometimes Crohn's disease symptoms are severe and a person may need to rest his or her bowel for a few days to several weeks. Bowel rest involves drinking only clear liquids or having no oral intake. To provide the patient with nutrition, a health care provider will deliver IV nutrition through a special catheter, or tube, inserted into a vein in the patient's arm. Some patients stay in the hospital, while other patients are able to receive the treatment at home. In most cases, the intestines are able to heal during bowel rest.

Surgery

Even with medication treatments, up to 20 percent of people will need surgery to treat their Crohn's disease. Although surgery will not cure Crohn's disease, it can treat complications and improve symptoms. Health care providers most often recommend surgery to treat

- fistulas

- bleeding that is life threatening

- bowel obstructions

- side effects from medications when they threaten a person's health

- symptoms when medications do not improve a person's condition

A surgeon can perform different types of operations to treat Crohn's disease:

- small bowel resection

- subtotal colectomy

- proctocolectomy and ileostomy

Patients will receive general anesthesia. Most patients will stay in the hospital for 3 to 7 days after the surgery. Full recovery may take 4 to 6 weeks.

Small bowel resection. Small bowel resection is surgery to remove part of a patient's small intestine. When a patient with Crohn's disease has a blockage or severe disease in the small intestine, a surgeon may need to remove that section of intestine. The two types of small bowel resection are

- laparoscopic—when a surgeon makes several small, half-inch incisions in the patient's abdomen. The surgeon inserts a laparoscope—a thin tube with a tiny light and video camera on the end—through the small incisions. The camera sends a magnified image from inside the body to a video monitor, giving the surgeon a close-up view of the small intestine. While watching the monitor, the surgeon inserts tools through the small incisions and removes the diseased or blocked section of small intestine. The surgeon will reconnect the ends of the intestine.

• open surgery—when a surgeon makes one incision about 6 inches long in the patient's abdomen. The surgeon will locate the diseased or blocked section of small intestine and remove or repair that section. The surgeon will reconnect the ends of the intestine.

Subtotal colectomy. A subtotal colectomy, also called a large bowel resection, is surgery to remove part of a patient's large intestine. When a patient with Crohn's disease has a blockage, a fistula, or severe disease in the large intestine, a surgeon may need to remove that section of intestine. A surgeon can perform a subtotal colectomy by

• laparoscopic colectomy—when a surgeon makes several small, half-inch incisions in the abdomen. While watching the monitor, the surgeon removes the diseased or blocked section of the large intestine. The surgeon will reconnect the ends of the intestine.

• open surgery—when a surgeon makes one incision about 6 to 8 inches long in the abdomen. The surgeon will locate the diseased or blocked section of small intestine and remove that section. The surgeon will reconnect the ends of the intestine.

Proctocolectomy and ileostomy. A proctocolectomy is surgery to remove a patient's entire colon and rectum. An ileostomy is a stoma, or opening in the abdomen, that a surgeon creates from a part of the ileum—the last section of the small intestine. The surgeon brings the end of the ileum through an opening in the patient's abdomen and attaches it to the skin, creating an opening outside of the patient's body. The stoma is about three-fourths of an inch to a little less than 2 inches wide and is most often located in the lower part of the patient's abdomen, just below the beltline.

A removable external collection pouch, called an ostomy pouch or ostomy appliance, connects to the stoma and collects intestinal contents outside the patient's body. Intestinal contents pass through the stoma instead of passing through the anus. The stoma has no muscle, so it cannot control the flow of intestinal contents, and the flow occurs whenever peristalsis occurs. Peristalsis is the movement of the organ walls that propels food and liquid through the GI tract.

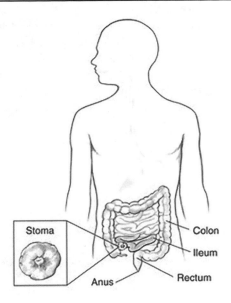

Figure 20.1. *Ileostomy*

People who have this type of surgery will have the ileostomy for the rest of their lives.

Eating, Diet, and Nutrition

Researchers have not found that eating, diet, and nutrition cause Crohn's disease symptoms. Good nutrition is important in the management of Crohn's disease, however. Dietary changes can help reduce symptoms. A health care provider may recommend that a person make dietary changes such as

- avoiding carbonated drinks

- avoiding popcorn, vegetable skins, nuts, and other high-fiber foods

- drinking more liquids

- eating smaller meals more often

- keeping a food diary to help identify troublesome foods

Health care providers may recommend nutritional supplements and vitamins for people who do not absorb enough nutrients.

To help ensure coordinated and safe care, people should discuss their use of complementary and alternative medical practices, including their use of dietary supplements and probiotics, with their health care provider.

Depending on a person's symptoms or medications, a health care provider may recommend a specific diet, such as a

- high-calorie diet

- lactose-free diet

- low-fat diet

- low-fiber diet

- low-salt diet

People should speak with a health care provider about specific dietary recommendations and changes.

What are the complications of Crohn's disease?

Complications of Crohn's disease can include

- **bowel obstruction.** Crohn's disease can thicken the wall of the intestine. Over time, the thickened areas of the intestine can narrow, which can block the intestine. A partial or complete obstruction, also called a bowel blockage, can block the movement of food or stool through the intestines. A complete bowel obstruction is life threatening and requires immediate medical attention and often surgery.

- **fistulas**—abnormal passages, or tunnels, between two organs, or between an organ and the outside of the body. How a health care provider treats fistulas depends on their type and severity. For some people, fistulas heal with medication and diet changes, while other people will need to have surgery.

- **anal fissures**—small tears in the anus that may cause itching, pain, or bleeding. Most anal fissures heal with medical treatment, including ointments, warm baths, and dietary changes.

- **ulcers.** Inflammation anywhere along the GI tract can lead to ulcers or open sores in a person's mouth, intestines, anus, and perineum—the area between the anus and the sex organs. In most cases, the treatment a health care provider prescribes for Crohn's disease will also treat the ulcers.

- **malnutrition**—a condition that develops when the body does not get the right amount of vitamins, minerals, and nutrients it needs to maintain healthy tissues and organ function. Some people may need IV fluids or feeding tubes to replace lost nutrients and fluids.

- **inflammation in other areas of the body.** The immune system can trigger inflammation in the

  - joints

  - eyes

  - skin

Health care providers can treat inflammation by adjusting medications or prescribing new medications.

Crohn's Disease and Colon Cancer

People with Crohn's disease in the large intestine may be more likely to develop colon cancer. People who receive ongoing treatment and remain in remission may reduce their chances of developing colon cancer.

People with Crohn's disease should talk with their health care provider about how often they should get screened for colon cancer. Screening can include colonoscopy with biopsies. Such screening does not reduce a person's chances of developing colon cancer. Instead, screening can help diagnose cancer early and improve chances for recovery.

Section 20.3

Ulcerative Colitis

Text in this section is excerpted from "Ulcerative Colitis," National
Institute of Diabetes and Digestive and Kidney Diseases (NIDDK),
September 2014.

What is ulcerative colitis?

Ulcerative colitis is a chronic, or long lasting, disease that causes
inflammation—irritation or swelling—and sores called ulcers on the
inner lining of the large intestine.

Ulcerative colitis is a chronic inflammatory disease of the gastrointestinal (GI) tract, called inflammatory bowel disease (IBD). Crohn's
disease and microscopic colitis are the other common IBDs.

Ulcerative colitis most often begins gradually and can become worse
over time. Symptoms can be mild to severe. Most people have periods of
remission—times when symptoms disappear—that can last for weeks
or years. The goal of care is to keep people in remission long term.

Most people with ulcerative colitis receive care from a gastroenterologist, a doctor who specializes in digestive diseases.

What causes ulcerative colitis?

The exact cause of ulcerative colitis is unknown. Researchers believe
the following factors may play a role in causing ulcerative colitis:

- overactive intestinal immune system

- genes

- environment

Overactive intestinal immune system. Scientists believe one
cause of ulcerative colitis may be an abnormal immune reaction in
the intestine. Normally, the immune system protects the body from
infection by identifying and destroying bacteria, viruses, and other
potentially harmful foreign substances. Researchers believe bacteria or
viruses can mistakenly trigger the immune system to attack the inner

lining of the large intestine. This immune system response causes the inflammation, leading to symptoms.

Genes. Ulcerative colitis sometimes runs in families. Research studies have shown that certain abnormal genes may appear in people with ulcerative colitis. However, researchers have not been able to show a clear link between the abnormal genes and ulcerative colitis.

Environment. Some studies suggest that certain things in the environment may increase the chance of a person getting ulcerative colitis, although the overall chance is low. Nonsteroidal anti-inflammatory drugs, antibiotics, and oral contraceptives may slightly increase the chance of developing ulcerative colitis. A high-fat diet may also slightly increase the chance of getting ulcerative colitis.

Some people believe eating certain foods, stress, or emotional distress can cause ulcerative colitis. Emotional distress does not seem to cause ulcerative colitis. A few studies suggest that stress may increase a person's chance of having a flare-up of ulcerative colitis. Also, some people may find that certain foods can trigger or worsen symptoms.

Who is more likely to develop ulcerative colitis?

Ulcerative colitis can occur in people of any age. However, it is more likely to develop in people

- between the ages of 15 and 30
- older than 60
- who have a family member with IBD
- of Jewish descent

What are the signs and symptoms of ulcerative colitis?

The most common signs and symptoms of ulcerative colitis are diarrhea with blood or pus and abdominal discomfort. Other signs and symptoms include

- an urgent need to have a bowel movement
- feeling tired
- nausea or loss of appetite
- weight loss

- fever
- anemia—a condition in which the body has fewer red blood cells than normal

  Less common symptoms include

- joint pain or soreness
- eye irritation
- certain rashes

The symptoms a person experiences can vary depending on the severity of the inflammation and where it occurs in the intestine. When symptoms first appear,

- most people with ulcerative colitis have mild to moderate symptoms
- about 10 percent of people can have severe symptoms, such as frequent, bloody bowel movements; fevers; and severe abdominal cramping

How is ulcerative colitis diagnosed?

A health care provider diagnoses ulcerative colitis with the following:

- medical and family history
- physical exam
- lab tests
- endoscopies of the large intestine

The health care provider may perform a series of medical tests to rule out other bowel disorders, such as irritable bowel syndrome, Crohn's disease, or celiac disease, that may cause symptoms similar to those of ulcerative colitis.

Medical and Family History

Taking a medical and family history can help the health care provider diagnose ulcerative colitis and understand a patient's symptoms. The health care provider will also ask the patient about current and past medical conditions and medications.

Physical Exam

A physical exam may help diagnose ulcerative colitis. During a physical exam, the health care provider most often

- checks for abdominal distension, or swelling
- listens to sounds within the abdomen using a stethoscope
- taps on the abdomen to check for tenderness and pain

Lab Tests

A health care provider may order lab tests to help diagnose ulcerative colitis, including blood and stool tests.

Blood tests. A blood test involves drawing blood at a health care provider's office or a lab. A lab technologist will analyze the blood sample. A health care provider may use blood tests to look for

- anemia
- inflammation or infection somewhere in the body
- markers that show ongoing inflammation
- low albumin, or protein—common in patients with severe ulcerative colitis

Stool tests. A stool test is the analysis of a sample of stool. A health care provider will give the patient a container for catching and storing the stool at home. The patient returns the sample to the health care provider or to a lab. A lab technologist will analyze the stool sample. Health care providers commonly order stool tests to rule out other causes of GI diseases, such as infection.

Endoscopies of the Large Intestine

Endoscopies of the large intestine are the most accurate methods for diagnosing ulcerative colitis and ruling out other possible conditions, such as Crohn's disease, diverticular disease, or cancer. Endoscopies of the large intestine include

- colonoscopy
- flexible sigmoidoscopy

How is ulcerative colitis treated?

A health care provider treats ulcerative colitis with

- medications
- surgery

Which treatment a person needs depends on the severity of the disease and the symptoms. Each person experiences ulcerative colitis differently, so health care providers adjust treatments to improve the person's symptoms and induce, or bring about, remission.

Medications

While no medication cures ulcerative colitis, many can reduce symptoms. The goals of medication therapy are

- inducing and maintaining remission
- improving the person's quality of life

Many people with ulcerative colitis require medication therapy indefinitely, unless they have their colon and rectum surgically removed.

Health care providers will prescribe the medications that best treat a person's symptoms:

- aminosalicylates
- corticosteroids
- immunomodulators
- biologics, also called anti-TNF therapies
- other medications

Depending on the location of the symptoms in the colon, health care providers may recommend a person take medications by

- enema, which involves flushing liquid medication into the rectum using a special wash bottle. The medication directly treats inflammation of the large intestine.
- rectal foam—a foamy substance the person puts into the rectum like an enema. The medication directly treats inflammation of the large intestine.
- suppository—a solid medication the person inserts into the rectum to dissolve. The intestinal lining absorbs the medication.
- mouth.
- IV.

Aminosalicylates are medications that contain 5-aminosalicyclic acid (5-ASA), which helps control inflammation. Health care providers typically use aminosalicylates to treat people with mild or moderate symptoms or help people stay in remission. Aminosalicylates can be prescribed as an oral medication or a topical medication—by enema or suppository. Combination therapy—oral and rectal—is most effective, even in people with extensive ulcerative colitis. Aminosalicylates are generally well tolerated.

Aminosalicylates include

- balsalazide
- mesalamine
- olsalazine
- sulfasalazine—a combination of sulfapyridine and 5-ASA

Some of the common side effects of aminosalicylates include

- abdominal pain
- diarrhea
- headaches
- nausea

Health care providers may order routine blood tests for kidney function, as aminosalicylates can cause a rare allergic reaction in the kidneys.

Corticosteroids, also known as steroids, help reduce the activity of the immune system and decrease inflammation. Health care providers prescribe corticosteroids for people with more severe symptoms and people who do not respond to aminosalicylates. Health care providers do not typically prescribe corticosteroids for long-term use.

Corticosteroids are effective in bringing on remission; however, studies have not shown that the medications help maintain long-term remission. Corticosteroids include

- budesonide
- hydrocortisone
- methylprednisone
- prednisone

Side effects of corticosteroids include

- acne
- a higher chance of developing infections

- bone mass loss
- death of bone tissue
- high blood glucose
- high blood pressure
- mood swings
- weight gain

People who take budesonide may have fewer side effects than with other steroids.

Immunomodulators reduce immune system activity, resulting in less inflammation in the colon. These medications can take several weeks to 3 months to start working. Immunomodulators include

- azathioprine
- 6-mercaptopurine, or 6-MP

Health care providers prescribe these medications for people who do not respond to 5-ASAs. People taking these medications may have the following side effects:

- abnormal liver tests
- feeling tired
- infection
- low white blood cell count, which can lead to a higher chance of infection
- nausea and vomiting
- pancreatitis
- slightly increased chance of lymphoma
- slightly increased chance of nonmelanoma skin cancers

Health care providers routinely test blood counts and liver function of people taking immunomodulators. People taking these medications should also have yearly skin cancer exams.

People should talk with their health care provider about the risks and benefits of immunomodulators.

Biologics—including adalimumab, golimumab, infliximab, and vedolizumab—are medications that target a protein made by the immune system called tumor necrosis factor (TNF). These medications decrease inflammation in the large intestine by neutralizing TNF. Anti-TNF therapies work quickly to bring on remission, especially in people who do not respond to other medications. Infliximab and vedolizumab are given through an IV; adalimumab and golimumab are given by injection.

Health care providers will screen patients for tuberculosis and hepatitis B before starting treatment with anti-TNF medications.

Side effects of anti-TNF medications may include

- a higher chance of developing infections—especially tuberculosis or fungal infection

- skin cancer—melanoma

- psoriasis

Other medications to treat symptoms or complications may include

- acetaminophen for mild pain. People with ulcerative colitis should avoid using ibuprofen, naproxen, and aspirin since these medications can make symptoms worse.

- antibiotics to prevent or treat infections.

- loperamide to help slow or stop diarrhea. In most cases, people only take this medication for short periods of time since it can increase the chance of developing megacolon. People should check with a health care provider before taking loperamide, because those with significantly active ulcerative colitis should not take this medication.

- cyclosporine—health care providers prescribe this medication only for people with severe ulcerative colitis because of the side effects. People should talk with their health care provider about the risks and benefits of cyclosporine.

Surgery

Some people will need surgery to treat their ulcerative colitis when they have

- colon cancer

- dysplasia, or precancerous cells in the colon

- complications that are life threatening, such as megacolon or bleeding

- no improvement in symptoms or condition despite treatment
- continued dependency on steroids
- side effects from medications that threaten their health

Removal of the entire colon, including the rectum, "cures" ulcerative colitis. A surgeon can perform two different types of surgery to remove a patient's colon and treat ulcerative colitis:

- proctocolectomy and ileostomy
- proctocolectomy and ileoanal reservoir

Full recovery from both operations may take 4 to 6 weeks.

Proctocolectomy and ileostomy. A proctocolectomy is surgery to remove a patient's entire colon and rectum. An ileostomy is a stoma, or opening in the abdomen, that a surgeon creates from a part of the ileum—the last section of the small intestine. The surgeon brings the end of the ileum through an opening in the patient's abdomen and attaches it to the skin, creating an opening outside of the patient's body. The stoma most often is located in the lower part of the patient's abdomen, just below the beltline.

A removable external collection pouch, called an ostomy pouch or ostomy appliance, connects to the stoma and collects intestinal contents outside the patient's body. Intestinal contents pass through the stoma instead of passing through the anus. The stoma has no muscle, so it cannot control the flow of intestinal contents, and the flow occurs whenever peristalsis occurs. Peristalsis is the movement of the organ walls that propels food and liquid through the GI tract.

People who have this type of surgery will have the ileostomy for the rest of their lives.

Proctocolectomy and ileoanal reservoir. An ileoanal reservoir is an internal pouch made from the patient's ileum. This surgery is a common alternative to an ileostomy and does not have a permanent stoma. Ileoanal reservoir is also known as a J-pouch, a pelvic pouch, or an ileoanal pouch anastamosis. The ileoanal reservior connects the ileum to the anus. The surgeon preserves the outer muscles of the patient's rectum during the proctocolectomy. Next, the surgeon creates the ileal pouch and attaches it to the end of the rectum. Waste is stored in the pouch and passes through the anus.

After surgery, bowel movements may be more frequent and watery than before the procedure. People may have fecal incontinence—the accidental passing of solid or liquid stool or mucus from the rectum. Medications can be used to control pouch function. Women may be infertile following the surgery.

Many people develop pouchitis in the ileoanal reservoir. Pouchitis is an irritation or inflammation of the lining of the ileoanal reservoir. A health care provider treats pouchitis with antibiotics. Rarely, pouchitis can become chronic and require long-term antibiotics or other medications.

The surgeon will recommend one of the operations based on a person's symptoms, severity of disease, expectations, age, and lifestyle. Before making a decision, the person should get as much information as possible by talking with

- health care providers

- enterostomal therapists, nurses who work with colon-surgery patients

- people who have had one of the surgeries

Patient-advocacy organizations can provide information about support groups and other resources.

Eating, Diet, and Nutrition

Researchers have not found that eating, diet, and nutrition play a role in causing ulcerative colitis symptoms. Good nutrition is important in the management of ulcerative colitis, however. Dietary changes can help reduce symptoms. A health care provider may recommend dietary changes such as

- avoiding carbonated drinks

- avoiding popcorn, vegetable skins, nuts, and other high-fiber foods while a person has symptoms

- drinking more liquids

- eating smaller meals more often

- keeping a food diary to help identify troublesome foods

Health care providers may recommend nutritional supplements and vitamins for people who do not absorb enough nutrients.

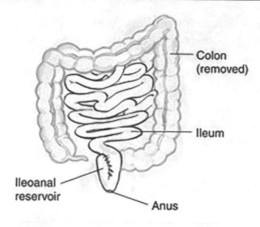

Figure 20.2. *Ileoanal reservoir*

To help ensure coordinated and safe care, people should discuss their use of complementary and alternative medical practices, including their use of dietary supplements and probiotics, with their health care provider.

Depending on a person's symptoms or medications, a health care provider may recommend a specific diet, such as a

- high-calorie diet
- lactose-free diet
- low-fat diet
- low-fiber diet
- low-salt diet

People should speak with a health care provider about specific dietary recommendations and changes.

What are the complications of ulcerative colitis?

Complications of ulcerative colitis can include

- **rectal bleeding**—when ulcers in the intestinal lining open and bleed. Rectal bleeding can cause anemia, which health care providers can treat with diet changes and iron supplements. People who have a large amount of bleeding in the intestine over a short period of time may require surgery to stop the bleeding. Severe bleeding is a rare complication of ulcerative colitis.

- **dehydration and malabsorbtion,** which occur when the large intestine is unable to absorb fluids and nutrients because of diarrhea and inflammation. Some people may need IV fluids to replace lost nutrients and fluids.

- **changes in bones.** Some corticosteroid medications taken to treat ulcerative colitis symptoms can cause

  - osteoporosis—the loss of bone
  - osteopenia—low bone density

Health care providers will monitor people for bone loss and can recommend calcium and vitamin D supplements and medications to help prevent or slow bone loss.

- **inflammation in other areas of the body.** The immune system can trigger inflammation in the

  - joints
  - eyes
  - skin
  - liver

Health care providers can treat inflammation by adjusting medications or prescribing new medications.

- **megacolon**—a serious complication that occurs when inflammation spreads to the deep tissue layers of the large intestine. The large intestine swells and stops working. Megacolon can be a life-threatening complication and most often requires surgery. Megacolon is a rare complication of ulcerative colitis.

Ulcerative Colitis and Colon Cancer

People with ulcerative colitis may be more likely to develop colon cancer when

- ulcerative colitis affects the entire colon
- a person has ulcerative colitis for at least 8 years
- inflammation is ongoing
- people also have primary sclerosing cholangitis, a condition that affects the liver
- a person is male

People who receive ongoing treatment and remain in remission may reduce their chances of developing colon cancer.

People with ulcerative colitis should talk with their health care provider about how often they should get screened for colon cancer. Screening can include colonoscopy with biopsies or a special dye spray called chromoendoscopy.

Health care providers may recommend colonoscopy every 1 to 3 years for people with ulcerative colitis who have

- the disease in one-third or more or of their colon
- had ulcerative colitis for 8 years

Such screening does not reduce a person's chances of developing colon cancer. Instead, screening can help diagnose cancer early and improve chances for recovery.
Surgery to remove the entire colon eliminates the risk of colon cancer.

Section 20.4

Microscopic Colitis

Text in this section is excerpted from "Microscopic Colitis: Collagenous Colitis and Lymphocytic Colitis," National Institute of Diabetes and Digestive and Kidney Diseases (NIDDK), May 2014.

What is microscopic colitis?

Microscopic colitis is an inflammation of the colon that a health care provider can see only with a microscope. Inflammation is the body's normal response to injury, irritation, or infection of tissues. Microscopic colitis is a type of inflammatory bowel disease—the general name for diseases that cause irritation and inflammation in the intestines.

The two types of microscopic colitis are collagenous colitis and lymphocytic colitis. Health care providers often use the term microscopic colitis to describe both types because their symptoms and treatments are the same. Some scientists believe that collagenous colitis and lymphocytic colitis may be different phases of the same condition rather than separate conditions.

In both types of microscopic colitis, an increase in the number of lymphocytes, a type of white blood cell, can be seen in the epithelium—the layer of cells that lines the colon. An increase in the number of white blood cells is a sign of inflammation. The two types of colitis affect the colon tissue in slightly different ways:

- **Lymphocytic colitis.** The number of lymphocytes is higher, and the tissues and lining of the colon are of normal thickness.

- **Collagenous colitis.** The layer of collagen, a threadlike protein, underneath the epithelium builds up and becomes thicker than normal.

When looking through a microscope, the health care provider may find variations in lymphocyte numbers and collagen thickness in different parts of the colon. These variations may indicate an overlap of the two types of microscopic colitis.

What is the colon?

The colon is part of the gastrointestinal (GI) tract, a series of hollow organs joined in a long, twisting tube from the mouth to the anus—a 1-inch-long opening through which stool leaves the body. Organs that make up the GI tract are the

- mouth
- esophagus
- stomach

- small intestine
- large intestine
- anus

The first part of the GI tract, called the upper GI tract, includes the mouth, esophagus, stomach, and small intestine. The last part of the GI tract, called the lower GI tract, consists of the large intestine and anus. The intestines are sometimes called the bowel.

The large intestine is about 5 feet long in adults and includes the colon and rectum. The large intestine changes waste from liquid to a solid matter called stool. Stool passes from the colon to the rectum. The rectum is 6 to 8 inches long in adults and is between the last part of the colon—called the sigmoid colon—and the anus. During a bowel movement, stool moves from the rectum to the anus and out of the body.

What causes microscopic colitis?

The exact cause of microscopic colitis is unknown. Several factors may play a role in causing microscopic colitis. However, most scientists believe that microscopic colitis results from an abnormal immune-system response to bacteria that normally live in the colon. Scientists have proposed other causes, including

- autoimmune diseases
- medications
- infections
- genetic factors
- bile acid malabsorption

Autoimmune Diseases

Sometimes people with microscopic colitis also have autoimmune diseases—disorders in which the body's immune system attacks the body's own cells and organs. Autoimmune diseases associated with microscopic colitis include

- celiac disease—a condition in which people cannot tolerate gluten because it damages the lining of the small intestine and prevents absorption of nutrients. Gluten is a protein found in wheat, rye, and barley.

- thyroid diseases such as

  - Hashimoto's disease—a form of chronic, or long lasting, inflammation of the thyroid.

  - Graves' disease—a disease that causes hyperthyroidism. Hyperthyroidism is a disorder that occurs when the thyroid gland makes more thyroid hormone than the body needs.

- rheumatoid arthritis—a disease that causes pain, swelling, stiffness, and loss of function in the joints when the immune system attacks the membrane lining the joints.

- psoriasis—a skin disease that causes thick, red skin with flaky, silver-white patches called scales.

Medications

Researchers have not found that medications cause microscopic colitis. However, they have found links between microscopic colitis and certain medications, most commonly

- nonsteroidal anti-inflammatory drugs such as aspirin, ibuprofen, and naproxen

- lansoprazole (Prevacid)

- acarbose (Prandase, Precose)

- ranitidine (Tritec, Zantac)

- sertraline (Zoloft)

- ticlopidine (Ticlid)

Other medications linked to microscopic colitis include

- carbamazepine

- clozapine (Clozaril, FazaClo)

- dexlansoprazole (Kapidex, Dexilant)

- entacapone (Comtan)

- esomeprazole (Nexium)

- flutamide (Eulexin)

- lisinopril (Prinivil, Zestril)

- omeprazole (Prilosec)

- pantoprazole (Protonix)

- paroxetine (Paxil, Pexeva)

- rabeprazole (AcipHex)

- simvastatin (Zocor)

- vinorelbine (Navelbine)

Infections

Bacteria. Some people get microscopic colitis after an infection with certain harmful bacteria. Harmful bacteria may produce toxins that irritate the lining of the colon.

Viruses. Some scientists believe that viral infections that cause inflammation in the GI tract may play a role in causing microscopic colitis.

Genetic Factors

Some scientists believe that genetic factors may play a role in microscopic colitis. Although researchers have not yet found a gene unique to microscopic colitis, scientists have linked dozens of genes to other types of inflammatory bowel disease, including

- Crohn's disease—a disorder that causes inflammation and irritation of any part of the GI tract

- ulcerative colitis—a chronic disease that causes inflammation and ulcers in the inner lining of the large intestine

Bile Acid Malabsorption

Some scientists believe that bile acid malabsorption plays a role in microscopic colitis. Bile acid malabsorption is the intestines' inability to completely reabsorb bile acids—acids made by the liver that work with bile to break down fats. Bile is a fluid made by the liver that carries toxins and waste products out of the body and helps the body digest fats. Bile acids that reach the colon can lead to diarrhea.

Who is more likely to get microscopic colitis?

People are more likely to get microscopic colitis if they

• are 50 years of age or older

• are female

• have an autoimmune disease

• smoke cigarettes, especially people ages 16 to 44

• use medications that have been linked to the disease

What are the signs and symptoms of microscopic colitis?

colitis may have long periods without diarrhea. Other signs and symptoms of microscopic colitis can include

• a strong urgency to have a bowel movement or a need to go to the bathroom quickly

• pain, cramping, or bloating in the abdomen—the area between the chest and the hips—that is usually mild

• weight loss

• fecal incontinence—accidental passing of stool or fluid from the rectum—especially at night

• nausea

• dehydration—a condition that results from not taking in enough liquids to replace fluids lost through diarrhea

The symptoms of microscopic colitis can come and go frequently. Sometimes, the symptoms go away without treatment.

How is microscopic colitis diagnosed?

A pathologist—a doctor who specializes in examining tissues to diagnose diseases—diagnoses microscopic colitis based on the findings of multiple biopsies taken throughout the colon. Biopsy is a procedure that involves taking small pieces of tissue for examination with a microscope. The pathologist examines the colon tissue samples in a lab. Many patients can have both lymphocytic colitis and collagenous colitis in different parts of their colon.

To help diagnose microscopic colitis, a gastroenterologist—a doctor who specializes in digestive diseases—begins with

- a medical and family history

- a physical exam

The gastroenterologist may perform a series of medical tests to rule out other bowel diseases—such as irritable bowel syndrome, celiac disease, Crohn's disease, ulcerative colitis, and infectious colitis—that cause symptoms similar to those of microscopic colitis. These medical tests include

- lab tests

- imaging tests of the intestines

- endoscopy of the intestines

Medical and Family History

The gastroenterologist will ask the patient to provide a medical and family history, a review of the symptoms, a description of eating habits, and a list of prescription and over-the-counter medications in order to help diagnose microscopic colitis. The gastroenterologist will also ask the patient about current and past medical conditions.

Physical Exam

A physical exam may help diagnose microscopic colitis and rule out other diseases. During a physical exam, the gastroenterologist usually

- examines the patient's body

- taps on specific areas of the patient's abdomen

Lab Tests

Lab tests may include

- blood tests

- stool tests

Blood tests. A blood test involves drawing blood at a health care provider's office or a commercial facility and sending the sample to a lab for analysis. A health care provider may use blood tests to help look for changes in red and white blood cell counts.

- **Red blood cells.** When red blood cells are fewer or smaller than normal, a person may have anemia—a condition that prevents the body's cells from getting enough oxygen.

- **White blood cells.** When the white blood cell count is higher than normal, a person may have inflammation or infection somewhere in the body.

Stool tests. A stool test is the analysis of a sample of stool. A health care provider will give the patient a container for catching and storing the stool. The patient returns the sample to the health care provider or a commercial facility that will send the sample to a lab for analysis. Health care providers commonly order stool tests to rule out other causes of GI diseases, such as different types of infections—including bacteria or parasites—or bleeding, and help determine the cause of symptoms.

Imaging Tests of the Intestines

Imaging tests of the intestines may include the following:

- computerized tomography (CT) scan
- magnetic resonance imaging (MRI)

Specially trained technicians perform these tests at an outpatient center or a hospital, and a radiologist—a doctor who specializes in medical imaging—interprets the images. A patient does not need anesthesia. Health care providers use imaging tests to show physical abnormalities and to diagnose certain bowel diseases, in some cases.

CT scan. CT scans use a combination of X-rays and computer technology to create images. For a CT scan, a health care provider may give the patient a solution to drink and an injection of a special dye, called contrast medium. CT scans require the patient to lie on a table that slides into a tunnel-shaped device where the technician takes the X-rays.

MRI. MRI is a test that takes pictures of the body's internal organs and soft tissues without using X-rays. Although a patient does not need anesthesia for an MRI, some patients with a fear of confined spaces may receive light sedation, taken by mouth. An MRI may include a solution to drink and injection of contrast medium. With most MRI machines, the patient will lie on a table that slides into a tunnel-shaped device that may be open ended or closed at one end. Some machines allow the patient to lie in a more open space. During an MRI, the patient, although usually awake, must remain perfectly still while the technician takes the images, which usually takes only a few minutes. The technician will take a sequence of images to create a detailed picture of the intestines. During sequencing, the patient will hear loud mechanical knocking and humming noises.

Upper GI series. This test is an X-ray exam that provides a look at the shape of the upper GI tract. Patients should ask their health care provider about how to prepare for an upper GI series. During the procedure, the patient will stand or sit in front of an X-ray machine and drink barium, a chalky liquid. Barium coats the upper GI tract so the radiologist and gastroenterologist can see the organs' shapes more clearly on X-rays. A patient may experience bloating and nausea for a short time after the test. For several days afterward, barium liquid in the GI tract causes white or light-colored stools. A health care provider will give the patient specific instructions about eating and drinking after the test.

Endoscopy of the Intestines

Endoscopy of the intestines may include

- colonoscopy with biopsy

- flexible sigmoidoscopy with biopsy

- upper GI endoscopy with biopsy

A gastroenterologist performs these tests at a hospital or an outpatient center.

Colonoscopy with biopsy. Colonoscopy is a test that uses a long, flexible, narrow tube with a light and tiny camera on one end, called a colonoscope or scope, to look inside the rectum and entire colon. In most cases, light anesthesia and pain medication help patients relax for the test. The medical staff will monitor a patient's vital signs and try to make him or her as comfortable as possible. A nurse or technician places an intravenous (IV) needle in a vein in the arm or hand to give anesthesia.

For the test, the patient will lie on a table while the gastroenterologist inserts a colonoscope into the anus and slowly guides it through the rectum and into the colon. The scope inflates the large intestine with air to give the gastroenterologist a better view. The camera sends a video image of the intestinal lining to a computer screen, allowing the gastroenterologist to carefully examine the tissues lining the colon and rectum. The gastroenterologist may move the patient several times and adjust the scope for better viewing. Once the scope has reached the opening to the small intestine, the gastroenterologist slowly withdraws it and examines the lining of the colon and rectum again. A colonoscopy can show irritated and swollen tissue, ulcers, and abnormal growths such as polyps—extra pieces of tissue that grow on the lining of the intestine. If the lining of the rectum and colon appears normal, the gastroenterologist may suspect microscopic colitis and will biopsy multiple areas of the colon.

A health care provider will provide written bowel prep instructions to follow at home before the test. The health care provider will also explain what the patient can expect after the test and give discharge instructions.

Flexible sigmoidoscopy with biopsy. Flexible sigmoidoscopy is a test that uses a flexible, narrow tube with a light and tiny camera on one end, called a sigmoidoscope or scope, to look inside the rectum and the sigmoid colon. A patient does not usually need anesthesia.

For the test, the patient will lie on a table while the gastroenterologist inserts the sigmoidoscope into the anus and slowly guides it through the rectum and into the sigmoid colon. The scope inflates the large intestine with air to give the gastroenterologist a better view. The camera sends a video image of the intestinal lining to a computer screen, allowing the gastroenterologist to carefully examine the tissues lining the sigmoid colon and rectum. The gastroenterologist may ask the patient to move several times and adjust the scope for better viewing. Once the scope reaches the end of the sigmoid colon, the gastroenterologist slowly withdraws it while carefully examining the lining of the sigmoid colon and rectum again.

The gastroenterologist will look for signs of bowel diseases and conditions such as irritated and swollen tissue, ulcers, and polyps. If the lining of the rectum and colon appears normal, the gastroenterologist may suspect microscopic colitis and will biopsy multiple areas of the colon.

A health care provider will provide written bowel prep instructions to follow at home before the test. The health care provider will also explain what the patient can expect after the test and give discharge instructions.

Upper GI endoscopy with biopsy. Upper GI endoscopy is a test that uses a flexible, narrow tube with a light and tiny camera on one end, called an endoscope or a scope, to look inside the upper GI tract. The gastroenterologist carefully feeds the endoscope down the esophagus and into the stomach and first part of the small intestine, called the duodenum. A small camera mounted on the endoscope transmits a video image to a monitor, allowing close examination of the intestinal lining. A health care provider may give a patient a liquid anesthetic to gargle or may spray anesthetic on the back of the patient's throat. A health care provider will place an IV needle in a vein in the arm or hand to administer sedation. Sedatives help patients stay relaxed and comfortable. This test can show blockages or other conditions in the upper small intestine. A gastroenterologist may biopsy the lining of the small intestine during an upper GI endoscopy.

How is microscopic colitis treated?

Treatment depends on the severity of symptoms. The gastroenterologist will

- review the medications the person is taking

- make recommendations to change or stop certain medications

- recommend that the person quit smoking

The gastroenterologist may prescribe medications to help control symptoms. Medications are almost always effective in treating microscopic colitis. The gastroenterologist may recommend eating, diet, and nutrition changes. In rare cases, the gastroenterologist may recommend surgery.

Medications

The gastroenterologist may prescribe one or more of the following:

- antidiarrheal medications such as bismuth subsalicylate (Kaopectate, Pepto-Bismol), diphenoxylate/atropine (Lomotil), and loperamide

- corticosteroids such as budesonide (Entocort) and prednisone

- anti-inflammatory medications such as mesalamine and sulfasalazine (Azulfidine)

- cholestyramine resin (Locholest, Questran)—a medication that blocks bile acids

- antibiotics such as metronidazole (Flagyl) and erythromycin

- immunomodulators such as mercaptopurine (Purinethol), azathioprine (Azasan, Imuran), and methotrexate (Rheumatrex, Trexall)

- anti-TNF therapies such as infliximab (Remicade) and adalimumab (Humira)

Corticosteroids are medications that decrease inflammation and reduce the activity of the immune system. These medications can have many side effects. Scientists have shown that budesonide is safer, with fewer side effects, than prednisone. Most health care providers consider budesonide the best medication for treating microscopic colitis.

Patients with microscopic colitis generally achieve relief through treatment with medications, although relapses can occur. Some patients may need long-term treatment if they continue to have relapses.

Eating, Diet, and Nutrition

To help reduce symptoms, a health care provider may recommend the following dietary changes:

- avoid foods and drinks that contain caffeine or artificial sugars

- drink plenty of liquids to prevent dehydration during episodes of diarrhea

- eat a milk-free diet if the person is also lactose intolerant

- eat a gluten-free diet

People should talk with their health care provider or dietitian about what type of diet is right for them.

Surgery

When the symptoms of microscopic colitis are severe and medications aren't effective, a gastroenterologist may recommend surgery to remove the colon. Surgery is a rare treatment for microscopic colitis.

The gastroenterologist will exclude other causes of symptoms before considering surgery.

How can microscopic colitis be prevented?

Researchers do not know how to prevent microscopic colitis. However, researchers do believe that people who follow the recommendations of their health care provider may be able to prevent relapses of microscopic colitis.

Does microscopic colitis increase the risk of colon cancer?

No. Unlike the other inflammatory bowel diseases, such as Crohn's disease and ulcerative colitis, microscopic colitis does not increase a person's risk of getting colon cancer.

Chapter 21

Appendicitis

Definition and Facts

What is appendicitis?

Appendicitis is inflammation of your appendix.

How common is appendicitis?

In the United States, appendicitis is the most common cause of acute abdominal pain requiring surgery. Over 5% of the population develops appendicitis at some point.

Who is more likely to develop appendicitis?

Appendicitis most commonly occurs in the teens and twenties but may occur at any age.

What are the complications of appendicitis?

If appendicitis is not treated, it may lead to complications. The complications of a ruptured appendix are

- peritonitis, which can be a dangerous condition. Peritonitis happens if your appendix bursts and infection spreads in your abdomen. If you have peritonitis, you may be very ill and have

---

Text in this chapter is excerpted from "Appendicitis," National Institute of Diabetes and Digestive and Kidney Diseases (NIDDK), November 13, 2014.

- fever
- nausea
- severe tenderness in your abdomen
- vomiting
- an abscess of the appendix called an appendiceal abscess.

Symptoms and Causes

What are the symptoms of appendicitis?

The most common symptom of appendicitis is pain in your abdomen. If you have appendicitis, you'll most often have pain in your abdomen that

- begins near your belly button and then moves lower and to your right
- gets worse in a matter of hours
- gets worse when you move around, take deep breaths, cough, or sneeze
- is severe and often described as different from any pain you've felt before
- occurs suddenly and may even wake you up if you're sleeping
- occurs before other symptoms

Other symptoms of appendicitis may include

- loss of appetite
- nausea
- vomiting
- constipation or diarrhea,
- an inability to pass gas
- a low-grade fever
- swelling in your abdomen
- the feeling that having a bowel movement will relieve discomfort

Symptoms can be different for each person and can seem like the following conditions that also cause pain in the abdomen:

- abdominal adhesions

- constipation

- inflammatory bowel disease, which includes Crohn's disease and ulcerative colitis, long-lasting disorders that cause irritation and ulcers in the GI tract

- intestinal obstruction

- pelvic inflammatory disease

What causes appendicitis?

Appendicitis can have more than one cause, and in many cases the cause is not clear. Possible causes include:

- Blockage of the opening inside the appendix

- enlarged tissue in the wall of your appendix, caused by infection in the gastrointestinal (GI) tract or elsewhere in your body

- inflammatory bowel disease

- stool, parasites, or growths that can clog your appendiceal lumen

- trauma to your abdomen

When should I seek a doctor's help?

Appendicitis is a medical emergency that requires immediate care. See a health care professional or go to the emergency room right away if you think you or a child has appendicitis. A doctor can help treat the appendicitis and reduce symptoms and the chance of complications.

Diagnosis

How do doctors diagnose appendicitis?

Most often, health care professionals suspect the diagnosis of appendicitis based on your symptoms, your medical history, and a physical exam. A doctor can confirm the diagnosis with an ultrasound, X-ray, or MRI exam.

Medical history

A health care professional will ask specific questions about your symptoms and health history to help rule out other health problems. The health care professional will want to know

- when your abdominal pain began
- the exact location and severity of your pain
- when your other symptoms appeared
- your other medical conditions, previous illnesses, and surgical procedures
- whether you use medicines, alcohol, or illegal drugs

Physical exam

Health care professionals need specific details about the pain in your abdomen to diagnose appendicitis correctly. A health care professional will assess your pain by touching or applying pressure to specific areas of your abdomen.

The following responses to touch or pressure may indicate that you have appendicitis:

- Rovsing's sign
- Psoas sign
- Obturator sign
- Guarding
- Rebound tenderness
- Digital rectal exam
- Pelvic exam

Lab tests

Doctors use lab tests to help confirm the diagnosis of appendicitis or find other causes of abdominal pain.

Blood tests. A health care professional draws your blood for a blood test at a doctor's office or a commercial facility. The health care professional sends the blood sample to a lab for testing. Blood tests can show a high white blood cell count, a sign of infection. Blood tests also may show dehydration or fluid and electrolyte imbalances.

Urinalysis. Urinalysis is testing of a urine sample. You will provide a urine sample in a special container in a doctor's office, a commercial facility, or a hospital. Health care professionals can test the urine in the same location or send it to a lab for testing. Doctors use urinalysis to rule out a urinary tract infection or a kidney stone.

Pregnancy test. For women, health care professionals also may order blood or urine samples to check for pregnancy.

Imaging tests

Doctors use imaging tests to confirm the diagnosis of appendicitis or find other causes of pain in the abdomen.

Abdominal ultrasound. In an ultrasound, a health care professional uses a device, called a transducer, to bounce safe, painless sound waves off of your organs to create an image of their structure. He or she can move the transducer to different angles to examine different organs.

In an abdominal ultrasound, a health care professional applies a gel to your abdomen and moves a hand-held transducer over your skin. A radiologist reviews the images, which can show signs of

- a blockage in your appendiceal lumen

- a burst appendix

- inflammation

- other sources of abdominal pain

Health care professionals use an ultrasound as the first imaging test for possible appendicitis in infants, children, young adults, and pregnant women.

Magnetic resonance imaging (MRI). MRI machines use radio waves and magnets to produce detailed pictures of your body's internal organs and soft tissues without using X-rays.

A health care professional performs the procedure in an outpatient center or a hospital. A radiologist reviews the images. Patients don't need anesthesia, although a health care professional may give light sedation, taken by mouth, to children and people with a fear of small spaces. A health care professional may inject a special dye, called contrast medium, into your body.

In most cases, you'll lie on a table that slides into a tunnel-shaped device. The tunnel may be open ended or closed at one end.

An MRI can show signs of

- a blockage in your appendiceal lumen

- a burst appendix

- inflammation

• other sources of abdominal pain

When diagnosing appendicitis and other sources of abdominal pain, doctors can use an MRI as a safe, reliable alternative to a computerized tomography (CT) scan.

CT scan. CT scans use X-rays and computer technology to create images.

A health care professional may give you a solution to drink and an injection of contrast medium. You'll lie on a table that slides into a tunnel-shaped device that takes the X-rays. X-ray technicians perform CT scans in an outpatient center or a hospital. Radiologists review the images.

Patients don't need anesthesia, although health care professionals may give children a sedative to help them fall asleep for the test.

A CT scan of the abdomen can show signs of inflammation, such as

• an enlarged or a burst appendix

• an appendiceal abscess

• a blockage in your appendiceal lumen

Women of childbearing age should have a pregnancy test before having a CT scan. The radiation from CT scans can be harmful to a developing fetus.

Treatment

How do doctors treat appendicitis?

Doctors typically treat appendicitis with surgery to remove the appendix. Surgeons perform the surgery in a hospital with general anesthesia. Your doctor will recommend surgery if you have continuous abdominal pain and fever, or signs of a burst appendix and infection. Prompt surgery decreases the chance that your appendix will burst.

Health care professionals call the surgery to remove the appendix an appendectomy. A surgeon performs the surgery using one of the following methods:

• **Laparoscopic surgery.** During laparoscopic surgery, surgeons use several smaller incisions and special surgical tools that they feed through the incisions to remove your appendix. Laparoscopic surgery leads to fewer complications, such as hospital-related infections, and has a shorter recovery time.

- **Laparotomy.** Surgeons use laparotomy to remove the appendix through a single incision in the lower right area of your abdomen.

After surgery, most patients completely recover from appendicitis and don't need to make changes to their diet, exercise, or lifestyle. Surgeons recommend that you limit physical activity for the first 10 to 14 days after a laparotomy and for the first 3 to 5 days after laparoscopic surgery.

What if the surgeon finds a normal appendix?

In some cases, a surgeon finds a normal appendix during surgery. In this case, many surgeons will remove it to eliminate the future possibility of appendicitis. Sometimes surgeons find a different problem, which they may correct during surgery.

Can doctors treat appendicitis without surgery?

Some cases of mild appendicitis may be cured with antibiotics alone. All patients suspected of having appendicitis are treated with antibiotics before surgery, and some patients may improve completely before surgery is performed.

How do doctors treat complications of a burst appendix?

Treating the complications of a burst appendix will depend on the type of complication. In most cases of peritonitis, a surgeon will remove your appendix immediately with surgery. The surgeon will use laparotomy to clean the inside of your abdomen to prevent infection and then remove your appendix. Without prompt treatment, peritonitis can cause death.

A surgeon may drain the pus from an appendiceal abscess during surgery or, more commonly, before surgery. To drain an abscess, the surgeon places a tube in the abscess through the abdominal wall. You leave the drainage tube in place for about 2 weeks while you take antibiotics to treat infection. When the infection and inflammation are under control, about 6 to 8 weeks later, surgeons operate to remove what remains of the burst appendix.

Eating, Diet, and Nutrition

How can your diet help prevent or relieve appendicitis?

Researchers have not found that eating, diet, and nutrition cause or prevent appendicitis.

Chapter 22

Gallstones

What are Gallstones?

Gallstones are hard particles that develop in the gallbladder. The gallbladder is a small, pear-shaped organ located in the upper right abdomen—the area between the chest and hips—below the liver.

Gallstones can range in size from a grain of sand to a golf ball. The gallbladder can develop a single large gallstone, hundreds of tiny stones, or both small and large stones. Gallstones can cause sudden pain in the upper right abdomen. This pain, called a gallbladder attack or biliary colic, occurs when gallstones block the ducts of the biliary tract.

What is the biliary tract?

The biliary tract consists of the gallbladder and the bile ducts. The bile ducts carry bile and other digestive enzymes from the liver and pancreas to the duodenum—the first part of the small intestine.

The liver produces bile—a fluid that carries toxins and waste products out of the body and helps the body digest fats and the fat-soluble vitamins A, D, E, and K. Bile mostly consists of cholesterol, bile salts, and bilirubin. Bilirubin, a reddish-yellow substance, forms when hemoglobin from red blood cells breaks down. Most bilirubin is excreted through bile.

Text in this chapter is excerpted from "Gallstones," National Institute of Diabetes and Digestive and Kidney Diseases (NIDDK), September 2013.

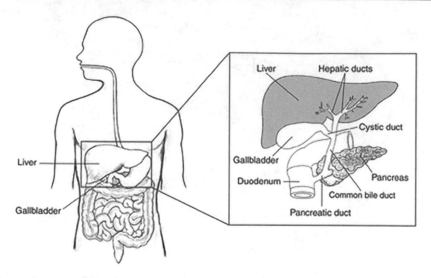

Figure 22.1. *The Biliary Tract*

The bile ducts of the biliary tract include the hepatic ducts, the common bile duct, the pancreatic duct, and the cystic duct. The gallbladder stores bile. Eating signals the gallbladder to contract and empty bile through the cystic duct and common bile duct into the duodenum to mix with food.

What causes gallstones?

Imbalances in the substances that make up bile cause gallstones. Gallstones may form if bile contains too much cholesterol, too much bilirubin, or not enough bile salts. Scientists do not fully understand why these imbalances occur. Gallstones also may form if the gallbladder does not empty completely or often enough.

The two types of gallstones are cholesterol and pigment stones:

- Cholesterol stones, usually yellow-green in color, consist primarily of hardened cholesterol. In the United States, more than 80 percent of gallstones are cholesterol stones.

- Pigment stones, dark in color, are made of bilirubin.

Who is at risk for gallstones?

Certain people have a higher risk of developing gallstones than others:

- Women are more likely to develop gallstones than men. Extra estrogen can increase cholesterol levels in bile and decrease gallbladder contractions, which may cause gallstones to form. Women may have extra estrogen due to pregnancy, hormone replacement therapy, or birth control pills.

- People over age 40 are more likely to develop gallstones than younger people.

- People with a family history of gallstones have a higher risk.

- American Indians have genetic factors that increase the amount of cholesterol in their bile. In fact, American Indians have the highest rate of gallstones in the United States—almost 65 percent of women and 30 percent of men have gallstones.

- Mexican Americans are at higher risk of developing gallstones.

Other factors that affect a person's risk of gallstones include

- **Obesity.** People who are obese, especially women, have increased risk of developing gallstones. Obesity increases the amount of cholesterol in bile, which can cause stone formation.

- **Rapid weight loss.** As the body breaks down fat during prolonged fasting and rapid weight loss, the liver secretes extra cholesterol into bile. Rapid weight loss can also prevent the gallbladder from emptying properly. Low-calorie diets and bariatric surgery—surgery that limits the amount of food a person can eat or digest— lead to rapid weight loss and increased risk of gallstones.

- **Diet.** Research suggests diets high in calories and refined carbohydrates and low in fiber increase the risk of gallstones. Refined carbohydrates are grains processed to remove bran and germ, which contain nutrients and fiber. Examples of refined carbohydrates include white bread and white rice.

- **Certain intestinal diseases.** Diseases that affect normal absorption of nutrients, such as Crohn's disease, are associated with gallstones.

- **Metabolic syndrome, diabetes, and insulin resistance.** These conditions increase the risk of gallstones. Metabolic syndrome also increases the risk of gallstone complications. Metabolic syndrome is a group of traits and medical conditions linked to being overweight or obese that puts people at risk for heart disease and type 2 diabetes.

Pigment stones tend to develop in people who have

- cirrhosis—a condition in which the liver slowly deteriorates and malfunctions due to chronic, or long lasting, injury

- infections in the bile ducts

- severe hemolytic anemias—conditions in which red blood cells are continuously broken down, such as sickle cell anemia

What are the symptoms and complications of gallstones?

Many people with gallstones do not have symptoms. Gallstones that do not cause symptoms are called asymptomatic, or silent, gallstones. Silent gallstones do not interfere with the function of the gallbladder, liver, or pancreas.

If gallstones block the bile ducts, pressure increases in the gallbladder, causing a gallbladder attack. The pain usually lasts from 1 to several hours. Gallbladder attacks often follow heavy meals, and they usually occur in the evening or during the night.

Gallbladder attacks usually stop when gallstones move and no longer block the bile ducts. However, if any of the bile ducts remain blocked for more than a few hours, complications can occur. Complications include inflammation, or swelling, of the gallbladder and severe damage or infection of the gallbladder, bile ducts, or liver.

A gallstone that becomes lodged in the common bile duct near the duodenum and blocks the pancreatic duct can cause gallstone pancreatitis—inflammation of the pancreas.

Left untreated, blockages of the bile ducts or pancreatic duct can be fatal.

When should a person talk with a health care provider about gallstones?

People who think they have had a gallbladder attack should notify their health care provider. Although these attacks usually resolve as gallstones move, complications can develop if the bile ducts remain blocked.

People with any of the following symptoms during or after a gallbladder attack should see a health care provider immediately:

- abdominal pain lasting more than 5 hours

- nausea and vomiting

- fever—even a low-grade fever—or chills

- yellowish color of the skin or whites of the eyes, called jaundice

- tea-colored urine and light-colored stools

These symptoms may be signs of serious infection or inflammation of the gallbladder, liver, or pancreas.

How are gallstones diagnosed?

A health care provider will usually order an ultrasound exam to diagnose gallstones. Other imaging tests may also be used.

- **Ultrasound exam.** If gallstones are present, they will be visible in the image. Ultrasound is the most accurate method to detect gallstones.

- **Computerized tomography (CT) scan.** CT scans can show gallstones or complications, such as infection and blockage of the gallbladder or bile ducts. However, CT scans can miss gallstones that are present.

- **Magnetic resonance imaging (MRI).** MRIs can show gallstones in the ducts of the biliary system.

- **Cholescintigraphy.** Cholescintigraphy is used to diagnose abnormal contractions of the gallbladder or obstruction of the bile ducts.

- **Endoscopic retrograde cholangiopancreatography (ERCP).** ERCP helps the health care provider locate the affected bile duct and the gallstone. The stone is captured in a tiny basket attached to the endoscope and removed. This test is more invasive than other tests and is used selectively.

Health care providers also use blood tests to look for signs of infection or inflammation of the bile ducts, gallbladder, pancreas, or liver. A blood test involves drawing blood at a health care provider's office or commercial facility and sending the sample to a lab for analysis.

Gallstone symptoms may be similar to those of other conditions, such as appendicitis, ulcers, pancreatitis, and gastroesophageal reflux disease.

Sometimes, silent gallstones are found when a person does not have any symptoms. For example, a health care provider may notice gallstones when performing ultrasound for a different reason.

How are gallstones treated?

If gallstones are not causing symptoms, treatment is usually not needed. However, if a person has a gallbladder attack or other symptoms, a health care provider will usually recommend treatment. A person may be referred to a gastroenterologist—a doctor who specializes in digestive diseases—for treatment. If a person has had one gallbladder attack, more episodes will likely follow.

The usual treatment for gallstones is surgery to remove the gallbladder. If a person cannot undergo surgery, nonsurgical treatments may be used to dissolve cholesterol gallstones. A health care provider may use ERCP to remove stones in people who cannot undergo surgery or to remove stones from the common bile duct in people who are about to have gallbladder removal surgery.

Surgery

Surgery to remove the gallbladder, called cholecystectomy, is one of the most common operations performed on adults in the United States.

The gallbladder is not an essential organ, which means a person can live normally without a gallbladder. Once the gallbladder is removed, bile flows out of the liver through the hepatic and common bile ducts and directly into the duodenum, instead of being stored in the gallbladder.

Surgeons perform two types of cholecystectomy:

- **Laparoscopic cholecystectomy.** In a laparoscopic cholecystectomy, the surgeon makes several tiny incisions in the abdomen and inserts a laparoscope—a thin tube with a tiny video camera attached. The camera sends a magnified image from inside the body to a video monitor, giving the surgeon a close-up view of organs and tissues. While watching the monitor, the surgeon uses instruments to carefully separate the gallbladder from the liver, bile ducts, and other structures. Then the surgeon removes the gallbladder through one of the small incisions. Patients usually receive general anesthesia.

Most cholecystectomies are performed with laparoscopy. Many laparoscopic cholecystectomies are performed on an outpatient basis, meaning the person is able to go home the same day. Normal physical activity can usually be resumed in about a week.

- **Open cholecystectomy.** An open cholecystectomy is performed when the gallbladder is severely inflamed, infected, or scarred from other operations. In most of these cases, open cholecystectomy is planned from the start. However, a surgeon may perform an open cholecystectomy when problems occur during a laparoscopic cholecystectomy. In these cases, the surgeon must switch to open cholecystectomy as a safety measure for the patient.

To perform an open cholecystectomy, the surgeon creates an incision about 4 to 6 inches long in the abdomen to remove the gallbladder. Patients usually receive general anesthesia. Recovery from open cholecystectomy may require some people to stay in the hospital for up to a week. Normal physical activity can usually be resumed after about a month.

A small number of people have softer and more frequent stools after gallbladder removal because bile flows into the duodenum more often. Changes in bowel habits are usually temporary; however, they should be discussed with a health care provider.

Though complications from gallbladder surgery are rare, the most common complication is injury to the bile ducts. An injured common bile duct can leak bile and cause a painful and possibly dangerous infection. One or more additional operations may be needed to repair the bile ducts. Bile duct injuries occur in less than 1 percent of cholecystectomies.

Nonsurgical Treatments for Cholesterol Gallstones

Nonsurgical treatments are used only in special situations, such as when a person with cholesterol stones has a serious medical condition that prevents surgery. Gallstones often recur within 5 years after nonsurgical treatment.

Two types of nonsurgical treatments can be used to dissolve cholesterol gallstones:

- **Oral dissolution therapy.** Ursodiol (Actigall) and chenodiol (Chenix) are medications that contain bile acids that can dissolve gallstones. These medications are most effective in dissolving small cholesterol stones. Months or years of treatment may be needed to dissolve all stones.

- **Shock wave lithotripsy.** A machine called a lithotripter is used to crush the gallstone. The lithotripter generates shock waves that pass through the person's body to break the gallstone into smaller pieces. This procedure is used only rarely and may be used along with ursodiol.

Eating, Diet, and Nutrition

Factors related to eating, diet, and nutrition that increase the risk of gallstones include

- obesity

- rapid weight loss

- diets high in calories and refined carbohydrates and low in fiber

People can decrease their risk of gallstones by maintaining a healthy weight through proper diet and nutrition.

Ursodiol can help prevent gallstones in people who rapidly lose weight through low-calorie diets or bariatric surgery. People should talk with their health care provider or dietitian about what diet is right for them.

Chapter 23

Diverticulosis and Diverticulitis

What is diverticular disease?

Diverticular disease is a condition that occurs when a person has problems from small pouches, or sacs, that have formed and pushed outward through weak spots in the colon wall. Each pouch is called a diverticulum. Multiple pouches are called diverticula.

The colon is part of the large intestine. The large intestine absorbs water from stool and changes it from a liquid to a solid form. Diverticula are most common in the lower part of the colon, called the sigmoid colon.

The problems that occur with diverticular disease include diverticulitis and diverticular bleeding. Diverticulitis occurs when the diverticula become inflamed, or irritated and swollen, and infected. Diverticular bleeding occurs when a small blood vessel within the wall of a diverticulum bursts.

What is diverticulosis?

When a person has diverticula that do not cause diverticulitis or diverticular bleeding, the condition is called diverticulosis. Most people with diverticulosis do not have symptoms. Some people with

Text in this chapter is excerpted from "Diverticular Disease," National Institute of Diabetes and Digestive and Kidney Diseases (NIDDK), September 2013.

diverticulosis have constipation or diarrhea. People may also have chronic

- cramping or pain in the lower abdomen—the area between the chest and hips
- bloating

Other conditions, such as irritable bowel syndrome and stomach ulcers, cause similar problems, so these symptoms do not always mean a person has diverticulosis. People with these symptoms should see their health care provider.

What causes diverticulosis and diverticular disease?

Scientists are not certain what causes diverticulosis and diverticular disease. For more than 50 years, the most widely accepted theory was that a low-fiber diet led to diverticulosis and diverticular disease. Diverticulosis and diverticular disease were first noticed in the United States in the early 1900s, around the time processed foods were introduced into the American diet. Consumption of processed foods greatly

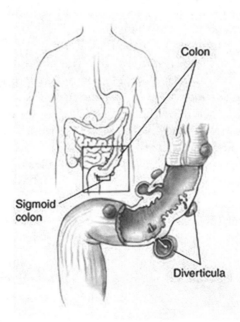

Figure 23.1. *Diverticula*

reduced Americans' fiber intake. Diverticulosis and diverticular disease are common in Western and industrialized countries—particularly the United States, England, and Australia—where low-fiber diets are common. The condition is rare in Asia and Africa, where most people eat high-fiber diets. Two large studies also indicate that a low-fiber diet may increase the chance of developing diverticular disease.

However, a recent study found that a low-fiber diet was not associated with diverticulosis and that a high-fiber diet and more frequent bowel movements may be linked to an increased rather than decreased chance of diverticula.

Other studies have focused on the role of decreased levels of the neurotransmitter serotonin in causing decreased relaxation and increased spasms of the colon muscle. A neurotransmitter is a chemical that helps brain cells communicate with nerve cells. However, more studies are needed in this area.

Studies have also found links between diverticular disease and obesity, lack of exercise, smoking, and certain medications including nonsteroidal anti-inflammatory drugs, such as aspirin, and steroids.

Scientists agree that with diverticulitis, inflammation may begin when bacteria or stool get caught in a diverticulum. In the colon, inflammation also may be caused by a decrease in healthy bacteria and an increase in disease-causing bacteria. This change in the bacteria may permit chronic inflammation to develop in the colon.

What is fiber?

Fiber is a substance in foods that comes from plants. Fiber helps soften stool so it moves smoothly through the colon and is easier to pass. Soluble fiber dissolves in water and is found in beans, fruit, and oat products. Insoluble fiber does not dissolve in water and is found in whole-grain products and vegetables. Both kinds of fiber help prevent constipation.

Constipation is a condition in which an adult has fewer than three bowel movements a week or has bowel movements with stools that are hard, dry, and small, making them painful or difficult to pass.

High-fiber foods also have many benefits in preventing and controlling chronic diseases, such as cardiovascular disease, obesity, diabetes, and cancer.

Who gets diverticulosis and diverticular disease?

Diverticulosis becomes more common as people age, particularly in people older than age 50. Some people with diverticulosis develop diverticulitis, and the number of cases is increasing. Although diverticular disease is generally thought to be a condition found in older adults, it is becoming more common in people younger than age 50, most of whom are male.

What are the symptoms of diverticular disease?

People with diverticulitis may have many symptoms, the most common of which is pain in the lower left side of the abdomen. The pain is usually severe and comes on suddenly, though it can also be mild and then worsen over several days. The intensity of the pain can fluctuate. Diverticulitis may also cause

- fevers and chills

- nausea or vomiting

- a change in bowel habits—constipation or diarrhea

- diverticular bleeding

In most cases, people with diverticular bleeding suddenly have a large amount of red or maroon-colored blood in their stool. Diverticular bleeding may also cause

- weakness

- dizziness or light-headedness

- abdominal cramping

How are diverticulosis and diverticular disease diagnosed?

Diverticulosis

Health care providers often find diverticulosis during a routine X-ray or a colonoscopy, a test used to look inside the rectum and entire colon to screen for colon cancer or polyps or to evaluate the source of rectal bleeding.

Diverticular Disease

Based on symptoms and severity of illness, a person may be evaluated and diagnosed by a primary care physician, an emergency department physician, a surgeon, or a gastroenterologist—a doctor who specializes in digestive diseases.

The health care provider will ask about the person's health, symptoms, bowel habits, diet, and medications, and will perform a physical exam, which may include a rectal exam. A rectal exam is performed in the health care provider's office; anesthesia is not needed. To perform the exam, the health care provider asks the person to bend over a table or lie on one side while holding the knees close to the chest. The health care provider slides a gloved, lubricated finger into the rectum. The exam is used to check for pain, bleeding, or a blockage in the intestine.

The health care provider may schedule one or more of the following tests:

- **Blood test.** A blood test involves drawing a person's blood at a health care provider's office, a commercial facility, or a hospital and sending the sample to a lab for analysis. The blood test can show the presence of inflammation or anemia—a condition in which red blood cells are fewer or smaller than normal, which prevents the body's cells from getting enough oxygen.

- **Computerized tomography (CT) scan.** A CT scan of the colon is the most common test used to diagnose diverticular disease. CT scans use a combination of X-rays and computer technology to create three-dimensional (3–D) images. For a CT scan, the person may be given a solution to drink and an injection of a special dye, called contrast medium. CT scans require the person to lie on a table that slides into a tunnel-shaped device where the X-rays are taken. The procedure is performed in an outpatient center or a hospital by an X-ray technician, and the images are interpreted by a radiologist—a doctor who specializes in medical imaging. Anesthesia is not needed. CT scans can detect diverticulosis and confirm the diagnosis of diverticulitis.

- **Lower gastrointestinal (GI) series.** A lower GI series is an X-ray exam that is used to look at the large intestine. The test is performed at a hospital or an outpatient center by an X-ray technician, and the images are interpreted by a radiologist. Anesthesia is not needed. The health care provider may provide written bowel prep instructions to follow at home before the test. The person may be asked to follow a clear liquid diet for 1 to 3 days before the procedure. A laxative or enema may be used before the test. A laxative is medication that loosens stool and increases bowel movements. An enema involves flushing water or laxative into the rectum using a special squirt bottle. These medications cause diarrhea, so the person should stay close to a bathroom during the bowel prep.

For the test, the person will lie on a table while the radiologist inserts a flexible tube into the person's anus. The colon is filled with barium, making signs of diverticular disease show up more clearly on X-rays.

For several days, traces of barium in the large intestine can cause stools to be white or light colored. Enemas and repeated bowel movements may cause anal soreness. A health care provider will provide specific instructions about eating and drinking after the test.

- **Colonoscopy.** The test is performed at a hospital or an outpatient center by a gastroenterologist. Before the test, the person's health care provider will provide written bowel prep instructions to follow at home. The person may need to follow a clear liquid diet for 1 to 3 days before the test. The person may also need to take laxatives and enemas the evening before the test.

In most cases, light anesthesia, and possibly pain medication, helps people relax for the test. The person will lie on a table while the gastroenterologist inserts a flexible tube into the anus. A small camera on the tube sends a video image of the intestinal lining to a computer screen. The test can show diverticulosis and diverticular disease.

Cramping or bloating may occur during the first hour after the test. Driving is not permitted for 24 hours after the test to allow the anesthesia time to wear off. Before the appointment, people should make plans for a ride home. Full recovery is expected by the next day, and people should be able to go back to their normal diet.

How are diverticulosis and diverticular disease treated?

A health care provider may treat the symptoms of diverticulosis with a high-fiber diet or fiber supplements, medications, and possibly probiotics. Treatment for diverticular disease varies, depending on whether a person has diverticulitis or diverticular bleeding.

Diverticulosis

High-fiber diet. Studies have shown that a high-fiber diet can help prevent diverticular disease in people who already have diverticulosis. A health care provider may recommend a slow increase in dietary fiber to minimize gas and abdominal discomfort.

Fiber supplements. A health care provider may recommend taking a fiber product such as methylcellulose (Citrucel) or psyllium (Metamucil) one to three times a day. These products are available as powders, pills, or wafers and provide 0.5 to 3.5 grams of fiber per dose. Fiber products should be taken with at least 8 ounces of water.

Medications. A number of studies suggest the medication mesalazine (Asacol), given either continuously or in cycles, may be effective at reducing abdominal pain and GI symptoms of diverticulosis. Research has also shown that combining mesalazine with the antibiotic rifaximin (Xifaxan) can be significantly more effective than using rifaximin alone to improve a person's symptoms and maintain periods of remission, which means being free of symptoms.4

Probiotics. Although more research is needed, probiotics may help treat the symptoms of diverticulosis, prevent the onset of diverticulitis, and reduce the chance of recurrent symptoms. Probiotics are live bacteria, like those normally found in the GI tract. Probiotics can be found in dietary supplements—in capsules, tablets, and powders—and in some foods, such as yogurt.

To help ensure coordinated and safe care, people should discuss their use of complementary and alternative medical practices, including their use of dietary supplements and probiotics, with their health care provider.

Diverticular Bleeding

Diverticular bleeding is rare. Bleeding can be severe; however, it may stop by itself and not require treatment. A person who has bleeding from the rectum—even a small amount—should see a health care provider right away.

To treat the bleeding, a colonoscopy may be performed to identify the location of and stop the bleeding. A CT scan or angiogram also may be used to identify the site of the bleeding. A traditional angiogram is a special kind of X-ray in which a thin, flexible tube called a catheter is threaded through a large artery, often from the groin, to the area of bleeding. Contrast medium is injected through the catheter so the artery shows up more clearly on the X-ray. The procedure is performed in a hospital or an outpatient center by an X-ray technician, and the images are interpreted by a radiologist. Anesthesia is not needed, though a sedative may be given to lessen anxiety during the procedure.

If the bleeding does not stop, abdominal surgery with a colon resection may be necessary. In a colon resection, the surgeon removes the affected part of the colon and joins the remaining ends of the colon together; general anesthesia is used. A blood transfusion may be needed if the person has lost a significant amount of blood.

Diverticulitis

Diverticulitis with mild symptoms and no complications usually requires a person to rest, take oral antibiotics, and be on a liquid diet for a period of time. If symptoms ease after a few days, the health care provider will recommend gradually adding solid foods back into the diet.

Severe cases of diverticulitis with acute pain and complications will likely require a hospital stay. Most cases of severe diverticulitis are treated with intravenous (IV) antibiotics and a few days without food or drink to help the colon rest. If the period without food or drink is longer, the person may be given parenteral nutrition—a method of providing an IV liquid food mixture through a special tube in the chest. The mixture contains proteins, carbohydrates, fats, vitamins, and minerals.

What are the complications of diverticulitis and how are they treated?

Diverticulitis can attack suddenly and cause complications, such as

- an abscess—a painful, swollen, pus-filled area just outside the colon wall—caused by infection

- a perforation—a small tear or hole in the diverticula

- peritonitis—inflammation of tissues inside the abdomen from pus and stool that leak through a perforation

- a fistula—an abnormal passage, or tunnel, between two organs, or between an organ and the outside of the body

- intestinal obstruction—partial or total blockage of movement of food or stool through the intestines

These complications need to be treated to prevent them from getting worse and causing serious illness. In some cases, surgery may be needed.

Abscess, perforation, and peritonitis. Antibiotic treatment of diverticulitis usually prevents or treats an abscess. If the abscess is large or does not clear up with antibiotics, it may need to be drained. After giving the person numbing medication, a radiologist inserts a needle through the skin to the abscess and then drains the fluid through a catheter. The procedure is usually guided by an abdominal ultrasound or a CT scan. Ultrasound uses a device, called a transducer, that bounces safe, painless sound waves off organs to create an image of their structure.

A person with a perforation usually needs surgery to repair the tear or hole. Sometimes, a person needs surgery to remove a small part of the intestine if the perforation cannot be repaired.

A person with peritonitis may be extremely ill, with nausea, vomiting, fever, and severe abdominal tenderness. This condition requires immediate surgery to clean the abdominal cavity and possibly a colon resection at a later date after a course of antibiotics. A blood transfusion may be needed if the person has lost a significant amount of blood. Without prompt treatment, peritonitis can be fatal.

Fistula. Diverticulitis-related infection may lead to one or more fistulas. Fistulas usually form between the colon and the bladder, small intestine, or skin. The most common type of fistula occurs between the colon and the bladder. Fistulas can be corrected with a colon resection and removal of the fistula.

Intestinal obstruction. Diverticulitis-related inflammation or scarring caused by past inflammation may lead to intestinal obstruction. If the intestine is completely blocked, emergency surgery is necessary, with possible colon resection. Partial blockage is not an emergency, so the surgery or other procedures to correct it can be scheduled.

When urgent surgery with colon resection is necessary for diverticulitis, two procedures may be needed because it is not safe to rejoin the colon right away. During the colon resection, the surgeon performs a temporary colostomy, creating an opening, or stoma, in the abdomen. The end of the colon is connected to the opening to allow normal eating while healing occurs. Stool is collected in a pouch attached to the stoma on the abdominal wall. In the second surgery, several months later, the surgeon rejoins the ends of the colon and closes the stoma.

Eating, Diet, and Nutrition

The *Dietary Guidelines for Americans*, 2010, recommends a dietary fiber intake of 14 grams per 1,000 calories consumed. For instance, for a 2,000-calorie diet, the fiber recommendation is 28 grams per day. The amount of fiber in a food is listed on the food's nutrition facts label. Some of the best sources of fiber include fruits; vegetables, particularly starchy ones; and whole grains. A health care provider or dietitian can help a person learn how to add more high-fiber foods into the diet.

Scientists now believe that people with diverticular disease do not need to eliminate certain foods from their diet. In the past, health care providers recommended that people with diverticular disease avoid

Table 23.1. Fiber-rich Foods

Beans, cereals, and breads	Amount of fiber
1/2 cup of navy beans	9.5 grams
1/2 cup of kidney beans	8.2 grams
1/2 cup of black beans	7.5 grams
Whole-grain cereal, cold	
1/2 cup of All-Bran	9.6 grams
3/4 cup of Total	2.4 grams
3/4 cup of Post Bran Flakes	5.3 grams
1 packet of whole-grain cereal, hot (oatmeal, Wheatena)	3.0 grams
1 whole-wheat English muffin	4.4 grams
Fruits	
1 medium apple, with skin	3.3 grams
1 medium pear, with skin	4.3 grams
1/2 cup of raspberries	4.0 grams
1/2 cup of stewed prunes	3.8 grams
Vegetables	
1/2 cup of winter squash	2.9 grams
1 medium sweet potato, with skin	4.8 grams
1/2 cup of green peas	4.4 grams
1 medium potato, with skin	3.8 grams
1/2 cup of mixed vegetables	4.0 grams
1 cup of cauliflower	2.5 grams
1/2 cup of spinach	3.5 grams
1/2 cup of turnip greens	2.5 grams

Source: U.S. Department of Agriculture and U.S. Department of Health and Human Services, Dietary Guidelines for Americans, *2010.*

nuts, popcorn, and sunflower, pumpkin, caraway, and sesame seeds because they thought food particles could enter, block, or irritate the diverticula. However, recent data suggest that these foods are not harmful. The seeds in tomatoes, zucchini, cucumbers, strawberries, and raspberries, as well as poppy seeds, are also fine to eat. Nonetheless, people with diverticular disease may differ in the amounts and types of foods that worsen their symptoms.

Chapter 24

Colon Polyps

Definition and Facts

What are colon polyps?

Colon polyps are growths on the lining of your colon and rectum. You can have more than one colon polyp.

Are colon polyps cancerous?

Colon and rectal cancer most often begins as polyps. Over time, some polyps can become cancerous. Removing polyps can help prevent cancer of the colon and rectum. Colon cancer is one the most common causes of death from cancer.

Who is more likely to develop colon polyps?

Everyone has a chance of developing colon polyps and colon cancer. However, some people are more likely to develop then than others. You may have a greater chance of developing polyps if

- someone in your family has had polyps or cancer of the colon or rectum

Text in this chapter is excerpted from "Colon Polyps," National Institute of Diabetes and Digestive and Kidney Diseases (NIDDK), November 13, 2014.

- you have inflammatory bowel disease such as ulcerative colitis and Crohn's disease

- you weigh too much or smoke cigarettes

When should I start colon polyp screening?

Screening is testing for diseases when you have no symptoms. Finding and removing polyps can help prevent cancer of the colon or rectum. Your doctor will recommend screening for colon and rectal cancer at age 50 if you don't have health problems or other factors that make you more likely to develop colorectal cancer.2

If you are at higher risk for colorectal cancer, your doctor may recommend screening at a younger age, and you may need to be tested more often.

If you are older than 75, talk with your doctor about whether you should be screened.

Symptoms and Causes

What are the symptoms of colon polyps?

Most people with colon polyps don't have symptoms, so you can't tell that you don't have polyps because you feel well. When colon polyps do cause symptoms, you may

- have bleeding from your rectum. You might notice blood on your underwear or on toilet paper after you've had a bowel movement.

- have blood in your stool. Blood can make stool look black, or blood can show up as red streaks in your stool.

- feel tired because you have anemia and a lack of iron in your body. Bleeding from colon polyps can lead to anemia and a lack of iron.

Many other problems can cause these symptoms. If you have bleeding from your rectum or blood in your stool, you should contact your doctor right away.

What causes colon polyps?

Experts aren't sure what causes colon polyps. However, research suggests that certain factors, such as age and family history can increase your chances of developing colon polyps.

Diagnosis

How does a doctor diagnose colon polyps?

Your doctor can only find colon polyps by using certain tests or procedures. Your doctor may also find polyps while testing you for other problems.

Medical and family history

Taking a medical and family history may help a doctor determine which test is best for you.

Physical exam

After taking a medical and family history, your doctor will perform a physical exam to help determine what testing is best for you.

Stool test

A stool test is the analysis of a sample stool.

Your doctor will give you a test kit and instructions for taking a sample at home. For some tests, you may need to change your diet for a few days before the test. You will receive instructions on where to send or take the kit for analysis.

Flexible sigmoidoscopy

Flexible sigmoidoscopy is a procedure that uses a flexible, narrow tube with a light and tiny camera (called a sigmoidoscope) on one end to look inside your rectum and lower colon.

The procedure can show irritated or swollen tissue, ulcers, and polyps. During the procedure, the doctor can take a biopsy. You won't feel the biopsy.

Colonoscopy

Colonoscopy is a procedure that uses a long, flexible, narrow tube with a light and tiny camera on one end to look inside your rectum and colon (called a colonoscope).

Colonoscopy can show irritated or swollen tissue, ulcers, polyps, and cancer. A trained specialist performs this procedure. The colonoscope has a tool that can remove polyps. A trained specialist typically removes polyps that he or she finds during colonoscopy. A pathologist will check the polyps for cancer.

Virtual colonoscopy

Virtual colonoscopy uses computerized tomography (CT) to look inside your rectum and colon. CT machines use a combination of X-rays and computer technology to create images. Virtual colonoscopy can show irritated or swollen tissue, ulcers, and polyps. Doctors can't remove polyps during virtual colonoscopy. If virtual colonoscopy shows a polyp, doctors will most often recommend a colonoscopy to confirm the diagnosis and remove the polyp.

Lower gastrointestinal (GI) series

A lower GI series is an X-ray that doctors use to look at your large intestine. For the procedure, you'll be asked to lie on a table while a health care professional inserts a flexible tube into your anus. Next, the health care professional fills your large intestine with barium, which makes polyps show up more clearly on X-rays. Doctors most often use lower GI series in combination with flexible sigmoidoscopy, because flexible sigmoidoscopy doesn't examine the entire colon.

Treatment

How do doctors treat colon polyps?

Doctors treat colon polyps by removing them.

In most cases, the doctor uses special tools to remove colon polyps during colonoscopy or flexible sigmoidoscopy. During some procedures, doctors may use a special method they call endoscopic mucosal resection to remove some larger polyps. In endoscopic mucosal resection, doctors inject a solution underneath the polyp or apply suction to lift the polyp away from the healthy colon tissue. Doctors then remove the polyp. After the doctor removes polyps, he or she sends them for testing. A pathologist will check the polyps for cancer. Doctors can remove almost all polyps without surgery.

If you have colon polyps, your doctor will ask you to have regular testing in the future because you have a higher chance of developing more polyps.

Seek Care Right Away

If you have any of the following symptoms after the removal of a colon polyp, you should call your doctor right away.

- severe pain in your abdomen
- fever
- bloody bowel movements that do not improve
- bleeding from your anus that does not stop

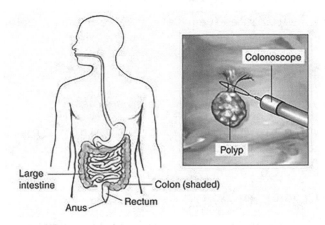

Figure 24.1. *Colon Polyps*

- dizziness
- weakness

How can I prevent colon polyps?

Researchers don't know of a sure way to prevent colon polyps. However, you can take steps to lower your chances of developing colon polyps.

Eating, diet, and nutrition

Eating, diet, and nutrition changes—such as eating more fruits, vegetables, and foods with vitamin D—may lower your chances of developing colon polyps.

Healthy lifestyle choices

You can make the following healthy lifestyle choices to help lower changes of colon polyps:

- exercise most days of the week
- don't smoke cigarettes, and if you smoke, quit smoking avoid drinking alcohol
- loose weight if you are overweight

Aspirin

Taking a low dose of aspirin every day might help prevent polyps. However, taking aspirin daily may cause side effects, such as bleeding in your stomach or intestines. Talk with your doctor before starting to take aspirin daily.

Eating, Diet, and Nutrition

What type of diet is best to prevent colon polyps?

Research suggests that the following changes may have health benefits and may lower your chances of developing colon polyps:

- eating more fruits and vegetables
- losing weight if you're overweight

Some research suggests that getting more calcium and vitamin D may lower your chances of developing polyps. Some foods rich in calcium are

- milk
- cheese
- yogurt
- broccoli

Foods that contain vitamin D include

- eggs
- liver
- certain kinds of fish, such as salmon

Some companies add vitamin D to their milk and milk products. Also, being outside in the sunlight helps your body make vitamin D. You can also talk with your doctor about taking calcium or vitamin D supplements. For safety reasons, talk with your doctor before using dietary supplements or any other nonmainstream medicine together with or in place of the treatment your doctor prescribes.

What should I avoid eating to prevent colon polyps?

Research suggests that eating less of the following foods may have health benefits and may lower your chances of developing polyps:

- fatty food
- red meat, such as beef and pork
- processed meat, such as bacon, sausage, hot dogs, and lunch meats

Chapter 25

Congenital and Pediatric Disorders of the Lower Gastrointestinal (GI) Tract

Chapter Contents

Section 25.1

Hirschsprung Disease

Text in this section is excerpted from "Hirschsprung disease,"
Genetics Home Reference (GHR), November 2, 2015.

What is Hirschsprung disease?

Hirschsprung disease is an intestinal disorder characterized by the absence of nerves in parts of the intestine. This condition occurs when the nerves in the intestine (enteric nerves) do not form properly during development before birth (embryonic development). This condition is usually identified in the first two months of life, although less severe cases may be diagnosed later in childhood.

Enteric nerves trigger the muscle contractions that move stool through the intestine. Without these nerves in parts of the intestine, the material cannot be pushed through, causing severe constipation or complete blockage of the intestine in people with Hirschsprung disease. Other signs and symptoms of this condition include vomiting, abdominal pain or swelling, diarrhea, poor feeding, malnutrition, and slow growth. People with this disorder are at risk of developing more serious conditions such as inflammation of the intestine (enterocolitis) or a hole in the wall of the intestine (intestinal perforation), which can cause serious infection and may be fatal.

There are two main types of Hirschsprung disease, known as short-segment disease and long-segment disease, which are defined by the region of the intestine lacking nerve cells. In short-segment disease, nerve cells are missing from only the last segment of the large intestine. This type is most common, occurring in approximately 80 percent of people with Hirschsprung disease. For unknown reasons, short-segment disease is four times more common in men than in women. Long-segment disease occurs when nerve cells are missing from most of the large intestine and is the more severe type. Long-segment disease is found in approximately 20 percent of people with Hirschsprung disease and affects men and women equally. Very rarely, nerve cells are missing from the entire large intestine and sometimes part of the small intestine (total colonic aganglionosis) or from all of the large and small intestine (total intestinal aganglionosis).

346

Hirschsprung disease can occur in combination with other conditions, such as Waardenburg syndrome, type IV; Mowat-Wilson syndrome; or congenital central hypoventilation syndrome. These cases are described as syndromic. Hirschsprung disease can also occur without other conditions, and these cases are referred to as isolated or nonsyndromic.

How common is Hirschsprung disease?

Hirschsprung disease occurs in approximately 1 in 5,000 newborns.

How do people inherit Hirschsprung disease?

Approximately 20 percent of cases of Hirschsprung disease occur in multiple members of the same family. The remainder of cases occur in people with no history of the disorder in their families.

Hirschsprung disease appears to have a dominant pattern of inheritance, which means one copy of the altered gene in each cell may be sufficient to cause the disorder. The inheritance is considered to have incomplete penetrance because not everyone who inherits the altered gene from a parent develops Hirschsprung disease.

What other names do people use for Hirschsprung disease?

- aganglionic megacolon
- congenital intestinal aganglionosis
- congenital megacolon
- Hirschsprung's disease
- HSCR

Section 25.2

Gastroschisis

Text in this section is excerpted from "Facts about Gastroschisis,"
Centers for Disease Control and Prevention (CDC), October 20, 2014.

Facts about Gastroschisis

Gastroschisis is a birth defect of the abdominal wall. The baby's
intestines stick outside of the baby's body, through a hole beside the
belly button.

What is Gastroschisis?

Gastroschisis is a birth defect of the abdominal (belly) wall. The
baby's intestines stick outside of the baby's body, through a hole beside
the belly button. The hole can be small or large and sometimes other
organs, such as the stomach and liver, can also stick outside of the
baby's body.

Gastroschisis occurs early during pregnancy when the muscles that
make up the baby's abdominal wall do not form correctly. A hole occurs
which allows the intestines and other organs to extend outside of the
body, usually to the right side of belly button. Because the intestines
are not covered in a protective sac and are exposed to the amniotic fluid,
the bowel can become irritated, causing it to shorten, twist, or swell.

Other Problems

Soon after the baby is born, surgery will be needed to place the
abdominal organs inside the baby's body and repair the abdominal
wall. Even after the repair, infants with gastroschisis can have problems with feeding, digestion of food, and absorption of nutrients.

Occurrence

The Centers for Disease Control and Prevention (CDC) estimates
that about 1,871 babies are born each year in the United States with
gastroschisis.

Causes and Risk Factors

The causes of gastroschisis among most infants are unknown. Some babies have gastroschisis because of a change in their genes or chromosomes. Gastroschisis might also be caused by a combination of genes and other factors, such as the things the mother comes in contact with in the environment or what the mother eats or drinks, or certain medicines she uses during pregnancy.

Like many families affected by birth defects, CDC wants to find out what causes them. Understanding factors that can increase the chance of having a baby with birth defects will help us learn more about the causes. We are currently working on one of the largest U.S. studies to understand the causes and risk factors for birth defects called the National Birth Defects Prevention Study. This study is looking at many possible risk factors for birth defects, like gastroschisis.

Recently, CDC researchers have reported important findings about some factors that affect the risk of having a baby with gastroschisis:

- Younger age: teenage mothers were more likely to have a baby with gastroschisis than older mothers, and White teenagers had higher rates than Black or African-American teenagers.

- Alcohol and tobacco: women who consumed alcohol or were a smoker were more likely to have a baby with gastroschisis.

CDC continues to study birth defects like gastroschisis in order to learn how to prevent them. If you are pregnant or thinking about getting pregnant, talk with your doctor about ways to increase your chance of having a healthy baby.

Diagnosis

Gastroschisis can be diagnosed during pregnancy or after the baby is born.

During Pregnancy

During pregnancy, there are screening tests (prenatal tests) to check for birth defects and other conditions. Gastroschisis might result in an abnormal result on a blood or serum screening test or it might be seen during an ultrasound (which creates pictures of the body).

After the Baby is Born

Gastroschisis is immediately seen at birth.

Treatments

Soon after the baby is born, surgery will be needed to place the abdominal organs inside the baby's body and repair the defect.

If the gastroschisis defect is small (only some of the intestine is outside of the belly), it is usually treated with surgery soon after birth to put the organs back into the belly and close the opening. If the gastroschisis defect is large (many organs outside of the belly), the repair might done slowly, in stages. The exposed organs might be covered with a special material and slowly moved back into the belly. After all of the organs have been put back in the belly, the opening is closed.

Babies with gastroschisis often need other treatments as well, including receiving nutrients through an IV line, antibiotics to prevent infection, and careful attention to control their body temperature.

Section 25.3

Omphalocele

Text in this section is excerpted from "Facts about Omphalocele," Centers for Disease Control and Prevention (CDC), September 14, 2015.

Facts about Omphalocele

Omphalocele is a birth defect of the abdominal (belly) wall. The infant's intestines, liver, or other organs stick outside of the belly through the belly button. The organs are covered in a thin, nearly transparent sac that hardly ever is open or broken.

What is Omphalocele?

Omphalocele, also known as exomphalos, is a birth defect of the abdominal (belly) wall. The infant's intestines, liver, or other organs stick outside of the belly through the belly button. The organs are covered in a thin, nearly transparent sac that hardly ever is open or broken.

As the baby develops during weeks six through ten of pregnancy, the intestines get longer and push out from the belly into the umbilical cord. By the eleventh week of pregnancy, the intestines normally go back into the belly. If this does not happen, an omphalocele occurs. The omphalocele can be small, with only some of the intestines outside of the belly, or it can be large, with many organs outside of the belly.

Other Problems

Because some or all of the abdominal (belly) organs are outside of the body, babies born with an omphalocele can have other problems. The abdominal cavity, the space in the body that holds these organs, might not grow to its normal size. Also, infection is a concern, especially if the sac around the organs is broken. Sometimes, an organ might become pinched or twisted, and loss of blood flow might damage the organ.

Occurrence

The Centers for Disease Control and Prevention (CDC) estimates that each year about 775 babies in the United States are born with an omphalocele. In other words, about 1 out of every 5,386 babies born in the United States each year is born with an omphalocele. Many babies born with an omphalocele also have other birth defects, such as heart defects, neural tube defects, and chromosomal abnormalities.

Causes and Risk Factors

Like many families affected by birth defects, we at CDC want to find out what causes them. Understanding factors that can increase the chance of having a baby with a birth defect will help us learn more about the causes. Currently, we are working on one of the largest U.S. studies-the National Birth Defects Prevention Study-to understand the causes of and risk factors for birth defects. This study is looking at many possible risk factors for birth defects, such as omphalocele.

Recently, CDC researchers have reported important findings about some factors that can affect the risk of having a baby with an omphalocele:

- Alcohol and tobacco: Women who consumed alcohol or were heavy smokers (more than 1 pack a day) were more likely to have a baby with omphalocele.

- Certain medications: Women who used selective serotonin-reuptake inhibitors (SSRIs) during pregnancy were more likely to have a baby with an omphalocele.

- Obesity: Women who were obese or overweight before pregnancy were more likely to have a baby with an omphalocele.

CDC continues to study birth defects such as omphaloceles and how to prevent them. If you consume alcohol or smoke cigarettes, take medications, or are obese, and you are pregnant or thinking about getting pregnant, talk with your doctor about ways to increase your chances of having a healthy baby.

Diagnosis

An omphalocele can be diagnosed during pregnancy or after a baby is born.

During Pregnancy

During pregnancy, there are screening tests (prenatal tests) to check for birth defects and other conditions. An omphalocele might result in an abnormal result on a blood or serum screening test or it might be seen during an ultrasound (which creates pictures of the baby).

After a Baby Is Born

In some cases, an omphalocele might not be diagnosed until after a baby is born. An omphalocele is seen immediately at birth.

Treatments

Treatment for infants with an omphalocele depends on a number of factors, including

- the size of the omphalocele,

- the presence of other birth defects or chromosomal abnormalities, and

- the baby's gestational age.

If the omphalocele is small (only some of the intestine is outside of the belly), it usually is treated with surgery soon after birth to put the intestine back into the belly and close the opening. If the omphalocele is large (many organs outside of the belly), the repair might be done in stages. The exposed organs might be covered with a special material, and slowly, over time, the organs will be moved back into the belly. When all the organs have been put back in the belly, the opening is closed.

Section 25.4

Necrotizing Enterocolitis (NEC)

Text in this section is excerpted from "Necrotizing Enterocolitis
(NEC)," National Institute of Child Health and Human Development
(NICHD), July 23, 2013.

What are the symptoms of necrotizing enterocolitis (NEC)

In NEC, some of the tissue lining an infant's intestine becomes
diseased and can die. The bacteria in the infant's intestine can then
penetrate the dead or decaying intestinal tissue, infect the wall of
the intestine, and enter the bloodstream, causing systemic or bloodstream infection. The surviving tissue becomes swollen and inflamed;
as a result, the infant is unable to digest food or otherwise move food
through the digestive tract. The symptoms of NEC can develop over
a period of days or appear suddenly. Commonly reported symptoms
include:

- Poor tolerance of feeding (not being able to digest food)

- Bloating or swelling of the stomach (abdominal distention)

- Stomach discoloration, usually bluish or reddish

- Pain when someone touches the abdomen

- Blood in the stools or a change in their volume or frequency

- Diarrhea, with change in the color and consistency of the stool,
  often containing frank (visible) blood

- Decreased activity (lethargy)

- Vomiting greenish-yellow liquid

- Inability to maintain normal temperature

- Episodes of low heart rate or apnea, a temporary stop in
  breathing

- In advanced cases, the blood pressure may drop and the pulse
  may become weak. Infants may develop fluid in the abdominal

cavity or infection of the tissue lining the stomach (a condition called peritonitis), or they could go into shock. The affected area of the intestine may develop a hole or perforation in the wall requiring emergency surgery. Pressure from the abdomen can cause a severe difficulty in breathing. In this case, the infant may need support from a breathing machine, or respirator.

How do health care providers diagnose necrotizing enterocolitis (NEC)?

The development of symptoms such as the inability to tolerate feeding, bloody stools, or distention of the abdomen could indicate NEC. The condition is usually confirmed by an abdominal X-ray. If the X-ray reveals a "bubbly" appearance in the wall of the intestine or air outside the infant's intestine (in the peritoneal cavity) the diagnosis is confirmed. Other X-ray signs include air in a vein of the liver called the portal vein, swollen intestines, or a lack of gas in the abdomen.

Other useful tests include looking for blood in the infant's stool. If necessary, the health care provider can use a chemical that reveals blood not visible to the eye.

In addition, health care providers may test the infant's blood to check for infection, which could suggest NEC. They may also use a blood test for lactic acid, which can indicate whether the body is getting enough oxygen or an infection that increases the metabolic rate and production of lactic acid.

Blood and stool tests, combined with the abdominal X-ray, can help the health care provider determine the seriousness of the infant's condition.

What are the common treatments for necrotizing enterocolitis (NEC)?

The treatment for NEC varies with the severity of the disease. Three stages (Bell stages) have been defined for NEC.

Stage 1, suspected NEC, includes symptoms such as bloody stools, diminished activity (lethargy), slow heart rate, an unstable temperature, mild abdominal bloating, and vomiting.

Stage 2, definite NEC, includes all the symptoms of stage 1 as well as slightly reduced blood platelet levels, a slight excess of lactic acid, no bowel sounds, pain when the abdomen is touched, reduced or no intestinal movement, and the growth of gas-filled spaces in the walls of the intestine.

Stage 3, advanced NEC, includes the symptoms of stages 1 and 2 plus periods of not breathing, low blood pressure, a lowered number of certain white blood cells, blood clot formation, a stop in urination, inflammation of tissue in the abdomen, increased pain when the abdomen is touched, redness in the abdomen, a build-up of fluid and gas in the abdominal cavity, and excess acid.

The treatment for stage 1 patients includes vigorous supportive care, resting the intestine by feeding through an intravenous tube instead of the mouth, and continued diagnostic and monitoring tests to ensure that the disease is not progressing. Treatments for stage 2 patients include continuation of stage 1 treatments and the use of antibiotics. Emergency surgery is sometimes performed for stage 3 patients.

Other treatments offered at all stages of NEC include:

- Inserting a tube through the nasal passages or mouth into the infant's stomach to remove air and fluid

- Taking blood samples to look for bacteria and giving antibiotic treatment through an intravenous tube

- Measuring and monitoring the infant's belly for swelling. If it becomes so swollen that it interferes with breathing, the infant may be given oxygen or put on a ventilator.

Many infants respond to treatment within 72 hours, and physicians may decide to put these infants back on regular feeding. (Generally, infants are not fed for up to 2 weeks or longer with confirmed NEC.) However, if the condition worsens or a hole develops in the intestine or bowel, surgery may be needed.

What causes necrotizing enterocolitis (NEC)?

The cause of NEC is not well known. In premature infants, the cause may be related to the immaturity of the child's digestive system. NEC involves infection and inflammation in the child's gut, which may stem from the growth of dangerous bacteria or the growth of bacteria in parts of the intestine where they do not usually live.

Other possible causes of NEC that are related to having an immature gut include:

- Inability to digest food and pass it through, allowing a buildup of toxic substances

- Inadequate blood circulation to the gut

- Inability of the infant's digestive system to keep out dangerous bacteria

- Inadequate ability of the immature intestine to provide an adequate structural barrier to bacteria. This barrier usually matures in the unborn infant starting about week 26 (11 to 12 weeks before a full-term birth).

- The inability of the immature gut to secrete its normal biochemical defenses

Because premature infants may lack any or all of these abilities, they may be more vulnerable to the types of inflammation that lead to NEC.

Full-term infants who get NEC almost always do so because they are already sick or, in some cases, have a low body weight for their gestational age. They might have congenital heart disease or have had vascular bypass surgery, for example, possibly affecting the blood supply to the intestines.

Full-term infants are usually diagnosed with NEC earlier than are premature infants (day 5 versus day 13 on average), possibly because they start feeding earlier. The condition is equally life threatening in premature and full-term infants.

A recent NICHD-supported study found that a common type of medication, sometimes given to infants for acid reflux and called "H2-blockers," was associated with a slight increase in the risk of NEC in preterm infants.

Other FAQs

How can NEC be prevented?

The most definitive step toward preventing NEC is to prevent preterm birth. However, some experts believe that the following steps have been shown to reduce the risk for NEC among those who are born preterm.

- **Early feeding with colostrum/human milk.** Because the colostrum and mother's milk contain many protective elements, even small quantities of a baby's mother's colostrum or early breast milk may have some protective effect.

- **Avoiding gut starvation.** Health care teams are mindful that feeding practices contribute to infant health. If an infant is very ill, they may need to withhold feedings because digestion is difficult. However, prolonged starvation is a risk factor for NEC, and therefore, early, small amounts of feeding are considered protective.

- **Some reports indicate that prophylactic use of probiotics can help prevent NEC.** However, no definitive studies have been conducted in the United States on probiotic use, and thus far, probiotics are not approved for use in sick newborn infants.

Are there disorders or conditions associated with NEC?

In full-term infants more often than in preterm infants, NEC is associated with congenital heart disease. Some researchers consider this type of NEC to be different from other types because infants who have NEC along with congenital heart disease have less of a chance of developing a hole in their intestine, which would require surgery. Thus the name "cardiogenic NEC," or NEC that stems from heart problems, has been suggested for this disease.

Other conditions that can predispose a full-term infant to NEC include severe asphyxia (lack of oxygen) suffered before, during, or immediately after birth and a condition known as polycythemia, in which the infant has higher than normal amount of red blood cells expressed as "hematocrit." Healthy infants have a hematocrit value between 45% and 65%. In infants with polycythemia, the hematocrit value is higher than 65%. Bursting of the intestine, which leads to a hole in its wall (called a perforation), as a result of infection and local tissue damage is the most serious complication of NEC. Removing the severely damaged or dead segment of the intestine is a major surgical procedure. Surgeons will hook the cut ends of the intestines to the abdominal wall, also known as an ostomy, until all signs of intestinal infection are healed. Later, in a second surgical procedure, the intestines are reconnected.

Areas of the intestine that were damaged from NEC may develop scar tissue, known as stricture. This can cause the intestine to narrow, making it difficult for bowel contents to pass through. Dilation or surgery of the intestine may be necessary.

A serious residual complication of removing dead and damaged intestine is called "short-gut syndrome." This syndrome causes problems with digestion if long portions of the small intestine that absorb nutrition have been removed. As the child gets older (over a span of 2 to 3 years), this digestive problem may improve. If it does not, it can cause under-nutrition, requiring prolonged nutritional support using intravenous routes. The latter can lead to liver failure. If the digestive problems do not resolve, infants with this complication may need a liver transplant and/or a small-bowel transplant.

Other possible complications of NEC include:

- Partial or complete blockage of the intestine due to abnormal tissue growth or scar tissue.

- Infection of the tissue lining the stomach (called peritonitis)

- Sepsis, a severe reaction of the child's body to infection.

Chapter 26

Hemorrhoids

What are hemorrhoids?

Hemorrhoids are swollen and inflamed veins around the anus or in the lower rectum. The rectum is the last part of the large intestine leading to the anus. The anus is the opening at the end of the digestive tract where bowel contents leave the body.

External hemorrhoids are located under the skin around the anus. Internal hemorrhoids develop in the lower rectum. Internal hemorrhoids may protrude, or prolapse, through the anus. Most prolapsed hemorrhoids shrink back inside the rectum on their own. Severely prolapsed hemorrhoids may protrude permanently and require treatment.

What are the symptoms of hemorrhoids?

The most common symptom of internal hemorrhoids is bright red blood on stool, on toilet paper, or in the toilet bowl after a bowel movement. Internal hemorrhoids that are not prolapsed are usually not painful. Prolapsed hemorrhoids often cause pain, discomfort, and anal itching.

Blood clots may form in external hemorrhoids. A blood clot in a vein is called a thrombosis. Thrombosed external hemorrhoids cause bleeding, painful swelling, or a hard lump around the anus. When the

Text in this chapter is excerpted from "Hemorrhoids," National Institute of Diabetes and Digestive and Kidney Diseases (NIDDK), November 27, 2013.

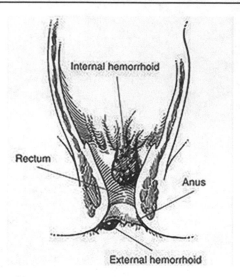

Figure 26.1. *Hemorrhoids*

blood clot dissolves, extra skin is left behind. This skin can become irritated or itch.

Excessive straining, rubbing, or cleaning around the anus may make symptoms, such as itching and irritation, worse.

Hemorrhoids are not dangerous or life threatening. Symptoms usually go away within a few days, and some people with hemorrhoids never have symptoms.

How common are hemorrhoids?

About 75 percent of people will have hemorrhoids at some point in their lives. Hemorrhoids are most common among adults ages 45 to 65. Hemorrhoids are also common in pregnant women.

What causes hemorrhoids?

Swelling in the anal or rectal veins causes hemorrhoids. Several factors may cause this swelling, including

- chronic constipation or diarrhea
- straining during bowel movements
- sitting on the toilet for long periods of time
- a lack of fiber in the diet

Another cause of hemorrhoids is the weakening of the connective tissue in the rectum and anus that occurs with age.

Pregnancy can cause hemorrhoids by increasing pressure in the abdomen, which may enlarge the veins in the lower rectum and anus. For most women, hemorrhoids caused by pregnancy disappear after childbirth.

How are hemorrhoids diagnosed?

The doctor will examine the anus and rectum to determine whether a person has hemorrhoids. Hemorrhoid symptoms are similar to the symptoms of other anorectal problems, such as fissures, abscesses, warts, and polyps.

The doctor will perform a physical exam to look for visible hemorrhoids. A digital rectal exam with a gloved, lubricated finger and an anoscope—a hollow, lighted tube—may be performed to view the rectum.

A thorough evaluation and proper diagnosis by a doctor is important any time a person notices bleeding from the rectum or blood in the stool. Bleeding may be a symptom of other digestive diseases, including colorectal cancer.

Additional exams may be done to rule out other causes of bleeding, especially in people age 40 or older:

- **Colonoscopy.** A flexible, lighted tube called a colonoscope is inserted through the anus, the rectum, and the upper part of the large intestine, called the colon. The colonoscope transmits images of the inside of the rectum and the entire colon.

- **Sigmoidoscopy.** This procedure is similar to colonoscopy, but it uses a shorter tube called a sigmoidoscope and transmits images of the rectum and the sigmoid colon, the lower portion of the colon that empties into the rectum.

- **Barium enema X-ray.** A contrast material called barium is inserted into the colon to make the colon more visible in X-ray pictures.

How are hemorrhoids treated?

At-home Treatments

Simple diet and lifestyle changes often reduce the swelling of hemorrhoids and relieve hemorrhoid symptoms. Eating a high-fiber diet can make stools softer and easier to pass, reducing the pressure on hemorrhoids caused by straining.

Fiber is a substance found in plants. The human body cannot digest fiber, but fiber helps improve digestion and prevent constipation. Good sources of dietary fiber are fruits, vegetables, and whole grains. On average, Americans eat about 15 grams of fiber each day. The American Dietetic Association recommends 25 grams of fiber per day for women and 38 grams of fiber per day for men.

Doctors may also suggest taking a bulk stool softener or a fiber supplement such as psyllium (Metamucil) or methylcellulose (Citrucel).

Other changes that may help relieve hemorrhoid symptoms include

- drinking six to eight 8-ounce glasses of water or other nonalcoholic fluids each day

- sitting in a tub of warm water for 10 minutes several times a day

- exercising to prevent constipation

- not straining during bowel movements

Over-the-counter creams and suppositories may temporarily relieve the pain and itching of hemorrhoids. These treatments should only be used for a short time because long-term use can damage the skin.

Medical Treatment

If at-home treatments do not relieve symptoms, medical treatments may be needed. Outpatient treatments can be performed in a doctor's office or a hospital. Outpatient treatments for internal hemorrhoids include the following:

- **Rubber band ligation.** The doctor places a special rubber band around the base of the hemorrhoid. The band cuts off circulation, causing the hemorrhoid to shrink. This procedure should be performed only by a doctor.

- **Sclerotherapy.** The doctor injects a chemical solution into the blood vessel to shrink the hemorrhoid.

- **Infrared coagulation.** The doctor uses heat to shrink the hemorrhoid tissue.

Large external hemorrhoids or internal hemorrhoids that do not respond to other treatments can be surgically removed.

What foods have fiber?

Table 26.1. Examples of foods that have fiber

Breads, cereals, and beans	Fiber
1/2 cup of navy beans	9.5 grams
1/2 cup of kidney beans	8.2 grams
1/2 cup of black beans	7.5 grams
Whole-grain cereal, cold	
1/2 cup of All-Bran	9.6 grams
3/4 cup of Total	2.4 grams
3/4 cup of Post Bran Flakes	5.3 grams
1 packet of whole-grain cereal, hot (oatmeal, Wheatena)	3.0 grams
1 whole-wheat English muffin	4.4 grams
Fruits	
1 medium apple, with skin	3.3 grams
1 medium pear, with skin	4.3 grams
1/2 cup of raspberries	4.0 grams
1/2 cup of stewed prunes	3.8 grams
Vegetables	
1/2 cup of winter squash	2.9 grams
1 medium sweet potato with skin	4.8 grams
1/2 cup of green peas	4.4 grams
1 medium potato with skin	3.8 grams
1/2 cup of mixed vegetables	4.0 grams
1 cup of cauliflower	2.5 grams
1/2 cup of spinach	3.5 grams
1/2 cup of turnip greens	2.5 grams

Source: U.S. Department of Agriculture and U.S. Department of Health and Human Services, Dietary Guidelines for Americans, *2010.*

Chapter 27

Abdominal Adhesions

What are abdominal adhesions?

Abdominal adhesions are bands of fibrous tissue that can form between abdominal tissues and organs. Normally, internal tissues and organs have slippery surfaces, preventing them from sticking together as the body moves. However, abdominal adhesions cause tissues and organs in the abdominal cavity to stick together.

What is the abdominal cavity?

The abdominal cavity is the internal area of the body between the chest and hips that contains the lower part of the esophagus, stomach, small intestine, and large intestine. The esophagus carries food and liquids from the mouth to the stomach, which slowly pumps them into the small and large intestines. Abdominal adhesions can kink, twist, or pull the small and large intestines out of place, causing an intestinal obstruction. Intestinal obstruction, also called a bowel obstruction, results in the partial or complete blockage of movement of food or stool through the intestines.

What causes abdominal adhesions?

Abdominal surgery is the most frequent cause of abdominal adhesions. Surgery-related causes include

---

Text in this section is excerpted from "Abdominal Adhesions," National Institute of Diabetes and Digestive and Kidney Diseases (NIDDK), September 2013.

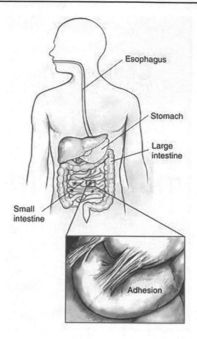

Figure 27.1. *Abdominal adhesions*

Abdominal adhesions are bands of fibrous tissue that can form between abdominal tissues and organs.

- cuts involving internal organs
- handling of internal organs
- drying out of internal organs and tissues
- contact of internal tissues with foreign materials, such as gauze, surgical gloves, and stitches
- blood or blood clots that were not rinsed away during surgery

Abdominal adhesions can also result from inflammation not related to surgery, including

- appendix rupture
- radiation treatment
- gynecological infections
- abdominal infections

Rarely, abdominal adhesions form without apparent cause.

How common are abdominal adhesions and who is at risk?

Of patients who undergo abdominal surgery, 93 percent develop abdominal adhesions. Surgery in the lower abdomen and pelvis, including bowel and gynecological operations, carries an even greater chance of abdominal adhesions. Abdominal adhesions can become larger and tighter as time passes, sometimes causing problems years after surgery.

What are the symptoms of abdominal adhesions?

In most cases, abdominal adhesions do not cause symptoms. When symptoms are present, chronic abdominal pain is the most common.

What are the complications of abdominal adhesions?

Abdominal adhesions can cause intestinal obstruction and female infertility—the inability to become pregnant after a year of trying.

Abdominal adhesions can lead to female infertility by preventing fertilized eggs from reaching the uterus, where fetal development takes place. Women with abdominal adhesions in or around their fallopian tubes have an increased chance of ectopic pregnancy—a fertilized egg growing outside the uterus. Abdominal adhesions inside the uterus may result in repeated miscarriages—a pregnancy failure before 20 weeks.

Seek Help for Emergency Symptoms

A complete intestinal obstruction is life threatening and requires immediate medical attention and often surgery. Symptoms of an intestinal obstruction include:

- severe abdominal pain or cramping
- nausea
- vomiting
- bloating
- loud bowel sounds
- abdominal swelling
- the inability to have a bowel movement or pass gas

- constipation—a condition in which a person has fewer than three bowel movements a week; the bowel movements may be painful

A person with these symptoms should seek medical attention immediately.

How are abdominal adhesions and intestinal obstructions diagnosed?

Abdominal adhesions cannot be detected by tests or seen through imaging techniques such as X-rays or ultrasound. Most abdominal adhesions are found during surgery performed to examine the abdomen. However, abdominal X-rays, a lower gastrointestinal (GI) series, and computerized tomography (CT) scans can diagnose intestinal obstructions.

- **Abdominal X-rays** use a small amount of radiation to create an image that is recorded on film or a computer. An X-ray is performed at a hospital or an outpatient center by an X-ray technician, and the images are interpreted by a radiologist—a doctor who specializes in medical imaging. An X-ray does not require anesthesia. The person will lie on a table or stand during the X-ray. The X-ray machine is positioned over the abdominal area. The person will hold his or her breath as the picture is taken so that the picture will not be blurry. The person may be asked to change position for additional pictures.

- A **lower GI series** is an X-ray exam that is used to look at the large intestine. The test is performed at a hospital or an outpatient center by an X-ray technician, and the images are interpreted by a radiologist. Anesthesia is not needed. The health care provider may provide written bowel prep instructions to follow at home before the test. The person may be asked to follow a clear liquid diet for 1 to 3 days before the procedure. A laxative or an enema may be used before the test. A laxative is medication that loosens stool and increases bowel movements. An enema involves flushing water or laxative into the rectum using a special squirt bottle.

For the test, the person will lie on a table while the radiologist inserts a flexible tube into the person's anus. The large intestine is filled with barium, making signs of underlying problems show up more clearly on X-rays.

- **CT scans** use a combination of X-rays and computer technology to create images. The procedure is performed at a hospital or an outpatient center by an X-ray technician, and the images are interpreted by a radiologist. Anesthesia is not needed. A CT scan may include the injection of a special dye, called contrast medium. The person will lie on a table that slides into a tunnel-shaped device where the X-rays are taken.

How are abdominal adhesions and intestinal obstructions treated?

Abdominal adhesions that do not cause symptoms generally do not require treatment. Surgery is the only way to treat abdominal adhesions that cause pain, intestinal obstruction, or fertility problems. More surgery, however, carries the risk of additional abdominal adhesions. People should speak with their health care provider about the best way to treat their abdominal adhesions.

Complete intestinal obstructions usually require immediate surgery to clear the blockage. Most partial intestinal obstructions can be managed without surgery.

How can abdominal adhesions be prevented?

Abdominal adhesions are difficult to prevent; however, certain surgical techniques can minimize abdominal adhesions.

Laparoscopic surgery decreases the potential for abdominal adhesions because several tiny incisions are made in the lower abdomen instead of one large incision. The surgeon inserts a laparoscope—a thin tube with a tiny video camera attached—into one of the small incisions. The camera sends a magnified image from inside the body to a video monitor. Patients will usually receive general anesthesia during this surgery.

If laparoscopic surgery is not possible and a large abdominal incision is required, at the end of surgery a special filmlike material can be inserted between organs or between the organs and the abdominal incision. The filmlike material, which looks similar to wax paper and is absorbed by the body in about a week, hydrates organs to help prevent abdominal adhesions.

Other steps taken during surgery to reduce abdominal adhesions include

- using starch- and latex-free gloves
- handling tissues and organs gently
- shortening surgery time
- using moistened drapes and swabs
- occasionally applying saline solution

Eating, Diet, and Nutrition

Researchers have not found that eating, diet, and nutrition play a role in causing or preventing abdominal adhesions. A person with a partial intestinal obstruction may relieve symptoms with a liquid or low-fiber diet, which is more easily broken down into smaller particles by the digestive system.

Chapter 28

Proctitis

What is proctitis?

Proctitis is inflammation of the lining of the rectum, the lower end of the large intestine leading to the anus. The large intestine and anus are part of the gastrointestinal (GI) tract. The GI tract is a series of hollow organs joined in a long, twisting tube from the mouth to the anus. The movement of muscles in the GI tract, along with the release of hormones and enzymes, allows for the digestion of food. With proctitis, inflammation of the rectal lining—called the rectal mucosa—is uncomfortable and sometimes painful. The condition may lead to bleeding or mucous discharge from the rectum, among other symptoms.

What causes proctitis?

Proctitis has many causes, including acute, or sudden and short-term, and chronic, or long-lasting, conditions. Among the causes are the following:

- **Sexually transmitted diseases (STDs)**. STDs that can be passed when a person is receiving anal sex are a common cause of proctitis. Common STD infections that can cause proctitis include gonorrhea, chlamydia, syphilis, and herpes. Herpes-induced proctitis may be particularly severe in people who are also infected with the HIV virus.

Text in this chapter is excerpted from "Proctitis," National Institute of Diabetes and Digestive and Kidney Diseases (NIDDK), October 2011. Reviewed December 2015.

- **Non-STD infections.** Infections that are not sexually transmitted also can cause proctitis. *Salmonella* and *Shigella* are examples of foodborne bacteria that can cause proctitis. Streptococcal proctitis sometimes occurs in children who have strep throat.

- **Anorectal trauma.** Proctitis can be caused by trauma to the anorectal area—which includes the rectum and anus—from anal sex or the insertion of objects or harmful substances into the rectum, including the chemicals in some enemas.

- **Ulcerative colitis and Crohn's disease.** Two forms of inflammatory bowel disease (IBD)—ulcerative colitis and Crohn's disease—can cause proctitis. Ulcerative colitis causes irritation and ulcers, also called sores, in the inner lining of the colon—part of the large intestine—and rectum. Crohn's disease usually causes irritation in the lower small intestine—also called the ileum—or the colon, but it can affect any part of the GI tract.

- **Radiation therapy.** People who have had radiation therapy that targets the pelvic area also may develop proctitis. Examples of those at risk are people with rectal, ovarian, or prostate cancer who have received radiation treatment directed to those areas. Symptoms of radiation proctitis, most commonly rectal bleeding, will typically occur within 6 weeks after beginning radiation therapy or more than 9 months after its completion.

- **Antibiotics.** Use of antibiotics may be associated with proctitis in some people. While meant to kill infectioncausing bacteria, antibiotics can also kill nonharmful, or commensal, bacteria in the GI tract. The loss of commensal bacteria can then allow other harmful bacteria known as *Clostridium difficile* to cause an infection in the colon and rectum.

What are the symptoms of proctitis?

Tenesmus—an uncomfortable and frequent urge to have a bowel movement—is one of the most common symptoms of proctitis. Other symptoms may include

- bloody bowel movements
- rectal bleeding
- a feeling of rectal fullness
- anal or rectal pain

- crampy abdominal pain

- rectal discharge of mucus or pus

- diarrhea or frequent passage of loose or liquid stools

How is proctitis diagnosed?

To diagnoso prootitis, a health care provider will take a complete medical history and do a physical exam. The health care provider will ask the patient about symptoms, current and past medical conditions, family history, and sexual behavior that increases the risk of STD-induced proctitis. The physical exam will include an assessment of the patient's vital signs, an abdominal exam, and a rectal exam.

Based on the patient's physical exam, symptoms, and other medical information, the doctor will decide which lab tests and diagnostic tests are needed. Lab tests may include blood tests such as a complete blood count to evaluate for blood loss or infection, stool tests to isolate and identify bacteria that may cause disease, and an STD screening. The doctor also may use one of the following diagnostic tests:

- **Rectal culture.** A cotton swab is inserted into the rectum to obtain a sample that can be used in tests that isolate and identify organisms that may cause disease.

- **Anoscopy.** This test allows examination of the anal canal and lower rectum by opening the anus using a special instrument called an anoscope.

- **Flexible sigmoidoscopy and colonoscopy.** These tests are used to help diagnose Crohn's disease. The tests are similar, but colonoscopy is used to view the entire colon and rectum, while flexible sigmoidoscopy is used to view just the lower colon and rectum. For both tests, a health care provider will provide written bowel prep instructions to follow at home before the test. The person may be asked to follow a clear liquid diet for 1 to 3 days before the test. A laxative may be required the night before the test. One or more enemas may be required the night before and about 2 hours before the test.

For either test, the person will lie on a table while the doctor inserts a flexible tube into the anus. A small camera on the tube sends a video image of the intestinal lining to a computer screen. The doctor can see inflammation, bleeding, or ulcers on the colon wall. The doctor may also perform a biopsy by snipping a bit of tissue from the intestinal lining. The person will not feel the biopsy. The doctor will look at the tissue with a microscope to confirm the diagnosis. In most cases, a light sedative, and possibly pain medication, helps people relax during a colonoscopy.

Cramping or bloating may occur during the first hour after the test. Driving is not permitted for 24 hours after a colonoscopy to allow the sedative time to wear off. Before the appointment, a person should make plans for a ride home. Full recovery is expected by the next day.

The above diagnostic tests may be performed at a hospital or out-patient center by a gastroenterologist—a doctor who specializes in digestive diseases.

How is proctitis treated?

Treatment of proctitis depends on its cause. The goal of treatment is to reduce inflammation, control symptoms, and eliminate infection, if it is present. Only a doctor can determine the cause of proctitis and the best course of treatment. With proper medical attention, proctitis can be successfully treated.

Proctitis from Infection

If lab tests confirm that an STD or non-STD infection is present, medication is prescribed based on the type of infection found. Antibiotics are prescribed to kill bacteria; antiviral medications are prescribed to treat viruses. Although some STD viruses cannot be eliminated, antivirals can control their symptoms.

Proctitis from Other Causes

If antibiotic use triggered proctitis, the doctor may prescribe a different antibiotic designed to destroy the harmful bacteria that have developed in the intestines.

If proctitis is caused by anorectal trauma, the activity causing the inflammation should be stopped. Healing usually occurs in 4 to 6 weeks. The doctor may recommend over-the-counter medications such as antidiarrheals and those used for pain relief, such as aspirin and ibuprofen.

Treatment of radiation proctitis is based on symptoms. Radiation proctitis causing only mild symptoms such as occasional bleeding or tenesmus may heal without treatment. For people with persistent or severe bleeding, thermal therapy may be used to stop bleeding and inflammation. Thermal therapy is done during flexible sigmoidoscopy or colonoscopy and targets the rectal lining with a heat probe, electric current, or laser. Argon plasma coagulation is the most common thermal therapy used to control bleeding in radiation proctitis. In many cases, several treatments are required. Obstruction that results from a stricture—a narrowing of the rectum—caused by radiation proctitis may be treated with stool softeners in mild cases. In people with narrower strictures, dilation to enlarge the narrow area may be required. Sucralfate, 5-aminosalicylic acid—known as 5-ASA—or corticosteroid enemas can also be used to ease pain and reduce inflammation from radiation proctitis, although their effectiveness is limited.

When a chronic IBD such as ulcerative colitis or Crohn's disease causes proctitis, treatment aims to reduce inflammation, control symptoms, and induce and maintain remission—a period when the person is symptom-free. Treatment depends on the extent and severity of the disease.

Anti-inflammation medications. Mild proctitis can often be effectively treated with topical mesalamine, either suppositories or enemas.

Some people with IBD and proctitis cannot tolerate—or may have an incomplete response to—rectal therapy with 5-ASA suppositories or enemas. For these people, the doctor may prescribe oral medications alone or in combination with rectal therapy. Oral medications commonly used for proctitis contain salicylate. These include sulfasalazine- or mesalamine-containing medications, such as Asacol, Dipentum, or Pentasa. Possible side effects of oral administration of sulfasalazine- or mesalaminecontaining medications include nausea, vomiting, heartburn, diarrhea, and headache. Improvement in symptoms, including a decrease in bleeding, can occur within a few days, although complete healing requires 4 to 6 weeks of therapy.

Cortisone or steroids. These medications, also called corticosteroids, are effective at reducing inflammation. Prednisone and budesonide are generic names of two medications in this group. Corticosteroids for proctitis may be taken in pill, suppository, or enema form. When symptoms are at their worst, corticosteroids are usually prescribed in a large dose. The dosage is then gradually lowered once symptoms are controlled. Corticosteroids can cause serious side effects, including greater susceptibility to infection and osteoporosis, or weakening of the bones.

Immune system suppressors. Medications that suppress the immune system—called immunosuppressive medications—are also used to treat proctitis. The most commonly prescribed medication is 6-mercaptopurine or a related medication, azathioprine. Immunosuppressive medications work by blocking the immune reaction that contributes to inflammation. These medications may cause side effects such as nausea, vomiting, and diarrhea and may lower a person's resistance to infection. Some patients are treated with a combination of corticosteroids and immunosuppressive medications. Some studies suggest that immunosuppressive medications may enhance the effectiveness of corticosteroids.

Infliximab (Remicade). Researchers have found that high levels of a protein produced by the immune system, called tumor necrosis factor (TNF), are present in people with Crohn's disease. Infliximab is the first of a group of medications that bind to TNF substances to block the body's inflammation response. The U.S. Food and Drug Administration approved the medication for the treatment of moderate to severe Crohn's disease that does not respond to standard therapies—mesalamine substances, corticosteroids, immunosuppressive medications—and for the treatment of open, draining fistulas. The medication is also given to people who have Crohn's disease with proctitis. Some studies suggest that infliximab may enhance the effectiveness of immunosuppressive medications.

Bacterial infection can occur with flare-ups of ulcerative colitis or Crohn's disease. Antibiotics may also be used to treat flare-ups in people with IBD and proctitis.

Eating, Diet, and Nutrition

Drinking plenty of fluids is important when diarrhea or frequent passage of loose or liquid stools occurs.

Avoiding caffeine and foods that are greasy, high in fiber, or sweet may lessen diarrhea symptoms. Some people also have problems digesting lactose—the sugar found in milk and milk products—during or after a bout of diarrhea. Yogurt, which has less lactose than milk, is often better tolerated. Yogurt with active, live bacterial cultures may even help people recover from diarrhea more quickly.

If diarrhea symptoms improve, soft, bland foods can be added to the diet, including bananas, plain rice, boiled potatoes, toast, crackers, cooked carrots, and baked chicken without the skin or fat. If the diarrhea stops, a normal diet may be resumed if tolerated.

What if proctitis is not treated?

Proctitis that is not treated or does not respond to treatment may lead to complications, including

- severe bleeding and anemia—a condition in which red blood cells are fewer or smaller than normal, which means less oxygen is carried to the body's cells

- abscesses—painful, swollen, pus-filled areas caused by infection

- ulcers on the intestinal lining

- fistulas—abnormal connections between two parts inside the body

People with proctitis symptoms need medical attention. If diagnosed with proctitis, patients should take all medications as prescribed and see their doctor for a followup appointment to be sure the cause of the inflammation has been treated successfully.

Can proctitis be prevented?

People who receive anal sex can avoid getting STD-related proctitis by having their partner use a condom. If anorectal trauma caused proctitis, stopping the activity that triggered inflammation often will stop the inflammation and prevent recurrence.

Other causes of proctitis cannot always be prevented. However, their symptoms can be treated by a doctor.

Part Five

Disorders of the Digestive System's Solid Organs: The Liver and Pancreas

Chapter 29

Pancreatitis

What is pancreatitis?

Pancreatitis is inflammation of the pancreas. The pancreas is a large gland behind the stomach and close to the duodenum—the first part of the small intestine. The pancreas secretes digestive juices, or enzymes, into the duodenum through a tube called the pancreatic duct. Pancreatic enzymes join with bile—a liquid produced in the liver and stored in the gallbladder—to digest food. The pancreas also releases the hormones insulin and glucagon into the bloodstream. These hormones help the body regulate the glucose it takes from food for energy.

Normally, digestive enzymes secreted by the pancreas do not become active until they reach the small intestine. But when the pancreas is inflamed, the enzymes inside it attack and damage the tissues that produce them.

Pancreatitis can be acute or chronic. Either form is serious and can lead to complications. In severe cases, bleeding, infection, and permanent tissue damage may occur.

The gallbladder and the ducts that carry bile and other digestive enzymes from the liver, gallbladder, and pancreas to the small intestine are called the biliary system.

Both forms of pancreatitis occur more often in men than women.

Text in this chapter is excerpted from "Pancreatitis," National Institute of Diabetes and Digestive and Kidney Diseases (NIDDK), August 16, 2012.

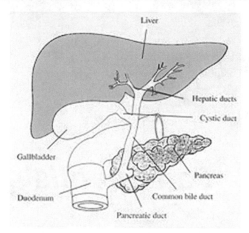

Figure 29.1. *Liver and Pancreas*

What is acute pancreatitis?

Acute pancreatitis is inflammation of the pancreas that occurs suddenly and usually resolves in a few days with treatment. Acute pancreatitis can be a life-threatening illness with severe complications. Each year, about 210,000 people in the United States are admitted to the hospital with acute pancreatitis. The most common cause of acute pancreatitis is the presence of gallstones—small, pebble-like substances made of hardened bile—that cause inflammation in the pancreas as they pass through the common bile duct. Chronic, heavy alcohol use is also a common cause. Acute pancreatitis can occur within hours or as long as 2 days after consuming alcohol. Other causes of acute pancreatitis include abdominal trauma, medications, infections, tumors, and genetic abnormalities of the pancreas.

Symptoms

Acute pancreatitis usually begins with gradual or sudden pain in the upper abdomen that sometimes extends through the back. The pain may be mild at first and feel worse after eating. But the pain is often severe and may become constant and last for several days. A person with acute pancreatitis usually looks and feels very ill and needs immediate medical attention. Other symptoms may include

- a swollen and tender abdomen

- nausea and vomiting

- fever

- a rapid pulse

Severe acute pancreatitis may cause dehydration and low blood pressure. The heart, lungs, or kidneys can fail. If bleeding occurs in the pancreas, shock and even death may follow.

Diagnosis

While asking about a person's medical history and conducting a thorough physical examination, the doctor will order a blood test to assist in the diagnosis. During acute pancreatitis, the blood contains at least three times the normal amount of amylase and lipase, digestive enzymes formed in the pancreas. Changes may also occur in other body chemicals such as glucose, calcium, magnesium, sodium, potassium, and bicarbonate. After the person's condition improves, the levels usually return to normal.

Diagnosing acute pancreatitis is often difficult because of the deep location of the pancreas. The doctor will likely order one or more of the following tests:

- Abdominal ultrasound

- Computerized tomography (CT) scan

- Endoscopic ultrasound (EUS)

- Magnetic resonance cholangiopancreatography (MRCP)

Treatment

Treatment for acute pancreatitis requires a few days' stay in the hospital for intravenous (IV) fluids, antibiotics, and medication to relieve pain. The person cannot eat or drink so the pancreas can rest. If vomiting occurs, a tube may be placed through the nose and into the stomach to remove fluid and air.

Unless complications arise, acute pancreatitis usually resolves in a few days. In severe cases, the person may require nasogastric feeding—a special liquid given in a long, thin tube inserted through the nose and throat and into the stomach—for several weeks while the pancreas heals.

Before leaving the hospital, the person will be advised not to smoke, drink alcoholic beverages, or eat fatty meals. In some cases, the cause of the pancreatitis is clear, but in others, more tests are needed after the person is discharged and the pancreas is healed.

Therapeutic Endoscopic Retrograde Cholangiopancreatography (ERCP) for Acute and Chronic Pancreatitis

ERCP is a specialized technique used to view the pancreas, gallbladder, and bile ducts and treat complications of acute and chronic pancreatitis—gallstones, narrowing or blockage of the pancreatic duct or bile ducts, leaks in the bile ducts, and pseudocysts—accumulations of fluid and tissue debris.

Soon after a person is admitted to the hospital with suspected narrowing of the pancreatic duct or bile ducts, a physician with specialized training performs ERCP.

After lightly sedating the patient and giving medication to numb the throat, the doctor inserts an endoscope—a long, flexible, lighted tube with a camera—through the mouth, throat, and stomach into the small intestine. The endoscope is connected to a computer and screen. The doctor guides the endoscope and injects a special dye into the pancreatic or bile ducts that helps the pancreas, gallbladder, and bile ducts appear on the screen while X-rays are taken.

The following procedures can be performed using ERCP:

- **Sphincterotomy.** Using a small wire on the endoscope, the doctor finds the muscle that surrounds the pancreatic duct or bile ducts and makes a tiny cut to enlarge the duct opening. When a pseudocyst is present, the duct is drained.

- **Gallstone removal.** The endoscope is used to remove pancreatic or bile duct stones with a tiny basket. Gallstone removal is sometimes performed along with a sphincterotomy.

- **Stent placement.** Using the endoscope, the doctor places a tiny piece of plastic or metal that looks like a straw in a narrowed pancreatic or bile duct to keep it open.

- **Balloon dilatation.** Some endoscopes have a small balloon that the doctor uses to dilate, or stretch, a narrowed pancreatic or bile duct. A temporary stent may be placed for a few months to keep the duct open.

People who undergo therapeutic ERCP are at slight risk for complications, including severe pancreatitis, infection, bowel perforation, or bleeding. Complications of ERCP are more common in people with acute or recurrent pancreatitis. A patient who experiences fever, trouble swallowing, or increased throat, chest, or abdominal pain after the procedure should notify a doctor immediately.

Complications

Gallstones that cause acute pancreatitis require surgical removal of the stones and the gallbladder. If the pancreatitis is mild, gallbladder removal—called cholecystectomy—may proceed while the person is in the hospital. If the pancreatitis is severe, gallstones may be removed using therapeutic endoscopic retrograde cholangiopancreatography (ERCP)—a specialized technique used to view the pancreas, gallbladder, and bile ducts and treat complications of acute and chronic pancreatitis. Cholecystectomy is delayed for a month or more to allow for full recovery.

If an infection develops, ERCP or surgery may be needed to drain the infected area, also called an abscess. Exploratory surgery may also be necessary to find the source of any bleeding, to rule out conditions that resemble pancreatitis, or to remove severely damaged pancreatic tissue.

Pseudocysts—accumulations of fluid and tissue debris—that may develop in the pancreas can be drained using ERCP or EUS. If pseudocysts are left untreated, enzymes and toxins can enter the bloodstream and affect the heart, lungs, kidneys, or other organs.

Acute pancreatitis sometimes causes kidney failure. People with kidney failure need blood-cleansing treatments called dialysis or a kidney transplant.

In rare cases, acute pancreatitis can cause breathing problems. Hypoxia, a condition that occurs when body cells and tissues do not get enough oxygen, can develop. Doctors treat hypoxia by giving oxygen to the patient. Some people still experience lung failure—even with oxygen—and require a respirator for a while to help them breathe.

What is chronic pancreatitis?

Chronic pancreatitis is inflammation of the pancreas that does not heal or improve—it gets worse over time and leads to permanent damage. Chronic pancreatitis, like acute pancreatitis, occurs when digestive enzymes attack the pancreas and nearby tissues, causing episodes of pain. Chronic pancreatitis often develops in people who are between the ages of 30 and 40.

The most common cause of chronic pancreatitis is many years of heavy alcohol use. The chronic form of pancreatitis can be triggered by one acute attack that damages the pancreatic duct. The damaged duct causes the pancreas to become inflamed. Scar tissue develops and the pancreas is slowly destroyed.

Other causes of chronic pancreatitis are

- hereditary disorders of the pancreas
- cystic fibrosis—the most common inherited disorder leading to chronic pancreatitis
- hypercalcemia—high levels of calcium in the blood
- hyperlipidemia or hypertriglyceridemia—high levels of blood fats
- some medicines
- certain autoimmune conditions
- unknown causes

Hereditary pancreatitis can present in a person younger than age 30, but it might not be diagnosed for several years. Episodes of abdominal pain and diarrhea lasting several days come and go over time and can progress to chronic pancreatitis. A diagnosis of hereditary pancreatitis is likely if the person has two or more family members with pancreatitis in more than one generation.

Symptoms

Most people with chronic pancreatitis experience upper abdominal pain, although some people have no pain at all. The pain may spread to the back, feel worse when eating or drinking, and become constant and disabling. In some cases, abdominal pain goes away as the condition worsens, most likely because the pancreas is no longer making digestive enzymes. Other symptoms include

- nausea
- vomiting
- weight loss
- diarrhea
- oily stools

People with chronic pancreatitis often lose weight, even when their appetite and eating habits are normal. The weight loss occurs because the body does not secrete enough pancreatic enzymes to digest food, so nutrients are not absorbed normally. Poor digestion leads to malnutrition due to excretion of fat in the stool.

Diagnosis

Chronic pancreatitis is often confused with acute pancreatitis because the symptoms are similar. As with acute pancreatitis, the doctor will conduct a thorough medical history and physical examination. Blood tests may help the doctor know if the pancreas is still making enough digestive enzymes, but sometimes these enzymes appear normal even though the person has chronic pancreatitis.

In more advanced stages of pancreatitis, when malabsorption and diabetes can occur, the doctor may order blood, urine, and stool tests to help diagnose chronic pancreatitis and monitor its progression.

After ordering X-rays of the abdomen, the doctor will conduct one or more of the tests used to diagnose acute pancreatitis—abdominal ultrasound, CT scan, EUS, and MRCP.

Treatment

Treatment for chronic pancreatitis may require hospitalization for pain management, IV hydration, and nutritional support. Nasogastric feedings may be necessary for several weeks if the person continues to lose weight.

When a normal diet is resumed, the doctor may prescribe synthetic pancreatic enzymes if the pancreas does not secrete enough of its own. The enzymes should be taken with every meal to help the person digest food and regain some weight. The next step is to plan a nutritious diet that is low in fat and includes small, frequent meals. A dietitian can assist in developing a meal plan. Drinking plenty of fluids and limiting caffeinated beverages is also important.

People with chronic pancreatitis are strongly advised not to smoke or consume alcoholic beverages, even if the pancreatitis is mild or in the early stages.

Complications

People with chronic pancreatitis who continue to consume large amounts of alcohol may develop sudden bouts of severe abdominal pain.

As with acute pancreatitis, ERCP is used to identify and treat complications associated with chronic pancreatitis such as gallstones, pseudocysts, and narrowing or obstruction of the ducts. Chronic pancreatitis also can lead to calcification of the pancreas, which means the pancreatic tissue hardens from deposits of insoluble calcium salts. Surgery may be necessary to remove part of the pancreas.

In cases involving persistent pain, surgery or other procedures are sometimes recommended to block the nerves in the abdominal area that cause pain.

When pancreatic tissue is destroyed in chronic pancreatitis and the insulin-producing cells of the pancreas, called beta cells, have been damaged, diabetes may develop. People with a family history of diabetes are more likely to develop the disease. If diabetes occurs, insulin or other medicines are needed to keep blood glucose at normal levels. A health care provider works with the patient to develop a regimen of medication, diet, and frequent blood glucose monitoring.

How common is pancreatitis in children?

Chronic pancreatitis in children is rare. Trauma to the pancreas and hereditary pancreatitis are two known causes of childhood pancreatitis. Children with cystic fibrosis—a progressive and incurable lung disease—may be at risk of developing pancreatitis. But more often the cause of pancreatitis in children is unknown.

Chapter 30

Autoimmune Hepatitis

What is autoimmune hepatitis?

Autoimmune hepatitis is a chronic—or long lasting—disease in which the body's immune system attacks the normal components, or cells, of the liver and causes inflammation and liver damage. The immune system normally protects people from infection by identifying and destroying bacteria, viruses, and other potentially harmful foreign substances.

Autoimmune hepatitis is a serious condition that may worsen over time if not treated. Autoimmune hepatitis can lead to cirrhosis and liver failure. Cirrhosis occurs when scar tissue replaces healthy liver tissue and blocks the normal flow of blood through the liver. Liver failure occurs when the liver stops working properly.

What are autoimmune diseases?

Autoimmune diseases are disorders in which the body's immune system attacks the body's own cells and organs with proteins called autoantibodies; this process is called autoimmunity.

The body's immune system normally makes large numbers of proteins called antibodies to help the body fight off infections. In some cases, however, the body makes autoantibodies. Certain environmental triggers can lead to autoimmunity. Environmental triggers are things originating outside the body, such as bacteria, viruses, toxins, and medications.

Text in this chapter is excerpted from "Autoimmune Hepatitis," National Institute of Diabetes and Digestive and Kidney Diseases (NIDDK), January 2014.

What causes autoimmune hepatitis?

A combination of autoimmunity, environmental triggers, and a genetic predisposition can lead to autoimmune hepatitis.

Who is more likely to develop autoimmune hepatitis?

Autoimmune hepatitis is more common in females. The disease can occur at any age and affects all ethnic groups.

What are the types of autoimmune hepatitis?

Autoimmune hepatitis is classified into several types. Type 1 autoimmune hepatitis is the most common form in North America. Type 1 can occur at any age; however, it most often starts in adolescence or young adulthood. About 70 percent of people with type 1 autoimmune hepatitis are female.

People with type 1 autoimmune hepatitis commonly have other autoimmune disorders, such as

- celiac disease, an autoimmune disease in which people cannot tolerate gluten because it damages the lining of their small intestine and prevents absorption of nutrients

- Crohn's disease, which causes inflammation and irritation of any part of the digestive tract

- Graves' disease, the most common cause of hyperthyroidism in the United States

- Hashimoto's disease, also called chronic lymphocytic thyroiditis or autoimmune thyroiditis, a form of chronic inflammation of the thyroid gland

- proliferative glomerulonephritis, or inflammation of the glomeruli, which are tiny clusters of looping blood vessels in the kidneys

- primary sclerosing cholangitis, which causes irritation, scarring, and narrowing of the bile ducts inside and outside the liver

- rheumatoid arthritis, which causes pain, swelling, stiffness, and loss of function in the joints

- Sjögren's syndrome, which causes dryness in the mouth and eyes

- systemic lupus erythematosus, which causes kidney inflammation called lupus nephritis

- type 1 diabetes, a condition characterized by high blood glucose, also called blood sugar, levels caused by a total lack of insulin

- ulcerative colitis, a chronic disease that causes inflammation and sores, called ulcers, in the inner lining of the large intestine

Type 2 autoimmune hepatitis is less common and occurs more often in children than adults. People with type 2 can also have any of the above autoimmune disorders.

What are the symptoms of autoimmune hepatitis?

The most common symptoms of autoimmune hepatitis are

- fatigue

- joint pain

- nausea

- loss of appetite

- pain or discomfort over the liver

- skin rashes

- dark yellow urine

- light-colored stools

- jaundice, or yellowing of the skin and whites of the eyes

Symptoms of autoimmune hepatitis range from mild to severe. Some people may feel as if they have a mild case of the flu. Others may have no symptoms when a health care provider diagnoses the disease; however, they can develop symptoms later.

How is autoimmune hepatitis diagnosed?

A health care provider will make a diagnosis of autoimmune hepatitis based on symptoms, a physical exam, blood tests, and a liver biopsy.

A health care provider performs a physical exam and reviews the person's health history, including the use of alcohol and medications that can harm the liver. A person usually needs blood tests for an exact diagnosis because a person with autoimmune hepatitis can have the same symptoms as those of other liver diseases or metabolic disorders.

Blood tests. A blood test involves drawing blood at a health care provider's office or a commercial facility and sending the sample to a lab for analysis. A person will need blood tests for autoantibodies to help distinguish autoimmune hepatitis from other liver diseases that have similar symptoms, such as viral hepatitis, primary biliary cirrhosis, steatohepatitis, or Wilson disease.

Liver biopsy. A liver biopsy is a procedure that involves taking a piece of liver tissue for examination with a microscope for signs of damage or disease. The health care provider may ask the patient to temporarily stop taking certain medications before the liver biopsy. He or she may also ask the patient to fast for 8 hours before the procedure.

During the procedure, the patient lies on a table, right hand resting above the head. A health care provider will apply a local anesthetic to the area where he or she will insert the biopsy needle. If needed, he or she will give sedatives and pain medication. Then, he or she will use a needle to take a small piece of liver tissue, and may use ultrasound, computerized tomography scans, or other imaging techniques to guide the needle. After the biopsy, the patient must lie on the right side for up to 2 hours and is monitored an additional 2 to 4 hours before being sent home.

A health care provider performs a liver biopsy at a hospital or an outpatient center. The liver sample is sent to a pathology lab where the pathologist—a doctor who specializes in diagnosing disease—looks at the tissue with a microscope and sends a report to the patient's health care provider.

A health care provider can use liver biopsy to diagnose autoimmune hepatitis and determine if cirrhosis is present. People often have cirrhosis at the time they are diagnosed with autoimmune hepatitis. A health care provider can also use liver biopsy to look for changes in the severity of liver damage prior to ending treatment for autoimmune hepatitis.

How is autoimmune hepatitis treated?

Treatment for autoimmune hepatitis includes medication to suppress, or slow down, an overactive immune system. Treatment may also include a liver transplant.

Treatment works best when autoimmune hepatitis is diagnosed early. People with autoimmune hepatitis generally respond to standard treatment and the disease can be controlled in most cases. Long-term response to treatment can stop the disease from getting worse and may even reverse some damage to the liver.

Medications

People with autoimmune hepatitis who have no symptoms or a mild form of the disease may or may not need to take medication. A health care provider will determine if a person needs treatment. In some people with mild autoimmune hepatitis, the disease may go into remission. Remission is a period when a person is symptom-free and blood tests and liver biopsy show improvement in liver function.

Corticosteroids. Corticosteroids are medications that decrease swelling and reduce the activity of the immune system. Health care providers treat both types of autoimmune hepatitis with a daily dose of a corticosteroid called prednisone. Treatment may begin with a high dose that is gradually lowered as the disease is controlled. The treatment goal is to find the lowest possible dose that helps control the disease.

Side effects of prednisone may include

- weight gain
- weakness of the bones, called osteoporosis or osteomalacia
- thinning of the hair and skin
- acne
- diabetes
- high blood pressure
- cataracts, a clouding in the lens of the eyes
- glaucoma, elevated pressure in the eyes
- anxiety and confusion

A health care provider will closely monitor and manage any side effects that may occur, as high doses of prednisone are often prescribed to treat autoimmune hepatitis.

Immune system suppressors. Medications that suppress the immune system prevent the body from making autoantibodies and block the immune reaction that contributes to inflammation. In most cases, health care providers use azathioprine (Azasan, Imuran) in conjunction with prednisone to treat autoimmune hepatitis. When using azathioprine, a health care provider can use a lower dose of prednisone, which may reduce prednisone's side effects.

Side effects of azathioprine include

- low white blood cell count

- nausea

- vomiting

- skin rash

- liver damage

- pancreatitis, or inflammation of the pancreas

Azathioprine is an immune system suppressor, so people taking the medication should undergo routine blood tests to monitor their white blood cell counts. A low white blood cell count can lead to bone marrow failure. Bone marrow is the tissue found inside bones that produces new blood cells, including platelets. A health care provider will also check the platelet count when blood tests are done.

A person may need to discontinue prednisone or azathioprine if they cause severe side effects. The risk of side effects is higher in people who also have cirrhosis.

A health care provider may gradually reduce the dose of medication in people who show improvement, although the symptoms can return. When a person discontinues treatment, a health care provider will perform routine blood tests and carefully monitor the person's condition for a return of symptoms. Treatment with low doses of prednisone or azathioprine may be necessary on and off for many years.

People who do not respond to standard immune therapy or who have severe side effects from the medications may benefit from other immunosuppressive agents such as mycophenolate mofetil (CellCept), cyclosporine, or tacrolimus (Hecoria, Prograf).

Medications that suppress the immune system may lead to various forms of cancer. People on low doses of azathioprine for long periods of time are at slight risk of developing cancer.

Liver Transplant

In some people, autoimmune hepatitis progresses to cirrhosis and end-stage liver failure, and a liver transplant may be necessary. Symptoms of cirrhosis and liver failure include the symptoms of autoimmune hepatitis and

- generalized itching

- a longer-than-usual amount of time for bleeding to stop

- easy bruising

- a swollen stomach or swollen ankles

- spiderlike blood vessels, called spider angiomas, that develop on the skin

- abdominal bloating due to an enlarged liver

- fluid in the abdomen—also called ascites

- forgetfulness or confusion

Liver transplant is surgery to remove a diseased or an injured liver and replace it with a healthy one from another person, called a donor. A team of surgeons performs a liver transplant in a hospital. When possible, the patient fasts for 8 hours before the surgery. The patient stays in the hospital about 1 to 2 weeks to be sure the transplanted liver is functioning properly. The health care provider will monitor the patient for bleeding, infections, and signs of liver rejection. The patient will take prescription medications long term to prevent infections and rejection. Liver transplant surgery for autoimmune hepatitis is successful in most cases.

What is a possible complication of autoimmune hepatitis and cirrhosis?

People with autoimmune hepatitis and cirrhosis are at risk of developing liver cancer. A health care provider will monitor the person with a regular ultrasound examination of the liver. Ultrasound uses a device, called a transducer, that bounces safe, painless sound waves off organs to create an image of their structure. A specially trained technician performs the procedure in a health care provider's office, an outpatient center, or a hospital, and a radiologist—a doctor who specializes in medical imaging—interprets the images; anesthesia is not needed. The images can show the liver's size and the presence of cancerous tumors.

Eating, Diet, and Nutrition

Researchers have not found that eating, diet, and nutrition play a role in causing or preventing autoimmune hepatitis.

Chapter 31

Biliary Atresia

What is biliary atresia?

Biliary atresia is a life-threatening condition in infants in which the bile ducts inside or outside the liver do not have normal openings.

Bile ducts in the liver, also called hepatic ducts, are tubes that carry bile from the liver to the gallbladder for storage and to the small intestine for use in digestion. Bile is a fluid made by the liver that serves two main functions: carrying toxins and waste products out of the body and helping the body digest fats and absorb the fat-soluble vitamins A, D, E, and K.

With biliary atresia, bile becomes trapped, builds up, and damages the liver. The damage leads to scarring, loss of liver tissue, and cirrhosis. Cirrhosis is a chronic, or long lasting, liver condition caused by scar tissue and cell damage that makes it hard for the liver to remove toxins from the blood. These toxins build up in the blood and the liver slowly deteriorates and malfunctions. Without treatment, the liver eventually fails and the infant needs a liver transplant to stay alive.

The two types of biliary atresia are fetal and perinatal. Fetal biliary atresia appears while the baby is in the womb. Perinatal biliary atresia is much more common and does not become evident until 2 to 4 weeks after birth. Some infants, particularly those with the fetal form, also have birth defects in the heart, spleen, or intestines.

Text in this chapter is excerpted from "Biliary Atresia," National Institute of Diabetes and Digestive and Kidney Diseases (NIDDK), July 2012.

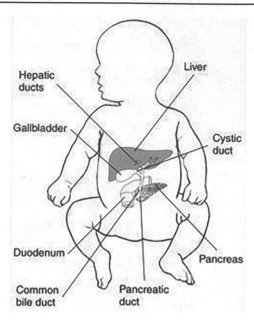

Figure 31.1. *Normal liver and biliary system*

Who is at risk for biliary atresia?

Biliary atresia is rare and only affects about one out of every 18,000 infants. The disease is more common in females, premature babies, and children of Asian or African American heritage.

What are the symptoms of biliary atresia?

The first symptom of biliary atresia is jaundice—when the skin and whites of the eyes turn yellow. Jaundice occurs when the liver does not remove bilirubin, a reddish-yellow substance formed when hemoglobin breaks down. Hemoglobin is an iron-rich protein that gives blood its red color. Bilirubin is absorbed by the liver, processed, and released into bile. Blockage of the bile ducts forces bilirubin to build up in the blood.

Other common symptoms of biliary atresia include

- dark urine, from the high levels of bilirubin in the blood spilling over into the urine

- gray or white stools, from a lack of bilirubin reaching the intestines

- slow weight gain and growth

What causes biliary atresia?

Biliary atresia likely has multiple causes, though none are yet proven. Biliary atresia is not an inherited disease, meaning it does not pass from parent to child. Therefore, survivors of biliary atresia are not at risk for passing the disorder to their children.

Biliary atresia is most likely caused by an event in the womb or around the time of birth. Possible triggers of the event may include one or more of the following:

- a viral or bacterial infection after birth, such as cytomegalovirus, reovirus, or rotavirus

- an immune system problem, such as when the immune system attacks the liver or bile ducts for unknown reasons

- a genetic mutation, which is a permanent change in a gene's structure

- a problem during liver and bile duct development in the womb

- exposure to toxic substances

How is biliary atresia diagnosed?

No single test can definitively diagnose biliary atresia, so a series of tests is needed. All infants who still have jaundice 2 to 3 weeks after birth, or who have gray or white stools after 2 weeks of birth, should be checked for liver damage.

Infants with suspected liver damage are usually referred to a

- pediatric gastroenterologist, a doctor who specializes in children's digestive diseases

- pediatric hepatologist, a doctor who specializes in children's liver diseases

- pediatric surgeon, a doctor who specializes in operating on children's livers and bile ducts

The health care provider may order some or all of the following tests to diagnose biliary atresia and rule out other causes of liver problems. If biliary atresia is still suspected after testing, the next step is diagnostic surgery for confirmation.

Blood test. A blood test involves drawing blood at a health care provider's office or commercial facility and sending the sample to a lab for analysis. High levels of bilirubin in the blood can indicate blocked bile ducts.

Abdominal X-rays. An X-ray is a picture created by using radiation and recorded on film or on a computer. The amount of radiation used is small. An X-ray is performed at a hospital or outpatient center by an X-ray technician, and the images are interpreted by a radiologist—a doctor who specializes in medical imaging. Anesthesia is not needed, but sedation may be used to keep infants still. The infant will lie on a table during the X-ray. The X-ray machine is positioned over the abdominal area. Abdominal X-rays are used to check for an enlarged liver and spleen.

Ultrasound. Ultrasound uses a device, called a transducer, that bounces safe, painless sound waves off organs to create an image of their structure. The procedure is performed in a health care provider's office, outpatient center, or hospital by a specially trained technician, and the images are interpreted a radiologist. Anesthesia is not needed, but sedation may be used to keep the infant still. The images can show whether the liver or bile ducts are enlarged and whether tumors or cysts are blocking the flow of bile. An ultrasound cannot be used to diagnose biliary atresia, but it does help rule out other common causes of jaundice.

Liver scans. Liver scans are special X-rays that use chemicals to create an image of the liver and bile ducts. Liver scans are performed at a hospital or outpatient facility, usually by a nuclear medicine technician. The infant will usually receive general anesthesia or be sedated before the procedure. Hepatobiliary iminodiacetic acid scanning, a type of liver scan, uses injected radioactive dye to trace the path of bile in the body. The test can show if and where bile flow is blocked. Blockage is likely to be caused by biliary atresia.

Liver biopsy. A biopsy is a procedure that involves taking a piece of liver tissue for examination with a microscope. The biopsy is performed by a health care provider in a hospital with light sedation and local anesthetic. The health care provider uses imaging techniques such as ultrasound or a computerized tomography scan to guide the biopsy needle into the liver. The liver tissue is examined in a lab by a pathologist—a doctor who specializes in diagnosing diseases. A liver biopsy can show whether biliary atresia is likely. A biopsy can also help rule out other liver problems, such as hepatitis—an irritation of the liver that sometimes causes permanent damage.

Diagnostic surgery. During diagnostic surgery, a pediatric surgeon makes an incision, or cut, in the abdomen to directly examine the liver and bile ducts. If the surgeon confirms that biliary atresia is the problem, a Kasai procedure will usually be performed immediately. Diagnostic surgery and the Kasai procedure are performed at a hospital or outpatient facility; the infant will be under general anesthesia during surgery.

How is biliary atresia treated?

Biliary atresia is treated with surgery, called the Kasai procedure, or a liver transplant.

Kasai Procedure

The Kasai procedure, named after the surgeon who invented the operation, is usually the first treatment for biliary atresia. During a Kasai procedure, the pediatric surgeon removes the infant's damaged bile ducts and brings up a loop of intestine to replace them. As a result, bile flows straight to the small intestine.

While this operation doesn't cure biliary atresia, it can restore bile flow and correct many problems caused by biliary atresia. Without surgery, infants with biliary atresia are unlikely to live past age 2. This procedure is most effective in infants younger than 3 months old, because they usually haven't yet developed permanent liver damage. Some infants with biliary atresia who undergo a successful Kasai procedure regain good health and no longer have jaundice or major liver problems.

If the Kasai procedure is not successful, infants usually need a liver transplant within 1 to 2 years. Even after a successful surgery, most infants with biliary atresia slowly develop cirrhosis over the years and require a liver transplant by adulthood.

Liver Transplant

Liver transplantation is the definitive treatment for biliary atresia, and the survival rate after surgery has increased dramatically in recent years. As a result, most infants with biliary atresia now survive. Progress in transplant surgery has also increased the availability and efficient use of livers for transplantation in children, so almost all infants requiring a transplant can receive one.

In years past, the size of the transplanted liver had to match the size of the infant's liver. Thus, only livers from recently deceased small children could be transplanted into infants with biliary atresia. New methods now make it possible to transplant a portion of a deceased adult's liver into an infant. This type of surgery is called a reduced-size or split-liver transplant.

Part of a living adult donor's liver can also be used for transplantation. Healthy liver tissue grows quickly; therefore, if an infant receives part of a liver from a living donor, both the donor and the infant can grow complete livers over time.

Infants with fetal biliary atresia are more likely to need a liver transplant—and usually sooner—than infants with the more common perinatal form. The extent of damage can also influence how soon an infant will need a liver transplant.

What are possible complications after the Kasai procedure?

After the Kasai procedure, some infants continue to have liver problems and, even with the return of bile flow, some infants develop cirrhosis. Possible complications after the Kasai procedure include ascites, bacterial cholangitis, portal hypertension, and pruritus.

Ascites. Problems with liver function can cause fluid to build up in the abdomen, called ascites. Ascites can lead to spontaneous bacterial peritonitis, a serious infection that requires immediate medical attention. Ascites usually only lasts a few weeks. If ascites lasts more than 6 weeks, cirrhosis is likely present and the infant will probably need a liver transplant.

Bacterial cholangitis. Bacterial cholangitis is an infection of the bile ducts that is treated with bacteria-fighting medications called antibiotics.

Portal hypertension. The portal vein carries blood from the stomach, intestines, spleen, gallbladder, and pancreas to the liver. In cirrhosis, scar tissue partially blocks and slows the normal flow of blood, which increases the pressure in the portal vein. This condition is called portal hypertension. Portal hypertension can cause gastrointestinal bleeding that may require surgery and an eventual liver transplant.

Pruritus. Pruritus is caused by bile buildup in the blood and irritation of nerve endings in the skin. Prescription medication may be recommended for pruritus, including resins that bind bile in the intestines and antihistamines that decrease the skin's sensation of itching.

What medical care is needed after a liver transplant?

After a liver transplant, a regimen of medications is used to prevent the immune system from rejecting the new liver. Health care providers may also prescribe blood pressure medications and antibiotics, along with special diets and vitamin supplements.

Eating, Diet, and Nutrition

Infants with biliary atresia often have nutritional deficiencies and require special diets as they grow up. They may need a higher calorie diet, because biliary atresia leads to a faster metabolism. The disease also prevents them from digesting fats and can lead to protein and vitamin deficiencies. Vitamin supplements may be recommended, along with adding medium-chain triglyceride oil to foods, liquids, and infant formula. The oil adds calories and is easier to digest without bile than other types of fats. If an infant or child is too sick to eat, a feeding tube may be recommended to provide high-calorie liquid meals.

After a liver transplant, most infants and children can go back to their usual diet. Vitamin supplements may still be needed because the medications used to keep the body from rejecting the new liver can affect calcium and magnesium levels.

Chapter 32

Cirrhosis of the Liver

What is cirrhosis?

Cirrhosis is a condition in which the liver slowly deteriorates and is unable to function normally due to chronic, or long lasting, injury. Scar tissue replaces healthy liver tissue and partially blocks the flow of blood through the liver.

The liver is the body's largest internal organ. The liver is called the body's metabolic factory because of the important role it plays in metabolism—the way cells change food into energy after food is digested and absorbed into the blood. The liver has many functions, including

- taking up, storing, and processing nutrients from food—including fat, sugar, and protein—and delivering them to the rest of the body when needed

- making new proteins, such as clotting factors and immune factors

- producing bile, which helps the body absorb fats, cholesterol, and fat-soluble vitamins

- removing waste products the kidneys cannot remove, such as fats, cholesterol, toxins, and medications

---

Text in this chapter is excerpted from "Cirrhosis," National Institute of Diabetes and Digestive and Kidney Diseases (NIDDK), March 2014.

A healthy liver is necessary for survival. The liver can regenerate most of its own cells when they become damaged. However, if injury to the liver is too severe or long lasting, regeneration is incomplete, and the liver creates scar tissue. Scarring of the liver, also called fibrosis, may lead to cirrhosis.

The buildup of scar tissue that causes cirrhosis is usually a slow and gradual process. In the early stages of cirrhosis, the liver continues to function. However, as cirrhosis gets worse and scar tissue replaces healthier tissue, the liver will begin to fail. Chronic liver failure, which is also called end-stage liver disease, progresses over months, years, or even decades. With end-stage liver disease, the liver can no longer perform important functions or effectively replace damaged cells.

Cirrhosis is a condition in which the liver slowly deteriorates and is unable to function normally due to chronic injury.

Cirrhosis is the 12th leading cause of death in the United States, accounting for nearly 32,000 deaths each year. More men die of cirrhosis than women.

What causes cirrhosis?

Cirrhosis has various causes. Many people with cirrhosis have more than one cause of liver damage.

The list below shows common causes of cirrhosis in the United States. While chronic hepatitis C and alcohol-related liver disease are the most common causes of cirrhosis, the incidence of cirrhosis caused by nonalcoholic fatty liver disease is rising due to increasing rates of obesity.

Most Common Causes of Cirrhosis

Chronic hepatitis C. Hepatitis C is due to a viral infection that causes inflammation, or swelling, and damage to the liver.

Alcohol-related liver disease. Alcoholism is the second most common cause of cirrhosis in the United States.

Nonalcoholic fatty liver disease (NAFLD) and nonalcoholic steatohepatitis (NASH). In NAFLD, fat builds up in the liver; however, the fat buildup is not due to alcohol use. When the fat accompanies inflammation and liver cell damage, the condition is called nonalcoholic steatohepatitis, or NASH, with "steato" meaning fat, and "hepatitis" meaning inflammation of the liver. The inflammation and damage can cause fibrosis, which eventually can lead to cirrhosis.

NASH now ranks as the third most common cause of cirrhosis in the United States.

Chronic hepatitis B. Hepatitis B, like hepatitis C, is due to a viral infection that causes inflammation and damage to the liver. Chronic infection can lead to damage and inflammation, fibrosis, and cirrhosis. In the United States, hepatitis B is somewhat uncommon, affecting less than 1 percent of the population, or fewer than one in 100 people.

Less Common Causes of Cirrhosis

Less common causes of cirrhosis include the following:

Autoimmune hepatitis. In this form of hepatitis, the body's immune system attacks liver cells and causes inflammation, damage, and eventually cirrhosis.

Diseases that damage, destroy, or block the bile ducts. Several diseases can damage, destroy, or block the ducts that carry bile from the liver to the small intestine, causing bile to back up in the liver and leading to cirrhosis. Long-term blockage of the bile ducts by gallstones can cause cirrhosis. Cirrhosis may also develop if the bile ducts are mistakenly tied off or injured during surgery on the gallbladder or liver.

Inherited diseases that affect the liver. Inherited diseases that interfere with how the liver produces, processes, and stores enzymes, proteins, metals, and other substances can cause cirrhosis.

Other causes. Other causes of cirrhosis may include

- reactions to medications taken over a period of time.
- prolonged exposure to toxic chemicals.
- parasitic infections.
- chronic heart failure with liver congestion, a condition in which blood flow out of the liver is slowed.

What are the signs and symptoms of cirrhosis?

Many people with cirrhosis have no symptoms in the early stages of the disease. However, as the disease progresses, a person may experience the following symptoms:

- fatigue, or feeling tired

- weakness

- itching

- loss of appetite

- weight loss

- nausea

- bloating of the abdomen from ascites—a buildup of fluid in the abdomen

- edema—swelling due to a buildup of fluid—in the feet, ankles, or legs

- spiderlike blood vessels, called spider angiomas, on the skin

- jaundice, a condition that causes the skin and whites of the eyes to turn yellow

What are the complications of cirrhosis?

As the liver fails, complications may develop. In some people, complications may be the first signs of the disease. Complications of cirrhosis may include the following:

Portal hypertension. The portal vein carries blood from the stomach, intestines, spleen, gallbladder, and pancreas to the liver. In cirrhosis, scar tissue partially blocks the normal flow of blood, which increases the pressure in the portal vein. This condition is called portal hypertension. Portal hypertension is a common complication of cirrhosis. This condition may lead to other complications, such as

- fluid buildup leading to edema and ascites

- enlarged blood vessels, called varices, in the esophagus, stomach, or both

- an enlarged spleen, called splenomegaly

- mental confusion due to a buildup of toxins that are ordinarily removed by the liver, a condition called hepatic encephalopathy

Edema and ascites. Liver failure causes fluid buildup that results in edema and ascites. Ascites can lead to spontaneous bacterial peritonitis, a serious infection that requires immediate medical attention.

Varices. Portal hypertension may cause enlarged blood vessels in the esophagus, stomach, or both. These enlarged blood vessels, called esophageal or gastric varices, cause the vessel walls to become thin and blood pressure to increase, making the blood vessels more likely to burst. If they burst, serious bleeding can occur in the esophagus or upper stomach, requiring immediate medical attention.

Splenomegaly. Portal hypertension may cause the spleen to enlarge and retain white blood cells and platelets, reducing the numbers of those cells and platelets in the blood. A low platelet count may be the first evidence that a person has developed cirrhosis.

Hepatic encephalopathy. A failing liver cannot remove toxins from the blood, so they eventually accumulate in the brain. The buildup of toxins in the brain is called hepatic encephalopathy. This condition can decrease mental function and cause stupor and even coma. Stupor is an unconscious, sleeplike state from which a person can only be aroused briefly by a strong stimulus, such as a sharp pain. Coma is an unconscious, sleeplike state from which a person cannot be aroused. Signs of decreased mental function include

- confusion
- personality changes
- memory loss
- trouble concentrating
- a change in sleep habits

Metabolic bone diseases. Some people with cirrhosis develop a metabolic bone disease, which is a disorder of bone strength usually caused by abnormalities of vitamin D, bone mass, bone structure, or minerals, such as calcium and phosphorous. Osteopenia is a condition in which the bones become less dense, making them weaker. When bone loss becomes more severe, the condition is referred to as osteoporosis. People with these conditions are more likely to develop bone fractures.

Gallstones and bile duct stones. If cirrhosis prevents bile from flowing freely to and from the gallbladder, the bile hardens into gallstones. Symptoms of gallstones include abdominal pain and recurrent bacterial cholangitis—irritated or infected bile ducts. Stones may also form in and block the bile ducts, causing pain, jaundice, and bacterial cholangitis.

Bruising and bleeding. When the liver slows the production of or stops producing the proteins needed for blood clotting, a person will bruise or bleed easily.

Sensitivity to medications. Cirrhosis slows the liver's ability to filter medications from the blood. When this slowdown occurs, medications act longer than expected and build up in the body. For example, some pain medications may have a stronger effect or produce more side effects in people with cirrhosis than in people with a healthy liver.

Insulin resistance and type 2 diabetes. Cirrhosis causes resistance to insulin. The pancreas tries to keep up with the demand for insulin by producing more; however, extra glucose builds up in the bloodstream, causing type 2 diabetes.

Liver cancer. Liver cancer is common in people with cirrhosis. Liver cancer has a high mortality rate. Current treatments are limited and only fully successful if a health care provider detects the cancer early, before the tumor is too large. For this reason, health care providers should check people with cirrhosis for signs of liver cancer every 6 to 12 months. Health care providers use blood tests, ultrasound, or both to check for signs of liver cancer.

Other complications. Cirrhosis can cause immune system dysfunction, leading to an increased chance of infection. Cirrhosis can also cause kidney and lung failure, known as hepatorenal and hepatopulmonary syndromes.

How is cirrhosis diagnosed?

A health care provider usually diagnoses cirrhosis based on the presence of conditions that increase its likelihood, such as heavy alcohol use or obesity, and symptoms. A health care provider may test for cirrhosis based on the presence of these conditions alone because many people do not have symptoms in the early stages of the disease. A health care provider may confirm the diagnosis with

- a medical and family history
- a physical exam
- a blood test
- imaging tests
- a liver biopsy

How is cirrhosis treated?

Treatment for cirrhosis depends on the cause of the disease and whether complications are present. In the early stages of cirrhosis, the goals of treatment are to slow the progression of tissue scarring in the liver and prevent complications. As cirrhosis progresses, a person may need additional treatments and hospitalization to manage complications. Treatment may include the following:

Avoiding Alcohol and Illegal Substances

People with cirrhosis should not drink any alcohol or take any illegal substances, as both will cause more liver damage.

Preventing Problems with Medications

People with cirrhosis should be careful about starting new medications and should consult a health care provider before taking prescription medications, over-the-counter medications, or vitamins. People with cirrhosis should avoid complementary and alternative medications, such as herbs.

Cirrhosis slows the liver's ability to filter medications from the blood. When this slowdown occurs, medications act longer than expected and build up in the body. Some medications and vitamins may also affect liver function.

Viral Hepatitis Vaccination and Screening

All people with cirrhosis should consider vaccination against hepatitis A and B. An infection with one of these hepatitis viruses can cause cirrhosis to get worse. Vaccination can easily prevent both infections.

People with cirrhosis should also get a screening blood test for hepatitis C.

Treating Causes of Cirrhosis

Health care providers can treat some causes of cirrhosis, for example, by prescribing antiviral medications for hepatitis B and C. In some instances, these medications cure the viral infection. Health care providers treat autoimmune hepatitis with corticosteroids and other medications that suppress the immune system. Health care providers can treat hemochromatosis and Wilson disease—inherited forms of liver disease caused by the buildup of iron or copper in the liver—if detected early.

411

Treating Symptoms and Complications of Cirrhosis

Itching and abdominal pain. A health care provider may give medications to treat various symptoms of cirrhosis, such as itching and abdominal pain.

Portal hypertension. A health care provider may prescribe a beta-blocker or nitrate to treat portal hypertension. Beta-blockers lower blood pressure by helping the heart beat slower and with less force, and nitrates relax and widen blood vessels to let more blood flow to the heart and reduce the heart's workload.

Varices. Beta-blockers can lower the pressure in varices and reduce the likelihood of bleeding. Bleeding in the stomach or esophagus requires an immediate upper endoscopy. People who have had varices in the past may need to take medication to prevent future episodes.

Edema and ascites. Health care providers prescribe diuretics—medications that remove fluid from the body—to treat edema and ascites. A health care provider may remove large amounts of ascitic fluid from the abdomen and check for spontaneous bacterial peritonitis. A health care provider may prescribe bacteria-fighting medications called antibiotics to prevent infection. He or she may prescribe oral antibiotics; however, severe infection with ascites requires intravenous (IV) antibiotics.

Hepatic encephalopathy. A health care provider treats hepatic encephalopathy by cleansing the bowel with lactulose, a laxative given orally or as an enema—a liquid put into the rectum. A health care provider may also add antibiotics to the treatment. Hepatic encephalopathy may improve as other complications of cirrhosis are controlled.

Hepatorenal syndrome. Some people with cirrhosis who develop hepatorenal syndrome must undergo regular dialysis treatment, which filters wastes and extra fluid from the body by means other than the kidneys. People may also need medications to improve blood flow through the kidneys.

Osteoporosis. A health care provider may prescribe bisphosphonate medications to improve bone density.

Gallstones and bile duct stones. A health care provider may use surgery to remove gallstones. He or she may use endoscopic retrograde cholangiopancreatography, which uses balloons and basketlike devices, to retrieve the bile duct stones.

Liver cancer. A health care provider may recommend screening tests every 6 to 12 months to check for signs of liver cancer. Screening tests can find cancer before the person has symptoms of the disease. Cancer treatment is usually more effective when the health care provider finds the disease early. Health care providers use blood tests, ultrasound, or both to screen for liver cancer in people with cirrhosis. He or she may treat cancer with a combination of surgery, radiation, and chemotherapy.

When is a liver transplant considered for cirrhosis?

A health care provider may consider a liver transplant when cirrhosis leads to liver failure or treatment for complications is ineffective. Liver transplantation is surgery to remove a diseased or an injured liver and replace it with a healthy whole liver or part of a liver from another person, called a donor.

Eating, Diet, and Nutrition

A healthy diet is important in all stages of cirrhosis because malnutrition is common in people with this disease. Malnutrition is a condition that occurs when the body does not get enough nutrients. Cirrhosis may lead to malnutrition because it can cause

- people to eat less because of symptoms such as loss of appetite

- changes in metabolism

- reduced absorption of vitamins and minerals

Health care providers can recommend a meal plan that is well balanced and provides enough calories and protein. If ascites develops, a health care provider or dietitian may recommend a sodium-restricted diet. To improve nutrition, the health care provider may prescribe a liquid supplement. A person may take the liquid by mouth or through a nasogastric tube—a tiny tube inserted through the nose and throat that reaches into the stomach.

A person with cirrhosis should not eat raw shellfish, which can contain a bacterium that causes serious infection. Cirrhosis affects the immune system, making people with cirrhosis more likely than healthy people to develop an infection after eating shellfish that contain this bacterium.

A health care provider may recommend calcium and vitamin D supplements to help prevent osteoporosis.

413

Chapter 33

Primary Sclerosing Cholangitis

What is primary sclerosing cholangitis?

Primary sclerosing cholangitis is a condition that affects the bile ducts. These ducts carry bile (a fluid that helps to digest fats) from the liver, where bile is produced, to the gallbladder, where it is stored, and to the small intestine, where it aids in digestion. Primary sclerosing cholangitis occurs because of inflammation in the bile ducts (cholangitis) that leads to scarring (sclerosis) and narrowing of the ducts. As a result, bile cannot be released to the gallbladder and small intestine, and it builds up in the liver.

Primary sclerosing cholangitis is usually diagnosed around age 40, and for unknown reasons, it affects men twice as often as women. Many people have no signs or symptoms of the condition when they are diagnosed, but routine blood tests reveal liver problems. When apparent, the earliest signs and symptoms of primary sclerosing cholangitis include extreme tiredness (fatigue), discomfort in the abdomen, and severe itchiness (pruritus). As the condition worsens, affected individuals may develop yellowing of the skin and whites of the eyes (jaundice) and an enlarged spleen (splenomegaly). Eventually, the buildup of bile damages the liver cells, causing chronic liver disease (cirrhosis) and liver failure. Without bile available to digest them, fats pass through

Text in this chapter is excerpted from "Primary Sclerosing Cholangitis," Genetics Home Reference (GHR), November 2, 2015.

the body. As a result, weight loss and shortages of vitamins that are absorbed with and stored in fats (fat-soluble vitamins) can occur. A fat-soluble vitamin called vitamin D helps absorb calcium and helps bones harden, and lack of this vitamin can cause thinning of the bones (osteoporosis) in people with primary sclerosing cholangitis.

Primary sclerosing cholangitis is often associated with another condition called inflammatory bowel disease, which is characterized by inflammation of the intestines that causes open sores (ulcers) in the intestines and abdominal pain. However, the reason for this link is unclear. Approximately 70 percent of people with primary sclerosing cholangitis have inflammatory bowel disease, most commonly a form of the condition known as ulcerative colitis. In addition, people with primary sclerosing cholangitis are more likely to have an autoimmune disorder, such as type 1 diabetes, celiac disease, or thyroid disease, than people without the condition. Autoimmune disorders occur when the immune system malfunctions and attacks the body's tissues and organs. People with primary sclerosing cholangitis also have an increased risk of developing cancer, particularly cancer of the bile ducts (cholangiocarcinoma).

How common is primary sclerosing cholangitis?

An estimated 1 in 10,000 people have primary sclerosing cholangitis, and the condition is diagnosed in approximately 1 in 100,000 people per year worldwide.

How do people inherit primary sclerosing cholangitis?

The inheritance pattern of primary sclerosing cholangitis is unknown because many genetic and environmental factors are likely to be involved. This condition tends to cluster in families, however, and having an affected family member is a risk factor for developing the disease.

Chapter 34

Other Liver Disorders

Chapter Contents

Section 34.1

Porphyria

Text in this section is excerpted from "Porphyria," National Institute
of Diabetes and Digestive and Kidney Diseases (NIDDK),
December 2013.

What are porphyrias?

Porphyrias are rare disorders that affect mainly the skin or nervous
system and may cause abdominal pain. These disorders are usually inherited, meaning they are caused by abnormalities in genes passed from
parents to children. When a person has a porphyria, cells fail to change
body chemicals called porphyrins and porphyrin precursors into heme,
the substance that gives blood its red color. The body makes heme mainly
in the bone marrow and liver. Bone marrow is the soft, sponge-like tissue
inside the bones; it makes stem cells that develop into one of the three
types of blood cells—red blood cells, white blood cells, and platelets.

The process of making heme is called the heme biosynthetic pathway. One of eight enzymes controls each step of the process. The body
has a problem making heme if any one of the enzymes is at a low level,
also called a deficiency. Porphyrins and porphyrin precursors of heme
then build up in the body and cause illness.

What is heme and what does it do?

Heme is a red pigment composed of iron linked to a chemical called
protoporphyrin. Heme has important functions in the body. The largest
amounts of heme are in the form of hemoglobin, found in red blood cells
and bone marrow. Hemoglobin carries oxygen from the lungs to all parts
of the body. In the liver, heme is a component of proteins that break down
hormones, medications, and other chemicals and keep liver cells functioning normally. Heme is an important part of nearly every cell in the body.

What are the types of porphyria?

Each of the eight types of porphyria corresponds to low levels of
a specific enzyme in the heme biosynthetic pathway. Experts often

classify porphyrias as acute or cutaneous based on the symptoms a person experiences:

- Acute porphyrias affect the nervous system. They occur rapidly and last only a short time.

- Cutaneous porphyrias affect the skin.

Two types of acute porphyrias, hereditary coproporphyria and variegate porphyria, can also have cutaneous symptoms.

Experts also classify porphyrias as erythropoietic or hepatic:

- In erythropoietic porphyrias, the body overproduces porphyrins, mainly in the bone marrow.

- In hepatic porphyrias, the body overproduces porphyrins and porphyrin precursors, mainly in the liver.

Table 36.1 lists each type of porphyria, the deficient enzyme responsible for the disorder, and the main location of porphyrin buildup.

How Common Is Porphyria?

The exact rates of porphyria are unknown and vary around the world. For example, porphyria cutanea tarda is most common in the United States, and variegate porphyria is most common in South America.

What causes porphyria?

Most porphyrias are inherited disorders. Scientists have identified genes for all eight enzymes in the heme biosynthetic pathway. Most porphyrias result from inheriting an abnormal gene, also called a gene mutation, from one parent. Some porphyrias, such as congenital erythropoietic porphyria, hepatoerythropoietic porphyria, and erythropoietic protoporphyria, occur when a person inherits two abnormal genes, one from each parent. The likeliness of a person passing the abnormal gene or genes to the next generation depends on the type of porphyria.

Porphyria cutanea tarda is usually an acquired disorder, meaning factors other than genes cause the enzyme deficiency. This type of porphyria can be triggered by

- too much iron

- use of alcohol or estrogen

Table 34.1. Types of Porphyria

Type of Porphyria	Deficient Enzyme	Main Location of Porphyrin Buildup
delta-aminolevulinate-dehydratase deficiency porphyria	delta-aminolevulinic acid dehydratase	liver
acute intermittent porphyria	porphobilinogen deaminase	liver
hereditary coproporphyria	coproporphyrinogen oxidase	liver
variegate porphyria	protoporphyrinogen oxidase	liver
congenital erythropoietic porphyria	uroporphyrinogen III cosynthase	bone marrow
porphyria cutanea tarda	uroporphyrinogen decarboxylase (~75% deficiency)	liver
hepatoerythropoietic porphyria	uroporphyrinogen decarboxylase (~90% deficiency)	bone marrow
erythropoietic protoporphyria*	ferrochelatase (~75% deficiency)	bone marrow

Protoporphyria XLPP is a variant of erythropoietic protoporphyria.

- smoking
- chronic hepatitis C—a long-lasting liver disease that causes inflammation, or swelling, of the liver
- HIV—the virus that causes AIDS
- abnormal genes associated with hemochromatosis—the most common form of iron overload disease, which causes the body to absorb too much iron

For all types of porphyria, symptoms can be triggered by

- use of alcohol
- smoking
- use of certain medications or hormones
- exposure to sunlight

- stress

- dieting and fasting

What are the symptoms of porphyria?

Some people with porphyria-causing gene mutations have latent porphyria, meaning they have no symptoms of the disorder. Symptoms of cutaneous porphyrias include

- oversensitivity to sunlight

- blisters on exposed areas of the skin

- itching and swelling on exposed areas of the skin

Symptoms of acute porphyrias include

- pain in the abdomen—the area between the chest and hips

- pain in the chest, limbs, or back

- nausea and vomiting

- constipation—a condition in which an adult has fewer than three bowel movements a week or a child has fewer than two bowel movements a week, depending on the person

- urinary retention—the inability to empty the bladder completely

- confusion

- hallucinations

- seizures and muscle weakness

Symptoms of acute porphyrias can develop over hours or days and last for days or weeks. These symptoms can come and go over time, while symptoms of cutaneous porphyrias tend to be more continuous. Porphyria symptoms can vary widely in severity.

How is porphyria diagnosed?

A health care provider diagnoses porphyria with blood, urine, and stool tests. These tests take place at a health care provider's office or a commercial facility. A blood test involves drawing blood and sending the sample to a lab for analysis. For urine and stool tests, the patient collects a sample of urine or stool in a special container. A health care provider tests the samples in the office or sends them to a lab for analysis. High levels of porphyrins or porphyrin precursors in blood, urine, or stool indicate porphyria. A health care provider may also recommend DNA testing of a blood sample to look for known gene mutations that cause porphyrias.

How is porphyria treated?

Treatment for porphyria depends on the type of porphyria the person has and the severity of the symptoms.

Acute Porphyrias

A health care provider treats acute porphyrias with heme or glucose loading to decrease the liver's production of porphyrins and porphyrin precursors. A patient receives heme intravenously once a day for 4 days. Glucose loading involves giving a patient a glucose solution by mouth or intravenously. Heme is usually more effective and is the treatment of choice unless symptoms are mild. In rare instances, if symptoms are severe, a health care provider will recommend liver transplantation to treat acute porphyria. In liver transplantation, a surgeon removes a diseased or an injured liver and replaces it with a healthy, whole liver or a segment of a liver from another person, called a donor. A patient has liver transplantation surgery in a hospital under general anesthesia. Liver transplantation can cure liver failure.

Cutaneous Porphyrias

The most important step a person can take to treat a cutaneous porphyria is to avoid sunlight as much as possible. Other cutaneous porphyrias are treated as follows:

- **Porphyria cutanea tarda.** A health care provider treats porphyria cutanea tarda by removing factors that tend to activate the disease and by performing repeated therapeutic phlebotomies to reduce iron in the liver. Therapeutic phlebotomy is the removal of about a pint of blood from a vein in the arm. A technician performs the procedure at a blood donation center, such as a hospital, clinic, or bloodmobile. A patient does not require anesthesia. Another treatment approach is low-dose hydroxychloroquine tablets to reduce porphyrins in the liver.

- **Erythropoietic protoporphyria.** People with erythropoietic protoporphyria may be given beta-carotene or cysteine to improve sunlight tolerance, though these medications do not lower porphyrin levels. Experts recommend hepatitis A and B vaccines and avoiding alcohol to prevent protoporphyric liver failure. A health care provider may use liver transplantation or a combination of medications to treat people who develop liver failure. Unfortunately, liver transplantation does not correct the primary defect, which is the continuous overproduction of protoporphyria by bone marrow. Successful bone marrow transplantations may successfully cure erythropoietic protoporphyria. A health care provider only considers bone marrow transplantation if the disease is severe and leading to secondary liver disease.

- **Congenital erythropoietic porphyria and hepatoerythropoietic porphyria.** People with congenital erythropoietic porphyria or hepatoerythropoietic porphyria may need surgery to remove the spleen or blood transfusions to treat anemia. A surgeon removes the spleen in a hospital, and a patient receives general anesthesia. With a blood transfusion, a patient receives blood through an intravenous (IV) line inserted into a vein. A technician performs the procedure at a blood donation center, and a patient does not need anesthesia.

Secondary Porphyrinurias

Conditions called secondary porphyrinurias, such as disorders of the liver and bone marrow, as well as a number of drugs, chemicals, and toxins are often mistaken for porphyria because they lead to mild or moderate increases in porphyrin levels in the urine. Only high—not mild or moderate—levels of porphyrin or porphyrin precursors lead to a diagnosis of porphyria.

Eating, Diet, and Nutrition

People with an acute porphyria should eat a diet with an average-to-high level of carbohydrates. The recommended dietary allowance for carbohydrates is 130 g per day for adults and children 1 year of age or older; pregnant and breastfeeding women need higher intakes.

People should avoid limiting intake of carbohydrates and calories, even for short periods of time, as this type of dieting or fasting can trigger symptoms. People with an acute porphyria who want to lose weight should talk with their health care providers about diets they can follow to lose weight gradually.

People undergoing therapeutic phlebotomies should drink plenty of milk, water, or juice before and after each procedure.

A health care provider may recommend vitamin and mineral supplements for people with a cutaneous porphyria.

Section 34.2

Glycogen Storage Disease Type I

Text in this section is excerpted from "Glycogen Storage Disease Type I," Genetics Home Reference (GHR), November 2, 2015.

What is glycogen storage disease type I?

Glycogen storage disease type I (also known as GSDI or von Gierke disease) is an inherited disorder caused by the buildup of a complex sugar called glycogen in the body's cells. The accumulation of glycogen in certain organs and tissues, especially the liver, kidneys, and small intestines, impairs their ability to function normally.

Signs and symptoms of this condition typically appear around the age of 3 or 4 months, when babies start to sleep through the night and do not eat as frequently as newborns. Affected infants may have low blood sugar (hypoglycemia), which can lead to seizures. They can also have a buildup of lactic acid in the body (lactic acidosis), high blood levels of a waste product called uric acid (hyperuricemia), and excess amounts of fats in the blood (hyperlipidemia). As they get older, children with GSDI have thin arms and legs and short stature. An enlarged liver may give the appearance of a protruding abdomen. The kidneys may also be enlarged. Affected individuals may also have diarrhea and deposits of cholesterol in the skin (xanthomas).

People with GSDI may experience delayed puberty. Beginning in young to mid-adulthood, affected individuals may have thinning of the bones (osteoporosis), a form of arthritis resulting from uric acid crystals in the joints (gout), kidney disease, and high blood pressure in the blood vessels that supply the lungs (pulmonary hypertension). Females with this condition may also have abnormal development of the ovaries (polycystic ovaries). In affected teens and adults, tumors called adenomas may form in the liver. Adenomas are usually noncancerous (benign), but occasionally these tumors can become cancerous (malignant).

Researchers have described two types of GSDI, which differ in their signs and symptoms and genetic cause. These types are known as glycogen storage disease type Ia (GSDIa) and glycogen storage disease type Ib (GSDIb). Two other forms of GSDI have been described, and they were originally named types Ic and Id. However, these types are now known to be variations of GSDIb; for this reason, GSDIb is sometimes called GSD type I non-a.

Many people with GSDIb have a shortage of white blood cells (neutropenia), which can make them prone to recurrent bacterial infections. Neutropenia is usually apparent by age 1. Many affected individuals also have inflammation of the intestinal walls (inflammatory bowel disease). People with GSDIb may have oral problems including cavities, inflammation of the gums (gingivitis), chronic gum (periodontal) disease, abnormal tooth development, and open sores (ulcers) in the mouth. The neutropenia and oral problems are specific to people with GSDIb and are typically not seen in people with GSDIa.

How common is glycogen storage disease type I?

The overall incidence of GSDI is 1 in 100,000 individuals. GSDIa is more common than GSDIb, accounting for 80 percent of all GSDI cases.

How do people inherit glycogen storage disease type I?

This condition is inherited in an autosomal recessive pattern, which means both copies of the gene in each cell have mutations. The parents of an individual with an autosomal recessive condition each carry one copy of the mutated gene, but they typically do not show signs and symptoms of the condition.

What other names do people use for glycogen storage disease type I?

- glucose-6-phosphate deficiency
- glucose-6-phosphate transport defect
- GSD I
- GSD type I
- hepatorenal form of glycogen storage disease

- hepatorenal glycogenosis
- von Gierke disease
- von Gierke's disease

Section 34.3

Hemochromatosis

Text in this section is excerpted from "Hemochromatosis," National Institute of Diabetes and Digestive and Kidney Diseases (NIDDK), March 2014.

What is hemochromatosis?

Hemochromatosis is the most common form of iron overload disease. Too much iron in the body causes hemochromatosis. Iron is important because it is part of hemoglobin, a molecule in the blood that transports oxygen from the lungs to all body tissues. However, too much iron in the body leads to iron overload—a buildup of extra iron that, without treatment, can damage organs such as the liver, heart, and pancreas; endocrine glands; and joints.

The three types of hemochromatosis are primary hemochromatosis, also called hereditary hemochromatosis; secondary hemochromatosis; and neonatal hemochromatosis.

What causes hemochromatosis?

Primary Hemochromatosis

Inherited genetic defects cause primary hemochromatosis, and mutations in the *HFE* gene are associated with up to 90 percent of cases. The *HFE* gene helps regulate the amount of iron absorbed from food. The two known mutations of *HFE* are *C282Y* and *H63D*. *C282Y* defects are the most common cause of primary hemochromatosis.

People inherit two copies of the *HFE* gene—one copy from each parent. Most people who inherit two copies of the *HFE* gene with the *C282Y* defect will have higher-than-average iron absorption. However, not all of these people will develop health problems associated with hemochromatosis. One recent study found that 31 percent of people with two copies of the *C282Y* defect developed health problems by their early fifties. Men who develop health problems from HFE defects typically develop them after age 40. Women who develop health problems from *HFE* defects typically develop them after menopause.

People who inherit two *H63D* defects or one *C282Y* and one *H63D* defect may have higher than-average iron absorption. However, they are unlikely to develop iron overload and organ damage.

Rare defects in other genes may also cause primary hemochromatosis. Mutations in the *hemojuvelin* or *hepcidin* genes cause juvenile hemochromatosis, a type of primary hemochromatosis. People with juvenile hemochromatosis typically develop severe iron overload and liver and heart damage between ages 15 and 30.

Secondary Hemochromatosis

Hemochromatosis that is not inherited is called secondary hemochromatosis. The most common cause of secondary hemochromatosis is frequent blood transfusions in people with severe anemia. Anemia is a condition in which red blood cells are fewer or smaller than normal, which means they carry less oxygen to the body's cells. Types of anemia that may require frequent blood transfusions include

- congenital, or inherited, anemias such as sickle cell disease, thalassemia, and Fanconi's syndrome

- severe acquired anemias, which are not inherited, such as aplastic anemia and autoimmune hemolytic anemia

Liver diseases—such as alcoholic liver disease, nonalcoholic steatohepatitis, and chronic hepatitis C infection—may cause mild iron overload. However, this iron overload causes much less liver damage than the underlying liver disease causes.

Neonatal Hemochromatosis

Neonatal hemochromatosis is a rare disease characterized by liver failure and death in fetuses and newborns. Researchers are studying the causes of neonatal hemochromatosis and believe more than one factor may lead to the disease.

Experts previously considered neonatal hemochromatosis a type of primary hemochromatosis. However, recent studies suggest genetic defects that increase iron absorption do not cause this disease. Instead,

427

the mother's immune system may produce antibodies—proteins made by the immune system to protect the body from foreign substances such as bacteria or viruses—that damage the liver of the fetus. Women who have had one child with neonatal hemochromatosis are at risk for having more children with the disease. Treating these women during pregnancy with intravenous (IV) immunoglobulin—a solution of antibodies from healthy people—can prevent fetal liver damage.

Researchers supported by the National Institute of Diabetes and Digestive and Kidney Diseases (NIDDK) recently found that a combination of exchange transfusion—removing blood and replacing it with donor blood—and IV immunoglobulin is an effective treatment for babies born with neonatal hemochromatosis.

Who is more likely to develop hemochromatosis?

Primary hemochromatosis mainly affects Caucasians of Northern European descent. This disease is one of the most common genetic disorders in the United States. About four to five out of every 1,000 Caucasians carry two copies of the *C282Y* mutation of the *HFE* gene and are susceptible to developing hemochromatosis. About one out of every 10 Caucasians carries one copy of *C282Y*.

Hemochromatosis is extremely rare in African Americans, Asian Americans, Hispanics/Latinos, and American Indians. *HFE* mutations are usually not the cause of hemochromatosis in these populations.

Both men and women can inherit the gene defects for hemochromatosis; however, not all will develop the symptoms of hemochromatosis. Men usually develop symptoms at a younger age than women. Women lose blood—which contains iron—regularly during menstruation; therefore, women with the gene defects that cause hemochromatosis may not develop iron overload and related symptoms and complications until after menopause.

What are the symptoms of hemochromatosis?

A person with hemochromatosis may notice one or more of the following symptoms:

- joint pain
- fatigue, or feeling tired
- unexplained weight loss
- abnormal bronze or gray skin color

- abdominal pain
- loss of sex drive

Not everyone with hemochromatosis will develop these symptoms.

What are the complications of hemochromatosis?

Without treatment, iron may build up in the organs and cause complications, including

- cirrhosis, or scarring of liver tissue
- diabetes
- irregular heart rhythms or weakening of the heart muscle
- arthritis
- erectile dysfunction

The complication most often associated with hemochromatosis is liver damage. Iron buildup in the liver causes cirrhosis, which increases the chance of developing liver cancer.

For some people, complications may be the first sign of hemochromatosis. However, not everyone with hemochromatosis will develop complications.

How is hemochromatosis diagnosed?

Health care providers use medical and family history, a physical exam, and routine blood tests to diagnose hemochromatosis or other conditions that could cause the same symptoms or complications.

- **Medical and family history.** Taking a medical and family history is one of the first things a health care provider may do to help diagnose hemochromatosis. The health care provider will look for clues that may indicate hemochromatosis, such as a family history of arthritis or unexplained liver disease.

- **Physical exam.** After taking a medical history, a health care provider will perform a physical exam, which may help diagnose hemochromatosis. During a physical exam, a health care provider usually

  - examines a patient's body
  - uses a stethoscope to listen to bodily sounds
  - taps on specific areas of the patient's body

- **Blood tests.** A blood test involves drawing blood at a health care provider's office or a commercial facility and sending the sample to a lab for analysis. Blood tests can determine whether the amount of iron stored in the body is higher than normal:

  - The **transferrin saturation test** shows how much iron is bound to the protein that carries iron in the blood. Transferrin saturation values above or equal to 45 percent are considered abnormal.

  - The **serum ferritin test** detects the amount of ferritin—a protein that stores iron—in the blood. Levels above 300 μg/L in men and 200 μg/L in women are considered abnormal. Levels above 1,000 μg/L in men or women indicate a high chance of iron overload and organ damage.

  If either test shows higher-than-average levels of iron in the body, health care providers can order a special blood test that can detect two copies of the *C282Y* mutation to confirm the diagnosis. If the mutation is not present, health care providers will look for other causes.

- **Liver biopsy.** Health care providers may perform a liver biopsy, a procedure that involves taking a piece of liver tissue for examination with a microscope for signs of damage or disease. The health care provider may ask the patient to temporarily stop taking certain medications before the liver biopsy. The health care provider may ask the patient to fast for 8 hours before the procedure.

  A health care provider performs a liver biopsy at a hospital or an outpatient center. The health care provider sends the liver sample to a pathology lab where the pathologist—a doctor who specializes in diagnosing disease—looks at the tissue with a microscope and sends a report to the patient's health care provider. The biopsy shows how much iron has accumulated in the liver and whether the patient has liver damage.

Hemochromatosis is rare, and health care providers may not think to test for this disease. Thus, the disease is often not diagnosed or treated. The initial symptoms can be diverse, vague, and similar to the symptoms of many other diseases. Health care providers may focus on the symptoms and complications caused by hemochromatosis rather than on the underlying iron overload. However, if a health care provider diagnoses and treats the iron overload caused by hemochromatosis before organ damage has occurred, a person can live a normal, healthy life.

Who should be tested for hemochromatosis?

Experts recommend testing for hemochromatosis in people who have symptoms, complications, or a family history of the disease.

Some researchers have suggested widespread screening for the *C282Y* mutation in the general population. However, screening is not cost-effective. Although the *C282Y* mutation occurs quite frequently, the disease caused by the mutation is rare, and many people with two copies of the mutation never develop iron overload or organ damage.

Researchers and public health officials suggest the following:

- Siblings of people who have hemochromatosis should have their blood tested to see if they have the *C282Y* mutation.

- Parents, children, and other close relatives of people who have hemochromatosis should consider being tested.

- Health care providers should consider testing people who have severe and continuing fatigue, unexplained cirrhosis, joint pain or arthritis, heart problems, erectile dysfunction, or diabetes because these health issues may result from hemochromatosis.

How is hemochromatosis treated?

Health care providers treat hemochromatosis by drawing blood. This process is called phlebotomy. Phlebotomy rids the body of extra iron. This treatment is simple, inexpensive, and safe.

Based on the severity of the iron overload, a patient will have phlebotomy to remove a pint of blood once or twice a week for several months to a year, and occasionally longer. Health care providers will test serum ferritin levels periodically to monitor iron levels. The goal is to bring serum ferritin levels to the low end of the average range and keep them there. Depending on the lab, the level is 25 to 50 μg/L.

After phlebotomy reduces serum ferritin levels to the desired level, patients may need maintenance phlebotomy treatment every few months. Some patients may need phlebotomies more often. Serum ferritin tests every 6 months or once a year will help determine how often a patient should have blood drawn. Many blood donation centers provide free phlebotomy treatment for people with hemochromatosis.

Treating hemochromatosis before organs are damaged can prevent complications such as cirrhosis, heart problems, arthritis, and diabetes. Treatment cannot cure these conditions in patients who already have them at diagnosis. However, treatment will help most of these conditions improve. The treatment's effectiveness depends on the degree of organ damage. For example, treating hemochromatosis can stop the progression of liver damage in its early stages and lead to a normal life expectancy. However, if a patient develops cirrhosis, his or her chance of developing liver cancer increases, even with phlebotomy treatment. Arthritis usually does not improve even after phlebotomy removes extra iron.

Eating, Diet, and Nutrition

Iron is an essential nutrient found in many foods. Healthy people usually absorb less than 10 percent of iron in the food they eat. People with hemochromatosis absorb up to 30 percent of that iron. People with hemochromatosis can help prevent iron overload by

- eating only moderate amounts of iron-rich foods, such as red meat and organ meat

- avoiding supplements that contain iron

- avoiding supplements that contain vitamin C, which increases iron absorption

People with hemochromatosis can take steps to help prevent liver damage, including

- limiting the amount of alcoholic beverages they drink because alcohol increases their chance of cirrhosis and liver cancer

- avoiding alcoholic beverages entirely if they already have cirrhosis

Section 34.4

Wilson Disease

Text in this section is excerpted from "Wilson Disease," National
Institute of Diabetes and Digestive and Kidney Diseases (NIDDK),
June 2014.

What is Wilson disease?

Wilson disease is a genetic disease that prevents the body from
removing extra copper. The body needs a small amount of copper from
food to stay healthy; however, too much copper is poisonous. Normally, the liver filters extra copper and releases it into bile. Bile is a
fluid made by the liver that carries toxins and wastes out of the body
through the gastrointestinal tract. In Wilson disease, the liver does not
filter copper correctly and copper builds up in the liver, brain, eyes, and
other organs. Over time, high copper levels can cause life-threatening
organ damage.

What causes Wilson disease?

Wilson disease is caused by an inherited autosomal recessive mutation, or change, in the ATP7B gene. In an autosomal recessive disease,
the child has to inherit the gene mutation from both parents to have
an increased likelihood for the disease. The chance of a child inheriting autosomal recessive mutations from both parents with a gene
mutation is 25 percent, or one in four. If only one parent carries the
mutated gene, the child will not get the disease, although the child may
inherit one copy of the gene mutation. The child is called a "carrier"
of the disease and can pass the gene mutation to the next generation.

Who is more likely to develop Wilson disease?

Men and women develop Wilson disease at equal rates. About one in
30,000 people have Wilson disease. Symptoms usually appear between
ages 5 and 35; however, new cases have been reported in people ages
3 to 72.

433

What are the signs and symptoms of Wilson disease?

The signs and symptoms of Wilson disease vary, depending on what organs of the body are affected. Wilson disease is present at birth; however, the signs and symptoms of the disease do not appear until the copper builds up in the liver, the brain, or other organs.

When people have signs and symptoms, they usually affect the liver, the central nervous system, or both. The central nervous system includes the brain, the spinal cord, and nerves throughout the body. Sometimes a person does not have symptoms and a health care provider discovers the disease during a routine physical exam or blood test, or during an illness. Children can have Wilson disease for several years before any signs and symptoms occur. People with Wilson disease may have

- liver-related signs and symptoms

- central nervous system-related signs and symptoms

- mental health-related signs and symptoms

- other signs and symptoms

Liver-Related Signs and Symptoms

People with Wilson disease may develop signs and symptoms of chronic, or long lasting, liver disease:

- weakness

- fatigue, or feeling tired

- loss of appetite

- nausea

- vomiting

- weight loss

- pain and bloating from fluid accumulating in the abdomen

- edema—swelling, usually in the legs, feet, or ankles and less often in the hands or face

- itching

- spiderlike blood vessels, called spider angiomas, near the surface of the skin

- muscle cramps

434

- jaundice, a condition that causes the skin and whites of the eyes to turn yellow

Some people with Wilson disease may not develop signs or symptoms of liver disease until they develop acute liver failure—a condition that develops suddenly.

Central Nervous System-Related Signs and Symptoms

Central nervous system-related symptoms usually appear in people after the liver has retained a lot of copper; however, signs and symptoms of liver disease may not be present. Central nervous system-related symptoms occur most often in adults and sometimes occur in children. Signs and symptoms include

- tremors or uncontrolled movements

- muscle stiffness

- problems with speech, swallowing, or physical coordination

A health care provider may refer people with these symptoms to a neurologist—a doctor who specializes in nervous system diseases.

Mental Health-Related Signs and Symptoms

Some people will have mental health-related signs and symptoms when copper builds up in the central nervous system. Signs and symptoms may include

- personality changes

- depression

- feeling anxious, or nervous, about most things

- psychosis—when a person loses contact with reality

Other Signs and Symptoms

Other signs and symptoms of Wilson disease may include

- anemia, a condition in which red blood cells are fewer or smaller than normal, which prevents the body's cells from getting enough oxygen

- arthritis, a condition in which a person has pain and swelling in one or more joints

- high levels of amino acids, protein, uric acid, and carbohydrates in urine

- low platelet or white blood cell count

- osteoporosis, a condition in which the bones become less dense and more likely to fracture

What are the complications of Wilson disease?

People who have Wilson disease that is not treated or diagnosed early can have serious complications, such as

- cirrhosis—scarring of the liver

- kidney damage—as liver function decreases, the kidneys may be damaged

- persistent nervous system problems when nervous system symptoms do not resolve

- liver cancer—hepatocellular carcinoma is a type of liver cancer that can occur in people with cirrhosis

- liver failure—a condition in which the liver stops working properly

- death, if left untreated

How is Wilson disease diagnosed?

A health care provider may use several tests and exams to diagnose Wilson disease, including the following:

- medical and family history

- physical exam

- blood tests

- urine tests

- liver biopsy

- imaging tests

Health care providers typically see the same symptoms of Wilson disease in other conditions, and the symptoms of Wilson disease do not occur together often, making the disease difficult to diagnose.

Medical and Family History

A health care provider may take a medical and family history to help diagnose Wilson disease.

Physical Exam

A physical exam may help diagnose Wilson disease. During a physical exam, a health care provider usually

- examines a patient's body

- uses a stethoscope to listen to sounds related to the abdomen

A health care provider will use a special light called a slit lamp to look for Kayser-Fleischer rings in the eyes.

Blood Tests

A nurse or technician will draw blood samples at a health care provider's office or a commercial facility and send the samples to a lab for analysis. A health care provider may

- perform liver enzyme or function tests—blood tests that may indicate liver abnormalities.

- check copper levels in the blood. Since the copper is deposited into the organs and is not circulating in the blood, most people with Wilson disease have a lower-than-normal level of copper in the blood. In cases of acute liver failure caused by Wilson disease, the level of blood copper is often higher than normal.

- check the level of ceruloplasmin—a protein that carries copper in the bloodstream. Most people with Wilson disease have a lower-than-normal ceruloplasmin level.

- conduct genetic testing. A health care provider may recommend genetic testing in cases of a known family history of Wilson disease.

Urine Tests

24-hour urine collection. A patient will collect urine at home in a special container provided by a health care provider's office or a commercial facility. A health care provider sends the sample to a lab for analysis. A 24-hour urine collection will show increased copper in the urine in most patients who have symptoms due to Wilson disease.

Liver Biopsy

A liver biopsy is a procedure that involves taking a small piece of liver tissue for examination with a microscope for signs of damage or disease. The health care provider may ask the patient to stop taking certain medications temporarily before the liver biopsy. He or she may also ask the patient to fast—eat or drink nothing—for 8 hours before the procedure.

Imaging Tests

A health care provider may order imaging tests to evaluate brain abnormalities in patients who have nervous system symptoms often seen with Wilson disease, or in patients diagnosed with Wilson disease. Health care providers do not use brain imaging tests to diagnose Wilson disease, though certain findings may suggest the patient has the disease.

Magnetic resonance imaging (MRI). An MRI is a test that takes pictures of the body's internal organs and soft tissues without using X-rays.

Computerized tomography (CT) scan. A CT scan uses a combination of X-rays and computer technology to create images.

How is Wilson disease treated?

A health care provider will treat Wilson disease with a lifelong effort to reduce and control the amount of copper in the body. Treatment may include

- medications

- changes in eating, diet, and nutrition

- a liver transplant

Medications

A health care provider will prescribe medications to treat Wilson disease. The medications have different actions that health care providers use during different phases of the treatment.

Chelating agents. Chelating agents are medications that remove extra copper from the body by releasing it from organs into the bloodstream. Once the cooper is in the bloodstream, the kidneys then filter the copper and pass it into the urine. A health care provider usually recommends chelating agents at the beginning of treatment. A potential side effect of chelating agents is that nervous system symptoms may become worse during treatment. The two medications available for this type of treatment include

- trientine (Syprine)—the risk for side effects and worsening nervous system symptoms appears to be lower with trientine than d-penicillamine. Researchers are still studying the side effects; however, some health care providers prefer to prescribe trientine as the first treatment of choice because it appears to be safer.

- d-penicillamine—people taking d-penicillamine may have other reactions or side effects, such as

  - fever

  - a rash

  - kidney problems

  - bone marrow problems

Zinc. A health care provider will prescribe zinc for patients who do not have symptoms, or after a person has completed successful treatment using a chelating agent and symptoms begin to improve. Zinc, taken by mouth as zinc salts such as zinc acetate (Galzin), blocks the digestive tract's absorption of copper from food. Although most people taking zinc usually do not experience side effects, some people may experience stomach upset. A health care provider may prescribe zinc for children with Wilson disease who show no symptoms. Women may take the full dosage of zinc safely during pregnancy.

Changes in Eating, Diet, and Nutrition

People with Wilson disease should reduce their dietary copper intake by avoiding foods that are high in copper, such as

- shellfish

- liver

- mushrooms

- nuts

- chocolate

People should not eat these foods during the initial treatment and talk with the health care provider to discuss if they are safe to eat in moderation during maintenance treatment.

People with Wilson disease whose tap water runs through copper pipes or comes from a well should check the copper levels in the tap water. Water that sits in copper pipes may pick up copper residue, but running water lowers the level to within acceptable limits. People with Wilson disease should not use copper containers or cookware to store or prepare food or drinks.

To help ensure coordinated and safe care, people should discuss their use of complementary and alternative medical practices, including their use of vitamins and dietary supplements, with their health care provider. If the health care provider recommends taking any type of supplement or vitamin, a pharmacist can recommend types that do not contain copper.

People should talk with a health care provider about diet changes to reduce copper intake.

Liver Transplant

A liver transplant may be necessary in people when

- cirrhosis leads to liver failure

- acute liver failure happens suddenly

- treatment is not effective

A liver transplant is an operation to remove a diseased or an injured liver and replace it with a healthy one from another person, called a donor. A successful transplant is a life-saving treatment for people with liver failure.

How can Wilson disease be prevented?

A person cannot prevent Wilson disease; however, people with a family history of Wilson disease, especially those with an affected sibling or parent, should talk with a health care provider about testing. A health care provider may be able to diagnose Wilson disease before symptoms appear. Early diagnosis and treatment of Wilson disease can reduce or even prevent organ damage.

Section 34.5

Sarcoidosis

Text in this section is excerpted from "What Is Sarcoidosis?"
National Heart, Lung, and Blood Institute (NHLBI), June 14, 2013.

What is sarcoidosis?

Sarcoidosis is a disease of unknown cause that leads to inflammation. This disease affects your body's organs.

Normally, your immune system defends your body against foreign or harmful substances. For example, it sends special cells to protect organs that are in danger.

These cells release chemicals that recruit other cells to isolate and destroy the harmful substance. Inflammation occurs during this process. Once the harmful substance is gone, the cells and the inflammation go away.

In people who have sarcoidosis, the inflammation doesn't go away. Instead, some of the immune system cells cluster to form lumps called granulomas in various organs in your body.

Overview

Sarcoidosis can affect any organ in your body. However, it's more likely to affect some organs than others. The disease usually starts in the lungs, skin, and/or lymph nodes (especially the lymph nodes in your chest).

Also, the disease often affects the eyes and liver. Although less common, sarcoidosis can affect the heart and brain, leading to serious complications.

If many granulomas form in an organ, they can affect how the organ works. This can cause signs and symptoms. Signs and symptoms vary depending on which organs are affected. Many people who have sarcoidosis have no signs or symptoms or mild ones.

Lofgren's syndrome is a classic set of signs and symptoms that is typical in some people who have sarcoidosis. Lofgren's syndrome may cause fever, enlarged lymph nodes, arthritis (usually in the ankles), and/or erythema nodosum.

Erythema nodosum is a rash of red or reddish-purple bumps on your ankles and shins. The rash may be warm and tender to the touch.

Treatment for sarcoidosis varies depending on which organs are affected. Your doctor may prescribe topical treatments and/or medicines to treat the disease. Not everyone who has sarcoidosis needs treatment.

Outlook

The outlook for sarcoidosis varies. Many people recover from the disease with few or no long-term problems.

More than half of the people who have sarcoidosis have remission within 3 years of diagnosis. "Remission" means the disease isn't active, but it can return.

Two-thirds of people who have the disease have remission within 10 years of diagnosis. People who have Lofgren's syndrome usually have remission. Relapse (return of the disease) 1 or more years after remission occurs in less than 5 percent of patients.

Sarcoidosis leads to organ damage in about one-third of the people diagnosed with the disease. Damage may occur over many years and involve more than one organ. Rarely, sarcoidosis can be fatal. Death usually is the result of problems with the lungs, heart, or brain.

Poor outcomes are more likely in people who have advanced disease and show little improvement from treatment.

Certain people are at higher risk for poor outcomes from chronic (long-term) sarcoidosis. This includes people who have lung scarring, heart or brain complications, or lupus pernio. Lupus pernio is a serious skin condition that sarcoidosis may cause.

What are the signs and symptoms of sarcoidosis?

Many people who have sarcoidosis have no signs or symptoms or mild ones. Often, the disease is found when a chest X-ray is done for another reason (for example, to diagnose pneumonia).

The signs and symptoms of sarcoidosis vary depending on which organs are affected. Signs and symptoms also may vary depending on your gender, age, and ethnic background.

Common Signs and Symptoms

In both adults and children, sarcoidosis most often affects the lungs. If granulomas (inflamed lumps) form in your lungs, you may wheeze, cough, feel short of breath, or have chest pain. Or, you may have no symptoms at all.

Some people who have sarcoidosis feel very tired, uneasy, or depressed. Night sweats and weight loss are common symptoms of the disease.

Common signs and symptoms in children are fatigue (tiredness), loss of appetite, weight loss, bone and joint pain, and anemia.

Children who are younger than 4 years old may have a distinct form of sarcoidosis. It may cause enlarged lymph nodes in the chest (which can be seen on chest X-ray pictures), skin lesions, and eye swelling or redness.

Other Signs and Symptoms

Sarcoidosis may affect your lymph nodes. The disease can cause enlarged lymph nodes that feel tender. Sarcoidosis usually affects the lymph nodes in your neck and chest. However, the disease also may affect the lymph nodes under your chin, in your armpits, or in your groin.

Sarcoidosis can cause lumps, ulcers (sores), or areas of discolored skin. These areas may itch, but they don't hurt. These signs tend to appear on your back, arms, legs, and scalp. Sometimes they appear near your nose or eyes. These signs usually last a long time.

Sarcoidosis may cause a more serious skin condition called lupus pernio. Disfiguring skin sores may affect your nose, nasal passages, cheeks, ears, eyelids, and fingers. These sores tend to be ongoing. They can return after treatment is over.

Sarcoidosis also can cause eye problems. If you have sarcoidosis, having an annual eye exam is important. If you have changes in your vision and can't see as clearly or can't see color, call 9–1–1 or have someone drive you to the emergency room.

You should call your doctor if you have any new eye symptoms, such as burning, itching, tearing, pain, or sensitivity to light.

Signs and symptoms of sarcoidosis also may include an enlarged liver, spleen, or salivary glands.

Although less common, sarcoidosis can affect the heart and brain. This can cause many symptoms, such as abnormal heartbeats, shortness of breath, headaches, and vision problems. If sarcoidosis affects the heart or brain, serious complications can occur.

Section 34.6

Primary Biliary Cirrhosis

Text in this section is excerpted from "Primary Biliary Cirrhosis,"
National Institute of Diabetes and Digestive and Kidney Diseases
(NIDDK), March 2014.

What is primary biliary cirrhosis?

Primary biliary cirrhosis is a chronic, or long lasting, disease that causes the small bile ducts in the liver to become inflamed and damaged and ultimately disappear.

The bile ducts carry a fluid called bile from the liver to the gallbladder, where it is stored. When food enters the stomach after a meal, the gallbladder contracts, and the bile ducts carry bile to the duodenum, the first part of the small intestine, for use in digestion. The liver makes bile, which is made up of bile acids, cholesterol, fats, and fluids. Bile helps the body absorb fats, cholesterol, and fat-soluble vitamins. Bile also carries cholesterol, toxins, and waste products to the intestines, where the body removes them. When chronic inflammation, or swelling, damages the bile ducts, bile and toxic wastes build up in the liver, damaging liver tissue.

This damage to the liver tissue can lead to cirrhosis, a condition in which the liver slowly deteriorates and is unable to function normally. In cirrhosis, scar tissue replaces healthy liver tissue, partially blocking the flow of blood through the liver.

What causes primary biliary cirrhosis?

The causes of primary biliary cirrhosis are unknown. Most research suggests it is an autoimmune disease. The immune system protects people from infection by identifying and destroying bacteria, viruses, and other potentially harmful foreign substances. An autoimmune disease is a disorder in which the body's immune system attacks the body's own cells and organs. In primary biliary cirrhosis, the immune system attacks the small bile ducts in the liver.

Genetics, or inherited genes, can make a person more likely to develop primary biliary cirrhosis. Primary biliary cirrhosis is more

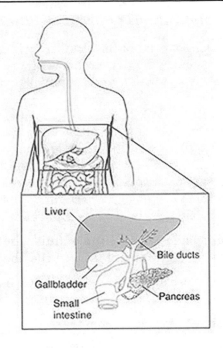

Figure 34.1. *Liver and Pancreas*

common in people who have a parent or sibling—particularly an identical twin—with the disease.

What are the symptoms of primary biliary cirrhosis?

The first and most common symptoms of primary biliary cirrhosis are

- fatigue, or feeling tired
- itching skin, and darkened skin in itching areas due to scratching
- dry eyes and mouth

Some people may have jaundice, a condition that causes the skin and whites of the eyes to turn yellow. Health care providers diagnose up to 60 percent of people with primary biliary cirrhosis before symptoms begin. Routine blood tests showing abnormal liver enzyme levels may lead a health care provider to suspect that a person without symptoms has primary biliary cirrhosis.

What are the complications of primary biliary cirrhosis?

Most complications of primary biliary cirrhosis are related to cirrhosis and start after primary biliary cirrhosis progresses to cirrhosis. In some cases, portal hypertension and esophageal varices may develop before cirrhosis.

Portal hypertension. The portal vein carries blood from the stomach, intestines, spleen, gallbladder, and pancreas to the liver. In cirrhosis, scar tissue partially blocks the normal flow of blood, which increases the pressure in the portal vein. This condition is called portal hypertension. Portal hypertension is a common complication of cirrhosis. This condition may lead to other complications, such as

- edema—swelling due to a buildup of fluid—in the feet, ankles, or legs, and ascites—a buildup of fluid in the abdomen

- enlarged blood vessels, called varices, in the esophagus, stomach, or both

- an enlarged spleen, called splenomegaly

- mental confusion due to a buildup of toxins that are ordinarily removed by the liver, a condition called hepatic encephalopathy

Edema and ascites. Liver failure causes fluid buildup that results in edema and ascites. Ascites can lead to spontaneous bacterial peritonitis, a serious infection that requires immediate medical attention.

Varices. Portal hypertension may cause enlarged blood vessels in the esophagus, stomach, or both. These enlarged blood vessels, called esophageal or gastric varices, cause the vessel walls to become thin and blood pressure to increase, making the blood vessels more likely to burst. If they burst, serious bleeding can occur in the esophagus or upper stomach, requiring immediate medical attention.

Splenomegaly. Portal hypertension may cause the spleen to enlarge and retain white blood cells and platelets, reducing the numbers of these cells and platelets in the blood. A low platelet count may be the first evidence that a person has developed cirrhosis.

Hepatic encephalopathy. A failing liver cannot remove toxins from the blood, so they eventually accumulate in the brain. The buildup of toxins in the brain is called hepatic encephalopathy. This condition can decrease mental function and cause stupor and even coma.

Metabolic bone diseases. Some people with cirrhosis develop a metabolic bone disease, which is a disorder of bone strength usually caused by abnormalities of vitamin D, bone mass, bone structure, or minerals, such as calcium and phosphorous.

Gallstones and bile duct stones. If cirrhosis prevents bile from flowing freely to and from the gallbladder, the bile hardens into gallstones. Symptoms of gallstones include abdominal pain and recurrent bacterial cholangitis—irritated or infected bile ducts. Stones may also form in and block the bile ducts, causing pain, jaundice, and bacterial cholangitis.

Steatorrhea. Steatorrhea is a condition in which the body cannot absorb fat, causing a buildup of fat in the stool and loose, greasy, and foul-smelling bowel movements. Steatorrhea may be caused by impairment of bile delivery to the small intestine or by the pancreas not producing enough digestive enzymes.

Liver cancer. Liver cancer is common in people with cirrhosis. Liver cancer has a high mortality rate. Current treatments are limited and only fully successful if a health care provider detects the cancer early, before the tumor is too large. For this reason, health care providers should check people with cirrhosis for signs of liver cancer every 6 to 12 months.

How is primary biliary cirrhosis diagnosed?

A health care provider may use the following tests to diagnose primary biliary cirrhosis:

- a medical and family history

- a physical exam

- blood tests

- imaging tests

- a liver biopsy

A health care provider usually bases a diagnosis of primary biliary cirrhosis on two out of three of the following criteria:

- a blood test showing elevated liver enzymes

- a blood test showing the presence of anti-mitochondrial antibodies (AMA)

- a liver biopsy showing signs of the disease

Health care providers may order additional tests to rule out other causes of symptoms. Health care providers diagnose the majority of people with primary biliary cirrhosis early in the course of the disease.

Medical and family history. Taking a medical and family history is one of the first things a health care provider may do to help diagnose primary biliary cirrhosis. He or she will ask a patient to provide a medical and family history.

Physical exam. A physical exam may help diagnose primary biliary cirrhosis. During a physical exam, a health care provider usually

- examines a patient's body
- uses a stethoscope to listen to sounds in the abdomen
- taps on specific areas of the patient's body

The health care provider will perform a physical exam to look for signs of the disease. For example, the liver may feel hard or ascites may cause the abdomen to enlarge.

Blood test. A blood test involves drawing blood at a health care provider's office or a commercial facility and sending the sample to a lab for analysis. The blood test can show elevated levels of liver enzymes, such as alkaline phosphatase. A routine blood test may show high levels of the liver enzyme alkaline phosphatase in people who have primary biliary cirrhosis and are not yet showing symptoms.

The health care provider will perform an AMA blood test to help confirm the diagnosis. A blood test will detect the presence of AMA in 90 to 95 percent of people with primary biliary cirrhosis.

Imaging tests. A health care provider may use the following imaging tests to examine the bile ducts. These tests can distinguish between primary biliary cirrhosis and other conditions that affect the bile ducts.

- Ultrasound
- Magnetic resonance cholangiopancreatography
- Endoscopic retrograde cholangiopancreatography

Liver biopsy. A liver biopsy is a procedure that involves taking a piece of liver tissue for examination with a microscope for signs of damage or disease. The health care provider may ask the patient to stop taking certain medications temporarily before the liver biopsy. The health care provider may ask the patient to fast for 8 hours before the procedure.

How is primary biliary cirrhosis treated?

Treatment for primary biliary cirrhosis depends on how early a health care provider diagnoses the disease and whether complications are present. In the early stages of primary biliary cirrhosis, treatment can slow the progression of liver damage to cirrhosis. In the early stages of cirrhosis, the goals of treatment are to slow the progression of tissue scarring in the liver and prevent complications. As cirrhosis progresses, a person may need additional treatments and hospitalization to manage complications.

Medications

Health care providers prescribe ursodiol (Actigall, Urso) to treat primary biliary cirrhosis. Ursodiol is a nontoxic bile acid that people can take orally. Ursodiol replaces the bile acids that are normally produced by the liver, which are more toxic and can harm the liver. Treatment with ursodiol can reduce levels of bilirubin and liver enzymes in the blood. Early treatment with this medication reduces the likelihood of needing a liver transplant and improves survival. Early treatment provides the most benefit; however, ursodiol treatment late in the course of the disease can still slow the progression of liver damage. While ursodiol treatment improves the outcome of primary biliary cirrhosis, it does not cure the disease.

Avoiding Alcohol and Other Substances

People with cirrhosis should not drink any alcohol or take any illegal substances, as both will cause more liver damage. People with cirrhosis should avoid complementary and alternative medications, such as herbs. People with cirrhosis should be careful about starting new medications and should consult a health care provider before taking prescription medications, over-the-counter medications, or vitamins. Many vitamins and prescription and over-the-counter medications can affect liver function.

Treatment of Symptoms and Complications

Health care providers treat symptoms and complications as follows:

Itching. Antihistamines may help with mild itching. However, antihistamines often cause drowsiness, and a person should take antihistamines just before bedtime to help with nighttime itching. A health care provider will treat more problematic itching with cholestyramine

(Locholest, Questran), which reduces cholesterol in the blood. Experts believe high levels of cholesterol let substances that cause itching build up in tissues.

Dry eyes and mouth. Health care providers usually treat dry eyes and mouth with artificial tears and saliva substitutes, respectively. These products are available without a prescription. A health care provider may treat people whose symptoms do not improve with pilocarpine (Salagen) or cevimeline (Evoxac). People who have difficulty with dry eyes should see an ophthalmologist—a doctor who diagnoses and treats all eye diseases and eye disorders—regularly. People with dry mouth should have regular dental exams.

Portal hypertension. A health care provider may prescribe a beta-blocker or nitrate to treat portal hypertension. Beta-blockers lower blood pressure by helping the heart beat slower and with less force, and nitrates relax and widen blood vessels to let more blood flow to the heart and reduce the heart's workload.

Varices. Beta-blockers can lower the pressure in varices and reduce the likelihood of bleeding. Bleeding in the stomach or esophagus requires an immediate upper endoscopy.

Edema and ascites. Health care providers prescribe diuretics—medications that remove fluid from the body—to treat edema and ascites.

Hepatic encephalopathy. A health care provider will treat hepatic encephalopathy by cleansing the bowel with lactulose, a laxative given orally or as an enema—a liquid put into the rectum. A health care provider may also add antibiotics to the treatment.

Osteoporosis. A health care provider may prescribe bisphosphonate medications to improve bone density.

Gallstones and bile duct stones. A health care provider may use surgery to remove gallstones. He or she may use endoscopic retrograde cholangiopancreatography, which uses balloons and basketlike devices, to retrieve the bile duct stones.

Liver cancer. A health care provider may recommend screening tests every 6 to 12 months to check for signs of liver cancer. Screening tests can find cancer before the person has symptoms of the disease.

When is a liver transplant considered for primary biliary cirrhosis?

A health care provider may consider a liver transplant when cirrhosis leads to liver failure or treatment for complications is ineffective. Liver transplantation is surgery to remove a diseased or an injured liver and replace it with a healthy liver or part of a liver from another person, called a donor.

Eating, Diet, and Nutrition

A healthy diet is important in all stages of cirrhosis because malnutrition is common in people with this disease. Malnutrition is a condition that occurs when the body does not get enough nutrients. Cirrhosis may lead to malnutrition because it can cause

- people to eat less because of symptoms such as loss of appetite

- changes in metabolism

- reduced absorption of vitamins and minerals

Health care providers can recommend a meal plan that is well balanced and provides enough calories and protein. If ascites develops, a health care provider or dietitian may recommend a sodium-restricted diet. To improve nutrition, the health care provider may prescribe a liquid supplement. A person may take the liquid by mouth or through a nasogastric tube—a tiny tube inserted through the nose and throat that reaches into the stomach.

A person with cirrhosis should not eat raw shellfish, which can contain a bacterium that causes serious infection. Cirrhosis affects the immune system, making people with cirrhosis more likely than healthy people to develop an infection after eating shellfish that contain this bacterium.

A health care provider may recommend calcium and vitamin D supplements to help prevent osteoporosis.

Section 34.7

Non-Alcoholic Steatohepatitis (NASH)

Text in this section is excerpted from "Non-Alcoholic Fatty Liver
Disease: A Patient's Guide," U.S. Department of Veterans Affairs
(VA), 2013.

What is fatty liver?

The buildup of fat in the liver not caused by an over use of alcohol.
Fatty liver (steatosis) occurs when the liver has more than 5-10% of its
weight in fat. Fatty liver does not damage the liver, however nonalcoholic
steatohepatitis (NASH) which is a severe form of Non-alcoholic fatty
liver disease (NAFLD) can cause inflammation and damage to the liver.

Who gets NAFLD?

- 20-30% of Americans have a form of NAFLD
  - 2-5% of Americans have NASH
  - About 25% of Americans have fatty liver
- Found in 80% of obese individuals
- Male and females
- Adults and children
- All ethnic groups

What happens when you have NAFLD?

Fatty Liver: Fat enters the liver cell. Next the cell swells and
changes which causes liver injury.

NASH: A bad case of liver injury which can progress to cirrhosis
or severe scarring of the liver. Not everyone with NASH will develop
cirrhosis.

Cirrhosis: A scarred liver from years of damage.

How do I know if I have NAFLD?

Routine blood tests your healthcare provider ordered may have shown to be high. Additional testing may be required to eliminate other possible causes of the high blood tests.

The healthcare provider may order an ultrasound, a computed tomography (CT) scan or magnetic resonance imaging (MRI) scan which can show a presence of fat in the liver or fatty liver.

The diagnosis of fatty liver versus NASH is done by liver biopsy.

What are the symptoms of NAFLD?

Non-alcoholic Fatty Liver Disease can be considered a silent disease in which the person may not notice any symptoms.

Symptoms may be divided in the following categories:

- **Early Symptoms:**
  - None
  - Tired / Fatigue
  - Pain in right upper abdomen
- **Late Symptoms:**
  - Weight loss
  - Fluid in the abdomen (Ascites)
  - Yellowing of skin (Jaundice)
  - Itchiness
- **Other Symptoms:**
  - Enlarged liver
  - Obesity

What are my risk factors for NAFLD?

The cause of NAFLD is not completely known, however NAFLD can take years to develop. Occurs most often in people with the following:

- **Central obesity** (around your abdomen)
- **Non insulin dependent diabetes**
- **Insulin resistance**
  - Cells in the body do not respond to insulin

- **Dyslipidemia** (fats found in blood which are needed for health, but sometimes become abnormal)
  - High triglycerides (a fatty substance in the blood)
  - High LDL (bad cholesterol)
  - Low HDL (good cholesterol)
- **Less Common Risk Factors**
  - Rapid and excessive weight loss
  - Poor diet and exercise habits
  - Middle age (but can be found in children)
  - Family or personal history
  - Polycystic Ovary Syndrome (PCOS) is a health problem that can affect a woman's menstrual cycle, ability to have children, hormones, heart, blood vessels, and appearance.

If more than one of the above risk factors are present than you may have metabolic syndrome. Metabolic syndrome is associated with a higher risk of developing NAFLD.

How is NAFLD/NASH treated?

- **Lifestyle Changes:** Key factor in treatment
  - **Physical Activity (Aerobic and Resistance)**
  - **Diet Changes**
  - **Weight Loss**
- **Physical Activity (Aerobic and Resistance)**
- Always check with your provider before beginning an exercise routine
- Increasing physical activity through aerobic and resistance type activities reduce risk factors
- If you aren't used to exercising start small and increase as tolerated
- Goal: 30 minutes of exercise 3 to 5 days per week
- Find ways to add more activity in your day
  - Take the stairs instead of the elevator

- Park further away at the grocery store
- Keep an exercise journal to track your progress

Diet Changes

- Good nutrition is part of an effective treatment for NAFLD

What Diet Changes Can I Make?

- Eat breakfast daily
  - Breakfast gives you energy to start the day
  - A healthy breakfast is important for everyone
- Watch portion sizes to manage your calorie intake
  - Using smaller plates, bowls and glasses can help you keep your portions under control
- Eat a diet rich in fruits and vegetables
  - Make fruits and vegetables cover at least half of your plate
  - Add fruits and vegetables to snacks
  - Aim for 2 1/2 cups of vegetables daily and 2 cups of fruit daily
- Reduce the amount of saturated fat in your diet
  - Select lean cuts of meat and low-fat dairy products
  - Switch to oils when preparing food
  - Select healthy unsaturated fats, such as those found in fish, olive oil and nuts
- Make at least half your grain servings whole grains
  - Choose whole grain breads and cereals, brown rice and whole wheat pasta

Weight Loss

- Weight loss is important in the treatment of NAFLD. However, too rapid of a loss can lead to worsening liver function.
- Recommend to have a 5% to 10% loss of body weight over 6 to 12 months of gradual weight loss not exceeding 2 pounds/week.

- Rapid weight loss may place you at risk for progression of liver disease and liver scarring.

Take Care of Your Liver

- Do not drink alcohol if you have NASH, abnormal liver enzymes or have Hepatitis B or C
- Before taking any medications including over the counter and herbal medications discuss with your health care provide
- Physical activity is important in treating fatty liver
- Eat a balanced diet low in saturated fats and high in fiber
- Keep your cholesterol, blood pressure and blood sugar under control

Part Six

Cancers of the
Gastrointestinal Tract

Chapter 35

Gastrointestinal Carcinoid Tumors

Overview

A gastrointestinal (GI) carcinoid tumor is a slow-growing tumor that forms in the neuroendocrine cells in the GI tract. The GI tract includes the stomach, small intestine, colon, rectum, appendix, and other organs. Most GI carcinoid tumors form in the rectum, small intestine, or appendix.

GI carcinoid tumors are a type of neuroendocrine tumor. Neuroendocrine cells release hormones into the blood when they receive a signal from the nervous system. The type of hormone released depends on where the tumor is found in the GI tract.

People who have a family history of multiple endocrine neoplasia type 1 (MEN1) syndrome or neurofibromatosis type 1 (NF1) syndrome have a higher risk of GI carcinoid tumors.

General Information about Gastrointestinal Carcinoid Tumors

A gastrointestinal carcinoid tumor is cancer that forms in the lining of the gastrointestinal tract.

The gastrointestinal (GI) tract is part of the body's digestive system. It helps to digest food, takes nutrients (vitamins, minerals,

---

Text in this chapter is excerpted from "Gastrointestinal Carcinoid Tumors—for Patients," National Cancer Institute (NCI), September 21, 2015.

carbohydrates, fats, proteins, and water) from food to be used by the body and helps pass waste material out of the body. The GI tract is made up of these and other organs:

- Stomach.

- Small intestine (duodenum, jejunum, and ileum).

- Colon.

- Rectum.

Gastrointestinal carcinoid tumors form from a certain type of neuroendocrine cell (a type of cell that is like a nerve cell and a hormone-making cell). These cells are scattered throughout the chest and abdomen but most are found in the GI tract. Neuroendocrine cells make hormones that help control digestive juices and the muscles used in moving food through the stomach and intestines. A GI carcinoid tumor may also make hormones and release them into the body.

GI carcinoid tumors are rare and most grow very slowly. Most of them occur in the small intestine, rectum, and appendix. Sometimes more than one tumor will form.

Health history can affect the risk of gastrointestinal carcinoid tumors.

Anything that increases a person's chance of developing a disease is called a risk factor. Having a risk factor does not mean that you will get cancer; not having risk factors doesn't mean that you will not get cancer. Talk to your doctor if you think you may be at risk.

Risk factors for GI carcinoid tumors include the following:

- Having a family history of multiple endocrine neoplasia type 1 (MEN1) syndrome or neurofibromatosis type 1 (NF1) syndrome.

- Having certain conditions that affect the stomach's ability to make stomach acid, such as atrophic gastritis, pernicious anemia, or Zollinger-Ellison syndrome.

Some gastrointestinal carcinoid tumors have no signs or symptoms in the early stages.

Signs and symptoms may be caused by the growth of the tumor and/or the hormones the tumor makes. Some tumors, especially tumors of the stomach or appendix, may not cause signs or symptoms. Carcinoid tumors are often found during tests or treatments for other conditions.

Carcinoid tumors in the small intestine (duodenum, jejunum, and ileum), colon, and rectum sometimes cause signs or symptoms as they grow or because of the hormones they make. Other conditions may cause the same signs or symptoms. Check with your doctor if you have any of the following:

Duodenum

Signs and symptoms of GI carcinoid tumors in the duodenum (first part of the small intestine, that connects to the stomach) may include the following:

- Abdominal pain.
- Constipation.
- Diarrhea.
- Change in stool color.
- Nausea.
- Vomiting.
- Jaundice (yellowing of the skin and whites of the eyes).
- Heartburn.

Jejunum and ileum

Signs and symptoms of GI carcinoid tumors in the jejunum (middle part of the small intestine) and ileum (last part of the small intestine, that connects to the colon) may include the following:

- Abdominal pain.
- Weight loss for no known reason.
- Feeling very tired.
- Feeling bloated
- Diarrhea.
- Nausea.
- Vomiting.

Colon

Signs and symptoms of GI carcinoid tumors in the colon may include the following:

- Abdominal pain.
- Weight loss for no known reason.

Rectum

Signs and symptoms of GI carcinoid tumors in the rectum may include the following:

- Blood in the stool.
- Pain in the rectum.
- Constipation.

Carcinoid syndrome may occur if the tumor spreads to the liver or other parts of the body.

The hormones made by gastrointestinal carcinoid tumors are usually destroyed by liver enzymes in the blood. If the tumor has spread to the liver and the liver enzymes cannot destroy the extra hormones made by the tumor, high amounts of these hormones may remain in the body and cause carcinoid syndrome. This can also happen if tumor cells enter the blood. Signs and symptoms of carcinoid syndrome include the following:

- Redness or a feeling of warmth in the face and neck.
- Abdominal pain.
- Feeling bloated.
- Diarrhea.
- Wheezing or other trouble breathing.
- Fast heartbeat.

These signs and symptoms may be caused by gastrointestinal carcinoid tumors or by other conditions. Talk to your doctor if you have any of these signs or symptoms.

Imaging studies and tests that examine the blood and urine are used to detect (find) and diagnose gastrointestinal carcinoid tumors.

The following tests and procedures may be used:

- **Physical exam and history:** An exam of the body to check general signs of health, including checking for signs of disease, such as lumps or anything else that seems unusual. A history of the patient's health habits and past illnesses and treatments will also be taken.

- **Blood chemistry studies:** A procedure in which a blood sample is checked to measure the amounts of certain substances, such as hormones, released into the blood by organs and tissues in the body.

- **Tumor marker test:** A procedure in which a sample of blood, urine, or tissue is checked to measure the amounts of certain substances, such as chromogranin A, made by organs, tissues, or tumor cells in the body. Chromogranin A is a tumor marker.

- **Twenty-four-hour urine test:** A test in which urine is collected for 24 hours to measure the amounts of certain substances, such as 5-HIAA or serotonin (hormone).

- **MIBG scan:** A very small amount of radioactive material called MIBG (metaiodobenzylguanidine) is injected into a vein and travels through the bloodstream. Carcinoid tumors take up the radioactive material and are detected by a device that measures radiation.

- **CT scan (CAT scan):** A procedure that makes a series of detailed pictures of areas inside the body, taken from different angles. A dye may be injected into a vein or swallowed to help the organs or tissues show up more clearly. This procedure is also called computed tomography, computerized tomography, or computerized axial tomography.

- **MRI (magnetic resonance imaging):** A procedure that uses a magnet, radio waves, and a computer to make a series of detailed pictures of areas inside the body. This procedure is also called nuclear magnetic resonance imaging

- **PET scan (positron emission tomography scan):** A small amount of radioactive glucose (sugar) is injected into a vein. The PET scanner rotates around the body and makes a picture of where glucose is being used in the body. Malignant tumor cells show up brighter in the picture because they are more active and take up more glucose than normal cells.

- **Endoscopic ultrasound (EUS):** A procedure in which an endoscope is inserted into the body, usually through the mouth or rectum. A probe at the end of the endoscope is used to bounce high-energy sound waves (ultrasound) off internal tissues or organs, such as the stomach, small intestine, colon, or rectum, and make echoes. The echoes form a picture of body tissues called a sonogram. This procedure is also called endosonography.

- **Upper endoscopy:** An endoscope is inserted through the mouth and passed through the esophagus into the stomach. Sometimes the endoscope also is passed from the stomach into the small intestine. It may also have a tool to remove tissue or lymph node samples, which are checked under a microscope for signs of disease.

- **Colonoscopy:** A colonoscope is inserted through the rectum into the colon. A colonoscope is a thin, tube-like instrument with a light and a lens for viewing. It may also have a tool to remove polyps or tissue samples, which are checked under a microscope for signs of cancer.

- **Capsule endoscopy:** The patient swallows a capsule that contains a tiny camera. As the capsule moves through the gastrointestinal tract, the camera takes pictures and sends them to a receiver worn on the outside of the body.

- **Biopsy:** The removal of cells or tissues so they can be viewed under a microscope to check for signs of cancer. Tissue samples may be taken during endoscopy and colonoscopy.

Certain factors affect prognosis (chance of recovery) and treatment options.

The prognosis (chance of recovery) and treatment options depend on the following:

- Where the tumor is in the gastrointestinal tract.

- The size of the tumor.

- Whether the cancer has spread from the stomach and intestines to other parts of the body, such as the liver or lymph nodes.

- Whether the patient has carcinoid syndrome or has carcinoid heart syndrome.

- Whether the cancer can be completely removed by surgery.

- Whether the cancer is newly diagnosed or has recurred.

Stages of Gastrointestinal Carcinoid Tumors

After a gastrointestinal carcinoid tumor has been diagnosed, tests are done to find out if cancer cells have spread within the stomach and intestines or to other parts of the body.

Staging is the process used to find out how far the cancer has spread. The information gathered from the staging process determines the stage of the disease. The results of tests and procedures used to diagnose gastrointestinal (GI) carcinoid tumors may also be used for staging.

A bone scan may be done to check if there are rapidly dividing cells, such as cancer cells, in the bone. A very small amount of radioactive material is injected into a vein and travels through the bloodstream. The radioactive material collects in the bones and is detected by a scanner.

There are three ways that cancer spreads in the body.

Cancer can spread through tissue, the lymph system, and the blood:

1. Tissue. The cancer spreads from where it began by growing into nearby areas.

2. Lymph system. The cancer spreads from where it began by getting into the lymph system. The cancer travels through the lymph vessels to other parts of the body.

3. Blood. The cancer spreads from where it began by getting into the blood. The cancer travels through the blood vessels to other parts of the body.

Cancer may spread from where it began to other parts of the body.

When cancer spreads to another part of the body, it is called metastasis. Cancer cells break away from where they began (the primary tumor) and travel through the lymph system or blood.

- Lymph system. The cancer gets into the lymph system, travels through the lymph vessels, and forms a tumor (metastatic tumor) in another part of the body.

- Blood. The cancer gets into the blood, travels through the blood vessels, and forms a tumor (metastatic tumor) in another part of the body.

The metastatic tumor is the same type of tumor as the primary tumor. For example, if a gastrointestinal (GI) carcinoid tumor spreads to the liver, the tumor cells in the liver are actually GI carcinoid tumor cells. The disease is metastatic GI carcinoid tumor, not liver cancer.

The plan for cancer treatment depends on where the carcinoid tumor is found and whether it can be removed by surgery.

For many cancers it is important to know the stage of the cancer in order to plan treatment. However, the treatment of gastrointestinal carcinoid tumors is not based on the stage of the cancer. Treatment depends mainly on whether the tumor can be removed by surgery and if the tumor has spread.

Treatment is based on whether the tumor:

- Can be completely removed by surgery.

- Has spread to other parts of the body.

- Has come back after treatment. The tumor may come back in the stomach or intestines or in other parts of the body.

- Has not gotten better with treatment.

Treatment Option Overview

There are different types of treatment for patients with gastrointestinal carcinoid tumors.

Different types of treatment are available for patients with gastrointestinal carcinoid tumor. Some treatments are standard (the currently used treatment), and some are being tested in clinical trials. A treatment clinical trial is a research study meant to help improve current treatments or obtain information on new treatments for patients with cancer. When clinical trials show that a new treatment is better than the standard treatment, the new treatment may become the standard treatment. Patients may want to think about taking part in a clinical trial. Some clinical trials are open only to patients who have not started treatment.

Four types of standard treatment are used:

1. Surgery

Treatment of GI carcinoid tumors usually includes surgery. One of the following surgical procedures may be used:

- **Endoscopic resection**: Surgery to remove a small tumor that is on the inside lining of the GI tract. An endoscope is inserted through the mouth and passed through the esophagus to the stomach and sometimes, the duodenum. An endoscope is a thin, tube-like instrument with a light, a lens for viewing, and a tool for removing tumor tissue.

- **Local excision**: Surgery to remove the tumor and a small amount of normal tissue around it.

- **Resection**: Surgery to remove part or all of the organ that contains cancer. Nearby lymph nodes may also be removed.

- **Cryosurgery**: A treatment that uses an instrument to freeze and destroy carcinoid tumor tissue. This type of treatment is also called cryotherapy. The doctor may use ultrasound to guide the instrument.

- **Radiofrequency ablation**: The use of a special probe with tiny electrodes that release high-energy radio waves (similar to microwaves) that kill cancer cells. The probe may be inserted through the skin or through an incision (cut) in the abdomen.

- **Liver transplant**: Surgery to remove the whole liver and replace it with a healthy donated liver.

- **Hepatic artery embolization**: A procedure to embolize (block) the hepatic artery, which is the main blood vessel that brings blood into the liver. Blocking the flow of blood to the liver helps kill cancer cells growing there.

2. Radiation Therapy

Radiation therapy is a cancer treatment that uses high-energy X-rays or other types of radiation to kill cancer cells. There are two types of radiation therapy. External radiation therapy uses a machine outside the body to send radiation toward the cancer. Internal radiation therapy uses a radioactive substance sealed in needles, seeds, wires, or catheters that are placed directly into or near the cancer. The way the radiation therapy is given depends on the type and stage of the cancer being treated.

Radiopharmaceutical therapy is a type of radiation therapy. Radiation is given to the tumor using a drug that has a radioactive substance, such as iodine I 131, attached to it. The radioactive substance kills the tumor cells.

3. Chemotherapy

Chemotherapy is a cancer treatment that uses drugs to stop the growth of cancer cells, either by killing the cells or by stopping the cells from dividing. When chemotherapy is taken by mouth or injected into a vein or muscle, the drugs enter the bloodstream and can reach cancer cells throughout the body (systemic chemotherapy). When chemotherapy is placed directly into the cerebrospinal fluid, an organ, or a body cavity such as the abdomen, the drugs mainly affect cancer cells in those areas (regional chemotherapy).

Chemoembolization of the hepatic artery is a type of regional chemotherapy that may be used to treat a gastrointestinal carcinoid tumor that has spread to the liver. The anticancer drug is injected into the hepatic artery through a catheter (thin tube). The drug is mixed with a substance that embolizes (blocks) the artery, and cuts off blood flow to the tumor. Most of the anticancer drug is trapped near the tumor and only a small amount of the drug reaches other parts of the body. The blockage may be temporary or permanent, depending on the substance used to block the artery. The tumor is prevented from getting the oxygen and nutrients it needs to grow. The liver continues to receive blood from the hepatic portal vein, which carries blood from the stomach and intestine.

The way the chemotherapy is given depends on the type and stage of the cancer being treated.

4. Hormone Therapy

Hormone therapy with a somatostatin analogue is a treatment that stops extra hormones from being made. GI carcinoid tumors are treated with octreotide or lanreotide which are injected under the skin or into the muscle. Octreotide and lanreotide may also have a small effect on stopping tumor growth.

Treatment for carcinoid syndrome may also be needed.

Treatment of carcinoid syndrome may include the following:

- Hormone therapy with a somatostatin analogue stops extra hormones from being made. Carcinoid syndrome is treated with octreotide or lanreotide to lessen flushing and diarrhea. Octreotide and lanreotide may also help slow tumor growth.

- Interferon therapy stimulates the body's immune system to work better and lessens flushing and diarrhea. Interferon may also help slow tumor growth.

- Taking medicine for diarrhea.

- Taking medicine for skin rashes.

- Taking medicine to breathe easier.

- Taking medicine before having anesthesia for a medical procedure.

Other ways to help treat carcinoid syndrome include avoiding things that cause flushing or difficulty breathing such as alcohol, nuts, certain cheeses and foods with capsaicin, such as chili peppers. Avoiding stressful situations and certain types of physical activity can also help treat carcinoid syndrome.

For some patients with carcinoid heart syndrome, a heart valve replacement may be done.

Treatment Options for Gastrointestinal Carcinoid Tumors

Carcinoid Tumors in the Stomach

Treatment of gastrointestinal (GI) carcinoid tumors in the stomach may include the following:

- Endoscopic surgery (resection) for small tumors.

- Surgery (resection) to remove part or all of the stomach. Nearby lymph nodes for larger tumors, tumors that grow deep into the stomach wall, or tumors that are growing and spreading quickly may also be removed.

For patients with GI carcinoid tumors in the stomach and MEN1 syndrome, treatment may also include:

- Surgery to remove tumors in the duodenum (first part of the small intestine, that connects to the stomach).

- Hormone therapy.

Carcinoid Tumors in the Small Intestine

It is not clear what the best treatment is for GI carcinoid tumors in the duodenum (first part of the small intestine, that connects to the stomach). Treatment may include the following:

- Endoscopic surgery (resection) for small tumors.

469

- Surgery (local excision) to remove the tumor, for slightly larger tumors.

- Surgery resection to remove the tumor and nearby lymph nodes.

Treatment of GI carcinoid tumors in the jejunum (middle part of the small intestine) and ileum (last part of the small intestine, that connects to the colon) may include the following:

- Surgery (resection) to remove the tumor and the membrane that connects the intestines to the back of the abdominal wall. Nearby lymph nodes are also removed.

- A second surgery to remove the membrane that connects the intestines to the back of the abdominal wall, if any tumor remains or the tumor continues to grow.

- Hormone therapy.

Carcinoid Tumors in the Appendix

Treatment of GI carcinoid tumors in the appendix may include the following:

- Surgery (resection) to remove the appendix.

- Surgery (resection) to remove the right side of the colon including the appendix. Nearby lymph nodes are also removed.

Carcinoid Tumors in the Colon

Treatment of GI carcinoid tumors in the colon may include the following:
Surgery (resection) to remove part of the colon and nearby lymph nodes, in order to remove as much of the cancer as possible.

Carcinoid Tumors in the Rectum

Treatment of GI carcinoid tumors in the rectum may include the following:

- Endoscopic surgery (resection) for tumors that are smaller than 1 centimeter.

- Surgery (resection) for tumors that are larger than 2 centimeters or that have spread to the muscle layer of the rectal wall. This may be either:

- surgery to remove part of the rectum; or

- surgery to remove the anus, the rectum, and part of the colon through an incision made in the abdomen.

It is not clear what the best treatment is for tumors that are 1 to 2 centimeters. Treatment may include the following:

- Endoscopic surgery (resection).

- Surgery to remove part of the rectum.

- Surgery to remove the anus, the rectum, and part of the colon through an incision made in the abdomen.

Metastatic Gastrointestinal Carcinoid Tumors

Distant metastases

Treatment of distant metastases of GI carcinoid tumors is usually palliative therapy to relieve symptoms and improve quality of life. Treatment may include the following:

- Surgery (resection) to remove as much of the tumor as possible.

- Hormone therapy.

- Radiopharmaceutical therapy.

- Radiation therapy for cancer that has spread to the bone, brain, or spinal cord.

- A clinical trial of a new treatment.

Liver metastases

Treatment of cancer that has spread to the liver may include the following:

- Surgery resection to remove the tumor from the liver.

- Hepatic artery embolization.

- Cryosurgery.

- Radiofrequency ablation.

- Liver transplant.

Recurrent Gastrointestinal Carcinoid Tumors

Treatment of recurrent GI carcinoid tumors may include the following:

- Surgery to remove part or all of the tumor.
- A clinical trial of a new treatment.

Chapter 36

Esophageal Cancer

Overview

Esophageal cancer is a disease in which malignant (cancer) cells form in the tissues of the esophagus. The esophagus is a muscular tube that moves food and liquids from the throat to the stomach.

The most common types of esophageal cancer are squamous cell carcinoma and adenocarcinoma. Squamous cell carcinoma begins in flat cells lining the esophagus. Adenocarcinoma begins in cells that make and release mucus and other fluids.

Smoking and heavy alcohol use increase the risk of esophageal squamous cell carcinoma. Gastroesophageal reflux disease and Barrett's esophagus may increase the risk of esophageal adenocarcinoma.

Esophageal cancer is often diagnosed at an advanced stage because there are no early signs or symptoms.

General Information about Esophageal Cancer

Esophageal cancer is a disease in which malignant (cancer) cells form in the tissues of the esophagus.

The esophagus is the hollow, muscular tube that moves food and liquid from the throat to the stomach. The wall of the esophagus is

---

Text in this chapter is excerpted from "Esophageal Cancer—for Patients," National Cancer Institute (NCI), May 12, 2015.

made up of several layers of tissue, including mucous membrane, muscle, and connective tissue. Esophageal cancer starts at the inside lining of the esophagus and spreads outward through the other layers as it grows.

> The esophagus and stomach are part of the upper gastrointestinal (digestive) system.

The two most common forms of esophageal cancer are named for the type of cells that become malignant (cancerous):

1. **Squamous cell carcinoma:** Cancer that forms in squamous cells, the thin, flat cells lining the esophagus. This cancer is most often found in the upper and middle part of the esophagus, but can occur anywhere along the esophagus. This is also called epidermoid carcinoma.

2. **Adenocarcinoma:** Cancer that begins in glandular (secretory) cells. Glandular cells in the lining of the esophagus produce and release fluids such as mucus. Adenocarcinomas usually form in the lower part of the esophagus, near the stomach.

Smoking, heavy alcohol use, and Barrett's esophagus can increase the risk of developing esophageal cancer.

Anything that increases your risk of getting a disease is called a risk factor. Having a risk factor does not mean that you will get cancer; not having risk factors doesn't mean that you will not get cancer. Talk with your doctor if you think you may be at risk. Risk factors include the following:

- Tobacco use.

- Heavy alcohol use.

- **Barrett's esophagus**: A condition in which the cells lining the lower part of the esophagus have changed or been replaced with abnormal cells that could lead to cancer of the esophagus. Gastric reflux (the backing up of stomach contents into the lower section of the esophagus) may irritate the esophagus and, over time, cause Barrett's esophagus.

- Older age.

- Being male.

- Being African-American.

Signs and symptoms of esophageal cancer are weight loss and painful or difficult swallowing.

These and other signs and symptoms may be caused by esophageal cancer or by other conditions. Check with your doctor if you have any of the following:

- Painful or difficult swallowing.

- Weight loss.

- Pain behind the breastbone.

- Hoarseness and cough.

- Indigestion and heartburn.

Tests that examine the esophagus are used to detect (find) and diagnose esophageal cancer.

The following tests and procedures may be used:

- **Physical exam and history:** An exam of the body to check general signs of health, including checking for signs of disease, such as lumps or anything else that seems unusual. A history of the patient's health habits and past illnesses and treatments will also be taken.

- **Chest X-ray:** An X-ray of the organs and bones inside the chest.

- **Barium swallow:** The patient drinks a liquid that contains barium (a silver-white metallic compound). The liquid coats the esophagus and stomach, and X-rays are taken. This procedure is also called an upper GI series.

- **Esophagoscopy:** An esophagoscope is inserted through the mouth or nose and down the throat into the esophagus. An esophagoscope is a thin, tube-like instrument with a light and a lens for viewing. It may also have a tool to remove tissue samples, which are checked under a microscope for signs of cancer. When the esophagus and stomach are looked at, it is called an upper endoscopy.

- **Biopsy:** The removal of cells or tissues so they can be viewed under a microscope by a pathologist to check for signs of cancer.

The biopsy is usually done during an esophagoscopy. Sometimes a biopsy shows changes in the esophagus that are not cancer but may lead to cancer.

Certain factors affect prognosis (chance of recovery) and treatment options.

The prognosis (chance of recovery) and treatment options depend on the following:

- The stage of the cancer (whether it affects part of the esophagus, involves the whole esophagus, or has spread to other places in the body).

- The size of the tumor.

- The patient's general health.

When esophageal cancer is found very early, there is a better chance of recovery. Esophageal cancer is often in an advanced stage when it is diagnosed. At later stages, esophageal cancer can be treated but rarely can be cured. Taking part in one of the clinical trials being done to improve treatment should be considered.

Stages of Esophageal Cancer

After esophageal cancer has been diagnosed, tests are done to find out if cancer cells have spread within the esophagus or to other parts of the body.

The process used to find out if cancer cells have spread within the esophagus or to other parts of the body is called staging. The information gathered from the staging process determines the stage of the disease. It is important to know the stage in order to plan treatment. The following tests and procedures may be used in the staging process:

- **Bronchoscopy:** A procedure to look inside the trachea and large airways in the lung for abnormal areas. A bronchoscope is inserted through the nose or mouth into the trachea and lungs. A bronchoscope is a thin, tube-like instrument with a light and a lens for viewing. It may also have a tool to remove tissue samples, which are checked under a microscope for signs of cancer.

- **CT scan (CAT scan):** A procedure that makes a series of detailed pictures of areas inside the body, such as the chest, abdomen, and pelvis, taken from different angles. The pictures are made by a computer linked to an X-ray machine. A dye may be injected into a vein or swallowed to help the organs or tissues show up more clearly. This procedure is also called computed tomography, computerized tomography, or computerized axial tomography.

- **PET scan (positron emission tomography scan):** A procedure to find malignant tumor cells in the body. A small amount of radioactive glucose (sugar) is injected into a vein. The PET scanner rotates around the body and makes a picture of where glucose is being used in the body. Malignant tumor cells show up brighter in the picture because they are more active and take up more glucose than normal cells do. A PET scan and CT scan may be done at the same time. This is called a PET-CT.

- **MRI (magnetic resonance imaging):** A procedure that uses a magnet, radio waves, and a computer to make a series of detailed pictures of areas inside the body. This procedure is also called nuclear magnetic resonance imaging (NMRI).

- **Endoscopic ultrasound (EUS):** A procedure in which an endoscope is inserted into the body, usually through the mouth or rectum. A probe at the end of the endoscope is used to bounce high-energy sound waves (ultrasound) off internal tissues or organs and make echoes. The echoes form a picture of body tissues called a sonogram. This procedure is also called endosonography.

- **Thoracoscopy:** An incision (cut) is made between two ribs and a thoracoscope is inserted into the chest. A thoracoscope is a thin, tube-like instrument with a light and a lens for viewing. It may also have a tool to remove tissue or lymph node samples, which are checked under a microscope for signs of cancer. In some cases, this procedure may be used to remove part of the esophagus or lung.

- **Laparoscopy:** A surgical procedure to look at the organs inside the abdomen to check for signs of disease. Small incisions (cuts) are made in the wall of the abdomen and a laparoscope (a thin, lighted tube) is inserted into one of the incisions. Other instruments may be inserted through the same or other incisions to perform procedures such as removing organs or taking tissue samples to be checked under a microscope for signs of disease.

There are three ways that cancer spreads in the body.

Cancer can spread through tissue, the lymph system, and the blood:

1. Tissue. The cancer spreads from where it began by growing into nearby areas.

2. Lymph system. The cancer spreads from where it began by getting into the lymph system. The cancer travels through the lymph vessels to other parts of the body.

3. Blood. The cancer spreads from where it began by getting into the blood. The cancer travels through the blood vessels to other parts of the body.

Cancer may spread from where it began to other parts of the body.

When cancer spreads to another part of the body, it is called metastasis. Cancer cells break away from where they began (the primary tumor) and travel through the lymph system or blood.

• Lymph system. The cancer gets into the lymph system, travels through the lymph vessels, and forms a tumor (metastatic tumor) in another part of the body.

• Blood. The cancer gets into the blood, travels through the blood vessels, and forms a tumor (metastatic tumor) in another part of the body.

The metastatic tumor is the same type of cancer as the primary tumor. For example, if esophageal cancer spreads to the lung, the cancer cells in the lung are actually esophageal cancer cells. The disease is metastatic esophageal cancer, not lung cancer.

The grade of the tumor is also used to describe the cancer and plan treatment.

The grade of the tumor describes how abnormal the cancer cells look under a microscope and how quickly the tumor is likely to grow and spread. Grades 1 to 3 are used to describe esophageal cancer:

- In grade 1, the cancer cells look more like normal cells under a microscope and grow and spread more slowly than grade 2 and 3 cancer cells.

- In grade 2, the cancer cells look more abnormal under a microscope and grow and spread more quickly than grade 1 cancer cells.

- In grade 3, the cancer cells look more abnormal under a microscope and grow and spread more quickly than grade 1 and 2 cancer cells.

The following stages are used for squamous cell carcinoma of the esophagus:

Stage 0 (High-grade Dysplasia)

In stage 0, abnormal cells are found in the mucosa or submucosa layer of the esophagus wall. These abnormal cells may become cancer and spread into nearby normal tissue. Stage 0 is also called high-grade dysplasia.

Stage I squamous cell carcinoma of the esophagus

Stage I is divided into Stage IA and Stage IB, depending on where the cancer is found.

- Stage IA: Cancer has formed in the mucosa or submucosa layer of the esophagus wall. The cancer cells are grade 1. Grade 1 cancer cells look more like normal cells under a microscope and grow and spread more slowly than grade 2 and 3 cancer cells.

- Stage IB: Cancer has formed:
  - in the mucosa or submucosa layer of the esophagus wall. The cancer cells are grade 2 and 3; or
  - in the mucosa or submucosa layer and spread into the muscle layer or the connective tissue layer of the esophagus wall. The cancer cells are grade 1. The tumor is in the lower esophagus or it is not known where the tumor is.

Grade 1 cancer cells look more like normal cells under a microscope and grow and spread more slowly than grade 2 and 3 cancer cells.

Stage II squamous cell carcinoma of the esophagus

Stage II is divided into Stage IIA and Stage IIB, depending on where the cancer has spread.

- Stage IIA: Cancer has spread:

  - into the muscle layer or the connective tissue layer of the esophagus wall. The cancer cells are grade 1. The tumor is in either the upper or middle esophagus; or

  - into the muscle layer or the connective tissue layer of the esophagus wall. The cancer cells are grade 2 and 3. The tumor is in the lower esophagus or it is not known where the tumor is.

Grade 1 cancer cells look more like normal cells under a microscope and grow and spread more slowly than grade 2 and 3 cancer cells.

- Stage IIB: Cancer:

  - has spread into the muscle layer or the connective tissue layer of the esophagus wall. The cancer cells are grade 2 and 3. Grade 2 and 3 cancer cells look more abnormal under a microscope and grow and spread more quickly than grade 1 cancer cells. The tumor is in either the upper or middle esophagus; or

  - is in the mucosa or submucosa layer and may have spread into the muscle layer of the esophagus wall. Cancer is found in 1 or 2 lymph nodes near the tumor.

Stage III squamous cell carcinoma of the esophagus

Stage III is divided into Stage IIIA, Stage IIIB, and Stage IIIC, depending on where the cancer has spread.

- Stage IIIA: Cancer:

  - is in the mucosa or submucosa layer and may have spread into the muscle layer of the esophagus wall. Cancer is found in 3 to 6 lymph nodes near the tumor; or

  - has spread into the connective tissue layer of the esophagus wall. Cancer is found in 1 or 2 lymph nodes near the tumor; or

  - has spread into the diaphragm, pleura (tissue that covers the lungs and lines the inner wall of the chest cavity), or sac around the heart. The cancer can be removed by surgery.

- Stage IIIB: Cancer has spread into the connective tissue layer of the esophagus wall. Cancer is found in 3 to 6 lymph nodes near the tumor.

- Stage IIIC: Cancer has spread:
  - into the diaphragm, pleura (tissue that covers the lungs and lines the inner wall of the chest cavity), or sac around the heart. The cancer can be removed by surgery. Cancer is found in 1 to 6 lymph nodes near the tumor; or
  - into other nearby organs such as the aorta, trachea, or spine, and the cancer cannot be removed by surgery, or
  - to 7 or more lymph nodes near the tumor.

Stage IV squamous cell carcinoma of the esophagus

In Stage IV, cancer has spread to other parts of the body.

The following stages are used for adenocarcinoma of the esophagus:

Stage 0 (High-grade Dysplasia)

In stage 0, abnormal cells are found in the mucosa or submucosa layer of the esophagus wall. These abnormal cells may become cancer and spread into nearby normal tissue. Stage 0 is also called high-grade dysplasia.

Stage I adenocarcinoma of the esophagus

Stage I is divided into Stage IA and Stage IB, depending on where the cancer is found.

- Stage IA: Cancer has formed in the mucosa or submucosa layer of the esophagus wall. The cancer cells are grade 1 or 2. Grade 1 and 2 cancer cells look more like normal cells under a microscope and grow and spread more slowly than grade 3 cancer cells.
- Stage IB: Cancer has formed:
  - in the mucosa or submucosa layer of the esophagus wall. The cancer cells are grade 3; or
  - in the mucosa or submucosa layer and spread into the muscle layer of the esophagus wall. The cancer cells are grade 1 or 2.

Grade 1 and 2 cancer cells look more like normal cells under a microscope and grow and spread more slowly than grade 3 cancer cells.

Stage II adenocarcinoma of the esophagus

Stage II is divided into Stage IIA and Stage IIB, depending on where the cancer has spread.

- Stage IIA: Cancer has spread into the muscle layer of the esophagus wall. The cancer cells are grade 3. Grade 3 cancer cells look more abnormal under a microscope and grow and spread more quickly than grade 1 and 2 cancer cells.

- Stage IIB: Cancer:
  - has spread into the connective tissue layer of the esophagus wall; or
  - is in the mucosa or submucosa layer and may have spread into the muscle layer of the esophagus wall. Cancer is found in 1 or 2 lymph nodes near the tumor.

Stage III adenocarcinoma of the esophagus

Stage III is divided into Stage IIIA, Stage IIIB, and Stage IIIC, depending on where the cancer has spread.

- Stage IIIA: Cancer:
  - is in the mucosa or submucosa layer and may have spread into the muscle layer of the esophagus wall. Cancer is found in 3 to 6 lymph nodes near the tumor; or
  - has spread into the connective tissue layer of the esophagus wall. Cancer is found in 1 or 2 lymph nodes near the tumor; or
  - has spread into the diaphragm, pleura (tissue that covers the lungs and lines the inner wall of the chest cavity), or sac around the heart. The cancer can be removed by surgery.

- Stage IIIB: Cancer has spread into the connective tissue layer of the esophagus wall. Cancer is found in 3 to 6 lymph nodes near the tumor.

- Stage IIIC: Cancer has spread:
  - into the diaphragm, pleura (tissue that covers the lungs and lines the inner wall of the chest cavity), or sac around the heart. The cancer can be removed by surgery. Cancer is found in 1 to 6 lymph nodes near the tumor; or
  - into other nearby organs such as the aorta, trachea, or spine, and the cancer cannot be removed by surgery; or
  - to 7 or more lymph nodes near the tumor.

Stage IV adenocarcinoma of the esophagus

In Stage IV, cancer has spread to other parts of the body.

Recurrent Esophageal Cancer

Recurrent esophageal cancer is cancer that has recurred (come back) after it has been treated. The cancer may come back in the esophagus or in other parts of the body.

Treatment Option Overview

There are different types of treatment for patients with esophageal cancer.

Different types of treatment are available for patients with esophageal cancer. Some treatments are standard (the currently used treatment), and some are being tested in clinical trials. A treatment clinical trial is a research study meant to help improve current treatments or obtain information on new treatments for patients with cancer. When clinical trials show that a new treatment is better than the standard treatment, the new treatment may become the standard treatment. Patients may want to think about taking part in a clinical trial. Some clinical trials are open only to patients who have not started treatment.

Patients have special nutritional needs during treatment for esophageal cancer.

Many people with esophageal cancer find it hard to eat because they have trouble swallowing. The esophagus may be narrowed by the tumor or as a side effect of treatment. Some patients may receive nutrients directly into a vein. Others may need a feeding tube (a flexible plastic tube that is passed through the nose or mouth into the stomach) until they are able to eat on their own.

Six types of standard treatment are used:

1. Surgery

Surgery is the most common treatment for cancer of the esophagus. Part of the esophagus may be removed in an operation called an esophagectomy.

The doctor will connect the remaining healthy part of the esophagus to the stomach so the patient can still swallow. A plastic tube or part of the intestine may be used to make the connection. Lymph nodes near the esophagus may also be removed and viewed under a microscope to see if they contain cancer. If the esophagus is partly blocked by the tumor, an expandable metal stent (tube) may be placed inside the esophagus to help keep it open.

2. Radiation Therapy

Radiation therapy is a cancer treatment that uses high-energy X-rays or other types of radiation to kill cancer cells or keep them from growing. There are two types of radiation therapy. External radiation therapy uses a machine outside the body to send radiation toward the cancer. Internal radiation therapy uses a radioactive substance sealed in needles, seeds, wires, or catheters that are placed directly into or near the cancer. The way the radiation therapy is given depends on the type and stage of the cancer being treated.

A plastic tube may be inserted into the esophagus to keep it open during radiation therapy. This is called intraluminal intubation and dilation.

3. Chemotherapy

Chemotherapy is a cancer treatment that uses drugs to stop the growth of cancer cells, either by killing the cells or by stopping them from dividing. When chemotherapy is taken by mouth or injected into a vein or muscle, the drugs enter the bloodstream and can reach cancer cells throughout the body (systemic chemotherapy). When chemotherapy is placed directly into the cerebrospinal fluid, an organ, or a body cavity such as the abdomen, the drugs mainly affect cancer cells in those areas (regional chemotherapy). The way the chemotherapy is given depends on the type and stage of the cancer being treated.

4. Chemoradiation Therapy

Chemoradiation therapy combines chemotherapy and radiation therapy to increase the effects of both.

5. Laser Therapy

Laser therapy is a cancer treatment that uses a laser beam (a narrow beam of intense light) to kill cancer cells.

6. Electrocoagulation

Electrocoagulation is the use of an electric current to kill cancer cells.

Treatment Options By Stage

Stage 0 (High-grade Dysplasia)

Treatment of stage 0 is usually surgery.

Stage I Esophageal Cancer

Treatment of stage I esophageal squamous cell carcinoma or adenocarcinoma may include the following:

- Surgery.
- Chemoradiation therapy followed by surgery.
- Clinical trials.

Stage II Esophageal Cancer

Treatment of stage II esophageal squamous cell carcinoma or adenocarcinoma may include the following:

- Chemoradiation therapy followed by surgery.
- Chemoradiation therapy alone.
- Surgery alone.

Stage III Esophageal Cancer

Treatment of stage III esophageal squamous cell carcinoma or adenocarcinoma may include the following:

- Chemoradiation therapy followed by surgery.
- Chemoradiation therapy alone.

Stage IV Esophageal Cancer

Treatment of stage IV esophageal squamous cell carcinoma or adenocarcinoma may include the following:

- An esophageal stent as palliative therapy to relieve symptoms and improve quality of life.

- External or internal radiation therapy as palliative therapy to relieve symptoms and improve quality of life.

- Laser surgery or electrocoagulation as palliative therapy to relieve symptoms and improve quality of life.

- Chemotherapy.

- Clinical trials of chemotherapy.

Treatment Options for Recurrent Esophageal Cancer

Treatment of recurrent esophageal cancer may include the following:

- Use of any standard treatments as palliative therapy to relieve symptoms and improve quality of life.

- Clinical trials.

Chapter 37

Gastric Cancer

Overview

Gastric (stomach) cancer is a disease in which malignant (cancer) cells form in the lining of the stomach. The stomach is in the upper abdomen and helps digest food.

Almost all gastric cancers are adenocarcinomas (cancers that begin in cells that make and release mucus and other fluids). Other types of gastric cancer are gastrointestinal carcinoid tumors, gastrointestinal stromal tumors, and lymphomas.

Infection with bacteria called *H. pylori* is a common cause of gastric cancer.

Gastric cancer is often diagnosed at an advanced stage because there are no early signs or symptoms.

General Information about Gastric Cancer

Gastric cancer is a disease in which malignant (cancer) cells form in the lining of the stomach.

The stomach is a J-shaped organ in the upper abdomen. It is part of the digestive system, which processes nutrients (vitamins, minerals, carbohydrates, fats, proteins, and water) in foods that are eaten and helps pass waste material out of the body. Food moves from the throat

Text in this chapter is excerpted from "Stomach (Gastric) Cancer—for Patients," National Cancer Institute (NCI), June 25, 2015.

to the stomach through a hollow, muscular tube called the esophagus. After leaving the stomach, partly-digested food passes into the small intestine and then into the large intestine.

The wall of the stomach is made up of 3 layers of tissue: the mucosal (innermost) layer, the muscularis (middle) layer, and the serosal (outermost) layer. Gastric cancer begins in the cells lining the mucosal layer and spreads through the outer layers as it grows.

Stromal tumors of the stomach begin in supporting connective tissue and are treated differently from gastric cancer.

Age, diet, and stomach disease can affect the risk of developing gastric cancer.

Anything that increases your risk of getting a disease is called a risk factor. Having a risk factor does not mean that you will get cancer; not having risk factors doesn't mean that you will not get cancer. Talk with your doctor if you think you may be at risk. Risk factors for gastric cancer include the following:

- Having any of the following medical conditions:
  - *Helicobacter pylori* (*H. pylori*) infection of the stomach.
  - Chronic gastritis (inflammation of the stomach).
  - Pernicious anemia.
  - Intestinal metaplasia (a condition in which the normal stomach lining is replaced with the cells that line the intestines).
  - Familial adenomatous polyposis (FAP) or gastric polyps.
- Eating a diet high in salted, smoked foods and low in fruits and vegetables.
- Eating foods that have not been prepared or stored properly.
- Being older or male.
- Smoking cigarettes.
- Having a mother, father, sister, or brother who has had stomach cancer.

Symptoms of gastric cancer include indigestion and stomach discomfort or pain.

These and other signs and symptoms may be caused by gastric cancer or by other conditions.

In the early stages of gastric cancer, the following symptoms may occur:

- Indigestion and stomach discomfort.
- A bloated feeling after eating.
- Mild nausea.
- Loss of appetite.
- Heartburn.

In more advanced stages of gastric cancer, the following signs and symptoms may occur:

- Blood in the stool.
- Vomiting.
- Weight loss for no known reason.
- Stomach pain.
- Jaundice (yellowing of eyes and skin).
- Ascites (build-up of fluid in the abdomen).
- Trouble swallowing.

Check with your doctor if you have any of these problems.

Tests that examine the stomach and esophagus are used to detect (find) and diagnose gastric cancer.

The following tests and procedures may be used:

- **Physical exam and history:** An exam of the body to check general signs of health, including checking for signs of disease, such as lumps or anything else that seems unusual. A history of the patient's health habits and past illnesses and treatments will also be taken.

- **Blood chemistry studies:** A procedure in which a blood sample is checked to measure the amounts of certain substances released into the blood by organs and tissues in the body. An unusual (higher or lower than normal) amount of a substance can be a sign of disease.

- **Complete blood count (CBC):** A procedure in which a sample of blood is drawn and checked for the following:

489

- • The number of red blood cells, white blood cells, and platelets.

- • The amount of hemoglobin (the protein that carries oxygen) in the red blood cells.

- • The portion of the sample made up of red blood cells.

- **Upper endoscopy:** A procedure to look inside the esophagus, stomach, and duodenum (first part of the small intestine) to check for abnormal areas. An endoscope (a thin, lighted tube) is passed through the mouth and down the throat into the esophagus.

- **Barium swallow:** A series of X-rays of the esophagus and stomach. The patient drinks a liquid that contains barium (a silver-white metallic compound). The liquid coats the esophagus and stomach, and X-rays are taken. This procedure is also called an upper GI series.

- **CT scan (CAT scan):** A procedure that makes a series of detailed pictures of areas inside the body, taken from different angles. The pictures are made by a computer linked to an X-ray machine. A dye may be injected into a vein or swallowed to help the organs or tissues show up more clearly. This procedure is also called computed tomography, computerized tomography, or computerized axial tomography.

- **Biopsy:** The removal of cells or tissues so they can be viewed under a microscope to check for signs of cancer. A biopsy of the stomach is usually done during the endoscopy.

The sample of tissue may be checked to measure how many *HER2* genes there are and how much HER2 protein is being made. If there are more *HER2* genes or higher levels of HER2 protein than normal, the cancer is called HER2 positive. HER2-positive gastric cancer may be treated with a monoclonal antibody that targets the HER2 protein.

Certain factors affect prognosis (chance of recovery) and treatment options.

The prognosis (chance of recovery) and treatment options depend on the following:

- • The stage of the cancer (whether it is in the stomach only or has spread to lymph nodes or other places in the body).

490

- The patient's general health.

When gastric cancer is found very early, there is a better chance of recovery. Gastric cancer is often in an advanced stage when it is diagnosed. At later stages, gastric cancer can be treated but rarely can be cured. Taking part in one of the clinical trials being done to improve treatment should be considered.

Stages of Gastric Cancer

After gastric cancer has been diagnosed, tests are done to find out if cancer cells have spread within the stomach or to other parts of the body.

The process used to find out if cancer has spread within the stomach or to other parts of the body is called staging. The information gathered from the staging process determines the stage of the disease. It is important to know the stage in order to plan treatment.

The following tests and procedures may be used in the staging process:

- **CEA (carcinoembryonic antigen) assay:** Tests that measure the level of CEA in the blood. This substance is released into the bloodstream from both cancer cells and normal cells. When found in higher than normal amounts, it can be a sign of gastric cancer or other conditions.

- **Endoscopic ultrasound (EUS):** A procedure in which an endoscope is inserted into the body, usually through the mouth or rectum. An endoscope is a thin, tube-like instrument with a light and a lens for viewing. A probe at the end of the endoscope is used to bounce high-energy sound waves (ultrasound) off internal tissues or organs and make echoes. The echoes form a picture of body tissues called a sonogram. This procedure is also called endosonography.

- **CT scan (CAT scan):** A procedure that makes a series of detailed pictures of areas inside the body, taken from different angles. The pictures are made by a computer linked to an X-ray machine. A dye may be injected into a vein or swallowed to help the organs or tissues show up more clearly. This procedure is also called computed tomography, computerized tomography, or computerized axial tomography.

- **PET scan (positron emission tomography scan):** A procedure to find malignant tumor cells in the body. A small amount of radioactive glucose (sugar) is injected into a vein. The PET scanner rotates around the body and makes a picture of where glucose is being used in the body. Malignant tumor cells show up brighter in the picture because they are more active and take up more glucose than normal cells do. A PET scan and CT scan may be done at the same time. This is called a PET-CT.

Cancer may spread from where it began to other parts of the body.

When cancer spreads to another part of the body, it is called metastasis.

The metastatic tumor is the same type of cancer as the primary tumor. For example, if gastric cancer spreads to the liver, the cancer cells in the liver are actually gastric cancer cells. The disease is metastatic gastric cancer, not liver cancer.

The following stages are used for gastric cancer:

Stage 0 (Carcinoma in Situ)

In stage 0, abnormal cells are found in the inside lining of the mucosa (innermost layer) of the stomach wall. These abnormal cells may become cancer and spread into nearby normal tissue. Stage 0 is also called carcinoma in situ.

Stage I

In stage I, cancer has formed in the inside lining of the mucosa (innermost layer) of the stomach wall. Stage I is divided into stage IA and stage IB, depending on where the cancer has spread.

- Stage IA: Cancer may have spread into the submucosa (layer of tissue next to the mucosa) of the stomach wall.

- Stage IB: Cancer:

  - may have spread into the submucosa (layer of tissue next to the mucosa) of the stomach wall and is found in 1 or 2 lymph nodes near the tumor; or

  - has spread to the muscle layer of the stomach wall.

Stage II

Stage II gastric cancer is divided into stage IIA and stage IIB, depending on where the cancer has spread.

- Stage IIA: Cancer:
  - has spread to the subserosa (layer of tissue next to the serosa) of the stomach wall; or
  - has spread to the muscle layer of the stomach wall and is found in 1 or 2 lymph nodes near the tumor; or
  - may have spread to the submucosa (layer of tissue next to the mucosa) of the stomach wall and is found in 3 to 6 lymph nodes near the tumor.

- Stage IIB: Cancer:
  - has spread to the serosa (outermost layer) of the stomach wall; or
  - has spread to the subserosa (layer of tissue next to the serosa) of the stomach wall and is found in 1 or 2 lymph nodes near the tumor; or
  - has spread to the muscle layer of the stomach wall and is found in 3 to 6 lymph nodes near the tumor; or
  - may have spread to the submucosa (layer of tissue next to the mucosa) of the stomach wall and is found in 7 or more lymph nodes near the tumor.

Stage III

Stage III gastric cancer is divided into stage IIIA, stage IIIB, and stage IIIC, depending on where the cancer has spread.

- Stage IIIA: Cancer has spread to:
  - the serosa (outermost) layer of the stomach wall and is found in 1 or 2 lymph nodes near the tumor; or
  - the subserosa (layer of tissue next to the serosa) of the stomach wall and is found in 3 to 6 lymph nodes near the tumor; or
  - the muscle layer of the stomach wall and is found in 7 or more lymph nodes near the tumor.

493

- Stage IIIB: Cancer has spread to:

  - nearby organs such as the spleen, transverse colon, liver, diaphragm, pancreas, kidney, adrenal gland, or small intestine, and may be found in 1 or 2 lymph nodes near the tumor; or

  - the serosa (outermost layer) of the stomach wall and is found in 3 to 6 lymph nodes near the tumor; or

  - the subserosa (layer of tissue next to the serosa) of the stomach wall and is found in 7 or more lymph nodes near the tumor.

- Stage IIIC: Cancer has spread to:

  - nearby organs such as the spleen, transverse colon, liver, diaphragm, pancreas, kidney, adrenal gland, or small intestine, and may be found in 3 or more lymph nodes near the tumor; or

  - the serosa (outermost layer) of the stomach wall and is found in 7 or more lymph nodes near the tumor.

Stage IV

In stage IV, cancer has spread to distant parts of the body.

Recurrent Gastric Cancer

Recurrent gastric cancer is cancer that has recurred (come back) after it has been treated. The cancer may come back in the stomach or in other parts of the body such as the liver or lymph nodes.

Treatment Option Overview

There are different types of treatment for patients with gastric cancer.

Different types of treatments are available for patients with gastric cancer. Some treatments are standard (the currently used treatment), and some are being tested in clinical trials. A treatment clinical trial is a research study meant to help improve current treatments or obtain information on new treatments for patients with cancer. When clinical trials show that a new treatment is better than the standard treatment, the new treatment may become the standard treatment.

Patients may want to think about taking part in a clinical trial. Some clinical trials are open only to patients who have not started treatment.

Five types of standard treatment are used:

1. Surgery

Surgery is a common treatment of all stages of gastric cancer. The following types of surgery may be used:

- **Subtotal gastrectomy**: Removal of the part of the stomach that contains cancer, nearby lymph nodes, and parts of other tissues and organs near the tumor. The spleen may be removed. The spleen is an organ in the upper abdomen that filters the blood and removes old blood cells.

- **Total gastrectomy:** Removal of the entire stomach, nearby lymph nodes, and parts of the esophagus, small intestine, and other tissues near the tumor. The spleen may be removed. The esophagus is connected to the small intestine so the patient can continue to eat and swallow.

If the tumor is blocking the stomach but the cancer cannot be completely removed by standard surgery, the following procedures may be used:

- **Endoluminal stent placement**: A procedure to insert a stent (a thin, expandable tube) in order to keep a passage (such as arteries or the esophagus) open. For tumors blocking the passage into or out of the stomach, surgery may be done to place a stent from the esophagus to the stomach or from the stomach to the small intestine to allow the patient to eat normally.

- **Endoluminal laser therapy**: A procedure in which an endoscope (a thin, lighted tube) with a laser attached is inserted into the body. A laser is an intense beam of light that can be used as a knife.

- **Gastrojejunostomy**: Surgery to remove the part of the stomach with cancer that is blocking the opening into the small intestine. The stomach is connected to the jejunum (a part of the small intestine) to allow food and medicine to pass from the stomach into the small intestine.

2. Chemotherapy

Chemotherapy is a cancer treatment that uses drugs to stop the growth of cancer cells, either by killing the cells or by stopping them from dividing. When chemotherapy is taken by mouth or injected into a vein or muscle, the drugs enter the bloodstream and can reach cancer cells throughout the body (systemic chemotherapy). When chemotherapy is placed directly into the cerebrospinal fluid, an organ, or a body cavity such as the abdomen, the drugs mainly affect cancer cells in those areas (regional chemotherapy). The way the chemotherapy is given depends on the type and stage of the cancer being treated.

3. Radiation Therapy

Radiation therapy is a cancer treatment that uses high-energy X-rays or other types of radiation to kill cancer cells or keep them from growing. There are two types of radiation therapy. External radiation therapy uses a machine outside the body to send radiation toward the cancer. Internal radiation therapy uses a radioactive substance sealed in needles, seeds, wires, or catheters that are placed directly into or near the cancer. The way the radiation therapy is given depends on the type and stage of the cancer being treated.

4. Chemoradiation

Chemoradiation therapy combines chemotherapy and radiation therapy to increase the effects of both. Chemoradiation given after surgery, to lower the risk that the cancer will come back, is called adjuvant therapy. Chemoradiation given before surgery, to shrink the tumor (neoadjuvant therapy), is being studied.

5. Targeted Therapy

Targeted therapy is a type of treatment that uses drugs or other substances to identify and attack specific cancer cells without harming normal cells. Monoclonal antibody therapy is a type of targeted therapy used in the treatment of gastric cancer.

Monoclonal antibody therapy uses antibodies made in the laboratory from a single type of immune system cell. These antibodies can identify substances on cancer cells or normal substances that may help cancer cells grow. The antibodies attach to the substances and kill the cancer cells, block their growth, or keep them from spreading. Monoclonal antibodies are given by infusion. They may be used alone or to carry drugs, toxins, or radioactive material directly to cancer cells. For stage IV gastric cancer and gastric cancer that has recurred, a monoclonal antibody such as trastuzumab may be given to block the effect of the growth factor protein HER2, which sends growth signals to gastric cancer cells.

Treatment Options by Stage

Stage 0 (Carcinoma in Situ)

Treatment of stage 0 is usually surgery (total or subtotal gastrectomy).

Stage I Gastric Cancer

Treatment of stage I gastric cancer may include the following:

- Surgery (total or subtotal gastrectomy).
- Surgery (total or subtotal gastrectomy) followed by chemoradiation therapy.
- A clinical trial of chemoradiation therapy given before surgery.

Stage II Gastric Cancer

Treatment of stage II gastric cancer may include the following:

- Surgery (total or subtotal gastrectomy).
- Surgery (total or subtotal gastrectomy) followed by chemoradiation therapy or chemotherapy.
- Chemotherapy given before and after surgery.
- A clinical trial of surgery followed by chemoradiation therapy testing new anticancer drugs.
- A clinical trial of chemoradiation therapy given before surgery.

Stage III Gastric Cancer

Treatment of stage III gastric cancer may include the following:

- Surgery (total gastrectomy).
- Surgery followed by chemoradiation therapy or chemotherapy.
- Chemotherapy given before and after surgery.
- A clinical trial of surgery followed by chemoradiation therapy testing new anticancer drugs.
- A clinical trial of chemoradiation therapy given before surgery.

Stage IV and Recurrent Gastric Cancer

Treatment of stage IV or recurrent gastric cancer may include the following:

- Chemotherapy as palliative therapy to relieve symptoms and improve the quality of life.

- Targeted therapy with a monoclonal antibody combined with chemotherapy.

- Endoluminal laser therapy or endoluminal stent placement to relieve a blockage in the stomach, or gastrojejunostomy to bypass the blockage.

- Radiation therapy as palliative therapy to stop bleeding, relieve pain, or shrink a tumor that is blocking the stomach.

- Surgery as palliative therapy to stop bleeding or shrink a tumor that is blocking the stomach.

- A clinical trial of new combinations of chemotherapy as palliative therapy to relieve symptoms and improve the quality of life.

Chapter 38

Small Intestine Cancer

Overview

The small intestine (also called small bowel) is part of the body's digestive system. It is a long, coiled tube that connects the stomach to the large intestine. The small intestine receives food from the stomach, helps break it down, and absorbs nutrients that are used by the body. The three parts of the small intestine are the duodenum, jejunum, and ileum. The duodenum connects to the stomach, and the ileum connects to the colon.

Small intestine cancer often starts in the duodenum. The most common type of small intestine cancer is adenocarcinoma (cancer that begins in cells that make and release mucus and other fluids). Other types of small intestine cancer are sarcomas, carcinoid tumors, gastrointestinal stromal tumors, and lymphomas.

General Information about Small Intestine Cancer

Small intestine cancer is a rare disease in which malignant (cancer) cells form in the tissues of the small intestine.

The small intestine is part of the body's digestive system, which also includes the esophagus, stomach, and large intestine. The digestive system removes and processes nutrients (vitamins, minerals,

Text in this chapter is excerpted from "Small Intestine Cancer—for Patients," National Cancer Institute (NCI), July 7, 2015.

carbohydrates, fats, proteins, and water) from foods and helps pass waste material out of the body. The small intestine is a long tube that connects the stomach to the large intestine. It folds many times to fit inside the abdomen.

There are five types of small intestine cancer.

The types of cancer found in the small intestine are adenocarcinoma, sarcoma, carcinoid tumors, gastrointestinal stromal tumor, and lymphoma. This summary discusses adenocarcinoma and leiomyosarcoma (a type of sarcoma).

Adenocarcinoma starts in glandular cells in the lining of the small intestine and is the most common type of small intestine cancer. Most of these tumors occur in the part of the small intestine near the stomach. They may grow and block the intestine.

Leiomyosarcoma starts in the smooth muscle cells of the small intestine. Most of these tumors occur in the part of the small intestine near the large intestine.

Diet and health history can affect the risk of developing small intestine cancer.

Anything that increases your risk of getting a disease is called a risk factor. Having a risk factor does not mean that you will get cancer; not having risk factors doesn't mean that you will not get cancer. Talk with your doctor if you think you may be at risk. Risk factors for small intestine cancer include the following:

- Eating a high-fat diet.

- Having Crohn's disease.

- Having celiac disease.

- Having familial adenomatous polyposis (FAP).

Signs and symptoms of small intestine cancer include unexplained weight loss and abdominal pain.

These and other signs and symptoms may be caused by small intestine cancer or by other conditions. Check with your doctor if you have any of the following:

- Pain or cramps in the middle of the abdomen.

- Weight loss with no known reason.

- A lump in the abdomen.

- Blood in the stool.

Tests that examine the small intestine are used to detect (find), diagnose, and stage small intestine cancer.

Procedures that make pictures of the small intestine and the area around it help diagnose small intestine cancer and show how far the cancer has spread. The process used to find out if cancer cells have spread within and around the small intestine is called staging.

In order to plan treatment, it is important to know the type of small intestine cancer and whether the tumor can be removed by surgery. Tests and procedures to detect, diagnose, and stage small intestine cancer are usually done at the same time. The following tests and procedures may be used:

- **Physical exam and history:** An exam of the body to check general signs of health, including checking for signs of disease, such as lumps or anything else that seems unusual. A history of the patient's health habits and past illnesses and treatments will also be taken.

- **Blood chemistry studies:** A procedure in which a blood sample is checked to measure the amounts of certain substances released into the blood by organs and tissues in the body. An unusual (higher or lower than normal) amount of a substance can be a sign of disease.

- **Liver function tests:** A procedure in which a blood sample is checked to measure the amounts of certain substances released into the blood by the liver. A higher than normal amount of a substance can be a sign of liver disease that may be caused by small intestine cancer.

- **Endoscopy:** A procedure to look at organs and tissues inside the body to check for abnormal areas. There are different types of endoscopy:

  - **Upper endoscopy:** A procedure to look at the inside of the esophagus, stomach, and duodenum (first part of the small intestine, near the stomach). An endoscope is inserted through the mouth and into the esophagus, stomach, and duodenum. An endoscope is a thin, tube-like instrument with a light and a lens for viewing. It may also have a tool to remove tissue samples, which are checked under a microscope for signs of cancer.

- **Capsule endoscopy:** A procedure to look at the inside of the small intestine. A capsule that is about the size of a large pill and contains a light and a tiny wireless camera is swallowed by the patient. The capsule travels through the digestive tract, including the small intestine, and sends many pictures of the inside of the digestive tract to a recorder that is worn around the waist or over the shoulder. The pictures are sent from the recorder to a computer and viewed by the doctor who checks for signs of cancer. The capsule passes out of the body during a bowel movement.

- **Double balloon endoscopy:** A procedure to look at the inside of the small intestine. A special instrument made up of two tubes (one inside the other) is inserted through the mouth or rectum and into the small intestine. The inside tube (an endoscope with a light and lens for viewing) is moved through part of the small intestine and a balloon at the end of it is inflated to keep the endoscope in place. Next, the outer tube is moved through the small intestine to reach the end of the endoscope, and a balloon at the end of the outer tube is inflated to keep it in place. Then, the balloon at the end of the endoscope is deflated and the endoscope is moved through the next part of the small intestine. These steps are repeated many times as the tubes move through the small intestine. The doctor is able to see the inside of the small intestine through the endoscope and use a tool to remove samples of abnormal tissue. The tissue samples are checked under a microscope for signs of cancer. This procedure may be done if the results of a capsule endoscopy are abnormal. This procedure is also called double balloon enteroscopy.

- **Laparotomy:** A surgical procedure in which an incision (cut) is made in the wall of the abdomen to check the inside of the abdomen for signs of disease. The size of the incision depends on the reason the laparotomy is being done. Sometimes organs or lymph nodes are removed or tissue samples are taken and checked under a microscope for signs of disease.

- **Biopsy:** The removal of cells or tissues so they can be viewed under a microscope to check for signs of cancer. This may be done during an endoscopy or laparotomy. The sample is checked by a pathologist to see if it contains cancer cells.

- **Upper GI series with small bowel follow-through:** A series of X-rays of the esophagus, stomach, and small bowel. The patient drinks a liquid that contains barium (a silver-white metallic compound). The liquid coats the esophagus, stomach, and small bowel. X-rays are taken at different times as the barium travels through the upper GI tract and small bowel.

- **CT scan (CAT scan):** A procedure that makes a series of detailed pictures of areas inside the body, taken from different angles. The pictures are made by a computer linked to an X-ray machine. A dye may be injected into a vein or swallowed to help the organs or tissues show up more clearly. This procedure is also called computed tomography, computerized tomography, or computerized axial tomography.

- **MRI (magnetic resonance imaging):** A procedure that uses a magnet, radio waves, and a computer to make a series of detailed pictures of areas inside the body. This procedure is also called nuclear magnetic resonance imaging (NMRI).

Certain factors affect prognosis (chance of recovery) and treatment options.

The prognosis (chance of recovery) and treatment options depend on the following:

- The type of small intestine cancer.
- Whether the cancer is in the inner lining of the small intestine only or has spread into or beyond the wall of the small intestine.
- Whether the cancer has spread to other places in the body, such as the lymph nodes, liver, or peritoneum (tissue that lines the wall of the abdomen and covers most of the organs in the abdomen).
- Whether the cancer can be completely removed by surgery.
- Whether the cancer is newly diagnosed or has recurred.

Stages of Small Intestine Cancer

Tests and procedures to stage small intestine cancer are usually done at the same time as diagnosis.

Staging is used to find out how far the cancer has spread, but treatment decisions are not based on stage.

Cancer may spread from where it began to other parts of the body.

When cancer spreads to another part of the body, it is called metastasis.

The metastatic tumor is the same type of cancer as the primary tumor. For example, if small intestine cancer spreads to the liver, the cancer cells in the liver are actually small intestine cancer cells. The disease is metastatic small intestine cancer, not liver cancer.

Small intestine cancer is grouped according to whether or not the tumor can be completely removed by surgery.

Treatment depends on whether the tumor can be removed by surgery and if the cancer is being treated as a primary tumor or is metastatic cancer.

Recurrent Small Intestine Cancer

Recurrent small intestine cancer is cancer that has recurred (come back) after it has been treated. The cancer may come back in the small intestine or in other parts of the body.

Treatment Option Overview

There are different types of treatment for patients with small intestine cancer.

Different types of treatments are available for patients with small intestine cancer. Some treatments are standard (the currently used treatment), and some are being tested in clinical trials. A treatment clinical trial is a research study meant to help improve current treatments or obtain information on new treatments for patients with cancer. When clinical trials show that a new treatment is better than the standard treatment, the new treatment may become the standard treatment. Patients may want to think about taking part in a clinical trial. Some clinical trials are open only to patients who have not started treatment.

Three types of standard treatment are used:

1. Surgery

Surgery is the most common treatment of small intestine cancer. One of the following types of surgery may be done:

- **Resection:** Surgery to remove part or all of an organ that contains cancer. The resection may include the small intestine and nearby organs (if the cancer has spread). The doctor may remove the section of the small intestine that contains cancer and perform an anastomosis (joining the cut ends of the intestine together). The doctor will usually remove lymph nodes near the small intestine and examine them under a microscope to see whether they contain cancer.

- **Bypass:** Surgery to allow food in the small intestine to go around (bypass) a tumor that is blocking the intestine but cannot be removed.

Even if the doctor removes all the cancer that can be seen at the time of the surgery, some patients may be given radiation therapy after surgery to kill any cancer cells that are left. Treatment given after the surgery, to lower the risk that the cancer will come back, is called adjuvant therapy.

2. Radiation Therapy

Radiation therapy is a cancer treatment that uses high-energy X-rays or other types of radiation to kill cancer cells or keep them from growing. There are two types of radiation therapy. External radiation therapy uses a machine outside the body to send radiation toward the cancer. Internal radiation therapy uses a radioactive substance sealed in needles, seeds, wires, or catheters that are placed directly into or near the cancer. The way the radiation therapy is given depends on the type and stage of the cancer being treated.

3. Chemotherapy

Chemotherapy is a cancer treatment that uses drugs to stop the growth of cancer cells, either by killing the cells or by stopping them from dividing. When chemotherapy is taken by mouth or injected into a vein or muscle, the drugs enter the bloodstream and can reach cancer cells throughout the body (systemic chemotherapy). When chemotherapy is placed directly into the cerebrospinal fluid, an organ, or a body cavity such as the abdomen, the drugs mainly affect cancer cells in those areas (regional chemotherapy). The way the chemotherapy is given depends on the type and stage of the cancer being treated.

Treatment Options for Small Intestine Cancer

Small Intestine Adenocarcinoma

When possible, treatment of small intestine adenocarcinoma will be surgery to remove the tumor and some of the normal tissue around it.

Treatment of small intestine adenocarcinoma that cannot be removed by surgery may include the following:

- Surgery to bypass the tumor.

- Radiation therapy as palliative therapy to relieve symptoms and improve the patient's quality of life.

- A clinical trial of radiation therapy with radiosensitizers, with or without chemotherapy.

- A clinical trial of new anticancer drugs.

- A clinical trial of biologic therapy.

Small Intestine Leiomyosarcoma

When possible, treatment of small intestine leiomyosarcoma will be surgery to remove the tumor and some of the normal tissue around it.

Treatment of small intestine leiomyosarcoma that cannot be removed by surgery may include the following:

- Surgery (to bypass the tumor) and radiation therapy.

- Surgery, radiation therapy, or chemotherapy as palliative therapy to relieve symptoms and improve the patient's quality of life.

- A clinical trial of new anticancer drugs.

- A clinical trial of biologic therapy.

Recurrent Small Intestine Cancer

Treatment of recurrent small intestine cancer that has spread to other parts of the body is usually a clinical trial of new anticancer drugs or biologic therapy.

Treatment of locally recurrent small intestine cancer may include the following:

- Surgery.

- Radiation therapy or chemotherapy as palliative therapy to relieve symptoms and improve the patient's quality of life.

- A clinical trial of radiation therapy with radiosensitizers, with or without chemotherapy.

Chapter 39

Colon Cancer

General Information about Colon Cancer

Colon cancer is a disease in which malignant (cancer) cells form in the tissues of the colon.

The colon is part of the body's digestive system. The digestive system removes and processes nutrients (vitamins, minerals, carbohydrates, fats, proteins, and water) from foods and helps pass waste material out of the body. The digestive system is made up of the esophagus, stomach, and the small and large intestines. The colon (large bowel) is the first part of the large intestine and is about 5 feet long. Together, the rectum and anal canal make up the last part of the large intestine and are about 6-8 inches long. The anal canal ends at the anus (the opening of the large intestine to the outside of the body).

Gastrointestinal stromal tumors can occur in the colon.

Health history can affect the risk of developing colon cancer.

Anything that increases your chance of getting a disease is called a risk factor. Having a risk factor does not mean that you will get cancer; not having risk factors doesn't mean that you will not get cancer. Talk with your doctor if you think you may be at risk. Risk factors include the following:

- A family history of cancer of the colon or rectum.

Text in this chapter is excerpted from "Colorectal Cancer—for Patients," National Cancer Institute (NCI), July 22, 2015.

- Certain hereditary conditions, such as familial adenomatous polyposis and hereditary nonpolyposis colon cancer (HNPCC; Lynch Syndrome).

- A history of ulcerative colitis (ulcers in the lining of the large intestine) or Crohn's disease.

- A personal history of cancer of the colon, rectum, ovary, endometrium, or breast.

- A personal history of polyps (small areas of bulging tissue) in the colon or rectum.

Signs of colon cancer include blood in the stool or a change in bowel habits.

These and other signs and symptoms may be caused by colon cancer or by other conditions. Check with your doctor if you have any of the following:

- A change in bowel habits.

- Blood (either bright red or very dark) in the stool.

- Diarrhea, constipation, or feeling that the bowel does not empty all the way.

- Stools that are narrower than usual.

- Frequent gas pains, bloating, fullness, or cramps.

- Weight loss for no known reason.

- Feeling very tired.

- Vomiting.

Tests that examine the colon and rectum are used to detect (find) and diagnose colon cancer.

The following tests and procedures may be used:

- **Physical exam and history:** An exam of the body to check general signs of health, including checking for signs of disease, such as lumps or anything else that seems unusual. A history of the patient's health habits and past illnesses and treatments will also be taken.

- **Digital rectal exam:** An exam of the rectum. The doctor or nurse inserts a lubricated, gloved finger into the rectum to feel for lumps or anything else that seems unusual.

- **Fecal occult blood test:** A test to check stool (solid waste) for blood that can only be seen with a microscope. Small samples of stool are placed on special cards and returned to the doctor or laboratory for testing.

- **Barium enema:** A series of X-rays of the lower gastrointestinal tract. A liquid that contains barium (a silver-white metallic compound) is put into the rectum. The barium coats the lower gastrointestinal tract and X-rays are taken. This procedure is also called a lower GI series.

- **Sigmoidoscopy:** A procedure to look inside the rectum and sigmoid (lower) colon for polyps (small areas of bulging tissue), other abnormal areas, or cancer. A sigmoidoscope is inserted through the rectum into the sigmoid colon. A sigmoidoscope is a thin, tube-like instrument with a light and a lens for viewing. It may also have a tool to remove polyps or tissue samples, which are checked under a microscope for signs of cancer.

- **Colonoscopy:** A procedure to look inside the rectum and colon for polyps, abnormal areas, or cancer. A colonoscope is inserted through the rectum into the colon. A colonoscope is a thin, tube-like instrument with a light and a lens for viewing. It may also have a tool to remove polyps or tissue samples, which are checked under a microscope for signs of cancer.

- **Virtual colonoscopy:** A procedure that uses a series of X-rays called computed tomography to make a series of pictures of the colon. A computer puts the pictures together to create detailed images that may show polyps and anything else that seems unusual on the inside surface of the colon. This test is also called colonography or CT colonography.

- **Biopsy:** The removal of cells or tissues so they can be viewed under a microscope by a pathologist to check for signs of cancer.

Certain factors affect prognosis (chance of recovery) and treatment options.

The prognosis (chance of recovery) and treatment options depend on the following:

- The stage of the cancer (whether the cancer is in the inner lining of the colon only or has spread through the colon wall, or has spread to lymph nodes or other places in the body).

- Whether the cancer has blocked or made a hole in the colon.

- Whether there are any cancer cells left after surgery.

- Whether the cancer has recurred.

- The patient's general health.

The prognosis also depends on the blood levels of carcinoembryonic antigen (CEA) before treatment begins. CEA is a substance in the blood that may be increased when cancer is present.

Stages of Colon Cancer

After colon cancer has been diagnosed, tests are done to find out if cancer cells have spread within the colon or to other parts of the body.

The process used to find out if cancer has spread within the colon or to other parts of the body is called staging. The information gathered from the staging process determines the stage of the disease. It is important to know the stage in order to plan treatment.

The following tests and procedures may be used in the staging process:

- **CT scan (CAT scan):** A procedure that makes a series of detailed pictures of areas inside the body, such as the abdomen or chest, taken from different angles. The pictures are made by a computer linked to an X-ray machine. A dye may be injected into a vein or swallowed to help the organs or tissues show up more clearly. This procedure is also called computed tomography, computerized tomography, or computerized axial tomography.

- **MRI (magnetic resonance imaging):** A procedure that uses a magnet, radio waves, and a computer to make a series of detailed pictures of areas inside the colon. A substance called gadolinium is injected into the patient through a vein. The gadolinium collects around the cancer cells so they show up brighter in the picture. This procedure is also called nuclear magnetic resonance imaging (NMRI).

- **PET scan (positron emission tomography scan):** A procedure to find malignant tumor cells in the body. A small amount of radioactive glucose (sugar) is injected into a vein. The PET scanner rotates around the body and makes a picture of where glucose is being used in the body. Malignant tumor cells show up brighter in the picture because they are more active and take up more glucose than normal cells do.

- **Chest X-ray:** An X-ray of the organs and bones inside the chest. An X-ray is a type of energy beam that can go through the body and onto film, making a picture of areas inside the body.

- **Surgery:** A procedure to remove the tumor and see how far it has spread through the colon.

- **Lymph node biopsy:** The removal of all or part of a lymph node. A pathologist views the tissue under a microscope to look for cancer cells.

- **Complete blood count (CBC):** A procedure in which a sample of blood is drawn and checked for the following:
  - The number of red blood cells, white blood cells, and platelets.
  - The amount of hemoglobin (the protein that carries oxygen) in the red blood cells.
  - The portion of the blood sample made up of red blood cells.

- **Carcinoembryonic antigen (CEA) assay:** A test that measures the level of CEA in the blood. CEA is released into the bloodstream from both cancer cells and normal cells. When found in higher than normal amounts, it can be a sign of colon cancer or other conditions.

Cancer may spread from where it began to other parts of the body.

When cancer spreads to another part of the body, it is called metastasis.

The metastatic tumor is the same type of cancer as the primary tumor. For example, if colon cancer spreads to the lung, the cancer cells in the lung are actually colon cancer cells. The disease is metastatic colon cancer, not lung cancer.

The following stages are used for colon cancer:

Stage 0 (Carcinoma in Situ)

In stage 0, abnormal cells are found in the mucosa (innermost layer) of the colon wall. These abnormal cells may become cancer and spread. Stage 0 is also called carcinoma in situ.

511

Stage I

In stage I, cancer has formed in the mucosa (innermost layer) of the colon wall and has spread to the submucosa (layer of tissue under the mucosa). Cancer may have spread to the muscle layer of the colon wall.

Stage II

Stage II colon cancer is divided into stage IIA, stage IIB, and stage IIC.

- Stage IIA: Cancer has spread through the muscle layer of the colon wall to the serosa (outermost layer) of the colon wall.

- Stage IIB: Cancer has spread through the serosa (outermost layer) of the colon wall but has not spread to nearby organs.

- Stage IIC: Cancer has spread through the serosa (outermost layer) of the colon wall to nearby organs.

Stage III

Stage III colon cancer is divided into stage IIIA, stage IIIB, and stage IIIC.

In stage IIIA:

- Cancer has spread through the mucosa (innermost layer) of the colon wall to the submucosa (layer of tissue under the mucosa) and may have spread to the muscle layer of the colon wall. Cancer has spread to at least one but not more than 3 nearby lymph nodes or cancer cells have formed in tissues near the lymph nodes; or

- Cancer has spread through the mucosa (innermost layer) of the colon wall to the submucosa (layer of tissue under the mucosa). Cancer has spread to at least 4 but not more than 6 nearby lymph nodes.

In stage IIIB:

- Cancer has spread through the muscle layer of the colon wall to the serosa (outermost layer) of the colon wall or has spread through the serosa but not to nearby organs. Cancer has spread to at least one but not more than 3 nearby lymph nodes or cancer cells have formed in tissues near the lymph nodes; or

- Cancer has spread to the muscle layer of the colon wall or to the serosa (outermost layer) of the colon wall. Cancer has spread to at least 4 but not more than 6 nearby lymph nodes; or

- Cancer has spread through the mucosa (innermost layer) of the colon wall to the submucosa (layer of tissue under the mucosa) and may have spread to the muscle layer of the colon wall. Cancer has spread to 7 or more nearby lymph nodes.

In stage IIIC:

- Cancer has spread through the serosa (outermost layer) of the colon wall but has not spread to nearby organs. Cancer has spread to at least 4 but not more than 6 nearby lymph nodes; or

- Cancer has spread through the muscle layer of the colon wall to the serosa (outermost layer) of the colon wall or has spread through the serosa but has not spread to nearby organs. Cancer has spread to 7 or more nearby lymph nodes; or

- Cancer has spread through the serosa (outermost layer) of the colon wall and has spread to nearby organs. Cancer has spread to one or more nearby lymph nodes or cancer cells have formed in tissues near the lymph nodes.

Stage IV

Stage IV colon cancer is divided into stage IVA and stage IVB.

- Stage IVA: Cancer may have spread through the colon wall and may have spread to nearby organs or lymph nodes. Cancer has spread to one organ that is not near the colon, such as the liver, lung, or ovary, or to a distant lymph node.

- Stage IVB: Cancer may have spread through the colon wall and may have spread to nearby organs or lymph nodes. Cancer has spread to more than one organ that is not near the colon or into the lining of the abdominal wall.

Recurrent Colon Cancer

Recurrent colon cancer is cancer that has recurred (come back) after it has been treated. The cancer may come back in the colon or in other parts of the body, such as the liver, lungs, or both.

Treatment Option Overview

There are different types of treatment for patients with colon cancer.

Different types of treatment are available for patients with colon cancer. Some treatments are standard (the currently used treatment), and some are being tested in clinical trials. A treatment clinical trial is a research study meant to help improve current treatments or obtain information on new treatments for patients with cancer. When clinical trials show that a new treatment is better than the standard treatment, the new treatment may become the standard treatment. Patients may want to think about taking part in a clinical trial. Some clinical trials are open only to patients who have not started treatment.

Six types of standard treatment are used:

1. Surgery

Surgery (removing the cancer in an operation) is the most common treatment for all stages of colon cancer. A doctor may remove the cancer using one of the following types of surgery:

- **Local excision**: If the cancer is found at a very early stage, the doctor may remove it without cutting through the abdominal wall. Instead, the doctor may put a tube with a cutting tool through the rectum into the colon and cut the cancer out. This is called a local excision. If the cancer is found in a polyp (a small bulging area of tissue), the operation is called a polypectomy.

- **Resection of the colon with anastomosis**: If the cancer is larger, the doctor will perform a partial colectomy (removing the cancer and a small amount of healthy tissue around it). The doctor may then perform an anastomosis (sewing the healthy parts of the colon together). The doctor will also usually remove lymph nodes near the colon and examine them under a microscope to see whether they contain cancer.

- **Resection of the colon with colostomy**: If the doctor is not able to sew the 2 ends of the colon back together, a stoma (an opening) is made on the outside of the body for waste to pass through. This procedure is called a colostomy. A bag is placed around the stoma to collect the waste. Sometimes the colostomy is needed only until the lower colon has healed, and then it can be reversed. If the doctor needs to remove the entire lower colon, however, the colostomy may be permanent.

Even if the doctor removes all the cancer that can be seen at the time of the operation, some patients may be given chemotherapy or radiation therapy after surgery to kill any cancer cells that are left. Treatment given after the surgery, to lower the risk that the cancer will come back, is called adjuvant therapy.

2. Radiofrequency Ablation

Radiofrequency ablation is the use of a special probe with tiny electrodes that kill cancer cells. Sometimes the probe is inserted directly through the skin and only local anesthesia is needed. In other cases, the probe is inserted through an incision in the abdomen. This is done in the hospital with general anesthesia.

3. Cryosurgery

Cryosurgery is a treatment that uses an instrument to freeze and destroy abnormal tissue. This type of treatment is also called cryotherapy.

4. Chemotherapy

Chemotherapy is a cancer treatment that uses drugs to stop the growth of cancer cells, either by killing the cells or by stopping them from dividing. When chemotherapy is taken by mouth or injected into a vein or muscle, the drugs enter the bloodstream and can reach cancer cells throughout the body (systemic chemotherapy). When chemotherapy is placed directly into the cerebrospinal fluid, an organ, or a body cavity such as the abdomen, the drugs mainly affect cancer cells in those areas (regional chemotherapy).

Chemoembolization of the hepatic artery may be used to treat cancer that has spread to the liver. This involves blocking the hepatic artery (the main artery that supplies blood to the liver) and injecting anticancer drugs between the blockage and the liver. The liver's arteries then deliver the drugs throughout the liver. Only a small amount of the drug reaches other parts of the body. The blockage may be temporary or permanent, depending on what is used to block the artery. The liver continues to receive some blood from the hepatic portal vein, which carries blood from the stomach and intestine.

The way the chemotherapy is given depends on the type and stage of the cancer being treated.

5. Radiation Therapy

Radiation therapy is a cancer treatment that uses high-energy X-rays or other types of radiation to kill cancer cells or keep them from growing. There are two types of radiation therapy. External radiation therapy uses a machine outside the body to send radiation toward the cancer. Internal radiation therapy uses a radioactive substance sealed in needles, seeds, wires, or catheters that are placed directly into or near the cancer. The way the radiation therapy is given depends on the type and stage of the cancer being treated.

6. Targeted Therapy

Targeted therapy is a type of treatment that uses drugs or other substances to identify and attack specific cancer cells without harming normal cells.

Types of targeted therapies used in the treatment of colon cancer include the following:

- **Monoclonal antibodies**: Monoclonal antibodies are made in the laboratory from a single type of immune system cell. These antibodies can identify substances on cancer cells or normal substances that may help cancer cells grow. The antibodies attach to the substances and kill the cancer cells, block their growth, or keep them from spreading. Monoclonal antibodies are given by infusion. They may be used alone or to carry drugs, toxins, or radioactive material directly to cancer cells.

- **Angiogenesis inhibitors**: Angiogenesis inhibitors stop the growth of new blood vessels that tumors need to grow.

Treatment Options for Colon Cancer

Stage 0 (Carcinoma in Situ)

Treatment of stage 0 (carcinoma in situ) may include the following types of surgery:

- Local excision or simple polypectomy.

- Resection and anastomosis. This is done when the tumor is too large to remove by local excision.

Stage I Colon Cancer

Treatment of stage I colon cancer usually includes the following:

• Resection and anastomosis.

Stage II Colon Cancer

Treatment of stage II colon cancer may include the following:

• Resection and anastomosis.

Stage III Colon Cancer

Treatment of stage III colon cancer may include the following:

• Resection and anastomosis which may be followed by chemotherapy.

• Clinical trials of new chemotherapy regimens after surgery.

Stage IV and Recurrent Colon Cancer

Treatment of stage IV and recurrent colon cancer may include the following:

• Local excision for tumors that have recurred.

• Resection with or without anastomosis.

• Surgery to remove parts of other organs, such as the liver, lungs, and ovaries, where the cancer may have recurred or spread. Treatment of cancer that has spread to the liver may also include the following:

  • Chemotherapy given before surgery to shrink the tumor, after surgery, or both before and after.

  • Radiofrequency ablation or cryosurgery, for patients who cannot have surgery.

  • Chemoembolization of the hepatic artery.

• Radiation therapy or chemotherapy may be offered to some patients as palliative therapy to relieve symptoms and improve quality of life.

• Chemotherapy and/or targeted therapy with a monoclonal antibody or an angiogenesis inhibitor.

• Clinical trials of chemotherapy and/or targeted therapy.

Chapter 40

Rectal Cancer

General Information about Rectal Cancer

Rectal cancer is a disease in which malignant (cancer) cells form in the tissues of the rectum.

The rectum is part of the body's digestive system. The digestive system takes in nutrients (vitamins, minerals, carbohydrates, fats, proteins, and water) from foods and helps pass waste material out of the body. The digestive system is made up of the esophagus, stomach, and the small and large intestines. The colon (large bowel) is the first part of the large intestine and is about 5 feet long. Together, the rectum and anal canal make up the last part of the large intestine and are 6-8 inches long. The anal canal ends at the anus (the opening of the large intestine to the outside of the body).

Age and family history can affect the risk of rectal cancer.

Anything that increases your chance of getting a disease is called a risk factor. Having a risk factor does not mean that you will get cancer; not having risk factors doesn't mean that you will not get cancer. Talk with your doctor if you think you may be at risk. The following are possible risk factors for rectal cancer:

- Being aged 50 or older.

Text in this chapter is excerpted from "Colorectal Cancer—for Patients," National Cancer Institute (NCI), June 30, 2015.

- Having certain hereditary conditions, such as familial adenomatous polyposis (FAP) and hereditary nonpolyposis colon cancer (HNPCC or Lynch syndrome).

- Having a personal history of any of the following:

  - Colorectal cancer.

  - Polyps (small pieces of bulging tissue) in the colon or rectum.

  - Cancer of the ovary, endometrium, or breast.

- Having a parent, brother, sister, or child with a history of colorectal cancer or polyps.

Signs of rectal cancer include a change in bowel habits or blood in the stool.

These and other signs and symptoms may be caused by rectal cancer or by other conditions. Check with your doctor if you have any of
the following:

- Blood (either bright red or very dark) in the stool.

- A change in bowel habits.

  - Diarrhea.

  - Constipation.

  - Feeling that the bowel does not empty completely.

  - Stools that are narrower or have a different shape than
    usual.

- General abdominal discomfort (frequent gas pains, bloating, fullness, or cramps).

- Change in appetite.

- Weight loss for no known reason.

- Feeling very tired.

Tests that examine the rectum and colon are used to detect (find) and diagnose rectal cancer.

Tests used to diagnose rectal cancer include the following:

- **Physical exam and history:** An exam of the body to check
  general signs of health, including checking for signs of disease,

such as lumps or anything else that seems unusual. A history of the patient's health habits and past illnesses and treatments will also be taken.

- **Digital rectal exam (DRE):** An exam of the rectum. The doctor or nurse inserts a lubricated, gloved finger into the lower part of the rectum to feel for lumps or anything else that seems unusual. In women, the vagina may also be examined.

- **Colonoscopy:** A procedure to look inside the rectum and colon for polyps (small pieces of bulging tissue), abnormal areas, or cancer. A colonoscope is a thin, tube-like instrument with a light and a lens for viewing. It may also have a tool to remove polyps or tissue samples, which are checked under a microscope for signs of cancer.

- **Biopsy:** The removal of cells or tissues so they can be viewed under a microscope to check for signs of cancer. Tumor tissue that is removed during the biopsy may be checked to see if the patient is likely to have the gene mutation that causes HNPCC. This may help to plan treatment. The following tests may be used:

  - **Reverse-transcription polymerase chain reaction (RT-PCR) test:** A laboratory test in which cells in a sample of tissue are studied using chemicals to look for certain changes in the structure or function of genes.

  - **Immunohistochemistry:** A test that uses antibodies to check for certain antigens in a sample of tissue. The antibody is usually linked to a radioactive substance or a dye that causes the tissue to light up under a microscope. This type of test may be used to tell the difference between different types of cancer.

- **Carcinoembryonic antigen (CEA) assay:** A test that measures the level of CEA in the blood. CEA is released into the bloodstream from both cancer cells and normal cells. When found in higher than normal amounts, it can be a sign of rectal cancer or other conditions.

Certain factors affect prognosis (chance of recovery) and treatment options.

The prognosis (chance of recovery) and treatment options depend on the following:

- The stage of the cancer (whether it affects the inner lining of the rectum only, involves the whole rectum, or has spread to lymph nodes, nearby organs, or other places in the body).

- Whether the tumor has spread into or through the bowel wall.

- Where the cancer is found in the rectum.

- Whether the bowel is blocked or has a hole in it.

- Whether all of the tumor can be removed by surgery.

- The patient's general health.

- Whether the cancer has just been diagnosed or has recurred (come back).

Stages of Rectal Cancer

After rectal cancer has been diagnosed, tests are done to find out if cancer cells have spread within the rectum or to other parts of the body.

The process used to find out whether cancer has spread within the rectum or to other parts of the body is called staging. The information gathered from the staging process determines the stage of the disease. It is important to know the stage in order to plan treatment.

The following tests and procedures may be used in the staging process:

- **Chest X-ray:** An X-ray of the organs and bones inside the chest. An X-ray is a type of energy beam that can go through the body and onto film, making a picture of areas inside the body.

- **Colonoscopy:** A procedure to look inside the rectum and colon for polyps (small pieces of bulging tissue). abnormal areas, or cancer. A colonoscope is a thin, tube-like instrument with a light and a lens for viewing. It may also have a tool to remove polyps or tissue samples, which are checked under a microscope for signs of cancer.

- **CT scan (CAT scan):** A procedure that makes a series of detailed pictures of areas inside the body, such as the abdomen, pelvis, or chest, taken from different angles. The pictures are made by a computer linked to an X-ray machine. A dye may be injected into a vein or swallowed to help the organs or tissues show up more clearly. This procedure is also called computed tomography, computerized tomography, or computerized axial tomography.

- **MRI (magnetic resonance imaging):** A procedure that uses a magnet, radio waves, and a computer to make a series of detailed pictures of areas inside the body. This procedure is also called nuclear magnetic resonance imaging (NMRI).

- **PET scan (positron emission tomography scan):** A procedure to find malignant tumor cells in the body. A small amount of radioactive glucose (sugar) is injected into a vein. The PET scanner rotates around the body and makes a picture of where glucose is being used in the body. Malignant tumor cells show up brighter in the picture because they are more active and take up more glucose than normal cells do.

- **Endorectal ultrasound:** A procedure used to examine the rectum and nearby organs. An ultrasound transducer (probe) is inserted into the rectum and used to bounce high-energy sound waves (ultrasound) off internal tissues or organs and make echoes. The echoes form a picture of body tissues called a sonogram. The doctor can identify tumors by looking at the sonogram. This procedure is also called transrectal ultrasound.

Cancer may spread from where it began to other parts of the body.

When cancer spreads to another part of the body, it is called metastasis.

The metastatic tumor is the same type of cancer as the primary tumor. For example, if rectal cancer spreads to the lung, the cancer cells in the lung are actually rectal cancer cells. The disease is metastatic rectal cancer, not lung cancer.

The following stages are used for rectal cancer:

Stage 0 (Carcinoma in Situ)

In stage 0, abnormal cells are found in the mucosa (innermost layer) of the rectum wall. These abnormal cells may become cancer and spread. Stage 0 is also called carcinoma in situ.

Stage I

In stage I, cancer has formed in the mucosa (innermost layer) of the rectum wall and has spread to the submucosa (layer of tissue under the mucosa). Cancer may have spread to the muscle layer of the rectum wall.

Stage II

Stage II rectal cancer is divided into stage IIA, stage IIB, and stage IIC.

- Stage IIA: Cancer has spread through the muscle layer of the rectum wall to the serosa (outermost layer) of the rectum wall.

- Stage IIB: Cancer has spread through the serosa (outermost layer) of the rectum wall but has not spread to nearby organs.

- Stage IIC: Cancer has spread through the serosa (outermost layer) of the rectum wall to nearby organs.

Stage III

Stage III rectal cancer is divided into stage IIIA, stage IIIB, and stage IIIC.

In stage IIIA:

- Cancer has spread through the mucosa (innermost layer) of the rectum wall to the submucosa (layer of tissue under the mucosa) and may have spread to the muscle layer of the rectum wall. Cancer has spread to at least one but not more than 3 nearby lymph nodes or cancer cells have formed in tissues near the lymph nodes; or

- Cancer has spread through the mucosa (innermost layer) of the rectum wall to the submucosa (layer of tissue under the mucosa). Cancer has spread to at least 4 but not more than 6 nearby lymph nodes.

In stage IIIB:

- Cancer has spread through the muscle layer of the rectum wall to the serosa (outermost layer) of the rectum wall or has spread through the serosa but not to nearby organs. Cancer has spread to at least one but not more than 3 nearby lymph nodes or cancer cells have formed in tissues near the lymph nodes; or

- Cancer has spread to the muscle layer of the rectum wall or to the serosa (outermost layer) of the rectum wall. Cancer has spread to at least 4 but not more than 6 nearby lymph nodes; or

- Cancer has spread through the mucosa (innermost layer) of the rectum wall to the submucosa (layer of tissue under the mucosa) and may have spread to the muscle layer of the rectum wall. Cancer has spread to 7 or more nearby lymph nodes.

In stage IIIC:

- Cancer has spread through the serosa (outermost layer) of the rectum wall but has not spread to nearby organs. Cancer has spread to at least 4 but not more than 6 nearby lymph nodes; or

- Cancer has spread through the muscle layer of the rectum wall to the serosa (outermost layer) of the rectum wall or has spread through the serosa but has not spread to nearby organs. Cancer has spread to 7 or more nearby lymph nodes; or

- Cancer has spread through the serosa (outermost layer) of the rectum wall and has spread to nearby organs. Cancer has spread to one or more nearby lymph nodes or cancer cells have formed in tissues near the lymph nodes.

Stage IV

Stage IV rectal cancer is divided into stage IVA and stage IVB

- Stage IVA: Cancer may have spread through the rectum wall and may have spread to nearby organs or lymph nodes. Cancer has spread to one organ that is not near the rectum, such as the liver, lung, or ovary, or to a distant lymph node.

- Stage IVB: Cancer may have spread through the rectum wall and may have spread to nearby organs or lymph nodes. Cancer has spread to more than one organ that is not near the rectum or into the lining of the abdominal wall.

Recurrent Rectal Cancer

Recurrent rectal cancer is cancer that has recurred (come back) after it has been treated. The cancer may come back in the rectum or in other parts of the body, such as the colon, pelvis, liver, or lungs.

Treatment Option Overview

There are different types of treatment for patients with rectal cancer.

Different types of treatment are available for patients with rectal cancer. Some treatments are standard (the currently used treatment), and some are being tested in clinical trials. A treatment clinical trial is a research study meant to help improve current treatments or obtain information on new treatments for patients with cancer. When clinical trials show that a new treatment is better than the standard treatment, the new treatment may become the standard treatment. Patients may want to think about taking part in a clinical trial. Some clinical trials are open only to patients who have not started treatment.

Four types of standard treatment are used:

1. Surgery

Surgery is the most common treatment for all stages of rectal cancer. The cancer is removed using one of the following types of surgery:

- **Polypectomy:** If the cancer is found in a polyp (a small piece of bulging tissue), the polyp is often removed during a colonoscopy.

- **Local excision:** If the cancer is found on the inside surface of the rectum and has not spread into the wall of the rectum, the cancer and a small amount of surrounding healthy tissue is removed.

- **Resection:** If the cancer has spread into the wall of the rectum, the section of the rectum with cancer and nearby healthy tissue is removed. Sometimes the tissue between the rectum and the abdominal wall is also removed. The lymph nodes near the rectum are removed and checked under a microscope for signs of cancer.

- **Radiofrequency ablation:** The use of a special probe with tiny electrodes that kill cancer cells. Sometimes the probe is inserted directly through the skin and only local anesthesia is needed. In other cases, the probe is inserted through an incision in the abdomen. This is done in the hospital with general anesthesia.

- **Cryosurgery:** A treatment that uses an instrument to freeze and destroy abnormal tissue. This type of treatment is also called cryotherapy.

- **Pelvic exenteration:** If the cancer has spread to other organs near the rectum, the lower colon, rectum, and bladder are removed. In women, the cervix, vagina, ovaries, and nearby lymph nodes may be removed. In men, the prostate may be removed. Artificial openings (stoma) are made for urine and stool to flow from the body to a collection bag.

After the cancer is removed, the surgeon will either:

- do an anastomosis (sew the healthy parts of the rectum together, sew the remaining rectum to the colon, or sew the colon to the anus);

or

- make a stoma (an opening) from the rectum to the outside of the body for waste to pass through. This procedure is done if the cancer is too close to the anus and is called a colostomy. A bag is placed around the stoma to collect the waste. Sometimes the colostomy is needed only until the rectum has healed, and then it can be reversed. If the entire rectum is removed, however, the colostomy may be permanent.

Radiation therapy and/or chemotherapy may be given before surgery to shrink the tumor, make it easier to remove the cancer, and help with bowel control after surgery. Treatment given before surgery is called neoadjuvant therapy. Even if all the cancer that can be seen at the time of the operation is removed, some patients may be given radiation therapy and/or chemotherapy after surgery to kill any cancer cells that are left. Treatment given after the surgery, to lower the risk that the cancer will come back, is called adjuvant therapy.

2. Radiation Therapy

Radiation therapy is a cancer treatment that uses high-energy X-rays or other types of radiation to kill cancer cells. There are two types of radiation therapy. External radiation therapy uses a machine outside the body to send radiation toward the cancer. Internal radiation therapy uses a radioactive substance sealed in needles, seeds, wires, or catheters that are placed directly into or near the cancer. The way the radiation therapy is given depends on the type and stage of the cancer being treated.

Short-course preoperative radiation therapy is used in some types of rectal cancer. This treatment uses fewer and lower doses of radiation than standard treatment, followed by surgery several days after the last dose.

3. Chemotherapy

Chemotherapy is a cancer treatment that uses drugs to stop the growth of cancer cells, either by killing the cells or by stopping the cells from dividing. When chemotherapy is taken by mouth or injected into a vein or muscle, the drugs enter the bloodstream and can reach cancer cells throughout the body (systemic chemotherapy). When chemotherapy is placed directly in the cerebrospinal fluid, an organ, or a body cavity such as the abdomen, the drugs mainly affect cancer cells in those areas (regional chemotherapy).

Chemoembolization of the hepatic artery is a type of regional chemotherapy that may be used to treat cancer that has spread to the liver. This is done by blocking the hepatic artery (the main artery that supplies blood to the liver) and injecting anticancer drugs between the blockage and the liver. The liver's arteries then carry the drugs into the liver. Only a small amount of the drug reaches other parts of the body. The blockage may be temporary or permanent, depending on what is used to block the artery. The liver continues to receive some blood from the hepatic portal vein, which carries blood from the stomach and intestine.

The way the chemotherapy is given depends on the type and stage of the cancer being treated.

4. Targeted Therapy

Targeted therapy is a type of treatment that uses drugs or other substances to identify and attack specific cancer cells without harming normal cells. Monoclonal antibody therapy is a type of targeted therapy being used for the treatment of rectal cancer.

Monoclonal antibody therapy uses antibodies made in the laboratory from a single type of immune system cell. These antibodies can identify substances on cancer cells or normal substances that may help cancer cells grow. The antibodies attach to the substances and kill the cancer cells, block their growth, or keep them from spreading. Monoclonal antibodies are given by infusion. They may be used alone or to carry drugs, toxins, or radioactive material directly to cancer cells.

Bevacizumab is a monoclonal antibody that binds to a protein called vascular endothelial growth factor (VEGF). This may prevent the growth of new blood vessels that tumors need to grow. Cetuximab and panitumumab are types of monoclonal antibodies that bind to a protein called epidermal growth factor receptor (EGFR) on the surface of some types of cancer cells. This may stop cancer cells from growing and dividing.

528

Treatment Options by Stage

Stage 0 (Carcinoma in Situ)

Treatment of stage 0 may include the following:

- Simple polypectomy.
- Local excision.
- Resection (when the tumor is too large to remove by local excision).

Stage I Rectal Cancer

Treatment of stage I rectal cancer may include the following:

- Local excision.
- Resection.
- Resection with radiation therapy and chemotherapy after surgery.

Stages II and III Rectal Cancer

Treatment of stage II and stage III rectal cancer may include the following:

- Surgery.
- Chemotherapy combined with radiation therapy, followed by surgery.
- Short-course radiation therapy followed by surgery and chemotherapy.
- Resection followed by chemotherapy combined with radiation therapy.
- A clinical trial of a new treatment.

Stage IV and Recurrent Rectal Cancer

Treatment of stage IV and recurrent rectal cancer may include the following:

- Surgery with or without chemotherapy or radiation therapy.
- Systemic chemotherapy with or without targeted therapy, such as bevacizumab, cetuximab, or panitumumab.

- Chemotherapy to control the growth of the tumor.

- Radiation therapy, chemotherapy, or a combination of both, as palliative therapy to relieve symptoms and improve the quality of life.

- Placement of a stent to help keep the rectum open if it is partly blocked by the tumor, as palliative therapy to relieve symptoms and improve the quality of life.

- A clinical trial of a new anticancer drug.

Treatment of rectal cancer that has spread to other organs depends on where the cancer has spread.

- Treatment for areas of cancer that have spread to the liver includes the following:

  - Surgery to remove the tumor. Chemotherapy may be given before surgery, to shrink the tumor.

  - Cryosurgery or radiofrequency ablation.

  - Chemoembolization and/or systemic chemotherapy.

  - A clinical trial of chemoembolization combined with radiation therapy to the tumors in the liver.

Chapter 41

Gallbladder Cancer

Overview

The gallbladder lies just under the liver in the upper abdomen. The gallbladder stores bile, a fluid made by the liver that helps digest fat.

Almost all gallbladder cancers are adenocarcinomas (cancers that begin in cells that make and release mucus and other fluids).

Gallbladder cancer is hard to diagnose in the early stages because there are no signs or symptoms. Gallbladder cancer may be found when the gallbladder is checked for gallstones or removed.

General Information about Gallbladder Cancer

Gallbladder cancer is a disease in which malignant (cancer) cells form in the tissues of the gallbladder.

Gallbladder cancer is a rare disease in which malignant (cancer) cells are found in the tissues of the gallbladder. The gallbladder is a pear-shaped organ that lies just under the liver in the upper abdomen. The gallbladder stores bile, a fluid made by the liver to digest fat. When food is being broken down in the stomach and intestines, bile is released from the gallbladder through a tube called the common bile

---

Text in this chapter is excerpted from "Gallbladder Cancer—for Patients," National Cancer Institute (NCI), September 21, 2015.

duct, which connects the gallbladder and liver to the first part of the small intestine.

The wall of the gallbladder has 3 main layers of tissue.

- Mucosal (inner) layer.

- Muscularis (middle, muscle) layer.

- Serosal (outer) layer.

Between these layers is supporting connective tissue. Primary gallbladder cancer starts in the inner layer and spreads through the outer layers as it grows.

Being female can increase the risk of developing gallbladder cancer.

Anything that increases your chance of getting a disease is called a risk factor. Having a risk factor does not mean that you will get cancer; not having risk factors doesn't mean that you will not get cancer. Talk with your doctor if you think you may be at risk. Risk factors for gallbladder cancer include the following:

- Being female.

- Being Native American.

Signs and symptoms of gallbladder cancer include jaundice, fever, and pain.

These and other signs and symptoms may be caused by gallbladder cancer or by other conditions. Check with your doctor if you have any of the following:

- Jaundice (yellowing of the skin and whites of the eyes).

- Pain above the stomach.

- Fever.

- Nausea and vomiting.

- Bloating.

- Lumps in the abdomen.

Gallbladder cancer is difficult to detect (find) and diagnose early.

Gallbladder cancer is difficult to detect and diagnose for the following reasons:

- There are no signs or symptoms in the early stages of gallbladder cancer.

- The symptoms of gallbladder cancer, when present, are like the symptoms of many other illnesses.

- The gallbladder is hidden behind the liver.

Gallbladder cancer is sometimes found when the gallbladder is removed for other reasons. Patients with gallstones rarely develop gallbladder cancer.

Tests that examine the gallbladder and nearby organs are used to detect (find), diagnose, and stage gallbladder cancer.

Procedures that make pictures of the gallbladder and the area around it help diagnose gallbladder cancer and show how far the cancer has spread. The process used to find out if cancer cells have spread within and around the gallbladder is called staging.

In order to plan treatment, it is important to know if the gallbladder cancer can be removed by surgery. Tests and procedures to detect, diagnose, and stage gallbladder cancer are usually done at the same time. The following tests and procedures may be used:

- **Physical exam and history:** An exam of the body to check general signs of health, including checking for signs of disease, such as lumps or anything else that seems unusual. A history of the patient's health habits and past illnesses and treatments will also be taken.

- **Liver function tests:** A procedure in which a blood sample is checked to measure the amounts of certain substances released into the blood by the liver. A higher than normal amount of a substance can be a sign of liver disease that may be caused by gallbladder cancer.

- **Carcinoembryonic antigen (CEA) assay:** A test that measures the level of CEA in the blood. CEA is released into the bloodstream from both cancer cells and normal cells. When

found in higher than normal amounts, it can be a sign of gallbladder cancer or other conditions.

- **CA 19-9 assay:** A test that measures the level of CA 19-9 in
  the blood. CA 19-9 is released into the bloodstream from both
  cancer cells and normal cells. When found in higher than normal amounts, it can be a sign of gallbladder cancer or other
  conditions.

- **Blood chemistry studies:** A procedure in which a blood sample is checked to measure the amounts of certain substances
  released into the blood by organs and tissues in the body. An
  unusual (higher or lower than normal) amount of a substance
  can be a sign of disease.

- **CT scan (CAT scan):** A procedure that makes a series of
  detailed pictures of areas inside the body, such as the chest,
  abdomen, and pelvis, taken from different angles. The pictures
  are made by a computer linked to an X-ray machine. A dye may
  be injected into a vein or swallowed to help the organs or tissues
  show up more clearly. This procedure is also called computed
  tomography, computerized tomography, or computerized axial
  tomography.

- **Ultrasound exam:** A procedure in which high-energy sound
  waves (ultrasound) are bounced off internal tissues or organs
  and make echoes. The echoes form a picture of body tissues
  called a sonogram. An abdominal ultrasound is done to diagnose
  gallbladder cancer.

- **PTC (percutaneous transhepatic cholangiography):** A
  procedure used to X-ray the liver and bile ducts. A thin needle is
  inserted through the skin below the ribs and into the liver. Dye
  is injected into the liver or bile ducts and an X-ray is taken. If
  a blockage is found, a thin, flexible tube called a stent is sometimes left in the liver to drain bile into the small intestine or a
  collection bag outside the body.

- **Chest X-ray:** An X-ray of the organs and bones inside the chest.
  An X-ray is a type of energy beam that can go through the body
  and onto film, making a picture of areas inside the body.

- **ERCP (endoscopic retrograde cholangiopancreatography):** A procedure used to X-ray the ducts (tubes) that carry
  bile from the liver to the gallbladder and from the gallbladder to

the small intestine. Sometimes gallbladder cancer causes these ducts to narrow and block or slow the flow of bile, causing jaundice. An endoscope (a thin, lighted tube) is passed through the mouth, esophagus, and stomach into the first part of the small intestine. A catheter (a smaller tube) is then inserted through the endoscope into the bile ducts. A dye is injected through the catheter into the ducts and an X-ray is taken. If the ducts are blocked by a tumor, a fine tube may be inserted into the duct to unblock it. This tube (or stent) may be left in place to keep the duct open. Tissue samples may also be taken.

- **Laparoscopy:** A surgical procedure to look at the organs inside the abdomen to check for signs of disease. Small incisions (cuts) are made in the wall of the abdomen and a laparoscope (a thin, lighted tube) is inserted into one of the incisions. Other instruments may be inserted through the same or other incisions to perform procedures such as removing organs or taking tissue samples for biopsy. The laparoscopy helps to find out if the cancer is within the gallbladder only or has spread to nearby tissues and if it can be removed by surgery.

- **Biopsy:** The removal of cells or tissues so they can be viewed under a microscope by a pathologist to check for signs of cancer. The biopsy may be done after surgery to remove the tumor. If the tumor clearly cannot be removed by surgery, the biopsy may be done using a fine needle to remove cells from the tumor.

Certain factors affect the prognosis (chance of recovery) and treatment options.

The prognosis (chance of recovery) and treatment options depend on the following:

- The stage of the cancer (whether the cancer has spread from the gallbladder to other places in the body).

- Whether the cancer can be completely removed by surgery.

- The type of gallbladder cancer (how the cancer cell looks under a microscope).

- Whether the cancer has just been diagnosed or has recurred (come back).

Treatment may also depend on the age and general health of the patient and whether the cancer is causing signs or symptoms.

Gallbladder cancer can be cured only if it is found before it has spread, when it can be removed by surgery. If the cancer has spread, palliative treatment can improve the patient's quality of life by controlling the symptoms and complications of this disease.

Stages of Gallbladder Cancer

Cancer may spread from where it began to other parts of the body.

When cancer spreads to another part of the body, it is called metastasis.

The metastatic tumor is the same type of cancer as the primary tumor. For example, if gallbladder cancer spreads to the liver, the cancer cells in the liver are actually gallbladder cancer cells. The disease is metastatic gallbladder cancer, not liver cancer.

The following stages are used for gallbladder cancer:

Stage 0 (Carcinoma in Situ)

In stage 0, abnormal cells are found in the inner (mucosal) layer of the gallbladder. These abnormal cells may become cancer and spread into nearby normal tissue. Stage 0 is also called carcinoma in situ.

Stage I

In stage I, cancer has formed and has spread beyond the inner (mucosal) layer to a layer of tissue with blood vessels or to the muscle layer.

Stage II

In stage II, cancer has spread beyond the muscle layer to the connective tissue around the muscle.

Stage IIIA

In stage IIIA, cancer has spread through the thin layers of tissue that cover the gallbladder and/or to the liver and/or to one nearby organ (such as the stomach, small intestine, colon, pancreas, or bile ducts outside the liver).

Stage IIIB

In stage IIIB, cancer has spread to nearby lymph nodes and:

- beyond the inner layer of the gallbladder to a layer of tissue with blood vessels or to the muscle layer; or

- beyond the muscle layer to the connective tissue around the muscle; or

- through the thin layers of tissue that cover the gallbladder and/or to the liver and/or to one nearby organ (such as the stomach, small intestine, colon, pancreas, or bile ducts outside the liver).

Stage IVA

In stage IVA, cancer has spread to a main blood vessel of the liver or to 2 or more nearby organs or areas other than the liver. Cancer may have spread to nearby lymph nodes.

Stage IVB

In stage IVB, cancer has spread to either:

- lymph nodes along large arteries in the abdomen and/or near the lower part of the backbone; or

- to organs or areas far away from the gallbladder.

For gallbladder cancer, stages are also grouped according to how the cancer may be treated. There are two treatment groups:

1. Localized (Stage I)

Cancer is found in the wall of the gallbladder and can be completely removed by surgery.

2. Unresectable, recurrent, or metastatic (Stage II, Stage III, and Stage IV)

Unresectable cancer cannot be removed completely by surgery. Most patients with gallbladder cancer have unresectable cancer.

Recurrent cancer is cancer that has recurred (come back) after it has been treated. Gallbladder cancer may come back in the gallbladder or in other parts of the body.

Metastasis is the spread of cancer from the primary site (place where it started) to other places in the body. Metastatic gallbladder cancer may spread to surrounding tissues, organs, throughout the abdominal cavity, or to distant parts of the body.

Treatment Option Overview

There are different types of treatment for patients with gallbladder cancer.

Different types of treatments are available for patients with gallbladder cancer. Some treatments are standard (the currently used treatment), and some are being tested in clinical trials. A treatment clinical trial is a research study meant to help improve current treatments or obtain information on new treatments for patients with cancer. When clinical trials show that a new treatment is better than the standard treatment, the new treatment may become the standard treatment. Patients may want to think about taking part in a clinical trial. Some clinical trials are open only to patients who have not started treatment.

Three types of standard treatment are used:

1. Surgery

Gallbladder cancer may be treated with a cholecystectomy, surgery to remove the gallbladder and some of the tissues around it. Nearby lymph nodes may be removed. A laparoscope is sometimes used to guide gallbladder surgery. The laparoscope is attached to a video camera and inserted through an incision (port) in the abdomen. Surgical instruments are inserted through other ports to perform the surgery. Because there is a risk that gallbladder cancer cells may spread to these ports, tissue surrounding the port sites may also be removed.

If the cancer has spread and cannot be removed, the following types of palliative surgery may relieve symptoms:

- **Surgical biliary bypass**: If the tumor is blocking the small intestine and bile is building up in the gallbladder, a biliary bypass may be done. During this operation, the gallbladder or bile duct will be cut and sewn to the small intestine to create a new pathway around the blocked area.

- **Endoscopic stent placement**: If the tumor is blocking the bile duct, surgery may be done to put in a stent (a thin, flexible tube) to drain bile that has built up in the area. The stent may be placed through a catheter that drains to the outside of the body or the stent may go around the blocked area and drain the bile into the small intestine.

- **Percutaneous transhepatic biliary drainage**: A procedure done to drain bile when there is a blockage and endoscopic stent placement is not possible. An X-ray of the liver and bile ducts is done to locate the blockage. Images made by ultrasound are used to guide placement of a stent, which is left in the liver to drain bile into the small intestine or a collection bag outside the body. This procedure may be done to relieve jaundice before surgery.

2. Radiation Therapy

Radiation therapy is a cancer treatment that uses high-energy X-rays or other types of radiation to kill cancer cells. There are two types of radiation therapy. External radiation therapy uses a machine outside the body to send radiation toward the cancer. Internal radiation therapy uses a radioactive substance sealed in needles, seeds, wires, or catheters that are placed directly into or near the cancer. The way the radiation therapy is given depends on the type and stage of the cancer being treated.

3. Chemotherapy

Chemotherapy is a cancer treatment that uses drugs to stop the growth of cancer cells, either by killing the cells or by stopping the cells from dividing. When chemotherapy is taken by mouth or injected into a vein or muscle, the drugs enter the bloodstream and can reach cancer cells throughout the body (systemic chemotherapy). When chemotherapy is placed directly into the cerebrospinal fluid, an organ, or a body cavity such as the abdomen, the drugs mainly affect cancer cells in those areas (regional chemotherapy). The way the chemotherapy is given depends on the type and stage of the cancer being treated.

Treatment Options for Gallbladder Cancer

Localized Gallbladder Cancer

Treatment of localized gallbladder cancer may include the following:

- Surgery to remove the gallbladder and some of the tissue around it. Part of the liver and nearby lymph nodes may also be removed. Radiation therapy with or without chemotherapy may follow surgery.

- Radiation therapy with or without chemotherapy.

- A clinical trial of radiation therapy with radiosensitizers.

Unresectable, Recurrent, or Metastatic Gallbladder Cancer

Treatment of unresectable, recurrent, or metastatic gallbladder cancer is usually within a clinical trial. Treatment may include the following:

- Percutaneous transhepatic biliary drainage or the placement of stents to relieve symptoms caused by blocked bile ducts. This may be followed by radiation therapy as palliative treatment.

- Surgery as palliative treatment to relieve symptoms caused by blocked bile ducts.

- Chemotherapy.

- A clinical trial of new ways to give palliative radiation therapy, such as giving it together with hyperthermia therapy, radiosensitizers, or chemotherapy.

- A clinical trial of new drugs and drug combinations.

Chapter 42

Pancreatic Cancer

Overview

The pancreas lies behind the stomach and in front of the spine. There are two kinds of cells in the pancreas. Exocrine pancreas cells make enzymes that are released into the small intestine to help the body digest food. Neuroendocrine pancreas cells (such as islet cells) make several hormones, including insulin and glucagon, that help control sugar levels in the blood.

Most pancreatic cancers form in exocrine cells. These tumors do not secrete hormones and do not cause signs or symptoms. This makes it hard to diagnose this type of pancreatic cancer early. For most patients with exocrine pancreatic cancer, current treatments do not cure the cancer.

Some types of malignant pancreatic neuroendocrine tumors, such as islet cell tumors, have a better prognosis than pancreatic exocrine cancers.

General Information about Pancreatic Cancer

Pancreatic cancer is a disease in which malignant (cancer) cells form in the tissues of the pancreas.

The pancreas is a gland about 6 inches long that is shaped like a thin pear lying on its side. The wider end of the pancreas is called

Text in this chapter is excerpted from "Pancreatic Cancer—for Patients," National Cancer Institute (NCI), July 2, 2015.

the head, the middle section is called the body, and the narrow end is called the tail. The pancreas lies between the stomach and the spine.

The pancreas has two main jobs in the body:

- To make juices that help digest (break down) food.

- To make hormones, such as insulin and glucagon, that help control blood sugar levels. Both of these hormones help the body use and store the energy it gets from food.

The digestive juices are made by exocrine pancreas cells and the hormones are made by endocrine pancreas cells. About 95% of pancreatic cancers begin in exocrine cells.

Smoking and health history can affect the risk of pancreatic cancer.

Anything that increases your risk of getting a disease is called a risk factor. Having a risk factor does not mean that you will get cancer; not having risk factors doesn't mean that you will not get cancer. Talk with your doctor if you think you may be at risk.

Risk factors for pancreatic cancer include the following:

- Smoking.

- Being very overweight.

- Having a personal history of diabetes or chronic pancreatitis.

- Having a family history of pancreatic cancer or pancreatitis.

- Having certain hereditary conditions, such as:

  - Multiple endocrine neoplasia type 1 (MEN1) syndrome.

  - Hereditary nonpolyposis colon cancer (HNPCC; Lynch syndrome).

  - von Hippel-Lindau syndrome.

  - Peutz-Jeghers syndrome.

  - Hereditary breast and ovarian cancer syndrome.

  - Familial atypical multiple mole melanoma (FAMMM) syndrome.

Signs and symptoms of pancreatic cancer include jaundice, pain, and weight loss.

Pancreatic cancer may not cause early signs or symptoms. Signs and symptoms may be caused by pancreatic cancer or by other conditions. Check with your doctor if you have any of the following:

- Jaundice (yellowing of the skin and whites of the eyes).
- Light-colored stools.
- Dark urine.
- Pain in the upper or middle abdomen and back.
- Weight loss for no known reason.
- Loss of appetite.
- Feeling very tired.

Pancreatic cancer is difficult to detect (find) and diagnose early.

Pancreatic cancer is difficult to detect and diagnose for the following reasons:

- There aren't any noticeable signs or symptoms in the early stages of pancreatic cancer.
- The signs and symptoms of pancreatic cancer, when present, are like the signs and symptoms of many other illnesses.
- The pancreas is hidden behind other organs such as the stomach, small intestine, liver, gallbladder, spleen, and bile ducts.

Tests that examine the pancreas are used to detect (find), diagnose, and stage pancreatic cancer.

Pancreatic cancer is usually diagnosed with tests and procedures that make pictures of the pancreas and the area around it. The process used to find out if cancer cells have spread within and around the pancreas is called staging. Tests and procedures to detect, diagnose, and stage pancreatic cancer are usually done at the same time. In order to plan treatment, it is important to know the stage of the disease and whether or not the pancreatic cancer can be removed by surgery.

The following tests and procedures may be used:

- **Physical exam and history:** An exam of the body to check general signs of health, including checking for signs of disease, such as lumps or anything else that seems unusual. A history of the patient's health habits and past illnesses and treatments will also be taken.

- **Blood chemistry studies:** A procedure in which a blood sample is checked to measure the amounts of certain substances, such as bilirubin, released into the blood by organs and tissues in the body. An unusual (higher or lower than normal) amount of a substance can be a sign of disease.

- **Tumor marker test:** A procedure in which a sample of blood, urine, or tissue is checked to measure the amounts of certain substances, such as CA 19-9, and carcinoembryonic antigen (CEA), made by organs, tissues, or tumor cells in the body. Certain substances are linked to specific types of cancer when found in increased levels in the body. These are called tumor markers.

- **MRI (magnetic resonance imaging):** A procedure that uses a magnet, radio waves, and a computer to make a series of detailed pictures of areas inside the body. This procedure is also called nuclear magnetic resonance imaging (NMRI).

- **CT scan (CAT scan):** A procedure that makes a series of detailed pictures of areas inside the body, taken from different angles. The pictures are made by a computer linked to an X-ray machine. A dye may be injected into a vein or swallowed to help the organs or tissues show up more clearly. This procedure is also called computed tomography, computerized tomography, or computerized axial tomography. A spiral or helical CT scan makes a series of very detailed pictures of areas inside the body using an X-ray machine that scans the body in a spiral path.

- **PET scan (positron emission tomography scan):** A procedure to find malignant tumor cells in the body. A small amount of radioactive glucose (sugar) is injected into a vein. The PET scanner rotates around the body and makes a picture of where glucose is being used in the body. Malignant tumor cells show up brighter in the picture because they are more active and take up more glucose than normal cells do. A PET scan and CT scan may be done at the same time. This is called a PET-CT.

- **Abdominal ultrasound:** An ultrasound exam used to make pictures of the inside of the abdomen. The ultrasound transducer is pressed against the skin of the abdomen and directs high-energy sound waves (ultrasound) into the abdomen. The sound waves bounce off the internal tissues and organs and make echoes. The transducer receives the echoes and sends them to a computer, which uses the echoes to make pictures called sonograms. The picture can be printed to be looked at later.

- **Endoscopic ultrasound (EUS):** A procedure in which an endoscope is inserted into the body, usually through the mouth or rectum. An endoscope is a thin, tube-like instrument with a light and a lens for viewing. A probe at the end of the endoscope is used to bounce high-energy sound waves (ultrasound) off internal tissues or organs and make echoes. The echoes form a picture of body tissues called a sonogram. This procedure is also called endosonography.

- **Endoscopic retrograde cholangiopancreatography (ERCP):** A procedure used to X-ray the ducts (tubes) that carry bile from the liver to the gallbladder and from the gallbladder to the small intestine. Sometimes pancreatic cancer causes these ducts to narrow and block or slow the flow of bile, causing jaundice. An endoscope (a thin, lighted tube) is passed through the mouth, esophagus, and stomach into the first part of the small intestine. A catheter (a smaller tube) is then inserted through the endoscope into the pancreatic ducts. A dye is injected through the catheter into the ducts and an X-ray is taken. If the ducts are blocked by a tumor, a fine tube may be inserted into the duct to unblock it. This tube (or stent) may be left in place to keep the duct open. Tissue samples may also be taken.

- **Percutaneous transhepatic cholangiography (PTC):** A procedure used to X-ray the liver and bile ducts. A thin needle is inserted through the skin below the ribs and into the liver. Dye is injected into the liver or bile ducts and an X-ray is taken. If a blockage is found, a thin, flexible tube called a stent is sometimes left in the liver to drain bile into the small intestine or a collection bag outside the body. This test is done only if ERCP cannot be done.

- **Laparoscopy:** A surgical procedure to look at the organs inside the abdomen to check for signs of disease. Small incisions (cuts) are made in the wall of the abdomen and a laparoscope (a thin, lighted tube) is inserted into one of the incisions. The laparoscope may have an ultrasound probe at the end in order to bounce high-energy sound waves off internal organs, such as the pancreas. This is called laparoscopic ultrasound. Other instruments may be inserted through the same or other incisions to perform procedures such as taking tissue samples from the pancreas or a sample of fluid from the abdomen to check for cancer.

- **Biopsy:** The removal of cells or tissues so they can be viewed under a microscope by a pathologist to check for signs of cancer. There are several ways to do a biopsy for pancreatic cancer. A fine needle or a core needle may be inserted into the pancreas during an X-ray or ultrasound to remove cells. Tissue may also be removed during a laparoscopy.

Certain factors affect prognosis (chance of recovery) and treatment options.

The prognosis (chance of recovery) and treatment options depend on the following:

- Whether or not the tumor can be removed by surgery.
- The stage of the cancer (the size of the tumor and whether the cancer has spread outside the pancreas to nearby tissues or lymph nodes or to other places in the body).
- The patient's general health.
- Whether the cancer has just been diagnosed or has recurred (come back).

Pancreatic cancer can be controlled only if it is found before it has spread, when it can be completely removed by surgery. If the cancer has spread, palliative treatment can improve the patient's quality of life by controlling the symptoms and complications of this disease.

Stages of Pancreatic Cancer

Tests and procedures to stage pancreatic cancer are usually done at the same time as diagnosis.

The process used to find out if cancer has spread within the pancreas or to other parts of the body is called staging. The information gathered from the staging process determines the stage of the disease. It is important to know the stage of the disease in order to plan treatment. The results of some of the tests used to diagnose pancreatic cancer are often also used to stage the disease.

Cancer may spread from where it began to other parts of the body.

When cancer spreads to another part of the body, it is called metastasis.

The metastatic tumor is the same type of cancer as the primary tumor. For example, if pancreatic cancer spreads to the liver, the cancer cells in the liver are actually pancreatic cancer cells. The disease is metastatic pancreatic cancer, not liver cancer.

The following stages are used for pancreatic cancer:

Stage 0 (Carcinoma in Situ)

In stage 0, abnormal cells are found in the lining of the pancreas. These abnormal cells may become cancer and spread into nearby normal tissue. Stage 0 is also called carcinoma in situ.

Stage I

In stage I, cancer has formed and is found in the pancreas only. Stage I is divided into stage IA and stage IB, based on the size of the tumor.

- Stage IA: The tumor is 2 centimeters or smaller.

- Stage IB: The tumor is larger than 2 centimeters.

Stage II

In stage II, cancer may have spread to nearby tissue and organs, and may have spread to lymph nodes near the pancreas. Stage II is divided into stage IIA and stage IIB, based on where the cancer has spread.

- Stage IIA: Cancer has spread to nearby tissue and organs but has not spread to nearby lymph nodes.

- Stage IIB: Cancer has spread to nearby lymph nodes and may have spread to nearby tissue and organs.

Stage III

In stage III, cancer has spread to the major blood vessels near the pancreas and may have spread to nearby lymph nodes.

Stage IV

In stage IV, cancer may be of any size and has spread to distant organs, such as the liver, lung, and peritoneal cavity. It may have also spread to organs and tissues near the pancreas or to lymph nodes.

Recurrent Pancreatic Cancer

Recurrent pancreatic cancer is cancer that has recurred (come back) after it has been treated. The cancer may come back in the pancreas or in other parts of the body.

Treatment Option Overview

There are different types of treatment for patients with pancreatic cancer.

Different types of treatment are available for patients with pancreatic cancer. Some treatments are standard (the currently used treatment), and some are being tested in clinical trials. A treatment clinical trial is a research study meant to help improve current treatments or obtain information on new treatments for patients with cancer. When clinical trials show that a new treatment is better than the standard treatment, the new treatment may become the standard treatment. Patients may want to think about taking part in a clinical trial. Some clinical trials are open only to patients who have not started treatment.

Five types of standard treatment are used:

1. Surgery

One of the following types of surgery may be used to take out the tumor:

- **Whipple procedure**: A surgical procedure in which the head of the pancreas, the gallbladder, part of the stomach, part of the small intestine, and the bile duct are removed. Enough of the pancreas is left to produce digestive juices and insulin.

- **Total pancreatectomy**: This operation removes the whole pancreas, part of the stomach, part of the small intestine, the common bile duct, the gallbladder, the spleen, and nearby lymph nodes.

- **Distal pancreatectomy**: The body and the tail of the pancreas and usually the spleen are removed.

If the cancer has spread and cannot be removed, the following types of palliative surgery may be done to relieve symptoms and improve quality of life:

- **Surgical biliary bypass**: If cancer is blocking the small intestine and bile is building up in the gallbladder, a biliary bypass may be done. During this operation, the doctor will cut the gallbladder or bile duct and sew it to the small intestine to create a new pathway around the blocked area.

- **Endoscopic stent placement**: If the tumor is blocking the bile duct, surgery may be done to put in a stent (a thin tube) to drain bile that has built up in the area. The doctor may place the stent through a catheter that drains to the outside of the body or the stent may go around the blocked area and drain the bile into the small intestine.

- **Gastric bypass**: If the tumor is blocking the flow of food from the stomach, the stomach may be sewn directly to the small intestine so the patient can continue to eat normally.

2. Radiation Therapy

Radiation therapy is a cancer treatment that uses high-energy X-rays or other types of radiation to kill cancer cells or keep them from growing. There are two types of radiation therapy. External radiation therapy uses a machine outside the body to send radiation toward the cancer. Internal radiation therapy uses a radioactive substance sealed in needles, seeds, wires, or catheters that are placed directly into or near the cancer. The way the radiation therapy is given depends on the type and stage of the cancer being treated.

3. Chemotherapy

Chemotherapy is a cancer treatment that uses drugs to stop the growth of cancer cells, either by killing the cells or by stopping them from dividing. When chemotherapy is taken by mouth or injected into a vein or muscle, the drugs enter the bloodstream and can reach cancer cells throughout the body (systemic chemotherapy). When chemotherapy is placed directly into the cerebrospinal fluid, an organ, or a body cavity such as the abdomen, the drugs mainly affect cancer cells in those areas (regional chemotherapy). Combination chemotherapy is treatment using more than one anticancer drug. The way the chemotherapy is given depends on the type and stage of the cancer being treated.

4. Chemoradiation Therapy

Chemoradiation therapy combines chemotherapy and radiation therapy to increase the effects of both.

5. Targeted Therapy

Targeted therapy is a type of treatment that uses drugs or other substances to identify and attack specific cancer cells without harming normal cells. Tyrosine kinase inhibitors (TKIs) are targeted therapy drugs that block signals needed for tumors to grow. Erlotinib is a type of TKI used to treat pancreatic cancer.

There are treatments for pain caused by pancreatic cancer.

Pain can occur when the tumor presses on nerves or other organs near the pancreas. When pain medicine is not enough, there are treatments that act on nerves in the abdomen to relieve the pain. The doctor may inject medicine into the area around affected nerves or may cut the nerves to block the feeling of pain. Radiation therapy with or without chemotherapy can also help relieve pain by shrinking the tumor.

Patients with pancreatic cancer have special nutritional needs.

Surgery to remove the pancreas may affect its ability to make pancreatic enzymes that help to digest food. As a result, patients may have problems digesting food and absorbing nutrients into the body. To prevent malnutrition, the doctor may prescribe medicines that replace these enzymes.

Treatment Options by Stage

Stages I and II Pancreatic Cancer

Treatment of stage I and stage II pancreatic cancer may include the following:

- Surgery.

- Surgery followed by chemotherapy.

- Surgery followed by chemoradiation.

- A clinical trial of combination chemotherapy.

- A clinical trial of chemotherapy and targeted therapy, with or without chemoradiation.

- A clinical trial of chemotherapy and/or radiation therapy before surgery.

Stage III Pancreatic Cancer

Treatment of stage III pancreatic cancer may include the following:

- Palliative surgery or stent placement to bypass blocked areas in ducts or the small intestine.

- Chemotherapy followed by chemoradiation.

- Chemoradiation followed by chemotherapy.

- Chemotherapy with or without targeted therapy.

- A clinical trial of new anticancer therapies together with chemotherapy or chemoradiation.

- A clinical trial of radiation therapy given during surgery or internal radiation therapy.

Stage IV Pancreatic Cancer

Treatment of stage IV pancreatic cancer may include the following:

- Palliative treatments to relieve pain, such as nerve blocks, and other supportive care.

- Palliative surgery or stent placement to bypass blocked areas in ducts or the small intestine.

- Chemotherapy with or without targeted therapy.

- Clinical trials of new anticancer agents with or without chemotherapy.

Treatment Options for Recurrent Pancreatic Cancer

Treatment of recurrent pancreatic cancer may include the following:

- Palliative surgery or stent placement to bypass blocked areas in ducts or the small intestine.

- Palliative radiation therapy to shrink the tumor.
- Other palliative medical care to reduce symptoms, such as nerve blocks to relieve pain.
- Chemotherapy.
- Clinical trials of chemotherapy, new anticancer therapies, or biologic therapy.

Chapter 43

Islet Cell Carcinoma

General Information about Pancreatic Neuroendocrine Tumors (Islet Cell Tumors)

Pancreatic neuroendocrine tumors form in hormone-making cells (islet cells) of the pancreas.

The pancreas is a gland about 6 inches long that is shaped like a thin pear lying on its side. The wider end of the pancreas is called the head, the middle section is called the body, and the narrow end is called the tail. The pancreas lies behind the stomach and in front of the spine.

There are two kinds of cells in the pancreas:

1. **Endocrine pancreas cells** make several kinds of hormones (chemicals that control the actions of certain cells or organs in the body), such as insulin to control blood sugar. They cluster together in many small groups (islets) throughout the pancreas. Endocrine pancreas cells are also called islet cells or islets of Langerhans. Tumors that form in islet cells are called islet cell tumors, pancreatic endocrine tumors, or pancreatic neuroendocrine tumors (pancreatic NETs).

2. **Exocrine pancreas cells** make enzymes that are released into the small intestine to help the body digest food. Most of

Text in this chapter is excerpted from "Pancreatic Cancer—for Patients," National Cancer Institute (NCI), July 30, 2015.

the pancreas is made of ducts with small sacs at the end of the ducts, which are lined with exocrine cells.

Pancreatic neuroendocrine tumors (NETs) may be benign (not cancer) or malignant (cancer). When pancreatic NETs are malignant, they are called pancreatic endocrine cancer or islet cell carcinoma.

Pancreatic NETs are much less common than pancreatic exocrine tumors and have a better prognosis.

Pancreatic NETs may or may not cause signs or symptoms.

Pancreatic NETs may be functional or nonfunctional:

- Functional tumors make extra amounts of hormones, such as gastrin, insulin, and glucagon, that cause signs and symptoms.

- Nonfunctional tumors do not make extra amounts of hormones. Signs and symptoms are caused by the tumor as it spreads and grows. Most nonfunctional tumors are malignant (cancer).

Most pancreatic NETs are functional tumors.

There are different kinds of functional pancreatic NETs.

Pancreatic NETs make different kinds of hormones such as gastrin, insulin, and glucagon. Functional pancreatic NETs include the following:

- **Gastrinoma:** A tumor that forms in cells that make gastrin. Gastrin is a hormone that causes the stomach to release an acid that helps digest food. Both gastrin and stomach acid are increased by gastrinomas. When increased stomach acid, stomach ulcers, and diarrhea are caused by a tumor that makes gastrin, it is called Zollinger-Ellison syndrome. A gastrinoma usually forms in the head of the pancreas and sometimes forms in the small intestine. Most gastrinomas are malignant (cancer).

- **Insulinoma:** A tumor that forms in cells that make insulin. Insulin is a hormone that controls the amount of glucose (sugar) in the blood. It moves glucose into the cells, where it can be used by the body for energy. Insulinomas are usually slow-growing tumors that rarely spread. An insulinoma forms in the head, body, or tail of the pancreas. Insulinomas are usually benign (not cancer).

- **Glucagonoma:** A tumor that forms in cells that make glucagon. Glucagon is a hormone that increases the amount of glucose in the blood. It causes the liver to break down glycogen. Too much glucagon causes hyperglycemia (high blood sugar). A glucagonoma usually forms in the tail of the pancreas. Most glucagonomas are malignant (cancer).

- **Other types of tumors:** There are other rare types of functional pancreatic NETs that make hormones, including hormones that control the balance of sugar, salt, and water in the body. These tumors include:
  - VIPomas, which make vasoactive intestinal peptide. VIPoma may also be called Verner-Morrison syndrome.
  - Somatostatinomas, which make somatostatin.

These other types of tumors are grouped together because they are treated in much the same way.

Having certain syndromes can increase the risk of pancreatic NETs.

Anything that increases your risk of getting a disease is called a risk factor. Having a risk factor does not mean that you will get cancer; not having risk factors doesn't mean that you will not get cancer. Talk with your doctor if you think you may be at risk.

Multiple endocrine neoplasia type 1 (MEN1) syndrome is a risk factor for pancreatic NETs.

Different types of pancreatic NETs have different signs and symptoms.

Signs or symptoms can be caused by the growth of the tumor and/ or by hormones the tumor makes or by other conditions. Some tumors may not cause signs or symptoms. Check with your doctor if you have any of these problems.

Signs and symptoms of a non-functional pancreatic NET

A non-functional pancreatic NET may grow for a long time without causing signs or symptoms. It may grow large or spread to other parts of the body before it causes signs or symptoms, such as:

- Diarrhea.
- Indigestion.

- A lump in the abdomen.
- Pain in the abdomen or back.
- Yellowing of the skin and whites of the eyes.

Signs and symptoms of a functional pancreatic NET

The signs and symptoms of a functional pancreatic NET depend on the type of hormone being made.

Too much gastrin may cause:

- Stomach ulcers that keep coming back.
- Pain in the abdomen, which may spread to the back. The pain may come and go and it may go away after taking an antacid.
- The flow of stomach contents back into the esophagus (gastro-esophageal reflux).
- Diarrhea.

Too much insulin may cause:

- Low blood sugar. This can cause blurred vision, headache, and feeling lightheaded, tired, weak, shaky, nervous, irritable, sweaty, confused, or hungry.
- Fast heartbeat.

Too much glucagon may cause:

- Skin rash on the face, stomach, or legs.
- High blood sugar. This can cause headaches, frequent urination, dry skin and mouth, or feeling hungry, thirsty, tired, or weak.
- Blood clots. Blood clots in the lung can cause shortness of breath, cough, or pain in the chest. Blood clots in the arm or leg can cause pain, swelling, warmth, or redness of the arm or leg.
- Diarrhea.
- Weight loss for no known reason.
- Sore tongue or sores at the corners of the mouth.

Too much vasoactive intestinal peptide (VIP) may cause:

- Very large amounts of watery diarrhea.

- Dehydration. This can cause feeling thirsty, making less urine, dry skin and mouth, headaches, dizziness, or feeling tired.

- Low potassium level in the blood. This can cause muscle weakness, aching, or cramps, numbness and tingling, frequent urination, fast heartbeat, and feeling confused or thirsty.

- Cramps or pain in the abdomen.

- Weight loss for no known reason.

Too much somatostatin may cause:

- High blood sugar. This can cause headaches, frequent urination, dry skin and mouth, or feeling hungry, thirsty, tired, or weak.

- Diarrhea.

- Steatorrhea (very foul-smelling stool that floats).

- Gallstones.

- Yellowing of the skin and whites of the eyes.

- Weight loss for no known reason.

Lab tests and imaging tests are used to detect (find) and diagnose pancreatic NETs.

The following tests and procedures may be used:

- **Physical exam and history:** An exam of the body to check general signs of health, including checking for signs of disease, such as lumps or anything else that seems unusual. A history of the patient's health habits and past illnesses and treatments will also be taken.

- **Blood chemistry studies:** A procedure in which a blood sample is checked to measure the amounts of certain substances, such as glucose (sugar), released into the blood by organs and tissues in the body. An unusual (higher or lower than normal) amount of a substance can be a sign of disease.

- **Chromogranin A test:** A test in which a blood sample is checked to measure the amount of chromogranin A in the blood. A higher than normal amount of chromogranin A and normal amounts of hormones such as gastrin, insulin, and glucagon can be a sign of a non-functional pancreatic NET.

- **Abdominal CT scan (CAT scan):** A procedure that makes a series of detailed pictures of the abdomen, taken from different angles. The pictures are made by a computer linked to an X-ray machine. A dye may be injected into a vein or swallowed to help the organs or tissues show up more clearly. This procedure is also called computed tomography, computerized tomography, or computerized axial tomography.

- **MRI (magnetic resonance imaging):** A procedure that uses a magnet, radio waves, and a computer to make a series of detailed pictures of areas inside the body. This procedure is also called nuclear magnetic resonance imaging (NMRI).

- **Somatostatin receptor scintigraphy:** A type of radionuclide scan that may be used to find small pancreatic NETs. A small amount of radioactive octreotide (a hormone that attaches to tumors) is injected into a vein and travels through the blood. The radioactive octreotide attaches to the tumor and a special camera that detects radioactivity is used to show where the tumors are in the body. This procedure is also called octreotide scan and SRS.

- **Endoscopic ultrasound (EUS):** A procedure in which an endoscope is inserted into the body, usually through the mouth or rectum. An endoscope is a thin, tube-like instrument with a light and a lens for viewing. A probe at the end of the endoscope is used to bounce high-energy sound waves (ultrasound) off internal tissues or organs and make echoes. The echoes form a picture of body tissues called a sonogram. This procedure is also called endosonography.

- **Endoscopic retrograde cholangiopancreatography (ERCP):** A procedure used to X-ray the ducts (tubes) that carry bile from the liver to the gallbladder and from the gallbladder to the small intestine. Sometimes pancreatic cancer causes these ducts to narrow and block or slow the flow of bile, causing jaundice. An endoscope is passed through the mouth, esophagus, and stomach into the first part of the small intestine. An endoscope is a thin, tube-like instrument with a light and a lens for viewing. A catheter (a smaller tube) is then inserted through the endoscope into the pancreatic ducts. A dye is injected through the catheter into the ducts and an X-ray is taken. If the ducts are blocked by a tumor, a fine tube may be inserted into the duct to unblock it. This tube (or stent) may be left in place to keep the duct open. Tissue samples may also be taken and checked under a microscope for signs of cancer.

- **Angiogram:** A procedure to look at blood vessels and the flow of blood. A contrast dye is injected into the blood vessel. As the contrast dye moves through the blood vessel, X-rays are taken to see if there are any blockages.

- **Laparotomy:** A surgical procedure in which an incision (cut) is made in the wall of the abdomen to check the inside of the abdomen for signs of disease. The size of the incision depends on the reason the laparotomy is being done. Sometimes organs are removed or tissue samples are taken and checked under a microscope for signs of disease.

- **Intraoperative ultrasound:** A procedure that uses high-energy sound waves (ultrasound) to create images of internal organs or tissues during surgery. A transducer placed directly on the organ or tissue is used to make the sound waves, which create echoes. The transducer receives the echoes and sends them to a computer, which uses the echoes to make pictures called sonograms.

- **Biopsy:** The removal of cells or tissues so they can be viewed under a microscope by a pathologist to check for signs of cancer. There are several ways to do a biopsy for pancreatic NETs. Cells may be removed using a fine or wide needle inserted into the pancreas during an X-ray or ultrasound. Tissue may also be removed during a laparoscopy (a surgical incision made in the wall of the abdomen).

- **Bone scan:** A procedure to check if there are rapidly dividing cells, such as cancer cells, in the bone. A very small amount of radioactive material is injected into a vein and travels through the blood. The radioactive material collects in bones where cancer cells have spread and is detected by a scanner.

Other kinds of lab tests are used to check for the specific type of pancreatic NETs.

The following tests and procedures may be used:

Gastrinoma

- **Fasting serum gastrin test:** A test in which a blood sample is checked to measure the amount of gastrin in the blood. This

559

test is done after the patient has had nothing to eat or drink for at least 8 hours. Conditions other than gastrinoma can cause an increase in the amount of gastrin in the blood.

- **Basal acid output test:** A test to measure the amount of acid made by the stomach. The test is done after the patient has had nothing to eat or drink for at least 8 hours. A tube is inserted through the nose or throat, into the stomach. The stomach contents are removed and four samples of gastric acid are removed through the tube. These samples are used to find out the amount of gastric acid made during the test and the pH level of the gastric secretions.

- **Secretin stimulation test:** If the basal acid output test result is not normal, a secretin stimulation test may be done. The tube is moved into the small intestine and samples are taken from the small intestine after a drug called secretin is injected. Secretin causes the small intestine to make acid. When there is a gastrinoma, the secretin causes an increase in how much gastric acid is made and the level of gastrin in the blood.

- **Somatostatin receptor scintigraphy:** A type of radionuclide scan that may be used to find small pancreatic NETs. A small amount of radioactive octreotide (a hormone that attaches to tumors) is injected into a vein and travels through the blood. The radioactive octreotide attaches to the tumor and a special camera that detects radioactivity is used to show where the tumors are in the body. This procedure is also called octreotide scan and SRS.

Insulinoma

- **Fasting serum glucose and insulin test:** A test in which a blood sample is checked to measure the amounts of glucose (sugar) and insulin in the blood. The test is done after the patient has had nothing to eat or drink for at least 24 hours.

Glucagonoma

- **Fasting serum glucagon test:** A test in which a blood sample is checked to measure the amount of glucagon in the blood. The test is done after the patient has had nothing to eat or drink for at least 8 hours.

Other tumor types

- VIPoma

  - **Serum VIP (vasoactive intestinal peptide) test:** A test in which a blood sample is checked to measure the amount of VIP.

  - **Blood chemistry studies:** A procedure in which a blood sample is checked to measure the amounts of certain substances released into the blood by organs and tissues in the body. An unusual (higher or lower than normal) amount of a substance can be a sign of disease. In VIPoma, there is a lower than normal amount of potassium.

  - **Stool analysis:** A stool sample is checked for a higher than normal sodium (salt) and potassium levels.

- Somatostatinoma

  - **Fasting serum somatostatin test:** A test in which a blood sample is checked to measure the amount of somatostatin in the blood. The test is done after the patient has had nothing to eat or drink for at least 8 hours.

  - **Somatostatin receptor scintigraphy:** A type of radionuclide scan that may be used to find small pancreatic NETs. A small amount of radioactive octreotide (a hormone that attaches to tumors) is injected into a vein and travels through the blood. The radioactive octreotide attaches to the tumor and a special camera that detects radioactivity is used to show where the tumors are in the body. This procedure is also called octreotide scan and SRS.

Certain factors affect prognosis (chance of recovery) and treatment options.

Pancreatic NETs can often be cured. The prognosis (chance of recovery) and treatment options depend on the following:

- The type of cancer cell.

- Where the tumor is found in the pancreas.

- Whether the tumor has spread to more than one place in the pancreas or to other parts of the body.

- Whether the patient has MEN1 syndrome.

- The patient's age and general health.

- Whether the cancer has just been diagnosed or has recurred (come back).

Stages of Pancreatic Neuroendocrine Tumors

The plan for cancer treatment depends on where the NET is found in the pancreas and whether it has spread.

The process used to find out if cancer has spread within the pancreas or to other parts of the body is called staging. The results of the tests and procedures used to diagnose pancreatic neuroendocrine tumors (NETs) are also used to find out whether the cancer has spread.

Although there is a standard staging system for pancreatic NETs, it is not used to plan treatment. Treatment of pancreatic NETs is based on the following:

- Whether the cancer is found in one place in the pancreas.

- Whether the cancer is found in several places in the pancreas.

- Whether the cancer has spread to lymph nodes near the pancreas or to other parts of the body such as the liver, lung, peritoneum, or bone.

Cancer may spread from where it began to other parts of the body.

When cancer spreads to another part of the body, it is called metastasis.

The metastatic tumor is the same type of tumor as the primary tumor. For example, if a pancreatic neuroendocrine tumor spreads to the liver, the tumor cells in the liver are actually neuroendocrine tumor cells. The disease is metastatic pancreatic neuroendocrine tumor, not liver cancer.

Recurrent Pancreatic Neuroendocrine Tumors

Recurrent pancreatic neuroendocrine tumors (NETs) are tumors that have recurred (come back) after being treated. The tumors may come back in the pancreas or in other parts of the body.

Treatment Option Overview

There are different types of treatment for patients with pancreatic NETs.

Different types of treatments are available for patients with pancreatic neuroendocrine tumors (NETs). Some treatments are standard (the currently used treatment), and some are being tested in clinical trials. A treatment clinical trial is a research study meant to help improve current treatments or obtain information on new treatments for patients with cancer. When clinical trials show that a new treatment is better than the standard treatment, the new treatment may become the standard treatment. Patients may want to think about taking part in a clinical trial. Some clinical trials are open only to patients who have not started treatment.

Six types of standard treatment are used:

1. Surgery

An operation may be done to remove the tumor. One of the following types of surgery may be used:

- **Enucleation:** Surgery to remove the tumor only. This may be done when cancer occurs in one place in the pancreas.

- **Pancreatoduodenectomy:** A surgical procedure in which the head of the pancreas, the gallbladder, nearby lymph nodes and part of the stomach, small intestine, and bile duct are removed. Enough of the pancreas is left to make digestive juices and insulin. The organs removed during this procedure depend on the patient's condition. This is also called the Whipple procedure.

- **Distal pancreatectomy:** Surgery to remove the body and tail of the pancreas. The spleen may also be removed.

- **Total gastrectomy:** Surgery to remove the whole stomach.

- **Parietal cell vagotomy:** Surgery to cut the nerve that causes stomach cells to make acid.

- **Liver resection:** Surgery to remove part or all of the liver.

- **Radiofrequency ablation:** The use of a special probe with tiny electrodes that kill cancer cells. Sometimes the probe is inserted directly through the skin and only local anesthesia is needed.

In other cases, the probe is inserted through an incision in the abdomen. This is done in the hospital with general anesthesia.

- **Cryosurgical ablation:** A procedure in which tissue is frozen to destroy abnormal cells. This is usually done with a special instrument that contains liquid nitrogen or liquid carbon dioxide. The instrument may be used during surgery or laparoscopy or inserted through the skin. This procedure is also called cryoablation.

2. Chemotherapy

Chemotherapy is a cancer treatment that uses drugs to stop the growth of cancer cells, either by killing the cells or by stopping them from dividing. When chemotherapy is taken by mouth or injected into a vein or muscle, the drugs enter the bloodstream and can reach cancer cells throughout the body (systemic chemotherapy). When chemotherapy is placed directly into the cerebrospinal fluid, an organ, or a body cavity such as the abdomen, the drugs mainly affect cancer cells in those areas (regional chemotherapy). Combination chemotherapy is the use of more than one anticancer drug. The way the chemotherapy is given depends on the type of the cancer being treated.

3. Hormone Therapy

Hormone therapy is a cancer treatment that removes hormones or blocks their action and stops cancer cells from growing. Hormones are substances made by glands in the body and circulated in the bloodstream. Some hormones can cause certain cancers to grow. If tests show that the cancer cells have places where hormones can attach (receptors), drugs, surgery, or radiation therapy is used to reduce the production of hormones or block them from working.

4. Hepatic Arterial Occlusion or Chemoembolization

Hepatic arterial occlusion uses drugs, small particles, or other agents to block or reduce the flow of blood to the liver through the hepatic artery (the major blood vessel that carries blood to the liver). This is done to kill cancer cells growing in the liver. The tumor is prevented from getting the oxygen and nutrients it needs to grow. The liver continues to receive blood from the hepatic portal vein, which carries blood from the stomach and intestine.

Chemotherapy delivered during hepatic arterial occlusion is called chemoembolization. The anticancer drug is injected into the hepatic artery through a catheter (thin tube). The drug is mixed with the substance that blocks the artery and cuts off blood flow to the tumor. Most of the anticancer drug is trapped near the tumor and only a small amount of the drug reaches other parts of the body.

The blockage may be temporary or permanent, depending on the substance used to block the artery.

5. *Targeted Therapy*

Targeted therapy is a type of treatment that uses drugs or other substances to identify and attack specific cancer cells without harming normal cells. Certain types of targeted therapies are being studied in the treatment of pancreatic NETs.

6. *Supportive Care*

Supportive care is given to lessen the problems caused by the disease or its treatment. Supportive care for pancreatic NETs may include treatment for the following:

- Stomach ulcers may be treated with drug therapy such as:
  - Proton pump inhibitor drugs such as omeprazole, lansoprazole, or pantoprazole.
  - Histamine blocking drugs such as cimetidine, ranitidine, or famotidine.
  - Somatostatin-type drugs such as octreotide.
- Diarrhea may be treated with:
  - Intravenous (IV) fluids with electrolytes such as potassium or chloride.
  - Somatostatin-type drugs such as octreotide.
- Low blood sugar may be treated by having small, frequent meals or with drug therapy to maintain a normal blood sugar level.
- High blood sugar may be treated with drugs taken by mouth or insulin by injection.

Treatment Options for Pancreatic Neuroendocrine Tumors

Gastrinoma

Treatment of gastrinoma may include supportive care and the following:
- For symptoms caused by too much stomach acid, treatment may be a drug that decreases the amount of acid made by the stomach.

- For a single tumor in the head of the pancreas:
  - Surgery to remove the tumor.
  - Surgery to cut the nerve that causes stomach cells to make acid and treatment with a drug that decreases stomach acid.
  - Surgery to remove the whole stomach (rare).
- For a single tumor in the body or tail of the pancreas, treatment is usually surgery to remove the body or tail of the pancreas.
- For several tumors in the pancreas, treatment is usually surgery to remove the body or tail of the pancreas. If tumor remains after surgery, treatment may include either:
  - Surgery to cut the nerve that causes stomach cells to make acid and treatment with a drug that decreases stomach acid; or
  - Surgery to remove the whole stomach (rare).
- For one or more tumors in the duodenum (the part of the small intestine that connects to the stomach), treatment is usually pancreatoduodenectomy (surgery to remove the head of the pancreas, the gallbladder, nearby lymph nodes and part of the stomach, small intestine, and bile duct).
- If no tumor is found, treatment may include the following:
  - Surgery to cut the nerve that causes stomach cells to make acid and treatment with a drug that decreases stomach acid.
  - Surgery to remove the whole stomach (rare).
- If the cancer has spread to the liver, treatment may include:
  - Surgery to remove part or all of the liver.
  - Radiofrequency ablation or cryosurgical ablation.
  - Chemoembolization.
- If cancer has spread to other parts of the body or does not get better with surgery or drugs to decrease stomach acid, treatment may include:
  - Chemotherapy.
  - Hormone therapy.
- If the cancer mostly affects the liver and the patient has severe symptoms from hormones or from the size of tumor, treatment may include:

- Hepatic arterial occlusion, with or without systemic chemotherapy.

- Chemoembolization, with or without systemic chemotherapy.

Insulinoma

Treatment of insulinoma may include the following:

- For one small tumor in the head or tail of the pancreas, treatment is usually surgery to remove the tumor.

- For one large tumor in the head of the pancreas that cannot be removed by surgery, treatment is usually pancreatoduodenectomy (surgery to remove the head of the pancreas, the gallbladder, nearby lymph nodes and part of the stomach, small intestine, and bile duct).

- For one large tumor in the body or tail of the pancreas, treatment is usually a distal pancreatectomy (surgery to remove the body and tail of the pancreas).

- For more than one tumor in the pancreas, treatment is usually surgery to remove any tumors in the head of the pancreas and the body and tail of the pancreas.

- For tumors that cannot be removed by surgery, treatment may include the following:

  - Combination chemotherapy.

  - Palliative drug therapy to decrease the amount of insulin made by the pancreas.

  - Hormone therapy.

  - Radiofrequency ablation or cryosurgical ablation.

- For cancer that has spread to lymph nodes or other parts of the body, treatment may include the following:

  - Surgery to remove the cancer.

  - Radiofrequency ablation or cryosurgical ablation, if the cancer cannot be removed by surgery.

- If the cancer mostly affects the liver and the patient has severe symptoms from hormones or from the size of tumor, treatment may include:

- Hepatic arterial occlusion, with or without systemic chemotherapy.

- Chemoembolization, with or without systemic chemotherapy.

Glucagonoma

Treatment may include the following:

- For one small tumor in the head or tail of the pancreas, treatment is usually surgery to remove the tumor.

- For one large tumor in the head of the pancreas that cannot be removed by surgery, treatment is usually pancreatoduodenectomy (surgery to remove the head of the pancreas, the gallbladder, nearby lymph nodes and part of the stomach, small intestine, and bile duct).

- For more than one tumor in the pancreas, treatment is usually surgery to remove the tumor or surgery to remove the body and tail of the pancreas.

- For tumors that cannot be removed by surgery, treatment may include the following:

  - Combination chemotherapy.

  - Hormone therapy.

  - Radiofrequency ablation or cryosurgical ablation.

- For cancer that has spread to lymph nodes or other parts of the body, treatment may include the following:

  - Surgery to remove the cancer.

  - Radiofrequency ablation or cryosurgical ablation, if the cancer cannot be removed by surgery.

- If the cancer mostly affects the liver and the patient has severe symptoms from hormones or from the size of tumor, treatment may include:

  - Hepatic arterial occlusion, with or without systemic chemotherapy.

  - Chemoembolization, with or without systemic chemotherapy.

Other Pancreatic Neuroendocrine Tumors (Islet Cell Tumors)

For VIPoma, treatment may include the following:

- Fluids and hormone therapy to replace fluids and electrolytes that have been lost from the body.

- Surgery to remove the tumor and nearby lymph nodes.

- Surgery to remove as much of the tumor as possible when the tumor cannot be completely removed or has spread to distant parts of the body. This is palliative therapy to relieve symptoms and improve the quality of life.

- For tumors that have spread to lymph nodes or other parts of the body, treatment may include the following:

  - Surgery to remove the tumor.

  - Radiofrequency ablation or cryosurgical ablation, if the tumor cannot be removed by surgery.

- For tumors that continue to grow during treatment or have spread to other parts of the body, treatment may include the following:

  - Chemotherapy.

  - Targeted therapy.

For somatostatinoma, treatment may include the following:

- Surgery to remove the tumor.

- For cancer that has spread to distant parts of the body, surgery to remove as much of the cancer as possible to relieve symptoms and improve quality of life.

- For tumors that continue to grow during treatment or have spread to other parts of the body, treatment may include the following:

  - Chemotherapy.

  - Targeted therapy.

Treatment of other types of pancreatic neuroendocrine tumors (NETs) may include the following:

- Surgery to remove the tumor.

- For cancer that has spread to distant parts of the body, surgery to remove as much of the cancer as possible or hormone therapy to relieve symptoms and improve quality of life.

- For tumors that continue to grow during treatment or have spread to other parts of the body, treatment may include the following:

    - Chemotherapy.

    - Targeted therapy.

Recurrent or Progressive Pancreatic Neuroendocrine Tumors (Islet Cell Tumors)

Treatment of pancreatic neuroendocrine tumors (NETs) that continue to grow during treatment or recur (come back) may include the following:

- Surgery to remove the tumor.
- Chemotherapy.
- Hormone therapy.
- Targeted therapy.
- For liver metastases:

    - Regional chemotherapy.

    - Hepatic arterial occlusion or chemoembolization, with or without systemic chemotherapy.

- A clinical trial of a new therapy.

Chapter 44

Liver Cancer

Overview

The liver has many important functions in the body. For example, it cleans toxins from the blood, makes bile that helps digest fat, makes substances that help blood clot, and makes, stores, and releases sugar for energy.

Primary liver cancer is cancer that starts in the liver. The most common type of primary liver cancer is hepatocellular carcinoma, which occurs in the tissue of the liver. When cancer starts in other parts of the body and spreads to the liver, it is called liver metastasis.

Liver cancer is rare in children and teenagers, but there are two types of liver cancer that can form in children. Hepatoblastoma occurs in younger children, and hepatocellular carcinoma occurs in older children and teenagers.

The bile ducts are tubes that carry bile between the liver and gallbladder and the intestine. Bile duct cancer is also called cholangiocarcinoma. When it begins in the bile ducts inside the liver, it is called intrahepatic cholangiocarcinoma. When it begins in the bile ducts outside the liver, it is called extrahepatic cholangiocarcinoma. Extrahepatic cholangiocarcinoma is much more common than intrahepatic cholangiocarcinoma.

Text in this chapter is excerpted from "Liver and Bile Duct Cancer—for Patients," National Cancer Institute (NCI), June 15, 2015.

General Information about Adult Primary Liver Cancer

Adult primary liver cancer is a disease in which malignant (cancer) cells form in the tissues of the liver.

The liver is one of the largest organs in the body. It has four lobes and fills the upper right side of the abdomen inside the rib cage. Three of the many important functions of the liver are:

1. To filter harmful substances from the blood so they can be passed from the body in stools and urine.

2. To make bile to help digest fat that comes from food.

3. To store glycogen (sugar), which the body uses for energy.

There are two types of adult primary liver cancer.

The two types of adult primary liver cancer are:

1. Hepatocellular carcinoma.

2. Cholangiocarcinoma (bile duct cancer).

The most common type of adult primary liver cancer is hepatocellular carcinoma. This type of liver cancer is the third leading cause of cancer-related deaths worldwide.

Primary liver cancer can occur in both adults and children. However, treatment for children is different than treatment for adults.

Having hepatitis or cirrhosis can affect the risk of adult primary liver cancer.

Anything that increases your chance of getting a disease is called a risk factor. Having a risk factor does not mean that you will get cancer; not having risk factors doesn't mean that you will not get cancer. Talk with your doctor if you think you may be at risk.

The following are risk factors for adult primary liver cancer:

*   Having hepatitis B or hepatitis C. Having both hepatitis B and hepatitis C increases the risk even more.

*   Having cirrhosis, which can be caused by:

    *   hepatitis (especially hepatitis C); or

- drinking large amounts of alcohol for many years or being an alcoholic.

- Having metabolic syndrome, a set of conditions that occur together, including extra fat around the abdomen, high blood sugar, high blood pressure, high levels of triglycerides and low levels of high-density lipoproteins in the blood.

- Having liver injury that is long-lasting, especially if it leads to cirrhosis.

- Having hemochromatosis, a condition in which the body takes up and stores more iron than it needs. The extra iron is stored in the liver, heart, and pancreas

- Eating foods tainted with aflatoxin (poison from a fungus that can grow on foods, such as grains and nuts, that have not been stored properly).

Signs and symptoms of adult primary liver cancer include a lump or pain on the right side.

These and other signs and symptoms may be caused by adult primary liver cancer or by other conditions. Check with your doctor if you have any of the following:

- A hard lump on the right side just below the rib cage.

- Discomfort in the upper abdomen on the right side.

- A swollen abdomen.

- Pain near the right shoulder blade or in the back.

- Jaundice (yellowing of the skin and whites of the eyes).

- Easy bruising or bleeding.

- Unusual tiredness or weakness.

- Nausea and vomiting.

- Loss of appetite or feelings of fullness after eating a small meal.

- Weight loss for no known reason.

- Pale, chalky bowel movements and dark urine.

- Fever.

Tests that examine the liver and the blood are used to detect (find) and diagnose adult primary liver cancer.

The following tests and procedures may be used:

- **Physical exam and history:** An exam of the body to check general signs of health, including checking for signs of disease, such as lumps or anything else that seems unusual. A history of the patient's health habits and past illnesses and treatments will also be taken.

- **Serum tumor marker test:** A procedure in which a sample of blood is examined to measure the amounts of certain substances released into the blood by organs, tissues, or tumor cells in the body. Certain substances are linked to specific types of cancer when found in increased levels in the blood. These are called tumor markers. An increased level of alpha-fetoprotein (AFP) in the blood may be a sign of liver cancer. Other cancers and certain noncancerous conditions, including cirrhosis and hepatitis, may also increase AFP levels. Sometimes the AFP level is normal even when there is liver cancer.

- **Liver function tests:** A procedure in which a blood sample is checked to measure the amounts of certain substances released into the blood by the liver. A higher than normal amount of a substance can be a sign of liver cancer.

- **CT scan (CAT scan):** A procedure that makes a series of detailed pictures of areas inside the body, such as the abdomen, taken from different angles. The pictures are made by a computer linked to an X-ray machine. A dye may be injected into a vein or swallowed to help the organs or tissues show up more clearly. This procedure is also called computed tomography, computerized tomography, or computerized axial tomography.

- **MRI (magnetic resonance imaging):** A procedure that uses a magnet, radio waves, and a computer to make a series of detailed pictures of areas inside the body, such as the liver. This procedure is also called nuclear magnetic resonance imaging (NMRI). To create detailed pictures of blood vessels in and near the liver, dye is injected into a vein. This procedure is called MRA (magnetic resonance angiography).

- **Ultrasound exam:** A procedure in which high-energy sound waves (ultrasound) are bounced off internal tissues or organs and make echoes. The echoes form a picture of body tissues called a sonogram. The picture can be printed to be looked at later.

- **Biopsy:** The removal of cells or tissues so they can be viewed under a microscope by a pathologist to check for signs of cancer. Procedures used to collect the sample of cells or tissues include the following:
  - **Fine-needle aspiration biopsy:** The removal of cells, tissue or fluid using a thin needle.
  - **Core needle biopsy:** The removal of cells or tissue using a slightly wider needle.
  - **Laparoscopy:** A surgical procedure to look at the organs inside the abdomen to check for signs of disease. Small incisions (cuts) are made in the wall of the abdomen and a laparoscope (a thin, lighted tube) is inserted into one of the incisions. Another instrument is inserted through the same or another incision to remove the tissue samples.

A biopsy is not always needed to diagnose adult primary liver cancer.

Certain factors affect prognosis (chance of recovery) and treatment options.

The prognosis (chance of recovery) and treatment options depend on the following:

- The stage of the cancer (the size of the tumor, whether it affects part or all of the liver, or has spread to other places in the body).
- How well the liver is working.
- The patient's general health, including whether there is cirrhosis of the liver.

Stages of Adult Primary Liver Cancer

After adult primary liver cancer has been diagnosed, tests are done to find out if cancer cells have spread within the liver or to other parts of the body.

The process used to find out if cancer has spread within the liver or to other parts of the body is called staging. The information gathered from the staging process determines the stage of the disease. It is important to know the stage in order to plan treatment. The following tests and procedures may be used in the staging process:

- **CT scan (CAT scan):** A procedure that makes a series of detailed pictures of areas inside the body, such as the chest, abdomen, and pelvis, taken from different angles. The pictures are made by a computer linked to an X-ray machine. A dye may be injected into a vein or swallowed to help the organs or tissues show up more clearly. This procedure is also called computed tomography, computerized tomography, or computerized axial tomography.

- **MRI (magnetic resonance imaging):** A procedure that uses a magnet, radio waves, and a computer to make a series of detailed pictures of areas inside the body. This procedure is also called nuclear magnetic resonance imaging (NMRI).

- **PET scan (positron emission tomography scan):** A procedure to find malignant tumor cells in the body. A small amount of radioactive glucose (sugar) is injected into a vein. The PET scanner rotates around the body and makes a picture of where glucose is being used in the body. Malignant tumor cells show up brighter in the picture because they are more active and take up more glucose than normal cells do.

Cancer may spread from where it began to other parts of the body.

When cancer spreads to another part of the body, it is called metastasis.

The metastatic tumor is the same type of cancer as the primary tumor. For example, if primary liver cancer spreads to the lung, the cancer cells in the lung are actually liver cancer cells. The disease is metastatic liver cancer, not lung cancer.

The Barcelona Clinic Liver Cancer Staging System may be used to stage adult primary liver cancer.

There are several staging systems for liver cancer. The Barcelona Clinic Liver Cancer (BCLC) Staging System is widely used and is described below. This system is used to predict the patient's chance of recovery and to plan treatment, based on the following:

- Whether the cancer has spread within the liver or to other parts of the body.

- How well the liver is working.

- The general health and wellness of the patient.

- The symptoms caused by the cancer.

The BCLC staging system has five stages:

1. Stage 0: Very early

2. Stage A: Early

3. Stage B: Intermediate

4. Stage C: Advanced

5. Stage D: End-stage

The following groups are used to plan treatment.

BCLC stages 0, A, and B

Treatment to cure the cancer is given for BCLC stages 0, A, and B.

BCLC stages C and D

Treatment to relieve the symptoms caused by liver cancer and improve the patient's quality of life is given for BCLC stages C and D. Treatments are not likely to cure the cancer.

Recurrent Adult Primary Liver Cancer

Recurrent adult primary liver cancer is cancer that has recurred (come back) after it has been treated. The cancer may come back in the liver or in other parts of the body.

Treatment Option Overview

There are different types of treatment for patients with adult primary liver cancer.

Different types of treatments are available for patients with adult primary liver cancer. Some treatments are standard (the currently used treatment), and some are being tested in clinical trials. A treatment clinical trial is a research study meant to help improve current treatments or obtain information on new treatments for patients with cancer. When clinical trials show that a new treatment is better than the standard treatment, the new treatment may become the standard treatment. Patients may want to think about taking part in a clinical trial. Some clinical trials are open only to patients who have not started treatment.

Patients with liver cancer are treated by a team of specialists who are experts in treating liver cancer.

The patient's treatment will be overseen by a medical oncologist, a doctor who specializes in treating people with cancer. The medical oncologist may refer the patient to other health professionals who have special training in treating patients with liver cancer. These may include the following specialists:

- Hepatologist (specialist in liver disease).

- Surgical oncologist.

- Transplant surgeon.

- Radiation oncologist.

- Interventional radiologist (a specialist who diagnoses and treats diseases using imaging and the smallest incisions possible).

- Pathologist.

Seven types of standard treatment are used:

1. Surveillance

Surveillance for lesions smaller than 1 centimeter found during screening. Follow-up every three months is common.

2. Surgery

A partial hepatectomy (surgery to remove the part of the liver where cancer is found) may be done. A wedge of tissue, an entire lobe, or a larger part of the liver, along with some of the healthy tissue around it is removed. The remaining liver tissue takes over the functions of the liver and may regrow.

3. Liver Transplant

In a liver transplant, the entire liver is removed and replaced with a healthy donated liver. A liver transplant may be done when the disease is in the liver only and a donated liver can be found. If the patient has to wait for a donated liver, other treatment is given as needed.

4. Ablation Therapy

Ablation therapy removes or destroys tissue. Different types of ablation therapy are used for liver cancer:

- **Radiofrequency ablation**: The use of special needles that are inserted directly through the skin or through an incision in the abdomen to reach the tumor. High-energy radio waves heat the needles and tumor which kills cancer cells.

- **Microwave therapy**: A type of treatment in which the tumor is exposed to high temperatures created by microwaves.

- This can damage and kill cancer cells or make them more sensitive to the effects of radiation and certain anticancer drugs.

- **Percutaneous ethanol injection**: A cancer treatment in which a small needle is used to inject ethanol (pure alcohol) directly into a tumor to kill cancer cells. Several treatments may be needed. Usually local anesthesia is used, but if the patient has many tumors in the liver, general anesthesia may be used.

- **Cryoablation**: A treatment that uses an instrument to freeze and destroy cancer cells. This type of treatment is also called cryotherapy and cryosurgery. The doctor may use ultrasound to guide the instrument.

- **Electroporation therapy**: A treatment that sends electrical pulses through an electrode placed in a tumor to kill cancer cells. Electroporation therapy is being studied in clinical trials.

5. Embolization Therapy

Embolization therapy is the use of substances to block or decrease the flow of blood through the hepatic artery to the tumor. When the tumor does not get the oxygen and nutrients it needs, it will not continue to grow. Embolization therapy is used for patients who cannot have surgery to remove the tumor or ablation therapy and whose tumor has not spread outside the liver.

The liver receives blood from the hepatic portal vein and the hepatic artery. Blood that comes into the liver from the hepatic portal vein usually goes to the healthy liver tissue. Blood that comes from the hepatic artery usually goes to the tumor. When the hepatic artery is blocked during embolization therapy, the healthy liver tissue continues to receive blood from the hepatic portal vein.

There are two main types of embolization therapy:

- **Transarterial embolization (TAE)**: A small incision (cut) is made in the inner thigh and a catheter (thin, flexible tube) is inserted and threaded up into the hepatic artery. Once the catheter is in place, a substance that blocks the hepatic artery and stops blood flow to the tumor is injected.

- **Transarterial chemoembolization (TACE)**: This procedure is like TAE except an anticancer drug is also given. The procedure can be done by attaching the anticancer drug to small beads that are injected into the hepatic artery or by injecting the anticancer drug through the catheter into the hepatic artery and then injecting the substance to block the hepatic artery. Most of the anticancer drug is trapped near the tumor and only a small amount of the drug reaches other parts of the body. This type of treatment is also called chemoembolization.

6. Targeted Therapy

Targeted therapy is a treatment that uses drugs or other substances to identify and attack specific cancer cells without harming normal cells. Adult liver cancer may be treated with a targeted therapy drug that stops cells from dividing and prevents the growth of new blood vessels that tumors need to grow.

7. Radiation Therapy

Radiation therapy is a cancer treatment that uses high-energy X-rays or other types of radiation to kill cancer cells or keep them from growing. Radiation therapy is given in different ways:

- External radiation therapy uses a machine outside the body to send radiation toward the cancer.

  - 3-D conformal radiation therapy uses a computer to create a 3-dimensional picture of the tumor. This allows doctors to give the highest possible dose of radiation to the tumor, while preventing damage to normal tissue as much as possible.

  - Stereotactic body radiation therapy uses special equipment to position a patient and deliver radiation directly to the tumors. The total dose of radiation is divided into smaller doses given over several days. This type of radiation therapy helps prevent damage to normal tissue. This type of radiation therapy is being studied in clinical trials.

- Proton-beam radiation therapy is a type of high-energy radiation therapy that uses streams of protons (small, positively-charged particles of matter) to kill tumor cells. This type of radiation therapy is being studied in clinical trials.

Treatment Options for Adult Primary Liver Cancer

Stages 0, A, and B Adult Primary Liver Cancer

Treatment of stages 0, A, and B adult primary liver cancer may include the following:

- Surveillance for lesions smaller than 1 centimeter.
- Partial hepatectomy.
- Total hepatectomy and liver transplant.
- Ablation of the tumor using one of the following methods:
  - Radiofrequency ablation.
  - Microwave therapy.
  - Percutaneous ethanol injection.
  - Cryoablation.
- A clinical trial of electroporation therapy.

Stages C and D Adult Primary Liver Cancer

Treatment of stages C and D adult primary liver cancer may include the following:

- Embolization therapy using one of the following methods:
  - Transarterial embolization (TAE).
  - Transarterial chemoembolization (TACE).
- Targeted therapy.
- Radiation therapy.
- A clinical trial of targeted therapy after chemoembolization or combined with chemotherapy.

- A clinical trial of new targeted therapy drugs.

- A clinical trial of targeted therapy with or without stereotactic body radiation therapy.

- A clinical trial of stereotactic body radiation therapy or proton-beam radiation therapy.

Treatment of Recurrent Adult Primary Liver Cancer

Treatment options for recurrent adult primary liver cancer may include the following:

- Total hepatectomy and liver transplant.

- Partial hepatectomy.

- Ablation

- Transarterial chemoembolization and targeted therapy with sorafenib, as palliative therapy to relieve symptoms and improve quality of life.

- A clinical trial of a new treatment.

Chapter 45

Anal Cancer

Overview

The anus is part of the body's digestive system and is the last part of the large intestine. Stool (solid waste) leaves the body through the anus.

The most common type of anal cancer is squamous cell carcinoma. Squamous cell carcinoma begins in flat cells lining the anal canal.

The number of cases of anal cancer diagnosed each year has been increasing over the last 10 years. Infection with human papillomavirus (HPV) is a major risk factor for anal cancer. Being vaccinated against HPV lowers the risk of anal cancer.

General Information about Anal Cancer

Anal cancer is a disease in which malignant (cancer) cells form in the tissues of the anus.

The anus is the end of the large intestine, below the rectum, through which stool (solid waste) leaves the body. The anus is formed partly from the outer skin layers of the body and partly from the intestine. Two ring-like muscles, called sphincter muscles, open and close the anal opening and let stool pass out of the body. The anal canal, the part of the anus between the rectum and the anal opening, is about 1-1½ inches long.

Text in this chapter is excerpted from "Anal Cancer–for Patients," National Cancer Institute (NCI), May 12, 2015.

The skin around the outside of the anus is called the perianal area. Tumors in this area are skin tumors, not anal cancer.

Being infected with the human papillomavirus (HPV) increases the risk of developing anal cancer.

Risk factors include the following:

- Being infected with human papillomavirus (HPV).
- Having many sexual partners.
- Having receptive anal intercourse (anal sex).
- Being older than 50 years.
- Frequent anal redness, swelling, and soreness.
- Having anal fistulas (abnormal openings).
- Smoking cigarettes.

Signs of anal cancer include bleeding from the anus or rectum or a lump near the anus.

These and other signs and symptoms may be caused by anal cancer or by other conditions. Check with your doctor if you have any of the following:

- Bleeding from the anus or rectum.
- Pain or pressure in the area around the anus.
- Itching or discharge from the anus.
- A lump near the anus.
- A change in bowel habits.

Tests that examine the rectum and anus are used to detect (find) and diagnose anal cancer.

The following tests and procedures may be used:

- **Physical exam and history:** An exam of the body to check general signs of health, including checking for signs of disease, such as lumps or anything else that seems unusual. A history of the patient's health habits and past illnesses and treatments will also be taken.

- **Digital rectal examination (DRE):** An exam of the anus and rectum. The doctor or nurse inserts a lubricated, gloved finger into the lower part of the rectum to feel for lumps or anything else that seems unusual.

- **Anoscop:** An exam of the anus and lower rectum using a short, lighted tube called an anoscope.

- **Proctoscopy:** An exam of the rectum using a short, lighted tube called a proctoscope.

- **Endo-anal or endorectal ultrasound:** A procedure in which an ultrasound transducer (probe) is inserted into the anus or rectum and used to bounce high-energy sound waves (ultrasound) off internal tissues or organs and make echoes. The echoes form a picture of body tissues called a sonogram.

- **Biopsy:** The removal of cells or tissues so they can be viewed under a microscope by a pathologist to check for signs of cancer. If an abnormal area is seen during the anoscopy, a biopsy may be done at that time.

Certain factors affect the prognosis (chance of recovery) and treatment options.

The prognosis (chance of recovery) depends on the following:

- The size of the tumor.
- Where the tumor is in the anus.
- Whether the cancer has spread to the lymph nodes.

The treatment options depend on the following:

- The stage of the cancer.
- Where the tumor is in the anus.
- Whether the patient has human immunodeficiency virus (HIV).
- Whether cancer remains after initial treatment or has recurred.

Stages of Anal Cancer

After anal cancer has been diagnosed, tests are done to find out if cancer cells have spread within the anus or to other parts of the body.

The process used to find out if cancer has spread within the anus or to other parts of the body is called staging. The information gathered from the staging process determines the stage of the disease. It is important to know the stage in order to plan treatment. The following tests may be used in the staging process:

- **CT scan (CAT scan):** A procedure that makes a series of detailed pictures of areas inside the body, such as the abdomen or chest, taken from different angles. The pictures are made by a computer linked to an X-ray machine. A dye may be injected into a vein or swallowed to help the organs or tissues show up more clearly. This procedure is also called computed tomography, computerized tomography, or computerized axial tomography. For anal cancer, a CT scan of the pelvis and abdomen may be done.

- **Chest X-ray :** An X-ray of the organs and bones inside the chest. An X-ray is a type of energy beam that can go through the body and onto film, making a picture of areas inside the body.

- **MRI (magnetic resonance imaging):** A procedure that uses a magnet, radio waves, and a computer to make a series of detailed pictures of areas inside the body. This procedure is also called nuclear magnetic resonance imaging (NMRI).

- **PET scan (positron emission tomography scan):** A procedure to find malignant tumor cells in the body. A small amount of radioactive glucose (sugar) is injected into a vein. The PET scanner rotates around the body and makes a picture of where glucose is being used in the body. Malignant tumor cells show up brighter in the picture because they are more active and take up more glucose than normal cells do.

There are three ways that cancer spreads in the body.

Cancer can spread through tissue, the lymph system, and the blood:

1. Tissue. The cancer spreads from where it began by growing into nearby areas.

2. Lymph system. The cancer spreads from where it began by getting into the lymph system. The cancer travels through the lymph vessels to other parts of the body.

3. Blood. The cancer spreads from where it began by getting into the blood. The cancer travels through the blood vessels to other parts of the body.

Cancer may spread from where it began to other parts of the body.

When cancer spreads to another part of the body, it is called metastasis. Cancer cells break away from where they began (the primary tumor) and travel through the lymph system or blood.

- Lymph system. The cancer gets into the lymph system, travels through the lymph vessels, and forms a tumor (metastatic tumor) in another part of the body.

- Blood. The cancer gets into the blood, travels through the blood vessels, and forms a tumor (metastatic tumor) in another part of the body.

The metastatic tumor is the same type of cancer as the primary tumor. For example, if anal cancer spreads to the lung, the cancer cells in the lung are actually anal cancer cells. The disease is metastatic anal cancer, not lung cancer.

The following stages are used for anal cancer:

Stage 0 (Carcinoma in Situ)

In stage 0, abnormal cells are found in the innermost lining of the anus. These abnormal cells may become cancer and spread into nearby normal tissue. Stage 0 is also called carcinoma in situ.

Stage I

In stage I, cancer has formed and the tumor is 2 centimeters or smaller.

Stage II

In stage II, the tumor is larger than 2 centimeters.

Stage IIIA

In stage IIIA, the tumor may be any size and has spread to either:

- lymph nodes near the rectum; or

- nearby organs, such as the vagina, urethra, and bladder.

Stage IIIB

In stage IIIB, the tumor may be any size and has spread:

- to nearby organs and to lymph nodes near the rectum; or
- to lymph nodes on one side of the pelvis and/or groin, and may have spread to nearby organs; or
- to lymph nodes near the rectum and in the groin, and/or to lymph nodes on both sides of the pelvis and/or groin, and may have spread to nearby organs.

Stage IV

In stage IV, the tumor may be any size and cancer may have spread to lymph nodes or nearby organs and has spread to distant parts of the body.

Recurrent Anal Cancer

Recurrent anal cancer is cancer that has recurred (come back) after it has been treated. The cancer may come back in the anus or in other parts of the body.

Treatment Option Overview

There are different types of treatment for patients with anal cancer.

Different types of treatments are available for patients with anal cancer. Some treatments are standard (the currently used treatment), and some are being tested in clinical trials. A treatment clinical trial is a research study meant to help improve current treatments or obtain information on new treatments for patients with cancer. When clinical trials show that a new treatment is better than the standard treatment, the new treatment may become the standard treatment. Patients may want to think about taking part in a clinical trial. Some clinical trials are open only to patients who have not started treatment.

Three types of standard treatment are used:

1. Radiation Therapy

Radiation therapy is a cancer treatment that uses high-energy X-rays or other types of radiation to kill cancer cells. There are two types of radiation therapy. External radiation therapy uses a machine outside the body to send radiation toward the cancer. Internal radiation therapy uses a radioactive substance sealed in needles, seeds, wires, or catheters that are placed directly into or near the cancer. The way the radiation therapy is given depends on the type and stage of the cancer being treated.

2. Chemotherapy

Chemotherapy is a cancer treatment that uses drugs to stop the growth of cancer cells, either by killing the cells or by stopping the cells from dividing. When chemotherapy is taken by mouth or injected into a vein or muscle, the drugs enter the bloodstream and can reach cancer cells throughout the body (systemic chemotherapy). When chemotherapy is placed directly into the cerebrospinal fluid, an organ, or a body cavity such as the abdomen, the drugs mainly affect cancer cells in those areas (regional chemotherapy). The way the chemotherapy is given depends on the type and stage of the cancer being treated.

3. Surgery

- **Local resection**: A surgical procedure in which the tumor is cut from the anus along with some of the healthy tissue around it. Local resection may be used if the cancer is small and has not spread. This procedure may save the sphincter muscles so the patient can still control bowel movements. Tumors that form in the lower part of the anus can often be removed with local resection.

- **Abdominoperineal resection**: A surgical procedure in which the anus, the rectum, and part of the sigmoid colon are removed through an incision made in the abdomen. The doctor sews the end of the intestine to an opening, called a stoma, made in the surface of the abdomen so body waste can be collected in a disposable bag outside of the body. This is called a colostomy. Lymph nodes that contain cancer may also be removed during this operation.

Having the human immunodeficiency virus can affect treatment of anal cancer.

Cancer therapy can further damage the already weakened immune systems of patients who have the human immunodeficiency virus (HIV). For this reason, patients who have anal cancer and HIV are usually treated with lower doses of anticancer drugs and radiation than patients who do not have HIV.

Treatment Options by Stage

Stage 0 (Carcinoma in Situ)

Treatment of stage 0 is usually local resection.

Stage I Anal Cancer

Treatment of stage I anal cancer may include the following:

- Local resection.

- External-beam radiation therapy with or without chemotherapy. If cancer remains after treatment, more chemotherapy and radiation therapy may be given to avoid the need for a permanent colostomy.

- Internal radiation therapy.

- Abdominoperineal resection, if cancer remains or comes back after treatment with radiation therapy and chemotherapy.

- Internal radiation therapy for cancer that remains after treatment with external-beam radiation therapy.

Patients who have had treatment that saves the sphincter muscles may receive follow-up exams every 3 months for the first 2 years, including rectal exams with endoscopy and biopsy, as needed.

Stage II Anal Cancer

Treatment of stage II anal cancer may include the following:

- Local resection.

- External-beam radiation therapy with chemotherapy. If cancer remains after treatment, more chemotherapy and radiation therapy may be given to avoid the need for a permanent colostomy.

- Internal radiation therapy.

- Abdominoperineal resection, if cancer remains or comes back after treatment with radiation therapy and chemotherapy.

- A clinical trial of new treatment options.

Patients who have had treatment that saves the sphincter muscles may receive follow-up exams every 3 months for the first 2 years, including rectal exams with endoscopy and biopsy, as needed.

Stage IIIA Anal Cancer

Treatment of stage IIIA anal cancer may include the following:

- External-beam radiation therapy with chemotherapy. If cancer remains after treatment, more chemotherapy and radiation therapy may be given to avoid the need for a permanent colostomy.

- Internal radiation therapy.

- Abdominoperineal resection, if cancer remains or comes back after treatment with chemotherapy and radiation therapy.

- A clinical trial of new treatment options.

Stage IIIB Anal Cancer

Treatment of stage IIIB anal cancer may include the following:

- External-beam radiation therapy with chemotherapy.

- Local resection or abdominoperineal resection, if cancer remains or comes back after treatment with chemotherapy and radiation therapy. Lymph nodes may also be removed.

- A clinical trial of new treatment options.

Stage IV Anal Cancer

Treatment of stage IV anal cancer may include the following:

- Surgery as palliative therapy to relieve symptoms and improve the quality of life.

- Radiation therapy as palliative therapy.

- Chemotherapy with radiation therapy as palliative therapy.

- A clinical trial of new treatment options.

Treatment Options for Recurrent Anal Cancer

Treatment of recurrent anal cancer may include the following:

- Radiation therapy and chemotherapy, for recurrence after surgery.

- Surgery, for recurrence after radiation therapy and/or chemotherapy.

- A clinical trial of radiation therapy with chemotherapy and/or radiosensitizers.

Part Seven

Food Intolerances and Infectious Disorders of the Gastrointestinal Tract

Chapter 46

Lactose Intolerance

What is lactose?

Lactose is a sugar found in milk and milk products. The small intestine—the organ where most food digestion and nutrient absorption take place—produces an enzyme called lactase. Lactase breaks down lactose into two simpler forms of sugar: glucose and galactose. The body then absorbs these simpler sugars into the bloodstream.

What is lactose intolerance?

Lactose intolerance is a condition in which people have digestive symptoms—such as bloating, diarrhea, and gas—after eating or drinking milk or milk products.

Lactase deficiency and lactose malabsorption may lead to lactose intolerance:

- **Lactase deficiency.** In people who have a lactase deficiency, the small intestine produces low levels of lactase and cannot digest much lactose.

- **Lactose malabsorption.** Lactase deficiency may cause lactose malabsorption. In lactose malabsorption, undigested lactose passes to the colon. The colon, part of the large intestine, absorbs water from stool and changes it from a liquid to a solid

Text in this chapter is excerpted from "Lactose Intolerance" National Institute of Diabetes and Digestive and Kidney Diseases (NIDDK), May 2014.

form. In the colon, bacteria break down undigested lactose and create fluid and gas. Not all people with lactase deficiency and lactose malabsorption have digestive symptoms.

People have lactose intolerance when lactase deficiency and lactose malabsorption cause digestive symptoms. Most people with lactose intolerance can eat or drink some amount of lactose without having digestive symptoms. Individuals vary in the amount of lactose they can tolerate.

People sometimes confuse lactose intolerance with a milk allergy. While lactose intolerance is a digestive system disorder, a milk allergy is a reaction by the body's immune system to one or more milk proteins. An allergic reaction to milk can be life threatening even if the person eats or drinks only a small amount of milk or milk product. A milk allergy most commonly occurs in the first year of life, while lactose intolerance occurs more often during adolescence or adulthood.

Four Types of Lactase Deficiency

Four types of lactase deficiency may lead to lactose intolerance:

- **Primary lactase deficiency,** also called lactase nonpersistence, is the most common type of lactase deficiency. In people with this condition, lactase production declines over time. This decline often begins at about age 2; however, the decline may begin later. Children who have lactase deficiency may not experience symptoms of lactose intolerance until late adolescence or adulthood. Researchers have discovered that some people inherit genes from their parents that may cause a primary lactase deficiency.
- **Secondary lactase deficiency** results from injury to the small intestine. Infection, diseases, or other problems may injure the small intestine. Treating the underlying cause usually improves the lactose tolerance.
- **Developmental lactase deficiency** may occur in infants born prematurely. This condition usually lasts for only a short time after they are born.
- **Congenital lactase deficiency** is an extremely rare disorder in which the small intestine produces little or no lactase enzyme from birth. Genes inherited from parents cause this disorder.

Who is more likely to have lactose intolerance?

In the United States, some ethnic and racial populations are more likely to have lactose intolerance than others, including African Americans, Hispanics/Latinos, American Indians, and Asian Americans. The condition is least common among Americans of European descent.

What are the symptoms of lactose intolerance?

Common symptoms of lactose intolerance include

- abdominal bloating, a feeling of fullness or swelling in the abdomen

- abdominal pain

- diarrhea

- gas

- nausea

Symptoms occur 30 minutes to 2 hours after consuming milk or milk products. Symptoms range from mild to severe based on the amount of lactose the person ate or drank and the amount a person can tolerate.

How does lactose intolerance affect health?

In addition to causing unpleasant symptoms, lactose intolerance may affect people's health if it keeps them from consuming enough essential nutrients, such as calcium and vitamin D. People with lactose intolerance may not get enough calcium if they do not eat calcium-rich foods or do not take a dietary supplement that contains calcium. Milk and milk products are major sources of calcium and other nutrients in the diet. Calcium is essential at all ages for the growth and maintenance of bones. A shortage of calcium intake in children and adults may lead to bones that are less dense and can easily fracture later in life, a condition called osteoporosis.

How is lactose intolerance diagnosed?

A health care provider makes a diagnosis of lactose intolerance based on

- medical, family, and diet history, including a review of symptoms

- a physical exam
- medical tests

Medical, family, and diet history. A health care provider will take a medical, family, and diet history to help diagnose lactose intolerance. During this discussion, the health care provider will review a patient's symptoms. However, basing a diagnosis on symptoms alone may be misleading because digestive symptoms can occur for many reasons other than lactose intolerance. For example, other conditions such as irritable bowel syndrome, celiac disease, inflammatory bowel disease, or small bowel bacterial overgrowth can cause digestive symptoms.

Physical exam. A physical exam may help diagnose lactose intolerance or rule out other conditions that cause digestive symptoms. During a physical exam, a health care provider usually

- checks for abdominal bloating
- uses a stethoscope to listen to sounds within the abdomen
- taps on the abdomen to check for tenderness or pain

A health care provider may recommend eliminating all milk and milk products from a person's diet for a short time to see if the symptoms resolve. Symptoms that go away when a person eliminates lactose from his or her diet may confirm the diagnosis of lactose intolerance.

Medical tests. A health care provider may order special tests to provide more information. Health care providers commonly use two tests to measure how well a person digests lactose:

- **Hydrogen breath test.** This test measures the amount of hydrogen in a person's breath. Normally, only a small amount of hydrogen is detectable in the breath when a person eats or drinks and digests lactose. However, undigested lactose produces high levels of hydrogen. For this test, the patient drinks a beverage that contains a known amount of lactose. A health care provider asks the patient to breathe into a balloon-type container that measures breath hydrogen level. Smoking and some foods and medications may affect the accuracy of the results. A health care provider will tell the patient what foods or medications to avoid before the test.

- **Stool acidity test.** Undigested lactose creates lactic acid and other fatty acids that a stool acidity test can detect in a stool sample. Health care providers sometimes use this test to check acidity in the stools of infants and young children. A child may also have glucose in his or her stool as a result of undigested lactose. The health care provider will give the child's parent or caretaker a container for collecting the stool specimen. The parent or caretaker returns the sample to the health care provider, who sends it to a lab for analysis.

How much lactose can a person with lactose intolerance have?

Most people with lactose intolerance can tolerate some amount of lactose in their diet and do not need to avoid milk or milk products completely. Avoiding milk and milk products altogether may cause people to take in less calcium and vitamin D than they need.

Individuals vary in the amount of lactose they can tolerate. A variety of factors—including how much lactase the small intestine produces—can affect how much lactose an individual can tolerate. For example, one person may have severe symptoms after drinking a small amount of milk, while another person can drink a large amount without having symptoms. Other people can easily eat yogurt and hard cheeses such as cheddar and Swiss, while they are not able to eat or drink other milk products without having digestive symptoms.

Research suggests that adults and adolescents with lactose malabsorption could eat or drink at least 12 grams of lactose in one sitting without symptoms or with only minor symptoms. This amount is the amount of lactose in 1 cup of milk. People with lactose malabsorption may be able to eat or drink more lactose if they eat it or drink it with meals or in small amounts throughout the day.

How is lactose intolerance managed?

Many people can manage the symptoms of lactose intolerance by changing their diet. Some people may only need to limit the amount of lactose they eat or drink. Others may need to avoid lactose altogether. Using lactase products can help some people manage their symptoms.

For people with secondary lactase deficiency, treating the underlying cause improves lactose tolerance. In infants with developmental lactase deficiency, the ability to digest lactose improves as the infants mature. People with primary and congenital lactase deficiency cannot change their body's ability to produce lactase.

Eating, Diet, and Nutrition

People may find it helpful to talk with a health care provider or a registered dietitian about a dietary plan. A dietary plan can help people manage the symptoms of lactose intolerance and make sure they get enough nutrients. Parents, caretakers, childcare providers, and others who serve food to children with lactose intolerance should follow the dietary plan recommended by the child's health care provider or registered dietitian.

Milk and milk products. Gradually introducing small amounts of milk or milk products may help some people adapt to them with fewer symptoms. Often, people can better tolerate milk or milk products by having them with meals, such as having milk with cereal or having cheese with crackers. People with lactose intolerance are generally more likely to tolerate hard cheeses, such as cheddar or Swiss, than a glass of milk. A 1.5-ounce serving of low-fat hard cheese has less than 1 gram of lactose, while a 1-cup serving of low-fat milk has about 11 to 13 grams of lactose.

However, people with lactose intolerance are also more likely to tolerate yogurt than milk, even though yogurt and milk have similar amounts of lactose.

Lactose-free and lactose-reduced milk and milk products. Lactose-free and lactose-reduced milk and milk products are available at most supermarkets and are identical nutritionally to regular milk and milk products. Manufacturers treat lactose-free milk with the lactase enzyme. This enzyme breaks down the lactose in the milk. Lactose-free milk remains fresh for about the same length of time or, if it is ultra-pasteurized, longer than regular milk. Lactose-free milk may have a slightly sweeter taste than regular milk.

Lactase products. People can use lactase tablets and drops when they eat or drink milk products. The lactase enzyme digests the lactose in the food and therefore reduces the chances of developing digestive symptoms. People should check with a health care provider before using these products because some groups, such as young children and pregnant and breastfeeding women, may not be able to use them.

Calcium and Vitamin D

Ensuring that children and adults with lactose intolerance get enough calcium is important, especially if their intake of milk and

Table 46.1. Recommended Dietary Allowance of calcium by age group

Age Group	Recommended Dietary Allowance (mg/day)
1–3 years	700 mg
4–8 years	1,000 mg
9–18 years	1,300 mg
19–50 years	1,000 mg
51–70 years, males	1,000 mg
51–70 years, females	1,200 mg
70+ years	1,200 mg
14–18 years, pregnant/breastfeeding	1,300 mg
19–50 years, pregnant/breastfeeding	1,000 mg

Source: Adapted from Dietary Reference Intakes for Calcium and Vitamin D, Institute of Medicine, National Academy of Sciences, November 2010.

milk products is limited. The amount of calcium a person needs to maintain good health varies by age. Table 48.1 illustrates recommendations for calcium intake.

A U.S. Recommended Dietary Allowance for calcium has not been determined for infants. However, researchers suggest 200 mg of calcium per day for infants age 0 to 6 months and 260 mg for infants age 6 to 12 months.

Many foods can provide calcium and other nutrients the body needs. Nonmilk products high in calcium include fish with soft bones, such as canned salmon and sardines, and dark green vegetables, such as spinach. Manufacturers may also add calcium to fortified breakfast cereals, fruit juices, and soy beverage—also called soy milk. Many fortified foods are also excellent sources of vitamin D and other essential nutrients, in addition to calcium.

Vitamin D helps the body absorb and use calcium. Some people with lactose intolerance may not get enough vitamin D. Foods such as salmon, tuna, eggs, and liver naturally contain vitamin D. Most milk sold in the United States is fortified with vitamin D, and vitamin D is added to some nonmilk beverages, yogurts, and breakfast cereals. People's bodies also make vitamin D when the skin is exposed to sunlight.

People may find it helpful to talk with a health care provider or a registered dietitian to determine if their diet provides adequate nutrients—including calcium and vitamin D. To help ensure coordinated and safe care, people should discuss their use of complementary and

Table 46.2. Calcium content in common foods

Nonmilk Products	Calcium Content
sardines, with bone, 3.75 oz.	351 mg
rhubarb, frozen, cooked, 1 cup	348 mg
soy milk, original and vanilla, with added calcium and vitamins A and D	299 mg
spinach, frozen, cooked, 1 cup	291 mg
salmon, canned, with bone, 3 oz.	181 mg
pinto beans, cooked, 1 cup	79 mg
broccoli, cooked, 1 cup	62 mg
soy milk, original and vanilla, unfortified, 1 cup	61 mg
orange, 1 medium	52 mg
lettuce, green leaf, 1 cup	13 mg
tuna, white, canned, 3 oz.	12 mg
Milk and Milk Products	
yogurt, plain, skim milk, 8 oz.	452 mg
milk, reduced fat, with added vitamins A and D, 1 cup	293 mg
Swiss cheese, 1 oz.	224 mg
cottage cheese, low fat, 1 cup	206 mg
ice cream, vanilla, 1/2 cup	84 mg

Source: Adapted from U.S. Department of Agriculture, Agricultural Research Service. 2013. USDA national nutrient database for standard reference, release 26.

alternative medical practices, including their use of dietary supplements, with their health care provider.

What products contain lactose?

Lactose is present in many food products and in some medications.

Food Products

Lactose is in all milk and milk products. Manufacturers also often add milk and milk products to boxed, canned, frozen, packaged, and prepared foods. People who have digestive symptoms after consuming a small quantity of lactose should be aware of the many food products that may contain even small amounts of lactose, such as

- bread and other baked goods

- waffles, pancakes, biscuits, cookies, and the mixes to make them

- processed breakfast foods such as doughnuts, frozen waffles and pancakes, toaster pastries, and sweet rolls

- processed breakfast cereals

- instant potatoes, soups, and breakfast drinks

- potato chips, corn chips, and other processed snacks

- processed meats such as bacon, sausage, hot dogs, and lunch meats

- margarine

- salad dressings

- liquid and powdered milk-based meal replacements

- protein powders and bars

- candies

- nondairy liquid and powdered coffee creamers

- nondairy whipped toppings

People can check the ingredients on food labels to find possible sources of lactose in food products. If a food label includes any of the following words, the product contains lactose:

- milk
- lactose
- whey
- curds

- milk by-products
- dry milk solids
- nonfat dry milk powder

Medications

Some medications also contain lactose, including prescription medications such as birth control pills and over-the-counter medications such as products to treat stomach acid and gas. These medications most often cause symptoms in people with severe lactose intolerance. People with lactose intolerance who take medications that contain lactose should speak with their health care provider about other options.

Chapter 47

Celiac Disease

What is celiac disease?

Celiac disease is an immune disorder in which people cannot tolerate gluten because it damages the inner lining of their small intestine and prevents it from absorbing nutrients. The small intestine is the tubeshaped organ between the stomach and large intestine. Gluten is a protein found in wheat, rye, and barley and occasionally in some products such as vitamin and nutrient supplements, lip balms, and certain medications.

The immune system is the body's natural defense system and normally protects the body from infection. However, when a person has celiac disease, gluten causes the immune system to react in a way that can cause intestinal inflammation—irritation or swelling—and long-lasting damage.

When people with celiac disease eat foods or use products containing gluten, their immune system responds by damaging or destroying villi—the tiny, fingerlike projections on the inner lining of the small intestine. Villi normally absorb nutrients from food and pass the nutrients through the walls of the small intestine and into the bloodstream. Without healthy villi, people can become malnourished, no matter how much food they eat.

Text in this chapter is excerpted from "Celiac Disease" National Institute of Diabetes and Digestive and Kidney Diseases (NIDDK), September 2014.

605

What causes celiac disease?

Researchers do not know the exact cause of celiac disease. Celiac disease sometimes runs in families. In 50 percent of people who have celiac disease, a family member, when screened, also has the disease.

A person's chances of developing celiac disease increase when his or her genes—traits passed from parent to child—have variants, or changes. In celiac disease, certain gene variants and other factors, such as a person's exposure to things in his or her environment, can lead to celiac disease.

For most people, eating something with gluten is harmless. For others, an exposure to gluten can cause, or trigger, celiac disease to become active. Sometimes surgery, pregnancy, childbirth, a viral infection, or severe emotional stress can also trigger celiac disease symptoms.

How common is celiac disease and who is affected?

As many as one in 141 Americans has celiac disease, although most remain undiagnosed. Celiac disease affects children and adults in all parts of the world and is more common in Caucasians and females.

Celiac disease is also more common among people with certain genetic diseases, including Down syndrome and Turner syndrome—a condition that affects girls' development.

What are the signs and symptoms of celiac disease?

A person may experience digestive signs and symptoms, or symptoms in other parts of the body. Digestive signs and symptoms are more common in children and can include

- abdominal bloating
- chronic diarrhea
- constipation
- gas
- pale, foul-smelling, or fatty stool
- stomach pain
- nausea
- vomiting

Being unable to absorb nutrients during the years when nutrition is critical to a child's normal growth and development can lead to other health problems, such as

- failure to thrive in infants
- slowed growth and short stature
- weight loss
- irritability or change in mood
- delayed puberty
- dental enamel defects of permanent teeth

Adults are less likely to have digestive signs and symptoms and may instead have one or more of the following:

- anemia
- bone or joint pain
- canker sores inside the mouth
- depression or anxiety
- dermatitis herpetiformis, an itchy, blistering skin rash
- fatigue, or feeling tired
- infertility or recurrent miscarriage
- missed menstrual periods
- seizures
- tingling numbness in the hands and feet
- weak and brittle bones, or osteoporosis
- headaches

Intestinal inflammation can cause other symptoms, such as

- feeling tired for long periods of time
- abdominal pain and bloating
- ulcers
- blockages in the intestine

Celiac disease can produce an autoimmune reaction, or a self-directed immune reaction, in which a person's immune system attacks healthy cells in the body. This reaction can spread outside of the gastrointestinal tract to affect other areas of the body, including the

- spleen
- skin
- nervous system
- bones
- joints

Recognizing celiac disease can be difficult because some of its symptoms are similar to those of other diseases and conditions. Celiac disease can be confused with

- irritable bowel syndrome (IBS)
- iron-deficiency anemia caused by menstrual blood loss
- lactose intolerance
- inflammatory bowel disease
- diverticulitis
- intestinal infections
- chronic fatigue syndrome

As a result, celiac disease has long been underdiagnosed or misdiagnosed. As health care providers become more aware of the many varied symptoms of the disease and reliable blood tests become more available, diagnosis rates are increasing, particularly for adults.

Dermatitis Herpetiformis

Dermatitis herpetiformis is a chronic, itchy, blistering skin rash—usually on the elbows, knees, buttocks, back, or scalp—that affects about 5 to 10 percent of people with celiac disease. Men with dermatitis herpetiformis may also have oral or genital lesions. People with dermatitis herpetiformis may have no other signs or symptoms of celiac disease. Skin deposits of antibodies—proteins that react against the body's own cells or tissues—common in celiac disease cause dermatitis herpetiformis. Ingesting gluten triggers these antibodies.

Why are celiac disease signs and symptoms so varied?

Signs and symptoms of celiac disease vary from person to person because of numerous factors, including

- the length of time a person was breastfed as an infant; some studies have shown that the longer an infant was breastfed, the later the symptoms of celiac disease appear
- the age a person started eating gluten
- the amount of gluten a person eats
- age—symptoms can vary between young children and adults
- the degree of damage to the small intestine

Some people with celiac disease have no signs or symptoms; however, they can still develop complications of the disease over time. Long-term complications include

- malnutrition
- liver diseases
- intestinal cancer
- lymphoma

What other diseases can people with celiac disease have?

People with celiac disease may also have autoimmune diseases, including

- type 1 diabetes
- autoimmune thyroid disease
- autoimmune liver disease
- rheumatoid arthritis
- Addison's disease, a condition in which the immune system damages the glands that produce critical hormones
- Sjögren's syndrome, a condition in which the immune system destroys the glands that produce tears and saliva

How is celiac disease diagnosed?

A health care provider diagnoses celiac disease with

- a medical and family history

- a physical exam
- blood tests
- an intestinal biopsy
- a skin biopsy

Medical and Family History

Taking a medical and family history may help a health care provider diagnose celiac disease. He or she will ask the patient or caregiver to provide a medical and family history, specifically if anyone in the patient's family has a history of celiac disease.

Physical Exam

A physical exam may help diagnose celiac disease. During a physical exam, a health care provider usually

- examines the patient's body for malnutrition or a rash
- uses a stethoscope to listen to sounds within the abdomen
- taps on the patient's abdomen checking for bloating and pain

Blood Tests

A blood test involves drawing blood at a health care provider's office or a commercial facility and sending the sample to a lab for analysis. A blood test can show the presence of antibodies that are common in celiac disease.

If blood test results are negative and a health care provider still suspects celiac disease, he or she may order additional blood tests, which can affect test results.

Before the blood tests, patients should continue to eat a diet that includes foods with gluten, such as breads and pastas. If a patient stops eating foods with gluten before being tested, the results may be negative for celiac disease even if the disease is present.

Intestinal Biopsy

If blood tests suggest that a patient has celiac disease, a health care provider will perform a biopsy of the patient's small intestine to confirm the diagnosis. A biopsy is a procedure that involves taking a piece of tissue for examination with a microscope. A health care provider performs the biopsy in an outpatient center or a hospital. He or she will give the patient light sedation and a local anesthetic. Some patients may receive general anesthesia.

During the biopsy, a health care provider removes tiny pieces of tissue from the patient's small intestine using an endoscope—a small, flexible camera with a light. The health care provider carefully feeds the endoscope down the patient's esophagus and into the stomach and small intestine. A small camera mounted on the endoscope transmits a video image to a monitor, allowing close examination of the intestinal lining. The health care provider then takes the samples using tiny tools that he or she passes through the endoscope. A pathologist—a doctor who specializes in examining tissues to diagnose diseases—examines the tissue in a lab. The test can show damage to the villi in the small intestine.

Skin Biopsy

When a health care provider suspects that a patient has dermatitis herpetiformis, he or she will perform a skin biopsy. A skin biopsy is a procedure that involves removing tiny pieces of skin tissue for examination with a microscope. A health care provider performs the biopsy in an outpatient center or a hospital. The patient receives a local anesthetic; however, in some cases, the patient will require general anesthesia.

A pathologist examines the skin tissue in a lab and checks the tissue for antibodies that are common in celiac disease. If the skin tissue tests positive for the antibodies, a health care provider will perform blood tests to confirm celiac disease. If the skin biopsy and blood tests both suggest celiac disease, the patient may not need an intestinal biopsy for diagnosis.

Genetic Tests

In some cases, a health care provider will order genetic blood tests to confirm or rule out a diagnosis of celiac disease. Most people with celiac disease have gene pairs that contain at least one of the human leukocyte antigen (HLA) gene variants. However, these variants are also common in people without celiac disease, so their presence alone cannot diagnose celiac disease.

If a biopsy and other blood tests do not give a clear diagnosis of celiac disease, a health care provider may test a patient for HLA gene variants. If the gene variants are not present, celiac disease is unlikely.

Do health care providers screen for celiac disease?

Health care providers in the United States do not routinely screen patients for celiac disease. However, since celiac disease sometimes runs in families, blood relatives of people with celiac disease should talk with their health care provider about their chances of getting the disease. Some researchers recommend the routine testing of all family members, such as parents and siblings, for celiac disease. However, routine genetic testing for celiac disease is not usually helpful when diagnosing the disease.

How is celiac disease treated?

Most people with celiac disease have a significant improvement in symptoms when they follow a gluten-free diet. Health care providers typically refer people to a dietitian who specializes in treating people with the disease. The dietitian will teach the person to avoid gluten while following a healthy and nutritious diet. The dietitian will give the person instructions for how to

- read food and product labels and identify ingredients that contain gluten
- make healthy choices about the types of foods to eat
- design everyday meal plans

For most people, following a gluten-free diet will stop symptoms, heal existing intestinal damage, and prevent further damage. Symptoms may improve within days to weeks of starting the diet. The small intestine usually heals in 3 to 6 months in children. Complete healing can take several years in adults. Once the intestine heals, the villi will absorb nutrients from food into the bloodstream normally.

Some people with celiac disease show no improvement after starting a gluten-free diet. The most common reason for poor response to dietary changes is that people are still consuming small amounts of gluten, which can damage the small intestine—even in people without symptoms. Most people start responding to the gluten-free diet once they find and eliminate hidden sources of gluten from their diet. Hidden sources of gluten include additives made with wheat, such as

- modified food starch
- preservatives
- stabilizers

Some people who continue to have symptoms even after changing their diet may have other conditions or disorders that are more common in people with celiac disease. These conditions may include

- small intestinal bacterial overgrowth, which happens when too many bacteria grow in the small intestine

- pancreatic exocrine insufficiency, in which the pancreas does not produce enough digestive juice

- microscopic colitis, an inflammation of the colon that a health care provider can see only with a microscope

- IBS

- lactose intolerance, a condition in which people have symptoms after consuming milk or milk products

- other food intolerances, which may occur because of continued damage to the intestine

Did you know that medications and nonfood products may contain gluten?

Medications, supplements, and other products may also contain lecithin, a hidden source of gluten. People with celiac disease should ask a pharmacist about the ingredients in

- prescription and over-the-counter medications
- vitamins and mineral supplements
- herbal and nutritional supplements

Other products can be ingested or transferred from a person's hands to his or her mouth. Reading product labels can help people avoid gluten exposure. If a product's label does not list its ingredients, the manufacturer should provide a list upon request.

Products that can contain gluten include

- lipstick, lip gloss, and lip balm
- cosmetics
- skin and hair products
- toothpaste and mouthwash
- glue on stamps and envelopes
- children's modeling dough, such as Play-Doh

In some cases, people continue to have difficulty absorbing nutrients despite following a strict gluten-free diet. People with this condition, known as refractory celiac disease, have severely damaged intestines that cannot heal. Their intestines are not absorbing enough nutrients, so they may need to receive nutrients intravenously. Researchers continue to evaluate medications to treat refractory celiac disease.

Depending on a person's age at diagnosis, some complications of celiac disease will not improve, such as short stature and dental enamel defects.

For people with dermatitis herpetiformis, skin symptoms generally respond to a gluten-free diet and may recur if a person adds gluten back into his or her diet. Medications such as dapsone can control the rash's symptoms. Dapsone does not treat intestinal symptoms or damage, so people with dermatitis herpetiformis should maintain a gluten-free diet, even if they don't have digestive symptoms. Even when a person follows a gluten-free diet, the skin lesions from dermatitis herpetiformis may take months or even years to fully heal and often recur over the years.

Eating, Diet, and Nutrition

Eating, diet, and nutrition play a significant role in treating celiac disease. People with the disease should maintain a gluten-free diet by avoiding products that contain gluten. In other words, a person with celiac disease should not eat most grains, pasta, and cereal, and many processed foods.

People with celiac disease can eat a wellbalanced diet with a variety of foods. They can use potato, rice, soy, amaranth, quinoa, buckwheat, or bean flour instead of wheat flour. They can buy gluten-free bread, pasta, and other products from stores, or order products from special food companies. Meanwhile, 'plain'—meaning no additives or seasonings—meat, fish, rice, fruits, and vegetables do not contain gluten, so people with celiac disease can eat these foods.

In the past, health care providers and dietitians advised people with celiac disease to avoid eating oats. Evidence suggests that most people with the disease can safely eat small amounts of oats, as long as the oats are not contaminated with wheat gluten during processing. People with celiac disease should talk with their health care team when deciding whether to include oats in their diet.

Eating out and shopping can be a challenge. Newly diagnosed people and their families may find support groups helpful as they adjust to a new approach to eating. People with celiac disease should

- read food labels—especially canned, frozen, and processed foods—for ingredients that contain gluten

- avoid ingredients such as hydrolyzed vegetable protein, also called lecithin or soy lecithin

- ask restaurant servers and chefs about ingredients and food preparation inquire whether a gluten-free menu is available

- ask a dinner or party host about glutenfree options before attending a social gathering

Foods that are packaged as gluten-free tend to cost more than the same foods containing gluten. People following a gluten-free diet may find that naturally gluten-free foods are less expensive. With practice, looking for gluten can become second nature.

The Gluten-free Diet: Some Examples

The Academy of Nutrition and Dietetics has published recommendations for a glutenfree diet. The following chart illustrates these recommendations. This list is not complete, so people with celiac disease should discuss gluten-free food choices with a dietitian or health care professional who specializes in celiac disease. People with celiac disease should always read food ingredient lists carefully to make sure the food does not contain gluten.

Table 47.1. Gluten-free foods and foods that contain gluten

Foods and Ingredients That Contain Gluten		
barley rye triticale (a cross between wheat and rye) wheat, including • including einkorn, emmer, spelt, kamut • wheat starch, wheat bran, wheat germ, cracked wheat, hydrolyzed wheat protein		brewer's yeast dextrin malt (unless a gluten-free source is named, such as corn malt) modified food starch oats (not labeled gluten-free) starch
Other Wheat Products That Contain Gluten		
bromated flour durum flour enriched flour farina	graham flour phosphated flour plain flour	self-rising flour semolina white flour

Table 47.1. Continued

Processed Foods That May Contain Wheat, Barley, or Rye*		
bouillon cubes brown rice syrup candy chewing gum chips/potato chips cold cuts, hot dogs, salami, sausage	communion wafers french fries gravies imitation fish matzo and matzo meal rice mixes	sauces seasoned tortilla chips self-basting turkey soups soy sauce vegetables in sauce

*Most of these foods can be found gluten-free. When in doubt, check with the food manufacturer.

Food Products and Ingredients Made from Barley*		
ale beer malt malt beverages	malted milk malt extract malt syrup malt vinegar	other fermented beverages porter stout

*People should only consume these foods if they are labeled gluten-free—such as sorghum-based beer—or they list a grain source other than barley, wheat, or rye—such as corn malt.

Foods That Do Not Contain Gluten			
amaranth arrowroot buckwheat cassava corn flax	legumes lentils millet nuts oats (labeled gluten-free) potatoes	quinoa rice sago seeds sorghum soy	tapioca tef (or teff) wild rice yucca

Adapted from: Thompson T. Celiac Disease Nutrition Guide. 3rd ed. Chicago: Academy of Nutrition and Dietetics; 2014.

Food Labeling Requirements

On August 2, 2013, the U.S. Food and Drug Administration (FDA) published a new regulation defining the term 'glutenfree' for voluntary food labeling. This new federal definition standardizes the meaning of 'gluten-free' foods regulated by the FDA. Foods regulated by the U.S. Department of Agriculture, including meat and egg products, are not subject to this regulation. The regulation requires that any food with the term 'gluten-free' on the label must meet all of the requirements of the definition, including that the food should contain fewer than 20 parts per million of gluten. The FDA rule also requires foods with the claims 'no gluten,' 'free of gluten,' and 'without gluten' to meet the definition for 'gluten-free.'

If a food that is labeled 'gluten-free' includes 'wheat' on the ingredients list or 'contains wheat' after the list, the following statement must be included on the label: 'The wheat has been processed to allow this food to meet the Food and Drug Administration requirements for gluten-free food.' If this statement is included, people with celiac disease may consume foods labeled 'gluten-free.'

Chapter 48

Food- and Water-Borne Diseases

Chapter Contents

Section 48.1

Foodborne Illnesses: An Overview

Text in this section is excerpted from "Foodborne Illnesses," National
Institute of Diabetes and Digestive and Kidney Diseases (NIDDK),
July 2012.

What are foodborne illnesses?

Foodborne illnesses are infections or irritations of the gastrointestinal (GI) tract caused by food or beverages that contain harmful bacteria, parasites, viruses, or chemicals. The GI tract is a series of hollow organs joined in a long, twisting tube from the mouth to the anus. Common symptoms of foodborne illnesses include vomiting, diarrhea, abdominal pain, fever, and chills.

Most foodborne illnesses are acute, meaning they happen suddenly and last a short time, and most people recover on their own without treatment. Rarely, foodborne illnesses may lead to more serious complications. Each year, an estimated 48 million people in the United States experience a foodborne illness. Foodborne illnesses cause about 3,000 deaths in the United States annually.

What causes foodborne illnesses?

The majority of foodborne illnesses are caused by harmful bacteria and viruses. Some parasites and chemicals also cause foodborne illnesses.

Bacteria

Bacteria are tiny organisms that can cause infections of the GI tract. Not all bacteria are harmful to humans.

Some harmful bacteria may already be present in foods when they are purchased. Raw foods including meat, poultry, fish and shellfish, eggs, unpasteurized milk and dairy products, and fresh produce often contain bacteria that cause foodborne illnesses. Bacteria can contaminate food—making it harmful to eat—at any time during growth, harvesting or slaughter, processing, storage, and shipping.

Foods may also be contaminated with bacteria during food preparation in a restaurant or home kitchen. If food preparers do not thoroughly wash their hands, kitchen utensils, cutting boards, and other kitchen surfaces that come into contact with raw foods, cross-contamination—the spread of bacteria from contaminated food to uncontaminated food—may occur.

If hot food is not kept hot enough or cold food is not kept cold enough, bacteria may multiply. Bacteria multiply quickly when the temperature of food is between 40 and 140 degrees. Cold food should be kept below 40 degrees and hot food should be kept above 140 degrees. Bacteria multiply more slowly when food is refrigerated, and freezing food can further slow or even stop the spread of bacteria. However, bacteria in refrigerated or frozen foods become active again when food is brought to room temperature. Thoroughly cooking food kills bacteria.

Many types of bacteria cause foodborne illnesses. Examples include

- *Salmonella*, a bacterium found in many foods, including raw and undercooked meat, poultry, dairy products, and seafood. Salmonella may also be present on egg shells and inside eggs.

- *Campylobacter jejuni (C. jejuni)*, found in raw or undercooked chicken and unpasteurized milk.

- *Shigella*, a bacterium spread from person to person. These bacteria are present in the stools of people who are infected. If people who are infected do not wash their hands thoroughly after using the bathroom, they can contaminate food that they handle or prepare. Water contaminated with infected stools can also contaminate produce in the field.

- *Escherichia coli (E. coli)*, which includes several different strains, only a few of which cause illness in humans. *E. coli O157:H7* is the strain that causes the most severe illness. Common sources of *E. coli* include raw or undercooked hamburger, unpasteurized fruit juices and milk, and fresh produce.

- *Listeria monocytogenes (L. monocytogenes)*, which has been found in raw and undercooked meats, unpasteurized milk, soft cheeses, and ready-to-eat deli meats and hot dogs.

- *Vibrio*, a bacterium that may contaminate fish or shellfish.

- *Clostridium botulinum (C. botulinum)*, a bacterium that may contaminate improperly canned foods and smoked and salted fish.

Viruses

Viruses are tiny capsules, much smaller than bacteria, that contain genetic material. Viruses cause infections that can lead to sickness. People can pass viruses to each other. Viruses are present in the stool or vomit of people who are infected. People who are infected with a virus may contaminate food and drinks, especially if they do not wash their hands thoroughly after using the bathroom.

Common sources of foodborne viruses include

• food prepared by a person infected with a virus

• shellfish from contaminated water

• produce irrigated with contaminated water

Common foodborne viruses include

• norovirus, which causes inflammation of the stomach and intestines

• hepatitis A, which causes inflammation of the liver

Parasites

Parasites are tiny organisms that live inside another organism. In developed countries such as the United States, parasitic infections are relatively rare.

Cryptosporidium parvum and *Giardia intestinalis* are parasites that are spread through water contaminated with the stools of people or animals who are infected. Foods that come into contact with contaminated water during growth or preparation can become contaminated with these parasites. Food preparers who are infected with these parasites can also contaminate foods if they do not thoroughly wash their hands after using the bathroom and before handling food.

Trichinella spiralis is a type of roundworm parasite. People may be infected with this parasite by consuming raw or undercooked pork or wild game.

Chemicals

Harmful chemicals that cause illness may contaminate foods such as

• fish or shellfish, which may feed on algae that produce toxins, leading to high concentrations of toxins in their bodies. Some types of fish, including tuna and mahi mahi, may be contaminated with bacteria that produce toxins if the fish are not properly refrigerated before they are cooked or served.

- certain types of wild mushrooms.
- unwashed fruits and vegetables that contain high concentrations of pesticides.

Who gets foodborne illnesses?

Anyone can get a foodborne illness. However, some people are more likely to develop foodborne illnesses than others, including

- infants and children
- pregnant women and their fetuses
- older adults
- people with weak immune systems

These groups also have a greater risk of developing severe symptoms or complications of foodborne illnesses.

What are the symptoms of foodborne illnesses?

Symptoms of foodborne illnesses depend on the cause. Common symptoms of many foodborne illnesses include

- vomiting
- diarrhea or bloody diarrhea
- abdominal pain
- fever
- chills

Symptoms can range from mild to serious and can last from a few hours to several days.

C. botulinum and some chemicals affect the nervous system, causing symptoms such as

- headache
- tingling or numbness of the skin
- blurred vision
- weakness

- dizziness

- paralysis

What are the complications of foodborne illnesses?

Foodborne illnesses may lead to dehydration, hemolytic uremic syndrome (HUS), and other complications. Acute foodborne illnesses may also lead to chronic—or long lasting—health problems.

Dehydration

When someone does not drink enough fluids to replace those that are lost through vomiting and diarrhea, dehydration can result. When dehydrated, the body lacks enough fluid and electrolytes—minerals in salts, including sodium, potassium, and chloride—to function properly. Infants, children, older adults, and people with weak immune systems have the greatest risk of becoming dehydrated.

Signs of dehydration are

- excessive thirst

- infrequent urination

- dark-colored urine

- lethargy, dizziness, or faintness

Signs of dehydration in infants and young children are

- dry mouth and tongue

- lack of tears when crying

- no wet diapers for 3 hours or more

- high fever

- unusually cranky or drowsy behavior

- sunken eyes, cheeks, or soft spot in the skull

Also, when people are dehydrated, their skin does not flatten back to normal right away after being gently pinched and released.

Severe dehydration may require intravenous fluids and hospitalization. Untreated severe dehydration can cause serious health problems such as organ damage, shock, or coma—a sleeplike state in which a person is not conscious.

Hemolytic Uremic Syndrome (HUS)

Hemolytic uremic syndrome is a rare disease that mostly affects children younger than 10 years of age. HUS develops when *E. coli* bacteria lodged in the digestive tract make toxins that enter the bloodstream. The toxins start to destroy red blood cells, which help the blood to clot, and the lining of the blood vessels.

In the United States, *E. coli O157:H7* infection is the most common cause of HUS, but infection with other strains of *E. coli*, other bacteria, and viruses may also cause HUS. A recent study found that about 6 percent of people with *E. coli O157:H7* infections developed HUS. Children younger than age 5 have the highest risk, but females and people age 60 and older also have increased risk.

Symptoms of *E. coli O157:H7* infection include diarrhea, which may be bloody, and abdominal pain, often accompanied by nausea, vomiting, and fever. Up to a week after *E. coli* symptoms appear, symptoms of HUS may develop, including irritability, paleness, and decreased urination. HUS may lead to acute renal failure, which is a sudden and temporary loss of kidney function. HUS may also affect other organs and the central nervous system. Most people who develop HUS recover with treatment. Research shows that in the United States between 2000 and 2006, fewer than 5 percent of people who developed HUS died of the disorder. Older adults had the highest mortality rate—about one-third of people age 60 and older who developed HUS died.

Studies have shown that some children who recover from HUS develop chronic complications, including kidney problems, high blood pressure, and diabetes.

Other Complications

Some foodborne illnesses lead to other serious complications. For example, C. botulinum and certain chemicals in fish and seafood can paralyze the muscles that control breathing. L. monocytogenes can cause spontaneous abortion or stillbirth in pregnant women.

Research suggests that acute foodborne illnesses may lead to chronic disorders, including

- **reactive arthritis**, a type of joint inflammation that usually affects the knees, ankles, or feet. Some people develop this disorder following foodborne illnesses caused by certain bacteria, including *C. jejuni* and *Salmonella*. Reactive arthritis usually lasts fewer than 6 months, but this condition may recur or become chronic arthritis.

- **irritable bowel syndrome (IBS)**, a disorder of unknown cause that is associated with abdominal pain, bloating, and diarrhea or constipation or both. Foodborne illnesses caused by bacteria increase the risk of developing IBS.

- **Guillain-Barré syndrome**, a disorder characterized by muscle weakness or paralysis that begins in the lower body and progresses to the upper body. This syndrome may occur after foodborne illnesses caused by bacteria, most commonly *C. jejuni*. Most people recover in 6 to 12 months.

A recent study found that adults who had recovered from E. coli O157:H7 infections had increased risks of high blood pressure, kidney problems, and cardiovascular disease.

When should people with foodborne illnesses see a health care provider?

People with any of the following symptoms should see a health care provider immediately:

- signs of dehydration

- prolonged vomiting that prevents keeping liquids down

- diarrhea for more than 2 days in adults or for more than 24 hours in children

- severe pain in the abdomen or rectum

- a fever higher than 101 degrees

- stools containing blood or pus

- stools that are black and tarry

- nervous system symptoms

- signs of HUS

If a child has a foodborne illness, parents or guardians should not hesitate to call a health care provider for advice.

How are foodborne illnesses diagnosed?

To diagnose foodborne illnesses, health care providers ask about symptoms, foods and beverages recently consumed, and medical history. Health care providers will also perform a physical examination to look for signs of illness.

Diagnostic tests for foodborne illnesses may include a stool culture, in which a sample of stool is analyzed in a laboratory to check for signs of infections or diseases. A sample of vomit or a sample of the suspected food, if available, may also be tested. A health care provider may perform additional medical tests to rule out diseases and disorders that cause symptoms similar to the symptoms of foodborne illnesses.

If symptoms of foodborne illnesses are mild and last only a short time, diagnostic tests are usually not necessary.

How are foodborne illnesses treated?

The only treatment needed for most foodborne illnesses is replacing lost fluids and electrolytes to prevent dehydration.

Over-the-counter medications such as loperamide (Imodium) and bismuth subsalicylate (Pepto-Bismol and Kaopectate) may help stop diarrhea in adults. However, people with bloody diarrhea—a sign of bacterial or parasitic infection—should not use these medications. If diarrhea is caused by bacteria or parasites, over-the-counter medications may prolong the problem. Medications to treat diarrhea in adults can be dangerous for infants and children and should only be given with a health care provider's guidance.

If the specific cause of the foodborne illness is diagnosed, a health care provider may prescribe medications, such as antibiotics, to treat the illness.

Hospitalization may be required to treat lifethreatening symptoms and complications, such as paralysis, severe dehydration, and HUS.

Eating, Diet, and Nutrition

The following steps may help relieve the symptoms of foodborne illnesses and prevent dehydration in adults:

- drinking plenty of liquids such as fruit juices, sports drinks, caffeine-free soft drinks, and broths to replace fluids and electrolytes

- sipping small amounts of clear liquids or sucking on ice chips if vomiting is still a problem

- gradually reintroducing food, starting with bland, easy-to-digest foods such as rice, potatoes, toast or bread, cereal, lean meat, applesauce, and bananas

- avoiding fatty foods, sugary foods, dairy products, caffeine, and alcohol until recovery is complete

Infants and children present special concerns. Infants and children are likely to become dehydrated more quickly from diarrhea and vomiting because of their smaller body size. The following steps may help relieve symptoms and prevent dehydration in infants and children:

- giving oral rehydration solutions such as Pedialyte, Naturalyte, Infalyte, and CeraLyte to prevent dehydration

- giving food as soon as the child is hungry

- giving infants breast milk or fullstrength formula, as usual, along with oral rehydration solutions

Older adults and adults with weak immune systems should also drink oral rehydration solutions to prevent dehydration.

How are foodborne illnesses prevented?

Foodborne illnesses can be prevented by properly storing, cooking, cleaning, and handling foods.

- Raw and cooked perishable foods—foods that can spoil—should be refrigerated or frozen promptly. If perishable foods stand at room temperature for more than 2 hours, they may not be safe to eat. Refrigerators should be set at 40 degrees or lower and freezers should be set at 0 degrees.

- Foods should be cooked long enough and at a high enough temperature to kill the harmful bacteria that cause illnesses. A meat thermometer should be used to ensure foods are cooked to the appropriate internal temperature:

    - 145 degrees for roasts, steaks, and chops of beef, veal, pork, and lamb, followed by 3 minutes of rest time after the meat is removed from the heat source

    - 160 degrees for ground beef, veal, pork, and lamb

    - 165 degrees for poultry

- Cold foods should be kept cold and hot foods should be kept hot.

- Fruits and vegetables should be washed under running water just before eating, cutting, or cooking. A produce brush can be used under running water to clean fruits and vegetables with firm skin.

- Raw meat, poultry, seafood, and their juices should be kept away from other foods.

- People should wash their hands for at least 20 seconds with warm, soapy water before and after handling raw meat, poultry, fish, shellfish, produce, or eggs. People should also wash their hands after using the bathroom, changing diapers, or touching animals.

- Utensils and surfaces should be washed with hot, soapy water before and after they are used to prepare food. Diluted bleach—1 teaspoon of bleach to 1 quart of hot water—can also be used to sanitize utensils and surfaces.

Traveler's Diarrhea

People who visit certain foreign countries are at risk for traveler's diarrhea, which is caused by eating food or drinking water contaminated with bacteria, viruses, or parasites. Traveler's diarrhea can be a problem for people traveling to developing countries in Africa, Asia, Latin America, and the Caribbean. Visitors to Canada, most European countries, Japan, Australia, and New Zealand do not face much risk for traveler's diarrhea.

To prevent traveler's diarrhea, people traveling from the United States to developing countries should avoid

- drinking tap water, using tap water to brush their teeth, or using ice made from tap water

- drinking unpasteurized milk or milk products

- eating raw fruits and vegetables, including lettuce and fruit salads, unless they peel the fruits or vegetables themselves

- eating raw or rare meat and fish

- eating meat or shellfish that is not hot when served

- eating food from street vendors

Travelers can drink bottled water, bottled soft drinks, and hot drinks such as coffee or tea.

People concerned about traveler's diarrhea should talk with a health care provider before traveling. The health care provider may recommend that travelers bring medication with them in case they develop diarrhea during their trip. Health care providers may advise some people—especially people with weakened immune systems—to take antibiotics before and during a trip to help prevent traveler's diarrhea. Early treatment with antibiotics can shorten a bout of traveler's diarrhea.

Section 48.2

Campylobacter *Infection*

Text in this section is excerpted from "Campylobacter," Centers for
Disease Control and Prevention (CDC), June 3, 2014.

What is campylobacteriosis?

Campylobacteriosis is an infectious disease caused by bacteria of
the genus *Campylobacter*. Most people who become ill with campylobacteriosis get diarrhea, cramping, abdominal pain, and fever within
two to five days after exposure to the organism. The diarrhea may be
bloody and can be accompanied by nausea and vomiting. The illness
typically lasts about one week. Some infected persons do not have any
symptoms. In persons with compromised immune systems, *Campylobacter* occasionally spreads to the bloodstream and causes a serious
life-threatening infection.

How common is Campylobacter?

Campylobacter is one of the most common causes of diarrheal illness
in the United States. Most cases occur as isolated, sporadic events,
not as part of recognized outbreaks. Active surveillance through the
Foodborne Diseases Active Surveillance Network (FoodNet) indicates
that about 14 cases are diagnosed each year for each 100,000 persons
in the population. Many more cases go undiagnosed or unreported, and
campylobacteriosis is estimated to affect over 1.3 million persons every
year. Campylobacteriosis occurs much more frequently in the summer
months than in the winter. The organism is isolated from infants and
young adults more frequently than from persons in other age groups
and from males more frequently than females. Although *Campylobacter*
infection does not commonly cause death, it has been estimated that
approximately 76 persons with *Campylobacter* infections die each year.

What sort of germ is Campylobacter?

Campylobacter organisms are spiral-shaped bacteria that can cause
disease in humans and animals. Most human illness is caused by one

species, called *Campylobacter jejuni*, but human illness can also be caused by other species. *Campylobacter jejuni* grows best at 37°C to 42°C, the approximate body temperature of a bird (41°C to 42°C), and seems to be well adapted to birds, who carry it without becoming ill. These bacteria are fragile. They cannot tolerate drying and can be killed by oxygen. They grow only in places with less oxygen than the amount in the atmosphere. Freezing reduces the number of *Campylobacter* bacteria on raw meat.

How is the infection diagnosed?

Many different kinds of infections can cause diarrhea and bloody diarrhea. *Campylobacter* infection is diagnosed when a culture of a stool specimen yields the bacterium.

How can campylobacteriosis be treated?

Almost all persons infected with *Campylobacter* recover without any specific treatment. Patients should drink extra fluids as long as the diarrhea lasts. Antimicrobial therapy is warranted only for patients with severe disease or those at high risk for severe disease, such as those with immune systems severely weakened from medications or other illnesses. Azithromycin and fluoroquinolones (e.g., ciprofloxacin) are commonly used for treatment of these infections, but resistance to fluoroquinolones is common. Antimicrobial susceptibility testing can help guide appropriate therapy.

Are there long-term consequences?

Most people who get campylobacteriosis recover completely within two to five days, although sometimes recovery can take up to 10 days. Rarely, *Campylobacter* infection results in long-term consequences. Some people develop arthritis. Others may develop a rare disease called Guillain-Barré syndrome that affects the nerves of the body beginning several weeks after the diarrheal illness. This occurs when a person's immune system is 'triggered' to attack the body's own nerves resulting in paralysis. The paralysis usually lasts several weeks and requires intensive medical care. It is estimated that approximately one in every 1,000 reported Campylobacter illnesses leads to Guillain-Barré syndrome. As many as 40% of Guillain-Barré syndrome cases in this country may be triggered by campylobacteriosis.

How do people get infected with this germ?

Campylobacteriosis usually occurs in single, sporadic cases, but it can also occur in outbreaks, when two or more people become ill from the same source. Most cases of campylobacteriosis are associated with eating raw or undercooked poultry meat or from cross-contamination of other foods by these items. Outbreaks of *Campylobacter* have most often been associated with unpasteurized dairy products, contaminated water, poultry, and produce. Animals can also be infected, and some people get infected from contact with the stool of an ill dog or cat. The organism is not usually spread from one person to another, but this can happen if the infected person is producing a large volume of diarrhea.

It only takes a very few *Campylobacter* organisms (fewer than 500) to make a person sick. Even one drop of juice from raw chicken meat can have enough *Campylobacter* in it to infect a person! One way to become infected is to cut poultry meat on a cutting board, and then use the unwashed cutting board or utensil to prepare vegetables or other raw or lightly cooked foods. The *Campylobacter* organisms from the raw meat can get onto the other foods.

How does food or water get contaminated with Campylobacter?

Many chicken flocks are infected with *Campylobacter* but show no signs of illness. *Campylobacter* can be easily spread from bird to bird through a common water source or through contact with infected feces. When an infected bird is slaughtered, *Campylobacter* organisms can be transferred from the intestines to the meat. In 2011, *Campylobacter* was found on 47% of raw chicken samples bought in grocery stores and tested through the National Antimicrobial Resistance Monitoring System (NARMS). *Campylobacter* can also be present in the giblets, especially the liver.

Unpasteurized milk can become contaminated if the cow has an infection with Campylobacter in her udder or if the milk is contaminated with manure. Surface water and mountain streams can become contaminated from infected feces from cows or wild birds. *Campylobacter* is common in the developing world, and travelers to foreign countries are at risk for becoming infected with *Campylobacter*. Approximately one-fifth (19%) of *Campylobacter* cases identified in FoodNet are associated with international travel.

What can be done to prevent **Campylobacter** *infection?*

Some simple food handling practices can help prevent *Campylobacter* infections.

- Cook all poultry products thoroughly. Make sure that the meat is cooked throughout (no longer pink) and any juices run clear. All poultry should be cooked to reach a minimum internal temperature of 165°F.

- If you are served undercooked poultry in a restaurant, send it back for further cooking.

- Wash hands with soap before preparing food

- Wash hands with soap after handling raw foods of animal origin and before touching anything else.

- Prevent cross-contamination in the kitchen by using separate cutting boards for foods of animal origin and other foods and by thoroughly cleaning all cutting boards, countertops, and utensils with soap and hot water after preparing raw food of animal origin.

- Do not drink unpasteurized milk or untreated surface water.

- Make sure that persons with diarrhea, especially children, wash their hands carefully and frequently with soap to reduce the risk of spreading the infection.

- Wash hands with soap after contact with pet feces.

Physicians who diagnose campylobacteriosis and clinical laboratories that identify this organism should report their findings to the local health department. If many cases occur at the same time, it may mean that an outbreak has occurred in which many people were exposed to a common contaminated food item or water source. If this food or water is still available, more people could get infected. Public health departments investigate outbreaks to identify the source so that action can be taken to prevent more cases.

Section 48.3

Escherichia Coli *Infection*

Text in this section is excerpted from "*E.coli (Escherichia coli)*,"
Centers for Disease Control and Prevention (CDC),
December 1, 2014.

General Information

Escherichia coli (E. coli) bacteria normally live in the intestines of people and animals. Most *E. coli* are harmless and actually are an important part of a healthy human intestinal tract. However, some *E. coli* are pathogenic, meaning they can cause illness, either diarrhea or illness outside of the intestinal tract. The types of *E. coli* that can cause diarrhea can be transmitted through contaminated water or food, or through contact with animals or persons.

E. coli consists of a diverse group of bacteria. Pathogenic *E. coli* strains are categorized into pathotypes. Six pathotypes are associated with diarrhea and collectively are referred to as diarrheagenic *E. coli.*

1. Shiga toxin-producing *E. coli* (STEC)—STEC may also be referred to as Verocytotoxin-producing *E. coli* (VTEC) or enterohemorrhagic *E. coli* (EHEC). This pathotype is the one most commonly heard about in the news in association with foodborne outbreaks.

2. Enterotoxigenic *E. coli* (ETEC)

3. Enteropathogenic *E. coli* (EPEC)

4. Enteroaggregative *E. coli* (EAEC)

5. Enteroinvasive *E. coli* (EIEC)

6. Diffusely adherent *E. coli* (DAEC)

Frequently Asked Questions

What are Escherichia coli?

Escherichia coli (abbreviated as *E. coli*) are a large and diverse group of bacteria. Although most strains of *E. coli* are harmless, others can make you sick. Some kinds of *E. coli* can cause diarrhea, while others cause urinary tract infections, respiratory illness and pneumonia, and other illnesses. Still other kinds of *E. coli* are used as markers for water contamination—so you might hear about *E. coli* being found in drinking water, which are not themselves harmful, but indicate the water is contaminated. It does get a bit confusing—even to microbiologists.

Are there important differences between E. coli O157 and other STEC?

Most of what we know about STEC comes from outbreak investigations and studies of *E. coli* O157 infection, which was first identified as a pathogen in 1982. The non-O157 STEC are not nearly as well understood, partly because outbreaks due to them are rarely identified. As a whole, the non-O157 serogroup is less likely to cause severe illness than *E. coli* O157; however, some non-O157 STEC serogroups can cause the most severe manifestations of STEC illness.

Who gets STEC infections?

People of any age can become infected. Very young children and the elderly are more likely to develop severe illness and hemolytic uremic syndrome (HUS) than others, but even healthy older children and young adults can become seriously ill.

What are the symptoms of STEC infections?

The symptoms of STEC infections vary for each person but often include severe stomach cramps, diarrhea (often bloody), and vomiting. If there is fever, it usually is not very high (less than 101?F/less than 38.5?C). Most people get better within 5–7 days. Some infections are very mild, but others are severe or even life-threatening.

What are the complications of STEC infections?

Around 5–10% of those who are diagnosed with STEC infection develop a potentially life-threatening complication known as hemolytic uremic syndrome (HUS). Clues that a person is developing HUS include decreased frequency of urination, feeling very tired, and losing pink color in cheeks and inside the lower eyelids. Persons with HUS should be hospitalized because their kidneys may stop working and they may develop other serious problems. Most persons with HUS recover within a few weeks, but some suffer permanent damage or die.

635

How soon do symptoms appear after exposure?

The time between ingesting the STEC bacteria and feeling sick is called the 'incubation period.' The incubation period is usually 3–4 days after the exposure, but may be as short as 1 day or as long as 10 days. The symptoms often begin slowly with mild belly pain or non-bloody diarrhea that worsens over several days. HUS, if it occurs, develops an average 7 days after the first symptoms, when the diarrhea is improving.

Where do STEC come from?

STEC live in the guts of ruminant animals, including cattle, goats, sheep, deer, and elk. The major source for human illnesses is cattle. STEC that cause human illness generally do not make animals sick. Other kinds of animals, including pigs and birds, sometimes pick up STEC from the environment and may spread it.

How are these infections spread?

Infections start when you swallow STEC—in other words, when you get tiny (usually invisible) amounts of human or animal feces in your mouth. Unfortunately, this happens more often than we would like to think about. Exposures that result in illness include consumption of contaminated food, consumption of unpasteurized (raw) milk, consumption of water that has not been disinfected, contact with cattle, or contact with the feces of infected people.

Some foods are considered to carry such a high risk of infection with *E. coli* O157 or another germ that health officials recommend that people avoid them completely. These foods include unpasteurized (raw) milk, unpasteurized apple cider, and soft cheeses made from raw milk. Sometimes the contact is pretty obvious (working with cows at a dairy or changing diapers, for example), but sometimes it is not (like eating an undercooked hamburger or a contaminated piece of lettuce). People have gotten infected by swallowing lake water while swimming, touching the environment in petting zoos and other animal exhibits, and by eating food prepared by people who did not wash their hands well after using the toilet. Almost everyone has some risk of infection.

Where did my infection come from?

Because there are so many possible sources, for most people we can only guess. If your infection happens to be part of the about 20% of cases that are part of a recognized outbreak, the health department might identify the source.

How common are STEC infections?

An estimated 265,000 STEC infections occur each year in the United States. STEC O157 causes about 36% of these infections, and non-O157 STEC cause the rest. Public health experts rely on estimates rather than actual numbers of infections because not all STEC infections are diagnosed, for several reasons. Many infected people do not seek medical care; many of those who do seek care do not provide a stool specimen for testing, and many labs do not test for non-O157 STEC. However, this situation is changing as more labs have begun using newer, simpler tests that can help detect non-O157 STEC.

How are STEC infections diagnosed and when should I contact my healthcare provider?

STEC infections are usually diagnosed through laboratory testing of stool specimens (feces). Identifying the specific strain of STEC is essential for public health purposes, such as finding outbreaks. Many labs can determine if STEC are present, and most can identify *E. coli* O157. Labs that test for the presence of Shiga toxins in stool can detect non-O157 STEC infections. However, for the O group (serogroup) and other characteristics of non-O157 STEC to be identified, Shiga tox-in-positive specimens must be sent to a state public health laboratory.

Contact your healthcare provider if you have diarrhea that lasts for more than 3 days, or is accompanied by high fever, blood in the stool, or so much vomiting that you cannot keep liquids down and you pass very little urine.

How long can an infected person carry STEC?

STEC typically disappear from the feces by the time the illiness is resolved, but may be shed for several weeks, even after symptoms go away. Young children tend to carry STEC longer than adults. A few people keep shedding these bacteria for several months. Good hand-washing is always a smart idea to protect yourself, your family, and other persons.

What is the best treatment for STEC infection?

Non-specific supportive therapy, including hydration, is import-ant. Antibiotics should not be used to treat this infection. There is no evidence that treatment with antibiotics is helpful, and taking antibiotics may increase the risk of HUS. Antidiarrheal agents like Imodium® may also increase that risk.

Should an infected person be excluded from school or work?

School and work exclusion policies differ by local jurisdiction. Check with your local or state health department to learn more about the laws where you live. In any case, good hand-washing after changing diapers, after using the toilet, and before preparing food is essential to prevent the spread of these and many other infections.

How can STEC infections be prevented?

- Wash your hands thoroughly after using the bathroom or changing diapers and before preparing or eating food. WASH YOUR HANDS after contact with animals or their environments (at farms, petting zoos, fairs, even your own backyard).

- Cook meats thoroughly. Ground beef and meat that has been needle-tenderized should be cooked to a temperature of at least 160°F/70?C. It's best to use a thermometer, as color is not a very reliable indicator of 'doneness.'

- Avoid raw milk, unpasteurized dairy products, and unpasteurized juices (like fresh apple cider).

- Avoid swallowing water when swimming or playing in lakes, ponds, streams, swimming pools, and backyard 'kiddie' pools.

- Prevent cross contamination in food preparation areas by thoroughly washing hands, counters, cutting boards, and utensils after they touch raw meat.

Section 48.4

Salmonellosis

Text in this section is excerpted from *"Salmonella,"* Centers for Disease Control and Prevention (CDC), March 9, 2015.

What is Salmonellosis?

Salmonella is a bacteria that makes people sick. It was discovered by an American scientist named Dr. Salmon, and has been known to cause illness for over 125 years.

Most people infected with *Salmonella* develop diarrhea, fever, and abdominal cramps between 12 and 72 hours after infection. The illness usually lasts 4 to 7 days, and most individuals recover without treatment. In some cases, diarrhea may be so severe that the patient needs to be hospitalized. In these patients, the *Salmonella* infection may spread from the intestines to the blood stream, and then to other body sites. In these cases, *Salmonella* can cause death unless the person is treated promptly with antibiotics. The elderly, infants, and those with impaired immune systems are more likely to have a severe illness.

How common is **Salmonella** *infection?*

CDC estimates that approximately 1.2 million illnesses and approximately 450 deaths occur due to non-typhoidal *Salmonella* annually in the United States.

There are many different kinds of *Salmonella* bacteria. *Salmonella* serotype Typhimurium and *Salmonella* serotype Enteritidis are the most common in the United States. *Salmonella* infections are more common in the summer than winter.

Who is at **Highest Risk** *for* **Salmonella** *infection?*

Children are at the highest risk for *Salmonella* infection. Children under the age of 5 have higher rates of *Salmonella* infection than any other age group. Young children, older adults, and people with weakened immune systems are the most likely to have severe infections.

Are there long-term consequences to a **Salmonella** *infection?*

People with diarrhea due to a *Salmonella* infection usually recover completely, although it may be several months before their bowel habits are entirely normal.

A small number of people with *Salmonella* develop pain in their joints. This is called reactive arthritis. Reactive arthritis can last for months or years and can lead to chronic arthritis, which can be difficult to treat. Antibiotic treatment of the initial *Salmonella* infection does not make a difference in whether or not the person develops arthritis. People with reactive arthritis can also develop irritation of the eyes and painful urination.

How can **Salmonella** *infections be diagnosed?*

Diagnosing salmonellosis requires testing a clinical specimen (such as stool or blood) from an infected person to distinguish it from other illnesses that can cause diarrhea, fever, and abdominal cramps. Once *Salmonella* is identified in the specimen, additional testing can be done to further characterize the *Salmonella*.

Prevention

More about Prevention

There is no vaccine to prevent salmonellosis. Because foods of animal origin may be contaminated with *Salmonella*, people should not eat raw or undercooked eggs, poultry, or meat. Raw eggs may be unrecognized in some foods, such as homemade Hollandaise sauce, Caesar and other homemade salad dressings, tiramisu, homemade ice cream, homemade mayonnaise, cookie dough, and frostings. Poultry and meat, including hamburgers, should be well-cooked, not pink in the middle. Persons also should not consume raw or unpasteurized milk or other dairy products. Produce should be thoroughly washed.

Cross-contamination of foods should be avoided. Uncooked meats should be kept separate from produce, cooked foods, and ready-to-eat foods. Hands, cutting boards, counters, knives, and other utensils should be washed thoroughly after touching uncooked foods. Hand should be washed before handling food, and between handling different food items.

People who have salmonellosis should not prepare food or pour water for others until their diarrhea has resolved. Many health departments require that restaurant workers with *Salmonella* infection have

Quick Tips for Preventing Salmonella

- Cook poultry, ground beef, and eggs thoroughly. Do not eat or drink foods containing raw eggs, or raw (unpasteurized) milk.

- If you are served undercooked meat, poultry or eggs in a restaurant, don't hesitate to send it back to the kitchen for further cooking

- Wash hands, kitchen work surfaces, and utensils with soap and water immediately after they have been in contact with raw meat or poultry.

- Be particularly careful with foods prepared for infants, the elderly, and the immunocompromised.

- Wash hands with soap after handling reptiles, birds, or baby chicks, and after contact with pet feces.

- Avoid direct or even indirect contact between reptiles (turtles, iguanas, other lizards, snakes) and infants or immuno-compromised persons.

- Don't work with raw poultry or meat, and an infant (e.g., feed, change diaper) at the same time.

- Mother's milk is the safest food for young infants. Breast-feeding prevents salmonellosis and many other health problems.

a stool test showing that they are no longer carrying the *Salmonella* bacterium before they return to work.

People should wash their hands after contact with animal feces. Because reptiles are particularly likely to have *Salmonella*, and it can contaminate their skin, everyone should immediately wash their hands after handling reptiles. Reptiles (including turtles) are not appropriate pets for small children and should not be in the same house as an infant. *Salmonella* carried in the intestines of chicks and ducklings contaminates their environment and the entire surface of the animal. Children can be exposed to the bacteria by simply holding, cuddling, or kissing the birds. Children should not handle baby chicks or other young birds. Everyone should immediately wash their hands after touching birds, including baby chicks and ducklings, or their environment.

Some prevention steps occur everyday without you thinking about it. Pasteurization of milk and treatment of municipal water supplies are highly effective prevention measures that have been in place for decades. In the 1970s, small pet turtles were a common source of salmonellosis in the United States, so in 1975, the sale of small turtles was banned in this country. However, in 2008, they were still being sold, and cases of *Salmonella* associated with pet turtles have been reported. Improvements in farm animal hygiene, in slaughter plant practices, and in vegetable and fruit harvesting and packing operations may help prevent salmonellosis caused by contaminated foods. Better education of food industry workers in basic food safety and restaurant inspection procedures may prevent cross-contamination and other food handling errors that can lead to outbreaks. Wider use of pasteurized egg in restaurants, hospitals, and nursing homes is an important prevention measure. In the future, irradiation or other treatments may greatly reduce contamination of raw meat.

Section 48.5

Shigellosis

Text in this section is excerpted from "*Shigella*—Shigellosis," Centers for Disease Control and Prevention (CDC), April 2, 2015.

Definitions and Symptoms

What is **Shigella?**

Shigellosis is a diarrheal disease caused by a group of bacteria called *Shigella*. *Shigella* causes about 500,000 cases of diarrhea in the United States annually. There are four different species of *Shigella*:

- *Shigella sonnei* (the most common species in the United States)
- *Shigella flexneri*
- *Shigella boydii*
- *Shigella dysenteriae*

S. dysenteriae and *S. boydii* are rare in the United States, though they continue to be important causes of disease in the developing world. *Shigella dysenteriae* type 1 can cause deadly epidemics.

What are the symptoms of **Shigella**?

Symptoms of shigellosis typically start 1–2 days after exposure and include:

- Diarrhea (sometimes bloody)
- Fever
- Abdominal pain
- Tenesmus (a painful sensation of needing to pass stools even when bowels are empty)

How long after infection do symptoms appear?

Symptoms of shigellosis generally begin 1 to 2 days after becoming infected with the bacteria.

How long will symptoms last?

In persons with healthy immune systems, symptoms usually last about 5 to 7 days. Persons with diarrhea usually recover completely, although it may be several months before their bowel habits are entirely normal. Once someone has had shigellosis, they are not likely to get infected with that specific type again for at least several years. However, they can still get infected with other types of *Shigella*.

Can there be any complications from **Shigella** *infections*?

Possible complications from *Shigella* infections include:

- **Post-infectious arthritis.** About 2% of persons who are infected with *Shigella flexneri* later develop pains in their joints, irritation of the eyes, and painful urination. This is called post-infectious arthritis. It can last for months or years, and can lead to chronic arthritis. Post-infectious arthritis is caused by a reaction to *Shigella* infection that happens only in people who are genetically predisposed to it.

- **Blood stream infections.** Although rare, blood stream infections are caused either by *Shigella* organisms or by other germs in the gut that get into the bloodstream when the lining of the intestines is damaged during shigellosis. Blood stream infections are most common among patients with weakened immune systems, such as those with HIV, cancer, or severe malnutrition.

- **Seizures.** Generalized seizures have been reported occasionally among young children with shigellosis, and usually resolve without treatment. Children who experience seizures while infected with *Shigella* typically have a high fever or abnormal blood electrolytes (salts), but it is not well understood why the seizures occur.

- **Hemolytic-uremic syndrome or HUS.** HUS occurs when bacteria enter the digestive system and produce a toxin that destroys red blood cells. Patients with HUS often have bloody diarrhea. HUS is only associated with Shiga-toxin producing *Shigella*, which is found most commonly in *Shigella dysenteriae*.

Diagnosis and Testing

How can Shigella *infections be diagnosed?*

Many different kinds of germs can cause diarrhea, so establishing the cause will help guide treatment. Healthcare providers can order laboratory tests to identify *Shigella* in the stools of an infected person. The laboratory can also do special tests to determine which antibiotics, if any, would be best to treat the infection.

Treatment

How can Shigella *infections be treated?*

Diarrhea caused by *Shigella* usually resolves without antibiotic treatment in 5 to 7 days. People with mild shigellosis may need only fluids and rest. Bismuth subsalicylate (e.g., Pepto-Bismol®) may be helpful but medications that cause the gut to slow down, such as loperamide (e.g., Imodium®) or diphenoxylate with atropine (e.g., Lomotil®), should be avoided. Antibiotics are useful for severe cases of shigellosis because they can reduce the duration of symptoms. However, *Shigella* is often resistant to antibiotics. If you require antibiotic treatment for shigellosis, your healthcare provider can culture your stool and determine which antibiotics are likely to work. Tell your healthcare provider if you do not get better within a couple of days after starting antibiotics. He or she can do additional tests to learn whether your strain of *Shigella* is resistant to the antibiotic you are taking.

Antibiotic Resistance

Is antibiotic resistance a problem with Shigella?

In 2013, CDC declared antibiotic-resistant *Shigella* an urgent threat in the United States. Resistance to traditional first-line antibiotics like ampicillin and trimethoprim-sulfamethoxazole is common among *Shigella* globally, and resistance to some other important antibiotics is increasing. While travelers to the developing world are at particular risk of acquiring antibiotic-resistant shigellosis, outbreaks of shigellosis resistant to ciprofloxacin or azithromycin—the two antibiotics most commonly used to treat shigellosis—have been reported recently within the United States and other industrialized countries. About 27,000 *Shigella* infections in the United States every year are resistant to one or both of these antibiotics. When pathogens are resistant to common antibiotic medications, patients may need to be treated with medications that may be less effective, but more toxic and expensive.

How will I know if I have an antibiotic-resistant Shigella *infection?*

Shigella infections are diagnosed through laboratory testing of stool specimens (feces). Healthcare providers can order tests to check which antibiotics are likely to help treat a particular patient's infection. If you were treated with antibiotics for shigellosis but do not feel better within a couple of days, tell your healthcare provider. You may need additional tests to check whether your *Shigella* strain is resistant to the antibiotics.

What should I do if I have an antibiotic-resistant Shigella *infection?*

Please follow the advice of your healthcare provider. If you do not feel better within a couple of days after beginning treatments, tell your healthcare provider. Protect others by washing your hands carefully with soap after using the toilet, and wait until your diarrhea has stopped before preparing food for others, swimming, or having sex.

How can we reduce the spread of antibiotic-resistant Shigella?

Reducing the spread of antibiotic-resistant *Shigella* requires a multi-pronged approach: preventing infections, tracking resistance, improving antibiotic use, and developing new treatments.

Transmission

How is **Shigella** *spread?*

Shigella germs are present in the stools of infected persons while they have diarrhea and for up to a week or two after the diarrhea has gone away. *Shigella* is very contagious; exposure to even a tiny amount of contaminated fecal matter—too small to see—can cause infection. Transmission of *Shigella* occurs when people put something in their mouths or swallow something that has come into contact with stool of a person infected with *Shigella*. This can happen when:

- Contaminated hands touch your food or mouth. Hands can become contaminated through a variety of activities, such as touching surfaces (e.g., toys, bathroom fixtures, changing tables, diaper pails) that have been contaminated by stool from an infected person. Hands can also become contaminated with *Shigella* while changing the diaper of an infected child or caring for an infected person.

- Eating food contaminated with *Shigella*. Food may become contaminated if food handlers have shigellosis. Produce can become contaminated if growing fields contain human sewage. Flies can breed in infected feces and then contaminate food when they land on it.

- Swallowing recreational (for example lake or river water while swimming) or drinking water that was contaminated by infected fecal matter.

- Exposure to feces through sexual contact.

Prevention

How can I reduce my risk of getting shigellosis?

Currently, there is no vaccine to prevent shigellosis. However, you can reduce your risk of getting shigellosis by:

- Carefully washing your hands with soap during key times:
  - Before eating.
  - After changing a diaper or helping to clean another person who has defecated (pooped).

- If you care for a child in diapers who has shigellosis, promptly discard the soiled diapers in a lidded, lined garbage can, and wash your hands and the child's hands carefully with soap and water immediately after changing the diapers. Any leaks or spills of diaper contents should be cleaned up immediately.

- Safe & Healthy Diapering in the Home
- Diaper-Changing Steps for Childcare Settings

- Avoid swallowing water from ponds, lakes, or untreated swimming pools.

- When traveling internationally, follow food and water precautions strictly and wash hands with soap frequently.

- Avoid sexual activity with those who have diarrhea or who recently recovered from diarrhea.

I was diagnosed with shigellosis. What can I do to avoid giving it to other people?

- Wash your hands with soap carefully and frequently, especially after using the toilet.

- Do not prepare food for others while you are sick. After you get better, wash your hands carefully with soap before preparing food for others.

- For those who work in healthcare, food service, or childcare facilities should not prepare or handle food for others until their local health department has authorized them to return to work. Improvements in worker sick leave policies and providing adequate hygiene facilities and education for food service workers may prevent shigellosis caused by contaminated foods.

- Avoid swimming until you have fully recovered.

- Don't have sex until several days after you no longer have diarrhea.

My child was diagnosed with shigellosis. How can I keep others from catching it?

- Supervise handwashing of toddlers and small children after they use the toilet. Wash infants' hands with soap and water after diaper changes.

- Dispose of soiled diapers properly, and clean diaper changing areas after using them.

- Safe & Healthy Diapering in the Home

- Keep the child out of childcare and group play settings while ill with diarrhea, and follow the guidance of your local health department about returning your child to his or her childcare facility.

- Avoid taking your child swimming or to group water play venues until after he or she has fully recovered.

Should an infected person be excluded from school or work?

School and work exclusion policies differ by local jurisdiction. Check with your local or state health department to learn more about the laws where you live. It is critical to practice good hand-washing after changing diapers, after using the toilet, and before preparing or eating food to prevent the spread of these and many other infections.

What else can be done to prevent shigellosis?

- Providing municipal water service, this may be lacking in many lower income countries. Making municipal water supplies available and safe and treating sewage are highly effective prevention measures that have been in place for many years.

- Following these guidelines to make your food safer to eat. People with shigellosis should not prepare food or drinks for others until they are well. Food service workers should not prepare or handle food for others until their local health department has authorized them to return to work. Improvements in worker sick leave policies and providing adequate hygiene facilities and education for food service workers may prevent shigellosis caused by contaminated foods.

- At swimming beaches, providing enough bathrooms and hand-washing stations with soap near the swimming area helps keep the water from becoming contaminated.

What can be done if an outbreak of **Shigella** occurs in the childcare setting?

- Exclude any child with diarrhea from the childcare setting until the diarrhea has stopped.

  - Children who have recently recovered from shigellosis can be grouped together in one classroom (cohorted) to minimize exposing uninfected children and staff to *Shigella*.

- Assign separate staff to change diapers and prepare or serve food.

- Reassign adults with diarrhea to jobs that minimize opportunities for spreading infection (for example, administrative work instead of food preparation).

- Establish, implement, and enforce policies on water-play and swimming that:

  - Exclude children ill with diarrhea from water-play and swimming activities.

  - Exclude children diagnosed with *Shigella* from water-play and swimming activities for an additional week after their diarrhea has resolved.

  - Have children and staff wash their hands before using water tables.

  - Have children and staff shower with soap before swimming in the water.

    - If a child is too young to shower independently, have staff wash the child, particularly the rear end, with soap and water.

  - Take frequent bathroom breaks or check their diapers often.

- Change children's diapers in a diaper-changing area or bathroom and not by the water.

  - Discourage children from getting the water in their mouths and swallowing it.

  - Prohibit the use of temporary inflatable or rigid fill-and-drain swimming pools and slides because they can spread germs in childcare facilities.

Section 48.6

Cryptosporidium *Infection*

Text in this section is excerpted from "Parasites—*Cryptosporidium*
(also known as 'Crypto')," Centers for Disease Control and Prevention
(CDC), April 20, 2015.

General Questions

What is cryptosporidiosis?

Cryptosporidiosis is a disease that causes watery diarrhea. It is
caused by microscopic germs—parasites called *Cryptosporidium*. *Cryptosporidium*, or 'Crypto' for short, can be found in water, food, soil or
on surfaces or dirty hands that have been contaminated with the feces
of humans or animals infected with the parasite. During 2001–2010,
Crypto was the leading cause of waterborne disease outbreaks, linked
to recreational water in the United States. The parasite is found in
every region of the United States and throughout the world.

How is cryptosporidiosis spread?

Crypto lives in the gut of infected humans or animals. An infected
person or animal sheds Crypto parasites in their poop. An infected
person can shed 10,000,000 to 100,000,000 Crypto germs in a single
bowel movement. Shedding of Crypto in poop begins when symptoms
like diarrhea begin and can last for weeks after symptoms stop. Swallowing as few as 10 Crypto germs can cause infection.

Crypto can be spread by:

- Swallowing recreational water (for example, the water in swimming pools, fountains, lakes, rivers) contaminated with Crypto

  - Crypto's high tolerance to chlorine enables the parasite to
    survive for long periods of time in chlorinated drinking and
    swimming pool water

- Drinking untreated water from a lake or river that is contaminated with Crypto

- Swallowing water, ice, or beverages contaminated with poop from infected humans or animals

- Eating undercooked food or drinking unpasteurized/raw apple cider or milk that gets contaminated with Crypto

- Touching your mouth with contaminated hands

  - Hands can become contaminated through a variety of activities, such as touching surfaces or objects (e.g., toys, bathroom fixtures, changing tables, diaper pails) that have been contaminated by poop from an infected person, changing diapers, caring for an infected person, and touching an infected animal

- Exposure to poop from an infected person through oral-anal sexual contact

Crypto is **not** spread through contact with blood.

What are the symptoms of cryptosporidiosis, when do they begin, and how long do they last?

Symptoms of Crypto generally begin 2 to 10 days (average 7 days) after becoming infected with the parasite. Symptoms include:

- Watery diarrhea
- Stomach cramps or pain
- Dehydration
- Nausea
- Vomiting
- Fever
- Weight loss

Symptoms usually last about 1 to 2 weeks (with a range of a few days to 4 or more weeks) in people with healthy immune systems.

The most common symptom of cryptosporidiosis is **watery diarrhea**. Some people with Crypto will have no symptoms at all.

Who is most at risk for cryptosporidiosis?

People who are most likely to become infected with *Cryptosporidium* include:

- Children who attend childcare centers, including diaper-aged children

- Childcare workers

- Parents of infected children

- People who take care of other people with Crypto

- International travelers

- Backpackers, hikers, and campers who drink unfiltered, untreated water

- People who drink from untreated shallow, unprotected wells

- People, including swimmers, who swallow water from contaminated sources

- People who handle infected calves or other ruminants like sheep

- People exposed to human poop through sexual contact

Contaminated water might include water that has not been boiled or filtered, as well as contaminated recreational water sources (e.g., swimming pools, lakes, rivers, ponds, and streams). Several community-wide outbreaks have been linked to drinking tap water or recreational water contaminated with *Cryptosporidium*. Crypto's high tolerance to chlorine enables the parasite to survive for long periods of time in chlorinated drinking and swimming pool water. This means anyone swallowing contaminated water could get ill.

Note: Although Crypto can infect all people, some groups are likely to develop more serious illness.

- **Young children and pregnant women** may be more likely to get dehydrated because of their diarrhea so they should drink plenty of fluids while ill.

- People with **severely weakened immune systems** are at risk for more serious disease. Symptoms may be more severe and could lead to serious or life-threatening illness. Examples of people with weakened immune systems include those with AIDS; those with inherited diseases that affect the immune system; and cancer and transplant patients who are taking certain immunosuppressive drugs.

What should I do if I think I might have cryptosporidiosis?

For diarrhea whose cause has not been determined, the following actions may help relieve symptoms: Individuals who have health concerns should talk to their healthcare provider.

- Drink plenty of fluids to remain well hydrated and avoid dehydration. Serious health problems can occur if the body does not maintain proper fluid levels. For some people, diarrhea can be severe resulting in hospitalization due to dehydration.

- Maintain a well-balanced diet. Doing so may help speed recovery.

- Avoid beverages that contain caffeine, such as tea, coffee, and many soft drinks.

- Avoid alcohol, as it can lead to dehydration.

Contact your healthcare provider if you suspect that you have cryptosporidiosis.

How is cryptosporidiosis diagnosed?

Cryptosporidiosis is a diarrheal disease that is spread through contact with the stool of an infected person or animal.

The disease is diagnosed by examining stool samples. People infected with Crypto can shed the parasite irregularly in their poop (for example, one day they shed parasite, the next day they don't, the third day they do) so patients may need to give three samples collected on three different days to help make sure that a negative test result is accurate and really means they do not have Crypto. Healthcare providers should specifically request testing for Crypto. Routine ova and parasite testing does not normally include Crypto testing.

What is the treatment for cryptosporidiosis?

Most people with healthy immune systems will recover from cryptosporidiosis without treatment. The following actions may help relieve symptoms. Individuals who have health concerns should talk to their healthcare provider.

- Drink plenty of fluids to remain well hydrated and avoid dehydration. Serious health problems can occur if the body does not maintain proper fluid levels. For some people, diarrhea can be severe resulting in hospitalization due to dehydration.

- Maintain a well-balanced diet. Doing so may help speed recovery.

- Avoid beverages that contain caffeine, such as tea, coffee, and many soft drinks.

- Avoid alcohol, as it can lead to dehydration.

Over-the-counter anti-diarrheal medicine might help slow down diarrhea, but a healthcare provider should be consulted before such medicine is taken.

A drug called nitazoxanide has been FDA-approved for treatment of diarrhea caused by *Cryptosporidium* in people with healthy immune systems and is available by prescription. Consult with your healthcare provider for more information about potential advantages and disadvantages of taking nitazoxanide.

Note: Infants, young children, and pregnant women may be more likely than others to suffer from dehydration. Losing a lot of fluids from diarrhea can be dangerous—and especially life-threatening in infants. These people should drink extra fluids when they are sick. Severe dehydration may require hospitalization for treatment with fluids given through your vein (intravenous or IV fluids). If you are pregnant or a parent and you suspect you or your child are severely dehydrated, contact a healthcare provider about fluid replacement options.

How should I clean my house to help prevent the spread of cryptosporidiosis?

No cleaning method is guaranteed to be completely effective against Crypto. However, you can lower the chance of spreading Crypto by taking the following precautions:

- **Wash linens, clothing, dishwasher—or dryer—safe soft toys, etc. soiled with poop or vomit as soon as possible.**

    - Flush excess vomit or poop on clothes or objects down the toilet.

    - Use laundry detergent, and wash in hot water: 113°F or hotter for at least 20 minutes or at 122°F or hotter for at least 5 minutes.

    - Machine dry on the highest heat setting.

- For other household object and surfaces (for example, diaper-change areas):

    - Remove all visible poop.

- Clean with soap and water.

- Let dry completely for at least 4 hours.

  - If possible, expose to direct sunlight during the 4 hours.

- Wash your hands with soap and water after cleaning objects or surfaces that could be contaminated with Crypto.

Note: The best way to prevent the spread of *Cryptosporidium* in the home is by practicing good hygiene. Wash your hands frequently with soap and water, especially after using the toilet, after changing diapers, and before eating or preparing food. **Alcohol-based hand sanitizers are not effective against Crypto.**

Section 48.7

Giardiasis

Text in this section is excerpted from "Parasites—*Giardia*," Centers for Disease Control and Prevention (CDC), July 21, 2015.

What is giardiasis?

Giardiasis is a diarrheal disease caused by the microscopic parasite *Giardia*. A parasite is an organism that feeds off of another to survive. Once a person or animal (for example, cats, dogs, cattle, deer, and beavers) has been infected with *Giardia*, the parasite lives in the intestines and is passed in feces (poop). Once outside the body, Giardia can sometimes survive for weeks or months. *Giardia* can be found within every region of the U.S. and around the world.

How do you get giardiasis and how is it spread?

Giardiasis can be spread by:

- Swallowing *Giardia* picked up from surfaces (such as bathroom handles, changing tables, diaper pails, or toys) that contain feces (poop) from an infected person or animal

- Drinking water or using ice made from water sources where *Giardia* may live (for example, untreated or improperly treated water from lakes, streams, or wells)

- Swallowing water while swimming or playing in water where *Giardia* may live, especially in lakes, rivers, springs, ponds, and streams

- Eating uncooked food that contains *Giardia* organisms

- Having contact with someone who is ill with giardiasis

- Traveling to countries where *giardiasis* is common

Anything that comes into contact with feces (poop) from infected humans or animals can become contaminated with the *Giardia* parasite. People become infected when they swallow the parasite. It is not possible to become infected through contact with blood.

What are the symptoms of giardiasis?

Giardia infection can cause a variety of intestinal symptoms, which include:

- Diarrhea

- Gas or flatulence

- Greasy stool that can float

- Stomach or abdominal cramps

- Upset stomach or nausea

- Dehydration

These symptoms may also lead to weight loss. Some people with *Giardia* infection have no symptoms at all.

How long after infection do symptoms appear?

Symptoms of giardiasis normally begin 1 to 3 weeks after becoming infected.

How long will symptoms last?

In otherwise healthy people, symptoms of giardiasis may last 2 to 6 weeks. Occasionally, symptoms last longer. Medications can help decrease the amount of time symptoms last.

Who is most at risk of getting giardiasis?

Though giardiasis is commonly thought of as a camping or back-packing-related disease and is sometimes called 'Beaver Fever,' anyone can get giardiasis. People more likely to become infected include:

- Children in childcare settings, especially diaper-aged children

- Close contacts of people with giardiasis (for example, people living in the same household) or people who care for those sick with giardiasis

- People who drink water or use ice made from places where *Giardia* may live (for example, untreated or improperly treated water from lakes, streams, or wells)

- Backpackers, hikers, and campers who drink unsafe water or who do not practice good hygiene (for example, proper handwashing)

- People who swallow water while swimming and playing in recreational water where *Giardia* may live, especially in lakes, rivers, springs, ponds, and streams

- International travelers

- People exposed to human feces (poop) through sexual contact

What should I do if I think I may have giardiasis?

Contact your healthcare provider.

How is giardiasis diagnosed?

Your healthcare provider will ask you to submit stool (poop) samples to see if you are infected. Because testing for giardiasis can be difficult, you may be asked to submit several stool specimens collected over several days.

What is the treatment for giardiasis?

Many prescription drugs are available to treat giardiasis. Although the *Giardia* parasite can infect all people, infants and pregnant women may be more likely to experience dehydration from the diarrhea caused by giardiasis. To prevent dehydration, infants and pregnant women should drink a lot of fluids while ill. Dehydration can be life threatening for infants, so it is especially important that parents talk to their healthcare providers about treatment options for their infants.

My child does not have diarrhea, but was recently diagnosed as having a Giardia infection. My healthcare provider says treatment is not necessary. Is this correct?

Your child does not usually need treatment if he or she has no symptoms. However, there are a few exceptions. If your child does not have diarrhea, but does have other symptoms such as nausea or upset stomach, tiredness, weight loss, or a lack of hunger, you and your healthcare provider may need to think about treatment. The same is true if many family members are ill, or if a family member is pregnant and unable to take the most effective medications to treat *Giardia*. Contact your healthcare provider for specific treatment recommendations.

What can I do to prevent and control giardiasis?

To prevent and control infection with the *Giardia* parasite, it is important to:

- Practice good hygiene
- Avoid water (drinking or recreational) that may be contaminated
- Avoid eating food that may be contaminated
- Prevent contact and contamination with feces (poop) during sex

Can I get giardiasis from my pet?

The risk of humans acquiring *Giardia* infection from dogs or cats is small. The exact type of *Giardia* that infects humans is usually not the same type that infects dogs and cats.

Chapter 49

Whipple Disease

What is Whipple disease?

Whipple disease is a rare bacterial infection that primarily affects the small intestine. The infection may spread to any organ in the body; however, it more commonly affects the

- joints
- central nervous system, which includes the brain, the spinal cord, and nerves located throughout the body
- heart
- eyes
- lungs

Left untreated, Whipple disease gets worse and is usually life threatening.

What is the small intestine?

The small intestine is part of the upper gastrointestinal (GI) tract and is a tube-shaped organ between the stomach and large intestine. The upper GI tract also includes the mouth, esophagus, stomach, and duodenum, or the first part of the small intestine.

Text in this chapter is excerpted from "Whipple Disease," National Institute of Diabetes and Digestive and Kidney Diseases (NIDDK), July 2014.

Most food digestion and nutrient absorption take place in the small intestine. The small intestine measures about 20 feet long and includes the duodenum, jejunum, and ileum. Villi—tiny, fingerlike protrusions—line the inside of the small intestine. Villi normally let nutrients from food be absorbed through the walls of the small intestine into the bloodstream.

What causes Whipple disease?

Bacteria called *Tropheryma whipplei (T. whipplei)* cause Whipple disease. *T. whipplei* infection can cause internal sores, also called lesions, and thickening of tissues in the small intestine. The villi take on an abnormal, clublike appearance and the damaged intestinal lining does not properly absorb nutrients, causing diarrhea and malnutrition. Diarrhea is frequent, loose, and watery bowel movements. Malnutrition is a condition that develops when the body does not get the right amount of vitamins, minerals, and other nutrients it needs to maintain healthy tissues and organ function. Over time, the infection spreads to other parts of the person's body and will damage other organs.

Who is more likely to develop Whipple disease?

Anyone can get Whipple disease. However, it is more common in Caucasian men between 40 and 60 years old. Whipple disease is rare and affects fewer than one in 1 million people. The condition appears to be more common in farmers and other people who work outdoors and have frequent contact with soil and sewage wastewater.

Experts are not sure how *T. whipplei* infects people; however, scientists have noted

- the bacteria are found in soil and sewage wastewater

- the bacteria are also found in people who are carriers of the disease—healthy individuals who have the bacteria, yet do not get sick

- Whipple disease is not transmitted from person to person

Some people may be more likely to develop Whipple disease because of genetic factors—related to genes, or traits passed from parent to child—that influence the body's immune system. The immune system normally protects people from infection by identifying and destroying bacteria, viruses, and other potentially harmful foreign substances.

What are the signs and symptoms of Whipple disease?

Signs and symptoms of Whipple disease can vary widely from person to person. The most common symptoms of Whipple disease are

- diarrhea

- weight loss caused by malabsorption

A person may not have diarrhea. Instead, other signs and symptoms of Whipple disease may appear, such as

- abnormal yellow and white patches on the lining of the small intestine

- joint pain, with or without inflammation, that may appear off and on for years before other symptoms

- fatty or bloody stools

- abdominal cramps or bloating felt between the chest and groin

- enlarged lymph nodes—the small glands that make infection-fighting white blood cells

- loss of appetite

- fever

- fatigue, or feeling tired

- weakness

- darkening of the skin

People with a more advanced stage of Whipple disease may have neurologic symptoms—those related to the central nervous system—such as

- vision problems.

- memory problems or personality changes.

- facial numbness.

- headaches.

- muscle weakness or twitching.

- difficulty walking.

- hearing loss or ringing in the ears.

- dementia—the name for a group of symptoms caused by disorders that affect the brain. People with dementia may not be able to think well enough to do normal activities such as getting dressed or eating.

Less common symptoms of Whipple disease may include

- chronic cough.

- chest pain.

- pericarditis—inflammation of the membrane surrounding the heart.

- heart failure—a long-lasting condition in which the heart cannot pump enough blood to meet the body's needs. Heart failure does not mean the heart suddenly stops working.

What are the complications of Whipple disease?

People with Whipple disease may have complications caused by malnutrition, which is due to damaged villi in the small intestine. As a result of delayed diagnosis or treatment, people may experience the following complications in other areas of the body:

- long-lasting nutritional deficiencies

- heart and heart valve damage

- brain damage

A person with Whipple disease may experience a relapse—a return of symptoms. Relapse can happen years after treatment and requires repeat treatments.

How is Whipple disease diagnosed?

A health care provider may use several tests and exams to diagnose Whipple disease, including the following:

- medical and family history

- physical exam

- blood tests

- upper GI endoscopy and enteroscopy

A patient may be referred to a gastroenterologist—a doctor who specializes in digestive diseases.

A health care provider may first try to rule out more common conditions with similar symptoms, including

- inflammatory rheumatic disease—characterized by inflammation and loss of function in one or more connecting or supporting structures of the body.

- celiac disease—a digestive disease that damages the small intestine and interferes with the absorption of nutrients from food. People who have celiac disease cannot tolerate gluten, a protein in wheat, rye, and barley.

- neurologic diseases—disorders of the central nervous system.

- intra-abdominal lymphoma—abdominal cancer in part of the immune system called the lymphatic system.

- *Mycobacterium avium* complex—an infection that affects people with AIDS.

Medical and Family History

Taking a family and medical history can help a health care provider diagnose Whipple disease.

Physical Exam

A physical exam may help diagnose Whipple disease. During a physical exam, a health care provider usually

- examines a patient's body

- uses a stethoscope to listen to sounds related to the abdomen

- taps on specific areas of the patient's body checking for pain or tenderness

Blood Tests

A technician or nurse draws a blood sample during an office visit or at a commercial facility and sends the sample to a lab for analysis. The health care provider may use blood tests to check for

- malabsorption. When the damaged villi do not absorb certain nutrients from food, the body has a shortage of protein, calories, and vitamins. Blood tests can show shortages of protein, calories, and vitamins in the body.

- abnormal levels of electrolytes. Electrolytes—chemicals in body fluids, including sodium, potassium, magnesium, and chloride—regulate a person's nerve and muscle function. A patient who has malabsorption or a lot of diarrhea may lose fluids and electrolytes, causing an imbalance in the body.

- anemia. Anemia is a condition in which the body has fewer red blood cells than normal. A patient with Whipple disease does not absorb the proper nutrients to make enough red blood cells in the body, leading to anemia.

- *T. whipplei* DNA. Although not yet approved, rapid polymerase chain reaction diagnostic tests have been developed to detect *T. whipplei* DNA and may be useful in diagnosis.

Upper Gastrointestinal Endoscopy and Enteroscopy

An upper GI endoscopy and enteroscopy are procedures that use an endoscope—a small, flexible tube with a light—to see the upper GI tract. A health care provider performs these tests at a hospital or an outpatient center. The health care provider carefully feeds the endoscope down the esophagus and into the stomach and duodenum.

Once the endoscope is in the duodenum, the health care provider will use smaller tools and a smaller scope to see more of the small intestine. These additional procedures may include

- push enteroscopy, which uses a long endoscope to examine the upper portion of the small intestine.

- double-balloon enteroscopy, which uses balloons to help move the endoscope through the entire small intestine.

- capsule enteroscopy, during which the patient swallows a capsule containing a tiny camera. As the capsule passes through the GI tract, the camera will transmit images to a video monitor. Using this procedure, the health care provider can examine the entire digestive tract.

A small camera mounted on the endoscope transmits a video image to a monitor, allowing close examination of the intestinal lining. A health care provider may give a patient a liquid anesthetic to gargle or may spray anesthetic on the back of the patient's throat. A health care provider will place an intravenous (IV) needle in a vein in the arm or hand to administer sedation. Sedatives help patients stay relaxed and comfortable. The test can show changes in the lining of the small intestine that can occur with Whipple disease.

The health care provider can use tiny tools passed through the endoscope to perform biopsies. A biopsy is a procedure that involves taking a piece of tissue for examination with a microscope. A pathologist—a doctor who specializes in examining tissues to diagnose diseases—examines the tissue from the stomach lining in a lab. The pathologist applies a special stain to the tissue and examines it for *T. whipplei*-infected cells with a microscope. Once the pathologist completes the examination of the tissue, he or she sends a report to the gastroenterologist for review.

How is Whipple disease treated?

The health care provider prescribes antibiotics to destroy the *T. whipplei* bacteria and treat Whipple disease. Health care providers choose antibiotics that treat the infection in the small intestine and cross the blood-brain barrier—a layer of tissue around the brain. Using antibiotics that cross the blood-brain barrier ensures destruction of any bacteria that may have entered the patient's brain and central nervous system.

The health care provider usually prescribes IV antibiotics for the first 2 weeks of treatment. Most patients feel relief from symptoms within the first week or two. A nurse or technician places an IV in the patient's arm to give the antibiotics. IV antibiotics used to treat Whipple disease may include

- ceftriaxone (Rocephin)

- meropenem (Merrem I.V.)

- penicillin G (Pfizerpen)

- streptomycin (Streptomycin)

After a patient completes the IV antibiotics, the health care provider will prescribe long-term oral antibiotics. Patients receive long-term treatment—at least 1 to 2 years—to cure the infection anywhere in the body. Oral antibiotics may include

- trimethoprim/sulfamethoxazole (Septra, Bactrim)—a combination antibiotic

- doxycycline (Vibramycin)

Patients should finish the prescribed course of antibiotics to ensure the medication destroyed all *T. whipplei* bacteria in the body. Patients who feel better may still have the bacteria in the small intestine or other areas of the body for 1 to 2 years. A health care provider will monitor the patient closely, repeat the blood tests, and repeat the upper GI endoscopy with biopsy during and after treatment to determine whether *T. whipplei* is still present.

People may relapse during or after treatment. A health care provider will prescribe additional or new antibiotics if a relapse occurs. Some people will relapse years after treatment, so it is important for patients to schedule routine follow-ups with the health care provider. Most patients have good outcomes with an early diagnosis and complete treatment.

Health care providers treat patients with neurologic symptoms at diagnosis or during relapse more aggressively. Treatment may include

- a combination of antibiotics
- hydroxychloroquine (Plaquenil)—an antimalarial medication
- weekly injections of interferon gamma—a substance made by the body that activates the immune system
- corticosteroids—medications that decrease inflammation

How can Whipple disease be prevented?

Experts have not yet found a way to prevent Whipple disease.

Eating, Diet, and Nutrition

A person with Whipple disease and malabsorption may need

- a diet high in calories and protein
- vitamins
- nutritional supplements

People with Whipple disease should discuss their nutritional needs with a dietitian or other health care professional and meet regularly with him or her to monitor changing nutritional needs.

Chapter 50

Rotavirus

Overview

Rotavirus is a contagious virus that can cause gastroenteritis (inflammation of the stomach and intestines). Symptoms include severe watery diarrhea, often with vomiting, fever, and abdominal pain. Infants and young children are most likely to get rotavirus disease. They can become severely dehydrated and need to be hospitalized and can even die.

Symptoms

Rotavirus disease is most common in infants and young children. However, older children and adults and can also become infected with rotavirus. Once a person has been exposed to rotavirus, it takes about 2 days for the symptoms to appear.

Children who get infected may have severe watery diarrhea, often with vomiting, fever, and abdominal pain. Vomiting and watery diarrhea can last from 3 to 8 days. Additional symptoms include loss of appetite and dehydration (loss of body fluids), which can be especially harmful for infants and young children.

Symptoms of dehydration include

- decrease in urination

Text in this chapter is excerpted from "Rotavirus," Centers for Disease Control and Prevention (CDC), May 12, 2014.

- dry mouth and throat

- feeling dizzy when standing up

A dehydrated child may also cry with few or no tears and be unusually sleepy or fussy.

Adults who get rotavirus disease tend to have milder symptoms.

Children, even those that are vaccinated, may develop rotavirus disease more than once. That is because neither natural infection with rotavirus nor rotavirus vaccination provides full immunity (protection) from future infections. Usually a person's first infection with rotavirus causes the most severe symptoms.

Transmission

Rotavirus spreads easily among infants and young children. Children can spread the virus both before and after they become sick with diarrhea. They can also pass rotavirus to family members and other people with whom they have close contact.

People who are infected with rotavirus shed rotavirus (passed from a person's body into the environment) in their feces (stool). They shed the virus most when they are sick and during the first 3 days after they recover from rotavirus disease.

The virus spreads by the fecal-oral route; this means that the virus must be shed by an infected person and then enter a susceptible person's mouth to cause infection. Rotavirus can be spread by contaminated

- Hands

- Objects (toys, surfaces)

- Food

- Water

Children are most likely to get rotavirus in the winter and spring (December through June).

Prevention

Rotavirus can spread easily. Good hygiene (handwashing) and cleanliness are important but are not enough to control the spread of the disease.

Rotavirus vaccines are very effective in preventing rotavirus gastroenteritis and the accompanying diarrhea and other symptoms. CDC recommends routine vaccination of infants with either of the two available vaccines:

- RotaTeq®(RV5), which is given in 3 doses at ages 2 months, 4 months, and 6 months; or

- Rotarix®(RV1), which is given in 2 doses at ages 2 months and 4 months.

Both rotavirus vaccines are given orally. The vaccines are very effective (85% to 98%) in preventing severe rotavirus disease in infants and young children, including rotavirus infection that requires hospitalization.

Rotavirus vaccines will not prevent diarrhea or vomiting caused by other viruses or pathogens.

Treatment

There is no antiviral drug to treat rotavirus infection. Antibiotic drugs will not help because antibiotics fight against bacteria not viruses.

Rotavirus infection can cause severe vomiting and diarrhea. This can lead to dehydration (loss of body fluids). During rotavirus infection, infants and young children, older adults, and people with other illnesses are most at risk becoming dehydrated.

Symptoms of dehydration include

- decrease in urination

- dry mouth and throat

- feeling dizzy when standing up

A dehydrated child may also cry with few or no tears and be unusually sleepy or fussy.

The best way to protect against dehydration is to drink plenty of liquids. Oral rehydration solutions that you can get over the counter in U.S. food and drug stores are most helpful for mild dehydration. Severe dehydration may require hospitalization for treatment with intravenous (IV) fluids, which are given to patients directly through their veins. If you think you or someone you are caring for is severely dehydrated, contact your doctor.

Chapter 51

Norovirus

Overview

Norovirus is a very contagious virus. You can get norovirus from an infected person, contaminated food or water, or by touching contaminated surfaces. The virus causes your stomach or intestines or both to get inflamed (acute gastroenteritis). This leads you to have stomach pain, nausea, and diarrhea and to throw up.

Anyone can be infected with norovirus and get sick. Also, you can have norovirus illness many times in your life. Norovirus illness can be serious, especially for young children and older adults.

Norovirus is the most common cause of acute gastroenteritis in the United States. Each year, it causes 19-21 million illnesses and contributes to 56,000–71,000 hospitalizations and 570–800 deaths. Norovirus is also the most common cause of foodborne-disease outbreaks in the United States.

The best way to help prevent norovirus is to practice proper hand washing and general cleanliness.

Symptoms

Norovirus causes inflammation of the stomach or intestines or both. This is called acute gastroenteritis.

Text in this chapter is excerpted from "Norovirus," Centers for Disease Control and Prevention (CDC), July 26, 2013.

Norovirus Has Many Names

You may hear norovirus illness called 'food poisoning' or 'stomach flu.' Food poisoning can be caused by noroviruses. But, other germs and chemicals can also cause food poisoning. Norovirus illness is not related to the flu (influenza), which is a respiratory illness caused by influenza virus.

The most common symptoms—

- diarrhea
- throwing up

- nausea
- stomach pain

Other symptoms—

- fever
- headache

- body aches

If you have norovirus illness, you can feel extremely ill and throw up or have diarrhea many times a day. This can lead to dehydration, especially in young children, older adults, and people with other illnesses.

A person usually develops symptoms 12 to 48 hours after being exposed to norovirus. Most people with norovirus illness get better within 1 to 3 days.

Symptoms of dehydration—

- decrease in urination
- dry mouth and throat
- feeling dizzy when standing up

Children who are dehydrated may cry with few or no tears and be unusually sleepy or fussy.

Transmission

Norovirus is a highly contagious virus. Anyone can get infected with norovirus and get sick. Also, you can get norovirus illness many times in your life. One reason for this is that there are many different types of noroviruses. Being infected with one type of norovirus may not protect you against other types.

Norovirus can be found in your stool (feces) even before you start feeling sick. The virus can stay in your stool for 2 weeks or more after you feel better.

You are most contagious

- when you are sick with norovirus illness, and

- during the first few days after you recover from norovirus illness.

You can become infected with norovirus by accidentally getting stool or vomit from infected people in your mouth. This usually happens by

- eating food or drinking liquids that are contaminated with norovirus,

- touching surfaces or objects contaminated with norovirus then putting your fingers in your mouth, or

- having contact with someone who is infected with norovirus (for example, caring for or sharing food or eating utensils with someone with norovirus illness).

Norovirus can spread quickly in closed places like daycare centers, nursing homes, schools, and cruise ships. Most norovirus outbreaks happen from November to April in the United States.

Norovirus and Food

Norovirus is the leading cause of illness and outbreaks from contaminated food in the United States. Most of these outbreaks occur in the food service settings like restaurants. Infected food workers are frequently the source of the outbreaks, often by touching ready-to-eat foods, such as raw fruits and vegetables, with their bare hands before serving them. However, any food served raw or handled after being cooked can get contaminated with norovirus.

Norovirus outbreaks can also occur from foods, such as oysters, fruits, and vegetables, that are contaminated at their source.

Treatment

There is no specific medicine to treat people with norovirus illness. Norovirus infection cannot be treated with antibiotics because it is a viral (not a bacterial) infection.

If you have norovirus illness, you should drink plenty of liquids to replace fluid lost from throwing up and diarrhea. This will help prevent dehydration.

Sports drinks and other drinks without caffeine or alcohol can help with mild dehydration. But, these drinks may not replace important nutrients and minerals. Oral rehydration fluids that you can get over the counter are most helpful for mild dehydration.

Dehydration can lead to serious problems. Severe dehydration may require hospitalization for treatment with fluids given through your vein (intravenous or IV fluids). If you think you or someone you are caring for is severely dehydrated, call the doctor.

Chapter 52

Clostridium difficile *Infection*

General Information about C. difficile

Clostridium difficile (C. difficile) is a bacterium that causes inflammation of the colon, known as colitis.

People who have other illnesses or conditions requiring prolonged use of antibiotics, and the elderly, are at greater risk of acquiring this disease. The bacteria are found in the feces. People can become infected if they touch items or surfaces that are contaminated with feces and then touch their mouth or mucous membranes. Healthcare workers can spread the bacteria to patients or contaminate surfaces through hand contact.

Symptoms of C. difficile

Symptoms include:

- Watery diarrhea (at least three bowel movements per day for two or more days)
- Fever
- Loss of appetite
- Nausea
- Abdominal pain/tenderness

Text in this chapter is excerpted from "Healthcare-associated Infections (HAIs)," Centers for Disease Control and Prevention (CDC), February 24, 2015.

Transmission of C. difficile

Clostridium difficile is shed in feces. Any surface, device, or material (e.g., toilets, bathing tubs, and electronic rectal thermometers) that becomes contaminated with feces may serve as a reservoir for the *Clostridium difficile* spores. *Clostridium difficile* spores are transferred to patients mainly via the hands of healthcare personnel who have touched a contaminated surface or item. *Clostridium difficile* can live for long periods on surfaces.

Treatment of C. difficile *Infection*

Whenever possible, other antibiotics should be discontinued; in a small number of patients, diarrhea may go away when other antibiotics are stopped. Treatment of primary infection caused by *C. difficile* is an antibiotic such as metronidazole, vancomycin, or fidaxomicin. While metronidazole is not approved for treating *C. difficile* infections by the FDA, it has been commonly recommended and used for mild *C. difficile* infections; however, it should not be used for severe *C. difficile* infections. Whenever possible, treatment should be given by mouth and continued for a minimum of 10 days.

One problem with antibiotics used to treat primary *C. difficile* infection is that the infection returns in about 20 percent of patients. In a small number of these patients, the infection returns over and over and can be quite debilitating. While a first return of a *C. difficile* infection is usually treated with the same antibiotic used for primary infection, all future infections should be managed with oral vancomycin or fidaxomicin.

Transplanting stool from a healthy person to the colon of a patient with repeat *C. difficile* infections has been shown to successfully treat *C. difficile*. These 'fecal transplants' appear to be the most effective method for helping patients with repeat *C. difficile* infections. This procedure may not be widely available and its long term safety has not been established.

Part Eight

Additional Help and Information

Chapter 53

Glossary of Terms Related to Gastrointestinal Disorders

acquired immune deficiency syndrome (AIDS): The illness caused by the HIV retrovirus. It affects your immunity by making you more susceptible to infections and to certain rare cancers. It is mostly transmitted by exposure to contaminated blood and semen.

alanine aminotransferase (ALT): An enzyme released from liver cells.

albumin (ALB): Is a protein made by the liver to keep body fluids in balance. Low levels can indicate poor health and nutrition or a failing liver.

alkaline phosphatase (alkphos): Is an enzyme made in the liver's bile ducts and also in bone, kidneys, and intestines. High levels can indicate liver or bone disease.

alpha-fetoprotein (AFP): is a protein that can be elevated in liver cancer.

anal fissure: A small tear in the anus that may cause itching, pain or bleeding.

anal fistula: A channel that develops between the anus and the skin. Most fistulas are the result of an abscess (infection) that spreads to the skin.

This glossary contains terms excerpted from documents produced by several sources deemed reliable.

anastomosis: An operation to connect two body parts. An example is an operation in which a part of the colon is removed and the two remaining ends are rejoined.

angiodysplasia: Abnormal or enlarged blood vessels in the gastrointestinal tract.

angiography: An X-ray that uses dye to detect bleeding in the gastrointestinal tract.

anoscopy: A test to look for fissures, fistulae, and hemorrhoids. The doctor uses a special instrument, called an anoscope, to look into the anus.

antacids: Medicines that balance acids and gas in the stomach.

antibodies: Are proteins produced by the body as a response to infections.

anticholinergics: Medicines that calm muscle spasms in the intestine.

antiemetics: Medicines that prevent and control nausea and vomiting.

antispasmodics: Medicines that help reduce or stop muscle spasms in the intestines.

appendectomy: An operation to remove the appendix.

appendicitis: Reddening, irritation (inflammation), and pain in the appendix caused by infection, scarring, or blockage.

appendix: A four-inch pouch attached to the first part of the large intestine (cecum). No one knows what function the appendix has, if any.

ascending colon: The part of the colon on the right side of the abdomen.

ascites: A buildup of fluid in the abdomen. Ascites is usually caused by severe liver disease such as cirrhosis.

aspartate aminotransferase (AST): An enzyme released from liver and muscle. A blood test that reveals AST levels above normal may indicate liver damage.

atresia: Lack of a normal opening from the esophagus, intestines, or anus.

atrophic gastritis: Chronic irritation of the stomach lining. Causes the stomach lining and glands to wither away.

autoimmune hepatitis: A liver disease caused when the body's immune system destroys liver cells for no known reason.

Barrett's esophagus: Peptic ulcer of the lower esophagus. It is caused by the presence of cells that normally stay in the stomach lining.

bezoar: A ball of food, mucus, vegetable fiber, hair, or other material that cannot be digested in the stomach. Bezoars can cause blockage, ulcers, and bleeding

bile ducts: Tubes that carry bile from the liver to the gallbladder for storage and to the small intestine for use in digestion.

bile: Fluid made by the liver and stored in the gallbladder. Bile helps break down fats and gets rid of wastes in the body.

biliary atresia: A condition present from birth in which the bile ducts inside or outside the liver do not have normal openings.

bilirubin: A bile pigment that is also created by the breakdown of heme pigments. Usually collected by the liver cells, its presence in blood or urine is often a sign of liver damage.

bloating: Fullness or swelling in the abdomen that often occurs after meals.

bulking agents: Laxatives that make bowel movements soft and easy to pass.

catheter: A thin, flexible tube that carries fluids into or out of the body.

cecum: The beginning of the large intestine. The cecum is connected to the lower part of the small intestine, called the ileum.

celiac disease: Inability to digest and absorb gliadin, the protein found in wheat. Undigested gliadin causes damage to the lining of the small intestine. This prevents absorption of nutrients from other foods.

cholangiography: A series of X-rays of the bile ducts.

cholangitis: Irritated or infected bile ducts.

cholecystectomy: An operation to remove the gallbladder.

chronic infection: An infection that persists indefinitely.

chyme: A thick liquid made of partially digested food and stomach juices. This liquid is made in the stomach and moves into the small intestine for further digestion.

cirrhosis: A chronic liver condition caused by scar tissue and cell damage. Cirrhosis makes it hard for the liver to remove poisons (toxins) like alcohol and drugs from the blood.

Clostridium difficile: Bacteria naturally present in the large intestine. These bacteria make a substance that can cause a serious infection called pseudomembranous colitis in people taking antibiotics.

colectomy: An operation to remove all or part of the colon.

colic: Attacks of abdominal pain, caused by muscle spasms in the intestines. Colic is common in infants.

colitis: Irritation of the colon.

collagenous colitis: A type of colitis. Caused by an abnormal band of collagen, a thread-like protein.

colon polyps: Small, fleshy, mushroom-shaped growths in the colon.

colon: The long, coiled, tube-like organ that removes water from digested food. The remaining material, solid waste called "stool," moves through the colon and the rectum and leaves the body through the anus.

colonoscope: A flexible, lighted instrument with a tiny built-in camera used to view the inside of the entire colon and rectum.

colonoscopy: An examination in which the doctor looks at the internal walls of the entire colon through a flexible, lighted instrument called a colonoscope. The doctor may collect samples of tissue or cells for closer examination.

colorectal cancer: Cancer that occurs in the colon (large intestine) or the rectum (the end of the large intestine).

colostomy: An operation that makes it possible for stool to leave the body after the rectum has been removed. The surgeon makes an opening in the abdomen and attaches the colon to it. A temporary colostomy may be done to let the rectum heal from injury or other surgery.

common bile duct: The tube that carries bile from the liver to the small intestine.

computed tomography (CT) scan: An X-ray that produces three-dimensional pictures of the body. Also known as computed axial tomography (CAT) scan.

continence: The ability to hold in a bowel movement or urine.

continent ileostomy: An operation to create a pouch from part of the small intestine. Stool that collects in the pouch is removed by inserting a small tube through an opening made in the abdomen.

corticosteroids: Medicines such as cortisone and hydrocortisone. These medicines reduce irritation from Crohn's disease and ulcerative colitis. They may be taken either by mouth or as suppositories.

Crohn's disease: A chronic form of inflammatory bowel disease. Crohn's disease causes severe irritation in the gastrointestinal tract. It usually affects the lower small intestine (called the ileum) or the colon, but it can affect the entire gastrointestinal tract.

cystic duct: The tube that carries bile from the gallbladder into the common bile duct and the small intestine.

defecography: An X-ray of the anus and rectum to see how the muscles work to move stool. The patient sits on a toilet placed inside the X-ray machine.

dermatitis herpetiformis: A skin disorder associated with celiac disease.

descending colon: The part of the colon where stool is stored. Located on the left side of the abdomen.

diverticulitis: A condition that occurs when small pouches in the colon (diverticula) become infected or irritated. Also called left-sided appendicitis.

diverticulosis: A condition that occurs when small pouches (diverticula) push outward through weak spots in the colon.

diverticulum: A small pouch in the colon. These pouches are not painful or harmful unless they become infected or irritated.

dumping syndrome: A condition that occurs when food moves too fast from the stomach into the small intestine. Symptoms are nausea, pain, weakness, and sweating.

duodenum: The first part of the small intestine.

dysphagia: Problems in swallowing food or liquid, usually caused by blockage or injury to the esophagus.

edema: The puffiness that occurs from abnormal amounts of fluid in the spaces between cells in the body, especially just below the skin.

electrocoagulation: A procedure that uses an electrical current passed through an endoscope to stop bleeding in the digestive tract and to remove affected tissue.

electrolytes: Chemicals such as salts and minerals needed for various functions in the body.

encephalopathy: A variety of brain function abnormalities experienced by some patients with advanced liver disease. These most commonly include confusion, disorientation, and insomnia, and may progress to coma.

endoscope: A small, flexible tube with a light and a lens on the end. It is used to look into the esophagus, stomach, duodenum, colon, or rectum. It can also be used to take tissue from the body for testing or to take color photographs of the inside of the body.

endoscopic retrograde cholangiopancreatography: A test using an X-ray to look into the bile and pancreatic ducts.

endoscopy: A procedure that uses an endoscope to diagnose or treat a condition.

enema: A liquid put into the rectum to clear out the bowel or to administer drugs or food.

enteroscopy: An examination of the small intestine with an endoscope. The endoscope is inserted through the mouth and stomach into the small intestine.

enzymes: A chemical substance in animals and plants that helps to cause natural processes (such as digestion). Helps chemical changes to take place in the plant or animals.

eosinophilic gastroenteritis: Infection and swelling of the lining of the stomach, small intestine, or large intestine. The infection is caused by white blood cells (eosinophils).

epithelium: The inner and outer tissue covering digestive tract organs.

erythema nodosum: Red swellings or sores on the lower legs during flare-ups of Crohn's disease and ulcerative colitis. These sores show that the disease is active. They usually go away when the disease is treated.

Escherichia coli: Bacteria that cause infection and irritation of the large intestine. The bacteria are spread by unclean water, dirty cooking utensils, or undercooked meat.

esophageal manometry: A test to measure muscle tone in the esophagus.

esophageal pH monitoring: A test to measure the amount of acid in the esophagus.

esophageal stricture: A narrowing of the esophagus often caused by acid flowing back from the stomach. This condition may require surgery.

esophageal varices: Stretched veins in the esophagus that occur when the liver is not working properly. If the veins burst, the bleeding can cause death.

esophagitis: An irritation of the esophagus, usually caused by acid that flows up from the stomach.

esophagogastroduodenoscopy: Exam of the upper digestive tract using an endoscope.

eatty liver: The buildup of fat in liver cells. The most common cause is alcoholism. Other causes include obesity, diabetes, and pregnancy. Also called steatosis.

fecal occult blood test: A test to check for hidden blood in stool.

fibrosis: is the first stage of scar formation in the liver. Scar tissue is an attempt to contain areas of the liver that have been damaged by alcohol, hepatitis C, or other factors.

fistula: An abnormal passage between two organs or between an organ and the outside of the body. Caused when damaged tissues come into contact with each other and join together while healing.

flatulence: Excessive gas in the stomach or intestine. May cause bloating.

flexible sigmoidoscopy: Also called proctosigmoidoscopy. A procedure in which the doctor looks inside the rectum and the lower portion of the colon (sigmoid colon) through a flexible, lighted tube called a sigmoidoscope.

galactose: A type of sugar in milk products and sugar beets.

galactosemia: Buildup of galactose in the blood. Caused by lack of one of the enzymes needed to break down galactose into glucose.

gallbladder: The organ that stores the bile made in the liver. Connected to the liver by bile ducts.

gallstones: The solid masses or stones made of cholesterol or bilirubin that form in the gallbladder or bile ducts.

gastrectomy: An operation to remove all or part of the stomach.

gastrin: A hormone released after eating. Gastrin causes the stomach to produce more acid.

gastritis: An inflammation of the stomach lining.

gastroenteritis: An infection or irritation of the stomach and intestines. May be caused by bacteria or parasites from spoiled food or unclean water.

gastroesophageal reflux disease: Flow of the stomach's contents back up into the esophagus. Happens when the muscle between the esophagus and the stomach (the lower esophageal sphincter) is weak or relaxes when it shouldn't. May cause esophagitis.

gastrointestinal tract: The large, muscular tube that extends from the mouth to the anus, where the movement of muscles and release of hormones and enzymes digest food.

gastroparesis: Nerve or muscle damage in the stomach. Causes slow digestion and emptying, vomiting, nausea, or bloating.

gastrostomy: An artificial opening from the stomach to a hole (stoma) in the abdomen where a feeding tube is inserted.

giardiasis: An infection with the parasite Giardia lamblia from spoiled food or unclean water. May cause diarrhea.

glycogen storage diseases: A group of birth defects. These diseases change the way the liver breaks down glycogen.

glycogen: A sugar stored in the liver and muscles. It releases glucose into the blood when cells need it for energy. Glycogen is the chief source of stored fuel in the body.

granuloma: A mass of red, irritated tissue in the GI tract found in Crohn's disease.

heartburn: A painful, burning feeling in the chest. Heartburn is caused by stomach acid flowing back into the esophagus. Changing the diet and other habits can help to prevent heartburn. Heartburn may be a symptom of GERD.

***Helicobacter pylori* (*H. pylori*):** A spiral-shaped bacterium found in the stomach. *H. pylori* damages stomach and duodenal tissue, causing ulcers. Previously called *Campylobacter pylori*.

hemochromatosis: A disease that occurs when the body absorbs too much iron. The body stores the excess iron in the liver, pancreas, and other organs. May cause cirrhosis of the liver. Also called iron overload disease.

hemorrhoids: Swollen blood vessels in and around the anus and lower rectum. Continual straining to have a bowel movement causes them to stretch and swell. They cause itching, pain, and sometimes bleeding.

hepatic: Related to the liver.

hepatitis: Irritation of the liver that sometimes causes permanent damage. Hepatitis may be caused by viruses or by medicines or alcohol.

hepatocellular carcinoma (HCC): Cancer stemming from the liver cells. Also called hepatoma.

hernia: The part of an internal organ that pushes through an opening in the organ's wall. Most hernias occur in the abdominal area.

hiatal hernia (Hiatus Hernia): A small opening in the diaphragm that allows the upper part of the stomach to move up into the chest. Causes heartburn from stomach acid flowing back up through the opening.

Hirschsprung disease: A birth defect in which some nerve cells are lacking in the large intestine. The intestine cannot move stool through, so the intestine gets blocked. Causes the abdomen to swell.

hydrogen breath test: A test for lactose intolerance. It measures breath samples for too much hydrogen. The body makes too much hydrogen when lactose is not broken down properly in the small intestine.

ileoanal reservoir: An operation to remove the colon, upper rectum, and part of the lower rectum. An internal pouch is created from the remaining intestine to hold stool. The operation may be done in two stages. The pouch may also be called a J-pouch or W-pouch.

ileostomy: An operation that makes it possible for stool to leave the body after the colon and rectum are removed. The surgeon makes an opening in the abdomen and attaches the bottom of the small intestine (ileum) to it.

ileum: The lower end of the small intestine.

inflammatory bowel disease (IBD): Long-lasting problems that cause irritation and ulcers in the GI tract. The most common disorders are ulcerative colitis and Crohn's disease.

inguinal hernia: A small part of the large or small intestine or bladder that pushes into the groin. May cause pain and feelings of pressure or burning in the groin. Often requires surgery.

insulin: A hormone released by the pancreas whose job is to help use or store glucose as glycogen.

interferon (IFN): are a group of proteins made by the body that have antiviral, antitumor, and immune system activity. They are also produced synthetically as a treatment of medical conditions, including hepatitis C and multiple sclerosis.

irritable bowel syndrome (IBS): A disorder that comes and goes. Nerves that control the muscles in the GI tract are too active. The GI tract becomes sensitive to food, stool, gas, and stress. Causes abdominal pain, bloating, and constipation or diarrhea. Also called spastic colon or mucous colitis.

jaundice: A symptom of many disorders. Jaundice causes the skin and eyes to turn yellow from too much bilirubin in the blood.

jejunostomy: An operation to create an opening of the jejunum to a hole (stoma) in the abdomen.

jejunum: The middle section of the small intestine between the duodenum and ileum.

lactase: An enzyme in the small intestine needed to digest milk sugar (lactose).

lactose intolerance: Being unable to digest lactose, the sugar in milk. This condition occurs because the body does not produce the lactase enzyme.

laparoscope: A thin tube with a tiny video camera attached. Used to look inside the body and see the surface of organs.

laparoscopic cholecystectomy: An operation to remove the gall-bladder. The doctor inserts a laparoscope and other surgical instruments through small holes in the abdomen. The camera allows the doctor to see the gallbladder on a television screen. The doctor removes the gallbladder through the holes.

laparoscopy: A test that uses a laparoscope to look at and take tissue from the inside of the body.

large intestine: The part of the intestine that goes from the cecum to the rectum. The large intestine absorbs water from stool and changes it from a liquid to a solid form. The large intestine includes the appendix, cecum, colon, and rectum. Also called colon.

laxatives: Medicines to relieve long-term constipation. Used only if other methods fail. Also called cathartics.

liver: The largest organ in the body. The liver carries out many important functions, such as making bile, changing food into energy, and cleaning alcohol and poisons from the blood.

lower esophageal ring: An abnormal ring of tissue that may partially block the lower esophagus. Also called Schatzki ring.

lower gastrointestinal series: X-rays of the rectum, colon, and lower part of the small intestine. A barium enema is given first. Barium coats the organs so they will show up on the X-ray. Also called barium enema X-ray.

magnetic resonance imaging (MRI): A test that takes pictures of the soft tissues in the body. The pictures are clearer than X-rays.

Mallory-Weiss tear: A tear in the lower end of the esophagus. Caused by severe vomiting. Common in alcoholics.

manometry: Tests that measure muscle pressure and movements in the GI tract.

megacolon: A huge, swollen colon. Results from severe constipation. In children, megacolon is more common in boys than girls.

Ménétrier disease: A long-term disorder that causes large, coiled folds in the stomach. Also called giant hypertrophic gastritis.

metabolic syndrome: A medical condition characterized by obesity, insulin resistance, hypertension and dyslipidemia.

motility: The movement of food through the digestive tract.

mucus: A clear liquid made by the intestines. Mucus coats and protects tissues in the gastrointestinal tract.

necrotizing enterocolitis: A condition in which part of the tissue in the intestines is destroyed. Occurs mainly in underweight newborn babies. A temporary ileostomy may be necessary.

neonatal hepatitis: Irritation of the liver with no known cause. Occurs in newborn babies. Symptoms include jaundice and liver cell changes.

neutropenia: means a decreased number of neutrophils. Neutrophils are a type of white blood cells that fights infections in the body.

Interferon treatment and chemotherapy can cause neutropenia. Neutropenia can increase risk of infections.

occult bleeding: Blood in stool that is not visible to the naked eye. May be a sign of disease such as diverticulosis or colorectal cancer.

oral dissolution therapy: A method of dissolving cholesterol gallstones. The patient takes the oral medications chenodiol (Chenix) and ursodiol (Actigall). These medicines are most often used for people who cannot have an operation.

ostomy: An operation that makes it possible for stool to leave the body through an opening made in the abdomen. An ostomy is necessary when part or all of the intestines are removed. Colostomy and ileostomy are types of ostomy.

pancreas: A gland that makes enzymes for digestion and the hormone insulin.

pancreatitis: Irritation of the pancreas that can make it stop working. Most often caused by gallstones or alcohol abuse.

parenteral nutrition: A way to provide a liquid food mixture through a special tube in the chest. Also called hyperalimentation or total parenteral nutrition.

polycystic ovary syndrome (PCOS): is a health problem that can affect a woman's menstrual cycle, ability to have children, hormones, heart, blood vessels, and appearance.

pepsin: An enzyme made in the stomach that breaks down proteins.

peptic ulcer: A sore in the lining of the esophagus, stomach, or duodenum. Usually caused by the bacterium Helicobacter pylori. An ulcer in the stomach is a gastric ulcer; an ulcer in the duodenum is a duodenal ulcer.

percutaneous transhepatic cholangiography: X-rays of the gallbladder and bile ducts. A dye is injected through the abdomen to make the organs show up on the X-ray.

perianal: The area around the anus.

perineum: The area between the anus and the sex organs.

peristalsis: A wavelike movement of muscles in the GI tract. Peristalsis moves food and liquid through the GI tract.

peritoneum: The lining of the abdominal cavity.

peritonitis: Infection of the peritoneum.

polymerase chain reaction (PCR): is a test used to determine the number of virus particles in the blood. It is one method to determine the "viral load."

polyp: An abnormal, often precancerous growth of tissue (colorectal polyps are growths of tissue inside the intestine).

polyposis: The presence of many polyps.

porphyria: A group of rare, inherited blood disorders. When a person has porphyria, cells fail to change chemicals (porphyrins) to the substance (heme) that gives blood its color.

portal hypertension: is high blood pressure in and around the liver. It is often caused by cirrhosis, and it can result in variceal bleeding and ascites.

portal vein: The large vein that carries blood from the intestines and spleen to the liver.

prescriptions: The number of prescriptions written annually for medications to treat a specific disease.

prevalence: The number of people affected by a specific disease or diseases.

primary biliary cirrhosis: A chronic liver disease. Slowly destroys the bile ducts in the liver. This prevents release of bile. Long-term irritation of the liver may cause scarring and cirrhosis in later stages of the disease.

primary sclerosing cholangitis (PSC): Irritation, scarring, and narrowing of the bile ducts inside and outside the liver. Bile builds up in the liver and may damage its cells. Many people with this condition also have ulcerative colitis.

proctitis: Irritation of the rectum.

proctocolectomy: An operation to remove the colon and rectum. Also called coloproctectomy.

proctoscope: A short, rigid metal tube used to look into the rectum and anus.

prolapse: A condition that occurs when a body part slips from its normal position.

prothrombin time (PT): is a test that measures how long your blood takes to clot. Prothrombin helps the blood to clot, so PT increases if the liver is not making enough of it.

proton pump inhibitors: Medicines that stop the stomach's acid pump. Examples are omeprazole (Prilosec) and lansoprazole (Prevacid).

pylorus: The opening from the stomach into the top of the small intestine (duodenum).

rectal prolapse: A condition in which the rectum slips so that it protrudes from the anus.

rectum: The lower end of the large intestine, leading to the anus.

reflux: A condition that occurs when gastric juices or small amounts of food from the stomach flow back into the esophagus and mouth. Also called regurgitation.

remission: Partial or complete disappearance--or a lessening of the severity--of symptoms of a disease. Remission may happen on its own or occur as a result of a medical treatment.

retching: Dry vomiting.

recombinant immunoblot assay (RIBA): A test that confirms the presence of hepatitis C antibodies in the bloodstream if the ELISA test results is in doubt.

risk factors: Certain behaviors (such as intravenous drug use or transfusions) linked to the development of an infection such as hepatitis.

ribonucleic acid (RNA): Molecules, found in all cells, that translate DNA genetic information into proteins.

rotavirus: The most common cause of infectious diarrhea in the United States, especially in children under age two.

Salmonella: A bacterium that may cause intestinal infection and diarrhea.

sarcoidosis: A condition that causes small, fleshy swellings in the liver, lungs, and spleen.

saturated fats: A type of fat commonly found in animal products that is thought to be less healthy than other kinds of fat from vegetable oils or fish.

sclerotherapy: A method of stopping upper GI bleeding. A needle is inserted through an endoscope to bring hardening agents to the place that is bleeding.

screening test: Tests used to check, or screen, for disease when there are no symptoms. Recommended screening tests for colorectal cancer include the fecal occult blood test, flexible sigmoidoscopy, and colonoscopy. (When a test is performed to find out why symptoms exist, it is called a "diagnostic" test.)

secretin: A hormone made in the duodenum. Causes the stomach to make pepsin, the liver to make bile, and the pancreas to make a digestive juice.

Shigellosis: Infection with the bacterium *Shigella*. Usually causes a high fever, acute diarrhea, and dehydration.

short bowel syndrome: Problems related to absorbing nutrients after removal of part of the small intestine. Symptoms include diarrhea, weakness, and weight loss. Also called short gut syndrome.

Shwachman syndrome: A digestive and respiratory disorder of children. Certain digestive enzymes are missing and white blood cells are few. Symptoms may include diarrhea and short stature.

sigmoid colon: The lower part of the colon that empties into the rectum.

sigmoidoscope: A flexible, lighted instrument with a tiny built-in camera that allows the doctor to view the lining of the rectum and lower portion of the colon.

sigmoidoscopy: Looking into the sigmoid colon and rectum with a flexible or rigid tube, called a sigmoidoscope.

small intestine: Organ where most digestion occurs. It measures about twenty feet and includes the duodenum, jejunum, and ileum.

somatostatin: A hormone in the pancreas. Somatostatin helps tell the body when to make the hormones insulin, glucagon, gastrin, secretin, and renin.

spasms: Muscle movements such as those in the colon that cause pain, cramps, and diarrhea.

sphincter: A ring-like band of muscle that opens and closes an opening in the body. An example is the muscle between the esophagus and the stomach known as the lower esophageal sphincter.

spleen: The organ that cleans blood and makes white blood cells. White blood cells attack bacteria and other foreign cells.

steatorrhea: A condition in which the body cannot absorb fat. Causes buildup of fat in the stool and loose, greasy, and foul bowel movements.

steatosis: Abnormal buildup of fat in the liver. Steatohepatitis

stricture: The abnormal narrowing of a body opening. Also called stenosis.

tenesmus: Straining to have a bowel movement. May be painful and continue for a long time without result.

thrombocytopenia: is a low level of platelets in the blood caused by cirrhosis and an enlarged spleen and can also be caused by interferon treatment.

transaminase: A term for alanine aminotransferase (ALT) and aminotransferases (AST), the two transaminases.

transverse colon: The part of the colon that goes across the abdomen from right to left.

triglycerides: One of the main fatty substances in the blood that can clog arteries.

triple therapy: Drugs that stop the body from making acid are often added to relieve symptoms.

ulcer: A sore on the skin surface or on the stomach lining.

ulcerative colitis: A serious disease that causes ulcers and irritation in the inner lining of the colon and rectum.

unsaturated fats: A type of fat found in food such as nuts, seeds, avocados, and fish.

upper GI endoscopy: Looking into the esophagus, stomach, and duodenum with an endoscope.

upper GI series: X-rays of the esophagus, stomach, and duodenum. The patient swallows barium first. Barium makes the organs show up on X-rays. Also called barium meal.

urea breath test: A test used to detect *Helicobacter pylori* infection. The test measures breath samples for urease, an enzyme *H. pylori* makes.

vagotomy: An operation to cut the vagus nerve. This causes the stomach to make less acid.

vagus nerve: The nerve in the stomach that controls the making of stomach acid.

varices: Stretched veins such as those that form in the esophagus from cirrhosis.

villi: The tiny, finger-like projections on the surface of the small intestine. Villi help absorb nutrients.

watermelon stomach: Parallel red sores in the stomach that look like the stripes on a watermelon. Frequently seen with cirrhosis.

Wilson disease: An inherited disorder. Too much copper builds up in the liver and is slowly released into other parts of the body. The overload can cause severe liver and brain damage if not treated with medication.

Zollinger-Ellison syndrome (ZES): A group of symptoms that occur when a tumor called a gastrinoma forms in the pancreas. The tumor, which may cause cancer, releases large amounts of the hormone gastrin. The gastrin causes too much acid in the duodenum, resulting in ulcers, bleeding, and perforation.

Chapter 54

Resources for Information about Gastrointestinal Conditions

Academy of Nutrition and Dietetics
120 S. Riverside Plz. Ste. 2000
Chicago, IL 60606–6995
Phone: 312-899-0040
Toll-Free: 800-877-1600
Website: www.eatright.org

Alagille Syndrome Alliance
10500 S.W. Starr Dr.
Tualatin, OR 97062
Phone: 503-885-0455
Website: www.alagille.org
E-mail: alagille@alagille.org

American Academy of Family Physicians
P.O. Box 11210
Shawnee Mission, KS 66207–1210
Phone: 913-906-6000
Fax: 913-906-6075
Toll-Free: 800-274-2237
Website: www.aafp.org
E-mail: fp@aafp.org

American Association for the Study of Liver Diseases
1001 N. Fairfax, Ste. 400
Alexandria, VA 22314
Phone: 703-299-9766
Fax: 703-299-9622
Website: www.aasld.org
E-mail: aasld@aasld.org

Resources in this chapter were compiled from several sources deemed reliable; all contact information was verified and updated in December 2015.

American Cancer Society Inc
250 Williams St. N.W.
Atlanta, GA 30303
Toll-Free: 800-227-2345
Website: www.cancer.org

American Celiac Disease Alliance
2504 Duxbury Pl.
Alexandria, VA 22308
Phone: 703-622-3331
Website: www.americanceliac.org
E-mail: info@americanceliac.org

American Celiac Society
Phone: 504-738-6165
Website: www.americanceliacsociety.org

American College of Gastroenterology
6400 Goldsboro Rd., Ste. 200
Bethesda, MD 20817
Phone: 301-263-9000
Website: gi.org
E-mail: info@acg.gi.org

American College of Surgeons
633 N. Saint Clair St.
Chicago, IL 60611–3211
Phone: 312-202-5000
Fax: 312-202-5001
Toll-Free: 800-621-4111
Website: www.facs.org
E-mail: postmaster@facs.org

American Diabetes Association
1701 N. Beauregard St.
Alexandria, VA 22311
Toll-Free: 800-342-2383
Website: www.diabetes.org

American Dietetic Association
120 S. Riverside Plaza, Ste. 2000
Chicago, IL 60606–6995
Fax: 312-899-4899
Website: www.eatright.org
E-mail: knowledge@eatright.org

American Gastroenterological Association
4930 Del Ray Ave.
Bethesda, MD 20814
Phone: 301-654-2055
Fax: 301-654-5920
Website: www.gastro.org
E-mail: member@gastro.org

American Hemochromatosis Society Inc
4044 W. Lake Mary Blvd., Ste. 104
Lake Mary, FL 32746–2012
Phone: 407-829-4488
Fax: 407-333-1284
Toll-Free: 888-655-4766
Website: www.americanhs.org
E-mail: mail@americanhs.org

American Liver Foundation
39 Broadway, Ste. 2700
New York, NY 10006
Phone: 212-668-1000
Fax: 212-483-8179
Toll-Free: 800-465-4837
Website: www.liverfoundation.
org

American Neurogastroenterology and Motility Society
45685 Harmony Ln.
Belleville, MI 48111
Phone: 734-699-1130
Fax: 734-699-1136
Website: www.motilitysociety.
org
E-mail: admin@motilitysociety.
org

American Pancreatic Association
P.O. Box 14906
Minneapolis, MN 55414
Phone: 612-626-9797
Fax: 612-625-7700
Website: www.american-
pancreatic-association.org
E-mail: apa@umn.edu

American Pediatric Surgical Association's (APSA)
One Parkview Plaza, Ste. 800
Oakbrook, IL 60181
Phone: 847-686-2237
Fax: 847-686-2253
Website: www.eapsa.org
E-mail: eapsa@eapsa.org

American Porphyria Foundation
4900 Woodway, Ste.780
Houston, TX 77506–1837
Phone: 713-266-9617
Fax: 713-840-9552
Toll-Free: 866-273-3635
Website: www.
porphyriafoundation.com
E-mail: porphyrus@aol.com

The American Society of Colon and Rectal Surgeons
85 W. Algonquin Rd., Ste. 550
Arlington Heights, IL 60005
Phone: 847-290-9184
Fax: 847-290-9203
Website: www.fascrs.org
E-mail: ascrs@fascrs.org

American Urogynecologic Society Foundation
2025 M St. N.W., Ste 800
Washington, DC 20036
Phone: 202-367-1167
Fax: 202-367-2167
Website: www.voicesforpfd.org
E-mail: info@augs.org

Association of Gastrointestinal Motility Disorders Inc (AGMD)
AGMD International Corporate Headquarters
12 Roberts Dr.
Bedford, MA 01730
Phone: 781-275-1300
Fax: 781-275-1304
Website: www.agmd-gimotility.org
E-mail: digestive.motility@
gmail.com

Celiac Disease Foundation
20350 Ventura Blvd., Ste. 240
Woodland Hills, CA 91364
Phone: 818-716-1513
Fax: 818-267-5577
Website: www.celiac.org
E-mail: info@celiac.org

Celiac Support Association
P.O. Box 31700
Omaha, NE 68131–0700
Phone: 402-558-0600
Fax: 402-643-4108
Toll-Free: 877-272-4272
Website: www.csaceliacs.org
E-mail: celiacs@csaceliacs.org

Centers for Disease Control and Prevention
1600 Clifton Rd.
Atlanta, GA 30333
Phone: 404-498-1515
Toll-Free: 800-311-3435
Website: www.cdc.gov

Children's Liver Association for Support Services
25379 Wayne Mills Pl., Ste. 143
Valencia, CA 91355
Phone: 661-263-9099
Fax: 661-263-9099
Toll-Free: 877-679-8256
Website: www.classkids.org
E-mail: info@classkids.org

Crohn's & Colitis Foundation of America
733 Third Ave., Ste. 510
New York, NY 10017
Toll-Free: 800-932-2423
Website: www.ccfa.org
E-mail: info@ccfa.org

Cyclic Vomiting Syndrome Association
P.O. Box 925
Elkhorn, WI 53121
Phone: 414-342-7880
Fax: 414-342-8980
Website: cvsaonline.org
E-mail: cvsa@cvsaonline.org

Department of Genetics and Genomic Sciences
The Porphyrias Consortium
1425 Madison Ave., 14–75A
New York, NY 10029
Phone: 212-659-6779
Fax: 212-659-6780
Toll-Free: 866-322-7968
Website: rarediseasesnetwork.
epi.usf.edu/porphyrias
E-mail: dana.doheny@mssm.edu

Digestive Disease National Coalition (DDNC)
507 Capitol Ct., N.E., Ste. 200
Washington, DC 20002
Phone: 202-544-7497
Fax: 202-546-7105
E-mail: psurio@hmcw.org

FoodSafety.gov
Website: www.foodsafety.gov

Genetic and Rare Diseases (GARD) Information Center
P.O. Box 8126
Gaithersburg, MD 20898–8126
Phone: 301-251-4925
Fax: 301-251-4911
Toll-Free: 888-205-2311
Website: rarediseases.info.nih.
gov

Gluten Intolerance Group
31214 124th Ave. S.E.
Auburn, WA 98092
Phone: 253-833-6655
Fax: 253-833-6675
Website: www.gluten.net
E-mail: CustomerService@
gluten.net

Hepatitis Foundation
International
504 Blick Dr.
Silver Spring, MD 20904
Phone: 301-879-6891
Fax: 301-879-6890
Toll-Free: 800-891-0707
Website: www.hepfi.org
E-mail: info@
hepatitisfoundation.org

International Foundation for
Functional Gastrointestinal
Disorders
P.O. Box 170864
Milwaukee, WI 53217–8076
Phone: 414-964-1799
Fax: 414-964-7176
Toll-Free: 888-964-2001
Website: www.iffgd.org
E-mail: iffgd@iffgd.org

Iron Disorders Institute
P.O. Box 675
Taylors, SC 29687
Phone: 864-292-1175
Toll-Free: 888-565-4766
Website: www.irondisorders.org
E-mail: cgarrison@irondisorders.
org

National Cancer Institute
9609 Medical Center Dr.
Bethesda, MD 20892
Toll-Free: 800–422–6237
Website: www.cancer.gov

National Digestive Diseases
Information Clearinghouse
2 Information Way
Bethesda, MD 20892–3570
Fax: 703-738-4929
Toll-Free: 800-891-5389
TTY: 866-569-1162
Website: www.digestive.niddk.
nih.gov
E-mail: nddic@info.niddk.nih.gov

National Foundation for
Celiac Awareness
P.O. Box 544
Ambler, PA 19002–0544
Phone: 215-325-1306
Fax: 215-643-1707
Website: www.celiaccentral.org
E-mail: info@celiaccentral.org

National Institute of
Child Health and Human
Development (NICHD)
31 Center Dr.
Bldg. 31, Rm. 2A32
Bethesda, MD 20892–2425
Fax: 866-760-5947
Toll-Free: 800-370-2943
TTY: 888-320-6942
Website: www.nichd.nih.gov
E-mail:
NICHDInformationResource
Center@mail.nih.gov

National Institute of Allergy and Infectious Diseases (NIAID)
5601 Fishers Ln.
Bethesda, MD 20892–9806
Phone: 301-496-5717
Fax: 301-402-3573
Toll-Free: 866-284-4107
Website: www.niaid.nih.gov
E-mail: ocpostoffice@niaid.nih.gov

National Institute of Neurological Disorders and Stroke (NINDS)
NIH Neurological Institute
P.O. Box 5801
Bethesda, MD 20824
Phone: 301-496-5751
Toll-Free: 800-352-9424
Website: www.ninds.nih.gov

National Institute on Deafness and Other Communication Disorders (NIDCD)
National Institutes of Health, DHHS
31 Center Dr.
Bethesda, MD 20892–2320
Phone: 301-496-7243
Fax: 301-402-0018
Toll-Free: 800-241-1044
Website: www.nidcd.nih.gov
E-mail: nidcdinfo@nidcd.nih.gov

The National Institute of Diabetes and Digestive and Kidney Diseases (NIDDK)
Bethesda, MD 20892–2560
Phone: 301-496-3583
Website: www.niddk.nih.gov/
Pages/default.aspx

National Institutes of Health
6100 Executive Blvd.
Rm. 3B01
Bethesda, MD 20892–7517
Phone: 301-435-2920
Fax: 301-480-1845
Website: ods.od.nih.gov
E-mail: ods@nih.gov

National Institutes of Health
9000 Rockville Pike
Bethesda, MD 20892
Phone: 301-496-4000
TTY: 301-402-9612
Website: www.nih.gov
E-mail: NIHinfo@od.nih.gov

National Organization for Rare Disorders
55 Kenosia Ave.
Danbury, CT 06810
Phone: 203-744-0100
Fax: 203-798-2291
Toll-Free: 800-999-6673
Website: www.carfintl.org
E-mail: info@carfintl.org

North American Society for Pediatric Gastroenterology, Hepatology and Nutrition
P.O. Box 6
Flourtown, PA 19031
Phone: 215-233-0808
Fax: 215-233-3918
Website: www.naspghan.org
E-mail: naspghan@naspghan.org

*North American Society for
Pediatric Gastroenterology,
Hepatology and Nutrition
(NASPGHAN)*
1501 Bethlehem Pike
P.O. Box 6
Flourtown, PA 19031
Phone: 215-233-0808
Fax: 215-233-3918
Website: www.naspghan.org
E-mail: naspghan@naspghan.org

*Office of Rare Diseases
Research*
National Center for Advancing
Translational Sciences (NCATS)
National Institutes of Health
(NIH)
6701 Democracy Blvd., Ste. 1001
Bethesda, MD 20892
Phone: 301-402-4336
Fax: 301-480-9655
Website: www.rarediseases.info.
nih.gov
E-mail: ordr@nih.gov

Office on Women's Health
Department of Health and
Human Services
200 Independence Ave., S.W.
Rm. 712E
Washington, DC 20201
Phone: 202-690-7650
Fax: 202-205-2631
Toll-Free: 800-994-9662
Website: womenshealth.gov

The Oley Foundation
Albany Medical Center
43 New Scotland Ave.
Albany, NY 12208–3478
Phone: 518-262-5079
Fax: 518-262-5528
Toll-Free: 800-776-6539
Website: www.oley.org
E-mail: bishopj@mail.amc.edu

*Pelvic Floor Disorders
Network*
Data Coordinating Center
6110 Executive Blvd., Ste. 420
Rockville, MD 20852
Phone: 301-230-4645
Fax: 301-230-4647
Website: pfdn.rti.org

*The Simon Foundation for
Continence*
P.O. Box 815
Wilmette, IL 60091
Phone: 847-864-3913
Fax: 847-864-9758
Toll-Free: 800-237-4666
Website: www.simonfoundation.
org

*Society of American
Gastrointestinal and
Endoscopic Surgeons*
11300 W. Olympic Blvd.
Ste. 600
Los Angeles, CA 90064
Phone: 310-437-0544
Website: www.sages.org
E-mail: webmaster@sages.org

U.S. Department of Agriculture (USDA)
1400 Independence Ave., S.W.
Washington, DC 20250
Phone: 202-720-2791
Website: www.usda.gov

U.S. Department of Health & Human Services
200 Independence Ave., S.W.
Washington, DC 20201
Toll-Free: 877-696-6775
Website: www.hhs.gov

U.S. Department of Veterans Affairs
810 Vermont Ave., N.W.
Washington, DC 20420
Toll-Free: 800-273-8255
Website: www.hepatitis.va.gov

U.S. Food and Drug Administration
10903 New Hampshire Ave.
Silver Spring, MD 20993–0002
Phone: 301-796-8240
Toll-Free: 888-463-6332
Website: www.fda.gov

United Network for Organ Sharing
P.O. Box 2484
Richmond, VA 23218
Phone: 804-782-4800
Fax: 804-782-4817
Toll-Free: 888-894-6361
Website: www.unos.org

United Ostomy Associations of America
P.O. Box 525
Kennebunk, ME 04043–0525
Toll-Free: 800-826-0826
Website: www.ostomy.org/Home.html

United Ostomy Associations of America Inc
2489 Rice St., Ste. 275
Roseville, MN 55113–3797
Toll-Free: 800-826-0826
Website: www.ostomy.org
E-mail: info@ostomy.org

Wilson Disease Association
5572 N. Diversey Blvd.
Milwaukee, WI 53217
Phone: 414-961-0533
Toll-Free: 866-961-0533
Website: www.wilsonsdisease.org
E-mail: info@wilsonsdisease.org

Wound, Ostomy and Continence Nurses Society (WOCN)
WOCN National Office
1120 Rt. 73, Ste. 200
Mount Laurel, NJ 08054
Fax: 856-439-0525
Toll-Free: 888-224-9626
Website: www.wocn.org
E-mail: info@wocn.org

Index

Index

Page numbers followed by 'n' indicate a footnote. Page numbers in *italics* indicate a table or illustration.

A

707

713